D0948810

WITHDRAWN

# SOUTH WEST AFRICA
## AND THE
## UNITED NATIONS

*Solomon Slonim*

# SOUTH WEST AFRICA AND THE UNITED NATIONS: AN INTERNATIONAL MANDATE IN DISPUTE

*The Johns Hopkins University Press*
BALTIMORE & LONDON

The Johns Hopkins University Press, Baltimore, Maryland 21218
The Johns Hopkins University Press Ltd., London

Library of Congress Catalog Card Number 72-4020
ISBN 0-8018-1431-6

Library of Congress Cataloging in Publication data
will be found on the last printed page of this book.

# CONTENTS

# ACKNOWLEDGMENTS

In writing this book I have incurred numerous intellectual debts and have had occasion to recall many earlier ones. Perhaps the first in order is that owed to my lecturers in the Faculty of Law of the University of Melbourne and, in particular, the late Dr. J. Leyser, who imparted to me an appreciation of both the scope and limitations of international law in the functioning of the world system. Major parts of this study were completed at Columbia University, and I am indebted to Professor Leland M. Goodrich who first suggested a study of the South West Africa problem and who read part of the original manuscript. I am grateful also to Professors Louis Henkin and Leon Gordenker for their helpful comments on an earlier version of this study. My greatest debt at Columbia undoubtedly is to Professor Oliver J. Lissitzyn, who was a constant source of guidance and inspiration. His door was always open to me and I regularly enjoyed the benefit of his excellent counsel and vast scholarship in international law. For all this I am deeply grateful. Professor Julius Stone, Challis Professor of International Law and Jurisprudence at the University of Sydney, read an earlier draft of this study and, besides making many helpful and penetrating comments on the work as it then stood, offered valuable suggestions for its further development. His advice, based on forty years of profound and prolific authorship in the law, was of incalculable benefit, and I thank him warmly.

Other scholars read this work and I profited greatly from their incisive comments. These include Dr. Yehuda Blum of the Hebrew University and Dr. Upendra Baxi of the University of Sydney. A very special note of appreciation is owed to Professor Jacob W. Landynski of the New School for Social Research for much sound advice in the writing and creation of this book.

Above all, I wish to express my deepest gratitude to my wife Michla for her invaluable assistance. An international legal scholar in her own right, she carefully reviewed and scrutinized every part of this study, from its earliest origins to its final stage, and made innumerable suggestions with reference to both substance and form which added immensely to whatever merit it may have.

I also take this opportunity to thank Mr. Keith Highet of the New York law firm of Curtis, Mallet-Prevost, Colt and Mosle, for his many kindnesses and especially for giving of his valuable time to discuss with me various aspects of the South West Africa litigation. Likewise, I wish to thank the members and staff of the Ethiopian, Liberian, South African, and United States missions to the United Nations for their help in obtaining essential United Nations documentation. Mrs. J. M. Noonan of the South African library was particularly helpful in locating long-forgotten documents and United Nations records.

Mrs. Bill, former director of Columbia University international law library, and her assistants, Mr. Popovitch and Mr. Lee, regularly met my numerous demands on their time with good cheer. At a later stage, the staff of the Hebrew University and National Library in Jerusalem, and especially, Mr. Yochai Goel, director of the lending division, assisted greatly in matters of research. Mrs. Malka Kroll worked speedily and accurately in converting a difficult script into neat typewritten form. And Mr. J. G. Goellner and Mrs. Nancy Middleton Gallienne of The Johns Hopkins University Press were more than kind and patient with an author who repeatedly found he had another note to add and another point to make in the manuscript. To all these people I wish to record my profound thanks.

Chapter I of this book originally appeared as a separate article in the *Canadian Yearbook of International Law* (1968), and I am grateful to the editors of the *Yearbook* for permission to reproduce it. I also wish to thank the Directors of the African Studies Center of the University of California, Los Angeles, for permission to quote from their Occasional Paper No. 5, which discusses the *South West Africa* cases.

I acknowledge with gratitude the generous financial assistance of Columbia University and the Faculty of the Social Sciences at the Hebrew University which made it possible for me to undertake and complete the necessary research.

Finally, I wish to emphasize that despite all the help I have received from the aforementioned scholars, I alone am responsible for the views expressed in this study. This standard disclaimer has particular relevance for a work dealing with a subject as controversial as South West Africa.

# ABBREVIATIONS

| | |
|---|---|
| *AJIL* | *American Journal of International Law.* |
| *BYB* | *British Yearbook of International Law.* |
| *Foreign Relations* | United States, Department of State, *Papers Relating to the Foreign Relations of the United States.* |
| GAOR | General Assembly, Official Records. |
| G.A. Res. | General Assembly Resolution. |
| Goodrich and Hambro | Leland M. Goodrich and Edvard Hambro, *Charter of the United Nations: Commentary and Documents.* 2nd rev. ed. Boston: World Peace Foundation, 1949. |
| *ICJ Reports* | International Court of Justice, *Reports of Judgments, Advisory Opinions and Orders.* |
| *ICLQ* | *International and Comparative Law Quarterly.* |
| L. of N. | League of Nations. |
| *Namibia Opinion* (1971) | *Legal Consequences for States of the Continued Presence of South Africa in Namibia (South West Africa) notwithstanding Security Council Resolution 276 (1970), Advisory Opinion, I.C.J. Reports 1971*, p. 16. |

| | |
|---|---|
| *Namibia Pleadings* | International Court of Justice, *Pleadings, Oral Arguments, Documents, Legal Consequences for States of the Continued Presence of South Africa in Namibia (South West Africa) notwithstanding Security Council Resolution 276 (1970)* (Request for Advisory Opinion), 2 vols. |
| *Oral Petitions Opinion (1956)* | *Admissibility of Hearings of Petitioners by the Committee on South West Africa, Advisory Opinion of June 1st, 1956, I.C.J. Reports 1956*, p. 23. |
| *1956 Oral Petitions Pleadings* | International Court of Justice, *Pleadings, Oral Arguments, Documents, Admissibility of Hearings of Petitioners by the Committee on South West Africa* (Request for Advisory Opinion). |
| PCIJ, Ser. A | Permanent Court of International Justice, Series A. Judgments and Orders. |
| PCIJ, Ser. B | Permanent Court of International Justice, Series B. Advisory Opinions. |
| P.M.C., Min. | Permanent Mandates Commission, Minutes. |
| SCOR | Security Council, Official Records. |
| S.C. Res. | Security Council Resolution. |
| *Status Opinion* (1950) | *International Status of South-West Africa, Advisory Opinion, I.C.J. Reports 1950*, p. 128. |
| *1950 Status Pleadings* | International Court of Justice, *Pleadings, Oral Arguments, Documents, International Status of South-West Africa* (Request for Advisory Opinion). |
| *SWA Judgment* (1962) | *South West Africa Cases (Ethiopia v. South Africa; Liberia v. South Africa), Preliminary Objections, Judgment of 21 December 1962, I.C.J. Reports 1962*, p. 319. |
| *SWA Judgment* (1966) | *South West Africa, Second Phase, Judgment, I.C.J. Reports 1966*, p. 6. |

| | |
|---|---|
| *SWA Pleadings* | International Court of Justice, *Pleadings, Oral Arguments, Documents, South West Africa Cases (Ethiopia* v. *South Africa; Liberia* v. *South Africa*), 12 vols. |
| TCOR | Trusteeship Council, Official Records. |
| UNCIO Docs. | *Documents of the United Nations Conference on International Organization.* 22 vols. New York and London: United Nations Information Organization, 1945. |
| U.N.P.C. | United Nations Preparatory Commission. |
| *Voting Procedure Opinion* (1955) | *South-West Africa—Voting Procedure, Advisory Opinion of June 7th, 1955, I.C.J. Reports 1955,* p. 67. |

# CHRONOLOGY

| | |
|---|---|
| 1883–84 | South West Africa becomes a German colony. |
| July 1915 | South African forces conquer South West Africa. |
| Jan. 30, 1919 | Mandate compromise finalized at Versailles Peace Conference (Article 22 of League Covenant). |
| May 7, 1919 | Principal Allied and Associated Powers formally distribute mandates and award South West Africa to South Africa. |
| June 28, 1919 | Treaty of Versailles signed. |
| Jan. 10, 1920 | Entry into force of Treaty of Versailles, including Covenant of League of Nations. |
| Dec. 17, 1920 | League Council adopts resolution confirming Mandate for South West Africa. |
| 1922 | Bondelzwarts incident. |
| 1925 | South African Parliament grants measure of political autonomy to South West Africa (White population). |
| 1933 | Permanent Mandates Commission objects to suggestions that South West Africa become a fifth province of Union. |
| 1937 | South Africa announces it has no plans to convert South West Africa into a fifth province of Union. |

| April 25, 1945 | San Francisco Conference convenes to draft United Nations Charter. |
| May 11, 1945 | South Africa at Conference reserves position with regard to future of South West Africa. |
| Nov.-Dec. 1945 | United Nations Preparatory Commission deliberations. Proposal for a temporary Trusteeship Council not accepted. |
| Jan. 1946 | South Africa, at first session of General Assembly, announces plans to consult population of South West Africa on proposed incorporation of territory into Union. |
| April 1946 | League of Nations Assembly holds final session at Geneva. No formal transfer of mandates to United Nations effected. |
| May-June 1946 | South Africa consults population of South West Africa on future status of territory. |
| Dec. 1946 | General Assembly adopts resolution 65 (I) rejecting South African proposal for incorporation. Invites South Africa to conclude trusteeship agreement. Invitation rejected. |
| Sept. 1947 | South Africa submits report on South West Africa to General Assembly. |
| Nov. 1947 | General Assembly requests Trusteeship Council to examine report. |
| May 1948 | Nationalist party enters into power in South Africa. |
| Nov. 1948 | General Assembly, on basis of Trusteeship Council report, criticizes South Africa's administration of territory. |
| July 1949 | South Africa announces no further reports to the United Nations will be submitted. |
| Dec. 1949 | General Assembly requests International Court of Justice to define status of South West Africa. |
| July 1950 | Court's *Status Opinion* rules that although South Africa is under no obligation to conclude trusteeship agreement, mandate continues in force with supervision to be exercised by General Assembly. |

| | |
|---|---|
| 1951-53 | Ad Hoc Committee negotiations with South Africa on implementation of *Status Opinion* prove abortive. |
| 1953 | General Assembly resolves to supervise mandate, even without South African cooperation, by means of Committee on South West Africa. |
| June 1955 | International Court, in *Voting Procedure Opinion*, confirms right of General Assembly to adopt resolutions on South West Africa by two-thirds majority. |
| June 1956 | International Court, in *Oral Petitions Opinion*, authorizes General Assembly to grant oral hearings to petitioners. |
| 1957 | General Assembly creates Good Offices Committee to undertake fresh negotiations with South Africa. |
| 1958 | General Assembly rejects suggestion of Good Offices Committee for possible partition of South West Africa. |
| 1959 | Subsequent efforts of Good Offices Committee to negotiate end in failure. |
| Nov. 1960 | Ethiopia and Liberia initiate contentious proceedings against South Africa before International Court. General Assembly endorses move. |
| Dec. 1960 | General Assembly adopts Declaration on the Granting of Independence to Colonial Countries and Peoples. |
| April 1961 | Ethiopia and Liberia submit Memorial to Court. |
| March 1962 | South Africa submits Preliminary Objections contesting jurisdiction of Court. |
| May 1962 | "Carpio incident," in which Chairman and Vice-Chairman of Special Committee on South West Africa visit territory and report no signs of threat to peace. |
| Sept. 1962 | South Africa establishes Odendaal Commission to make recommendations for promoting welfare of non-White population of South West Africa. |

| | |
|---|---|
| Oct. 1962 | Oral proceedings on Preliminary Objections held. |
| Dec. 1962 | General Assembly transfers South West Africa issue to Special Committee on Colonialism. |
| Dec. 1962 | Court, in *SWA Judgment*, dismisses Preliminary Objections and assumes jurisdiction. |
| Nov. 1963 | General Assembly adopts Declaration on the Elimination of All Forms of Racial Discrimination. |
| Jan. 1964 | South Africa submits its Counter-Memorial on the merits to Court. |
| May 1964 | Odendaal Commission recommends early creation of Bantustans in South West Africa and proposes a five-year economic and social plan for the territory. |
| June 1964 | Ethiopia and Liberia submit Reply to Court. |
| March–July; Sept.–Nov. 1964 | Oral proceedings on merits held, including hearing of witnesses and experts. |
| July 1966 | Court in *SWA Judgment* (Second Phase) declares that Ethiopia and Liberia lack standing to obtain a judgment on the merits. |
| Oct. 1966 | General Assembly adopts resolution 2145(XXI) revoking South Africa's mandate over South West Africa. South Africa denies Assembly competence. |
| May 1967 | United Nations Council for South West Africa created to administer the territory. |
| Jan. 1968 | Security Council enters picture by adopting resolution condemning South West Africa terrorist trial. |
| April 1968 | South West Africa renamed Namibia by General Assembly. |
| 1968–69 | South Africa moves to establish Bantustans in South West Africa with initial emphasis on Ovamboland. |
| March 1969 | Security Council formally recognizes General Assembly termination of South Africa's mandate. |

| | |
|---|---|
| July 1970 | Security Council requests advisory opinion on legal consequences for states of South Africa's continued presence in Namibia. |
| June 1971 | Court in *Namibia Opinion* rules that South Africa's continued presence in Namibia is illegal. South Africa rejects opinion. |
| Nov. 1971 | Ovambos strike to protest labor-contract system in South West Africa. |
| Feb. 1972 | Security Council, meeting at Addis Ababa, requests Secretary-General to initiate contacts with all parties concerned, for exercise of self-determination in Namibia. |
| March 1972 | Secretary-General Waldheim visits South and South West Africa and holds discussions with government officials in Pretoria. |

# SOUTH WEST AFRICA
## AND THE
# UNITED NATIONS

# INTRODUCTION

As the United Nations advances into the second quarter century of its existence it continues to be embroiled in a controversy which emerged with the creation of the new world organization in 1945—the problem of South West Africa. Repeatedly the United Nations has sought to exercise some form of control or supervision over the territory, only to be as regularly rebuffed in its efforts by the administering authority, South Africa. As a result, South West Africa is the only former mandated territory which was neither brought under the United Nations trusteeship system nor granted its independence. And, as of now, South Africa remains in control of South West Africa no less effectively than when the mandates system of the League came to an end just over two-and-a-half decades ago. Today, because of parallel disputes which have arisen between the United Nations and the White regimes holding sway in southern Africa, the conflict over South West Africa must be regarded as part of the general international crisis which has enveloped that corner of the globe.

The territory of South West Africa[1] lies on the Atlantic coast and is bounded by South Africa to the south, Portuguese Angola to the north, and Botswana (formerly Bechuanaland) to the east. At its northeastern tip, South West Africa also borders upon Zambia and Rhodesia. In strategic terms South West Africa constitutes a valuable buffer between the Black independent states of Africa north of the Zambesi River and South Africa. The territory of some 318,000 square miles, much of it desert, is rich in mineral wealth—diamonds, copper, lead, zinc, and,

---

1. For a comprehensive review of the geographic, demographic, and economic facts of South West Africa, see J. H. Wellington, *South West Africa and its Human Issues* (Oxford: Clarendon Press, 1967); and *South West Africa Survey 1967* (Department of Foreign Affairs of the Republic of South Africa, March 1967).

more recently, uranium—and thus represents a valuable economic asset to South Africa as well. About 90 percent of South West Africa's import trade and 50 percent of its export trade are conducted with South Africa. In 1966 the population was estimated at 610,000, of which some 95,000 were Whites (i.e., a ratio of about 6:1).

Administratively, ever since the period of German rule, South West Africa is divided into two main sections—the Police Zone, in the south and center, comprising two-thirds of the territory and reserved primarily for White settlement; and the northern Tribal Areas, constituting the remaining one-third of the territory and exclusively occupied by non-Whites. This administrative framework serves as the basis for the operation of the policy of apartheid, since Natives within the Police Zone are permitted to reside in designated areas only. Travel beyond these areas is regulated by means of a comprehensive pass system which controls all matters of Native residence, occupation, and status.

From 1883 to 1915 South West Africa constituted part of the German colonial empire; but in the latter year, in concert with the allied war effort, South African forces under Generals Botha and Smuts conquered the territory. The 1919 Versailles Peace Conference, in accordance with the principle of "no annexation of enemy territories" granted a Class C Mandate over South West Africa to South Africa. This arrangement represented a compromise between annexation, as desired by South Africa, and implementation of the principle of self-determination, as desired by President Woodrow Wilson of the United States. In practical terms South Africa was accorded full control of the territory subject to the ultimate, but barely imposing, supervision of the League of Nations. In 1946 South Africa renewed its proposal to annex South West Africa and sought formal recognition of this step from the United Nations General Assembly. The South African proposal, however, was categorically rejected by the members of the United Nations who were dedicated to the implementation of a reverse process in international relations, namely, the emancipation of dependent territories to self-government and independence. The conflict between South Africa and the World Organization which arose at that time, so far from abating, has progressively sharpened as the impact of the newly emancipated states of Africa and Asia has made itself increasingly felt at the United Nations.

But South West Africa stands for much more than the mere durability or intractability of an international dispute. For it encompasses and, in fact, has come to symbolize, many of the critical problems of the postwar world—colonialism and self-determination; racialism and human rights; apartheid and equality; minority rule and democracy. Furthermore, it represents a noteworthy instance of an attempt by the

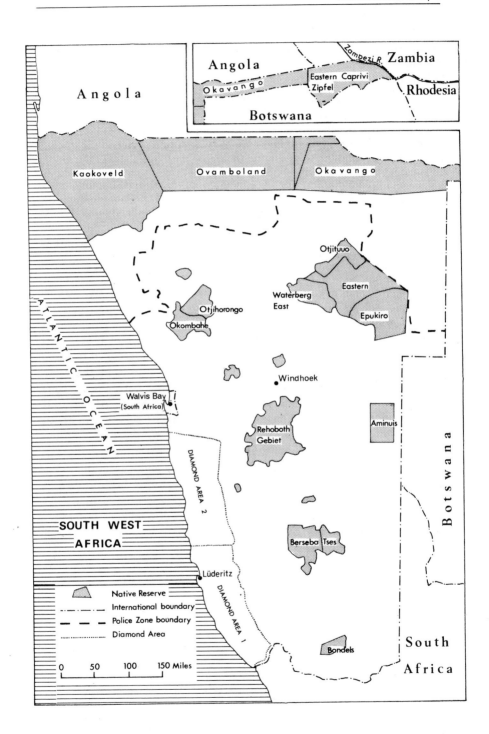

organized international community to impose its consensus upon a defiant member state.

In the initial phase, the dispute over South West Africa centered on the issue of the continuance of international accountability with respect to the territory. A majority of the United Nations held from the start that no state should be permitted to administer a dependent territory without holding itself accountable before the organized international community for its administration. *A fortiori* was this so in the case of an international mandate, which, unlike outright colonies, had been impressed with an international status since the aftermath of World War I. South Africa had been accountable to the League for its administration of South West Africa because the League represented the organized international community. No less a measure of international accountability was, therefore, owed to the new representative of the world community, the United Nations.

In contrast, South Africa contended that accountability for the administration of the mandate was owed exclusively to a specific international organization, the League of Nations. Upon that organization's demise the mandate lapsed and South Africa was henceforth obligated to no international body. Nonetheless, South Africa pledged itself to continue to administer South West Africa "in the spirit of the Mandate." But this did not prevent it from moving ahead at the same time with plans to tie South West Africa ever closer to South Africa itself and to establish it, in fact, as a real fifth province of the Union. In justification of its steps, South Africa pointed to the fact that the Mandate permitted it to administer the territory "as an integral portion of the Union" with "full power of administration and legislation." One of the by-products of integrating the administration in both areas was that South Africa's distinctive system of race relations, apartheid, was automatically extended to South West Africa. A critical new dimension was thereby added to the conflict between South Africa and the United Nations over South West Africa.

Apartheid, with all its detested elements—Native reserves, color bar acts, Bantustans, pass laws, and influx control measures (with resultant separation of families)—represented to most member states a direct challenge to human dignity. To the African states, racialism was far worse—it was an unspeakable personal humiliation and degradation; it was, in the words of Julius Nyerere, "the ultimate horror."[2] The operation of apartheid in South Africa was odious enough; its introduction into a territory impressed with an international status was totally insufferable. Racialism was now combined with colonialism to produce a

2. "Rhodesia in the Context of Southern Africa," *Foreign Affairs* XLIV (1966): 386.

two-headed monster of "unfreedom."[3] South Africa's effort to portray its racial policy of "separate development" (the advanced stage of apartheid) as an enlightened method for ensuring self-determination to each racial or national group was dismissed as a transparent attempt to disguise a ruthless scheme for White domination.

But the practice of colonialism and racialism in South West Africa presented the United Nations with an opportunity as well as a challenge. The special international status of the territory offered the United Nations scope for summoning to its aid (to an extent not possible in relation to apartheid within South Africa) international law and the International Court of Justice. In fact, the notable intermeshing of law and politics and the interaction between the political and judicial organs of the United Nations in relation to South West Africa must be reckoned among the distinctive features of the entire dispute. To date the Court has been called upon to deliver no less than six pronouncements on the matter: four advisory opinions—the fourth rendered at the request of the Security Council—and two judgments in contentious proceedings. It was upon the judgments that the greatest hopes had, in fact, been pinned. The mandate status—the continuance of which was affirmed by the Court in 1950—and the presence of a compulsory adjudicatory clause in the Mandate instrument (which clause the 1950 Court held also continues in force) seemed to allow an unprecedented opportunity to bring into play legally binding decisions with, if necessary, Security Council enforcement. And in this way, it was thought, the flank of the White minority regimes in southern Africa might be turned.

It must be recognized that the states prompting recourse to the Court's compulsory jurisdiction were not really sanguine about the prospects of voluntary South African compliance with any Court judgment. Nor, for that matter, were they seriously concerned with elucidating, so as to be guided by, the relevant international law. The undisguised purpose of all the legal proceedings (even the advisory) was to confront the Western powers with a Court ruling which they would be strongly pressured to uphold. In short, by posing the question of South West Africa as one for or against "the rule of law," it was hoped that the major powers, and through them, ultimately, the Security Council, could be galvanized into taking the necessary steps to compel South Africa to adjust its policies in South West Africa to the wishes of the United Nations.

This is the background to the lengthy contentious proceedings conducted by Ethiopia and Liberia on behalf of the United Nations, which

3. The metaphor of a multiheaded "monster of 'unfreedom' " is taken from Nyerere, ibid., p. 376.

lasted from 1960 to 1966 and which eventuated in a much maligned and misunderstood Court judgment when the Court ruled that the Applicants lacked the necessary right or interest to obtain a decision on the merits. The nations of the Third World, in particular, had been led to harbor totally unrealistic expectations of what the Court could, or should, do and were completely unaware of the manner in which the case had actually unfolded before the Court.

But whatever the reasons or reasoning behind the 1966 judgment, its delivery signified that the pattern of fruitful cooperation developed over the years between the General Assembly and the Court in relation to South West Africa was, temporarily at least, at an end. With the path of judicial action thus blocked, the General Assembly resolved that there was, in any case, no further purpose in attempting to exact international accountability from South Africa in regard to its administration of the territory. Henceforth, South Africa must be compelled to accord South West Africa direct independence, in accordance with the Assembly's fundamental resolution of 1960, calling for immediate independence for all colonial territories. To this end, the Assembly, in October 1966, moved to revoke the mandate, and subsequently, it announced that South West Africa, "in accordance with the desires of its people," would thereafter be known as Namibia. These moves heralded a new stage in the confrontation between the United Nations and South Africa and coincided with a generally more militant atmosphere in the United Nations in relation to the White minority regimes in southern Africa—in the Portuguese colonies of Angola and Mozambique, in Rhodesia, and in South Africa itself. The Assembly majority, ever more impatient with the existing situation, sought to enlist the forceful involvement of the Security Council in defeating the vestiges of colonialism and racialism in southern Africa.

Thus, in the face of continued South African intransigence over South West Africa, the Assembly turned several times to the Security Council to "take all effective measures" to secure South Africa's withdrawal. Despite these invitations, the Security Council was slow to become embroiled in this dispute. Formal recognition by the Council of the Assembly's termination of the mandate was not forthcoming until 1969. In retrospect, the initial hesitancy of the Council in the matter of South West Africa does not seem to have been unjustified, for to date the Council—after repeated and express calls to South Africa to evacuate the territory—remains no less frustrated in its efforts to dislodge South Africa than the General Assembly itself. Again, as on previous occasions in which an impasse had been reached in the relevant political organ, the South West Africa question was referred to the Court. The Security Council—employing for the first time its power to request advisory opinions of the International Court of Justice—sought judicial elucidation of the question of "the legal consequences for States of the continued presence of South Africa in Namibia." The opinion of the Court, delivered on June 21, 1971, placed the seal of judicial approval upon the previous actions of the General Assembly and the Security Council in revoking the mandate and in demanding immediate South African withdrawal from the territory. It remains to be seen, however, to what degree this latest pronouncement of the principal judicial organ of the United Nations will contribute to an effective resolution of the long-standing South West Africa dispute.

For an appreciation of the unique features of the South West Africa dispute in the legal-political field it is necessary first to understand the historical context of the conflict—the diplomatic compromise by means of which the mandates system was formed and South West Africa became a mandated territory; the operation of the mandates system in practice; and the significance of the creation of a new system of international accountability under the United Nations. On the basis of this historical review, it will then fall to trace the manner in which the dispute arose between South Africa and the United Nations over international accountability for South West Africa; United Nations efforts to unilaterally exercise supervisory authority over the territory; and the role and pronouncements of the Court in the course of the controversy, with particular emphasis upon the final decision in the contentious litigation which emerged from the great forensic struggle of the 60's. The stage is then set for an examination of the United Nations act of revocation of the mandate—an act endorsed by the latest opinion of the Court—and its aftermath—the direct confrontation between the United Nations and South Africa over the future of the territory.

# I.

# THE
# HISTORICAL
# BACKGROUND

# I.

## CREATION OF THE LEAGUE OF NATIONS MANDATES SYSTEM: A DIPLOMATIC COMPROMISE

The roots of the South West Africa dispute relate back to the events that transpired at the end of World War I and led to the creation of the League of Nations mandates system. More particularly, the conflict between the United Nations and South Africa cannot be understood except by tracing the manner in which South West Africa became a part of the mandates system. The "great compromise" hammered out by President Wilson and the Dominion ministers at the Paris Peace Conference in 1919, produced a three-tiered system of mandates which reflected in a sliding scale a varied balancing of national and international interests. The result of the compromise was a divergency of interpretation that has endured to this day and in considerable measure has fostered and sustained the dispute in its present-day dimensions.

### ALLIED WAR AIMS AND SELF-DETERMINATION

The historical roots of the mandates system undoubtedly stretch back to the concepts and principles enunciated in such earlier international arrangements as the 1885 Treaty of Berlin and the 1906 Algeciras Act.[1]

1. For a review of the historical antecedents of the mandates system, see Pittman B. Potter, "Origin of the System of Mandates under the League of Nations," *American Political Science Review* XVI (1922): 563–83; Potter, "Further Notes," ibid. XX (1926): 842–46; Luther H. Evans, "Some Legal and Historical Antecedents of the Mandatory System," *Proceedings of the Southwestern Political Association* V (1924): 143–61; Evans, "The Mandates System and the Administration of Territories Under C Mandate" (Ph.D. dissertation, Dept. of Political Science, Stanford University, 1927), Part I; H. W. V. Temperley (ed.), *A History of the Peace Conference of Paris*, 6 vols. (London: Frowde, Hodder and Stoughton, 1920–24), II: 236; VI, Part IV; Elizabeth van Maanen-Helmer, *The Mandates System in Relation to Africa and the Pacific Islands* (London: King, 1929), chaps. I and II; William Roger Louis, "African Origins of the Mandates Idea," *International Organization* XIX (1965): 20–36; *The Mandates System: Origin—Principles—Application*, League of Nations Publication, 1945. VI.A.1 (Geneva: 1945), pp. 7–13; Quincy Wright, *Mandates Under the League of Nations* (Chicago: University of Chicago Press, 1930), chap. I.

Nonetheless, it is quite clear that the mandates system came about not as a result of organic development in international relations, but rather as a direct result of the diplomatic events of World War I and the Paris Peace Conference.

From 1914 to 1916 allied leaders, in anticipation of victory, had concluded a series of secret treaties for dividing up colonial and other territories severed from Germany and Turkey.[2] Dramatic events in the course of the year 1917, however, caused the Allies to lay increasing emphasis on the moral and liberal goals of their struggle.[3] The Russian Revolution, followed by United States entry into the war, produced a climate that was antagonistic to greedy annexationist schemes such as those formulated in the secret treaties. Now, such progressive ideals as democracy, the right of self-determination of peoples, and protection for minority rights were proclaimed as the true aims of the allied cause. The Bolshevik Revolution added impetus to this development and gave cause to the principle of self-determination to be extended to the peoples of Africa and Asia as well as of Europe.

This was the background to the famous Fourteen Points enunciated by President Wilson before a joint session of Congress on January 8, 1918.[4] Point V called for "a free, open-minded, and absolutely impartial adjustment of all colonial claims," based on the principle "that in determining all such questions of sovereignty the interests of the populations concerned must have equal weight with the equitable claims of the government whose title is to be determined."[5] In similar vein, Lloyd George, in the course of an address before the Trade Unions Congress on January 5, 1918,[6] had acknowledged that peoples under

2. For a detailed summary of the secret treaties, see Ray Stannard Baker, *Woodrow Wilson and World Settlement*, 3 vols. (Garden City: Doubleday, Page, 1922), I, chaps. III and IV. See also Samuel Flagg Bemis, *A Diplomatic History of the United States* (4th ed., rev; New York: Holt, Rinehart and Winston, 1955), pp. 619–21. On the subject generally, see W. W. Gottlieb, *Studies in Secret Diplomacy during the First World War* (London: Allen and Unwin, 1957).

3. See generally, Arno J. Mayer, *Political Origins of the New Diplomacy 1917–1918* (New Haven: Yale University Press, 1959), passim.

4. On the origins and significance of the Fourteen Points, see ibid., pp. 341–44, 352–53; Charles Seymour, *The Intimate Papers of Colonel House*, 4 vols. (Boston and New York: Houghton Mifflin, 1926–28), III, chap. XI; Seth P. Tillman, *Anglo-American Relations at the Paris Peace Conference of 1919* (Princeton, N.J.: Princeton University Press, 1961), pp. 24–32. For text, see James Brown Scott (ed.), *Official Statements of War Aims and Peace Proposals, December 1916 to November 1918* (Washington, D.C.: Carnegie Endowment for International Peace, 1921), pp. 234–39.

5. Note that this language in Point V does not at all refer to mandates. On the contrary, it clearly implies that territories will be annexed, but that the various claims shall be equitably settled, taking into account the interests of the native population as well. Smuts in his initial work on the League of Nations also interpreted Point V in this manner. See below, p. 7. The Commentary to the Fourteen Points, however, did interpret this passage to refer to mandates. See below, p. 14.

6. On the background to Lloyd George's address, see Baker, *Wilson and World Settlement*, I: 40; Mayer, *New Diplomacy*, pp. 322–28; Tillman, *Anglo-American Relations*, pp. 26–28.

Turkish control were entitled to a "recognition of their separate national condition," and that the German colonies should be placed "at the disposal of a conference whose decisions must have primary regard to the wishes and interests of the native inhabitants of such colonies," the principle of self-determination being "as applicable in their cases as in those of occupied European territories."[7]

By early 1918, then, the allied leaders were basically committed in their peace program to the right of self-determination of peoples. By this time, too, they envisioned creation of a permanent world organization to preserve peace. However, they did not yet relate a solution for the enemy colonies to any such projected international institution. At this stage, the measure of international involvement was to be limited to the deliberations of the Peace Conference which would seek to apply the basic principle of self-determination. No permanent scheme relating to colonies was yet devised. In short, although the principle of self-determination was already enunciated, the effective means for instituting and confirming this right through the provision of international accountability was not yet conceived of.

## FROM SELF-DETERMINATION TO MANDATES SYSTEM

During the course of the year 1918, the original commitment to the principle of self-determination in the disposition of enemy colonies matured gradually into a full-scale conception of a League of Nations mandates system. A consensus gradually developed to the effect that the enemy colonies issue could best be resolved by some permanent tie-in with the projected world organization. A review of certain key elements which progressively contributed to this development provides the necessary background for an appreciation of the events at Paris.

The first (and perhaps most significant) contribution was that of G. L. Beer, a former Columbia University professor, who was a specialist on colonial affairs.[8] At the time of his writing, January 1918, Beer was a member of the Inquiry, the group of United States experts selected in late 1917 by Colonel House, President Wilson's adviser, to collect data and offer considered opinions on various questions that could be expected to arise at the Peace Conference.[9]

Beer recommended that the "administration of the derelict territories and peoples freed from German and Turkish rule must, in general,

---

7. For text, see Scott, *War Aims and Peace Proposals*, pp. 225–33.
8. George Louis Beer, *African Questions at the Paris Peace Conference*, ed. Louis Herbert Gray (New York: Macmillan, 1923).
9. For a description of the formation and work of the Inquiry, see Sidney Edward Mezes, "Preparations for Peace," *What Really Happened at Paris*, ed. Edward Mandel House and Charles Seymour (New York: Scribners', 1921), p. 1; Baker, *Wilson and World Settlement*, I: 97; Charles Seymour, *Papers of Colonel House*, III: 168; Lawrence E. Gelfand, *The Inquiry: American Preparations for Peace, 1917–1919* (New Haven: Yale University Press, 1963).

be entrusted to different states acting as mandatories of the League of Nations." But these mandates were not to be "uniform"; they were to "vary with the circumstances of the different cases." Prime attention was to be given to the welfare of the native populations; the open door was to be ensured "by an arrangement like that of the Six-Powers Group in China and that of the Algeciras Act of 1906"; and provision was to be made for arbitration relating to the maintenance of the open door.[10] According to Beer, it may be noted, neither South West Africa nor New Guinea would be placed under a mandate regime; they would be annexed by South Africa and Australia respectively.[11]

Beer's outline is the first clear prototype of the mandates system and in fact bears remarkable resemblance to the scheme ultimately adopted. However, it is not fully clear to what extent Beer's work was directly instrumental in guiding President Wilson's thoughts along the path of trusteeship. Nonetheless, before the war was over the President was definitely convinced that some such concept of mandates should be instituted for former enemy territories.

In October 1918, he told Sir William Wiseman, ambassador of the United Kingdom to the United States, that while he had little faith in international administration for the German colonies and was absolutely opposed to their restoration to Germany, he favored administration by single states "in trust." "In trust for whom?" Wiseman asked. "Well for the League of Nations, for instance," Wilson replied.[12]

The principle of international accountability was more formally expressed in the official United States Commentary to the Fourteen Points adopted in October 1918.[13] On Point V, the Commentary declared:

> It would seem as if the principle involved in this proposition is that a colonial power acts not as owner of its colonies but as trustees for the natives and for the interests of the society of nations, that the terms on which the colonial administration is conducted are a matter of international concern and may legitimately be the subject of international inquiry and that the peace conference may, therefore, write a code of colonial conduct binding upon all colonial powers.[14]

10. Beer, *African Questions*, pp. 424–25; 431–32.
11. Ibid., pp. 443–44; 457–58.
12. Cited in Tillman, *Anglo-American Relations*, p. 87.
13. Seymour, *Papers of Colonel House*, IV: 192–200.
14. Ibid., p. 195. President Wilson confirmed his acceptance of the Commentary as "a satisfactory interpretation of the principles involved" on October 30, 1918. Ibid., p. 153.
   The reference in the concluding sentence to "a code binding on all colonial powers" relates (according to the opening paragraph of the Commentary on this Point) only to "those colonial claims . . . created by the war"; it has no relationship to general colonial policy. Ibid., p. 194.

On November 11, 1918, the war ended, and three weeks later President Wilson set sail for Europe. In the course of a meeting with members of the Inquiry aboard ship, the President stated that "the German colonies should be declared the common property of the League of Nations and administered by small nations." "Nothing," he said, "stabilizes an institution as well as the possession of property."[15]

In the meantime, the British government was also moving toward acceptance of the mandates idea.[16] In October 1918, Colonel House had met with Lloyd George and had gained British acceptance of the trusteeship principle for all enemy territories, with the exception of South West Africa and the Asiatic islands. These, the British Prime Minister indicated, would have to go to South Africa and Australia respectively, lest he "be confronted by a revolution in those dominions."[17]

In early November 1918, a British Foreign Office memorandum on the League dealt with the mandates issue in the following terms:

> The treaty should give precision to the idea of the responsibility of the civilised States to the more backward peoples. Trusts or, to speak more precisely, charters should be drawn up for the various territories for whose future government the signatory Powers have to issue a mandate, and particular areas handed over to individual States who would be responsible to the League for the discharge of that mandate. Arrangements of this kind will require to be made for tropical Africa, for the Pacific Islands and for Western Asia.[18]

On November 28, the subject of mandates was fully discussed at a meeting of the Imperial War Cabinet.[19] Lloyd George records that two

15. Notes taken by Dr. Isaiah Bowman, December 10, 1918. Dr. Bowman's memorandum may be found in James T. Shotwell, *At the Paris Peace Conference* (New York: Macmillan, 1937), pp. 73–78; Seymour, *Papers of Colonel House*, IV: 280–83; David Hunter Miller, *The Drafting of the Covenant*, 2 vols. (New York: G. P. Putnam's Sons, 1928), I: 41–44.

16. On this topic generally, see Wm. Roger Louis, *Great Britain and Germany's Lost Colonies, 1914–1919* (Oxford: Clarendon Press, 1967), chaps. III and IV.

17. House to Wilson, October 30, 1918, *Foreign Relations, 1919, The Paris Peace Conference* I: 407. At this meeting Lloyd George also expressed the hope that the United States would see fit to become trustee for German East Africa colonies. For a review of the attempts to have the United States assume a mandate under the League Covenant, see William Roger Louis, "The United States and the African Peace Settlement of 1919: The Pilgrimage of George Louis Beer," *Journal of African History* IV (1963): 413–33.

18. Quoted in Alfred Zimmern, *The League of Nations and the Rule of Law, 1918–1935* (London: MacMillan, 1936), pp. 202–3. For the full text of the memorandum see ibid., pp. 196–208. This memorandum is particularly important since it was to be the starting point of the Smuts draft. It is to be noted, however, that the memorandum does not envisage a regime for South West Africa and the Pacific Islands different from that of the other colonies. Ibid., p. 209. See also H. Duncan Hall, *Mandates, Dependencies and Trusteeship* (Washington, D.C.: Carnegie Endowment for International Peace, 1948), p. 110 n. 13.

19. David Lloyd George, *The Truth About the Peace Treaties*, 2 vols. (London: Gollancz, 1938), I: 114.

basic facts emerged from this meeting. First, the Dominions were not prepared to give up any of the colonies conquered by them and contiguous to their own territories. Second, Great Britain herself was not desirous of annexing any territory and was fully prepared to accept the former German colonies in the form of mandates.

At a subsequent cabinet meeting (undated), the distinction between the occupation of a territory in a "possessory" and in a "mandatory" capacity was outlined. The definition adopted is of major significance for the scope of power it concedes to the League (embracing even a right of revocation) and for the dedication to the principle of self-determination that it embodies.

"Mandatory occupation," it was agreed, would involve "administration by a single power on certain general lines laid down by the League of Nations." These lines would include guarantees for an open-door policy and prohibitions against militarization and fortification.

> There would be a right of appeal from the mandatory Power to the League of Nations on the part of anyone who considered himself illtreated, or claimed that the conditions laid down by the League of Nations were not being fulfilled. Subject to such appeal, which might involve the League of Nations withdrawing the mandate in the case of deliberate and persistent violation of its conditions, the mandate would be continuous until such time as the inhabitants of the country themselves were fit for self-government.[20]

The mandates doctrine was unanimously accepted by the Cabinet in respect of all enemy territories except South West Africa and the Pacific islands.[21]

On December 16, 1918, General Jan Smuts published a small pamphlet entitled, "The League of Nations: A Practical Suggestion," which was destined to have a profound influence on the formulation of the mandates system.[22] Almost a third of Smuts's tract was devoted to the subject of mandates. The key point was that the collapse of the old empires should not be made the occasion for "national annexation" of derelict territories. "Europe," he declared, "is being liquidated, and the League of Nations must be the heir to this great estate." The League of Nations must be made the reversionary, in the broadest sense, of the

---

20. Ibid., p. 118.
21. Ibid., p. 123. Smuts appears to have opposed application of the mandates system to any part of Africa, and not just to South West Africa. This would coincide with the viewpoint expressed in his League of Nations pamphlet that Africa was not suited to the institution of mandates. See further, below.
22. Jan C. Smuts, *The League of Nations: A Practical Suggestion* (London: Hodder and Stoughton, 1918). Reproduced in full in Miller, *Drafting of the Covenant*, II, Doc. 5, pp. 23–60.

peoples and territories formerly belonging to Russia, Austria–Hungary and Turkey; the League must be clothed with the right of ultimate disposal in accordance with certain fundamental principles. These principles, he went on to say, "have been summed up . . . in the general formula of 'No annexations, and the self-determination of nations'."[23] Since the peoples involved differed in their preparedness for self-government, a scheme of graded mandates was called for. The terms of each mandate would be spelled out in a special charter which would not only reserve ultimate control to the League, but would call for periodic reports and even allow for appeal against gross breach of the mandate by the people of the mandated territory. In such event the League would be entitled to "assert its authority to the full, even to the extent of removing the mandate, and entrusting it to some other State, if necessary."[24] Provision would be made for observance of the open door and guarantees against militarization.

Smuts, however, expressly excluded Africa and the Pacific islands from the mandates principle by declaring: "The German colonies in the Pacific and Africa are inhabited by barbarians who not only cannot possibly govern themselves but to whom it would be impracticable to apply any idea of political self-determination in the European sense. . . . The disposal of these colonies should be decided on the basis of the principles which President Wilson has laid down in the fifth of his celebrated fourteen points."[25]

Toward the end of December 1918, President Wilson arrived in London and met with Lloyd George.[26] The British Prime Minister presented Wilson with a copy of the Smuts pamphlet and raised the topic of mandates for discussion.[27] There was basic agreement on the principle to be applied, but when Lloyd George presented the case for South African annexation of South West Africa and Australian annexation of the Pacific islands, the President objected. His objection regarding South West Africa was not serious. Wilson was prepared to recognize some merit, based upon contiguity of territory, in that case. But he

23. Smuts, *The League of Nations*, p. 12. The reference to the peoples and territories of Russia, Austria–Hungary, and Turkey, coupled with exclusion from the plan of the peoples of Africa and the Pacific islands (as noted below) has been interpreted in some quarters to mean that Smuts's plan, far from being a "plan for the betterment of backward peoples" was rather "something not very far removed from a twentieth-century Holy Alliance." Zimmern, *League of Nations*, p. 212. D. H. Miller likewise considers Smuts's ideas on mandates to have been quite opposite to those of President Wilson. "The Origin of the Mandates System," *Foreign Affairs* VI (1928): 281.

24. Smuts, *The League of Nations*, pp. 21–22. This passage was cited by the Court in the *Namibia Opinion* (1971): 48 as evidence that a mandate was inherently revocable.

25. Ibid., p. 12. Wilson's fifth point, as noted above, made no reference to mandates, and in the words of Hall, "definitely implied annexation." *Mandates*, p. 112. This interpretation of Point V differs, of course, from the one presented in the Commentary. See above, p. 14.

26. Lloyd George, *Peace Treaties*, pp. 184 ff.

27. Ibid., pp. 190 ff.

was not prepared to accept annexation of the Pacific islands by Australia on grounds of security. If Australian claims were to be conceded, then "a case on similar grounds might be made for every other captured territory." Furthermore, reports Lloyd George: "In answer to the argument that we had definitely promised to Japan the islands in the Northern Pacific, and that it would be impossible to deny to Australia and New Zealand what was given to Japan, the President had shown that he was by no means prepared to accept the Japanese treaty, and was doubtful whether Japan could be admitted there even in the capacity of a mandatory Power."[28]

Mr. Bonar Law, who was present at that part of the discussion, said that President Wilson had remarked in that connection that "he regarded it as his function to act as a buffer to prevent disagreeable things, such as the Japanese retention of the islands, being carried out."[29] The matter was not resolved, and Lloyd George indicated to the President that the question would have to be fought out at the Conference, where the Dominions would be able to present their own case.

President Wilson's strong opposition to Japanese control of the islands north of the equator demonstrates that Wilson, for all his idealism, was not unmindful of American security interests. Further evidence that this consideration engaged his thoughts during the negotiations on the mandates issue is revealed by the following comments by the President.

Upon being presented with the Smuts compromise resolution, involving the creation of an additional category of mandates (Class C), Wilson penned the following observation: "I could agree to this if the interpretation were in practice to come from General Smuts. My difficulty is with the demands of men like Hughes and the certain difficulties with Japan. The latter loom large. A line of islands in her possession would be very dangerous to the United States."[30]

Similar misgivings were expressed by Wilson in his remarks to David Hunter Miller on January 30, following completion of the agreement on the mandates issue. Wilson first spoke of his general distrust of the Japanese, particularly in the face of their broken promises with respect to Siberia. Then, referring to the islands to be mandated to Japan, the President noted that they "lie athwart the path from Hawaii to the

28. Ibid., p. 191.
29. Ibid.
30. Cited in Arthur Walworth, *Woodrow Wilson*, 2 vols. (New York: Longmans Green, 1958), II: 250.

Philippines and that they were nearer to Hawaii than the Pacific coast was and they could be fortified and made naval bases by Japan; that indeed they were of little use for anything else and that we had no naval base except at Guam."[31]

Appreciation of this set of circumstances permits speculation as to whether President Wilson would have fought as tenaciously as he did to generalize the mandates system had these security considerations not been present. Wilson would apparently have preferred to bar the Japanese completely from the islands; as a minimum he was prepared to accept a system of international control which would prohibit militarization and fortification. If this sort of regime was to be applied to the islands north of the equator, it had to be equally applied both to the islands south of the equator and to South West Africa, since the various territories were basically bracketed together. As a result, no exceptions could be allowed for annexation, even in the case of South West Africa, where Wilson was at first prepared to recognize the contiguity argument, as noted earlier.[32]

It might be mentioned, incidentally, that such a strategy regarding the Japanese had been advocated by Beer early in 1918. He had suggested that the smaller South Pacific islands be mandated to Australia and New Zealand, not because this was really necessary, but in order to bind Japan with mandatory commitments with regard to the islands north of the equator. Japan could only be thus bound if the principle were generalized.[33] New Guinea and South West Africa, as noted earlier, would, according to Beer, best be annexed by Australia and South Africa respectively.

When Lloyd George reported on his meeting with the President to the Imperial Cabinet, Dominion representatives, and particularly Prime Minister Hughes of Australia, were bitterly critical of the President's

---

31. David Hunter Miller, *My Diary at the Conference of Paris*, privately printed, 21 vols. (New York: Appeal Printing Co., 1924), I: 100. See also Miller, *The Drafting of the Covenant*, I: 114.

American officials, it is clear, had repeatedly stressed the potential danger posed to United States interests by Japanese retention of the islands. See Russell H. Fifield, *Woodrow Wilson and the Far East: The Diplomacy of the Shantung Question* (New York: Crowell, 1952), pp. 120–39; and see also Tillman, *Anglo-American Relations*, pp. 98–100.

32. Cf. the comment by Temperley in connection with South West Africa: "As it was feared that an exception made in one case—no matter how valid it might be—might open the door to others, a general application of the system was insisted upon." *Peace Conference of Paris*, II: 233.

33. See Beer, *African Questions*, pp. 453–58; Paul Birdsall, *Versailles Twenty Years After* (London: Allen and Unwin, 1941), p. 75. See also contemporary newspaper opinion in Australia and New Zealand, as analyzed in Louis, *Great Britain And Germany's Lost Colonies*, pp. 141–43.

objections to their plans for annexation.[34]   They called upon Lloyd
George to "resolutely insist upon such terms of peace as were necessary
for the safety of the Empire, through whose sacrifices and efforts victory had been won." Other members of the Cabinet, however, reminded their companions of the overriding importance of reaching an
understanding with the United States.[35]

This dichotomy of interests, as reflected in the Cabinet debates,
explains much of the subsequent British conduct toward the mandates
issue at the Paris Peace Conference. On the one hand, the British were
desirous of cooperating with the United States to the fullest extent
possible, consistent with their own national interests. Moreover, Great
Britain, independently of the United States, had attained a keen appreciation of the responsibilities of mandatory powers as reflected in the
Cabinet discussions and Foreign Office memoranda. The British were,
therefore, fully prepared to accept the mandates system for the territories that had come under their own control. On the other hand, Great
Britain, the head of a vast empire, found itself committed to supporting
Dominion claims for annexation, based upon grounds of security and
contiguity of territory. Lloyd George resolved that the matter could
best be settled by having the Dominion representatives themselves present the issue directly to the President at a session of the Conference.[36]

After his meeting with Lloyd George in London, Wilson returned to
Paris and proceeded to draw up a draft Covenant, incorporating therein
much of the thought and language of General Smuts. His reliance on
Smuts's draft was particularly evident in regard to the mandates section, which was appended as a supplementary agreement to the body of

34. Hughes scorned the attempt of the President "to dictate . . . how the world was to be
governed." America, he declared, had entered the war late and had suffered very little. "If the
saving of civilization had depended on the United States, it would have been in tears and chains
today." Above all, he thought the President was talking of a problem which he did not really
understand. See Lloyd George, *Peace Treaties*, I: 194-97.
35. See particularly the remarks of Lord Reading, ibid., p. 198, and Lord Robert Cecil,
ibid., pp. 200-1.
36. Ernst B. Haas, in an article entitled, "The Reconciliation of Conflicting Colonial
Policy Aims: Acceptance of the League of Nations Mandate System," *International Organization* VI (1952): 521-36, has argued that the mandates system, and particularly the Class C
mandates, were conceived partly as a compromise formula to reconcile the clash between
Empire elements seeking annexation and those objecting to any further expansion of British
territory. Judge Jessup in his dissenting opinion in the *SWA Judgment* (1966): 398-99, quotes
Haas approvingly and refers to the final "compromise" of January 30, 1919 as "a domestic
matter concerning the internal arrangements of the British Empire." Ibid., p. 397. It is respectfully submitted that the foregoing material demonstrates quite clearly that opposition to extending British colonial territory was not at all related to the question of Dominion annexation
of the colonies adjoining their own territories. Domestic opposition may have induced acceptance of the mandates principle for Britain itself. The Dominion drive for annexation was not in
issue and was in fact fully supported by the British government both before and during the
Conference. The Class C mandates came about not because of internal opposition to the
expansion of the British Empire, but solely to accommodate President Wilson's demands for
generalized application of the mandates principle. See below, pp. 22-32.

the draft Covenant.[37] The President's plan, however, extended the mandates system, with a clear pledge to the principle of self-determination, to all German colonies—including those in Africa and the Pacific—something which Smuts had specifically excluded. Whereas Smuts had envisaged a mandates system purely as a means of resolving the nationality problem of Eastern Europe and the Near East, the President regarded it as a concept of general applicability and one that could resolve the colonial problem of Africa and the Pacific as well.[38] The first official American draft of the Covenant was circulated to the allied governments on January 10, 1919.[39]

On January 25, 1919, David Hunter Miller, the United States legal adviser in Paris, received a British "Draft Convention regarding Mandates" from Lord Cecil, which went into considerable detail regarding the proposed mandates system.[40] Among other things, it referred to two categories of mandates—the territories close to independence, called "assisted states," and the areas requiring direct administration by the mandatory power, called "vested territories." The state placed in charge of a "vested territory" would be "invested with all powers and rights of a sovereign government"; such state would hold the territory "upon trust to afford to the . . . inhabitants peace, order and good government."[41] The British draft also provided for annual reports by the mandatory power and included a provision for the creation of a Commission to assist the League in its supervisory role and to receive the annual reports.[42]

37. The extent to which the President drew upon the Smuts draft is analyzed by Potter, "Origin of the System of Mandates," pp. 563–83. See also George Curry, "Woodrow Wilson, Jan Smuts, and the Versailles Settlement," *American Historical Review* LXVI (1961): 968–86.
38. See Wright, *Mandates*, p. 32.
39. For the text of this first Paris draft (which was actually Wilson's second draft), see Miller, *Drafting of the Covenant*, II, Doc. 7, p. 65; and Baker, *Wilson and World Settlement*, III, Doc. 12, p. 100.
40. For the text, see Miller, *Drafting of the Covenant*, I: 106–7.
41. Ibid. It is to be noted that the provisions on "vested territories" contained no reference to independence, or even self-determination.
42. Ernst B. Haas, "Conflicting Colonial Policy Aims," p. 535, maintains that inclusion of the Permanent Mandates Commission clause in Article 22 of the Covenant, came about as a result of "the insistent demand of the American delegation." It was instituted solely at the behest of President Wilson. He cites no evidence. The material cited by Applicants in the *South West Africa* cases (*SWA Pleadings* VIII: 144) in support of a similar thesis proves on examination to be quite irrelevant. Both Haas and the Applicants apparently overlooked Miller's comment on the subject. "The provision for a Mandate Commission . . . seems to have its origin in Clause 7 of the British Draft Convention." Miller, *Drafting of the Covenant* I: 111–12. Judge Jessup, in his dissenting opinion in *SWA Judgment* (1966): 399, in the course of rejecting South Africa's argument that the compromise worked out on January 30, 1919 (analyzed below) was the sum total of obligation to which South Africa had been prepared to subscribe, points out that that compromise had not contained the provision for the Permanent Mandates Commission, which was only added at a later date. It is evident, however, that South Africa and the remaining Dominions were familiar with this provision, since it was part of Cecil's draft, completed on January 24. The provision in fact was reinserted into the mandates article by General Smuts himself, when he presented the final version of that article to the Commission

In effect, then, there was basic agreement between the United States and Great Britain on the mandates principle. During the course of 1918, both nations had advanced from a simple commitment to the ideal of self-determination to a recognition that this ideal could best be implemented through the creation of a mandates system integrally linked with the League of Nations. The general features of the system were also agreed upon.[43] The outstanding difference centered on the extent of the mandates system, and particularly the question of whether annexation would be allowed in certain exceptional cases. This issue was to be the chief source of controversy on the topic of mandates at the Paris Conference.

## THE CLASS C COMPROMISE

The Peace Conference opened in Paris on January 18, 1919. Disposition of colonial territories was the first major issue dealt with by the Conference.[44]

Lloyd George opened the discussion on Friday, January 24, amid early and general concurrence on not returning the colonies to Germany.[45] Great Britain, he declared, was prepared to accept the mandates system for those territories that had come under British control. The mandates system, with its concern for native interest and equality of commercial access was, in essence, already a part of the British colonial system. But the territories conquered by the Dominions, he felt, should be treated differently. South West Africa was a wilderness and could only be developed as an integral part of South Africa, upon which it bordered. New Guinea and Samoa likewise could best be administered if they became part of Australia and New Zealand respectively. In these cases, therefore, annexation was advisable.

Each of the Dominion ministers then stated his case. Hughes argued that control of New Guinea was vital to Australian security. Pointing to

---

on the League of Nations on February 8, 1919. See Miller, *Drafting of the Covenant* I: 185; II, Doc. 19, pp. 272–75.

43. The similarity between British and American views was, of course, not due to mere coincidence, but rather to their common derivation from the Smuts plan.

44. Wilson actually favored giving precedence to European territorial questions since these, he felt, were more demanding. Lloyd George, however, pushed for prior consideration of the colonial question. The matter was resolved by allotting ten days for the submission of all territorial claims. Since the Dominion claims were ready the next day, these were taken up first. Baker, in accordance with his conspiratorial interpretation of events at Paris, maintains that this maneuver by Lloyd George was deliberately designed to obtain "a division of the spoils before discussion of the League or of the mandatory system could even be begun." *Wilson and World Settlement*, I: 251.

45. Council of Ten, January 24, 1919, 3 P.M., *Foreign Relations, 1919, The Paris Peace Conference* III: 718; Lloyd George, *Peace Treaties* I: 513; Baker, *Wilson and World Settlement*, I: 257–58; Birdsall, *Versailles*, pp. 60–61.

a map, he demonstrated that the Pacific islands encompassed Australia like a fortress and in unfriendly hands constituted a direct menace. Massey of New Zealand likewise emphasized the strategic importance of Samoa for his country; he did not believe the world had seen the last of war. Smuts claimed South West Africa on grounds of contiguity to the Union and the undesirability of a separate administrative system. Borden of Canada endorsed the arguments of his fellow ministers, pointing out, at the same time, that Canada itself sought no territory. Neither the French, Italians, nor Japanese, all of whom were basically opposed to the mandates system, intervened in the debate. Only the Japanese had a really vital stake in the issue, "and they were content to let the British Empire present the case for annexations."[46]

At the second meeting on this issue, on Monday, January 27, President Wilson outlined his concept of the mandatory system.[47] The basis of the idea, he said, was worldwide opposition to further annexation. Since it was agreed that the colonies should not be returned to Germany, mandatories acting on behalf of the League would have to take care of the inhabitants of these territories. This guardianship would operate not only to protect the welfare of the people but also to promote their political development until such time as they were qualified "to express a wish as to their ultimate relations—perhaps [even] lead[ing] them to desire their union with the mandatory power." In case administration of the mandate became a financial burden, "it was clearly proper that the League of Nations should bear a proportion of the expense.[48] The fundamental idea would be that the world was acting as trustee through a mandatory, and would be in charge of the whole administration until the day when the true wishes of the inhabitants could be ascertained.[49] It was up to the Union of South Africa to make it so attractive that South West Africa would come into the Union of their [sic] own free will."

Turning to Australia's security arguments, Wilson charged that they were "based on a fundamental lack of faith in the League of Nations."

46. Tillman, *Anglo-American Relations*, p. 91.
47. Council of Ten, January 27, 1919, 3 P.M., *Foreign Relations, 1919, The Paris Peace Conference* III: 740-43. Over the weekend, the plenary meeting of the Conference had adopted a resolution for establishing the League of Nations.
48. On this point, see Wilson's Third Draft, January 20, 1919, in Miller, *Drafting of the Covenant* II, Doc. 9, p. 104.
49. In this regard Wilson's third draft (in common with his other Paris drafts) reserved to the League "complete power of supervision," including authority, upon appeal from the people of the territory, to substitute, in event of a breach of the mandate, "some other State or agency, as mandatory." "The object of all such tutelary oversight" was the development of "a political unit which can take charge of its own affairs." In accordance with this purpose, the people of the territory would be entitled to petition the League to set up their territory "as an independent unit." Ibid.

Any nation attempting to take the mandated territory from the mandatory power would be an "outlaw," subject to the concerted action of the League members who "would be pledged, with the United States in the lead, to take up arms for the mandatory."[50] Australia, because of its contiguity to New Guinea, might very well be appointed mandatory there. But, "if the process of annexation went on, the League of Nations would be discredited from the beginning." Above all, the Peace Conference should not appear as a meeting "to divide up the spoils."

The Dominion ministers, however, remained firm in their campaign to obtain the territories outright, without mandatory obligations. Lloyd George pointed out that the President's suggestion for League assumption of ultimate financial responsibility for the mandates, with the possibility of assessments upon members, invited a host of practical difficulties which required careful consideration. At this point the meeting adjourned.[51]

The third meeting, on Tuesday, January 28, opened with Lloyd George reiterating British acceptance of the mandate principle.[52] It was, he said, not very different from the principles laid down by the Berlin Conference which had also covered such subjects as the open door and the prohibition on arms and liquor traffic. The only new feature was the provision of external machinery for enforcement. With regard to the Dominion requests, Lloyd George again asked the President to consider them as a special case.

Massey of New Zealand followed through with a dramatic presentation of the case for annexing Samoa. He compared the island in strategic terms to the American West, and inquired whether President Washington, after independence, would have accepted a mandatory system for those western lands.[53]

Wilson, in reply, ignored the historical analogy and discounted the strategic value of Samoa by noting that United States control of one of the islands of the Samoan group made it impossible for any power "to

50. But cf. Wilson's own anxieties with respect to Japan's role as the mandatory power for the Pacific islands.

51. That evening, January 27, Arthur Balfour, British Foreign Secretary, presented a memorandum to Lloyd George which seriously questioned the feasibility of the President's proposal regarding finances. The necessity for checking on both expenditures and budget of a mandate, plus the requirement of assessing members, would make for "an almost unworkable fiscal system." He was also critical of that aspect of the President's plan which would empower the League to dispossess a mandatory power upon application of the inhabitants of the mandated territory. Absence of fixity of tenure would seriously weaken the whole system and could well "supply a perpetual incentive to agitation and intrigue." Finally, independent powers of inspection by the League—which Balfour acknowledged was an essential element in any effective mandate system—raised the constant peril of collision between the League and the mandatory power. Lloyd George, *Peace Treaties*, I: 554-57.

52. Council of Ten, January 28, 1919, 11 A.M., *Foreign Relations, 1919, The Paris Peace Conference* III: 749-50.

53. Ibid., pp. 751-53.

play in Samoa the part played by Germany without attracting the attention of the United States."[54]

In the fourth meeting that afternoon, M. Simon, the French minister for colonies, in a lengthy memorandum, presented his country's case for annexation.[55] It was obvious that Wilson was becoming more and more isolated in his insistence upon universal application of the mandates principle. Matters became very strained as the President observed that the discussions, so far, had been "a negation in detail—one case at a time—of the whole principle of mandatories." "It looked," he said, "as if their roads diverged." There was serious danger that the Conference might reach an impasse before it had hardly begun. At this point, Mr. Balfour, in an attempt to iron things out, sought to explain to the President some of the difficulties which troubled the delegates. One issue was the problem of League financing of mandated territories. Another was the question of permanency of tenure for the mandatory power. Wilson thereupon acknowledged that practical aspects of the system had yet to be worked out, but that unless the "quality of trusteeship" was imparted to the League it would be reduced to "a laughing stock." "The world would say that the Great Powers first portioned out the helpless parts of the world, and then formed a League of Nations." He appealed to the delegates to agree on the principle and to leave resolution of specific problems to the practical determination of the League.[56]

This passionate plea by the President induced Orlando and Clemenceau to express reserved acceptance of the mandates principle on behalf of their respective countries. Both statesmen, however, acknowledged the merits of the Dominion claims and would allow annexation in those cases. At this point, Clemenceau, in seeking to clarify the role of the League in the mandates system, inquired whether the

54. Ibid., pp. 753–54. Was this a veiled hint that any Japanese threat to New Zealand would automatically involve the United States, and that reliance on American involvement would offer New Zealand far more security than mere procurement of a small Pacific island?

55. Ibid., pp. 758–63. In the course of arguing against a mandates arrangement M. Simon made the following statement: "The mandatory system consisted of empowering one nation to act on behalf of another. Every mandate was revocable, and there would therefore be no guarantee for its continuance." Ibid., pp. 760–61.

In the 1971 Namibia pleadings the representative of Finland cited this statement as evidence that in 1919, when the mandates agreement was concluded, it was "tacitly understood" that a mandate was inherently revocable. It was only "out of tact towards the mandatory powers [that] the possibility of revocation was not dealt with either in the Covenant or in the texts of the actual mandates concluded." *Namibia Pleadings* II: 75. See also the statement of the representative of Pakistan. Ibid. p. 137. In response, the representative of South Africa argued that "Mr. Simon's opinion was expressed relative to President Wilson's proposals [on revocability] . . . and . . . intended to demonstrate why [these] . . . proposals were unacceptable to the French Government." Ibid., p. 309. South Africa's interpretation of events was discounted by the Court majority in *Namibia Opinion* (1971): 47–48. But cf. the sharp criticism of the Finnish line of argument by dissenting Judge Fitzmaurice, ibid., p. 275, n. 56.

56. Ibid., pp. 766–67.

League's authority over a mandatory power would not really constitute an exercise of legislative-executive power.[57] Lloyd George undertook to define the true nature of the League's authority. Clemenceau's interpretation, he said, was unwarranted. The system merely amounted to "general trusteeship upon defined conditions." Only if conditions were scandalously abused would the League call for an explanation and insist on a remedy of the abuse. Hitherto, diplomatic correspondence between the powers had fulfilled this function. Now it would be the task of the League to ensure compliance.[58] President Wilson assented to this definition,[59] and the form of the mandates system began to take shape.

Thereupon, Lloyd George went a step further and, addressing himself to the President, asked that the selection of mandatories not be delayed. The Council of Ten was practically the League of Nations, and acceptance of the principle of trusteeship would resolve the matter now.[60] As the end of the meeting approached, it appeared that a consensus on the mandates principle was being reached. Even Hughes and Massey seemed to be going along on the issue. But Lloyd George's request for immediate designation of the mandatories changed the whole atmosphere, and the previously developing consensus was shattered. President Wilson, as desirous as he was of gaining general acceptance of the mandates principle, was not prepared to finalize the matter there and then. He rejected Lloyd George's request by stating that his difficulty lay in preventing the assignment of mandatories "from appearing to the world as a mere distribution of the spoils."[61]

Lloyd George's drive to gain immediate confirmation of the mandatories went far beyond the "acceptance in principle" which the President had sought to achieve; in fact, it might have negated that very principle. The mandate territories would be delivered into the hands of the mandatory powers, free of any international obligations or controls. As one writer comments, "it amounted to the thinnest disguise of annexation. There was as yet no constitution for [Wilson's] League of Nations, much less any formal code of mandatory responsibilities."[62] By the time the League would come into operation it would be confronted with entrenched powers ruling the new territories as fully annexed provinces of their own countries. The President was not prepared to acquiesce in any such arrangement, merely on the basis of a vague pledge to the mandates cause. In fact, Wilson was so displeased and agitated over the course of the discussions, that he even contem-

57. Ibid., pp. 768–69.
58. Ibid., pp. 769–70.
59. Ibid., p. 769.
60. Ibid., p. 770.
61. Ibid., p. 771.
62. Birdsall, *Versailles*, p. 64.

plated the possibility of bringing the whole matter to the attention of the public.[63] Clearly, he was going to stand firm on the issue. And Lloyd George, for one, recognized this only too clearly. His stratagem had failed badly. Apparently he had only been able to persuade the Dominion ministers to join him in support of the mandates proposal at this session, in the belief that immediate endorsement of the principle would help resolve the whole matter. Wilson would get his mandates system, and the Dominions would still be free to assume full control in their respective territories. But Wilson had foiled the scheme and matters were back where they started.

The next morning, January 29, the Imperial War Cabinet met and "all hell broke loose."[64] Hughes, recognizing now that Wilson was unprepared to acquiesce in any vague arrangement which could amount to an immediate grant of title, free of obligation, reverted to his original demand for outright annexation of New Guinea. No matter what mandatory standards were adopted for other areas, he was determined that Australia should receive its Pacific possessions unencumbered by international controls. He was particularly opposed to any open-door regime which might tend to affect Australia's restrictive immigration policies. And he now wanted Lloyd George to do battle with the President in Australia's cause. At this, "Lloyd George lost his temper and told Hughes that he had fought Australia's battles for three days but that he would not quarrel with the United States for [the] Solomon Islands."[65] Lloyd George warned his fellow cabinet members of the danger of a deadlock, with the possibility that President Wilson might leave the country before an agreement could be reached, and called upon them to endorse a draft resolution which had been worked out in the interval by General Smuts.[66]

---

63. Telephone conversation with Colonel House, January 28, 1919: see Seymour, *Papers of Colonel House*, IV: 297.

64. Birdsall, *Versailles*, p. 68. See also Tillman, *Anglo-American Relations*, p. 93; Ernest Scott, *Australia During the War*, Vol. XI of *The Official History of Australia in the War of 1914-1918*, 12 vols. (Sydney: Angus and Robertson, 1936), pp. 783-84.

65. Henry Borden (ed.), *Robert Laird Borden: His Memoirs*, 2 vols. (New York: Macmillan, 1938), II: 906. Hughes, in describing this scene, relates, "For the first time we gave up English and went into Welsh." Ernest Scott, *Australia*, p. 784.

66. General Smuts, after formulating the draft resolution, had consulted with Colonel House who approved of the document as a "fair compromise." Seymour, *Papers of Colonel House*, IV: 298. Parenthetically, it is noteworthy that Colonel House intimated in conversations with Lord Cecil (with Wiseman and Miller also present) that, if the Dominions would be willing meanwhile to accept the colonies as mandates, they would probably be able to arrange for annexation within a short time. In the light of subsequent developments this trend of thought is rather significant, particularly since the idea is attributed to President Wilson. The accuracy of this House–Cecil conversation is confirmed from various sources. In a Wiseman Memorandum dated January 27, 1919, it is reported as follows: "House argues that the League of Nations must reserve the right to cancel the mandate in cases of gross mismanagement, but says the President would agree that the peoples concerned should be able at any time to vote themselves part of Australia and South Africa, thereby cancelling the mandate." *Ibid.*, p. 294. In the House

The draft resolution was heavily predicated on the earlier British Draft Convention, which in turn had been developed from the original Smuts plan. But in contrast to that plan, no explicit reference was made to the principle of self-determination, nor was the League classified as the ultimate reversionary. The purpose of the mandates was couched in broad general terms. As a compromise proposal it was designed, on the one hand, to meet the President's demands by defining specific international obligations to be assumed by the mandatory power. On the other hand, it would not impose a uniform set of standards upon all mandatories indiscriminately. The degree of obligation would vary in accordance with the type of mandate. Three categories of mandates were designated, depending upon the stage of development attained. The first, covering the territories severed from the Turkish Empire, were deemed to have reached a stage of provisional independence, so that the rule of the mandatory power would be limited to "the rendering of administrative advice and assistance"[67] until such time as the mandate would be able to stand alone. (This category resembled the "assisted states" of the British draft.) The second category, made up of former German colonies in Central Africa, would require the mandatory to be responsible for administration, subject to conditions guaranteeing preservation of the open door as well as prohibition of the slave trade, traffic in arms and liquor, militarization and fortification. (This group was akin to the "vested territories" of the British draft.) The third group—whose inclusion formed the heart of the compromise resolution—was composed of

diary the concluding thought is expressed in the following manner: "I convinced him that it was best for Great Britain as a whole to take what we had proposed rather than what the Dominions proposed. The result I thought would be presumably the same and in the end the Mandatory Power would in a short time persuade the colony to annex itself." Ibid., p. 296. Similarly, in David Hunter Miller's diary the entry for January 27, 1919 reads: "Colonel House said . . . that the President's plan was that the Colonies should not go back to Germany but that they should be held by Australia, New Zealand, South Africa, Great Britain, France, etc., with a provision permitting them to be annexed when the inhabitants so wished. He thought this would result in annexation in a few years of good management." In a footnote, Miller comments: "This reads like a very free translation of the President's ideas." Miller, *My Diary at the Conference of Paris* I: 94, 341. Later in London, during the Milner Commission discussion on the Mandate agreements, a draft clause for the C Mandate agreements was submitted on July 9, 1919 (origin not clear), which would have permitted the natives of a mandated territory to express a desire to be united to the mandatory power and would have permitted incorporation of the mandate into the territory of the mandatory power. This proposal was dropped in the face of the objections of M. Simon, the French delegate, who expressed the view that the envisaged procedure would be a pure mockery. *Conférence de la Paix 1919–20, Recueil des Actes de la Conférence* (Paris: Impr. Nationale, 1934), Partie 4B(1), pp. 354–56. The idea for such a proposal arose, no doubt, out of the discussions that had taken place at this stage of the Paris negotiations. Cf. *SWA Pleadings* VIII: 141.

The Smuts resolution, with minor modifications, was ultimately adopted as Article 22 of the Covenant. The text of the Smuts resolution may be found in Miller, *The Drafting of the Covenant* I: 109–10; *Foreign Relations, 1919, The Paris Peace Conference* III: 795–96; Lloyd George, *Peace Treaties*, I: 538–41.

67. Clause 6.

such territories as South West Africa and the islands of the South Pacific which were, "owing to the sparseness of their populations, or their small size, or their remoteness from the centers of civilization" to be "administered under the laws of the mandatory state as integral portions thereof subject to the safeguards above mentioned in the interests of the indigenous population."[68]

Despite the fact that the gradations within the mandates system were attributed primarily to the different stages of development attained by the respective territories, it is obvious that they reflected, more significantly, different degrees of national interest in annexing the territories concerned. Thus, an inverse relationship existed between national interest in annexation and the measure of international involvement to be introduced. In the case of the Class C mandates, the Dominions' interest in annexation would result in a minimal measure of obligation to the international community and maximal concession to national authority. The principle of international accountability, however, was to be retained throughout.

Lloyd George told the Dominion ministers that "if they persisted in asking for more than this compromise, they must go on without the help of the British government with all that this implied."[69] The Australian Prime Minister was still deeply dissatisfied; he felt that Australia's security was imperiled. Lloyd George devoted considerable efforts to convincing him that a Class C mandate for New Guinea was tantamount to Australian ownership of the island, subject only to certain conditions on behalf of the natives.[70] Finally, Mr. Hughes asked: "Is this the equivalent of a 999 years' lease as compared with a freehold?" Assured that it was, Hughes notified Lloyd George in writing of his

68. Clause 8. The principal obligation omitted from the Class C group was the open-door requirement. Most writers credit General Smuts with exclusive authorship of this compromise resolution. However, Ernest Scott, *Australia*, p. 781, claims that an Australian officer, Lieut. Commander Latham, in fact originated the concept of a Class C group of mandates. Latham, Scott says, pointed out that the term "open door" was undefined and could mean "whatever the conference said it meant. For example, in the case of the territories that were so important to South Africa and Australia, it could be given a connotation which, so far as their interest was concerned, was equivalent to ownership." Latham drafted a paragraph spelling out what he meant. Colonel Hankey then added Latham's new category of mandate to the two groups already outlined in the British draft convention, and he submitted the entire revised proposal to Lloyd George and General Smuts. The latter then showed it to Colonel House who found it a satisfactory compromise. Only then did Lloyd George present it to the Cabinet for endorsement. Ibid., p. 783; see also Seymour, *Papers of Colonel House*, IV: 298; Birdsall, *Versailles*, pp. 66-68.

69. Ernest Scott, *Australia*, p. 784.

70. In the course of the discussion this dialogue resulted. Lloyd George: "Did Mr. Hughes object to the prohibition of both slavery and the sale of strong drink to the natives?" No, Mr. Hughes did not object. "Are you prepared to receive missionaries?" "Of course," replied Hughes, "the natives are very short of food and for some time past they have not had enough missionaries to eat."! *Lord Riddell's Intimate Diary of the Peace Conference and After, 1918-1923* (London: Gollancz, 1933), January 30, 1919, p. 17; Birdsall, *Versailles*, p. 69.

acceptance of the draft, and the British Prime Minister prepared to present it to the Conference the next morning, Thursday, January 30.[71]

At this fifth meeting, Lloyd George introduced the Smuts resolution by noting that although it did not represent the "real views" of the Dominions, "they had agreed to this compromise rather than face the catastrophe of a break-up."[72] In reply, President Wilson indicated that he considered it a very gratifying paper. He was prepared to accept it "as a precursor of agreement, [but] it did not constitute a rock foundation, as the League of Nations had not yet been fixed, on which this superstructure would rest." "What would [a mandate] involve? No one could . . . answer. . . . In every instance the mandate should fit the case as the glove fits the hand."[73]

The President was obviously not going to be pressured. He had defeated Lloyd George's original thrust for distributing mandates free of international commitment. Nor was he now willing to accede to an immediate allotment merely because certain international obligations had been spelled out in the mandates draft. In his eyes, the Smuts plan was rather more in the nature of a working paper than a finalized document. Clearly, in the President's view, neither the list of mandatory powers nor the terms upon which they would assume their mandates had been really determined. This spelt particular "danger" for the vague obligations referred to in Clause 8, dealing with Class C mandates.

Mindful of the apprehensions of the Dominion ministers, Lloyd George remarked that the words of the President "filled him with despair." He candidly admitted that only with the greatest difficulty had the ministers been prevailed upon to accept the Smuts draft, even provisionally. Postponement of the mandates issue until the League was established would signify that no final decision could ever be reached on this or any other question. He strongly appealed for provisional acceptance of the resolution.[74]

In response, Wilson agreed to accept the Smuts scheme as a provisional arrangement, with the League acting as a final court of appeal on this as on other issues.[75] This was a significant concession on the part of the President to meet Lloyd George's wishes.

Hughes, however, was not satisfied. Provisional acceptance did not by any means amount to a definite confirmation of the mandates on the limited terms outlined in the plan. He wanted this Conference—

71. Ernest Scott, *Australia*, p. 784.
72. Lloyd George, I: 541; see also Council of Ten, January 30, 1919, 11 A.M. *Foreign Relations, 1919, The Paris Peace Conference* III: 785.
73. Ibid., pp. 786–89.
74. Ibid., pp. 789–90.
75. Ibid., p. 791.

which amounted to a *de facto* League—to act as an executive and assign the mandates. What settlement was there, he asked, if all they knew was that "the arrangements would be such that the scheme would fit like a glove to the hand?" Hughes and Wilson were fast moving to a showdown.

That afternoon, matters came to a head in a sharp clash.[76] Massey of New Zealand was the first to speak. He cited the specific international obligations which related to Class C mandates and called upon the President to confirm that this would be the sum total of obligation. Basically, said Massey, he favored annexation; but if he were to accept the Smuts plan, he at least awaited a clear word from the President on the finality of Clause 8. This statement by Massey provoked the President to anger. He demanded to know whether New Zealand and Australia had presented an ultimatum to the Conference. Was he to understand that Clause 8 was the most that they were prepared to concede "and if they could not get that definitely now, they proposed to do what they could to stop the whole agreement?" At this peremptory challenge, Massey backed down somewhat, and indicated that he had not meant anything in the nature of an ultimatum. Hughes, however, remained quite undismayed. He did not hear the question clearly, and the President repeated it to him in the following terms: "Mr. Hughes, am I to understand that if the whole civilized world asks Australia to agree to a mandate in respect of these islands, Australia is prepared still to defy the appeal of the whole civilized world?"; to which Hughes replied, "That's about the size of it."[77]

At this critical juncture, Botha of South Africa delivered an eloquent address appealing to both sides to strive toward "the higher ideal." He expressed appreciation of the ideals of President Wilson, which, he said, "were the ideals of the people of the world," and which would succeed.

> Personally he felt very strongly about the question of German South West Africa. He thought that it differed entirely from any question that they had to decide in this conference, but he would be prepared to say that he was a supporter of the document handed in that morning, because he knew that, if the idea fructified, the League of Nations would consist mostly of the same people who were present there that day, who understood the position and who would not make it impossible for any mandatory to govern the country. That was why he said he would accept it.

76. Council of Ten, January 30, 1919, 3:30 P.M., ibid., pp. 797–803; Miller, *Drafting of the Covenant* II: 204–16; Lloyd George, *Peace Treaties*, I: 541–46.
77. Ibid., p. 542.

He called for a spirit of cooperation and compromise and sincerely hoped that the President would see fit to support Lloyd George's resolution which was the result of long and serious efforts.[78] Botha's conciliatory speech made a deep and memorable impression upon the President,[79] and the situation eased considerably.

Matters now moved rapidly toward agreement. Massey offered renewed assurances that he had not implied anything in the nature of a threat. Lloyd George then modified his earlier request that the President accept the Smuts resolution at once without qualification, and so commit himself to immediate distribution of the mandates upon the terms specified. Instead, he now proposed that this be taken as a provisional decision "subject to the right of reconsideration if the Covenant of the League as finally drafted did not fit in."[80] No formal vote was taken on the resolution, but at the suggestion of President Wilson it was agreed that a communique be issued stating that the Conference had arrived at a satisfactory provisional arrangement with regard to dealing with the German and Turkish territory outside Europe.[81] Implicitly, then, it was agreed that the Dominions would receive the territories in question as Class C mandates upon the terms specified.

At a subsequent meeting early in May, President Wilson confirmed that the tacit arrangement had settled the matter "to all intents and purposes . . . the mandate for German South West Africa should be given to South Africa, for New Guinea and the adjacent islands to Australia, for Samoa to New Zealand."[82] A formal resolution presented by Great Britain confirming these and the other mandates was adopted and published (with minor changes) on May 7, 1919.[83]

78. Council of Ten, January 30, 1919, 3:30 P.M., *Foreign Relations, 1919, The Paris Peace Conference* III: 800-2. South Africa repeatedly cited Botha's statement in the pleadings in the *South West Africa* cases, as an indication of the restricted nature of the commitment undertaken by South Africa. See, e.g., *SWA Pleadings* I: 222; II: 12, 119; VIII: 335, 347.

79. Lloyd George, *Peace Treaties*, I: 546.

80. Ibid., p. 546; Council of Ten, January 30, 1919, 3:30 P.M., *Foreign Relations, 1919, The Paris Peace Conference* III: 802; Miller, *Drafting of the Covenant* II: 215; Birdsall, *Versailles*, p. 73. Lloyd George's interpretation of the provisional nature of the decision was quite different from that which the President had suggested at the morning session. According to the President, the decision was a mere "precursor of agreement," and thus the whole issue would be open to reconsideration upon creation of the League. Lloyd George, on the other hand, implied that the agreement was the sum total of the matter and would only be modified to the extent that it would be necessary to fit it in with the Covenant of the League. Birdsall, mistakenly, it is submitted, equates the two interpretations.

81. Council of Ten, January 30, 1919, 3:30 P.M. *Foreign Relations, 1919, The Paris Peace Conference* III: 816.

82. Council of Four, May 5, 1919, 11 A.M., ibid., V: 472-73. Note omission of any reference to the islands to be mandated to Japan. This omission was probably deliberate. See discussion, above, pp. 17-19, on Wilson's attitude toward Japan.

83. Council of Four, May 7, 1919, 4:15 P.M., *Foreign Relations, 1919, The Paris Peace Conference* V: 507-8.

## THE NATURE OF THE COMPROMISE

Wilson's acceptance of the Class C compromise in the Council of Ten ensured that the principle of international accountability would have universal application in the postwar colonial settlement. This principle was confirmed for even the most backward German colony, with no exceptions allowed for considerations of contiguity, security, common economic interest, or advantages of administrative unity. In this respect the mandates system represented a new creation of a genre previously unknown in international relations. As Beer records in Temperley, "The experience of the past affords no counterpart to the Mandatory System. . . . What sharply distinguishes the Mandate System from all such international arrangements of the past, is the unqualified right of intervention possessed by the League of Nations."[84] All previous commitments undertaken by states with reference to colonial areas simply amounted to pious declarations of intention. There was no set procedure or form for checking on violations of the commitments, and only other states, parties to the original agreement, were individually entitled under international law to raise the matter with the offending state. The mandates system was unique in that it linked defined obligations in international law with a continuing international organization which was empowered to supervise the operation of the system and to ensure that the legal obligations were faithfully observed.

The compromise agreement firmly established the principle of international accountability, but the question remained, to what extent had it actually incorporated the principle of self-determination and how far had it gone in barring future annexation of the respective territories.[85] The compromise document itself did not (in contrast to previous formulations) enunciate the principle of self-determination in any clear

84. Temperley, *Peace Conference of Paris*, II: 236.
85. At a later date, further questions would be posed with respect to the nature and content of international accountability:

First, was it an obligation owed exclusively to a specific international organization, namely, the League of Nations, or was it owed to the organized international community in the abstract, so that substitution of one international organization for the other would not affect the basic obligation of the mandatory?

Second, was there an obligation on the part of the mandatory power to hold itself accountable to each and every member state individually or was there responsibility only to the League of Nations (or the United Nations) in its organizational capacity?

Third, did the principle of international accountability entail a right on the part of the international organization to prescribe standards binding on the mandatory power for the administration of the territory?

Lastly, did the function of international supervision carry with it an implied right to revoke the mandate in the event of material breach by the mandatory power of its obligations under the mandate.

But these questions only assumed actual significance after the League of Nations had ceased to exist. See below, chaps. IX, X, XI, and XII.

or categorical terms. It certainly did not postulate independence as the definite goal of all mandates. Only paragraph 4 contained a reference to independence, by describing the A mandates as having "reached a stage of development where their existence as independent nations can be provisionally recognized." Otherwise, the purpose or design of the mandates system was dealt with in a series of broad rhetorical and imprecise phrases, such as: "peoples not yet able to stand by themselves"; "the well-being and development of such peoples form a sacred trust of civilization"; "securities for the performance of this trust," etc. Nor was the provision in the Class C mandates allowing administration as "integral portions of [the Mandatory's] territory" clearly defined. It was evident that the draftsmen had purposely avoided using any precise legal language for fear that too much or too little might be committed. The vague phraseology allowed for a variety of different, and even conflicting, interpretations. Whereas to some it represented a pledge to promote self-government for all peoples, black as well as white, to others it merely instituted a more effective device for protecting the native welfare from specific abuses. The latter restricted concept of the mandates system was oft expressed by Lloyd George during meetings of the Council of Ten. In his view it would not amount to much more than the international obligations already incumbent upon colonial powers as a result of earlier international treaties. He did not consider that involvement of the League would very radically affect the colonial set-up. The Prime Minister in fact frequently declared that the mandates system was already basically in effect in British colonial practice, with its enlightened outlook regarding native welfare. The final version of Article 22 of the Covenant of the League of Nations did nothing to clarify the matter, since the ambiguous phraseology was faithfully preserved throughout all discussions.

The compromise document accepted provisionally on January 30, 1919, was taken up on February 8 by the Commission on the League of Nations for insertion in the Covenant.[86] The draft introduced by General Smuts was identical with the text of the compromise document, except for the elimination of two introductory paragraphs and the addition of two supplementary paragraphs at the end. The latter two were what later became paragraphs 8 and 9 of Article 22. The first of these paragraphs empowered the League Council to define "the degree of authority, control, or administration" of the Mandatory if this was not "previously agreed upon by the High Contracting Parties."[87] This

86. See Miller, *Drafting of the Covenant* I: 185–90; II: 271–76.
87. Ibid., I: 111; II: 275. Subsequently, the term, "High Contracting Parties" was replaced by "Members of the League." Ibid., p. 680. Whether or not this change signified a

paragraph was derived from clause 6 of the original Smuts Plan and had its counterpart in Wilson's various Paris drafts. However, in contrast to these earlier texts, paragraph 8 of Article 22 did not reserve "complete power of supervision" to the League, nor did it refer to the possibility of League substitution of one Mandatory for another. The second paragraph provided for the establishment of "a Mandatory Commission to receive and examine the annual reports . . . and to assist the League in ensuring the observance of the terms of all Mandates."[88]

The deliberations in the Commission on the League of Nations reveal that Wilson and the British Empire delegates were primarily concerned with one thing—preserving intact both the substance and form of the compromise agreement concluded in the Council of Ten. When Mr. Orlando (Italy) and Mr. Bourgeois (France) suggested certain amendments to the text, President Wilson (supported by Lord Cecil) emphasized "that General Smuts' text was based upon a decision of the Conference of the five Powers."[89] The only significant (if small) changes that were accepted were designed to restore the original compromise to its exact earlier text. The word "yet" which Smuts had now dropped from the phrase "peoples not *yet* able to stand for themselves" was reinserted.[90] And the word "if" which Smuts had now included into the phrase "as *if* integral portions" (of the Mandatory's territory) was dropped from the Class C paragraph, since it was said that it had not figured there in the original agreement, and, in effect, modified it. At the same time, an amendment proposed by Mr. Vesnitch, the

---

substantive change in meaning was an issue of contention in the subsequent 1962 and 1966 judgments. See below, pp. 40–42.

88. Miller, *Drafting of the Covenant* II: 275. The latter part of this draft provision was retained intact throughout all the readings of the Covenant, but was changed by Hurst and Miller in the text which they presented to the Drafting Committee on March 31, 1919, to read: "and to advise the Council on all matters relating to the observance of the mandates" (the final form). No explanation is given for this substitution; but by its terms the revised text modifies the power of the Commission and tones down the spirit of compulsion in supervision, which the previous version seemed to reflect. This writer has not found any reference to the significance of this modification in any of the judgments or separate opinions in the 1962 or 1966 *South West Africa* cases, nor in the extensive pleadings in the case. Curiously enough, South Africa even while adverting to the text of the relevant basic instruments as evidence against the alleged authority of the supervisory body to set binding standards for the administration of the mandate (see, e.g., *SWA Pleadings* IX: 591–97), failed to make anything of the above-mentioned drafting change (or even to make any reference at all to paragraph 9 of Article 22).

In any event, the modification in wording would appear to lend some weight to the view of the 1966 Court that the idea of compulsion was quite alien to the constitution and operation of the mandates system, and would tend to confirm the view of that Court that the provision for an adjudicatory clause in the mandates was not designed to impart compulsory supervisory power to the Court. See below, chaps. IX, X, and XI.

89. Miller, *Drafting of the Covenant* II: 272.

90. Ibid., p. 306. For an analysis of the significance of this change see John F. Crawford, "South West Africa: Mandate Termination in Historical Perspective," *Columbia Journal of Transnational Law* VI (1967): 95 n. 15. See also separate opinion of Judge de Castro in *Namibia Opinion* (1971): 207–8.

Serbian representative, designed expressly to facilitate the complete emancipation of the mandated peoples and their admission to the League was not accepted.[91]

The Commission was obviously not prepared to accept any changes which would either strengthen or weaken the ideals incorporated in the text or that might even attempt to spell them out. The vague general ideals enunciated in the compromise agreement satisfied all parties, and it would be a precarious undertaking to introduce any modifications. As Smuts is reported to have said to Makino (Japan): "If you pull out a single plank, the whole edifice, miserable as it is, will come crashing down."[92] This warning was heeded by the Commission and the compromise document was confirmed.

In summary, then, Article 22 of the League of Nations Covenant establishing the mandates system passed through the following stages until it reached its final form in 1919. In early 1918, Wilson and Lloyd George postulated the principle of self-determination in the settlement of the colonial problem. They did not, however, link that principle with the proposed League, and so the concept of international accountability was not yet born. It was in the respective works of Smuts and Beer that the principle of international accountability to a going world organization was first clearly enunciated. But neither Smuts, nor even Beer, regarded the proposed mandates system as capable of universal application to the former German colonies. Smuts, in fact, expressly excluded the African colonies from the proposed mandates system, since he considered the inhabitants of those territories completely remote from the exercise of self-determination. Wilson adopted the Smuts plan, but universalized it—with confirmation of the principle of self-determination for even the most backward German colony. Smuts and the other Dominion ministers then recognized that they could not obtain their respective territories totally free of international obligations. But if the mandates principle was to be thus generalized, then it would have to have a variable content with a graded system of man-

91. Ibid., I:188–90; II: 273. The text of the amendment read as follows: "The Mandatory Commission may also, when it shall deem the time proper, suggest that the independence of any such people may be proclaimed and recognized with a view to the eventual admission of such people as a member of the League." Ibid., I: 188.

92. Stephen Bonsal, *Unfinished Business* (New York: Doubleday, Doran, 1944), p. 36. Bonsal's is the only verbatim record of that meeting in existence, since Miller's record merely presents the minutes. According to Bonsal, Smuts, in presenting the mandates draft article, apologized for the ambiguity and lack of clarity, saying: "We admit that the original purpose with which we set out upon our task is not easily recognizable, but upon patient scrutiny you will find that it is there and that while it may not be an ideal solution, it is, I can assure you, the best that your delegates will agree to at this junction in world history." Ibid., p. 35. Bonsal notes that Wilson was quite pleased with Smuts's performance. "He is not so insistent now upon details as he was a few weeks ago. He is pinning his faith to the cooling-off influences of time and the interpretive work of the League." Ibid., p. 36.

dates, in which Class C mandates would be as close to annexation as one can go without formal annexation. This meant that the League could no longer be clothed with absolute power over the mandates. Earlier references to the League as the ultimate reversionary would have to be dropped and Wilson's specific proposals regarding a possible substitution of Mandatories would likewise have to be omitted. Moreover, the goals and purposes would have to be so worded that for the Class A mandates independence would be assumed, while for the Class C mandates a process of ultimate absorption into the metropolitan country would be envisaged. This meant that the mandates article could no longer postulate the principle of self-determination as a definitive goal. The earlier reference to self-determination would have to be omitted. A skillfully drafted document, which was to imply different things for different situations, was what finally emerged as Article 22. Starting off with self-determination without international accountability, it had finished up as international accountability without self-determination (as an express goal).

Article 22 had gone through a process, aptly described by Hudson, as one in which "it is sometimes less profitable to seek clarity than to arrive at acceptable ambiguity."[93] The resultant wording could satisfy annexationists and internationalists simultaneously; indeed, this was its purpose. As a result, to Hughes, Australia was obtaining a 999 year lease on New Guinea;[94] and to Smuts, "in effect the relations between the South West Protectorate and the Union amount to annexation in all but name";[95] while to President Wilson, the mandates system represented "the universal application of a principle . . . of Colonies [being] lifted into the sphere of complete self-government."[96] The extent to

93. Manley O. Hudson, *The Permanent Court of International Justice, 1920–1942* (New York: Macmillan, 1943), p. 229.

94. See above, p. 29. In a memorandum dated May 5, 1919, to Colonel House, Hughes referred to the differences between the various mandates. "Whereas a Mandate under Class 1 looks to the mandated country being ultimately 'able to stand alone' the Mandate under Class 3 provides for the mandated territory being administered as an 'integral portion of the territory' of the Mandatory, and looks to its ultimate incorporation by the free will of its inhabitants." Miller, *Diary* IX: 291, Doc. 936.

95. P.M.C., Min. II (1922), Annex 6, p. 92. In similar vein, Lord Balfour subsequently referred to mandates as "self imposed limitations by the conquerors on the sovereignty which they obtained over conquered territory." Cited in Wright, *Mandates*, p. 62, n. 115.

96. Plenary Sess., February 14, 1919, *Foreign Relations, 1919, The Paris Peace Conference* III: 214. See also Miller, *Drafting of the Covenant* II: 564. At a subsequent meeting of the Council of Four, Wilson said: "The whole theory of mandates is not the theory of permanent subordination. It is the theory of development, of putting upon the mandatory the duty of assisting in the development of the country under mandate, in order that it may be brought to a capacity for self-government and self-dependence which for the time being it has not reached, and that therefore the countries under mandate are candidates, so to say, for full membership in the family of nations." Council of Four, May 17, 1919, 4:30 P.M., *Foreign Relations, 1919, The Paris Peace Conference* V: 700.

Notwithstanding the thesis presented in the text regarding the nature of the mandates compromise ultimately worked out, it may be noted that Smuts is reported by Bonsal to have

which either interpretation would prevail was left to be determined by the future operation of the system.

---

presented the compromise to the Conference in the following very Wilsonian terms: "If you give your sanction to our work you will demonstrate that world public opinion is in favor of the ultimate self-government of all peoples, without distinction as to race, religion, or color, or previous condition of servitude. It also provides for a careful supervision and scrutiny as to the way in which the mandates are exercised." *Unfinished Business*, p. 35.

Remarkably enough, Ethiopia and Liberia, in presenting their case against the application of apartheid to South West Africa before the International Court in the *South West Africa* cases, made no reference to the foregoing statement.

# OPERATION
# OF THE LEAGUE
# MANDATES SYSTEM

## ESTABLISHMENT OF THE SYSTEM

The League Covenant came into force as part of the Treaty of Versailles on January 10, 1920. Article 22 of the Covenant provided for the establishment of the mandates system, but it did not of itself bring that system into operation; nor did it spell out the detailed form of administration applicable to each mandate. According to paragraph 8 of Article 22, it was for the League Council to define "the degree of authority, control, or administration" to be exercised by the Mandatory in each case, if this had not previously been agreed upon by "the Members of the League." The reference to "the Members of the League" in this special context clearly meant the members of the Supreme Allied Council.[1] In effect, the provision envisaged alternative procedures for promulgating the mandates. Either they would be constituted in the form of treaties, with the members of the Supreme Council and the mandatory power as parties, or they would be formulated by an act of the League Council. The Milner (or Mandates) Commission, which met in London in July 1919, drew up draft treaties for the mandates, but these were never published or adopted in that precise form, because a number of governments objected to certain terms in the Mandates.[2] In the end,

---

1. See report of M. Hymans, L. of N., Official Journal (1920): 338. Apparently the authors of the Covenant had at first intended inserting the terms of the mandates into the treaties of peace. Moreover, it was thought that only the Principal Allied and Associated Powers would be the original members of the League. Ibid. See also Quincy Wright, *Mandates Under the League of Nations* (Chicago: University of Chicago Press, 1930), p. 43; *The Mandates System: Origin—Principles—Application*, League of Nations Publication, 1945.VI.A.1 (Geneva: 1945), p. 20; *SWA Pleadings* II: 19; and separate opinion of Judge Jessup, *SWA Judgment* (1962): 390–91.

2. See *Foreign Relations, 1919, The Paris Peace Conference* VI: 649ff. The most serious objection was that of the Japanese, who protested the absence of an "open-door" requirement from the Class C mandates—a fact which would operate as a bar to Japanese immigration and

the two procedures were somewhat coalesced: while basic agreement was earlier reached among the Allied Powers, it was the League Council which issued the Mandates in the form of Council resolutions after making certain modifications in the draft proposals.[3]

The Class C mandates, including the one for South West Africa, were confirmed by the League Council on December 17, 1920. The South West Africa Mandate, composed of a four-paragraph preamble and seven articles, defined the scope of authority South Africa was to exercise in the territory and the obligations incumbent upon it as the mandatory power.[4]

In the preamble, the following consideranda were recited:

1) that by Article 119 of the Treaty of Versailles, "Germany renounced in favour of the Principal Allied and Associated Powers all her rights over her oversea possessions," including South West Africa;

2) that the Principal Allied and Associated Powers had agreed that, in accordance with Article 22 of the Covenant, a mandate over South West Africa be awarded to the Union of South Africa and that they had "proposed that the Mandate should be formulated in the following terms";

3) that the Union government had agreed to accept the mandate and had undertaken "to exercise it on behalf of the League of Nations in accordance with the following provisions"; and

4) that by Article 22, paragraph 8, of the Covenant it was provided "that the degree of authority, control or administration to be exercised by the Mandatory not having been previously agreed upon by the Members of the League, shall be explicitly defined by the Council."

On the basis of these consideranda, it was stated that the Council "confirming the said Mandate, defines its terms as follows":

In the *South West Africa* cases of 1962 and 1966, differences of opinion between majority and minority judges (in particular between Judge Jessup, on the one hand, and Judges Spender and Fitzmaurice, on the other) centered in part on the proper interpretation to be accorded to the Mandate's fourth preambular paragraph (reproducing, as it does, Article 22 [8] of the Covenant) and to the manner in which the Mandate agreement for South West Africa was finally adopted. At stake was the application of Article 37 of the Statute of the Interna-

---

trade. Despite the Japanese efforts, the "open door" was not incorporated into any of the Class C mandates. See Wright, *Mandates*, p. 478.

3. For a discussion of the significance of the coalescence of these procedures, see below, pp. 40–42.

4. For the full text of the South West Africa Mandate, see Appendix II.

tional Court of Justice relied upon by Ethiopia and Liberia to confer jurisdiction on the Court. By its terms, this article requires that jurisdiction be based on a "treaty or convention in force," and one of the matters in dispute was whether the South West Africa Mandate had *ever* qualified as a "treaty or convention." As a corollary to this point, there was too the problem of identifying the parties to the treaty in question.

Judges Spender and Fitzmaurice contended, *inter alia*, that promulgation of the Mandates in the form of League Council resolutions signified the abandonment of the attempt (by the Milner Commission) to embody the Mandates in treaties (the first alternative mentioned in paragraph 8 of Article 22 of the Covenant). Instead, the second alternative mentioned in paragraph 8—definition of the mandate terms by the League Council—was adopted; and this fact is attested to by the Mandate's preamble, which stresses that the terms of the Mandate had not "been previously agreed upon by the Members of the League." Thus, the Mandates were *ab initio* not "treaties," but merely quasi-legislative acts of the League Council. And "the Members of the League," who, in the first alternative were to be parties to the mandate, were in the end not given such a role. In brief, the "treaty" requirement of Article 37 remained unfulfilled, and the article could thus not operate to confer jurisdiction on the Court.[5]

Judge Jessup, on the other hand, argued that the original intention for an agreement between the Allied Powers was never abandoned. The act of the League in passing a resolution on the constitution of the mandate was merely a formal ratification of the prior agreement reached between the respective parties to the mandate, i.e., the Allied Powers and the Mandatory. There was, therefore, a fully valid treaty in existence before, and independent of, any action of the League Council. In accordance with this interpretation, the Council "defined" the terms of the Mandate only in the sense that it "made definite," and gave approval to, the prior agreements.

As for the term "the Members of the League" both in Article 22 and in the Mandate's preamble, this was a mere substitute for the term "the High Contracting Parties" which had originally appeared in paragraph 8 of Article 22 of the Covenant.[6] In both cases the expression referred to the Principal Allied and Associated Powers who were

5. See *SWA Judgment* (1962): 482-503. In 1966, the recital in the Mandate's preamble of the fact that the terms of the Mandate had "not . . . been previously agreed upon by the Members of the League," was cited in the judgment as evidence that the individual members of the League were never intended to play a separate supervisory role in the functioning of the mandate. Supervision was exclusively a matter for the appropriate League organs in their corporate capacity. *SWA Judgment* (1966): 26-27. Judge Jessup vigorously challenged this interpretation of the Mandate's preamble. Ibid., pp. 394-95.

6. See above, chap. I, n. 87.

expected to be the original parties to the Covenant and the original members of the League. The term, therefore, bore no relationship to the individual members of the League. In any event, the Mandate, exclusive of the action of the Council, was a distinct treaty within the terms of Article 37 of the Court's Statute.[7]

The operative part of the mandate resolution, as noted earlier, consisted of seven articles.

Article 1 identified the territory over which the mandate was conferred.

Article 2, in its first paragraph, declared that "the Mandatory shall have full power of administration and legislation over the territory . . . as an integral portion of the Union of South Africa . . . and may apply the laws of the Union . . . to the territory." (These terms, it will be noted, closely followed the language of Article 22 of the Covenant.) The second paragraph committed South Africa to "promote to the utmost the material and moral well-being and the social progress of the inhabitants of the territory."

This juxtaposition of the enabling power alongside the commitment to promote the welfare of the inhabitants to the utmost gave rise in the subsequent litigation on apartheid in the *South West Africa* cases to the question of what was the exact legal relationship between these two sets of provisions. Was one part of the article subordinated to the other, and what was the resulting legal situation?[8] Both parties to the litigation conceded that the power granted was subordinate to the purpose for which it was granted. South Africa, as will be seen below,[9] preferred to rest its case for apartheid on the claim that this policy in fact constituted *fulfillment* of the purposes of the mandate, not the negation thereof.

Article 3 committed the Mandatory to prohibit the slave trade in the territory, to control the traffic in arms, and to prohibit the supply of intoxicating spirits to the natives.

Article 4 barred the military training of the natives other than for police or local defense purposes. It also forbade the establishment in the territory of military or naval bases and the erection of fortifications.

7. See *SWA Judgment* (1962): 387–401. The Court adopted reasoning somewhat similar to that of Judge Jessup, but based itself more on the preamble of the Mandate than on the *travaux préparatoires* in reaching the conclusion that the Mandate was as much an agreement or treaty as it was a declaration. Ibid., pp. 330–31.

8. See question No. 10 posed by Judge Fitzmaurice to Applicants and Respondent on May 7, 1965. *SWA Pleadings* VIII: 32–33.

9. See pp. 228–37.

Article 5 guaranteed freedom of conscience and worship and obliged the Mandatory to permit all missionaries to enter and prosecute their calling in the territory.

Article 6 required the Mandatory to make an annual report to the League Council "to the satisfaction of the Council, containing full information with regard to the territory, and indicating the measures taken to carry out the obligations assumed under Articles 2, 3, 4, and 5."

Article 7 contained a clause requiring Council consent for any modification of the terms of the Mandate. It also contained an adjudicatory clause which committed the Mandatory to accept the jurisdiction of the Permanent Court of International Justice in respect of "any dispute whatever" which might arise between the Mandatory and another Member of the League "relating to the interpretation or the application of the provisions of the Mandate," if such dispute could not be settled by negotiation.

It is appropriate to note that this adjudicatory or compromissory clause arose out of a United States draft proposal which originally contained two parts. The first part was almost identical to the final version, just outlined. The second part, strikingly novel, conferred a right upon "citizens of States Members of the League" to bring claims concerning infractions of their individual rights—either economic or religious—before the Court for decision. During the Milner Commission discussions, opposition was expressed to the conferment of adjudicatory rights directly upon individuals, and so the second paragraph was changed to read: "The Members of the League . . . will also be entitled on behalf of their subjects . . . to refer claims" etc. Ultimately, however, this latter paragraph failed to be incorporated in the adjudicatory clause of any of the Mandates—with the single exception of the Tanganyika Mandate. All the rest, including the South West Africa Mandate, contained only the first paragraph, relating to inter-state disputes.

Subsequently, in the two phases of the *South West Africa* cases, the correct interpretation to be accorded to the origins and historical development of the adjudicatory clause became a focal matter of contention between members of the Court. Judge Jessup, on the one hand, pointed to the Tanganyika clause as evidence that a principle of judicial supervision was instituted under the Mandate. Since the second paragraph of the Tanganyika clause empowered a state to initiate action in defense of the economic or material interests of its nationals, the first paragraph must have meant something more; it must have embraced the right of a state to bring an action in reference to the general conduct of the mandate, in matters affecting the welfare of the inhabitants.[10] On the other hand, Judges Spender and Fitzmaurice in 1962[11] and the judgment of the Court in 1966[12] dismissed the evidentiary value of the Tanganyika clause, which, they claimed, resulted merely from a drafting quirk.[13] That clause could not overweigh the substantial evidence pointing to the absence of any grant of supervisory power to individual states under the Mandates. The adjudicatory clause, it was said, had arisen only in conjunction with the enunciation of economic and religious rights to be accorded states, Members of the League, and their nationals. So far from endowing individual states with the power to invoke judicial supervision of the mandate, the clause was designed for the strictly limited function of protecting the material or economic interests of states. In his 1966 dissent, Judge Jessup, on the basis of an extensive analysis of the *travaux préparatoires*, vigorously contested the foregoing interpretation of the historical record.[14]

While the Class C mandates were, as noted earlier, confirmed by the League Council on December 17, 1920, formulation of the remaining mandates (Classes A and B) was somewhat delayed. Certain differences, primarily those arising from the failure of the United States to join the League, needed to be ironed out; and the various mandates were only confirmed during 1922 and 1923.[15] Notwithstanding this delay, the Permanent Mandates Commission contemplated by paragraph 9 of Article 22 of the Covenant, was already constituted by the Council in December 1920, and began operation in October 1921.

The role of the Permanent Mandates Commission was "to receive and examine the annual reports of the Mandatories and to advise the

10. *SWA Judgment* (1962): 431; *SWA Judgment* (1966): 356-67.
11. *SWA Judgment* (1962): 554-60. See also the remarks of Judge Winiarski, ibid., p. 454.
12. *SWA Judgment* (1966): 43-44.
13. South Africa, in the course of its pleadings, sought to discount the evidentiary value of the Tanganyika clause in a different manner. The existence of a two-paragraph compromissory clause in the Tanganyika Mandate, argued South Africa, provided no evidence that Article 7(2) of the South West Africa Mandate related of necessity to the "general conduct" of the mandate. The "Tanganyika clause" related to claims brought by states *on behalf of their nationals*, while the counterpart to Article 7(2) of the Mandate related to claims involving the *rights of states themselves.* But nowhere was there any evidence which would necessitate attributing to the latter clause a wider ambit of operation so as to cover "general conduct" provisions as well. *SWA Pleadings* II: 191-92.
14. *SWA Judgment* (1966): 356-67.
15. See, generally, League of Nations, *The Mandates System*, pp. 20-21; Wright, *Mandates*, pp. 43-63, 109-19; H. Duncan Hall, *Mandates, Dependencies and Trusteeship* (Washington, D.C.: Carnegie Endowment for International Peace, 1948), pp. 135-57; H.W.V. Temperley (ed.), *A History of the Peace Conference of Paris*, 6 vols. (London: Frowde, Hodder and Stoughton, 1920-24), VI, chap. VI. The Mandate for Iraq, it might be noted, took the form of a treaty concluded between the United Kingdom and the King of Iraq, which was communicated to the League of Nations.

Council on all matters relating to the observance of the mandates." In point of fact, the task of supervision was by and large carried out by the Permanent Mandates Commission. The Council rarely departed from the recommendations or attitudes adopted by the Commission.

Under its constitution, the Commission was composed of ten members.[16] A majority of the members had to be nationals of nonmandatory powers, i.e., only four out of the ten could be nationals of mandatory powers. Since nationals of Britain, France, Belgium, and Japan were always on the Commission, this meant that no nationals of the remaining three mandatory powers (Australia, New Zealand, and South Africa) ever sat on the Commission. But, in any case, members of the Commission were appointed by the League Council on the basis of personal competence and expertise and were in no way the representatives of their respective governments.[17]

## MEANS OF SUPERVISION[18]

The scope of League supervision of the mandates was outlined in 1920 by Council adoption of a report which referred to the issue in the following terms:

> What will be the responsibility of the mandatory Power before the League of Nations, or in other words, in what direction will the League's right of control be exercised? Is the Council to content itself with ascertaining that the mandatory Power has remained within the limits of the powers which were conferred upon it, or is it to ascertain also whether the mandatory Power has made a good use of these powers and whether its administration has conformed to the interests of the native population?
>
> It appears . . . that the wider interpretation should be adopted . . . [and] the Council should also examine the question of the whole administration. In this matter the Council will obviously have to display extreme prudence so that the exercise of its right of

16. Initially there were only nine members, but in 1927 a German member was added to the Commission. Earlier, in 1924, Professor Rappard of Switzerland was appointed as an extraordinary member. On the constitution and composition of the Permanent Mandates Commission, see Temperley, *Peace Conference of Paris*, VI: 512–14; Wright, *Mandates*, pp. 137–43; League of Nations, *The Mandates System*, pp. 35–37; Hall, *Mandates, Dependencies and Trusteeship*, pp. 178–84.

17. With a view to ensuring genuine detachment, members of the Commission were paid for their services, granted permanent tenure, and forbidden to hold any governmental positions. See ibid., pp. 177–80.

18. See generally, League of Nations, *The Mandates System*, pp. 33–50; Wright, *Mandates*, Chap. VI; Hall, *Mandates, Dependencies and Trusteeship*, chaps. XI, XII, and XIII.

It might be noted that the Mandates Section of the League Secretariat played an important role in the system of supervision by supplementing the general information available to the Permanent Mandates Commission in regard to each mandate. See on this point William E. Rappard, "The Mandates and the International Trusteeship Systems," *Political Science Quarterly* LXI (1946): 411. And see the citation of Rappard's views in the dissenting opinion of Judge Jessup, *SWA Judgment* (1966): 405–6.

control should not provoke any justifiable complaints, and thus increase the difficulties of the task undertaken by the Mandatory Power.[19]

The wider ambit of League supervision was fulfilled through the following procedures:

1) **Annual reports.** These reports covered the complete administration of the mandatory power, indicating at the same time the measures taken to fulfill the obligations assumed under the mandate. A lengthy questionnaire (60 questions) formed the framework of the report and indicated to the Commission the relative progress made annually in any given field. An attempt in 1926 to expand the number of questions from 60 to 300 was rejected by the mandatory powers. Sir Austen Chamberlain, foreign secretary of Great Britain, objected to the "immense" questionnaire which, he said, was "infinitely more detailed, infinitely more inquisitorial than the questionnaire which had hitherto been in force. . . . It seemed to him . . . that there was a tendency on the part of the Commission to extend its authority to a point where the government would no longer be vested in the mandatory Power but in the Mandates Commission. He was sure that was not the intention of the Covenant."[20] A subsequent British note (speaking for the Dominions as well) charged that the proposal was "based on a misconception of the duties and responsibilities of the Commission and the Council." It was not for the Council "to check and examine every detail of administration. . . . Its duty [was] to see that the administration . . . [was] conducted generally in accordance with the ideas enunciated in Article 22."[21]

2) **Questioning of accredited representatives of mandatory powers.** When the annual report of a particular mandatory power was to be examined by the Commission, an accredited representative of that power would be present to answer questions, to clear up obscure or doubtful points, and generally to make good any deficiencies in the written information. In time, the practice developed of having the actual administrator of the territory in question available during the examination of the annual report. This facilitated the work of the Commission considerably, and also enabled the administrator to appreciate the spirit animating the activities of the Commission.

Furthermore, in accordance with Article 4, paragraph 5, of the Covenant, mandatory powers who were not Council members, were standardly invited to send representatives to Council meetings at which

19. Report by M. Hymans of August 5, 1920. L. of N., Assembly Doc. 20/48/161.
20. L. of N., Official Journal (1926): 1233.
21. Ibid., p. 1651.

matters relating to their mandates were discussed. It is to be noted that by force of Article 5 of the Covenant, which prescribed that decisions of the Council required "the agreement of all the Members of the League represented at the meeting," the mandatory power would, in effect, have a veto over any Council decision.[22] Such a veto power was, however, never put to the test, since all decisions concerning mandates were in practice adopted unanimously.

3) **Petitions.** The right of petition was not expressly referred to in either the Covenant or the texts of the Mandates. It was first instituted by the Council on January 31, 1923, with the adoption of Procedure in Respect of Petitions.[23] In accordance with this Procedure any petition reaching the Commission from the inhabitants of one of the mandated territories could be considered only if it was transmitted by the mandatory power concerned. Petitions emanating from sources outside the territory, if not frivolous, were to be communicated to the mandatory government, which had six months within which to make any comments it thought desirable. The petitions not only served the democratic function of allowing for expression of grievances with request for redress but also provided the Commission with an additional and valuable source of information.

However, when the Commission attempted to expand the procedure so as to allow for oral hearings by petitioners, the proposal was unanimously rejected by the mandatory powers. "They pointed out that, with such a procedure—which would involve the hearing at the same time of a representative of the mandatory Power—the parties would, in fact, be engaged in a controversy before the Commission and that any procedure which would seem to transform the Commission

22. See the separate opinion of Judge Klaestad in *Voting Procedure Opinion* (1955): 85–86. But cf. the views of Judge Lauterpacht, ibid., pp. 98–106. For a critical comment on Judge Lauterpacht's views, see R. Y. Jennings, "The International Court's Advisory Opinion on the Voting Procedure on Questions Concerning South-West Africa," *Transactions of the Grotius Society* XLII (1956): 90–92. It should be noted, however, that Judge Lauterpacht himself was not free of doubts in the matter. See *Voting Procedure Opinion* (1955): 105–6 and 123.

In both the 1962 and 1966 phases of the *South West Africa* cases the Court accepted that the mandatory power possessed a right of veto in the period of the League. *SWA Judgment* (1962): 336–37; *SWA Judgment* (1966): 31, 44–45, and 46. See also the dissenting opinion of Judge Wellington Koo, ibid., pp. 218–19.

In the 1971 Namibia proceedings, the unanimity rule was cited by South Africa as further evidence that the power to revoke a mandate never resided in the League Council. *Namibia Pleadings* I: 580 and n. 1; II: 313–16. Judge Fitzmaurice in his dissenting opinion accepted this line of reasoning. *Namibia Opinion* (1971): 272–73. The Court majority, however, denied the strength of the argument. Ibid., p. 49. See also the comment of President Zafrulla Khan, ibid., pp. 59–60 and the full discussion by Judge de Castro, ibid., pp. 199–207.

For scholarly consideration of the veto question (prior to delivery of the Namibia Opinion) see John Dugard, "The Revocation of the Mandate for South West Africa," *AJIL* LXII (1968): 89–91 and the authorities cited therein.

23. L. of N., Official Journal (1923): 300. L. of N. Doc. C.44(I).M.73.1923.VI. Reproduced in Hall, *Mandates, Dependencies and Trusteeship*, Annex VIII, p. 314.

into a court of law would be inconsistent with the very nature of the mandatory system."[24] In short, the mandatory powers felt their prestige would suffer from being placed on an equal footing with petitioners as adversaries. In recognition of this vehement opposition, the Council, in 1927, expressed the opinion that there was "no occasion to modify the procedure which has hitherto been followed by the Commission."[25] This, however, was not regarded as barring any member of the Commission, individually and in his private capacity, from granting an interview to any person anxious to express a grievance in relation to a mandate.

Similar considerations to those which led to the rejection of the proposal for granting oral hearings to petitioners also operated against instituting a procedure for visits of inspection to the mandated territories. The question of on-site inspections as a regular procedure of investigation was never discussed by the League Council. (On a number of exceptional occasions, special commissions were appointed by the Council to investigate *in situ* a specific point in dispute.)[26] The Mandates Commission, however, in 1925, did discuss the matter. Most members, in theory, recognized the merit of a procedure for on-the-spot investigations. The British member, however, considered that such a proposal was "quite impracticable." "No mandatory Power could accept such a procedure," he claimed. "Its prestige would inevitably suffer, for the Commission or subcommittee would be in the position of a court of inquiry in which the mandatory Power was the defendant."[27]

The attitude of the mandatory powers on the question was never sought, probably out of advance recognition of the negative nature of any forthcoming reply.

## OBJECTIVES OF SUPERVISION

The general policy line followed by the Permanent Mandates Commission in its relationship with the mandatory powers was, in the words of a 1926 report, "one of supervision and of co-operation."[28] In examining the annual reports, the Commission felt obliged not only "to determine how far the principles of the Covenant and of the Mandates [had] been truly applied in the administration of the different territories" but

24. League of Nations, *The Mandates System*, p. 41. In contrast, Sir Frederick Lugard of the Commission argued: "I found it difficult to reconcile an attitude of complete impartiality with a denial of audience to a petitioner while hearing the representative of the Mandatory, unless there were special reasons for the denial." P.M.C., Min. IX (1926): 190.

25. L. of N., Official Journal (1927): 438.

26. League of Nations, *The Mandates System*, p. 45.

27. Ibid., p. 44.

28. P.M.C., Min. VIII (1926): 200.

also "to assist the mandatory Governments in carrying out the important and difficult tasks which they [were] accomplishing on behalf of the League."[29] This task required a careful balancing of both the faculty of inquiry and of praise, of modest (never sharp) criticism and commendation, and above all a recognition that it was the mandatory power and not the Commission that was confronted with the immediate problems of administration. As a result, the Commission basically advised, and only rarely made recommendations which had a bearing on the future.[30]

Essentially, three main objectives were fulfilled by the supervisory function of the Commission.[31]

1) **Protection of the native welfare.** The Commission was concerned with the political and moral education of the natives, the improvement of their living conditions (including the provision of health and educational facilities), and, in general, the protection of the interests of the native population. It also sought to ensure the freedom of the natives to retain their own customs (insofar as this was compatible with the Mandatory's "civilizing" mission). And it attempted to guard against violations of any of the specific prohibitions in the Mandate touching on native welfare.

2) **Protection of the interests of other member states.** This involved the Commission in ascertaining that the military status of the mandated territory was faithfully observed and that the right of entry and practice for missionaries of all denominations was maintained. Moreover, in the A and B mandates, the "open-door" guarantee in commercial and industrial matters required the Commission to make certain that the mandatory power was not taking undue advantage of its position to derive special benefits.

3) **Preservation of the legal status, integrity, and individuality of the territory as a distinct international entity.** There is little doubt that the action of the Commission in preserving the international status of the mandates through effective use of the instrumentality of international accountability, represents the most dramatic and far-reaching achievement of the whole mandates system. It ensured that the commonly awaited stage of formal annexation would not materialize. More significantly, however, by demonstrating the efficacy of a system of international accountability under the aegis of an international organization, it set the stage for the evolutionary development of the United Nations Trusteeship System and the ultimate emancipation of colonial territories.

29. Ibid.
30. Hall, *Mandates, Dependencies and Trusteeship*, p. 207.
31. See generally, League of Nations, *The Mandates System*, p. 50.

It has been justly observed that "had there been no Permanent Mandates Commission the disposition of the former German colonies would so unquestionably have been equivalent to annexation that the mandates system would no longer have been heard of. Only the devotion of the members of the Commission to the belief that there was something real and workable in this new idea . . . saved it from the role of a mere pious aspiration."[32] A review of some of the more notable events in the history of the Permanent Mandates Commission—with particular emphasis on South West Africa—amply demonstrates the truth of this observation and reveals how attentive the Commissioners were to the issue of native welfare and to possible infractions of the mandatory status of a territory.

In 1922 an uprising took place among the Bondelzwarts, a native tribe in South West Africa. The members of this tribe had become incensed at the imposition of an exorbitant dog tax designed to divert native tribesmen from hunting to rural work on white farms. Other grievances related to refusal to restore part of the tribe's traditional lands and the banishment of certain leaders from the tribe. In order to suppress the uprising the Administrator took the unusual step of dispatching planes to bomb the lager in which the natives had congregated. In the process, men, women, and children were killed. South Africa was called upon to furnish the Mandates Commission with a comprehensive report on the incident. South Africa instituted an investigation, but its report was considered inadequate by the Commission; it contained conflicting interpretations with no indication of the official South African view. It was also deemed too one-sided to allow the Commission to express an opinion as to whether the Administrator's measures of repression had been excessive. Nevertheless, after receiving supplementary written and oral testimony from the South African representative at Geneva, the majority of the Commission adopted an attitude critical of the Administrator in respect of the fundamental and immediate causes of the uprising. The Bondelzwarts, it was said, were "driven to exasperation" by real (if exaggerated) grievances against the white population, which the Administrator had failed to redress; and the final outbreak of hostilities stemmed from the Administrator's mishandling of negotiations to forestall violence. Moreover, the Commission was "unable to convince itself" that the "treatment of the natives" which lay at the root of their discontent was such as could be "justified in a territory under mandate." The Chairman of the Mandates Commission, in a separate statement, adopted an even more critical stance by charg-

32. Elizabeth van Maanen-Helmer, *The Mandates System in Relation to Africa and the Pacific Islands* (London: King, 1929), p. 203.

ing "that the Administration has pursued a policy of force rather than of persuasion, and, further, that this policy has always been conceived and applied in the interests of the colonists rather than in the interests of the natives." And, in his view, the principle established in the mandates, as opposed to the principle of general "colonial law," was the primacy of the interests of the natives.[33] (It should be noted that the thesis of the Chairman regarding the precedence of the interests of the natives over those of the white population was not acceptable to the majority of the Commission.)[34]

The Bondelzwarts episode demonstrated for the first time the authority of the League to call a mandatory power to account for events transpiring within the mandated territory. It confirmed that a mandate was not simply a colony under a different name; that the mandatory power was indeed answerable to the League for its treatment of the native population; and that international accountability might be a potent force in international affairs.[35]

The question of the application of color-bar legislation to South West Africa furnished yet another example of the Commission's vigilance regarding native welfare. Color-bar legislation, which restricted certain types of employment to whites, was of long standing in South Africa; and the Commission wished to know whether its application extended to South West Africa. In response to this question, the Administrator indicated briefly that a color bar was being observed, but only with regard to work done by the administration itself and the Railway Department.[36] In its report to the League Council, the Commission noted this reply and expressed its criticism in the following terms: "The Commission considers that this Act, the effect of which is to limit the occupations open to native and coloured workers and thus

33. For the report of the Mandates Commission and the separate statement of the chairman, M. Theodoli, see P.M.C., Min. III (1923): 290–96. For the subsequent discussion and resolution of the League Council, see L. of N., Official Journal (1924): 339–41.
The unfortunate plight of the Bondelzwarts and the Commission's handling of the issue is reviewed in detail in J. H. Wellington, *South West Africa and Its Human Issues* (Oxford: Clarendon Press, 1967), pp. 283–89. See also van Maanen-Helmer, *The Mandates System*, pp. 232–35; Freda White, *Mandates* (London: Jonathan Cape, 1926), pp. 136–40; Wright, *Mandates*, pp. 209–10; and I. Goldblatt, *History of South West Africa From the Beginning of the Nineteenth Century* (Cape Town: Juta, 1971), pp. 215–17.
34. P.M.C., Min. III (1923): 206–7.
35. It is illuminating, in this respect, to contrast South Africa's treatment of the Bondelzwart uprising with its subsequent handling of a clash with the Rehoboth tribe in South West Africa. In 1924–25, the Rehobothers seemed set on launching an armed revolt against the administration. A show of force coupled with patient handling of the dispute averted a major tragedy. Knowledge that the administration's action would be "scrutinized by the world body" presumably led to a more cautious and restrained policy. See Wellington, *South West Africa*, pp. 289–90. See also Wright, *Mandates*, p. 211; White, *Mandates*, pp. 140–41; and Goldblatt, *History of South West Africa*, p. 223.
36. P.M.C., Min. XIV (1928): 106.

place them at a disadvantage with white workers in the area under mandate, is based upon considerations which are not compatible with the principles laid down in the mandate."[37]

In reaction to this criticism, the Administrator, in a letter to the Commission dated November 19, 1928, indicated that a misunderstanding had taken place and that, in fact, the true position was as follows:

> The Colour Bar Act of the Union is not in force in South-West Africa. There is therefore no statutory colour bar. Owing, however, to the present low state of civilisation among the natives, no native is at present employed either by the Administration or by the Railway Department on work involving the risk of human life, such as driving a motor-car or working an engine. A certain colour bar is therefore being observed in practice, but it is certainly not a statutory enactment and is purely temporary, that is, until such time as the native is sufficiently advanced to be able to undertake this responsible work.
>
> I hope that this explanation will satisfy the Commission and remove all ground for the observation which it has made.[38]

It has been observed that South Africa, by this announcement, "admitted, albeit tacitly, that she did not believe the mandate authorized her to apply all her domestic policies to South West Africa."[39]

In addition to its concern for native welfare, the Commission was ever alert to any sign, in word or deed, which might imply that the mandatory power was treating the mandate as an incorporated part of its own state. When, in 1922, the South African Parliament passed a South West Africa Railways and Harbours Act which referred to the railways and harbours as being under the Union in "full dominion," the Commission called for an explanation of the term. The South African reply proved satisfactory to the Commission which, nonetheless, suggested amendment of the Act.[40] This was ultimately undertaken in 1930.

The Commission regularly insisted that the finances of the mandate and those of the mandatory power be kept separate and distinct.[41] This

---

37. Ibid., p. 275.

38. Ibid., p. 278.

39. R. W. Imishue, *South West Africa: An International Problem* (London: Pall Mall Press, 1965), p. 9.

Interestingly enough, Ethiopia and Liberia in their exhaustive pleadings in the *South West Africa* cases did not advert to this color-bar episode in the period of the League except once very obliquely. *SWA Pleadings* I: 122. They did not refer to the South African letter at all. Since the Applicants' case against apartheid was ultimately premised upon the capacity of the Permanent Mandates Commission to set binding standards for mandated territories, Applicants' complete failure to make anything of the material cited in the text is the more surprising.

40. P.M.C., Min. VI (1925): 63–64, 178.

41. Wright, *Mandates*, p. 214; van Maanen-Helmer, *The Mandates System*, p. 219.

was a corollary of the rule that all revenue and profits from the mandate must be used solely for the benefit of its inhabitants. In like manner, the Commission emphasized that the Mandatory did not possess title to public lands except in its capacity as mandatory power.[42] Similarly, the Commission insisted that the nationality status of inhabitants of a mandated territory be distinguished from that of the nationals of the mandatory power.[43] In each of these respects, the Commission ensured that the separate identity of the mandate would not be lost sight of.

Suggested changes in the constitutional regime of a mandate regularly called forth the firm opposition of the Mandates Commission. In 1933 the question of a closer administrative customs and fiscal union between the mandated territory of Tanganyika and the neighboring British colonies of Kenya and Uganda arose. As a result of the Commission's opposition, the British government announced it would not introduce any changes, since the time was "not yet ripe for the introduction of closer political or constitutional Union." The Commission took exception to this qualified concession to its stand. In a resolution, the Commission noted Britain's abandonment of its proposal, which would have had

> the effect of destroying or endangering for the future the existence of the mandatory territory as a distinct entity in international law.
>
> With reference to the expression "the time is not yet ripe," the Commission considers that [such] a ... union ... cannot be carried out as long as the present mandate is in force.
>
> It also considers ... that any measures tending during that period towards the *de facto* establishment of such "closer union" should be avoided.[44]

The constitutional relationship between South West Africa and the Union was another area in which the Permanent Mandates Commission acted to prevent any change in the status of a mandate.[45] (The discussions between the Commission and South Africa adumbrate, to some

42. Wright, *Mandates*, p. 447; van Maanen-Helmer, *The Mandates System*, p. 178. The League, however, never undertook to settle the intricate legal question, long debated in juristic circles, of the locus of sovereignty in mandated territories. An answer to this question was by no means essential to the successful operation of the mandates system. For a review of the various theories on the subject, see Wright, *Mandates*, pp. 319-39; L. Oppenheim, *International Law*, 2 vols., ed. H. Lauterpacht (8th ed.; London: Longmans, Green, 1955), I: 222, n. 5; Oral Statement of Mr. Kerno (United Nations), in *1950 Status Pleadings*, pp. 192-203.

43. Wright, *Mandates*, pp. 461-62; van Maanen-Helmer, *The Mandates System*, pp. 225-27.

44. P.M.C., Min. XXIII (1933): 189.

45. For divergent interpretations of what transpired, see *SWA Pleadings* I: 39-40, 231-34; II: 29-30; IV: 78-81, 252. See also *SWA Judgment* (1962): 337. For a fuller discussion of some of the events involved, see I. Goldblatt, *The Mandated Territory of South West Africa in Relation to the United Nations* (Cape Town: C. Struik, 1961), pp. 14-16.

degree, the subsequent controversy between South Africa and the United Nations over the possible incorporation of South West Africa into the Union.)

In 1925 the South African Parliament enacted the South West Africa Constitution Act which granted the white population of the territory a considerable measure of responsible government. A Legislative Assembly, composed of twelve elected and six nominated members, was constituted with powers to enact ordinances in matters of local concern, subject to the approval of the Union government. "Native affairs" and matters warranting a "national" policy, such as defense and posts, were excluded from the competence of the Assembly. The Assembly was to be composed of, and elected by, Europeans. Members of the Commission were immediately concerned that South West Africa (i.e., the white population) might be granted full autonomy, or, alternatively, that the territory might be incorporated into the Union. In either case it would put an end to the mandate status "since the mandatory Power would no longer be responsible for the administration for which it was accountable to the League of Nations." Furthermore, fulfillment of the wishes of the white minority was hardly consonant with the purposes of the mandate, which was specifically designed to promote the welfare of the natives, including their advancement toward self-government.[46]

The issue assumed more urgency in 1933, when the Legislative Assembly of South West Africa passed a resolution which, inter alia, requested the South African government to amend the 1925 Constitution Act so as to provide : (a) that South West Africa be administered as a fifth province of the Union subject to the provisions of the Mandate; and (b) that the territory be represented in the South African Parliament. Members of the Mandates Commission expressed serious concern at the import of this resolution, seeing that it tended "to undermine the principles of the mandate."[47] They sought to ascertain the Union government's attitude on the resolution. The Chairman explained that, as desirous as the Commission was of collaborating with the mandatory power, it was most anxious to avoid being faced with a fait accompli. At the next session the Union delegate sought to reassure the Commission of the complete loyalty of his government in its administration of the mandate. A quasi-judicial commission, he indicated, had been appointed to investigate the whole question.[48]

The South African commission, as it turned out, favored the process of integration. In a report dated March 2, 1936, it concluded: "(a) The present form of government of the Territory is a failure and

46. Comments of M. Rappard, in P.M.C., Min. VI (1925): 58–61.
47. Ibid., XXVI (1934): 63.
48. Ibid., XXVII (1935): 160.

should be abolished. (b) There is no legal obstacle to the government of the mandated Territory as a province of the Union subject to the Mandate."[49] In its annual report to the Permanent Mandates Commission (1936), the Union government also expressed the view that administration of South West Africa as a "fifth province" of the Union subject to the terms of the Mandate would not represent a violation of the mandate. It stated, however, that "sufficient grounds had not been adduced for taking such a step."[50] The Mandates Commission, in turn, decided not to express an opinion at that time, confining itself to "making all legal reservations on the question."[51]

The foregoing review demonstrates very effectively the manner in which the Permanent Mandates Commission gave life to the principle of international accountability. By assuming the role of a vigilant watchdog, the Commission strove to improve the condition of the native inhabitants and to bar any attempt to alter the status of a mandate. The Commission called for explanations from the mandatory powers on any disturbances or unrest that occurred in the mandated territory; and it objected to certain policies which tended to discriminate against, rather than promote, the welfare of the native population. To highlight the separate status of a mandate, the Commission insisted on a separate system of land tenure for the mandate, a distinct national status for the inhabitants of the mandate, and a financial system that was not interwoven with that of the mandatory power. Above all, the Commission sought to bar any moves which might tend to alter the constitutional relationship between a mandate and neighboring territories, whether these latter were adjoining colonies or the national territory of the mandatory power. The mandated territories were never allowed to slip into a state of *de facto* annexation.

## THE MEANING OF INTERNATIONAL ACCOUNTABILITY UNDER THE LEAGUE

Such success as was achieved by the League of Nations mandates system was grounded in the spirit of cooperation and mutual confidence that governed the relations between mandatory powers and the organs

49. *Report of South West Africa Commission* (Pretoria, 1936), p. 77.

50. *Report of Union of South Africa to the Council of the League of Nations Concerning the Administration of South West Africa, for Year 1936* (Pretoria, 1937), p. 4.

51. P.M.C., Min. XXXI (1937): 192. The foregoing episodes reveal the persistence of South Africa's twin arguments with respect to South West Africa: first, that the mandates system envisioned incorporation, rather than independence, for the territory; and second, that the administration of the territory as a fifth province of South Africa was fully in accordance with the Mandate, which authorized South Africa to administer the territory "as an integral portion of . . . South Africa." On the other hand, the Mandates Commission (or, at least, a majority of its members) consistently deemed such arrangements incompatible with the mandate.

of the League. In approaching their task, members of the Permanent Mandates Commission, aside from their commitment to "absolute independence and impartiality," pledged themselves at their very first session, to exercise their authority "less as judges from whom critical pronouncements are expected, than as collaborators who are resolved to devote their experience and their energies to a joint endeavour."[52] In short, the Commission set out to be "a useful ally" rather than a "censorious critic."[53] Consequently, it did not seek to define policy for the mandates, nor did it direct governments (except on rare occasions) to a given course of action. Its function was to advise the Council; and in doing that it sought to elicit the cooperation of the mandatory power, not to engage in conflict with it. As expressed by Hall:"[The mandates system] achieved its main objectives . . . on the whole without crises, deadlocks, or very serious international friction. Governments never met in head-on collisions in the Mandates Commission. The Commission was never used by governments as a platform for attacking each other or as a forum for ideological disputes."[54] According to Lord Lugard, a long-time member of the Commission, the success of the Commission was due to its observance of three principles: (1) abstention from direct advice or criticism of administration and policy; (2) arrival at a collective opinion only after full discussion; and (3) recognition by members of their duty to maintain an attitude of political impartiality devoid of any national bias.[55]

It is clear, therefore, that the Mandates Commission and the League generally, envisaged their role as a modest one in promoting the ideals of "tutelage" and the "sacred trust." It was their aim to enable the peoples in the various mandates "to stand for themselves," but this could only be achieved by reserving to the mandatory powers the initiative in promoting this goal. The function of the Mandates Commission was to impress upon the mandatories the fact that they were internationally accountable for their conduct of the mandates and that their administration should be directed toward fulfillment of the ideals enunciated in Article 22 of the Covenant and the respective mandates. In a sense, then, the Commission acted something like a tutor to the tutors. But it did so essentially from a negative rather than a positive standpoint. It did not make demands of the mandatories; it offered guidance by pointing out what was inconsistent with the mandate status and by encouraging whatever was consistent therewith—particularly in the field of improvement of the native welfare. It made no dramatic moves to

52. L. of N., Official Journal (1921): 1125.
53. Wright, *Mandates*, p. 587.
54. Hall, *Mandates, Dependencies and Trusteeship*, p. 209.
55. Cited, ibid.

facilitate political autonomy for the mandates and it certainly did not act as a timekeeper for their attainment of independent status. The mandates system operated as a safeguard of the international status of mandates; it did not operate as the great emancipator. This definition of the Commission's role is borne out by the fact that by 1939 only one mandate had emerged into independence and that was the unique case of Iraq, an A Class mandate which, to all intents and purposes, had been independent before it ever became a mandate.[56] The Class B and C mandates were not appreciably closer to independence in 1939 than they had been in 1919.

League practice saw the realization neither of the Wilsonian vision of the mandates system nor of the Dominion ministers' expectations with respect to that system. None of the parties at Paris accurately foresaw the actual mode of development. On the one hand, the mandates did not slip into a condition of *de facto* annexation; but, on the other hand, neither did they achieve any major or dramatic progress toward self-determination and independence. The compromise of 1919 had operated so as to establish a new international status for the mandated territories, and the Permanent Mandates Commission, together with the other organs of the League, effectively sustained that unique regime; but they were not capable of moving radically beyond that level. Perhaps it was radical enough that states at that time should even consider themselves internationally accountable for territories under their control. Given the prevailing state of world affairs, this was as far as matters could go.

In the light of these facts it is not really surprising that the mandates system operated so smoothly and without any serious friction. It did so because mandatory powers never felt themselves confronted with what they might have considered exorbitant demands. If the mandates were not simply colonies under another name, they were at least close enough to that denomination (particularly in the case of the Class C mandates) so as not to pose any notable difficulties to the mandatory power in its administration of the territory. The examination of the annual reports was on occasion bothersome, but not overly so. The Mandatory could not always institute changes it felt desirable, but by the same token, neither could it be compelled to adopt measures contrary to its own national interests. After all, it reserved a veto in the

---

56. Two other Class A mandates, Syria and Lebanon, had negotiated treaties of friendship and alliance with France in 1936. The treaties were to enter into operation when the independence of these two countries was established. However, these actions were not deemed by France to have finally terminated the mandate status. See Leland M. Goodrich and Edvard Hambro, *Charter of the United Nations: Commentary and Documents* (2nd ed., rev.; Boston: World Peace Foundation, 1949), pp. 429–30. (Hereinafter referred to as Goodrich and Hambro—see abbreviations.)

League Council.[57] The Mandatory could in fact assimilate its policy in the mandated territory sufficiently to its own national policy so that it never felt it was confronted with a serious and major dichotomy of interests. Moreover, the mandatory powers were never faced with a formidable ideological antagonist, bent on challenging their very right to exercise control over the mandated territories. The atmosphere of the League was, relatively speaking, a calm and serene one for the mandatories, and for this reason it was understandably tolerable.[58] It was World War II and its aftermath which shattered the harmonious and "club-like" atmosphere dominating mandatory and colonial affairs generally.

57. See above, n. 22.
58. The attitude of critics of the mandates system in the League period was summed up by Salvador de Madariaga in 1938, in a rather vivid phrase: "The old hag of colonization puts on a fig leaf and calls itself mandate." *The World's Design* (London: Allen and Unwin, 1938), p. 7. Cited by Inis L. Claude, Jr., *Swords into Plowshares* (3rd ed., rev.; New York: Random House, 1964), p. 321.

# III.

## THE UNITED NATIONS TRUSTEESHIP SYSTEM

### SAN FRANCISCO

The events of World War II set in motion powerful ideological forces destined to bring sweeping changes to the whole structure of colonial relations. Nationalism emerged as a potent force amongst Asian and African peoples. As Rupert Emerson has said, "Self-determination [became] a living principle for the non-European world, opening the door to a full assertion of the nationalist claims which had been mounting in the interwar decades."[1] The strength of this new drive for self-assertion was reflected in the drafting of the United Nations Charter at San Francisco in 1945.[2]

In contrast to the situation at Paris in 1919, when Wilson alone fought valiantly for a "new deal" for the peoples of Africa and Asia, at San Francisco these peoples now had their own representatives and spokesmen actively campaigning on their behalf in the hallways of diplomacy.[3] States such as India, Egypt, China, and the Philippines worked diligently to fashion the Charter into an instrument for the total elimination of dependency—whether of colonial or trusteeship form—in as speedy a manner as possible. Their efforts were basically

---

1. *From Empire to Nation: The Rise to Self-Assertion of Asian and African Peoples* (Cambridge, Mass.: Harvard University Press, 1960), p. 4.
2. On this topic generally, see Ernst B. Haas, "The Attempt to Terminate Colonialism: Acceptance of the United Nations Trusteeship System," *International Organization* VII (1953): 1–21; Inis L. Claude, Jr., *Swords into Plowshares* (3rd ed., rev.; New York: Random House, 1964), chap. XVI; Leland M. Goodrich, *The United Nations* (New York: Crowell, 1959), chap. XIII.
3. In its main outlines the Charter, like the League Covenant, was fashioned primarily by the big powers. Nevertheless, at San Francisco, the smaller powers, including the newly independent states, were able to introduce significant modifications into the scheme of the Charter agreed upon earlier by the great powers at Dumbarton Oaks. See Goodrich, *The United Nations*, pp. 26–27.

supported by the Latin American bloc, as well as the two superpowers, the United States and the Soviet Union, and resulted in a notable strengthening of the whole system of international accountability.[4] The advance over the League mandates system was reflected both in the scope and objectives of the new system and in the machinery for supervision instituted in the Charter.[5]

In striking contrast to Article 22 of the Covenant, Article 76 of the Charter enumerates the "basic objectives" of the trusteeship system in precise categorical (and even elaborate) terms. Foremost among these is the commitment of the trust authority "to promote the political, economic, social and educational advancement of the inhabitants of the trust territories, and their progressive development towards self-government or independence."[6] This clear pledge to the right of self-determination, although it was hedged about with certain qualifications, reflects the great advance made in the United Nations Charter with regard to the principle and purposes of international accountability. In contrast to the Covenant, which subsumed "political development" under the general term "tutelage," the Charter formulated a clear and abiding duty to guide the peoples of the trust territories "towards self-government or independence." Special circumstances such as "the stage of development of the people, the geographical situation of the territory [or] its economic conditions," were not permitted to modify this basic commitment. Even security considerations, which prompted a change of supervisory agency from General Assembly to Security Council for certain trust territories, did not affect the pledge to promote the basic objectives enumerated in Article 76.[7] Enunciation of these goals in such clear terms foreshadowed the active and radical role which the United Nations, or, more accurately, the anticolonial group within the United Nations, would assume in promoting the cause of national independence.

The supervisory powers of the international organization were fashioned with the goal of the emancipation of trust territories in

---

4. It might be mentioned that Australia, under the leadership of Dr. Evatt, also campaigned strongly for the same cause. Subsequently, Australia became less enchanted with the anticolonial drive.

On the attitude of the United States, before and during the San Francisco Conference, and the changes brought about by security considerations, see Ruth B. Russell and Jeannette E. Muther, *A History of the United Nations Charter* (Washington, D.C.: The Brookings Institution, 1958), passim; James N. Murray, Jr., *The United Nations Trusteeship System* (Urbana, Ill.: University of Illinois Press, 1957), chap. II.

5. For a detailed analysis of the changes, see Goodrich and Hambro, chaps. XI, XII, and XIII.

6. Article 76 (b). See Appendix III. For the history of this provision, see Russell and Muther, *United Nations Charter*, pp. 830–33.

7. See Article 83, paragraph 2, of Charter.

view.[8] In contrast to the Permanent Mandates Commission, the Trusteeship Council was purposely designed as a political organ, and, moreover, was constituted as one of the "principal" organs of the new world body. It was meant to function as the right arm of the plenary representative organ, the General Assembly, which in turn would operate under a two-thirds majority rule and not under a unanimity requirement as did the League Council. The representatives on the Trusteeship Council would be delegates of their respective countries, rather than colonial experts. Their job was not simply to "advise," but to promote actively the attainment of certain defined goals. The Trusteeship Council was given considerable power to interfere directly in trusteeship affairs.[9] It was empowered, for instance, to accept any and all petitions, both written and oral, without any special procedure for prior consideration of the petition by the administering authority.[10] It could also make periodic visits to the trust territories.[11] As a former member of the Mandates Commission wrote rather prophetically, in 1946: "What is certain . . . is that in the intentions of the drafters of the Charter, persuasion and the discreet political pressure of emulation, which were the main motives of the Mandate System, are to be supplemented and even, if need be, replaced by coercive and direct intervention."[12]

Furthermore, the Charter confirmed the principle of international accountability not only for trust territories, but for all dependent territories alike. It did this by means of Chapter XI, the "Declaration Regarding Non-Self-Governing Territories."[13] This chapter, it is true, did not postulate self-government or independence as specific goals. At most it pledged colonial powers "to *develop* self-government in their respective territories."[14] Nor did it confer supervisory powers on the international organization as such. Even the commitment to transmit information to the United Nations did not include a requirement to

8. For the elements entering into the formulation of the trusteeship machinery, see Russell and Muther, *United Nations Charter*, pp. 838–42.

9. Articles 87 and 88.

10. See discussion in Goodrich and Hambro, pp. 467–69.

11. See ibid., pp. 469–72.

12. William E. Rappard, "The Mandates and the International Trusteeship Systems," *Political Science Quarterly* LXI (1946): 416.

13. In the League Covenant, the only general commitment undertaken by colonial powers, was that recorded in Article 23 (b), "to secure just treatment of the native inhabitants of territories under their control." This provision, which, in accordance with the terms of Article 23, was limited to the operation of international conventions, remained very much a dead letter as far as League action was concerned. See H. Duncan Hall, *Mandates, Dependencies and Trusteeship* (Washington, D.C.: Carnegie Endowment for International Peace, 1948), pp. 223–28.

14. Emphasis supplied. At San Francisco, the Chinese delegate moved to include independence as a specific goal. The amendment was subsequently withdrawn. See Goodrich and Hambro, p. 410; Russell and Muther, *United Nations Charter*, pp. 814–22.

supply information on political development. Nonetheless, "is not the Declaration . . . to be read in close conjunction with the succeeding two chapters . . . [on] . . . the Trusteeship System, and are they not the twin children of the same parents?"[15] The very fact that a set of ideals for dependent territories was incorporated into a constitutional document of the nature of the United Nations Charter could not be viewed otherwise than as conferment of some authority on the world body to promote positively the ideals enumerated.[16] As one writer has said: "While [Chapter XI] provided only the vaguest hint of measures for the institutionalization of international accountability, it nevertheless ratified the doctrine that all colonies, whether subjected to the formal authority of the Trusteeship System or not, are minor wards of the human family to be brought to self-respecting and self-reliant adulthood."[17]

In summary, then, if the Paris Peace Conference gave birth to the principle of international accountability, and the Permanent Mandates Commission sustained it in life during the frail period of its youth, then the San Francisco Conference, it may be said, saw this doctrine mature into a powerful and vigorous principle in international affairs with universal application. No state was to be permitted to control a territory and a people other than its own, unless it did so for the express purpose of leading that people toward self-government—and this responsibility had to be discharged to the satisfaction of the world organization.

## THE PREPARATORY COMMISSION

Despite the fact that the Charter formulated such a grand scheme for the operation of international accountability, there was no guarantee that the most ambitious and important part of this project—the trusteeship system—would necessarily come into early operation. The provisions of the Charter made clear, certainly in the eyes of the mandatory powers, that the formulation of trusteeship agreements was to be an entirely voluntary undertaking.[18] And unlike Chapter XI of the Char-

15. Rappard, "Mandates and International Trusteeship," p. 413. It might be noted, incidentally, that Judges Spender and Fitzmaurice regarded Chapter XI as being based fundamentally on Article 22 of the Covenant. *SWA Judgment* (1962): 541.

16. See on this point Hans Kelsen, *The Law of the United Nations* (London: Stevens, 1950), pp. 553–55; L. Oppenheim, *International Law*, ed. H. Lauterpacht (8th ed.; London: Longmans, Green, 1955), I: 240–42.

17. Claude, *Swords into Plowshares*, p. 330; see also Goodrich, *The United Nations*, p. 300.

18. According to Article 77, paragraph 1, "the trusteeship system shall apply to . . . (a) territories now held under mandate." But paragraph 2 provided: "It will be a matter for subsequent agreement as to which territories in the foregoing categories will be brought under the trusteeship system and upon what terms."

Subsequently, it was argued that the clearly permissive nature of this provision was modified by other provisions of the Charter. See below, chaps. IV and V. There is, however, no

ter, which was to begin operating upon entry into force of the Charter, the trusteeship system could not begin to function until trusteeship agreements were concluded. In theory, then, there was always the possibility that the creation of a trusteeship system might be seriously delayed. This was one of the problems taken up by the Preparatory Commission of the United Nations.

The Preparatory Commission was established at San Francisco for the purpose of arranging and preparing for the convocation of the first session of the General Assembly.[19] When the Commission met in London on November 24, 1945, it had before it a recommendation of its Executive Committee that the General Assembly create a Temporary Trusteeship Committee "to carry out certain of the functions assigned in the Charter to the Trusteeship Council, pending its establishment."[20] One of the functions proposed for such a committee was to "advise the General Assembly on any matters that might arise with regard to the transfer to the United Nations of any functions and responsibilities hitherto exercised under the Mandates System."[21] Opposition was, however, expressed by certain delegates (particularly the Soviet Union) on the grounds that the creation of a Temporary Trusteeship Committee might only serve to delay the actual establishment of the Trusteeship Council, and that, moreover, such a committee would be of doubtful constitutionality under the Charter. As a result, the proposal was replaced by a recommendation that the General Assembly should adopt a resolution calling on the mandatory powers to undertake practical steps for submitting trusteeship agreements in respect of the mandate territories "preferably not later than during the Second Part of the First Session of the General Assembly."[22] South Africa, it should be noted, abstained in the vote on this proposal at each stage of the Preparatory Commission's deliberations, since it wished to reserve its position with respect to South West Africa.[23]

The Preparatory Commission was also concerned with the possible transfer of certain functions from the League of Nations to the United Nations. During the drafting of the Charter and thereafter, it was made

---

doubt that at San Francisco the mandatory powers themselves were under the impression that the conclusion of trusteeship agreements was strictly a voluntary affair. To this end they had joined in defeating an Egyptian proposal for applying the trusteeship system automatically to all mandates. See Russell and Muther, *United Nations Charter*, pp. 824-26; *SWA Pleadings* I: 244.

19. See Goodrich and Hambro, pp. 44-46.
20. U.N. Doc. PC/EX/113/Rev. 1, chap. IV, sec. 2, para. 3, p. 55.
21. Ibid., para. 4 (iv), p. 56.
22. U.N. Doc. PC/20, chap. IV, sec. 1, p. 49.
23. See U.N.P.C., Ctte. 4, *Summary Records*, p. 40; U.N.P.C., *Journal*, p. 131. The text of both reservations is reproduced in *SWA Pleadings* II: 141.

very clear that the United Nations was not simply the League of Nations under a new name, nor was it the automatic successor in title to the earlier international organization. (The United States, it will be recalled, had never been a member of the League, and the Soviet Union had been expelled from membership in 1939. These two powers were therefore most insistent that the separate and distinct identity of the new world organization be clearly established. The Charter, of course, did not include any reference to the Covenant; moreover, both world organizations existed side by side until April 1946, when the League was formally disbanded.) Consequently, any assumption of League functions by the United Nations would be done on a selective basis. With this end in view, the Preparatory Commission was bidden to:

> Formulate recommendations concerning the possible transfer of certain functions, activities, and assets of the League of Nations which it may be considered desirable for the new Organization to take over on terms to be arranged.[24]

After careful consideration, the Executive Committee recommended

> 1. That the functions, activities and assets of the League of Nations be transferred to the United Nations with [certain] exceptions and qualifications . . . with the understanding that the contemplated transfer does not include the political functions of the League, which have in fact already ceased, but solely the technical and non-political functions.[25]

A footnote relative to exceptions and qualifications read in part:

> The Committee recommends that no political questions should be included in the transfer. It makes no recommendation to transfer the activities concerning refugees, mandates, or international bureaux.[26]

The Preparatory Commission basically adopted the recommendations of the Executive Committee, except that the word "transfer" was replaced by the phrase "the assumption of responsibility," since the former term could "imply a legal continuity which would not in fact exist."[27]

The Preparatory Commission's report was acted upon by the General Assembly at the First Part of its First Session in January–February 1946. Resolutions were adopted, both with reference to the creation of

24. UNCIO Docs., V: 316, item (c).
25. U.N. Doc. PC/EX/113/Rev. 1, chap. IX, sec. 3, p. 108.
26. Ibid.
27. U.N.P.C., Ctte. 7, *Summary Records*, para. 3, pp. 2–3.

the Trusteeship Council and the transfer of certain functions from the League to the United Nations.

During the discussions each of the mandatory powers, except South Africa, expressed an intention to negotiate a trusteeship agreement for its mandated territory.[28] South Africa reserved its position in the following terms:

> The Union Government considers that it is incumbent upon it, as indeed upon all other mandatory Powers, to consult the people of the mandated territory regarding the form which their own future government should take, since they are the people chiefly concerned. Arrangements are now in train for such consultations to take place and, until they have been concluded, the South African Government must reserve its position concerning the future of the mandate, together with its right of full liberty of action, as provided for in paragraph 1 of Article 80 of the Charter. . . .
>
> South West Africa occupies a special position in relation to the Union which differentiates that territory from any other under a C mandate. This special position should be given full consideration in determining the future status of the territory.[29]

The General Assembly, in the course of a comprehensive resolution on the subject of dependent peoples, welcomed the declarations made by the various states regarding their intention to negotiate trusteeship agreements and extended a general invitation to

> the States administering territories now held under mandate to undertake practical steps . . . for the implementation of Article 79 of the Charter (which provides for the conclusion of agreements on the terms of trusteeship for each territory to be placed under the trusteeship system), in order to submit these agreements for approval, preferably not later than during the second part of the first session of the General Assembly.[30]

Furthermore, in the course of a comprehensive resolution entitled, "Transfer of Certain Functions, Activities and Assets of the League of Nations," the General Assembly declared that it

> will itself examine, or will submit to the appropriate organ of the United Nations, any request from the parties that the United Na-

28. See the statements of the United Kingdom, GAOR, 1st Sess., 1st Part, Plen., 11th Mtg., Jan. 17, 1946, pp. 166–67; New Zealand, ibid., 14th Mtg., Jan. 18, 1946, p. 227; Australia, ibid., p. 233; Belgium, ibid., 15th Mtg., Jan. 18, 1946, p. 238; France, ibid., 16th Mtg., Jan. 19, 1946, p. 251.

29. Ibid., 12th Mtg., Jan. 7, 1946, pp. 185–86. See also ibid., 4th Ctte., 3rd Mtg., Jan. 22, 1946, p. 10.

30. G. A. Res. 11 (I), Feb. 9, 1946, in U.N. Doc. A/64.

tions should assume the exercise of functions or powers entrusted to the League of Nations by treaties, international conventions, agreements and other instruments having a political character.[31]

The upshot of all this would appear to be as follows: Throughout 1945 and at least until April 1946, when the League of Nations was disbanded, the mandates system continued in full force. In actual fact there was no form of supervision over mandates; annual reports were not rendered nor were petitions transmitted. But this did not affect the continuing force of the legal obligations and responsibilities involved. The members of the United Nations were moving toward the early establishment of the trusteeship system and were desirous of speeding up the process of concluding trusteeship agreements. They were therefore not interested in assuming the League of Nations' responsibilities in relation to the functioning of the mandates system, as such. They wanted to have their own system of international accountability in operation as soon as possible. Consequently, no formal program was instituted for transferring the mandates system—as a going concern—to the United Nations. Rather, the expectation was that the component parts of the mandates system, i.e., the individual mandates, would become United Nations trust territories, and with the creation of the one system the other system would automatically dissolve. It would be neither wise nor expeditious to assume that a lengthy lapse would ensue before the trusteeship agreements were concluded, and anything which might tend to confirm such a delay was to be avoided. (After all, Article 80 of the United Nations Charter was specifically designed to expedite the process of concluding trusteeship agreements.) Therefore, the United Nations should not undertake to supervise the mandates in that form, nor should a Temporary Trusteeship Committee be established. The Assembly should move "with all deliberate speed" to the creation of the Trusteeship Council. In the event that any of the mandatory powers would not conclude a trusteeship agreement—and South Africa had, indeed, repeatedly reserved its position regarding South West Africa—the United Nations would have time to consider the matter at that point.

In the contentious proceedings in the *South West Africa* cases, three "new facts," allegedly not brought to the attention of the 1950 Court, were cited by South Africa as evidence that the United Nations had not succeeded to the supervisory functions of the League with regard to mandates. One of these "new facts" involved the foregoing set

31. G. A. Res. 14 (I), Feb. 12, 1946, in U.N. Doc. A/64.

of events in the Preparatory Commission. South Africa noted, first, that the proposal for a temporary trusteeship committee had been turned down, with nothing substituted for it. Second, South Africa claimed, the fact that one of the proposed Committee's duties would have been to "advise the General Assembly on any matters that might arise with regard to the *transfer* to the United Nations of . . . functions . . . under the Mandates System," denoted that no automatic transfer had or could have taken place. A transfer of such a nature could only take place if all parties agreed—and no such transfer arrangements were ever concluded.

In addition to this "new" fact, South Africa pointed to the fact already noted in its 1950 pleadings, that the United Nations had refused to designate itself heir to the League of Nations and had rather decided upon a selective assumption of League functions. The Assembly resolved to examine any request from the parties to a political treaty to determine if the United Nations should assume the functions of the League under such treaty. But with respect to the mandates system—manifestly of a political character—no such "request" had ever been made by the parties; nor had the General Assembly ever undertaken any such "examination." Furthermore, as far as South West Africa was concerned, South Africa had reserved its position with regard to the future of the territory at each critical point of the United Nations deliberations. Consequently, it could not be said, argued South Africa, that the United Nations succeeded to the supervisory functions of the League.

According to South Africa, the 1950 advisory opinion had been premised on tacit consent on South Africa's part to United Nations supervision of the mandate. But had the foregoing "new" evidence negativing such consent been brought to the attention of the Court, the Court majority would undoubtedly have agreed with Judges McNair and Read, that no transfer of supervisory authority from the League to the United Nations had ever been effected.[32] (In response to Applicants' denial of the "newness" of the evidence, South Africa emphasized that while the text of the General Assembly resolutions had been brought before the 1950 Court the proposal of the Executive Committee of the Preparatory Commission and the Commission's reaction to that proposal had not been raised. And these particular points, South Africa claimed, were crucial.)[33]

32. For the South African arguments, see *SWA Pleadings* I: 239–47, 325–28, 345–46; II: 35–43, 141–48; VII: 79–82, 97–98, 335–37; VIII: 287–89, 376–87, 547–62; IX: 390–411, 415–17. For the arguments of Ethiopia and Liberia dismissing the significance of this evidence, see ibid., I: 430–33; IV: 552; VII: 289–91, 361–62; VIII: 152–53; IX: 141–60, 187–88.

33. See, especially, ibid., VII: 289–90, 335–36; and II: 147, n. 4. Cf. also the dissenting opinion of Judge Jessup, *SWA Judgment* (1966): 341. Inexplicably, the Applicants, in contend-

In 1962 dissenting Judges Spender, Fitzmaurice, and van Wyk accepted the South African thesis.[34] On the other hand, the Court majority implicitly did not regard the material cited by South Africa as sufficiently crucial to outweigh other evidence demonstrating that the United Nations was qualified to exercise supervisory functions with respect to the South West Africa mandate. The Court did not advert expressly to the acts of the Preparatory Commission, but the evidence was later discussed and discounted by Judge Jessup in his dissenting opinion in the South West Africa Judgment of 1966.[35]

## FINAL SESSION OF LEAGUE ASSEMBLY

The League Assembly met for the last time in April 1946 to formally dissolve the League of Nations.[36] The representatives of the various mandatory powers, other than South Africa, once again expressed their governments' intention to place the respective mandates under United Nations trusteeship. The representatives (including the South African representative) also pledged that the territories would, in the meantime, continue to be administered in accordance with the principles of the mandates system.[37]

The statement of the South African representative, incorporating both his government's reservations and intentions regarding the future administration of the mandate read in part as follows:

It is the intention of the Union Government, at the forth-coming session of the United Nations General Assembly in New York, to formulate its case for according South-West Africa a status under which it would be internationally recognised as an integral part of the Union. . . . In the meantime, the Union will continue to administer the territory scrupulously in accordance with the obligations of the Mandate, for the advancement and promotion of the interests of the inhabitants, as she has done during the past six years when meetings of the Mandates Commission could not be held.

The disappearance of those organs of the League concerned with the supervision of mandates, primarily the Mandates Commis-

___

ing that the Preparatory Commission material had been before the Court, cited the statement of M. Kerno, the representative of the Secretary-General, in the *1950 Status Pleadings*, p. 161, but stopped short of citing the crucial sentence, beginning: "Le Comité exécutif proposa à la Commission préparatoire . . . ." See *SWA Pleadings* VII: 289–90.

34. *SWA Judgment* (1962): 531–38, 619–26. See also Separate Opinion of Judge van Wyk, *SWA Judgment* (1966): 96–105.

35. Ibid., pp. 341–47. Cf. joint dissenting opinion of Judges Badawi, Basdevant, Hsu Mo, Armand Ugon, and Moreno Quintana, in *Oral Petitions Opinion* (1956): 65.

36. This session of the League, it might be noted, took place in the interval between the first and second parts of the first session of the U.N. General Assembly. The first part had concluded in February 1946, and the second part was to open in November 1946.

On the formal dissolution of the League generally, see *The League Hands Over* (Geneva: 1946).

37. L. of N., Official Journal (1946) Spec. Suppl. no. 194, pp. 28–47.

sion and the League Council, will necessarily preclude complete compliance with the letter of the Mandate. The Union Government will nevertheless regard the dissolution of the League as in no way diminishing its obligations under the Mandate, which it will continue to discharge with the full and proper appreciation of its responsibilities until such time as other arrangements are agreed upon concerning the future status of the territory.[38]

The Assembly proceeded to adopt various resolutions relating to the United Nations assumption of functions and activities hitherto performed by the League. Several resolutions were adopted with regard to technical and nonpolitical activities.[39] The subject of mandates was handled separately.

In the course of the discussion, the Chinese representative, on April 9, 1946, indicated he wished to submit a draft resolution in the following terms:

*The Assembly*
*Considering* that the Trusteeship Council of the United Nations has not yet been constituted and that all mandated territories under the League have not been transformed into territories under trusteeship;

*Considering* that the League functions as supervisory organ for mandated territories should be transferred to the United Nations after the dissolution of the League in order to avoid a period of *interregnum* in the supervision of the mandated territories;

*Recommends* that the mandatory powers as well as those administering ex-enemy mandated territories shall continue to submit annual reports on these territories to the United Nations and to submit to inspection by the same until the Trusteeship Council shall have been constituted.[40]

The Chairman of the Assembly, however, considered that the Chinese suggestion was not relevant at that particular time, and the matter was deferred.[41]

Following this event, informal discussions were held on the subject and a new draft resolution was formulated, which was submitted by the

38. Ibid., pp. 32–33. Subsequently, in 1950, the Court held that the latter part of this statement constituted recognition by the Union government of the continuance of its obligations under the mandate, and not a mere indication of its future conduct (as South Africa attempted to portray it). *Status Opinion* (1950): 135. See also Written Statement of the United States, *1950 Status Pleadings*, pp. 100–1, and the Statement of the South African Representative, ibid., pp. 279–80. The Court in 1950 also held that the first part of the foregoing statement signified recognition by the Union government that it was competent to modify the international status of South West Africa, *only* with the consent of the United Nations. *Status Opinion* (1950): 142. See further below, pp. 115, 118.

39. L. of N., Official Journal (1946), Spec. Suppl. no. 194, p. 278.

40. See L. of N., 21st Ass., 1st Ctte., 2nd Mtg., Provisional Record. Cited in *SWA Pleadings* I: 253; II: 49.

41. L. of N., Official Journal (1946), Spec. Suppl. no. 194, p. 76.

Chinese delegate on April 12, 1946.[42] In proposing the new draft resolution, the Chinese delegate recalled that he had already drawn the Committee's attention "to the complicated problems arising in regards to mandates from the transfer of functions from the League to the United Nations." The Charter, he said, established

> a system of trusteeship based largely upon the principles of the mandates system, but the functions of the League in that respect were not transferred automatically to the United Nations. The Assembly should therefore take steps to secure the continued application of the principles of the mandates system . . . [and] would wish to be assured as to the future of mandated territories.

The final resolution, which was identical with the second Chinese draft, was adopted on April 18, 1946, and read as follows:

> *The Assembly:*
> . . . . . . . . . . . . . . . . . . . . . . . . . . . . . . . . . . . . . . . . . . .
> 3. Recognises that, on the termination of the League's existence, its functions with respect to the mandated territories will come to an end, but notes that Chapters XI, XII and XIII of the Charter of the United Nations embody principles corresponding to those declared in Article 22 of the Covenant of the League;
> 4. Takes note of the expressed intentions of the Members of the League now administering territories under mandate to continue to administer them for the well-being and development of the peoples concerned in accordance with the obligations contained in the respective Mandates, until other arrangements have been agreed between the United Nations and the respective mandatory Powers.[43]

The correct interpretation to be accorded the foregoing events in the League Assembly and the question whether they supported United Nations succession to the League's supervisory powers over mandates, became one of the central points of conflict in the South West Africa controversy.

South Africa argued in the 1950 advisory proceedings (without referring to the Chinese draft proposals) that the League resolution merely "noted" that the Charter embodies principles corresponding to those of Article 22 of the Covenant. It did not purport to transfer anything.[44] The Court, in its 1950 Advisory Opinion, held, however, that the League resolution signified an intention by the League of

---

42. Ibid., pp. 78–79.
43. Ibid., pp. 58, 278–79. In the vote, Egypt abstained, on the ground "that mandates have terminated with the dissolution of the League of Nations, and that, in so far as Palestine is concerned, there should be no question of putting that country under trusteeship." Ibid., pp. 58–59.
44. *1950 Status Pleadings*, pp. 76–77.

Nations that its supervisory authority over mandates be assumed by the United Nations.[45] Only Judges McNair and Read found merit in the South African argument.[46]

In the contentious proceedings in the *South West Africa* cases, South Africa's arguments centered on the Chinese draft proposal episode, which constituted the second of the "new facts" which failed to be drawn to the 1950 Court's attention. South Africa maintained that the withdrawal of the original Chinese draft proposal and its replacement by the final version of the resolution clearly revealed that the members of the League had not been prepared to accord the United Nations supervisory power over mandates. And had the 1950 Court been aware of the drafting history of the final resolution, it would, no doubt, have ruled otherwise than it did.[47]

The 1962 Court, however, apparently did not find anything of significance in the "new" evidence. It proceeded to reaffirm the 1950 Advisory Opinion (in so far as that was necessary for the assumption of jurisdiction) without referring to the first Chinese proposal. In dissent, Judges Spender, Fitzmaurice, and van Wyk laid great stress upon the Chinese episode; they considered it conclusive evidence that the mandatory powers in 1945–46 had not in any way consented to a transfer of supervisory functions from the League to the United Nations.[48] Judge Jessup, in his 1966 dissenting opinion, discounted the weight of this evidence.[49]

In the course of the final oral pleadings in the *South West Africa* cases, in 1965, Mr. Gross, agent for Applicants, in order to overcome Respondent's "new facts" argument, presented a radically novel interpretation of the events of 1945–46 in the United Nations Preparatory Commission and in the final League Assembly Session.[50] According to this interpretation, it was the mandatory powers, including South Africa, who actually desired United Nations supervision of the mandates, while the nonmandatory states objected. As a compromise, a system of pledges was instituted whereby the mandatory powers "were to carry out all the obligations of the mandate, including the obligation to submit to international supervision."[51] Consequently, declared Mr. Gross, the "facts" of 1945–46, far from proving that the 1950 Ad-

45. *Status Opinion* (1950): 134–37 (see discussion below, pp. 116, 118–19).
46. *Status Opinion* (1950): 161–62, 168, 173.
47. *SWA Pleadings* I: 247–55, 328–33; II: 43–52, 146–47; VII: 82–88, 97–98, 337–41; VIII: 289, 392–426, 557–58; IX: 411–16.
48. *SWA Judgment* (1962): 534, 540, 627–34. See also separate opinion of Judge van Wyk, *SWA Judgment* (1966): 106–19.
49. Ibid., pp. 347–48. See also the arguments presented by Ethiopia and Liberia, *SWA Pleadings* I: 431–33; VII: 291–94, 362–63; VIII: 147–52; IX: 160–61, 188–89.
50. See, generally, ibid., pp. 140–50, 159–61, 187–90, 241. For Respondent's reaction, see ibid., pp. 384–416.
51. Ibid., p. 146.

visory Opinion had reached mistaken conclusions on United Nations succession to the supervisory powers of the League, actually confirmed those conclusions. So much was this so, that even dissenting Judges McNair and Read might have gone along with the majority in according the United Nations the requisite supervisory authority over South West Africa.

Mr. Gross' interpretation of the facts was, however, unsubstantiated by any evidentiary support and at vital points seemed to be in direct conflict with the facts. It is, therefore, not surprising that this belatedly presented thesis failed to receive the endorsement of even a single member of the Court in the 1966 judgment.

In the course of the years 1946–48 all the mandated territories were either granted independence or converted into trust territories, with the exception of South West Africa. South Africa had already indicated that its plans for the territory pointed in a very different direction. It now moved toward implementing that intention.

# II.

# THE
# TRUSTEESHIP
# STRUGGLE

# IV.

UNITED NATIONS
EFFORTS TO CONVERT
THE MANDATE OF
SOUTH WEST AFRICA
INTO A TRUST
TERRITORY

## SOUTH AFRICAN PROPOSALS FOR INCORPORATION

During World War II, in 1944, General Smuts remarked in the South African Parliament that "there is a feeling in many quarters that the Mandatory System has outlived its time and that another arrangement must be made that will have to be decided in the future."[1] This statement, despite its reference to the mandates system as a whole, actually reflected South Africa's concern regarding the future of South West Africa. President Wilson, with his insistence on a generalized mandates system, had frustrated South Africa's desire to annex South West Africa in 1919. South Africa had administered the territory under the mandate in the interwar years, but it had never been very satisfied with the arrangement. Agitation among the formerly German population had been a cause for tension in the territory and had posed a threat to South Africa's security. In general, in South Africa's view, the mandates system had operated as an artificial divide between South West Africa and the Union and had, in effect, hindered rather than promoted the territory's natural development.

The war was putting an end to the League of Nations and its mandates system, and a new world organization was being formed which undoubtedly would institute its own trusteeship system, with increased international obligations for the trust authorities. South Africa considered any such international regime totally inappropriate for South West Africa. Rather, it considered the time ripe for bringing South West Africa into a more natural and more complete association with the Union, by means of incorporation.

1. Quoted in "The Future of the Mandates: A Symposium," *African Affairs* XLIII (1944): 159.

To this end, at the San Francisco Conference during the discussions on the proposed trusteeship system, the South African representative made the following statement:[2]

I wish to point out that there are territories already under Mandate where the Mandatory principle cannot be achieved.

As an illustration, I would refer to the former German territory of South West Africa held by South Africa under a "C" Mandate.

The facts with regard to this territory are set out in a memorandum filed with the Secretariat, which I now read:

. . . . . . . . . . . . . . . . . . . . . . . . . . . . . . . . . . . . .

The territory is in a unique position when compared with other territories under the same form of Mandate.

It is geographically and strategically a part of the Union of South Africa, . . .

It is in large measure economically dependent upon the Union, whose railways serve it and from which it draws the great bulk of its supplies.

Its dependent native peoples spring from the same ethnological stem as the great mass of the native peoples of the Union.

Two-thirds of the European population are of Union origin and are Union Nationals, and the remaining one-third are Enemy Nationals.

The territory has its own Legislative Assembly granted to it by the Union Parliament, and this Assembly has submitted a request for incorporation of the territory as part of the Union.

The Union has introduced a progressive policy of Native Administration, including a system of local government through Native Councils giving the Natives a voice in the management of their own affairs; and under Union Administration Native Reserves have reached a high state of economic development.

In view of contiguity and similarity in composition of the native peoples in South West Africa the native policy followed in South West Africa must always be aligned with that of the Union, three-fifths of the population of which is native.

There is no prospect of the territory ever existing as a separate state, and the ultimate objective of the Mandatory principle is therefore impossible of achievement.[3]

The Delegation of the Union of South Africa therefore claims that the Mandate should be terminated and that the territory should be incorporated as part of the Union of South Africa.

2. This statement summarizes the various arguments South Africa subsequently adduced in support of its case for incorporation. See below, p. 79. The statement is also significant because South Africa has steadfastly maintained that it represented a clear reservation to the trusteeship provisions of the Charter. See also below, n. 4.
3. On the implication of this paragraph see below, p. 80.

As territorial questions are however reserved for handling at the later Peace Conference where the Union of South Africa intends to raise this matter, it is here only mentioned for the information of the Conference in connection with the Mandates question.[4]

As noted in the previous chapter,[5] similar expressions of intention were voiced by South African representatives at each stage of the deliberations leading up to the creation of the United Nations trusteeship system. In the Preparatory Commission meeting of December 23, 1945, the South African representative noted the special situation of South West Africa and reserved his government's position on its future.[6] When the report of the Preparatory Commission was taken up by the General Assembly in the first part of its first session in January 1946, the South African delegate once again reiterated his government's stand.[7] Noting that consultation with the population of South West Africa was then in progress, he reserved his government's position pending the outcome of the consultation. Later, in the Fourth Committee, in answer to objections raised by certain members that the Charter had envisaged a trusteeship system embracing all mandates, he pointed to Articles 77 and 80, paragraph 1, of the Charter, which, in his view, clearly established the voluntary nature of conversion of a mandate into a trust territory. Nor was Article 80, paragraph 2, intended to mitigate the purely voluntary nature of such an undertaking. In conclusion, he said: "There would be no attempt to draw up an agreement until the freely expressed will of both the European and native populations had been

4. The official records of the San Francisco Conference contain only a summary of this document. The Chairman disallowed the South African attempt to record the matter officially in the minutes, since he held that references to specific territories were not in order. UNCIO Docs., X, Doc. 260 (May 11, 1945), p. 434. The full text is available in the South African memorandum presented to the General Assembly in 1946. GAOR, 1st Sess., 2nd Part, 4th Ctte., Part 1, Annex 13, p. 200. It is also reproduced in the Written Statement of the United States, *1950 Status Pleadings*, p. 114, n. 10. In the *SWA Pleadings* 1: 237–38, and II: 33–34, South Africa, in presenting the full text, emphasized that it had been entered as a reservation. In support, South Africa cited an additional paragraph, which it claimed was part of the original typewritten document read to the Committee on Trusteeship by Dr. D. L. Smit, the South African representative, on May 11, 1945, to the following effect: "As stated in the Memorandum, this is not a matter that can be decided here, but I am directed to mention it for the information of the Conference so that South Africa may not afterwards be held to have acquiesced in the continuance of the Mandate or the inclusion of the territory in any form of trusteeship under the new International Organization." Judges Spender and Fitzmaurice in the *SWA Judgment* (1962): 533, gave recognition to the South African statement as a clear reservation. Moreover, the two judges found no reason to doubt the veracity of the additional paragraph. Judge Jessup, in the *SWA Judgment* (1966): 340, referred to the verbatim transcript of the meeting to establish that "there is no indication that the extra paragraph was pronounced." See also the Oral Statement of the Representative of the Philippines, *1950 Status Pleadings*, pp. 250–51, and the Oral Statement of the Representative of South Africa, ibid., p. 293.

5. See above, pp. 63, 65, and 68–69.
6. U.N.P.C., *Journal*, p. 131; and cf. U.N.P.C., Ctte. 4, *Summary Records*, p. 40.
7. GAOR, 1st Sess., 1st Part, Plen., 12th Mtg., Jan. 7, 1946, pp. 185–86.

ascertained. When that had been done, the decision of the Union would be submitted to the General Assembly for judgment."[8]

During the final session of the League Assembly, held in Geneva in April 1946, South Africa once again had occasion to outline its plans with regard to South West Africa.[9] It confirmed its intention, after due consultation with the population, to formulate its case before the General Assembly "for according South West Africa a status under which it would be internationally recognised as an integral part of the Union."

In the interim between the first and second parts of the first session of the General Assembly, the Union government proceeded to canvass the attitude of the European and non-European populations of South West Africa on the question of incorporation. The decision of the European population was voiced by means of a unanimous resolution adopted by the Legislative Assembly of South West Africa on May 8, 1946. This resolution formally requested the Union government to terminate the mandate status of South West Africa and to annex the territory and incorporate it as part of the Union.[10] The non-European population was consulted by means of tribal meetings at which each tribe was asked whether it favored or opposed becoming part of the Union of South Africa. This form of referendum was conducted by Native Commissioners and Magistrates "familiar with the traditions and customs" of the different tribes. The chiefs and headmen of each tribe were called upon to attest to the decision of their respective tribe or group (voting as a unit) by signing a memorial of the vote. The results of the vote were:

| For | 208,850 |
|---|---|
| Against | 33,520 |
| Not consulted | 56,790 |
| Grand Total | 299,160[11] |

8. Ibid., 4th Ctte., 3rd Mtg., Jan. 22, 1946, p. 10. Mr. Fraser of New Zealand sought to gain some elucidation of this latter remark, but the South African delegate refused to be drawn on. Ibid. The Court in 1950 referred to this remark as recognition by the Union government of the General Assembly's competence in the matter of South West Africa. *Status Opinion* (1950): 142.

9. L. of N., Official Journal, Spec. Suppl., no. 194, pp. 32–33 (April 9, 1946).

10. For the text of this resolution, see GAOR, 1st Sess., 2nd Part, 4th Ctte., Annex 13, p. 232 (1946).

11. Ibid., pp. 232–34. It is to be noted that no foreign observers were present during these consultations. Shortly after they were completed, Lord Hailey, a former member of the Permanent Mandates Commission, visited South West Africa on behalf of the British government, and basically affirmed the accuracy of the results. This conclusion of an expert in the field provided grounds for British support of South Africa's position before the General Assembly. See below, p. 82. For a detailed examination of the consultations, and the significance of Lord Hailey's visit, see Richard Dale, "The Evolution of the South West African Dispute before the United Nations, 1945–1950" (Ph.D. dissertation, Princeton University, 1962).

Armed with this data, the South African government prepared to present its case for incorporation before the General Assembly. The agenda of the second part of the first session listed the following item *at the request of South Africa*: "Statement by the Union of South Africa on the outcome of their consultations with the peoples of South West Africa as to the future status of the mandated Territory and implementation to be given to the wishes thus expressed."[12]

In support of its proposal, South Africa submitted in October 1946 a lengthy and comprehensive memorandum which outlined in great detail all the reasons for incorporating the territory into the Union.[13] The memorandum covered the historical formulation of the Class C group of mandates in 1919, with the doubts expressed at the time whether a mandatory status was actually suitable for South West Africa.[14] It elaborated in considerable detail the geographical and strategic considerations affecting South Africa and South West Africa, the degree of administrative integration that had been achieved, the close ethnological relationship between native tribes in both areas and the extent to which South West Africa was economically dependent on the Union. In conclusion, the memorandum held that a continued system of trusteeship was not suitable for South West Africa for the following reasons:

a) The fundamental principle of the mandates and trusteeship systems is "ultimate self-government and separate statehood"; but the low economic potential of the territory and "the backwardness of the vast majority of the population" render this impossible of achievement.

b) Development of the territory would involve great expense for the Mandatory, which in the nature of things it could not undertake.

c) Uncertainty as to the ultimate future of the territory militated against racial tranquillity and optimum development of the territory.[15]

The people of South West Africa, it was said, had freely and unequivocally expressed themselves in favor of incorporation, and they had thereby underscored the strength of all the foregoing considerations.

12. GAOR, 1st Sess., 2nd Part, Plen., p. LII (1946). South Africa's unilateral act in bringing the question of South West Africa's future before the United Nations was deemed significant by the Court in 1950. It constituted additional recognition by the Union government of "the competence of the General Assembly in the matter." *Status Opinion* (1950): 142.

13. GAOR, 1st Sess., 2nd Part, 4th Ctte. (Part 1), Annex 13, pp. 199–235 (1946).

14. Particular emphasis was placed on the views of G. L. Beer, who had recommended that South West Africa be annexed by South Africa. Ibid., p. 204. See also above, chap. I, p. 14. Reference was also made to the statement of Prime Minister Botha during the Class C crisis at Paris, in which he predicated South Africa's willingness to accept a League mandate on the understanding that the League "would consist mostly of the same people who were present there that day, who understood the position, and who would not make it impossible for any mandatory to govern the country." See above, p. 31.

15. GAOR, 1st Sess., 2nd Part, 4th Ctte. (Part 1), Annex 13, p. 231.

As can be readily observed, South Africa's primary focus in the memorandum was on the unsuitability of a system of international accountability and ultimate independence for the successful development of South West Africa. In this submission, South Africa was not denying that the original intent of the mandates system was "political self-government and separate statehood." By the same token, it was not challenging the general applicability of the principle of international accountability for dependent territories. It was merely asserting that South West Africa was unique and warranted international confirmation of a different arrangement. A quarter of a century's experience under the mandates system had confirmed original doubts regarding the merits of an international status for this territory, and introduction of a trusteeship arrangement would be even more ill-suited. Reference to the views of the population was only ancillary to this basic argument. In the course of the General Assembly debates emphasis was placed on two alternative themes. First, that for the Class C mandates, in contrast to those in the other two classes, incorporation with the metropolitan state, rather than independence, had been envisaged as the normal goal. Second, that the consultations that had taken place with the population, did in fact represent implementation of the principle of self-determination.

These two additional points were highlighted by General Smuts in an address before the Fourth Committee in November 1946.[16] He reminded the Committee that President Wilson had envisaged that South West Africa "would come into the Union of their [sic] own free will." "The uniting of South West Africa's destiny has been a process lasting over many years, but it has been an inevitable one—as inevitable as was the union of Wales and Scotland with England, of Texas and Louisiana with the American Union." He referred to the reservation made by South Africa at the San Francisco Conference as to the future of the territory and concluded by saying he was confident that the United Nations

> will recognize that to give effect to the wishes of the population of South West Africa in the manner indicated will primarily be the logical application of the democratic principles of self-determination. But it will be more than that. It will also be the inevitable fulfillment of an historical evolution which is in itself designed to promote the best interests of the Territory and confer upon it the benefits of the membership of a larger community without loss of those individual rights and responsibilities which the Territory enjoyed under the mandate.[17]

16. Ibid., Annex 13a, pp. 236–44, U.N. Doc. A/C. 4/41 (Nov. 4, 1946).
17. Ibid., p. 244.

South Africa's proposal regarding the future of South West Africa evoked a fiercely hostile reception from the members of the Fourth Committee. At the very moment that the world community was moving in the direction of an enhanced system of international accountability,[18] South Africa was moving toward elimination of whatever measure of international accountability yet existed. The paths of South Africa and the world organization were bound to clash. The Indian representative, setting the tone for the Fourth Committee's reaction, castigated the proposal as "retrograde" in comparison with the spirit of the Charter.[19] What advantages, he asked, would accrue to the population of South West Africa from incorporation, in the light of the racial discrimination practiced in the Union itself?[20] Considering the state of development of the native population in South West Africa, and in particular, recognizing that they had no share in the executive or legislative administration of the territory, he failed to see what meaningfulness could be accorded the "consultations" that had taken place. The only appropriate step would be to place South West Africa under the trusteeship system, whereby it would be led progressively toward political independence.

It was clear that the serene and tranquil times of the League had passed. The days of the "club" were over, and an atmosphere of sharpening conflict would be ushered in.[21]

The sharply critical tone set by the Indian representative was taken up by other representatives,[22] including those of the Soviet Union and the Soviet bloc generally,[23] the Latin American states,[24] and members of the Arab–Asian bloc.[25] South Africa was accused of attempting to justify its proposal for "annexation" by advancing a fictitious demon-

---

18. Trusteeship agreements for all those former mandates that were to come under the trusteeship system, except for the Pacific islands formerly under Japan, were concluded during the course of this second part of the first session of the General Assembly in 1946. See Goodrich and Hambro, p. 431. The United States submitted a trusteeship agreement for the islands in 1947. Ibid., p. 432.

19. GAOR, 1st Sess., 2nd Part, 4th Ctte., Part 1, 15th Mtg., Nov. 5, 1946, pp. 69–71.

20. India, it should be noted, was already at loggerheads with South Africa over the latter's treatment of Indians. See the letter dated June 22, 1946, from the Indian delegate to the Secretary-General, requesting that the item, "Treatment of Indians in the Union of South Africa," be added to the agenda of the General Assembly. U.N. Doc. A/149.

21. In the light of the stormy reception which South Africa's proposal received, one can only wonder whether the Union government canvassed the views of member states before submitting the issue to the General Assembly. Needless to say, the matter would sooner or later have been raised before that body in any case.

22. The topic of South West Africa was discussed during Meetings 15–20, November 5–14, 1946.

23. See, e.g., the remarks of the representatives of Czechoslovakia, the Soviet Union, the Ukraine, and Byelorussia, ibid., pp. 86–87, 87–92, 102, and 106–7, respectively.

24. See the remarks of the delegates of Haiti, Venezuela, and Mexico, ibid., pp. 84, 104, and 108, respectively.

25. See e.g., the remarks of the delegates of China and Syria, ibid., pp. 98, 113.

stration of the will of the people of South West Africa.[26] Why, it was asked, could the white population be consulted by means of "normal democratic processes" and the rest of the population only by "abnormal democratic processes?"[27] Did "the right of peoples to self-determination" include "the right to commit suicide," and could the United Nations sanction such a step?[28] Even the representative of the United States expressed the view that the available data did not justify approval of the plan for incorporation "during *this* session of the General Assembly."[29] The United Kingdom alone supported South Africa's proposal, by stressing that there was no reason to doubt the fairness and accuracy of the results of the consultations with the natives.[30] But the overwhelming majority of delegates were violently opposed to the South African proposal. It was inconceivable in their eyes that any move along the lines advocated by South Africa should be sanctioned by the United Nations, an organization dedicated to the "self-determination of peoples."[31]

A subcommittee was established to formulate the views of the Committee members. At this point, Field-Marshal Smuts addressed the Fourth Committee once again and indicated that "it would not be possible for the Union Government as a former mandatory to submit a trusteeship agreement in conflict with the clearly expressed wishes of the inhabitants."

> If . . . the Assembly did not agree that the clear wishes of the inhabitants should be implemented, the Union Government could take no other course than to abide by the declaration it had made to the last Assembly of the League of Nations to the effect that it would continue to administer the territory as heretofore as an integral part of the Union, and to do so in the spirit of the principles laid down in the mandate.

> In particular the Union would, in accordance with Article 73, paragraph (e) of the Charter, transmit regularly to the Secretary-General of the United Nations "for information purposes, subject to such limitations as security and constitutional regulations might require, statistical and other information of a technical nature relating to economic, social, and educational conditions" in South West Africa. There was nothing in the relevant clauses of the Charter, nor was it in the minds of those who drafted these clauses, to support the contention that the Union Government could be

26. Ibid., pp. 87–92. Remarks of the Soviet delegate.
27. Ibid., p. 98. Remarks of the Cuban delegate.
28. Ibid., pp. 86–87. Remarks of the Czech delegate.
29. Ibid., p. 107 (emphasis supplied).
30. Ibid., pp. 99–101. The United Kingdom delegate referred to the independent survey conducted by Lord Hailey.
31. Article 1 of the Charter.

compelled to enter into a trusteeship agreement even against its own view or those of the people concerned.[32]

The subcommittee, after rejecting one draft resolution proposed by the Soviet Union and another sponsored jointly by India and Cuba, adopted a Danish-United States draft resolution.[33] In contrast to the others, this draft did not state that incorporation was contrary to the Charter, nor that it was the intention of the Charter that the trusteeship system shall apply to mandated territories. Instead, it simply noted that the data before the General Assembly did not justify action approving incorporation. However, when the matter was considered by the Fourth Committee as a whole, in place of the Danish-United States text, it adopted an Indian draft-resolution which was no less peremptory than the aforementioned Indian-Cuban draft.[34] As adopted, the draft resolution rejected incorporation as being inconsistent with the Charter which, it was said, intended the conversion of mandates into trust territories. Accordingly, South Africa was to be "requested" to submit a trusteeship agreement for South West Africa. In plenary, however, the Fourth Committee's proposal was in turn replaced by a new joint-draft resolution sponsored by the delegations of India, the United States, and Denmark.[35] As might be expected, the compromise text was more forceful than the Danish-United States version of the subcommittee, but less so than the Indian version accepted by the Fourth Committee.

(The foregoing pattern of events, it may be noted, was to be regularly repeated throughout the fifties whenever the South West Africa issue arose in the United Nations. India, Cuba, and the Philippines were invariably at the head of an activist group bent on taking drastic political steps against South Africa, while Denmark and the United States were regularly at the head of a group of Western states intent on promoting a more moderate approach to the issue [with particular emphasis on international law and the role of the International Court]. Each group prepared separate draft resolutions, and these were ultimately combined in order to command the necessary majorities. [The Soviet bloc generally adopted a more extreme position than that of the activist group, but its suggested course was never followed by the Assembly.] Subsequently, in the late 1950's with the influx of Afro-

32. GAOR, 1st Sess., 2nd Part, 4th Ctte., Part 1, 19th Mtg., Nov. 13, 1946, p. 102.
33. For a review of the work of the subcommittee and the text of the various draft resolutions, see ibid., Annex 21, Part II, pp. 285-89 and 295. U N. Doc. A/C. 4/68.
34. GAOR, 1st Sess., 2nd Part, 4th Ctte., Part 1, 21st Mtg., Dec. 8, 1946, p. 123. For text, see U.N. Doc. A/250.
35. Discussed in GAOR, 1st Sess., 2nd Part, Plen., 64th Mtg., Dec. 14, 1946, pp. 1323-27. The vote was 37 to 0, with 9 abstentions. Presumably India recognized that its draft resolution would not receive a two-thirds majority in Plenary. The question of the vote required was to be debated in the second General Assembly session. See below, p. 90.

Asian states, the moderate elements lost most, if not all, of their effective influence.)

In the preambular part of the resolution (Resolution 65 [I]), as adopted, the General Assembly, *inter alia*, noted with satisfaction South Africa's recognition of United Nations interest and concern in the future status of South West Africa; recalled that the Charter provided that the trusteeship system shall apply to territories under mandate *"as may be subsequently agreed"*;[36] expressed a desire for an agreement between the United Nations and South Africa on the future status of the territory, and accepted South Africa's assurance that it would continue in the meantime to administer the territory in the spirit of the mandate. However, considering that the peoples of South West Africa had not yet reached a stage of political development enabling them to express a considered opinion on the question of incorporation, it was stated that:

> *The General Assembly therefore,*
> *Is unable to accede* to the incorporation of the territory of South West Africa in the Union of South Africa; and
> *Recommends that the* mandated territory of South West Africa be placed under the international trusteeship system and invites the Government of the Union of South Africa to propose for the consideration of the General Assembly a trusteeship agreement for the aforesaid territory.

Prior to the vote, the South African representative indicated his inability to accept the draft resolution, as a result of which he would abstain from voting. He would, however, report back to the peoples of South West Africa and acquaint them with the contents of the resolution.[37]

South Africa's reply to the General Assembly's recommendations was contained in a letter to the Secretary-General, dated July 23, 1947.[38] The posture of the Union government, as reflected in this communication, represented a combination of compliance and recalcitrance. On the one hand, that government conveyed its willingness not to proceed with incorporation, in deference to the General Assembly's wishes. But on the other hand, it indicated its inability to comply with the Assembly's recommendation for concluding a trusteeship agreement, which course would, in its view, flout the clearly expressed wishes of the inhabitants of the territory. At the same time, the

---

36. Emphasis supplied. The phrase was added at the behest of the group of states that had supported the Danish–United States proposal. This group denied that the Charter obligated the conversion of mandates into trust territories.

37. GAOR, 1st Sess., 2nd Part, Plen., 64th Mtg., Dec. 14, 1946, p. 1326.

38. U.N. Doc. A/334, in GAOR, 2nd Sess., 4th Ctte., Annex 3a, p. 135.

Union government indicated that, in accordance with a resolution of its Parliament, it was taking steps to furnish reports on the administration of the territory for the information of the United Nations, and also to secure direct representation for South West Africa in the Union Parliament. In South Africa's view these latter moves were not inconsistent with one another. Both moves were related to South Africa's decision to "maintain the *status quo* and to continue to administer the territory in the spirit of the existing mandate."[39]

A copy of the resolution adopted by the House of Assembly of the Union Parliament was included in the South African letter. In the resolution, the House considered, first, that full power of legislation and administration was conferred on the Union in respect of South West Africa, "subject only to the rendering of reports to the League"; second, that the League had ceased to exist and that it was neither empowered to nor did it in fact transfer its rights and powers to the United Nations; third, that the Union had never surrendered its rights and powers regarding the territory; and finally, that the overwhelming desire of the territory's population was in favor of incorporation. On this basis, it was concluded:

> Therefore this House is of opinion that the Territory should be represented in the Parliament of the Union as an integral portion thereof and requests the Government to introduce legislation, after consultation with the inhabitants of the territory, providing for its representation in the Union Parliament, and that the Government should continue to render reports to the United Nations Organization as it has done heretofore under the Mandate.[40]

39. This sentence in the South African letter, including the reference to "the existing mandate," was cited by the Court in 1950, as "recognition by the Union Government of the continuance of its obligations under the Mandate." *Status Opinion* (1950): 135.

40. U.N. Doc. A/334, in GAOR, 2nd Sess., 4th Ctte., Annex 3a, p. 134. The final sentence in this resolution was also cited by the 1950 Court as acknowledgment by South Africa of the continued existence of the mandate. But the Court did not cite this resolution as evidence that South Africa had acquiesced in United Nations supervision of the mandate. *Status Opinion* (1950): 135–38. See also *SWA Pleadings* IX: 427. Ethiopia and Liberia, however, in the pleadings in the *South West Africa* cases high-lighted the fact that this resolution directed the Union government "to continue to render reports to the United Nations Organization as it has done heretofore under the Mandate." "This resolution," Applicants argued, "makes explicit Respondent's awareness of its responsibility to report to the United Nations 'as it has done heretofore under the Mandate.'" Ibid., p. 172. It was, therefore, evidence of South African recognition of the transfer of supervisory powers over South West Africa from the League to the United Nations. Respondent's attempt to dismiss this evidence by noting that it was merely "a resolution of one of the Houses of the Union Parliament" (ibid., VIII: 464) was countered by Applicants, who pointed out that the resolution was referred to, and its text even included, in the official communication of South Africa to the Secretary-General on July 23, 1947. (Ibid., IX: 172.) In response, South Africa emphasized that its letter had explicitly indicated that submission of its report was for the purpose of "the information of the United Nations," a clear reference to the terms of Article 73(e) of the Charter. There was never any acceptance on South Africa's part of United Nations supervision of South West Africa *as a mandated territory*. See ibid., VIII: 464–66; IX: 424–27.

## THE SECOND SESSION OF THE GENERAL ASSEMBLY

The General Assembly at its Second Session was faced with two distinct issues. (1) What action should it take upon the announced intention of South Africa to disregard the 1946 General Assembly recommendation that South West Africa be placed under the trusteeship system? (2) In the meantime, how should it deal with the report on South West Africa submitted during the session by South Africa? Was it appropriate that the Trusteeship Council consider the report, even though no trusteeship agreement existed, or would it be more advisable for a special committee of the General Assembly to handle the matter? Furthermore, what form of procedure should be followed in the actual consideration of the report?

*1) South Africa's Refusal to Negotiate a Trusteeship Agreement.*

The question of what attitude the Assembly should adopt on this point revolved basically around divergent interpretations of the provisions of the Charter and whether they created a legal obligation for each mandatory power to negotiate a trusteeship agreement. The South African representative in the debate in the Fourth Committee emphatically denied the existence of any such legal obligation. The Charter had clearly established the optional nature of the trusteeship arrangements, and the mere fact that other mandatory powers had concluded trusteeship agreements could not impose a moral obligation on South Africa to do likewise; nor could the "recommendations" of the General Assembly establish a legal obligation.[41]

The countervailing viewpoint, endorsed by members of the Soviet bloc, Arab–Asian states, and some Latin–American states, was that South Africa was under a clear legal and moral obligation to negotiate a trusteeship agreement.[42] The following legal arguments were adduced in support:[43] The language of Article 77 (1) is mandatory: "The trusteeship system *shall* apply to . . . . (a) territories now held under

41. GAOR, 2nd Sess., 4th Ctte., 31st Mtg., Sept. 25, 1947, pp. 3–4; 38th Mtg., Oct. 7, 1947, pp. 47–49. Moreover, a trusteeship agreement "would create between the Union and South West Africa, a relation less integrated than was contemplated by, and in fact existed, under the Treaty of Versailles and the League Covenant." Again he reminded the Committee that President Wilson had envisaged South West Africa as a self-governing unit integrated into the Union. Ibid., pp. 48–49.

42. The remarks of the Indian delegate are representative. Ibid., 31st Mtg., Sept. 25, 1947, pp. 4–5.

43. The legal arguments, both pro and con, presented at this session of the General Assembly were repeated and expanded upon in subsequent Assembly sessions. Ultimately, they constituted the heart of the pleadings presented to the Court in 1950. See below, chap. V. See also *Repertory of Practice of United Nations Organs* IV: 162–68 (1955). The debate in the Fourth Committee took place during Meetings 31–33, 38–40, and 45, held from September 25–October 15, 1947. GAOR, 2nd Sess., 4th Ctte., pp. 3–98.

Mandate."[44] The fact that the word "voluntarily" was found only in paragraph (c) of Article 77 (1), confirmed that mandates, covered in paragraph (a), were the subject of a legal duty;[45] Article 80 (2) stipulated that the negotiation and conclusion of agreements for placing mandated territories under the trusteeship system should not be postponed;[46] were South Africa's argument adopted, the Trusteeship Council, a principal organ of the United Nations, might never have come into being;[47] since the League no longer existed, South Africa could no longer administer the territory as a mandate and had no choice but to convert it to a trust territory.[48] The Charter provided for only two alternatives—trusteeship or independence; it did not envisage the coexistence of the mandates and trusteeship systems.[49]

On the other hand, South Africa's view that there was no legal obligation to convert the mandate into a trust territory was endorsed by representatives of Australia, Belgium, Bolivia, Canada, Denmark, France, Greece, the Netherlands, New Zealand, the United Kingdom, and the United States. In support, they cited the following considerations: Article 75 in its terms was clearly permissive. The trusteeship system was to be established for the administration of "such territories as *may* be placed thereunder by subsequent individual agreements";[50] Article 77 (1) was similarly permissive by its reference to "territories . . . as *may* be placed thereunder." An attempt by Egypt at San Francisco to eliminate the permissive quality of this provision was rejected.[51] Article 77 (2) was crystal clear on the issue: "It will be a matter for subsequent agreement as to which territories in the foregoing categories will be brought under the trusteeship system and upon what terms";[52] inclusion of the word "voluntarily" in Article 77 (1)c, did not mean that mandates, covered in (1)a, were subject to a legal obligation to be brought under the trusteeship system. The word "voluntarily" was also omitted in (1)b, and yet it could hardly be claimed that territories detached from enemy states were the subject of a legal obli-

44. Emphasis supplied. See the remarks of the delegates of China, Guatemala, Cuba, Byelorussia, and Colombia. Ibid., pp. 6, 8, 10, 12–13, and 14, respectively.

45. See the remarks of the delegates of China, the Philippines, and the Soviet Union, ibid., pp. 6–7, 9.

46. See the remarks of the delegates of China, Uruguay, and Colombia, ibid., pp. 6, 14.

47. See the remarks by the delegates of Poland, Byelorussia, and Mexico, ibid., pp. 6–7, 13, and 17.

48. See the remarks of the delegates of Guatemala and Colombia, ibid., pp. 8 and 14.

49. See the remarks of the delegate of China, ibid., p. 6.

50. See, e.g., the remarks of the delegates of the Netherlands, France, the United States, and Australia, ibid., pp. 8, 11, 50, and 58 (emphasis supplied).

51. Ibid., p. 58. See also the remarks of the delegates of South Africa and Canada. Ibid., pp. 15, 56.

52. Ibid., p. 56. See also the remarks of the delegate of France, ibid., pp. 11–12.

gation.[53] The word "voluntarily" was only included in (1)c, *ex abundanti cautela*. Article 80 (1) safeguarded the existing rights of members; Article 80 (2) could not be given an interpretation which would nullify the effect of Article 80 (1) or the clearly permissive quality of all other provisions. Article 80 (2) only related to the instance where a state has already decided to submit an agreement. Any other interpretation would make it compulsory for every non-self-governing territory to be converted into a trust territory, since Article 80 (2) would have to modify all of Article 77 (1), including (1)c.[54]

During the course of the debate a suggestion was made for the General Assembly to request an advisory opinion from the International Court of Justice on the question of legal obligation; but no action was taken on the suggestion at that time.[55]

### 2) Handling of the Report on South West Africa.

In his opening statement to the Fourth Committee, the South African representative had confirmed that his government would not proceed with the incorporation of South West Africa, but would continue to maintain the *status quo* by administering the territory in the spirit of the mandate; it would also transmit to the United Nations for its information an annual report on the administration of the territory of South West Africa.[56] Subsequently, the representative explained that the annual report would contain the same type of information as is required for non-self-governing territories under Article 73 (e) of the Charter. It was the assumption of his government, he said, that the report would not be considered by the Trusteeship Council and would not be dealt with as if a trusteeship agreement had in fact been concluded. He further explained that since the League of Nations had ceased to exist, the right to submit petitions could no longer be exercised, since that right presupposes a jurisdiction which would only exist where there is a right of control or supervision, and in the view of the Union of South Africa no such jurisdiction is vested in the United Nations with regard to South West Africa.[57]

South Africa presumably envisioned that the report on South West Africa, submitted in September, would be taken up by the *Ad Hoc*

53. Ibid. See the question posed by the representative of South Africa to the Soviet delegate on these lines, with reference to Soviet control of East Prussia. GAOR, 3rd Sess., 4th Ctte., 81st Mtg., Nov. 16, 1948, pp. 341 ff.

54. See the remarks of the delegate of South Africa, GAOR, 2nd Sess., Plen., 105th Mtg., Nov. 1, 1947, pp. 631–32.

55. See the remarks of the delegates of the Netherlands, Greece, and Argentina, ibid., 4th Ctte., 31st Mtg., Sept. 27, 1947, p. 8; 33rd Mtg., Sept. 27, 1947, p. 14; and 38th Mtg., Oct. 7, 1947, p. 52, respectively.

56. Ibid., 31st Mtg., Sept. 25, 1947, p. 3.

57. U.N. Doc. A/422, in GAOR, 2nd Sess., Plen., Vol. II, Annex 13, p. 1538.

Committee set up by the General Assembly to assist it in considering information on non-self-governing territories. This suggestion, however, was totally unacceptable to the members of the General Assembly, since it would put South West Africa, a mandated territory, on a level with colonies—a category of dependent territory with the least measure of international accountability. The vast majority of states favored consideration of the report by the Trusteeship Council, since in their eyes South West Africa was closest in status to a trust territory (whether a legal obligation to conclude a trusteeship agreement existed or not).[58] On similar grounds, they were opposed to its examination by a special committee, since this might imply that South West Africa was something *sui generis*.[59] Other states, however, considered that it would be appropriate for the Fourth Committee or a subcommittee thereof to handle the matter.[60]

Once again India[61] and Denmark[62] presented separate draft resolutions, reflecting a divergency of approach both on the issue of South Africa's refusal to negotiate a trusteeship agreement and the proper organ for handling the report. The Danish draft resolution was far less forceful than the Indian version. It expressed regret at, rather than disapproval of, South Africa's failure to act in accordance with Resolution 65 (1); it expressed the hope that South Africa would soon see fit to comply, but did not impose a time limit for such compliance as the Indian draft did; and, finally, it recommended that a special committee, rather than the Trusteeship Council, consider the report on South West Africa. Despite modifications from both sides, agreement on a unified text proved impossible. The revised versions of the respective draft resolutions[63] agreed on authorizing the Trusteeship Council to examine the report and urging South Africa to submit a trusteeship agreement, but continued to differ over the imposition of a time limit. The Indian draft resolution, by specifying a time limit, i.e., the third General Assembly session, clearly implied that South Africa was under a legal duty to submit an agreement. This Denmark refused to accept.[64] The Fourth Committee, after accepting a Polish amendment, adopted the Indian draft resolution by a vote of 27 to 20, with 4 abstentions.[65] The

58. See, for example, the remarks of the delegates of China, France, Egypt, the Soviet Union, Cuba, and the Ukraine, GAOR, 2nd Sess., 4th Ctte., pp. 6, 12, 51, 52, 56, and 60, respectively.
59. See the remarks of Mexican delegate, ibid., p. 55.
60. See the remarks of the delegates of the United States, Denmark, and Australia, ibid., pp. 6, 47, and 58.
61. Ibid., Annex, 3 (h), p. 197.
62. Ibid., Annex, 3 (m), pp. 200–1.
63. Ibid., Annex, 3 (1) and 3 (p), pp. 199–202.
64. See the remarks of the representatives of Denmark and the Netherlands, GAOR, 2nd Sess., 4th Ctte., p. 94.
65. Ibid., p. 98.

amendment declared categorically that it was the clear intention of Chapter XII of the Charter that all mandates shall, until granted self-government or independence, be brought under the trusteeship system.[66] This stamped South Africa's position as one of rank illegality.

In Plenary,[67] the Danish representative proposed amendments by which both the Polish amendment and the time limit would be eliminated.[68] At this point, a lengthy debate ensued on whether a resolution calling upon a state to submit a trusteeship agreement constituted a "question relating to the operation of the trusteeship system," such as would, in accordance with Article 18 (2) of the Charter, require a two-thirds majority for acceptance.[69] By a vote of 31 to 20, with 5 abstentions, the Assembly decided to accept the ruling of the President of the General Assembly that the resolution involved an important question requiring a two-thirds majority.[70] This fact precluded General Assembly adoption of the Fourth Committee's draft resolution, and led the Indian representative to endorse the Danish amendments. The draft resolution, as amended, was then adopted by a vote of 41 to 10, with 4 abstentions.[71]

This resolution referred to earlier General Assembly recommendations that South West Africa be placed under the trusteeship system and noted South Africa's failure to comply therewith. The Assembly reaffirmed its earlier recommendation, urged the Union government to propose a trusteeship agreement and expressed the hope that the Union government might find it possible to do this in time for Assembly consideration at the third session. Finally, the Resolution authorized the Trusteeship Council to examine the report on South West Africa and to submit its observations thereon to the General Assembly. Most significantly, however, the General Assembly had eliminated any implication that South Africa was under a legal *duty* to negotiate a trusteeship agreement.[72]

66. Ibid., p. 96. For the full text of the Fourth Committee resolution, see ibid., pp. 97–98.

67. Ibid., Plen., 104th Mtg., Nov. 1, 1947, pp. 574–77.

68. U.N. Doc. A/429.

69. GAOR, 2nd Sess., Plen., 104th and 105th Mtgs., Nov. 1, 1947, pp. 574–648. In support of a simple majority it was argued that a request for a trusteeship agreement did not relate to the "operation" of the trusteeship system and that the present resolution merely confirmed a previous resolution. In response, it was emphasized that if the "operation" of the trusteeship system was sufficiently important to warrant a two-thirds majority, then *a fortiori* a question relating to the introduction of a territory into the system required such a majority. Moreover, the role of the Trusteeship Council under the proposed resolution was noted. Other delegates simply emphasized that a resolution adopted with anything less than a two-thirds majority would carry very little weight.

70. Ibid., 105th Mtg., Nov. 1, 1947, p. 648.

71. Ibid., pp. 650–51. G. A. Res. 141 (II), Nov. 1, 1947.

72. See the discussion relating to adoption of this resolution in the Written Statement of the United States, *1950 Status Pleadings*, pp. 118–19, 122–24; see also Goodrich and Hambro, pp. 433, 436.

## CONSIDERATION OF THE 1946 REPORT ON SOUTH WEST AFRICA BY THE TRUSTEESHIP COUNCIL

The Trusteeship Council,[73] in entering upon a consideration of the report on South West Africa,[74] was first confronted with a relatively simple question, which in turn raised a series of legal and technical problems. The first preliminary question was: Should the Union government be invited to have a representative present during examination of the report?[75] This in turn raised two more fundamental questions, one substantive and the other procedural.

1. What was the substantive nature of the report referred to the Trusteeship Council? Was the report simply a collection of factual material for information purposes only, as intimated by South Africa, or was it, properly speaking, an international accounting on a dependent territory?

2. If the report was considered a formal accounting, what procedures should be adopted in its examination? Could the Trusteeship Council handle it as it would a report from a trust territory, or was it required to follow the procedure of the Permanent Mandates Commission?

The first question was the subject of debate between the Australian and Chinese representatives at the Council session.[76] According to the Australian representative, the Council was bound to take due notice of the limited purpose for which South Africa had submitted the report. South West Africa was, for the moment, not a trust territory, and the Trusteeship Council could not exercise a supervisory authority over the territory. In reply, the Chinese representative noted that the General Assembly had purposely selected the Trusteeship Council rather than some other body to examine the report, and had thereby recognized "the propriety of a thorough examination of the report from the point of view of the interest of the inhabitants." Authority was granted "to examine the report and not just to look at it for information purposes."[77] No formal determination of the issue was ever made, but in the nature of things the Chinese interpretation prevailed, as evidenced by the action of the Council and the form of the report ultimately presented to the General Assembly.

73. The Trusteeship Council at this time consisted of representatives of Australia, Belgium, China, France, Iraq, Mexico, New Zealand, Soviet Union, United Kingdom, United States, Costa Rica, and the Philippines.
74. See *Report by the Government of the Union of South Africa on the Administration of South West Africa for the Year 1946* (Pretoria: Government Printer, 1947).
75. See the discussions in TCOR, 2nd Sess., 1st Part, 6th Mtg., Dec. 1, 1947, pp. 120–33; 15th Mtg., Dec. 12, 1947, pp. 470–513; and 18th Mtg., Dec. 16, 1947, pp. 575–81.
76. Ibid., 15th Mtg., Dec. 12, 1947, pp. 473–78.
77. Ibid., pp. 476–77.

As regards the procedural issue, a consensus was more or less reached that the Trusteeship Council would examine this report as it would any other, but would in principle endeavor to follow as closely as possible the practice of the Permanent Mandates Commission.[78] This would exclude oral petitions and periodic visits to the territory.[79]

The questions and doubts raised at this early stage are illustrative of the type of legal and procedural problems that were to successively plague the world organization in its endeavors to handle a remarkably anomalous situation, namely, the United Nations acting in place of the League of Nations to control a League instrumentality. It was anomalous, because a mandate was something of a fossilized remnant of an earlier colonial age, and the United Nations was not equipped to handle relics. How does a gasoline station service a horse and buggy?

The Union government was informed of the date on which the report would be considered and that it would be welcome to send a representative to be present, if it desired to do so.[80] In reply, the Union government informed the Council that it did not propose to avail itself of the invitation, but would be prepared to supplement the report with other available data in writing, if clarifying material was requested.[81]

Council consideration of the report prompted a number of delegates to instance numerous areas where the report seemed to lack adequate particularization or clarification.[82] Ultimately, a resolution was unanimously adopted noting this incompleteness and inviting South Africa to provide supplementary information before June 1948.[83] A comprehensive list of fifty questions was attached to the resolution for transmission to the Union government.[84] The list was subdivided into the following seven heads: Government, Financial and Economic, Land and Reserves, Labor, Education, Health, and Hereros. The questions were quite incisive and clearly designed to ascertain the extent to which

78. See the remarks of the representatives of Belgium, et al., ibid., 6th Mtg., pp. 124-25.

79. See general discussion, ibid., 15th Mtg., pp. 473-85. A suggestion by the Mexican representative that the Reverend Michael Scott, a minister bearing petitions from certain African chiefs in South West Africa, be heard was not accepted. In withdrawing his proposal, the Mexican delegate reserved the right to reintroduce it at a later date. See general discussion, ibid., 18th Mtg., Dec. 16, 1947, pp. 593-605.

This marked the first occasion upon which the name of the Rev. Michael Scott arose in connection with the South West Africa issue at the United Nations. Henceforth it was to be regularly and intimately associated with that subject during every stage of the dispute. The Rev. Scott is an Anglican priest from South Africa, now resident in England, who has made it his life task to speak and act on behalf of the cause of independence for South West Africa. South Africa has castigated him as a misinformed agitator.

80. Ibid., 6th Mtg., pp. 132-33.

81. See ibid., 10th Mtg., Dec. 5, 1947, p. 294, and 15th Mtg., Dec. 12, 1947, p. 471.

82. Ibid., pp. 485-508.

83. Ibid., pp. 508-9.

84. For the text of the resolution and the annexed questions, see Resolutions of the Trusteeship Council, 2nd Sess., Res. 28 (II), Dec. 11, 1947, pp. 15-21.

South Africa was actually promoting the welfare of the non-Europeans and to probe the degree to which discriminatory practices were permitted to interfere with that purpose.[85]

The detailed reply of the South African government was transmitted on May 31, 1948.[86] In an accompanying letter,[87] it was recalled that in the view of the Union government, the transmission to the United Nations of information on South West Africa, in the form of an annual report or any other form, was done on a voluntary basis and for the purposes of information only. South Africa recognized no obligation to transmit this information to the United Nations. Submission of the original report had been done on the basis of the provisions of Article 73 (e) of the Charter, which only refers to "statistical and other information of a technical nature," but which excludes reference to information on questions of policy. Nevertheless, the Union government, anxious to be as helpful and as cooperative as possible, had, on this occasion, replied in full to the questions dealing with various aspects of policy. This, however, should not be regarded as a precedent. Furthermore, these replies should not be construed as a commitment as to future policy or as implying any measure of accountability to the United Nations on the part of the Union government. The declared intention to administer the territory in the spirit of the mandate "has been construed in some quarters as implying a measure of international accountability. This construction the Union Government cannot accept and they would again recall that the League of Nations at its final session in April 1946 explicitly refrained from transferring its functions in respect of Mandates to the United Nations."[88]

On July 23, 1948, the Trusteeship Council resumed consideration of the report on South West Africa and of the supplementary informa-

---

85. The government was asked, for instance, to provide details regarding: the steps planned toward fuller participation by non-Europeans in the government of the territory; the total amount spent directly on non-European administration and welfare; the nature of the pass laws; government expenditure on European, African, and Coloured education, respectively; and the number of hospital beds provided per 1,000 of the population for Europeans and non-Europeans, respectively.

86. U.N. Doc. T/175. TCOR, 3rd Sess., Supp., pp. 51–152 (1948). The Council had requested submission of the information before June 1948.

In the South African elections of May 26, 1948, the Smuts government was defeated by the Nationalist party. Smuts resigned forthwith, and in the next few days Dr. D. F. Malan appointed his ministry. See Eric A. Walker, *A History of Southern Africa* (3rd ed.; London: Longmans, Green, 1957), pp. 772–73. As noted in the text, South Africa's reply was transmitted on May 31, 1948. It is interesting to speculate whether the material, which was certainly prepared under the Smuts government, was actually conveyed in accordance with instructions from that government or was transmitted as a result of a decision taken by the new government. (As will be seen below, the Nationalist government refused to submit any further reports to the world organization.) An inquiry on the subject addressed by this writer to the South African Ministry for Foreign Affairs did not elicit any clarification.

87. U.N. Doc. T/175. TCOR, 3rd Sess., Supp., pp. 51–54 (1948).

88. Ibid., p. 52.

tion furnished by South Africa in response to the Council's question-naire.[89] The material was subjected to a detailed and critical analysis to determine the degree to which South Africa was promoting the welfare of the indigenous inhabitants and ensuring their political, economic, social, and educational advancement.[90] In the end, a severely critical report was adopted.[91] Certain members had earlier argued that the report, in accordance with the original Assembly resolution, should contain "observations" only, not recommendations, since South West Africa was, after all, not a trust territory. Moreover, it was feared that sharp criticism of South Africa might only induce that state to refrain from submitting further reports.[92] In response, it was pointed out that the General Assembly, in requesting "observations," had undoubtedly wished for "an expression of opinion." "Those who maintained," said the Mexican delegate, "that the submission of a completely neutral report to the General Assembly would encourage the [Union] Govern-ment . . . to place South West Africa under the Trusteeship System were deluding themselves. Nothing but an aroused world public opinion would compel the Union of South Africa to take that step." For this reason it was the duty of the Council to present "both an analysis and a diagnosis of conditions in South West Africa."[93]

In its Report to the General Assembly,[94] the Trusteeship Council observed that although the indigenous inhabitants represented 90 per-cent of the South West African population, barely 10 percent of the budget was expended on their administration and welfare. The disparity was particularly evident in the fields of education and medical services. There was little provision for primary education and none at all for secondary or higher education. There were no arrangements for training indigenous medical personnel. The indigenous inhabitants were denied the franchise, eligibility to office, and representation in the governing bodies or in the administration of the territory. Non-Europeans were restricted both in their ownership of land and of livestock. The report

89. TCOR, 3rd Sess., 31st Mtg., p. 406.

90. Ibid., pp. 410 ff.

91. Ibid., 42nd Mtg., Aug. 4, 1948, p. 552.

92. See the remarks of the representatives of the United Kingdom, Australia, Belgium, and the United States. Ibid., 41st Mtg., Aug. 4, 1948, pp. 531-35.

93. Ibid., p. 533. The hope that an aroused "world public opinion" would ultimately prevail upon South Africa to modify its stand guided much United Nations thinking up until the late 1950's.

94. Report of the Trusteeship Council Covering its Second and Third Sessions, 29 April 1947-5 August 1948. GAOR, 3rd Sess. Supp. No. 4 (A/603), 1948, pp. 42-45.

This report has significance, not only for its substantive findings and the immediate effect which it had on the relationship between South Africa and the United Nations but also because it constituted the model followed by all subsequent committees charged with drawing up annual reports on conditions in South West Africa.

criticized various aspects of the labor situation, such as the hiring of convict labor, the low scale of wages paid to workers in the mines, the imposition of criminal penalties for breach of contract by employees, and the fact that no conventions of the International Labor Organization had been applied to the territory. But above all, the report declared its opposition to the system of racial segregation and considered that great efforts should be made, through education and other positive measures, to alter the situation.

As can readily be seen, the "observations" of the Trusteeship Council amounted to a blistering attack on South Africa's conduct of the South West Africa mandate. Every single facet of its administration was criticized for failing, in effect, to fulfill the injunction of Article 2 of the Mandate to "promote to the utmost the material and moral well-being and the social progress of the inhabitants of the territory." Despite the fact that the views of the Council were not couched in the form of recommendations, they were clearly designed to promote change and, in this respect, represented quite consciously an exercise of supervision over the territory of South West Africa.

## THE THIRD SESSION OF THE GENERAL ASSEMBLY

Consideration of the Trusteeship Council's report on South West Africa opened in the Fourth Committee on November 9, 1948.[95] On that occasion, Mr. Louw, the new South African representative, made his first appearance before the Committee. In the period since the previous General Assembly session, a change of government had taken place in South Africa, with the Nationalists, under the leadership of D. F. Malan, replacing the Smuts government. The new government had been elected on a platform of more rigorous racial segregation under a system known under its Afrikaans title as *apartheid*. Mr. Louw criticized the Trusteeship Council's handling of the report submitted by the South African government.[96] South Africa maintained its earlier stand: it recognized no measure of accountability to the United Nations with respect to South West Africa, its previous report and subsequent replies having been supplied voluntarily and for information purposes only. Therefore, by assuming for itself the right to determine whether or not South Africa had adequately discharged its responsibilities under the mandate, the Trusteeship Council had, in the opinion of South Africa, clearly exceeded its powers. Moreover, the Trusteeship Council was very unlike the Permanent Mandates Commission, which "had been

95. GAOR, 3rd Sess., Part 1, 4th Ctte., 76th Mtg., pp. 287 ff.
96. Ibid., pp. 287–94.

characterized by a spirit of understanding and a genuine desire to take full account of the special conditions arising in the territories," and "had never been influenced by political or ideological motives."[97]

After reviewing once again the historical and legal considerations underlying his government's stand, he declared that the territory would be administered, as in the past, "with due regard to the material and moral well-being of all sections of its population." He informed the General Assembly that steps were under way to institute representation of South West Africa in the Union Parliament as well as to accord the territory increased powers of autonomy. The new arrangement was not incorporation, he insisted, for, in fact, it would confer on South West Africa a greater measure of self-government than was accorded to other provinces of the Union. Nonetheless, the agreement would provide for "a closer association and integration of South West Africa with the Union of South Africa along the lines envisaged in the previous Mandate, since expired." Such, he declared, was the vision and intention of President Wilson and other Allied leaders at Versailles, and the actions of the Union government were in accordance with that vision.[98]

This was the first occasion upon which South Africa claimed that the mandate, as such, had come to an end. Up until this point, South Africa had not denied that the mandate, as an institution, continued to exist. It merely claimed that there was no longer an organ to report to, once the League was disbanded. Now, however, South Africa was arguing that it was no longer subject to *any* obligations under the mandate, even as regards its obligations toward the indigenous population. Its action, henceforth, would be based not on a legal duty, but simply on a subjective desire to sustain the spirit of the mandate.[99]

South Africa's announcement that it was in the process of initiating measures which would tie South West Africa closer to the Union amounted to a firm denial of the authority of the United Nations to intervene in this whole question. Those delegates who had consistently called upon South Africa to place the territory under the trusteeship system saw ominous signs in this latest development. The Chinese repre-

97. Ibid., pp. 288–89.
98. Ibid., pp. 292–93.
99. Applicants, during the proceedings in the *South West Africa* cases, referred a number of times to the fact that "in the period 1946–1949 the Union's policy concerning the Mandate underwent a marked change." *SWA Pleadings* I: 48; VIII: 163–65. In the Counter-Memorial South Africa denied that its policy had undergone any change. Ibid., II: 63–64. However, in the subsequent oral proceedings, Respondent conceded that South Africa's earlier and later positions represented the divergent views of the Smuts and Malan governments on the question of the continued existence of the mandate, *as an institution*. Nevertheless, neither government, Respondent stressed, acknowledged any right of United Nations supervision of the mandate. Ibid., VIII: 428–30.

sentative charged that "steps had been taken which virtually constituted an annexation of the Territory."[100] Madame Pandit, the Indian
delegate, declared that "on these facts she had no hesitation in asserting
that the absorption of South West Africa into the Union was imminent
if not already complete."[101] The representative of Uruguay challenged
the assertion that the mandate was ended, by citing the Union letter of
July 23, 1947, in the course of which reference was made to the "existing Mandate."[102] International accountability, he maintained, did not
end with the League. The Council of the League had studied reports in
its capacity as an organ of the international community. In this respect
it acted as a coordinating center for all states. With the disappearance of
the League, the United Nations assumed the role of a coordinating
center, acting on behalf of the members of the civilized and organized
collectivity. It was to the international community, rather than to any
particular organization *per se*, that international accountability was
owed.[103] (This concept of an international community to which legal
obligations are owed is one that received considerable attention in the
course of the South West Africa dispute.)[104]

In reply, Mr. Louw insisted that South Africa predicated its stand
on "the legal position, namely on the provisions of the Charter." That
the United Nations was not the legatee of the League was amply demonstrated by the final resolution of the League Assembly. Paragraph 4
of that resolution spoke of the intents of mandatory powers "to continue to administer the ex-mandated territories[105] 'until other arrangements have been agreed between the United Nations and the respective
Mandatory Powers,' not until Trusteeship agreements had been drawn
up." This wording, he said, had been carefully tailored to reflect the

100. GAOR, 3rd Sess., Part 1, 4th Ctte., 76th Mtg., Nov. 9, 1948, p. 295.
101. Ibid., 77th Mtg., Nov. 10, 1948, p. 301.
102. Ibid., p. 306. See above pp. 84-85.
103. GAOR, 3rd Sess., Part 1, 4th Ctte., 78th Mtg., Nov. 11, 1948, p. 312.
104. See the argument presented to this effect by Mr. Ingles of the Philippines in the
*1950 Status Pleadings*, pp. 270-72. See also the statement of Mr. Kerno, ibid., p. 235; and see
South Africa's denial of the concept, ibid., pp. 277-78. The Court, in its 1950 advisory
opinion, made no express reference to any such concept, but it may well have underlain the
reasoning of the Court in that case. See below, p. 121. In the preliminary objections
phase of the *South West Africa* cases, Ethiopia and Liberia analyzed the 1950 opinion along
these lines. *SWA Pleadings* I: 440-46. Once again South Africa strenuously contested the
notion. Ibid., VII: 111-17. The 1962 Judgment implied some support of this notion by
referring to the League as an "organized international community." *SWA Judgment* (1962):
329. And cf. separate opinion of Judge Bustamante, ibid., pp. 335-36. Ethiopia and Liberia
thereafter laid great stress upon this line of reasoning. See *SWA Pleadings* IV: 233-42, 524-40;
VIII: 169, 197-208; IX: 246, 255-59, 304, 310, 346. For the counterarguments of South
Africa, see ibid., V: 31-53; VIII: 298, 310-12; IX: 463-64, 485-86, 613-19.
105. The expression "ex-mandated territories," is, of course, not part of the League
resolution. Actually, the resolution refers to "Members of the League now administering territories under mandate." See above p. 70.

fact that South Africa was not prepared to conclude a trusteeship agreement and would instead propose incorporation of the territory of South West Africa into the Union.[106]

The question of what reaction the General Assembly should adopt toward South Africa's rather defiant stand, once again prompted the placing of two divergent draft resolutions before the Fourth Committee. Those states that had throughout claimed that South Africa was under a legal duty to convert South West Africa into a trust territory regarded South Africa's action as tantamount to a declaration of war on the organization. The organization, in response, must take a forceful stand and must establish its right to supervise the territory as if it were a trust territory. As summed up by the Philippine delegate: "So long as the issue was coming to a head, as it was bound to, it was the duty of the Committee to establish its position unequivocally."[107] Those states, however, who questioned whether South Africa was violating a legal duty in refusing to negotiate a trusteeship agreement, adopted a more modest view of the scope of General Assembly authority under the circumstances. In their view, the focus of any resolution must be the retention of an effective link between the United Nations and South West Africa and insurance that South Africa would continue to hold itself internationally accountable in reference to the territory. In the words of the United States delegate: "It was upon the continuation of reports that any chance of helping the people of South West Africa in their progress towards self-government or independence would depend."[108]

One draft resolution was submitted by India,[109] and the other by Denmark, Norway, and Uruguay, jointly.[110] The major differences between the two draft resolutions were: while the former "endorsed," the latter merely "took note of" the Trusteeship Council's observations; while the former expressed "regret" and "grave concern" over South Africa's attitude, the latter merely took note of South Africa's commitment to administer the territory in the spirit of the mandate and to refrain from incorporation; while the former declared categorically that South Africa should propose a trusteeship agreement, the latter simply reaffirmed the Assembly's earlier view that South West Africa should come under the trusteeship system and recommended, in the meantime, that South Africa continue to submit reports on the territory, to be examined by the Trusteeship Council. Finally, in con-

106. GAOR, 3rd Sess., Part 1, 4th Ctte., 81st Mtg., Nov. 16, 1948, p. 340.
107. Ibid., 82nd Mtg., Nov. 17, 1948, p. 361.
108. Ibid., p. 363.
109. U.N. Doc. A/C. 4/164.
110. U.N. Doc. A/C.4/163/Corr. 1. Both draft resolutions are reproduced in Report of Fourth Committee, GAOR, 3rd Sess., Part 1, Plen., Annexes, pp. 405–8.

trast to the Indian version, the Danish draft did not seek to appoint a commission to visit the territory. The essential difference between the two draft resolutions was that whereas one looked to the mandate for the basis of United Nations supervisory authority, the other regarded the territory as falling in essence under the trusteeship system, so that the General Assembly was entitled to exercise supervision as if it was already a trust territory, even to the extent of arranging for a visit of inspection.[111]

The joint draft resolution was adopted by the Fourth Committee,[112] after the Danish delegate reminded the Committee members that although a simple majority was sufficient in Committee, in Plenary a two-thirds majority was required.[113] The draft resolution was adopted basically intact by the General Assembly.[114]

South Africa's response to the resolution of the General Assembly was furnished in a letter dated July 11, 1949.[115] In that communication addressed to the Secretary-General, the Union government reaffirmed its earlier assurances that it would continue to administer South West Africa in the spirit of the mandate and that the new arrangements for closer association did not constitute incorporation or absorption of the territory into the Union. As for the General Assembly recommendation that South Africa continue to furnish information on its administration of the territory to the United Nations, the Union government, after careful consideration, had decided regretfully that no further reports should be delivered. It was recalled that the Union government had at no time recognized any legal obligation on its part to supply information on South West Africa to the United Nations, but, in a spirit of good will, cooperation, and helpfulness, had offered to provide reports "with the clear stipulation that this would be done on a voluntary

111. See the criticism leveled by the representative of the United States at this Indian proposal. Ibid., 4th Ctte., 81st Mtg., Nov. 16, 1948, pp. 350-51. In response, the Indian delegate referred to the "extraordinary" nature of the situation and the fact that events had shown "the impossibility of returning ... to the narrow legalistic interpretation of the Charter." Ibid., pp. 352-54. The delegate of Costa Rica maintained that the United Nations was fully entitled to send a mission to South West Africa, since the mandates system no longer existed, and could not rule the United Nations from the grave. Ibid., 82nd Mtg., Nov. 17, 1948, p. 365.

112. Ibid.

113. Ibid., 81st Mtg., Nov. 16, 1948, p. 349. He also mentioned the possibility of referring certain questions to the International Court of Justice, but did not think it was necessary at that time.

114. G.A. Res. 227 (III), Nov. 26, 1948. The vote was 43 to 1, with 5 abstentions. GAOR, 3rd Sess., Part 1, Plen., 164th Mtg., Nov. 26, 1948, p. 592. Prior to the vote the Indian delegate charged that the draft resolution "was lifeless and almost seemed to condone an act which amounted to a violation of the Charter itself." The Assembly and its committees, she said, were rapidly being reduced to the status of law courts in which different legal angles were discussed. Such an approach could spell disaster for an organization "which should give effect to the hopes and aspirations of mankind." Ibid., p. 586.

115. U.N. Doc. A/929 in GAOR, 4th Sess., 4th Ctte., Annex, pp. 7-8.

basis, for purposes of information only, and on the distinct under-standing that the United Nations had no supervisory jurisdiction in South West Africa." Confidence had been expressed that the Trustee-ship Council would approach its task "in the same spirit of goodwill, co-operation and helpfulness as had motivated the Union in making the information available." These hopes, however, had unfortunately not been realized. Instead, the submission of information had provided opportunity "to utilize the Trusteeship Council and the Trusteeship Committee as a forum for unjustified criticism and censure of the Union Government's administration, not only in South West Africa but in the Union as well. . . . Furthermore, the very act of submitting a report had created in the minds of a number of Members of the United Nations an impression that the Trusteeship Council was competent to make recommendations on matters of internal administration of South West Africa," and had given rise to "other misconceptions regarding the status of this Territory." In the circumstances, the Union government could no longer see any real benefit to be derived from the submission of reports and had therefore decided to discontinue this practice. Factual and other information regarding South West Africa would con-tinue to be available to the general public through the usual govern-mental publications. At the same time, the letter indicated that a copy of the South West Africa Affairs Amendment Act No. 23 of 1949, which, it was said, was fully in accord with the spirit of the mandate, was attached for information purposes only.[116]

In brief, the act provided for South West African representation in the Union Parliament by means of six members in the House of Assembly and four senators.[117] It also accorded the Legislative Assembly of the territory increased powers of autonomy. The franchise was limited to persons of European descent. Specific references to the mandate, contained in the original 1925 Act and in the oath to be administered to members of the Legislative Assembly, were deleted.

From a reading of the United Nations record, one might be led to believe that South Africa's decision to accord South West Africa repre-sentation in the Union Parliament was primarily intended as a show of

116. Ibid., pp. 8–12.

117. In the contentious proceedings in the *South West Africa* cases, Applicants charged that the adoption and application of this statute constituted one of four actions whereby South Africa violated the separate international status of South West Africa (Submission 5). *SWA Pleadings* I: 192–93; IV: 579–81. For Respondent's answer to the charge, see ibid., pp. 101–4; VI: 405–9. Ultimately, all four of the specific charges were dropped from Submission 5, when Applicants eliminated all elements of disputed facts from the case. Final Submission 5 was based purely on South Africa's refusal to submit to international supervision. This fact in itself, it was said, "alters and fundamentally impairs the international status of the Territory." Ibid., IX: 238.

defiance of the United Nations. Actually, however, this step might well have been motivated by considerations stemming from South Africa's domestic politics.[118] Although the Nationalists entered into power in 1948, they did so only at the head of a coalition government and were dependent upon at least five members of the Afrikaner party for an absolute majority. Creation of six new Parliamentary seats for South West Africa (a disproportionate number for the population represented) may have been designed to strengthen the hand of the Nationalists, who may, justifiably, have expected to win most of the new seats. (In the 1950 elections the Nationalists, in fact, captured all six seats.)

Regardless of South Africa's motivation in this respect, in its letter to the United Nations, South Africa was, in effect, claiming that it was absolved from any further obligation of international accountability with reference to South West Africa. The League of Nations had failed to transfer its powers relative to mandates to the United Nations; and under the United Nations Charter, South Africa's obligations with regard to the territory were limited to those embraced by Article 73 (e). But since the United Nations had taken the material furnished under that provision "for information purposes only," and had illegally and unconstitutionally applied it for the purpose of exercising supervision, South Africa was henceforth freed of any obligation to furnish information under Article 73 (e).[119]

South Africa's action in discontinuing submission of further annual reports and its moves for closer association with South West Africa represented for the first time an attempt to exclude the United Nations totally from any role in South West Africa—whether in respect of supervision or consent to modification of status. A new phase in the South West Africa dispute was thus opened. Technically speaking, there had been no dispute up to that date—merely a difference of opinion. The United Nations, in its resolutions, had *invited* South Africa to negotiate a trusteeship agreement, and South Africa had not acted upon that invitation. The view that South Africa was under a *legal obligation* to effect this move had never prevailed in the General Assembly. At the same time, however, the members were in agreement that South Africa was subject to a legal obligation of international accountability toward the United Nations. (Whatever difference of opinion existed among

118. See Leo Marquard, *The Peoples and Policies of South Africa* (4th ed.; London: Oxford University Press, 1969), pp. 152, 240–41; Walker, *History of Southern Africa*, pp. 784–85.

119. In the *SWA Judgment* (1966), Judge van Wyk raised the question whether the United Nations' disregard of the provisions of Chapter XI was not "tantamount to a breach or repudiation which entitles members affected thereby to refuse to comply with the reporting provision of the Chapter" (pp. 117, n. 1, and 138, n. 1). See also the view of dissenting Judge Fitzmaurice, *Namibia Opinion* (1971): 296.

members on this point centered on the measure and form of that accountability and whether it was based on the mandate or on a postulated trusteeship status, or again, as several members claimed, on Chapter XI of the Charter.) But South Africa was now denying that it owed the United Nations any measure of international accountability at all. By the same token, South Africa claimed it was free to introduce constitutional changes in South West Africa, affecting its international status, without the need for prior United Nations consent.

The lines of the first stage of the conflict were thus drawn. The United Nations could not be expected to sit idly by and acquiesce in South Africa's attempt to sever the last link between South West Africa and the world organization and to eliminate the last vestige of international accountability with respect to that territory.

## THE FOURTH SESSION OF THE GENERAL ASSEMBLY

The fourth session of the General Assembly commenced its deliberations on the South West Africa question on November 18, 1949.[120] The issues posed by South Africa's latest acts were now analyzed by the Philippine representative in the course of a comprehensive review of the South West Africa problem.[121] He surveyed the deterioration of relations that had taken place between South Africa and the United Nations over the past four years. South Africa had consistently refused to comply with General Assembly resolutions requesting that South West Africa be placed under the trusteeship system. Now it had further compounded its defiance of the General Assembly, and even violated its own pledges. It had repudiated its commitment to furnish annual information, as required by the Mandate and Article 73 of the Charter, and by passing the 1949 South West Africa Affairs Amendment Act had effected virtual annexation of the territory. As a result, the General Assembly was now faced with new issues, in addition to the problem arising from failure to convert South West Africa into a trust territory, viz., South Africa's failure to hold itself internationally accountable to the United Nations for its administration of South West Africa, its unilateral repudiation of the mandate, and the incorporation of South West Africa into the Union. The Philippine delegate endorsed the moves that were being made for submission of these latter issues to the

120. GAOR, 4th Sess., 4th Ctte., 128th Mtg., pp. 199 ff. On July 20, 1949, the Trusteeship Council had taken note of South Africa's letter and had adopted a resolution notifying the Assembly of the Council's inability to examine any reports on South West Africa, since none had been forthcoming. TCOR, 5th Sess., 25th–27th Mtgs., July 20–21, 1949, pp. 309–33. Res. 111 (V), July 21, 1949. For text, see TCOR, 5th Sess., Resolutions, p. 19.

121. GAOR, 4th Sess., 4th Ctte., 128th Mtg., Nov. 18, 1949, pp. 203–7.

International Court of Justice for determination,[122] and concluded by calling upon the remaining Principal Allied and Associated Powers to use their good offices, as states directly concerned, to give effect to Article 79 of the Charter and the standing resolutions of the General Assembly.

The impact of these remarks was two-fold. First, South Africa's latest actions in moving toward "closer association" and its refusal to submit reports and petitions had converted the disagreement from one involving a single issue—whether South Africa was morally and/or legally obliged to convert the mandate into a trust territory—into the broader issues of international accountability and whether the international status of the mandate survived. Obviously, any clarification to be requested from the Court would, therefore, have to include the broader issues involving definition of the status of South West Africa, if it were to be truly useful. Second, these remarks denoted that the Assembly's resolutions had made little impact on the problem. South Africa's intransigence had been quite unaffected and would remain unaffected, if the only pressure brought to bear would be that arising from formalistic reiteration of Assembly resolutions. Far from influencing South Africa to move closer to United Nations supervision, the actions of the General Assembly had only induced the Union government to sever whatever ties had previously existed between South West Africa and the world organization.

These conclusions dictated that outside influences would have to be brought to bear on the issue if any change was to ensue. It was in this vein that the Philippine delegate referred to the possible role of the Principal Allied and Associated Powers, and more significantly, to the proposed reference of the legal questions to the International Court of Justice. Determination of these questions by the supreme judicial organ of the United Nations would prevent South Africa from justifying its negative attitude under a "façade of legalism," and would put an end to the rather arid discussions revolving around legal interpretations. It would furnish the necessary outside authority to clarify the matter once and for all. Even states which, to date, had opposed reference of any aspect of the South West Africa question to an outside body, had come around to the recognition that no effective solution could be found without prior settlement of the legal issue. Moreover, even if such states themselves could dispense with such a step, other states, and particularly the United States, the United Kingdom, and France, the

122. Two draft resolutions were presented that day for requesting an advisory opinion (A/C.4/L.54 and 55). Ibid., p. 208 and ibid., 129th Mtg., Nov. 18, 1949, p. 211. Ultimately, the two versions were consolidated (A/C.4/L.64). Ibid., 140th Mtg., Nov. 29, 1949, p. 273.

former Principal Allied and Associated Powers, could not be induced to take a firmer stand against South Africa in the absence of an authoritative judicial determination of the international law questions involved. The Assembly, therefore, moved to formulate the legal questions involved for presentation to the International Court of Justice for an advisory opinion.

In the meantime, however, many member states were not content to let the matter ride for any period of time without reassertion of continued United Nations authority in the matter. The delegates of these states felt that the world organization had to manifest a continuous claim to international accountability, if it was not subsequently to be confronted with the argument that the control and interest of the United Nations had lapsed. Furthermore, these delegates felt that it was urgent for the world organization to maintain *some* tie to South West Africa, nominal as it might be. Since South Africa was resorting to extraordinary tactics to alter the international status of the territory, the United Nations was, likewise, entitled and compelled to adopt extraordinary procedures to confirm international involvement in the territory. It was in this spirit that two decisions were taken in this session, which contrasted with the decision to request an advisory opinion.

The first involved the granting of a hearing by the Fourth Committee to the Reverend Michael Scott, acting as a petitioner on behalf of certain tribes in South West Africa.[123] It will be recalled that in 1947 the Trusteeship Council had not considered itself justified in authorizing such a step.[124] The representative of France referred to this fact now, and noted that South West Africa was not a trust territory and not subject to Chapters XII and XIII of the Charter.[125] And, if it was the mandate which furnished the basis for United Nations supervisory power over South West Africa, then it must be borne in mind that the Permanent Mandates Commission had never permitted oral hearings for petitioners.[126] These "technical" arguments, however, carried little weight. "The Committee was dealing with a special situation which necessitated recourse to special methods," said the Yugoslav delegate.[127] The only dangerous precedent that might be established, in the view of the Cuban delegate, was "the fact that the General Assembly had not received further information on . . . South West Africa and that

123. GAOR, 4th Sess., 4th Ctte., 138th Mtg., Nov. 26, 1949, pp. 258-67.

124. See above, n. 79.

125. GAOR, 4th Sess., 4th Ctte., 130th Mtg., Nov. 21, 1949, pp. 217-18. See general discussion, ranging from 130th to 138th Mtgs., Nov. 21-26, 1949, pp. 217-28.

126. Ibid., pp. 217-18. See also the remarks of the representatives of the United States, South Africa and Belgium, ibid., pp. 221, 224-26, 227-28.

127. Ibid., p. 221.

the Mandate was to be set aside through unilateral action."[128] These same delegates were also little impressed with the argument that granting such a hearing would, in effect, amount to a prejudgment of the question regarding the legal status of South West Africa, to be submitted to the Court.[129]

The Reverend Michael Scott addressed the Fourth Committee on November 26, 1949. Prior to the meeting, the South African representative announced he would not attend, since "his presence might be interpreted as consent."[130] In his statement, the Reverend Scott recited a series of petitions from tribal chiefs and others in South West Africa, calling on the United Nations to bar South African incorporation of the territory and to strive for South African accountability to the world organization, so that the lot of the indigenous population might be improved. The operation of the pass laws and the consequences of the alienation of land were vividly described. In general, the petitions amounted to a harsh indictment of South Africa's administration of the territory.[131]

The second contentious step taken during this session was adoption of a resolution which, *inter alia*, reiterated all previous General Assembly resolutions on the subject of South West Africa (requesting South Africa to conclude a trusteeship agreement).[132] In the Fourth Committee, representatives of the United States, France, and the United Kingdom argued against the reiteration of earlier Assembly resolutions since it "might prejudge the legal questions which it was expected would be referred to the International Court of Justice."[133] In reply, the Mexican delegate maintained that "if the Assembly's position were not reaffirmed, the Union Government and its supporters might claim that the previous resolutions lacked authority, and everything that had been gained might be lost."[134] The Indian delegate maintained that a renewal of the request to South Africa to negotiate a trusteeship agreement

128. Ibid., p. 222. The Cuban delegate also referred to Article 80(1) of the Charter and argued that the right of petition was one of the rights preserved by that provision, pending the territory's being placed under the trusteeship system. Ibid., p. 217.
129. This point had been raised by the representatives of the United States, Canada, Israel, France, and the United Kingdom. Ibid., pp. 221, 229, 230–31, and 233–34.
130. Ibid., 137th Mtg., p. 258.
131. Ibid., 138th Mtg., pp. 258–65. At the next meeting, the South African representative announced his delegation's withdrawal from further discussion on South West Africa in the Fourth Committee for the remainder of the session. Ibid., 139th Mtg., Nov. 28, 1949, p. 270. Reverend Scott's statement was made a part of the official records, ibid., 138th Mtg., Nov. 26, 1949, p. 267.
132. The resolution also expressed regret at South Africa's withdrawal of its previous undertaking to submit reports, and invited South Africa to resume submission. This part of the resolution was more or less acceptable to the Western states, since it was premised on South Africa's own pledges, rather than an interpretation of law.
133. Ibid., 139th Mtg., Nov. 28, 1949, pp. 268–69.
134. Ibid., p. 268.

would not invade the realm of the Court. The latter's sphere was the legal one, whereas that of the Assembly was political.[135] The draft resolution as amended was adopted by the Fourth Committee. (It was draft resolution I in the Committee report.)[136]

Attention was then focused on formulation of the request for an advisory opinion. According to the new joint draft resolution,[137] the Assembly would have requested the Court to clarify the international status of South West Africa and, more particularly, to determine:

a) whether South Africa continued to have obligations under the Mandate;

b) whether South Africa was obligated to convert the mandate into a trust territory;

c) in the event of a negative reply to (b), whether Chapter XI of the Charter applied to South West Africa;

d) whether South Africa could unilaterally modify the international status of South West Africa.

Certain states objected to questions (b) and (c), which they claimed had already been decided by the resolutions of the General Assembly. It would be most inappropriate, they maintained, "for the General Assembly to express doubt as to the validity of measures already taken."[138] Once again, the Indian representative argued that the Court, in any case, would only decide the legal issue and, therefore, nothing would prevent the Assembly "from invoking political reasons for again recommending to . . . South Africa the negotiation of a trusteeship agreement even if the . . . Court . . . considered that, legally, the Government of that country was not obliged to do so."[139] Notwithstanding, subparagraphs (b) and (c) were deleted.[140] The draft resolution, as amended, was thereupon adopted. (It was draft resolution II in the Committee report.)[141]

135. Ibid., p. 269.

136. Ibid., p. 273. The vote was 31 to 11, with 4 abstentions. For text, see U.N. Doc. A/1180, Report of the 4th Ctte. in GAOR, 4th Sess., Plen., Annex, Agenda Item 34, p. 110 (1949).

137. U.N. Doc. A/C.4/L.64 in ibid., p. 108. The sponsoring states were Denmark, India, Norway, Syria, and Thailand. The diversified sponsorship of the draft resolution reveals the general consensus that had evolved among the membership for obtaining a judicial opinion. It reflected the common belief that "an authoritative statement on the legal aspects was necessary before any progress could be made in the matter." Statement of representative of Thailand, ibid., 4th Ctte., 128th Mtg., Nov. 18, 1949, p. 208. See also the remarks of the Belgian representative: "The only solution would . . . be to consult a higher authority which could be none other than the International Court." Ibid., 129th Mtg., Nov. 18, 1949, p. 211. South Africa, it might be noted, was not averse to obtaining an advisory opinion, although it was critical of the formulation of the request. Ibid., Plen., 269th Mtg., Dec. 6, 1949, pp. 528-29.

138. Remarks of the representative of Guatemala, ibid., 4th Ctte., 140th Mtg., Nov. 29, 1949, p. 273. See also the remarks of the representatives of Brazil, ibid., p. 275, and Mexico, ibid., p. 277, opposing any reference to Chapter XI.

139. Ibid., p. 277.

140. Ibid., pp. 281-82.

141. Ibid. For text, see Report of 4th Ctte., in GAOR, 4th Sess., Plen., Annex, Agenda Item 34, p. 110 (1949).

In Plenary a number of the foregoing issues became the subject of further debate. The South African delegate charged that draft resolution I anticipated, and could prejudice, the projected opinion of the Court.[142] The Belgian delegate claimed that "if both resolutions were adopted, the Assembly would, on the one hand, express something in the nature of a vote of censure, thereby affirming its right to take decisions . . . binding on . . . South Africa; while on the other hand, by consulting the Court on the point, it would admit its ignorance of the legal status of the Territory and of the obligations of . . . South Africa."[143]

The majority of delegates, however, held otherwise. As explained by the representative of Guatemala: "The Assembly had no doubts about the problem. It must be solved by placing the Territory under the . . . Trusteeship System. . . . South Africa's duty to comply with the wishes of the General Assembly was evident. The Court was to be consulted simply in order to meet certain moral or legal scruples of some delegations. . . . The decision of the General Assembly must be upheld until the Court handed down its opinion. The two draft resolutions were not . . . inconsistent."[144] In other words, according to these states, the real view of the Assembly was reflected in draft resolution I, and draft resolution II was merely an accommodation to the wishes of certain (important) states. Adoption of the latter could not be permitted to negative the strength of the former. With slight modifications, draft resolution I was adopted by the General Assembly.[145]

Discussion on draft resolution II opened with the Danish delegate presenting a seventeen-power amendment designed to restore the question of an obligation to negotiate a trusteeship agreement to the request.[146] This new subparagraph (b) would ask whether Chapter XII of the Charter was applicable to South West Africa and in what manner. This would enable the Court to analyze all aspects of the South West Africa problem. In the words of the Danish representative: "At its fifth session [the Assembly] would have before it an authoritative opinion on the legal aspects of the South West African problem and would thus be in a better position to reach a solution."[147] The Brazilian delegate, who, in the Fourth Committee had opposed inclusion of this third question, now supported the amendment. His delegation, he indicated,

142. Ibid., Plen., 269th Mtg., Dec. 6, 1949, pp. 523–29.
143. Ibid., p. 533. See also the remarks of the representatives of Greece, the United States, and the United Kingdom, ibid., pp. 530, 534.
144. Ibid., p. 533.
145. Ibid., p. 536. The vote was 33 to 9, with 10 abstentions. G.A. Res. 337 (IV), Dec. 6, 1949. Those voting against the resolution were France, Greece, Luxembourg, the Netherlands, Norway, Sweden, South Africa, the United States, and Belgium. The states abstaining included the United Kingdom, Canada, Australia, and New Zealand.
146. Introduced orally, GAOR, 4th Sess., Plen., 269th Mtg., Dec. 6, 1949, p. 529.
147. Ibid.

had never entertained any doubts as to the real obligations of the Union, but considered it "advisable to ask the Court for an advisory opinion, if only to dispel the doubts of certain other delegations and to settle the matter once and for all."[148] Draft resolution II, as amended, was adopted by a vote of 40 to 7, with 4 abstentions.[149]

The questions, as finally formulated, were:

What is the international status of the Territory of South West Africa and what are the international obligations of the Union of South Africa arising therefrom, in particular:

(a) Does the Union of South Africa continue to have international obligations under the Mandate for South West Africa and, if so, what are those obligations?

(b) Are the provisions of Chapter XII of the Charter applicable and, if so, in what manner, to the Territory of South West Africa?

(c) Has the Union of South Africa the competence to modify the international status of the Territory of South West Africa, or, in the event of a negative reply, where does competence rest to determine and modify the international status of the Territory?

Three basic issues had engaged the attention of the General Assembly since South Africa first brought the South West Africa problem before the United Nations in 1946. The initial issue had been whether South Africa was under a legal obligation to negotiate a trusteeship agreement. Since the General Assembly had never officially endorsed the view that South Africa was under such an obligation, this issue could not be classified as a straight-out United Nations v. South Africa issue. Rather, it reflected a general difference of opinion among the United Nations membership or, alternatively, a conflict between South Africa and a considerable segment of the United Nations membership. The second issue that arose related to the more basic problem of international accountability, and whether South Africa was obligated to submit reports and petitions to the United Nations. This issue centered

148. Ibid. At the same time, however, the Assembly was not prepared to reinsert a question on the relevance of Chapter XI. Such a step, said the Brazilian delegate, would have been "extremely dangerous" since it would practically recognize South African sovereignty over the territory. Ibid., p. 530.

149. Ibid., p. 537. G.A. Res. 339 (IV)., Dec. 6, 1949. Amongst those voting in opposition were the Soviet, Cuban, Polish, Yugoslavian, and Liberian delegates. The Liberian delegate claimed that reference of the question to the Court "would throw doubt upon the legality of the General Assembly's previous action. . . . [The General Assembly's] chief concern was not with the legal aspect of the question but rather with the political and moral aspect." Ibid., p. 532.

The opposition of the Soviet Union accorded with its traditional unwillingness to have matters referred to the Court. On this topic generally, see Oliver J. Lissitzyn, *International Law Today and Tomorrow* (Dobbs Ferry, New York: Oceana, 1965), p. 62; and Julius Stone, "The International Court and World Crisis," *International Conciliation*, No. 536 (January 1962): 3, 34–36.

on the two-pronged question whether the mandate continued in force, and whether, and how, the United Nations succeeded to the supervisory powers of the League. (Another possible question was, of course, that of the applicability of Chapter XI. The Assembly had avoided premising its authority on this chapter and had, as indicated, deleted reference to the chapter from the list of questions submitted to the Court.)[150] The third issue was whether South Africa was competent to unilaterally modify the international status of South West Africa by bringing the territory into closer association with the Union. Each of these issues now constituted a separate question posed to the Court for judicial determination.

---

150. See further, on the matter of the applicability of Chapter XI, below, p. 117 and n. 27.

# V.

# THE 1950 ADVISORY OPINION OF THE INTERNATIONAL COURT: THE STATUS OF THE TERRITORY DEFINED

## THE OPINION

The International Court of Justice handed down its advisory opinion on July 11, 1950.[1]

With reference to the original question which had engaged the attention of the Assembly, the Court held, by a vote of 8 to 6, that the provisions of Chapter XII of the Charter do *not* impose a legal obligation on the Union of South Africa to place the territory of South West Africa under the trusteeship system.[2] The Court reached this decision by noting that the language used in Articles 75 and 77 was clearly permissive ("as may be placed thereunder"). The procedure for placing a territory under the trusteeship system requires an agreement, the Court said, and an agreement implies consent of the parties concerned. "The parties must be free to accept or reject the terms of a contemplated agreement." Moreover, Article 77 (2) clearly presupposes agreement not only as to the terms but also as to which territories would be brought under the trusteeship system.

1. The Union government participated in the pleadings with both written and oral statements. In addition, the governments of Egypt, the United States, India, and Poland submitted written statements. Oral statements were delivered by Dr. Ivan Kerno, on behalf of the Secretary-General of the United Nations; by Judge Jose D. Ingles, on behalf of the government of the Philippines; and by Dr. L. Steyn, K.C., on behalf of the government of the Union of South Africa.
2. *Status Opinion* (1950): 140. This conclusion concurred with the view of most publicists. See J. L. Brierly, *The Law of Nations* (4th ed.; Oxford: Oxford University Press, 1949), p. 155; H. Duncan Hall, *Mandates, Dependencies and Trusteeship* (Washington, D.C.: Carnegie Endowment for International Peace, 1948), p. 274; Hall, "The Trusteeship System and the Case of South West Africa," *BYB* XXIV (1947): 385-89; Huntington Gilchrist, "Colonial Questions at the San Francisco Conference," *American Political Science Review* XXXIX (1945): 274; Hans Kelsen, *The Law of the United Nations* (London: Stevens, 1950), pp. 571-75; Goodrich and Hambro, pp. 433, 435-36; Francis B. Sayre, "Legal Problems Arising from the United Nations Trusteeship System," *AJIL* XLII (1948): 279-81.

The Court rejected each of the arguments adduced in support of the proposition that mandatory powers were legally obligated to negotiate trusteeship agreements.[3] Article 80, paragraph 2, which declares that paragraph 1 of that article shall not be interpreted as giving grounds for delaying "the negotiation and conclusion" of trusteeship agreements, framed as it is in negative terms, could not create a positive obligation to conclude an agreement. Neither could it be said that this provision creates an obligation for mandatory states to at least enter into negotiations on the subject of a trusteeship agreement. The provision refers to both negotiation and conclusion; and since, as shown, it does not compel the latter, it equally does not compel the former.[4] The fact that the trusteeship system would have had no more than a theoretical existence if mandatory powers were not obligated to enter into negotiations on trusteeship agreements was not deemed pertinent to a question of legal obligation.[5] Similarly, the fact that the Charter had "contemplated and regulated only a single system, the International Trusteeship System" and "did not contemplate or regulate a co-existing Mandate System," merely indicated an expectation that the mandatory states would follow the normal course outlined by the Charter and conclude trusteeship agreements; but this could not in itself establish a legal obligation. The Court was obviously not free to pronounce on "the political or moral duties" which these considerations might involve.[6] For these reasons, the Court concluded that South Africa was

3. *Status Opinion* (1950): 139–40. For a summary of the arguments see above, pp. 86–87.

4. In the pleadings before the Court, the Philippine representative had argued that Article 80 (2), as a minimum, created a *pactum de contrahendo*—a duty to negotiate in good faith toward an agreement. See *1950 Status Pleadings*, pp. 241–43, 247–48. Judge de Visscher (in a dissent concurred in by Judges Guerrero, Zoriĉić, and Badawi Pasha), accepted the rationale of the Philippine argument. He maintained that each article of the Charter must be interpreted so as to give it full meaning, consistent with all other articles. Consequently, if Articles 75, 77, and 79 denoted a permissive quality, and Article 80 (2) a mandatory quality, the sound means of reconciling these provisions was to recognize "that the mandatory Power, while remaining free to reject the particular terms of a proposed agreement, has the legal obligation to be ready to take part in negotiations and to conduct them in good faith with a view to concluding an agreement." *Status Opinion* (1950): 188. Judge Krylov adopted a similar position. Ibid., pp. 191–92. Judge Alvarez, on the basis of his postulated "new international law" went a step further and determined that South Africa is obligated to negotiate "and conclude" a trusteeship agreement. Ibid., p. 184.

5. Cf. dissenting opinion of Judge de Visscher. Ibid., p. 189.

6. Ibid., p. 140. The Court thus rejected the approach of Judge Alvarez who, in accordance with his conception of the "new international law," maintained that the Court should take into account not only legal considerations but concepts of political and social values as well. Ibid., pp. 174–85. Two writers who have basically adopted the views of Judge Alvarez in criticizing the decision of the Court on the trusteeship agreement question are C.V. Lakshminarayan, *Analysis of the Principles and System of International Trusteeship in the Charter* (Geneva: Imprimeries Populaires, 1951), pp. 100–1; and R. N. Chowdhuri, *International Mandates and Trusteeship Systems: A Comparative Study* (The Hague: Nijhoff, 1955), pp. 170–71. For further discussion of the trusteeship issue (as of the opinion generally), see J. H. W. Verzijl, *The Jurisprudence of the World Court* (Leyden: Sijthoff, 1966), II; 47–64.

not subject to a legal obligation to place South West Africa under the trusteeship system.[7]

The fact, however, that South Africa could not be legally compelled to negotiate a trusteeship agreement did not mean that the Union government was free of international accountability with regard to the territory of South West Africa. The new pattern of international accountability in the form of the trusteeship system could not be imposed, but the previous pattern could be continued, in that the mandate status persisted. Furthermore, the supervisory role formerly exercised by the Council of the League of Nations was now assumed by the General Assembly of the United Nations. On similar grounds, the Court concluded that South Africa could only modify the international status of South West Africa with the consent of the United Nations.[8]

The Court reached its decision on international accountability in two steps.[9] In the first step, the Court analyzed the *nature* of the mandate as a "sacred trust of civilization."[10] Article 22 of the Covenant, together with the Mandate, created a "new international institution" for South West Africa, which did not involve any cession of territory or transfer of sovereignty to the Union of South Africa. The

7. The Court however repeatedly stressed that "the normal way of modifying the international status of the Territory would be to place it under the Trusteeship System by means of a Trusteeship Agreement." *Status Opinion* (1950): 141.
8. The operative part of the opinion read as follows:
"The Court is of opinion,
"*On the General Question:*
"unanimously,
"that South-West Africa is a territory under the international Mandate assumed by the Union of South Africa on December 17th, 1920;
"*On Question (a):*
"by twelve votes to two,
"that the Union of South Africa continues to have the international obligations stated in Article 22 of the Covenant of the League of Nations and in the Mandate for South-West Africa as well as the obligation to transmit petitions from the inhabitants of that Territory, the supervisory functions to be exercised by the United Nations, to which the annual reports and the petitions are to be submitted, and the reference to the Permanent Court of International Justice to be replaced by a reference to the International Court of Justice, in accordance with Article 7 of the Mandate and Article 37 of the Statute of the Court;
"*On Question (b):*
"unanimously,
"that the provisions of Chapter XII of the Charter are applicable to the Territory of South-West Africa in the sense that they provide a means by which the Territory may be brought under the Trusteeship System;
"and by eight votes to six,
"that the provisions of Chapter XII of the Charter do not impose on the Union of South Africa a legal obligation to place the Territory under the Trusteeship System;
"*On Question (c):*
"unanimously,
"that the Union of South Africa acting alone has not the competence to modify the international status of the Territory of South-West Africa, and that the competence to determine and modify the international status of the Territory rests with the Union of South Africa acting with the consent of the United Nations." Ibid., pp. 143–44.
9. Ibid., pp. 131–38.
10. Ibid., pp. 131–33. This part of the decision was unanimous.

Union government was simply empowered "to exercise an international function of administration on behalf of the League, with the object of promoting the well-being and development of the inhabitants." The mandate, having been created in the interests of the inhabitants of the territory and of humanity in general, was an "international institution with an international object—a sacred trust of civilization." Such an international status, with its attendant rights and obligations, was not subject to the regular vicissitudes to which normal treaties were subject. The objective nature of a mandate enabled it to continue beyond the lifetime of the institutions and organs that were normally associated with its functioning. Consequently, the territory of South West Africa continued to be a mandated territory even after the dissolution of the League of Nations.[11] The argument presented by South Africa to the effect that once the League was dissolved the mandate lapsed, as would any other contractual arrangement where one of the two contracting parties ceased to exist, was not valid. "The object of the Mandate . . . far exceeded that of contractual relations regulated by national law."[12] Moreover,

> The authority which the Union Government exercises over the Territory is based on the Mandate. If the Mandate lapsed, as the Union Government contends, the latter's authority would equally have lapsed. To retain the rights derived from the Mandate and to deny the obligations thereunder could not be justified.[13]

11. The concept of an international status, or regime, was analyzed even more elaborately in the separate opinion of Judge McNair. Ibid., pp. 146–57. "From time to time it happens that a group of great Powers, or a large number of States both great and small, assume a power to create by a multipartite treaty some new international regime or status, which soon acquires a degree of acceptance and durability extending beyond the limits of the actual contracting parties and giving it an objective existence. This power is used when some public interest is involved, and its exercise often occurs in the course of the peace settlement at the end of a great war." As instances of judicially recognized "objective law" Judge McNair cited the Aaland Islands and S. S. Wimbledon cases. The mandates system was a further example of such a new international regime which, in addition to the usual personal rights and obligations arising from a contractual relationship, created certain "real" rights and obligations, valid *in rem*—against the whole world. "This status—valid *in rem*—supplied the element of permanence which would enable the legal condition of the Territory to survive the disappearance of the League. . . . 'Real' rights created by an international agreement have a greater degree of permanence than personal rights because these rights acquire an objective existence which is more resistant than are personal rights to the dislocating effects of international events."

12. Ibid., p. 132. According to South Africa, "the dissolution of the League had the effect of extinguishing all international legal rights and obligations under the Mandate System." Oral Statement of South Africa, *1950 Status Pleadings*, p. 290. See also, ibid., pp. 275, 277. Kelsen, *Law of the United Nations*, pp. 596, 598–99 supports the South African position. In fact, he goes even further by claiming that it would have been legally impossible for the mandatory powers who concluded trusteeship agreements to have done so had the mandates system not come to an end. This event conferred sovereignty on the former mandatory powers and enabled them to conclude trusteeship agreements. Ibid., pp. 592–96, 603.

13. *Status Opinion* (1950): 133. This point was argued by the representative of the Philippines, *1950 Status Pleadings*, pp. 267–68. See also Written Statement of the United States, ibid., p. 104.

The Court, in its second step, analyzed the *constituent elements* of the mandate and concluded that the obligations assumed by South Africa were of two kinds, both of which survived as part of the mandate institution.[14]

1. The first group of obligations, defined by Article 22 of the Covenant and Articles 2 to 5 of the Mandate, related to the administration of the territory for the benefit of its inhabitants. These obligations were reflected in the general commitment "to promote to the utmost the material and moral well-being and the social progress of the inhabitants." Since these obligations represent the "very essence of the sacred trust, their *raison d'être* and original object" remained, and their fulfillment could not depend on the existence of the League or its supervisory organs.

The Court confirmed its view that this group of substantive obligations continued in force by reference to:

a) Article 80 (1) of the Charter,[15] which was intended "to safeguard the rights of States and peoples under all circumstances and in all respects, until each territory shall be placed under the Trusteeship System;"[16]

b) The final resolution of the League Assembly of April 18, 1946, which noted that "the League's functions with respect to man-

---

In the contentious proceedings in the *South West Africa* cases, South Africa endeavored to meet the argument that it lacks any rights in South West Africa other than on the basis of the mandate, by contending that the lapse of the mandate in 1946 revived the *status quo ante* as it had existed at the end of 1918. South Africa's right to administer the territory was thus premised on conquest. See *SWA Pleadings* V: 82-84; IX: 476-79. This argument was dismissed by Judge Jessup in *SWA Judgment* (1966): 418-19, as being "devoid of legal foundation." Conquest alone, without subjugation, could never confer title. Cf. separate opinion of Judge van Wyk, ibid., p. 127.

With reference to the comment by Judge Jessup, it should be noted that South Africa never asserted actual *title* to South West Africa on the basis of conquest. It merely claimed that restoration of the *status quo ante* revived "the same legal right of administration as had existed prior to the mandate." *SWA Pleadings* IX: 479. There is little doubt that a conqueror, even in the absence of full legal title, has full power of administration. See Julius Stone, *Legal Controls of International Conflict* (London: Stevens, 1954), chap. XXVI. Cf. South Africa's statement in *Namibia Pleadings* II: 549-52. But see the Court's rejection of South Africa's stand. *Namibia Opinion* (1971): 42-43.

14. *Status Opinion* (1950): 133.

15. "Except as may be agreed upon in individual trusteeship agreements, made under Articles 77, 79, and 81, placing each territory under the trusteeship system, and until such agreements have been concluded, nothing in this chapter shall be construed in or of itself to alter in any manner the rights whatsoever of any states or any peoples or the terms of existing international instruments to which Members of the United Nations may respectively be parties."

16. *Status Opinion* (1950): 133-34. The Court acknowledged that this provision only says that nothing in *Chapter XII of the Charter* shall affect such rights, and says nothing of the effect of other incidents, such as the dissolution of the League. "But," said the Court, "as far as mandated territories are concerned . . . this provision presupposes that the rights of States and peoples shall not lapse automatically on the dissolution of the League."

dated territories would come to an end; it did not say that the Mandates themselves came to an end. . . . The Assembly manifested its understanding that the Mandates were to continue in existence until 'other arrangements' were established."[17]

c) Unilateral declarations of the Union government which, in effect, confirmed that government's recognition "that its obligations under the Mandate continued after the disappearance of the League." [18] "Interpretations placed upon legal instruments by the parties to them," said the Court, "though not conclusive as to their meaning, have considerable probative value."[19] The foregoing considerations were adduced to confirm the view that the administrative obligations of the mandate relating to the welfare of the territory's inhabitants continued in full force.

---

The Court's reliance on Article 80 (1) to sustain any aspect of the mandate has been critically attacked. Judge McNair, in dissent, declared: "The cause of the lapse . . . is not anything in Chapter XII . . . but is the dissolution of the League, so that it is difficult to see the relevance of this article." Ibid., p. 160. See also Manley O. Hudson, "The Twenty-ninth Year of the World Court," *AJIL* XLV (1951): 14; Joseph Nisot, "The Advisory Opinion of the International Court of Justice on the International Status of South West Africa," *South African Law Journal* LXVIII (1951): 274, 278-79; Ellison Kahn, "The International Court's Advisory Opinion on the International Status of South West Africa," *International Law Quarterly* IV (1951): 78, 91; Georg Schwarzenberger, *International Law* (3rd ed.; London: Stevens, 1957), I: 101-2.

In the pleadings on the preliminary objections in the *South West Africa* cases, Ethiopia and Liberia placed heavy reliance on Article 80 (1) to sustain the Court's jurisdiction. *SWA Pleadings* VII: 295-98, 304-10, 321, 324. However, the 1962 Court judgment, in confirming its jurisdiction, made no reference to this provision. This silence was noted in the dissenting opinion of Judge Basdevant. *SWA Judgment* (1962): 459. Dissenting Judges Spender and Fitzmaurice severely criticized the 1950 Court's use of Article 80 (1). This provision, they argued, was merely a saving clause, of a kind standard in many treaties, and it could not operate to "conserve" any rights. Ibid., pp. 515-16. See also dissenting opinion of Judge van Wyk, ibid., pp. 615-19, 646-50. Ultimately, the Applicants themselves abandoned any reliance on Article 80 (1), and in effect acknowledged that the Court's interpretation of the provision as having a positive effect was not well-founded. See *SWA Pleadings* VIII: 223-27. Nevertheless, Applicants argued, the "common assumption" underlying Article 80 (1) was that the mandate regime would continue "*until* superseded by other arrangements." Ibid., pp. 226-27. See the subsequent comments of Respondent, ibid., pp. 294-304, 552-54.

In the 1971 Namibia case the Court went even beyond the 1950 opinion in according a positive effect to Article 80 (1). In the view of the Court this provision, in conjunction with Article 10 of the Charter, operated to establish a "relationship" between South Africa and the United Nations, under which South Africa "agreed to submit its administration of South West Africa to the scrutiny of the General Assembly." *Namibia Opinion* (1971): 33-37, 45-46. (Subsequent South African conduct, it was said, constituted a breach of this "relationship.") The Court's reliance upon Article 80 (1) was severely challenged by dissenting Judge Fitzmaurice, who claimed that it was an attempt to give "an exaggerated and misplaced effect" to the provision which "cannot bear the weight thus put upon it." Ibid., pp. 238-41.

17. *Status Opinion* (1950): 134.
18. Ibid., pp. 134-36. The Court referred to the statement before the Assembly of the League on April 9, 1946; the memorandum submitted to the United Nations on October 17, 1946; the statement of Prime Minister Smuts before the Fourth Committee on November 4, 1946, and the letter of July 23, 1947 to the Secretary-General of the United Nations. See above, pp. 68-69, 79-80, 84-85.
19. In this respect the statements represented a source of evidence rather than a complete estoppel.

2. The second group of obligations related to the machinery for implementation, or system of international supervision of the mandate, with particular reference to the submission of annual reports.[20] This set of obligations was likewise an integral part of the mandates system and must also be deemed to have continued in force beyond the life of the League of Nations as part of the mandate institution.

> When the authors of the Covenant created this system, they considered that the effective performance of the sacred trust of civilization by the mandatory Powers required that the administration of mandated territories should be subject to international supervision. The authors of the Charter had in mind the same necessity when they organized an International Trusteeship System. The necessity for supervision continues to exist despite the disappearance of the supervisory organ under the Mandates System. It cannot be admitted that the obligation to submit to supervision has disappeared merely because the supervisory organ has ceased to exist, when the United Nations has another international organ performing similar, though not identical, supervisory functions.[21]

The Court confirmed these "general considerations" by reference, once again, to Article 80(1) of the Charter and the final resolution of the League Assembly.[22] The former was designed to safeguard the rights of peoples of mandated territories, and this included the right to have the mandatory power subject to international supervision even after dissolution of the League. The latter gave expression to a corresponding view, by noting that Chapters XI, XII, and XIII of the Charter embodied principles corresponding to those declared in Article 22 of the Covenant. "This resolution presupposes that the supervisory functions exercised by the League would be taken over by the United Nations."[23] Thus, in effect, the United Nations expressed intent to assume the supervisory functions of the League, and the League in its Assembly resolution endorsed that assumption of authority. These actions, therefore, confirmed the general argument of the necessity of continued international supervision.

20. *Status Opinion* (1950): 136–38.
21. Ibid., p. 136.
22. Ibid., pp. 136–37. It should be noted, however, that the Court, in finding that the supervisory powers of the League were transferred to the United Nations, did not sustain its conclusion by reference to South Africa's actions. This is in marked contrast to its citation of South Africa's statements for supportive evidence of the continuation of the mandate as an institution. See above, p. 115. For the significance of this point, see *SWA Pleadings* VII: 89–90.
23. *Status Opinion* (1950): 137. For criticism of this interpretation of the League Assembly resolution, see Hudson, "Twenty-ninth Year of World Court," *AJIL* XLV (1951): 13; Nisot, "International Status of South West Africa," pp. 279–80. See also dissenting opinion of Judges Spender and Fitzmaurice, *SWA Judgment* (1962): 535–40; dissenting opinion of Judge van Wyk, ibid., pp. 650–52; separate opinion of Judge van Wyk, *SWA Judgment* (1966): 106–19. Cf. dissenting opinion of Judge Jessup, ibid., pp. 347–48.

As for the competence of the General Assembly to exercise supervision and to receive and examine reports, this was derived from Article 10 of the Charter, which authorizes the Assembly to discuss any questions within the scope of the Charter and make recommendations thereon.[24]

Since South West Africa was still to be considered as a territory held under the Mandate of December 17, 1920, the Court declared:

> The degree of supervision to be exercised by the General Assembly should not therefore exceed that which applied under the Mandates System, and should conform as far as possible to the procedure followed in this respect by the Council of the League of Nations. These observations are particularly applicable to annual reports and petitions.[25]

The Court also indicated that South Africa was still subject to the compulsory jurisdiction of the International Court in any dispute between the Union government and another member of the League of Nations, relating to the interpretation or application of the provisions of the mandate. The continuance of this obligation arose from the joint operation of Article 7 of the Mandate, Article 37 of the statute of the Court and Article 80 (1) of the Charter, as a result of which the International Court of Justice replaced the Permanent Court of International Justice in reference to any such dispute.[26]

In accordance with its conclusions on the continuing operation of the mandate, the Court indicated that it was not necessary for it to consider the applicability of Chapter XI of the Charter.[27]

24. *Status Opinion* (1950): 137. Sir Gerald Fitzmaurice in an article entitled, "Judicial Innovation—Its Uses and Its Perils," *Cambridge Essays in International Law* (London: Stevens, 1965), p. 38, n. 42, maintains that Article 10, empowering the General Assembly to make recommendations, is quite an inadequate source of power to exercise supervision over a mandate.

25. *Status Opinion* (1950): 138. This passage, although not incorporated into the formal answers of the Court, was substantially more than an *obiter dictum*; it was to be a focal source of controversy in endeavors to implement the advisory opinion. See below, chap. VII.

As to the right of petition, the Court considered that although it was not provided for in either the Covenant or the Mandate, it was an "acquired" right of the inhabitants of South West Africa, as a result of Council rules adopted in 1923. *Status Opinion* (1950): 137.

26. Ibid., p. 138. The majority opinion made no reference to the concept of "judicial supervision," as did Judges McNair and Read. As a result, the exact scope of this jurisdictional clause is undefined in the majority opinion. Nor is it clear which states would be eligible to invoke the jurisdiction of the Court. Each of these issues was to assume central importance in the preliminary objections stage of the *South West Africa* cases. See below chap. IX. Judge Winiarski, in the *SWA Judgment* (1962): 451, maintained that the viewpoint of the majority, of which he was a member, was not the same as that of Judges McNair and Read. The 1962 Court, however, adopted the position that the 1950 majority viewpoint also reflected a concept of "judicial supervision."

27. *Status Opinion* (1950): 138. In the proceedings in the *South West Africa* cases, the relevance of Chapter XI to South West Africa came up for consideration upon various occasions. Judges Spender and Fitzmaurice, in their joint dissent in 1962, severely criticized the

Finally, since the mandate constituted an international status it was quite clear that the Union did not have the "competence to modify unilaterally the international status of the Territory."[28] Article 7 of the Mandate stipulated, in its first paragraph, that the consent of the League Council, the supervisory organ, was necessary for any modification of the terms of the mandate. The powers of supervision now "belonged" to the General Assembly of the United Nations, and it, therefore, was also the appropriate organ to authorize modification of the terms of the mandate.[29]

The Court corroborated this conclusion by citing the actions taken by the General Assembly and the attitude adopted by the Union of South Africa in requesting the United Nations to ratify its proposals for incorporation of South West Africa into the Union. "By thus submitting the question of the future international status of the territory to the 'judgment' of the General Assembly as the 'competent international organ,' the Union Government recognized the competence of the General Assembly in the matter."[30] Likewise, the General Assembly, by means of its subsequent resolutions, affirmed its competence in the matter.

On the basis of these considerations, the Court concluded that "competence to determine and modify the international status of South West Africa rests with the Union of South Africa acting with the consent of the United Nations."[31]

Judges McNair and Read, although they were in agreement with the Court majority both on the question of the continued existence of the mandate status and the need for United Nations consent to any modification of that status, vigorously dissented from the majority view on

_____

1950 opinion for failure to take account of the applicability of Chapter XI to South West Africa. They noted, *inter alia*, that the final League Assembly resolution expressly referred to this chapter along with the chapters on trusteeship. See *SWA Judgment* (1962): 541–45. Subsequently, in the course of the oral proceedings on the merits, Judge Jessup asked the parties directly whether Chapter XI was applicable to South West Africa. *SWA Pleadings* VIII: 16–17. Judge Spender, President of the Court, requested the parties, in formulating their replies to Judge Jessup's question, to take into account "certain facts" (nine in number) relating to the *travaux préparatoires* of Chapter XI. Ibid., pp. 38–40. For Applicants' answer, see ibid., IX: 124–42, 156–59, 217–20. South Africa respectfully declined to answer Judge Jessup's question on the ground that "as a matter of law and as a matter of fact," it was not one "submitted to the Court for determination." Ibid., p. 471. But see the reply of the representative of South Africa to the question of Judge Jiménez de Aréchaga in *Namibia Pleadings* II: 567–70, to the effect that Chapter XI was intended to apply to colonial territories exclusively and not to former mandated territories; the latter were provided for "only within the context of the trusteeship system." Ibid., p. 569. Cf., however, the view of dissenting Judge Fitzmaurice, *Namibia Opinion* (1971): 248–49, 296, that Chapter XI continues to apply to South West Africa, since "on any view [it] is a non-self-governing territory." Ibid., p. 296.

28. *Status Opinion* (1950): 141.
29. Ibid., p. 142
30. Ibid.
31. Ibid., p. 143.

the matter of United Nations succession to the supervisory powers of the League.[32] In their view, the duty to submit to administrative supervision involving annual reports and petitions had died with the League, and no succession had ever been arranged between the League and the United Nations. To attempt to require South Africa to submit to United Nations' supervision would, in the words of Judge McNair, "amount to imposing a new obligation upon the Union Government and would be a piece of judicial legislation."[33] Nevertheless, South Africa was not totally free from all forms of international control. If it was free of *administrative* supervision, it was not free of *judicial* supervision. Every state which was a member of the League at the date of its dissolution retained "a legal interest in the proper exercise of the Mandate" and was qualified to implead South Africa before the Court for its conduct of the mandate. Judicial supervision had been expressly preserved by means of Article 37 of the Statute of the Court operating in conjunction with Article 7 of the Mandate.[34]

## SIGNIFICANCE OF THE OPINION

The most noteworthy feature of the opinion was, of course, the fact that the Court had found a means for confirming the United Nations as successor to the League of Nations with reference to the supervision of mandates. This decision was, in turn, based on the finding that the mandate, as an institution, had survived the demise of the League. But this latter fact alone could not impart authority to the United Nations. All the provisions of Article 22 of the Covenant and the Mandate referred expressly and exclusively to the League and its organs as the supervisory authority, and for the United Nations to be qualified to replace the League, some act of transfer had to have taken place; and no express transfer was ever instituted. Nevertheless, despite the absence of any formal arrangements, the Court found, as part of its "general considerations," that "decisive reasons" existed for replacing the League by the United Nations in the "machinery for implementation" of the sacred trust. The Court pointed out that the authors of the mandates system had regarded international supervision as a vital element in that system. The "same necessity" was present in the minds of the authors of the trusteeship system—a fact which enabled the United

---

32. See the separate opinion of Judge McNair, ibid., at pp. 158-62; and the separate opinion of Judge Read, ibid., at pp. 165-66, 169-73. For an analysis of Judge McNair's views on the failure of the United Nations to succeed to the administrative supervision of the League, see Fitzmaurice, "Judicial Innovation," pp. 35-39.

33. *Status Opinion* (1950): 162.

34. Ibid., pp. 158-59; and see pp. 165-66, 169.

Nations to supervise the mandate.[35] The Court, however, did not explain how it bridged the gap from one organization to another.[36]

Three basic interpretations have been suggested by commentators to explain the rationale of the Court's opinion.[37]

1. The trusteeship system was fundamentally a continuation and extension of the mandates system—and of the principle of international accountability and supervision that it incorporated. Moreover, the General Assembly's supervisory role in the trusteeship system implied a derivative link with the role of the League Council in the functioning of the mandates system, since the one system was predicated on the disappearance of the other. As a result, the General Assembly was automatically qualified to assume the mantle of the League Council in fulfilling the latter's supervisory role in the operation of the mandates system. This rule of automatic succession has been characterized as an instance of functional succession in the international organizational field, comparable to the rule of state succession in general international law.

> Just as a territorial area passing from one state to another carries with it all rights and obligations specifically appertaining to that area in a territorial manner, so a functional field "passing" [with or without the operation of an instrument] from one international organization to another (in the sense that the former is extinguished but the latter is created expressly to fulfill the same general purposes, and the extinction of the former is carried out largely on that basis) carries with it the rights, obligations, and functions connected with that field, and appertaining to the capacity to act in it.[38]

35. See discussion above, p. 116. In particular note the extract from p. 136 of the *Status Opinion.*

36. The Court's "general considerations" were confirmed by reference to Article 80 (1) and the final resolution of the League Assembly, but this did not serve to clarify the intent of the "general considerations."

37. South Africa rejected each of these interpretations of the 1950 opinion, since in its view there was no rule of international law which would enable one international organization to succeed another automatically. According to South Africa, the 1950 opinion was based on a reading of the events of 1945–46 as implying tacit consent by South Africa to United Nations supervision of the mandate. And in the pleadings in the *South West Africa* cases, South Africa sought to rebut this assumption on the basis of "new facts" which had come to light after delivery of the opinion, and which, it was claimed, negatived any possibility of tacit consent on South Africa's part. *SWA Pleadings* I: 345–46; II: 141–48; VII: 91–98; VIII: 383, 550–62. See above, pp. 66–68, 70–72; and see also below, pp. 128–29, 194, 217.

38. G. Fitzmaurice, "The Law and Procedure of the International Court of Justice: International Organizations and Tribunals," *BYB* XXIX (1952): 8–9. This however did not mean that the United Nations had succeeded to *all* League functions. The case of the mandates system was essentially different because of the commitment to international accountability. As Fitzmaurice cautions: "The Court's view that there had been an automatic succession in the present case derived from their view as to the nature and effect of the Mandate." Ibid., p. 10, n. 2.

Some notion of automatic succession was apparently endorsed by the 1956 Court in the *Oral Petitions Opinion.* See below, pp. 158–62. In the preliminary objections phase of the

2. The primary focus of the Court was actually on the status of the international community as an enduring entity in international law.[39] According to this interpretation, the principle of international accountability, first formulated in connection with the mandates system, was in reality an acknowledgment of answerability to the *international community—in its organized form.* Under the mandates system, that obligation was fulfilled through submission of reports to the League Council; under the trusteeship system, it is fulfilled through submission of reports to the United Nations General Assembly. But in each case, the particular institution is nothing more than the agency of the international community to which the basic obligation is owed. The international community, needless to say, is constant throughout, and the normal difficulties associated with succession do not arise. As the contemporary representative institution of the international community, the United Nations was fully qualified to supervise the mandate.[40]

3. The Court's ruling on United Nations succession resulted from application of the rule of effectiveness to the original treaties which set up the mandates system.[41] The Court recognized that the removal of international supervision would effectively put an end to the whole mandates status. Consequently, in order to give effect to the original obligations assumed under the mandate, the Court was compelled to read into the original documents a principle of succession in international organization. Only by this means could the initial commitment assumed by South Africa be effectively preserved. As explained by Lauterpacht, this interpretation arose from "the requirement of continuity of international life." It was, he says, an application of the *cy-pres* doctrine which common law courts apply "in order to render effective a general charitable intention in face of the impossibility of

---

South West Africa cases, Applicants argued that the 1950 opinion was based on a principle of automatic succession. *SWA Pleadings* I: 429; 443–46; VII: 319. But the 1962 majority failed to endorse any such interpretation; and Applicants subsequently abandoned this line of argument. Instead, they adopted the reasoning employed by the 1956 minority for interpreting the 1950 opinion. See ibid., VIII: 132–33. For the comments of Respondent, see ibid., pp. 311–18.

39. See discussion above, p. 97, n. 104.

40. This interpretation of the 1950 opinion, centering on the conception of an international community, was the one basically adopted by Ethiopia and Liberia in the *South West Africa* cases. *SWA Pleadings* I: 440–46; IV: 533–40. See also Alexander J. Pollock, "The South West Africa Cases and the Jurisprudence of International Law," *International Organization* XXIII (1969): 772.

41. This is the approach of Sir Hersch Lauterpacht, *The Development of International Law by the International Court* (London: Stevens, 1958), pp. 278–79. See also L. Oppenheim, *International Law*, ed. H. Lauterpacht (8th ed.; London: Longmans, Green, 1955), I: 168. This concept of the 1950 opinion, as being premised on the principle of effectiveness, was subsequently applied and expounded by Lauterpacht, in his capacity as judge, in the *Voting Procedure Opinion* (1955): 90 ff.; and in the *Oral Petitions Opinion* (1956): 35 ff. See below, pp. 152–53, and 162. This line of reasoning was urged by Applicants in the *South West Africa* cases. *SWA Pleadings* I: 445–46; VIII: 189. For the reaction of Respondent, see ibid., VII: 118–21; VIII: 524–25.

applying it according to the literal language of its author." And "seldom was there a more compelling occasion for applying [this] doctrine."[42]

Regardless of the interpretation adopted, the essential point was that the International Court had concurred with the opinion of the overriding majority of the Assembly and had provided a legal basis for United Nations supervision of the mandate of South West Africa. The succession between League Council and United Nations General Assembly, as postulated by the Court, was a limited or functional, rather than a total, succession. The Court did not say that the mandate had matured into a United Nations entity; rather it remained a League institution, to be supervised by the United Nations as it had been supervised by the League. As a result, the General Assembly could not do all that its own Charter might permit it to do. It was bound by the Court's stipulation that "The degree of supervision . . . should not . . . exceed that which applied under the Mandates System" and the procedure to be followed "should conform as far as possible to the procedure followed" by the League Council. In effect, then, the Court established a new regime for the mandate, composed of elements of the Covenant, the Mandate, and the United Nations Charter.[43] This compound structure was essentially of judicial origin, and the action of the Court in formulating such a regime and in conferring supervisory powers on the General Assembly represented fulfillment by the Court of an essentially creative, and not just an interpretative, role in its capacity as the principal judicial organ of the United Nations. It signified a close interaction between the judicial and political organs of the world organization. While it was true that the Court could not find legal authority in the Charter to convert the mandate into a full United Nations entity, this could not be regarded as crucial, for, as Lauterpacht has said: "Once the Court had affirmed the principle of continuing international supervision—as well as of the international status of the territory, unmodified and unmodifiable except in accordance with the Charter—the problem of the formal conclusion of trusteeship agreements acquired a symbolic rather than practical significance."[44] At the same time, however, the very *sui generis* character of the new regime, based on novel judicial interpretations, was bound to create complications in application, unless all parties were dedicated to abiding by the opinion of the court.

42. Lauterpacht, *Development of International Law by the International Court*, p. 279.
43. As expressed by Judge Lauterpacht in his separate opinion in the *Oral Petitions Opinion* (1956): 47: "The Opinion of 11 July 1950 did no more than to formulate a regime resulting from two multilateral conventional instruments, namely, the Covenant . . . and the Charter." This regime was "in the nature of an objective law." Ibid., p. 46.
44. *The Development of International Law by the International Court*, p. 281.

# III.

## ATTEMPTS
## TO IMPLEMENT
## THE ADVISORY
## OPINION

# VI.

# THE ATTEMPT
# TO NEGOTIATE:
# THE *AD HOC*
# COMMITTEE

## CONSTITUTION OF THE *AD HOC* COMMITTEE

The history of the next period of United Nations-South African relations in reference to South West Africa was marked by an effort (ultimately vain) to implement the 1950 advisory opinion of the International Court of Justice with the cooperation of South Africa.

The opinion, as noted, represented simultaneously an affirmation of the General Assembly's authority with respect to South West Africa and a limitation of that authority. In exercising supervision, the Assembly was not permitted to equate the territory to a trust territory; its task was to supervise a *mandate*. This meant that annual reports could not be examined by the Trusteeship Council, nor could the Assembly adopt procedures that were unknown to the Permanent Mandates Commission. In essence, the General Assembly had to constitute itself into something like the Council of the League and also create a special supervisory organ to parallel the Permanent Mandates Commission. These facts were universally recognized by United Nations members, as discussions commenced in the Fifth Session of the General Assembly.[1] However, two schools of thought developed over the appropriate means to implement the advisory opinion and over the necessity and desirability of consultation with South Africa. The activist anticolonial states were bent on giving immediate and direct effect to the Court's ruling. The Court having confirmed the Assembly's authority in the matter, South Africa was, in their view, automatically and unqualifiedly obligated to submit reports immediately to the world organization. What need was there for negotiations with South Africa and

---

1. GAOR, 5th Sess., 4th Ctte., 190th Mtg., Nov. 29, 1950, pp. 314 ff.

what purpose could be served thereby? The suggestion was, moreover, positively dangerous, since it would imply a need for South Africa's consent. It could only cause delay without compensatory benefits.

In contrast, Western states, reflecting a more moderate stand on colonial issues, emphasized that the Court's ruling was neither a fiat nor a self-implementing ordinance so crystal clear in its guidelines that there was no room for consultation or discussion. The United Nations was, after all, not the League in fact, and a certain measure of adjustment would be necessary in order for the one organization to create and institute organs and procedures appropriate to the other organization. Unilateral imposition of supervisory machinery would not prove effective, and the whole effort to implement the Court's opinion might prove abortive. For all these reasons, consultation—not real negotiation—was warranted.

Two draft resolutions reflecting the divergent views were presented to the Fourth Committee. One draft resolution, sponsored by the delegations of Brazil, India, Cuba, Mexico, Syria, and Uruguay,[2] would have "noted" the advisory opinion and would have provided, *inter alia*, for an *ad hoc* committee for South West Africa composed of ten experts (in similar manner to the Mandates Commission)[3] to assist the General Assembly in its supervision of the mandate. South Africa would be requested to submit reports on its administration of the territory for the years 1947–50, in accordance with the Mandates Commission questionnaire, together with any relevant petitions. South Africa would also be invited to appoint a representative to meet with the Committee upon examination of the reports.

In contrast, a draft resolution sponsored by the United States, Denmark, El Salvador, Iraq, Peru, Thailand, and Venezuela, would have, *inter alia*, accepted and endorsed the advisory opinion, urged the Union government to take the necessary steps to give effect to the opinion, and established a Committee of three to confer with the Union government concerning measures for implementing the opinion.[4]

The United States representative emphasized that a solution to the South West Africa problem could best be attained by means of "consultation" rather than "arbitrary decisions."[5] He warned the

2. U.N. Doc. A/C.4/L.116/Rev. 1, in Report of 4th Ctte., Doc. A/1643, GAOR, 5th Sess., Annexes, Agenda Item 35, pp. 3–4 (1950–51).

3. Originally, a "Commission for South West Africa" had been envisaged, but since this might imply an air of permanence the title was changed. As explained by the Indian delegate, "the establishment of an *ad hoc* committee . . . to examine petitions and annual reports was simply an interim measure pending the preparation of a trusteeship agreement." A second draft resolution, recommending the latter step, was submitted. GAOR, 5th Sess., 4th Ctte., 191st Mtg., Nov. 30, 1950, p. 321. See below, p. 129.

4. U.N. Doc. A/C.4/L.142, in Report of 4th Ctte., Doc. A/1643, pp. 1–2.

5. GAOR, 5th Sess., 4th Ctte., 191st Mtg., Nov. 30, 1950, pp. 323–24.

Committee against adopting impractical methods which could only jeopardize the objective sought. The United Kingdom delegate stressed that what was involved was a "delicate adjustment" of two international systems. The South African government could hardly be expected to accept the Brazilian-Indian plan, since "the essential part of the new procedure," namely, "the limits of the supervision to be exercised and the appropriate machinery to be instituted were not really defined."[6] In response, the Indian representative noted that four years had gone by without any action and that the people of South West Africa had been deprived of their lawful rights, particularly the right of petition, for that period. The United States-Danish draft resolution would only delay matters for another year.[7]

After a close vote, the Fourth Committee adopted the Brazilian-Indian draft resolution.[8] In Plenary session, however, this draft resolution could not muster sufficient votes, and a compromise resolution was adopted in its place.[9] The latter resolution,[10] after reciting the various conclusions of the Court, accepted the Court's opinion,[11] urged South Africa to take the necessary steps to give effect to the opinion, including the transmission of reports and petitions; established an *ad hoc* committee of five states to confer with South Africa "concerning the procedural measures necessary for implementing the advisory opinion," and authorized the Committee, "as an interim measure" and "as far as possible in accordance with the procedure of the former Mandates system," to examine reports and petitions that may be submitted to the Secretary-General. Thus, although the Committee was established as a negotiating body, it nonetheless had the power to act as a supervisory organ in the interval.[12]

6. Ibid., pp. 319-20. See also the remarks of the Belgian delegate (ibid., pp. 324-27), who noted that the Assembly, no more than South Africa, could unilaterally modify the status of South West Africa. Yet, requiring South Africa to submit reports to an organ whose functions and powers would be determined by the Assembly alone would, he said, represent a unilateral modification of the mandate. See also the remarks of the French representative, ibid., p. 327.

7. Ibid., p. 326. See also the remarks of the Brazilian delegate (ibid., 192nd Mtg., Dec. 1, 1950, p. 336), and those of the Chinese delegate (ibid., 196th Mtg., Dec. 4, 1950, pp. 364-65).

8. Ibid., pp. 366-67. For text, see Report of 4th Ctte., Doc. A/1643, GAOR, 5th Sess., Annexes, Agenda Item 35, pp. 9-10. Draft Resolution I.

9. GAOR, 5th Sess., Plen., 322nd Mtg., Dec. 13, 1950, p. 628.

10. G.A. Res. 449A (V), Dec. 13, 1950.

11. As observed earlier, the Brazilian-Indian draft would only "note" the opinion, reflecting, presumably, dissatisfaction with the Court's conclusion on the voluntary character of Chapter XII. According to the United States-Danish draft, the Assembly would "accept and endorse" the opinion. In the resultant compromise, the opinion was accepted but not endorsed. Subsequent advisory opinions in 1955 and 1956 were both accepted and endorsed by the General Assembly. See below p. 154. In 1971 the Security Council declared it "takes note with appreciation" of the Namibia opinion and "agrees with" the operative paragraph in the opinion. For the significance of this terminology see below chap. XII, p. 344.

12. The five states appointed to the Committee were Denmark, Syria, Thailand, Uruguay, and the United States.

Notwithstanding its compromise character, the resolution was sharply criticized by the South African representative.[13] He was especially critical of the interim power given the committee to examine reports before any set procedure had been agreed upon through consultation with South Africa. If it was necessary to establish a committee for purposes of consultation, he maintained, then surely it was somewhat premature and contradictory to empower this same committee to examine reports before any consultations had taken place. Moreover, he objected to the fact that the members of the Committee would serve as representatives of states rather than in an individual capacity.[14] "Instead of creating the machinery to ensure the calm and objective consideration of the problem . . . this compromise resolution practically closes the door to this method of approach."[15]

These remarks of the South African representative did not augur well for the forthcoming negotiations. Earlier, in the Fourth Committee, the Union representative had noted that "the nature of the resolution [adopted] would have an important influence on the decision" of his government.[16] He had also stated his government's view regarding the Court's advisory opinion: first, it was merely "advisory" and in no way binding on South Africa; second, important "new facts," not brought to the Court's attention, demonstrated conclusively that no transfer had ever been effected between the League and the United Nations with reference to the supervision of mandates. In connection with the second point, he discussed in detail the original Chinese proposal at the final session of the League Assembly and its replacement by the draft resolution finally adopted.[17] Quite clearly, he said, the express purpose of the revised resolution was to avoid, rather than to imply, a transfer of supervisory functions from the League to the United Nations. "If the resolution had indeed intended such a transfer of functions . . . it would not have received the unanimous vote of the League Assembly . . . as South Africa, at any rate, would have voted against it with the result that no resolution would have been adopted." South Africa's negative vote would have been assured, since it had by then made clear its intention to incorporate South West Africa as an integral part of the Union—a policy quite inconsistent with the continued submission of annual reports and

13. GAOR, 5th Sess., Plen., 322nd Mtg., Dec. 13, 1950, pp. 629–30.
14. This objection was, of course, based on the contrast between the projected political role of the committee and the nonpartisan nature of the Permanent Mandates Commission composed of individual experts.
15. Ibid.
16. Ibid., 4th Ctte., 196th Mtg., Dec. 4, 1950, pp. 362–64. The full text of the statement was later distributed as U.N. Doc. A/C. 4/185.
17. See discussion above, pp. 69–72.

petitions. Had the Court been aware of this evidence, it would undoubtedly have reached a different decision, "because the very basis . . . on which the Court found that there had been such a transfer is destroyed by the facts" presented.[18] If the Court's decision had been delivered in a judgment, South Africa would have requested a revision in accordance with Article 61 of the Court's Statute. There was, however, no set procedure for revising advisory opinions.[19] Nevertheless, South Africa was entitled to take this new development into consideration, together with the attitude reflected in any Assembly resolution, in formulating its own viewpoint on the whole question.[20]

This lengthy discourse challenging the validity of the Court's opinion could hardly have inspired much confidence that the Court's opinion would really provide a firm basis for a solution to the South West Africa problem. If South Africa from its side did not seem inclined to adopt the opinion of the Court as a final determination of the legal status of South West Africa, many member states, and particularly those in the anticolonial group, were likewise not content to let the matter rest, with South West Africa continuing as a "permanent Mandate."[21] These states placed key emphasis on the statement of the Court that "the normal way of modifying the international status of the Territory would be to place it under the Trusteeship System by means of a Trusteeship Agreement in accordance with the provisions of Chapter XII of the Charter." Under their inspiration, the General Assembly adopted a second resolution in this Fifth Session, which reiterated earlier Assembly resolutions and invited South Africa to negotiate a trusteeship agreement for South West Africa. In the Committee several delegates argued that adoption of the resolution would only exacerbate relations between South Africa and the world organization, since the former clearly had no intention of negotiating a trusteeship agreement. In any case, the earlier invitations were still valid, and there was little purpose in repeating worn-out invitations.[22] The Committee, however, was obviously in agreement with

18. The Chinese representative rejected the view "that the Court had been ignorant of the facts." GAOR, 5th Sess., 4th Ctte., 196th Mtg., Dec. 4, 1950, pp. 364–65. See also separate opinion of Judge Jessup, *SWA Judgment* (1966): 348.

19. Cf. statement of Judge Jessup, ibid., p. 339.

20. GAOR, 5th Sess., 4th Ctte., 196th Mtg., Dec. 4, 1950, p. 364. The South African delegate also adverted to the fact that the mandate status of Nauru had not ended until November 1947, and that of Palestine until May 1948, and yet no reports were ever submitted or even requested in reference to those territories—something which again confirmed absence of any transfer of supervisory power from League to United Nations. This evidence, he noted, had also not been drawn to the attention of the Court. Ibid.

21. Ibid., 198th Mtg., Dec. 5, 1950, pp. 378–79.

22. See the remarks of the representative of Australia, ibid., p. 375. See also the remarks of the representatives of Belgium, Canada, the United States, and the United Kingdom, ibid., 197th Mtg., Dec. 5, 1950, pp. 371–72.

the observation of the Indian delegate at the Fourth Assembly Session to the effect that the Court's pronouncement on the legal issue could not affect South Africa's distinct moral and political obligation to negotiate an agreement.[23]

Subsequent to the vote in the Plenary, the South African delegate reaffirmed the view of his government, that it was under no obligation, legal or moral, to negotiate a trusteeship agreement. "In these circumstances," he declared, "no good purpose could be served by a resolution of this nature."[24]

If mutual agreements spring from mutual confidence, then the events of the Fifth Session of the General Assembly did not provide much cause for sanguineness.

## AD HOC COMMITTEE NEGOTIATIONS (1951)

Negotiations between the *Ad Hoc* Committee and the Union government got under way on June 27, 1951.[25] On that occasion, Mr. Jooste, the South African delegate, presented his country's proposals for a solution of the South West Africa problem.[26] He prefaced his remarks by defining his government's views on the Court's advisory opinion. That opinion had no binding force; nor could South Africa concur in the substantive views therein expressed, which had been endorsed by the majority of the United Nations. Rather it considered that the mandate had lapsed, and in consequence South Africa had no legal obligations whatsoever thereunder. In particular, it was not in any way accountable to the United Nations for implementation of the mandate.[27]

But notwithstanding South Africa's stand on the legal position, in deference to the wishes of the United Nations, it was prepared to

23. See, in particular, the remarks of the Brazilian representative, ibid., pp. 370-71. In Plenary, the resolution was adopted at the 322nd Mtg., Dec. 13, 1950, pp. 631-32, and became G.A. Res. 449B(V).

24. GAOR, 5th Sess., Plen., 322nd Mtg., Dec. 13, 1950, p. 632. A similar resolution inviting South Africa to negotiate a trusteeship agreement was standardly adopted at subsequent General Assembly sessions. In the *SWA Pleadings* I: 273, South Africa referred to this procedure in the following terms: "The inconsistency of on the one hand offering 'negotiations' with a view to amicable settlement of a dispute, while on the other hand making what in effect amounted to an extreme demand relative to that dispute, namely United Nations Trusteeship for South West Africa, was to become a regularly recurring feature in the history of this matter." These "extreme demands," argued South Africa, foreclosed at the outset any possibility of settlement by means of negotiation. Hence, the implicit requirement of Article 7 of the Mandate, that a realistic attempt to negotiate precede submission of a dispute to the Court was never fulfilled; and the Court was precluded from exercising jurisdiction. Ibid., p. 402. See below, p. 208.

25. See U.N. Doc. A/AC.49/SR.2, pp. 1-2 (1951).

26. Ibid., pp. 3 ff. In his view the differences that had arisen over South West Africa had no relation to the manner in which South Africa had fulfilled the mandate, but rather derived from political developments within the United Nations. Ibid., p. 5.

27. U.N. Doc. A/AC.49/SR.3, p. 3 (1951).

compromise and negotiate a *new* international instrument whereby it would *"reassume"*[28] the obligations covered in Articles 2 to 5 of the original Mandate. (These, in the view of the Court, had related directly to the sacred trust.) "The United Nations wished to ensure that that sacred trust continue and the Union Government in fact was carrying out that sacred trust. It was here that common ground could be found between the Government of the Union of South Africa, the United Nations and the International Court of Justice."[29] The agreement would be concluded between South Africa on the one hand, and the three remaining Principal Allied and Associated Powers (France, the United Kingdom, and the United States), on the other. The South African delegation emphasized that the suggested participation of these powers in the new arrangement was derived from historical not legal association with South West Africa. All legal ties to the territory had been lost by those states in their capacity as Principal Allied and Associated Powers once the mandate was conferred in 1919. (This stand, it might be noted, was consistent with the view already espoused by South Africa in the 1950 proceedings before the Court, that once "the mandate had been conferred and confirmed," the Principal Powers were *"functi officio."*)[30] In the course of subsequent discussions it became evident that South Africa was not prepared to accord the United Nations any significant role either in the conclusion or operation of the new agreement. The agreement would be concluded with the three states as principals, not as agents of the United Nations, and South Africa would not be responsible to the United Nations in any way. In fact, there would be no arrangements for submission of reports or petitions to any body. South Africa would be responsible to the three powers solely for the substantive obligations to be assumed.

28. Emphasis supplied. In line with its stand on the legal issue, it refused to substitute "reaffirm" for "reassume." See discussions in U.N. Doc. A/AC.49/SR.4, pp. 4–6, 9.

29. U.N. Doc. A/AC.49/SR.3, p. 3.

30. *SWA Status Pleadings*, p. 276. Subsequently, however, in the *South West Africa* cases proceedings, South Africa hesitated to commit itself categorically to the view that the Principal Powers had lost all legal ties to the territory. Judge Fitzmaurice posed to the parties the question whether the Principal Powers retained any residual rights in reference to the mandates "which would revive . . . in the event . . . of a termination of the mandate." *SWA Pleadings* VIII: 36. In response, Mr. de Villiers, Counsel for Respondent, asserted that while South Africa's right to administer the territory would be ensured in the event of a lapse of the mandate, the problem of rights accruing to the Principal Powers entailed "very difficult questions of law." But since, in any case, Applicants' entire claim was premised on the continuance of the mandate, Mr. de Villiers thought it was not necessary for South Africa to determine the rights of either South Africa or the Principal Powers in the absence of the mandate; he, therefore, respectfully declined "to express any view" on the question. Ibid., IX: 476–80. (For Applicants' response to Judge Fitzmaurice's question, see ibid., pp. 365–66.) South Africa's new-found reticence in the matter stemmed perhaps from the fact that Judges Spender and Fitzmaurice in their 1962 dissenting opinion had expressed the view that the Principal Powers may have retained "and may still retain on a dormant basis a residual or reversionary interest in the actual territories concerned." *SWA Judgment* (1962): 482, n. 1. Judge Jessup, in his 1966 dissenting opinion, totally dismissed the possibility that the Principal Powers retained any reversionary rights. *SWA Judgment* (1966): 421–23.

The role of the United Nations would be limited to authorizing the three powers to conclude the agreement.

Despite South Africa's attempt to portray these proposals as a partial fulfillment of the Court's opinion, the Committee members recognized them as a fundamental negation of that opinion.[31] The essence of the opinion was the substitution of the United Nations for the League in the continued operation of the mandate so as to preserve the principle of international accountability, and this was precisely what South Africa wished to exclude. Doubt was expressed as to whether the South African proposal actually came within the Committee's terms of reference. It was decided, however, to see whether common ground might not yet be found.[32]

As the talks progressed, South Africa modified its position somewhat by agreeing to accord the United Nations authority not only to initially authorize the negotiations but also to confirm the final agreement.[33] Moreover, as a concession to the Committee's wishes on "implementation," South Africa was prepared to accept "judicial supervision" as part of the proposed agreement. Any two of the three powers could, under this scheme, invoke the compulsory jurisdiction of the International Court for any alleged violation of the "sacred trust" provisions.[34]

These concessions, as significant as they might have been in South Africa's eyes, did not radically alter the situation. The Committee had been designated to work out procedures for a United Nations role in the supervision of the mandate, not a method for abandoning that role.[35] It had not been appointed to preside over the liquidation of international accountability in reference to South West Africa.[36] The Committee deemed consideration of South Africa's plan beyond its terms of reference and in its place suggested a new agreement composed of the seven basic provisions of the Mandate, plus an eighth provision which would institute new organs to assist the General Assembly in supervision of the mandate.[37] As a counterpart of the League Council a

31. See the remarks of the United States and Danish representatives, U.N. Doc. A/AC.49/SR.3, p. 7.
32. Ibid.
33. U.N. Doc. A/AC.49/SR.4 and 5.
34. Ibid., SR.7, p. 5. According to South Africa, this would revive all provisions of the Mandate, including "judicial supervision," with only Article 6 relating to reports excluded. For the significance of South Africa's recognition of Article 7 as incorporating a principle of "judicial supervision," see below, chap. IX, n. 69.
35. As expressed by the Uruguayan delegate, "The Committee's task was not to study a modification of the existing situation or of the concepts or ideas of the various parties, but to confer with South Africa in order to find a procedure for the implementation of the Court's opinion." U.N. Doc. A/AC.49/SR.5, p. 4.
36. Needless to say, from South Africa's viewpoint, it was not obliged to revive a scheme of international accountability which had already died.
37. U.N. Doc. A/AC.49/SR.10. For the text, see Report of *Ad Hoc* Committee, in GAOR, 6th Sess., Annexes, Agenda Item 38, pp. 5–7 (1951) (A/1901).

Committee on South West Africa would be established to be composed of fifteen members, including the Union of South Africa. This Committee, in turn, would set up a Special Commission on South West Africa composed of experts, which would fulfill the functions of the Permanent Mandates Commission in the examination of reports and petitions. The Committee on South West Africa would report annually to the General Assembly.[38] In effect, the new agreement was designed to formally substitute the United Nations for the League in the operation of the mandate. Similarly, power to invoke the compulsory jurisdiction of the Court (provided for in Article 7 of the original Mandate) would now be extended to all members of the United Nations.

The South African representative indicated, however, that his government was not willing to hold itself accountable to the United Nations in any form or manner,[39] because such accountability would inevitably increase the obligations South Africa had assumed under the mandate. This was so, particularly in view of United Nations voting procedure which, unlike the League, did not require unanimity.[40]

In a letter dated September 20, 1951, South Africa formally notified the Committee of its unwillingness to accept the counterproposals as a basis for discussion.[41] *Inter alia*, the letter pointed out that the Committee's proposals "would confer certain rights in respect of South West Africa on states now members of the United Nations which had no such rights under the League."[42] This was particularly directed at the widening of the compulsory jurisdiction clause. At this point the negotiations were suspended.

As will be recalled, the *Ad Hoc* Committee had been empowered by the General Assembly, not only to confer with South Africa but also to examine in the interim any reports or petitions that might be submitted. Not unexpectedly, no report was presented by South Africa on its administration of South West Africa; and this fact was duly recorded in the Committee report.[43] The report also noted receipt of two communications, one from the Reverend Michael Scott and the other from the British Section of the Women's International League for Peace and Freedom, both of which urged United Nations supervision of South Africa's administration of the territory. The documents were

38. The General Assembly would thus retain ultimate supervisory authority, although this would be exercised in a less direct manner than, for instance, in the case of trust territories.

39. U.N. Doc. A/AC.49/SR.11, p. 7.

40. Ibid. He also referred to the widened membership of the United Nations which had particular significance in the light of basic ideological differences that had arisen.

41. For text, see Report of *Ad Hoc* Committee, U.N. Doc. A/1901, in GAOR, 6th Sess., Annexes, Agenda Item 38, pp. 7–8.

42. Ibid.

43. Ibid., p. 9.

treated as petitions, and in accordance with mandates procedure, were transmitted to the Union government for comment. The text of the two petitions was appended to the *Ad Hoc* Committee's report.[44]

The dismal failure of the negotiations between the *Ad Hoc* Committee and the Union government advanced the conflict between that government and the United Nations one step further. It was now abundantly clear that the advisory opinion had not really settled the matter at all. South Africa was denying the validity of that opinion (except in so far as it confirmed that South Africa was under no obligation to negotiate a trusteeship agreement) and was obviously not prepared to join in any scheme for its implementation. International accountability, as far as South Africa was concerned, had died with the League, and there was no legal duty to submit reports or petitions to the new world organization. At most, South Africa was prepared to pledge itself to observance of the obligations of the "sacred trust" (i.e., the administrative duties alone without international accountability), and this commitment would be undertaken not to the world organization but only toward three major powers in their individual capacity. Quite obviously, the essential prerequisite to the success of any negotiations—viz., agreement on the purpose of the negotiations—was totally absent. For the Committee, which regarded the question of international accountability as settled by the advisory opinion, the purpose was to evolve procedural rules to implement that opinion. On the other hand, for South Africa, which considered the question of international accountability as negotiable, the purpose was to formulate a new agreement in place of the one that had lapsed. That agreement, as noted, would have involved merely a unilateral pledge to promote the welfare of the indigenous population—with no role for the Organization in assuring observance of that pledge. In the view of the Committee, South Africa was attempting to revert to the pre-Covenant days, when international obligations were assumed not toward a permanent international organization but toward individual states, parties to a treaty. This could only mean that international accountability, as it was understood from Versailles on, would be effectively removed from the South West African scene.

The failure of the negotiations only served to promote a keen sense of impatience and frustration among United Nations members. This new mood was reflected in the debates of the Fourth Committee.

---

44. Ibid., pp. 9–11. Eight other communications were received subsequent to the issuance of the report. They were dealt with in the same manner as the early communications and were added as special appendices. Ibid., pp. 11–16.

## THE SIXTH SESSION OF THE GENERAL ASSEMBLY

On November 16, 1951, the Fourth Committee voted, over the protest of the South African delegate, to accord hearings to spokesmen of various tribes in South West Africa.[45] The South African representative had argued that the Committee was obliged to adhere to League procedures, since the Assembly had accepted the advisory opinion. Oral hearings for petitioners were never permitted by the League, and petitions were always processed through the mandatory power. Adoption of the proposed draft resolution, he said, could only "reveal a serious lack of respect towards the South African Government."[46] South West Africa, according to the mandate, was to be administered as an integral part of the Union. Could it be conceived that a part of the population of a member state having a grievance could appeal directly to the United Nations? "No nation, great or small could allow its rights or dignity to be attacked," he concluded.[47]

The argument that the granting of hearings was inconsistent with the advisory opinion was supported by various Western States.[48] The representatives of the United Kingdom, Denmark, and the United States warned against precipitate action which might close the door to further negotiation.[49]

In reply,[50] it was said that the hearings were designed to accord the Committee information on South West Africa rather than to afford an opportunity for the expression of grievances. Consequently, no question of petitions was involved. But, in any case, South Africa could not forever interdict petitions directed toward the world organization. And, finally, it was vain to refer to the advisory opinion as ground for barring the hearings, when it was only South Africa's refusal to accept and apply that opinion in the first place which had engendered the present crisis.

On November 24, 1951, the head of the South African delegation addressed a letter to the president of the General Assembly, Luis Padilla Nervo of Mexico, charging the Fourth Committee with having acted illegally in authorizing the hearings.[51] He announced that the South

45. GAOR, 6th Sess., 4th Ctte., 204th Mtg., Nov. 16, 1951, p. 19. The draft resolution had been submitted by the delegations of Brazil, Cuba, Ecuador, Egypt, Guatemala, India, Indonesia, Pakistan, and the Philippines. For text, see U.N. Doc. A/C.4/190, in Report of 4th Ctte., Doc. A/2066 and Corr. 1, GAOR, 6th Sess., Annexes, Agenda Item 38, p. 27.
46. Ibid., 4th Ctte., 203rd Mtg., Nov. 16, 1951, pp. 11–13.
47. Ibid.
48. See the remarks of the delegates of France, Belgium, Australia, the Netherlands, and Norway, ibid., 203rd and 204th Mtgs., Nov. 16, 1951, passim.
49. Ibid.
50. See generally the remarks of the delegates of the Philippines, Guatemala, Syria, and Brazil, ibid.
51. U.N. Doc. A/C.4/196, in GAOR, 6th Sess., Annexes, Agenda Item 38, pp. 18–19 (1951). The resolution, he indicated, was contrary to (a) the Charter; (b) G.A. Res. 449(V);

African delegation would, as a result of this illegality, "withdraw from further participation in the work of the Fourth Committee, pending review of the constitutionality of the resolution in question by the General Assembly." He requested the President to take the necessary steps to arrange for this constitutional review by the General Assembly. In reply, Mr. Padilla Nervo indicated that from the text of the Committee resolution, as well as the surrounding proceedings, it was clear "that the decision . . . to grant a hearing was not taken with the purpose of considering a petition, but . . . in order that the Committee may enjoy the fullest information on this question." He would therefore be unable to follow the course advocated.[52] As a result, the South African delegation was absent from further Fourth Committee discussions on South West Africa during this session. When the South West Africa topic reached the Plenary, the South African delegate once again raised the issue of the hearings,[53] but the Assembly did not even enter into a discussion on the subject.

As part of the hearings, the Reverend Michael Scott addressed the Fourth Committee on December 8, 1951. He reviewed the situation in South West Africa and referred to the frustrations suffered by tribal leaders in their efforts to leave the territory and appear before the Committee personally. He hoped that a means would yet be found for the Committee to hear these leaders, who would be able to describe in vivid detail the nature of the laws and confinements under which they and their peoples lived.[54]

---

(c) the advisory opinion of the International Court; and (d) the authority of the *Ad Hoc* Committee.

52. Ibid. In 1965 South Africa applied to the International Court in relation "to the composition of the Court" for the purposes of the *South West Africa* cases (*SWA Judgment* [1966]: 9). After two days of closed hearings, the Court decided by a vote of 8 to 6, not to accede to the application. (Order of Mar. 18, 1965, *ICJ Reports 1965*, p. 3.) There are good grounds for believing that South Africa's challenge was directed at the ability of Judge Padilla Nervo to adjudicate in an unprejudiced manner in relation to the South West Africa issue. (Cf. in this connection, the comment of Jeremy D. Morley, "Relative Incompatibility of Functions in the International Court," *ICLQ* XIX (1970): 321–22 and n. 27.)

Perhaps Padilla Nervo's actions as President of the Assembly, and especially his rejection of South Africa's request for an Assembly review of the legality of the Fourth Committee's action, furnished one of various grounds for the aforementioned challenge.

In the 1971 Namibia proceedings South Africa submitted to the Court that the past political involvement of certain judges, including Judge Padilla Nervo, in the South West Africa issue, was *inter alia* reason for the Court not to accede to the request for an advisory opinion. See written statement of South Africa, *Namibia Pleadings*, I: 438. The Court rejected South Africa's objection on the ground that it found no reason to depart from the 1965 decision of the Court in the *South West Africa* cases. *Namibia Opinion* (1971): 18.

53. GAOR, 6th Sess., Plen., 361st Mtg., Jan. 18, 1952, pp. 356–63.

54. Ibid., 4th Ctte., 222nd Mtg., pp. 126–28. Reverend Scott appeared twice more before the Committee during this session. See records of the 244th and 247th meetings. He appealed to the Committee to acquaint itself at first hand with the racial conditions in South West Africa, by arranging for a commission to visit the territory. The United Nations, he declared, was being challenged to establish its jurisdiction and he hoped that the world organization would succeed in bringing the message of the Charter to South West Africa. The

After general discussion on the report of the *Ad Hoc* Committee, the Fourth Committee adopted two draft resolutions on the subject of South West Africa.[55] The first, *inter alia*, regretted South Africa's "unwillingness to give adequate expression ... to the supervisory responsibility of the United Nations," and appealed solemnly to South Africa to reconsider its position. The *Ad Hoc* Committee was reconstituted for the purpose of "conferring" with South Africa "concerning means of implementing the Advisory Opinion."[56] At the same time, the Committee was again authorized to examine reports and petitions. The second draft resolution reaffirmed previous Assembly resolutions, calling on South Africa to negotiate a trusteeship agreement for South West Africa. In Plenary, both draft resolutions were adopted by the General Assembly without change.[57]

## *AD HOC* COMMITTEE NEGOTIATIONS (1952-1953)

Negotiations were resumed on September 10, 1952.[58] Upon that occasion, the South African representative reviewed the course of negotiations of the previous year.[59] He attributed the Committee's inability to accept his government's proposals to the Committee's narrow terms of reference. Since the Committee now had "a much freer hand," he was resubmitting the previous proposals for further consideration.[60] For its part, South Africa was prepared to go beyond its earlier position and would be prepared to institute a system of annual reports. These reports would be submitted to the three powers, the other parties to the agreement, and would include all the information covered in the Mandates Commission questionnaire. This would "bridge the remaining gap."[61]

Members of the Committee, however, remained unimpressed. The slight modification in the original proposals did nothing to remedy the chief shortcoming, namely, failure to institute the principle of accountability to the United Nations. International accountability

Fourth Committee adopted a resolution expressing its "admiration and gratitude" for Reverend Scott's statements and its "regrets" at the inability of the tribal chiefs to appear before the Committee. See Report of 4th Ctte., Doc. A/2066 and Corr. 1, p. 30.

55. Ibid., pp. 30-32.

56. The terms of reference were somewhat broader than those of the previous year, which read: "concerning the procedural measures for implementing the advisory opinion." There is no indication in the debates that the change was deliberately instituted. The South African delegation, however, subsequently referred to the change as a positive factor promoting chances of agreement.

57. G.A. Res. 570A and B (VI), January 19, 1952.

58. U.N. Doc. A/AC.49/SR.21, pp. 1-2.

59. Ibid., pp. 2-7.

60. U.N. Doc. A/AC.49/SR.23, p. 4.

61. Ibid., p. 8. South Africa, however, would not accept that this information or report be formally conveyed to the United Nations. U.N. Doc. A/C.49/SR.25, p. 9.

could not be fulfilled by accountability to a fragment of the international community.[62]

The negotiations had extended from September 10, 1952, to mid-November, but the gap had been narrowed very little, if at all. Since the *Ad Hoc* Committee was due to make its report to the General Assembly, the discussions were suspended. The report, dated November 18, 1952, classified the state of negotiations as "inconclusive."[63] The report also listed various points of agreement and disagreement. The two points of disagreement were:

1. How supervision of the administration should be carried out. The Committee, although it agreed that such supervision "should not exceed that which applied under the Mandates System," insisted that it be exercised by the United Nations. South Africa, on the other hand, maintained that United Nations supervision would inevitably be "more onerous than that existing under the Mandates System."

2. The identity of the second party to the proposed agreement to replace the mandate. The Committee insisted that the agreement be concluded with the United Nations directly or with an agency appointed by and responsible to it, while South Africa was only prepared to allow the United Nations to sanction the agreement with the three powers.

With reference to the examination of reports and petitions, the Committee noted that no report had been received and that communications had been dealt with in accordance with the procedure referred to in the 1951 report, viz., they were accepted as petitions and transmitted to the Union government for comment. The report indicated that South Africa's failure to cooperate would not prevent the Committee from examining the petitions, but that "it was for the General Assembly to recommend any practical steps which could be taken."[64]

In the light of the *Ad Hoc* Committee's statement that negotiations were still under way, the Assembly resolved to postpone consideration of the South West Africa question until the Eighth Assembly Session in 1953. In the meantime, it requested the *Ad Hoc* Committee to pursue its negotiations.[65]

---

62. Ibid., pp. 2–8. The Uruguayan representative charged South Africa with wishing "to conclude an agreement with former members of a defunct organization and to restore discarded machinery," to which the Union delegate replied, that "being accountable to the United Nations was not the only possible form of international accountability." Ibid., pp. 5–8.

63. Report of *Ad Hoc* Committee, U.N. Doc. A/2261, in GAOR, 8th Sess., Annexes, Agenda Item 36, p. 5.

64. Ibid., p. 6.

65. G.A. Res. 651 (VII), Dec. 20, 1952.

Negotiations were resumed on June 25, 1953, and entered a state of deadlock almost immediately. The Committee from the very outset made clear its inability to "entertain . . . any proposals which do not . . . make provision for the supervision of the administration of the Territory by the United Nations as envisaged in the advisory opinion."[66] The South African representative, in turn, again reiterated his government's view that any scheme involving United Nations supervision would *ipso facto* extend South Africa's obligations. As such, it would conflict with the stipulation in the opinion that the degree of supervision by the United Nations not exceed that which had obtained under the mandates system.[67] There was no way, for example, in which the principle of unanimity could be safeguarded under the United Nations. "The United Nations acted in virtue of the Charter and could not agree to measures which would be in contravention of the Charter."[68] The South African representative also noted that under the terms of the Committee's counterproposals, any member of the United Nations would have the right to summon South Africa before the International Court. He wondered how the Committee proposed to cope with the constitutional difficulties involved.

The Committee, however, was unwilling to discuss this aspect of implementation until South Africa had accepted the principle of United Nations supervision. Committee members expressed confidence that a means could be found to reconcile the limited extent of South Africa's obligations with United Nations supervision, but basic acceptance of that supervision was a prior necessity. However, South Africa was unwilling to commit itself unless it could be first shown a scheme for United Nations supervision which would in fact not extend its obligations. The negotiations ended at this point of deadlock.

The *Ad Hoc* Committee report, besides its review of the fruitless negotiations, noted receipt of further communications which, it indicated, were dealt with in accordance with the established procedure.[69]

66. U.N. Doc. A/AC.49/SR.37, p. 3.
67. U.N. Doc. A/AC.49/SR.38/Part III, p. 13.
68. Ibid.
69. Among the communications was a memorandum from Reverend Scott analyzing in considerable detail the possibility of invoking the compulsory jurisdiction of the International Court in reference to South Africa's obligations under the Mandate. "A world renowned authority on international law," who preferred to remain anonymous, was cited as authority for the legal analysis presented. This memorandum, dated March 15, 1953, appears to be the first occasion in which use of the Court's compulsory jurisdiction in the South West Africa issue was publicly advocated. See Report of *Ad Hoc* Committee, U.N. Doc. A/2475, in GAOR, 8th Sess., Annexes, Agenda Item 36, Appendix VII, pp. 43–44. The identity of the "anonymous authority" was subsequently revealed in the course of testimony before the Fourth Committee in 1960, when Reverend Scott indicated that Professor Hersch Lauterpacht had, as early as

When the Fourth Committee opened discussions on the South West Africa issue on November 6, 1953, the South African delegate called upon that body to broaden the terms of reference of the *Ad Hoc* Committee so that "a final settlement of the question could be reached."[70] He attributed the failure of the negotiations to the fact that the *Ad Hoc* Committee considered itself bound by the advisory opinion. But that opinion, he emphasized, was purely advisory. In its place South Africa had proposed a practical solution for preserving the sacred trust. Under the proposed new agreement, "the Union . . . [would] reassume international accountability towards the three nations, which would undoubtedly be not less diligent in supervision than any organ of the United Nations."[71]

South Africa's suggestion was as little acceptable to the Fourth Committee as it had been to the *Ad Hoc* Committee. International accountability, it was made clear, meant accountability to the United Nations. In the words of the Pakistani delegate: "It could hardly be said that the three Powers alone formed 'the sacred trust of civilization' referred to in Article 22 of the Covenant, or that they alone could act as trustees for the world in general."[72]

In the view of the majority of delegates, the impasse that had been reached demonstrated quite clearly that South Africa would not cooperate with the United Nations in any real implementation of the advisory opinion. But this lack of cooperation could not be allowed to render nugatory the supervisory authority imparted to the Assembly by the Court. The supervision of the territory must be carried on, with or without the support of the mandatory power, in order to assure for the international community an effective role in protecting the interests of the people of South West Africa.

---

1950, proffered the foregoing advice with regard to compulsory jurisdiction. GAOR, 15th Sess., 4th Ctte., 1051st Mtg., Nov. 15, 1960, p. 307.

70. GAOR, 8th Sess., 4th Ctte., 357th Mtg., Nov. 6, 1953, pp. 265–67.

71. Ibid., p. 267.

72. Ibid., 358th Mtg., Nov. 9, 1953, p. 270. With reference to the South African call for compromise, the Venezuelan delegate stated: "The South African representative had asked the General Assembly to make concessions; but the Assembly had already made a great concession by accepting the Court's advisory opinion which was more conservative than the views held by many delegations." Ibid., 363rd Mtg., Nov. 12, 1953, p. 307.

# VII.

## THE ATTEMPT TO SUPERVISE: THE COMMITTEE ON SOUTH WEST AFRICA

### CONSTITUTION OF THE COMMITTEE ON SOUTH WEST AFRICA

The new phase in United Nations efforts to assert an effective role with respect to South West Africa was marked by the abolition of the *Ad Hoc* Committee and the creation of a new organ specifically designed to supervise the administration of the territory. In the resolution establishing the South West Africa Committee,[1] the General Assembly also commended the *Ad Hoc* Committee for its efforts to find a mutually satisfactory basis of agreement; recorded with deep regret South Africa's frustration of those efforts and its failure to submit annual reports and petitions; appealed solemnly to South Africa to reconsider its position and to continue negotiations with the South West Africa Committee so that an agreement could be reached for implementing the advisory opinion.[2] Until such an agreement was reached, the Committee, composed of seven members was to:

a) examine, within the scope of the Questionnaire adopted by the Permanent Mandates Commission of the League of Nations in 1926, such information and documentation as may be available in respect of the Territory of South West Africa;

b) examine, as far as possible in accordance with the procedure of the former Mandates System, reports and petitions which may be submitted to the Committee or to the Secretary-General;

c) transmit to the General Assembly a report concerning conditions in the Territory taking into account, as far as possible, the

1. G.A. Res. 749A (VIII), Nov. 28, 1953.
2. The contrast between the *Ad Hoc* and South West Africa Committees is high-lighted by the fact that whereas the primary role of the former was negotiation, and only secondarily, supervision (on an interim basis), in the case of the latter, the emphasis was reversed.

scope of the reports of the Permanent Mandates Commission of the League of Nations;

d) prepare, for the consideration of the General Assembly, a procedure for the examination of reports and petitions which should conform as far as possible to the procedure followed in this respect by the Assembly, the Council and the Permanent Mandates Commission of the League of Nations.

At the same time, the General Assembly adopted another resolution repeating the by now standard invitation to South Africa to place South West Africa under the trusteeship system.[3]

In the light of South Africa's total objection to any United Nations control of its administration of South West Africa, what purpose could the creation of a supervisory organ such as the South West Africa Committee and the repetition of worn-out resolutions requesting a trusteeship agreement serve? In the absence of any commitment to international accountability on the part of the supervised state, would not all the resolutions, in the words of the Belgian delegate, "remain a dead letter?"[4] Was there any reason to believe that South Africa would suddenly become more cooperative and do what it had refused to do all along, namely, accept the guidance of the world organization and furnish reports and petitions?

The United Nations, it must be assumed, was not deluding itself regarding its ability to exercise direct supervisory powers in any real sense. But neither was it willing to allow even the appearance of acquiescence in South Africa's actions. By its resolutions, it hoped to assert international concern over the territory and to confirm for the inhabitants of South West Africa the right of ultimate self-determination. Moreover, the reports of the South West Africa Committee, by spotlighting deficiencies in South Africa's administration of the territory, would serve to mobilize world public opinion in support of United Nations efforts, and in particular, would place pressure on the Western powers to induce South Africa to alter its stand. In a sense then, the idea of establishing some supervisory machinery was designed to produce change—but in a much more indirect manner than would appear on the surface.

A further explanation of the purpose of the Committee was outlined in the remarks of the Philippine representative:

> The Philippine delegation did not intend for the time being to propose that the United Nations should call upon former Members of the League of Nations . . . to initiate the proper proceedings be-

3. G.A. Res. 749B (VIII), Nov. 28, 1953.
4. GAOR, 8th Sess., 4th Ctte., 364th Mtg., Nov. 12, 1953, p. 309.

fore the International Court of Justice under Article 7 of the Mandate. The purpose of the submission of annual reports and the transmission of petitions was to give the international community information from which it could ascertain whether or not the mandated territory was being administered in accordance with the terms of the Mandate. If the information which would be made available under the terms of [the] resolution showed that the territory of South West Africa was being administered in accordance with the spirit of the Mandate, as the Government of . . . South Africa claimed, the failure of that Government to submit annual reports, though reprehensible, would be only a technical violation of the Mandate. On the other hand, if the General Assembly was unable to appraise the real situation because of the failure of South Africa to cooperate, or if the information available showed that the territory was not being administered in accordance with the terms of the Mandate, the way would be clear for the United Nations to recommend proceedings under Article 7 of the Mandate which, in the unanimous opinion of the International Court of Justice, had been preserved under Article 37 of its Statute.[5]

In these telling sentences, the Philippine delegate not only explained the immediate role of the South West Africa Committee but, more significantly, outlined its possible long-range purpose as an instrument for marshalling evidence for possible use in contentious proceedings. In the latter sphere, the Committee's activities would, in effect, lay the groundwork for invoking the compulsory jurisdiction of the Court, by detailing violations of the mandate committed by South Africa. Creation of the South West Africa Committee might, therefore, be accurately described as the first positive step toward the major Court battle that was to be waged from 1960 to 1966.

## OPERATION OF THE COMMITTEE ON SOUTH WEST AFRICA

The South West Africa Committee, composed of representatives of Brazil, Mexico, Norway, Pakistan, Syria, Thailand, and Uruguay, commenced its work on January 20, 1954.[6] An immediate invitation was extended to the South African government to resume negotiations on implementation of the advisory opinion.[7] South Africa was also requested to furnish a report on its administration of South West Africa for the year past, together with information covering the years since the

5. Ibid., 361st Mtg., Nov. 11, 1953, p. 290.
6. Report of the Committee on South West Africa, GAOR, 9th Sess., Supp. No. 14 (A/2666).
7. For text of the Committee's letter, see ibid., Annex I(a), p. 6.

last report, i.e., 1949. In a letter dated March 25, 1954, South Africa declined the invitation to resume negotiations.[8] Attributing the failure of the earlier negotiations with the *Ad Hoc* Committee to that committee's narrow terms of reference, South Africa had concluded that negotiations with the present Committee would be clearly futile, since its terms of reference "appear to be even more inflexible." Nor was it prepared to submit reports and petitions, since it recognized no obligation to do so.

In view of South Africa's attitude, the Committee undertook to assess the situation in the territory independently. On the basis of official documentation issued by the South African government, and on the basis of other relevant information derived from various sources, the Committee issued a comprehensive report on conditions in South West Africa covering the period from 1949.[9] The report, which surveyed in detail political, economic, and social conditions in South West Africa, was generally critical of South Africa's administration of the mandate. It cited, *inter alia*, racially discriminatory legislation and a serious disparity between expenditures on education for European, Colored, and Native children. In its concluding remarks, the Committee observed that "after thirty-five years of administration under the Mandates System, the Native inhabitants are still not participating in the political development of the Territory, that their participation in the economic development is restricted to that of labourers and that the social and educational services for their benefit are far from satisfactory."[10]

The General Assembly, in a resolution adopted on November 23, 1954, expressed appreciation for the work done by the Committee, and noted "*with concern* that, in the opinion of the Committee, the administration of South West Africa is in several aspects not in conformity with the obligations of the Government of . . . South Africa under the Mandate."[11]

## VOTING PROCEDURE CRISIS

The Committee on South West Africa, it will be recalled, had also been given the task of drawing up rules of procedure for the General Assembly's examination of the reports and petitions which it would receive from the Committee. These rules were to be framed so as to accord as much as possible with the procedure followed by the organs of the League. Little difficulty was experienced by the Committee in proposing special rules A to E, for Assembly *examination* of the reports and

8. Ibid., Annex I(c), pp. 6–7.
9. Ibid., Annex V, pp. 14–31.
10. Ibid., p. 31.
11. G.A. Res. 851 (IX).

petitions on South West Africa.[12] Special rule F, however, dealing with General Assembly *voting procedure* on these questions, became a matter of serious debate. The Court had indicated that "the degree of supervision . . . should not . . . exceed that which applied under the Mandates System, and should conform as far as possible to the procedure followed . . . by the [League] Council." Did this mean, as South Africa insisted, that supervision could only function under the unanimity rule as it operated under the League—with the implication that the mandatory power would always retain a veto power on every nonprocedural question bearing on the mandate? Or could it be assumed that the Court, by its proviso "should conform as far as possible" with League procedure, had obviously not intended to affect the United Nations voting procedure as prescribed by Article 18 of the Charter? Accordingly, a two-thirds majority would be the maximum majority required.[13]

As a means of resolving the legal doubts on this point, the South West Africa Committee recommended that the Assembly adopt special rule F, providing for a two-thirds majority on questions relating to reports and petitions on South West Africa, subject to the concurrence of South Africa, "as the State most directly concerned." In the absence of South African concurrence, the question of the conformity of special rule F with the 1950 advisory opinion should be submitted to the Court for clarification. The various rules of procedure, including special rule F, constituted draft resolution A, and the suggested request for an advisory opinion (if necessary) constituted draft resolution B.[14]

The whole proposal excited considerable controversy in the Fourth Committee, when the report of the South West Africa Committee came up for consideration. Many considered the granting of a veto to a single state, under any circumstances, highly irregular and in contravention of Charter principles.[15]

Notwithstanding the reservations of these delegates, the Fourth Committee accepted the recommendation of the South West Africa Committee and adopted (with certain technical changes) both draft resolutions, A and B.[16]

12. Report of the Committee on South West Africa, GAOR, 9th Sess., Supp. No. 14 (A/2666), Annexes III and IV, pp. 11-13.
13. This was the viewpoint of the Mexican and Pakistani representatives on the Committee. The Norwegian delegate, however, held that the Court's awareness of United Nations voting procedure did not necessarily, "as a matter of law," have to be read into the Court's opinion, and the preceding view (in favor of a two-thirds majority) "might be construed as an unwarranted interpretation of that opinion." Ibid., Annex III, p. 12.
14. Ibid., Annex IV, pp. 13-14.
15. See, for instance, the remarks of the representatives of Israel, Colombia, and Uruguay, GAOR, 9th Sess., 4th Ctte., 401st Mtg., Oct. 6, 1954, pp. 24-29.
16. For text, see Report of the 4th Ctte. (Part I), ibid., Annexes, Agenda Item 34, pp. 8-9.

Since Fourth Committee consideration of the substantive portion of the South West Africa Committee report was dependent on adoption of the procedural rules, the General Assembly, in Plenary, immediately turned its attention to the matters raised.[17] Various delegates supported the Fourth Committee proposals, calling attention to the fact that the legal effect of South Africa's objection to special rule F (anticipating that it would object) could only be resolved by the International Court.[18] Determination of the issue by the latter body would remove any legal doubts that might exist in the minds of certain delegates (albeit a minority) regarding the voting procedure. Many delegates, however, reiterated the aforementioned objection regarding conferral of a veto power.[19] The Peruvian delegate requested a separate vote on the condition attached to adoption of special rule F, viz., "subject to the acceptance by the Union of South Africa, as the Mandatory for South West Africa."[20] In the result, this phrase failed of adoption.[21] Special rule F, prescribing a two-thirds majority for questions on South West Africa, *minus the conditional phrase*, was then adopted as part of the rules of procedure listed in draft resolution A.[22] This meant that the General Assembly had resolved all doubts on the voting issue by prescribing a two-thirds majority for the South West Africa question and without making adoption of this rule in any way conditional on South Africa's affirmative vote. Clearly, then, draft resolution B, relating to a request for an advisory opinion in the event of a negative vote from South Africa on special rule F, was no longer relevant, since the adoption of the rule had not been made conditional in the first place. The Assembly President ruled accordingly that draft resolution B need no longer be considered, and his ruling was upheld by the Assembly.[23]

With the procedural question now settled by the General Assembly, the Fourth Committee turned its attention to the substantive aspects of the South West Africa Committee report.[24] Sharp criticism was voiced at South Africa's administration of the mandate generally, and its practice of racial discrimination in the territory, in particular. In reply, the Union delegate charged that the report was marked by inaccuracies and omissions.[25]

17. GAOR, 9th Sess., Plen., 494th Mtg., Oct. 11, 1954, pp. 243 ff.
18. See the remarks of the representatives of Lebanon, Iraq and Mexico, ibid., pp. 244–48.
19. See the remarks of the representatives of Indonesia, Ethiopia, Iraq, Israel, Liberia, and Colombia, ibid., pp. 244–46.
20. Ibid., p. 245.
21. Ibid., p. 248. The vote, 13 to 8, with 29 abstentions, fell short of the required two-thirds.
22. Ibid., p. 249. The vote was 33 to 3, with 15 abstentions. G.A. Res. 844 (IX), Oct. 11, 1954.
23. GAOR, 9th Sess., Plen., 494th Mtg., p. 250. The vote was 30 to 8, with 13 abstentions.
24. Ibid., 4th Ctte., 404th Mtg., Oct. 12, 1954, pp. 41 ff.
25. Ibid., 407th Mtg., Oct. 15, 1954, pp. 66–70.

During the debate a number of delegates reverted to the procedural issue and expressed regret that the General Assembly had not been given the opportunity to vote on draft resolution B, requesting an advisory opinion from the Court. Failure to gain the necessary legal clarification, they insisted, placed in doubt the validity of any resolution adopted with reference to South West Africa. As expressed by the United States representative: "Action on the report of the Committee on South West Africa would be incomplete without an advisory opinion from the International Court on its recommendations."[26] He announced that under the circumstances his delegation would be unable to participate in any vote on the South West Africa issue. Other delegates expressed similar reservations, and the Norwegian and Thai representatives announced their states' withdrawal from the South West Africa Committee.[27]

These actions posed a serious challenge to the relative value of any resolutions to be adopted on the subject. As a result, a special subcommittee was delegated to review the whole issue and report back to the Fourth Committee.

The report of the subcommittee recommended "that the question of submitting special rule F to an advisory opinion . . . be reopened."[28] This recommendation was, however, defeated by the Fourth Committee in a tie vote: 18 to 18 with 16 abstentions.[29]

The Fourth Committee thereupon proceeded to adopt four draft resolutions on South West Africa.[30] Of these, two dealt with specific petitions; another reiterated previous Assembly invitations to South Africa to place the territory under the trusteeship system; and a fourth related to the work of the South West Africa Committee. This last draft resolution expressed appreciation for the work of the Committee and noted "*with concern* that, in the opinion of the Committee, the administration of South West Africa is in several aspects not in conformity

26. Ibid., 409th Mtg., Oct. 19, 1954, p. 77.
27. See the remarks of the representatives of Norway, New Zealand, and Thailand, ibid., pp. 78-79. For the text of the letters of resignation, see Report of 4th Ctte. (A/2747) in GAOR, 9th Sess., Annexes, Agenda Item 34, p. 12 (1954).
28. Report of Sub-Committee on South West Africa to 4th Ctte., ibid., p. 10. The reason offered for this recommendation was that a number of delegations had informally noted, that their vote for draft resolution A, which included special rule F (now minus the contingent phrase), had been premised on the belief that they would be given an opportunity to vote on draft resolution B, requesting an advisory opinion on the very legality of special rule F. Had they known that draft resolution B would in fact not be put to the vote, they would not have supported draft resolution A at all. As a result, said the report, doubt existed whether draft resolution A might not have failed to obtain the necessary two-thirds majority. "In the circumstances Members of the General Assembly did not have a complete opportunity to vote on the two resolutions which many regarded as substantively forming a whole." Ibid. This reasoning, of course, failed to take into account the overwhelming vote (30 to 8, with 13 abstentions) by which the President's ruling not to vote on draft resolution B was upheld.
29. GAOR, 9th Sess., 4th Ctte., 425th Mtg., Nov. 8, 1954, p. 195.
30. Report of 4th Ctte., Part II (A/2747) in GAOR, 9th Sess., Annexes, Agenda Item 34, pp. 13-17 (1954).

with the obligations of the Government of . . . South Africa under the Mandate."

In the meantime, however, the United States representative, in the wake of the second defeat of the proposal for an advisory opinion, announced his country's reservations regarding future participation in the work of the South West Africa Committee.[31] Similar reservations were expressed by the representatives of Sweden, Mexico, and Pakistan.[32] The Iraqi delegate scored the members of the Fourth Committee for rejecting the proposal of the subcommittee. "He wondered whether all the members realized the seriousness of the situation. Furthermore, few of them realized how difficult it had been to induce the United States delegation to participate in the Committee's work."[33]

When the General Assembly, in Plenary, resumed consideration of the South West Africa question on November 23, 1954, it had before it, aside from the four draft resolutions of the Fourth Committee, a joint proposal of Guatemala and Lebanon for requesting an advisory opinion on the consistency of voting rule F with the 1950 advisory opinion.[34] In presenting his proposal, the Guatemalan delegate stressed that his delegation, together with a majority of members, entertained no doubts whatsoever regarding the absolute legality of special rule F, and its conformity to the 1950 opinion. However, only by obtaining a clear pronouncement from the Court on the issue could the doubts expressed by some key members of the South West Africa Committee be resolved, thereby enabling those members to again join in the work of the Committee. The joint proposal was adopted by a roll-call vote of 25 to 11, with 21 abstentions.[35]

Having decided to seek judicial guidance on the proper voting procedure for South West Africa questions, the Assembly deferred in the meantime its vote on the two draft resolutions dealing with South West Africa petitions "until such time as it is seized of the advisory opinion

31. Ibid., 4th Ctte., 426th Mtg., Nov. 9, 1954, p. 197.
32. Ibid., p. 198.
33. Ibid., p. 197.
34. Ibid., Plen., 500th Mtg., Nov. 23, 1954, p. 309.
35. Ibid., 501st Mtg., Nov. 23, 1954, p. 326. G.A. Res. 904 (IX), Nov. 23, 1954. The request, as framed, read as follows: "*The General Assembly*,
. . . . . . . . . . . . . . . . . . . . . . . . . . . . . . . . . . . . . . . . . . . . . . . . . . . . . .
"*Requests* the International Court of Justice to give an advisory opinion on the following questions:
"a) Is the following rule on the voting procedure to be followed by the General Assembly a correct interpretation of the advisory opinion of the International Court of Justice of 11 July 1950:
" 'Decisions of the General Assembly on questions relating to reports and petitions concerning the Territory of South West Africa shall be regarded as important questions within the meaning of Article 18, paragraph 2, of the Charter of the United Nations'?
"b) If this interpretation of the advisory opinion of the Court is not correct, what voting procedure should be followed by the General Assembly in taking decisions on questions relating to reports and petitions concerning the Territory of South West Africa?"

of the International Court."[36] But this did not prevent the Assembly from voting on draft resolution C, which endorsed the report of the South West Africa Committee condemning South Africa's administration of the territory.[37] A South African motion to postpone the vote on this draft resolution was rejected. The South African representative had argued that since special rule F covered both petitions and reports, deferral of the vote on the one necessitated similar treatment for the other.

Obviously, the Assembly was not going to be deterred from voting on the South West Africa question at this late stage of the game. The General Assembly had regularly adopted resolutions bearing on South West Africa by a two-thirds majority, whether they were appeals for a trust agreement or requests to negotiate implementation of the advisory opinion; and the Assembly was not now prepared to relinquish that practice. While a vote on draft resolution C was, in truth, hardly consistent with the decision to defer the vote on the draft resolutions related to petitions, the Assembly was not overly concerned with proceeding in neat, consistent fashion. In submitting the voting question to the International Court it was not motivated by a really objective concern with the international law on the subject—for the majority of members entertained no doubts on that score. The chief purpose was to stem the tide of defection by an important minority of states, who were unwilling to assume responsibilities unless the legal issue was first judicially resolved. In deference to the wishes of this minority, the General Assembly agreed to refer the matter to the Court and to delay the vote on the petitions. But these actions were not to be permitted to place in doubt the very plenary measure of United Nations authority over South West Africa. It was practical necessity, not legal niceties, which had dictated recourse to the Court. Legal niceties could certainly not cause the General Assembly to abdicate, even for one session, its supervisory role with respect to the territory.

## THE 1955 ADVISORY OPINION ON VOTING PROCEDURE

The International Court of Justice handed down a unanimous opinion on June 7, 1955, confirming the right of the General Assembly to take decisions on questions relating to reports and petitions concerning South West Africa, by a two-thirds majority vote. This voting rule, the Court said, was a correct interpretation of the 1950 advisory opinion.[38]

36. GAOR, 9th Sess., Plen., 501st Mtg., Nov. 23, 1954, p. 329.
37. It also adopted the standard resolution calling on South Africa to negotiate a trusteeship agreement.
38. *Voting Procedure Opinion* (1955): 78. South Africa did not participate in the pleadings in this case, since it held that it related solely to an opinion which it had never accepted

In reaching this decision the Court focused its attention on the crucial passage in the 1950 opinion:

The degree of supervision to be exercised by the General Assembly should not therefore exceed that which applied under the Mandates System, and should conform as far as possible to the procedure followed in this respect by the Council of the League of Nations.[39]

Adopting a textual interpretative approach, the Court indicated that the voting rules of a supervisory organ really had nothing to do either with the *degree* of supervision or the *procedure* of supervision, but formed rather "one of the characteristics of the constitution of the supervisory organ."[40] The Court was saying, in effect, that "a voting system is no more a question of procedure than it is one of substance, being related rather to a third question, that of the composition and functions of the organ concerned."[41] Just as the unanimity rule was one of the distinguishing features of the League, so also were the simple majority and two-thirds rules part and parcel of the General Assembly structure. To attempt to impose a different system of voting on the Assembly, other than that ordained for it under the Charter, "would not be simply the introduction of a new procedure, but would amount to a disregard of one of the characteristics of the General Assembly."[42] Moreover, the authority of the Assembly to exercise supervision over South West Africa was based on the provisions of the *Charter* (i.e., Article 10), and this same document prescribed the voting rules of the Assembly (i.e., Article 18). "It would be legally impossible for the General Assembly, on the one hand, to rely on the Charter in receiving and examining reports and petitions concerning South West Africa, and, on the other hand, to reach decisions relating to those reports and petitions in accordance with a voting system entirely alien to that pre-

---

and which, in its view, had reached incorrect conclusions. There were no oral proceedings in the case, and only three governments submitted written statements, namely, the United States, Poland, and India, all three arguing for the validity of special rule F. The argument of the United States was the most elaborate.

For discussion and analysis of the opinion, see J. H. W. Verzijl, *The Jurisprudence of the World Court*, 2 vols. (Leyden: Sijthoff, 1965), II: 218-29; R. Y. Jennings, "The International Court's Advisory Opinion on the Voting Procedure on Questions Concerning South-West Africa," *Transactions of the Grotius Society* XLII (1956): 85-97; Manley O. Hudson, "The Thirty-Fourth Year of the World Court," *AJIL* L (1956): 5-9; Shabtai Rosenne, *The Law and Practice of the International Court*, 2 vols. (Leyden: Sijthoff, 1965), II: 719-24; Rosenne, "Sir Hersch Lauterpacht's Concept of the Task of the International Judge," *AJIL* LV (1961): 825-62, passim.; Sir Gerald Fitzmaurice, "Hersch Lauterpacht—The Scholar as Judge," part I, *BYB* XXXVII (1961): 1-71, passim.; part II, ibid., XXXVIII (1962): 1-83, passim.; part III, ibid., XXXIX (1963): 133-88, passim.

39. *Status Opinion* (1950): 138.
40. *Voting Procedure Opinion* (1955): 75.
41. Verzijl, *Jurisprudence of World Court*, II: 233.
42. *Voting Procedure Opinion* (1955): 75.

scribed by the Charter."[43] These legal and practical considerations dictated that the Assembly must abide by its own voting system, and rule F was, therefore, not inconsistent with the 1950 opinion.[44]

The Court had approached the question as one of interpretation of the constitutional powers of the Assembly, and had treated the operative passage of its 1950 opinion as if it were another article of the Charter requiring detailed textual interpretation. By so doing, the Court avoided and evaded a critical analysis of the underlying problem that prompted the request, namely, the conflict between the new world organization and an individual state over the correct formula to be applied so as to sustain, but not increase, the measure of international accountability originally assumed by that state. The reply of the Court was merely a cryptic confirmation of the validity of rule F, rather than a careful analysis of what international accountability amounted to under League procedures and how a similar measure of international responsibility could be effectively instituted within the framework of the United Nations.

This shortcoming of the majority opinion was high-lighted by Judges Klaestad and Lauterpacht in their separate opinions. Judge Klaestad indicated that the task of the Court was to determine "whether decisions of the General Assembly on questions relating to reports and petitions concerning the Territory of South-West Africa would, by the operation of the voting procedure indicated in the Request, subject the Union of South Africa to other or more onerous legal obligations than the Union had previously under the supervision of the League of Nations."[45] This, in turn, necessitated an examination of two particular questions relating to: (1) the respective voting procedures under the League and the United Nations; (2) the legal effect of such decisions. Judge Klaestad determined that absolute unanimity was required under the League, and since this included the mandatory power's affirmative vote, the decision was legally binding. In contrast, decisions of the General Assembly, although they could be adopted by a vote less than unanimous, only amounted to nonbinding recommendations. Only the affirmative vote of South Africa could convert these decisions into legal obligations. In that respect, the legal situation

43. Ibid., p. 76.
44. Ibid., p. 77. Cf. also the separate opinion of Judge Basdevant, who while acknowledging that South Africa was subject only to the supervisory obligations it had incurred under the Mandate, held that the question of voting in the General Assembly concerned South Africa not as a mandatory power, but as a member of the United Nations. In this respect South Africa had "the rights and duties flowing from the Charter and not those flowing from the Mandate." Moreover, the method of voting was, in any case, not one in which the Assembly possessed any discretion. Ibid., p. 82.
45. Ibid., p. 85.

under the United Nations and the League was identical. Consequently, a two-thirds voting rule in the General Assembly would not impose on South Africa any legal obligations additional to those to which it had been subject under the League.[46]

Judge Lauterpacht likewise eschewed the approach of the Court, which he described as the "method of pure construction." The term "degree of supervision," said Judge Lauterpacht, covers not only the *means* of supervision, but relates also to the methods of ensuring compliance with the means thus adopted.[47] If one has agreed to accept a tax obligation in pursuance of unanimous decisions, then this obligation is increased if the tax can be imposed by majority vote. "The procedure of voting determines the degree of supervision."[48] Consequently,

> there is room for the view that the Union of South Africa is legally entitled to resist any attempted extension of the scope of its accountability and of the corresponding degree of scrutiny, interference and supervision by the United Nations, even if such extension is of a procedural nature, for instance, by way of a particular system of voting, so long as no conclusive proof has been adduced that such extension is unavoidable on account of an imperative necessity of relying on the procedure in force in the General Assembly and unalterable in any circumstances.[49]

In Judge Lauterpacht's view, the issue of whether rule F represented a modification of the supervisory arrangements current under the League could only be elucidated by seeking answers to the following three questions:

1) "Did the Rule of Absolute Unanimity obtain in the Council of the League acting as a Supervisory Organ of the Mandates System?"[50]

After a careful examination of the record, Judge Lauterpacht somewhat cautiously determined that there was "no conclusive or convincing evidence in support of the view that as a matter of practice the rule of unanimity operated and was interpreted in a manner substantiating any right of veto on the part of the mandatory Power."[51]

---

46. Ibid., pp. 88–89.
47. Ibid., p. 94.
48. Ibid., p. 95.
49. Ibid., p. 96.
50. Ibid., p. 98. And see the discussion of this question, ibid., pp. 98–106.
51. Ibid., p. 103. Judge Klaestad, as noted earlier, reached a contrary conclusion with respect to League practice. "I am not aware," he said, "of a single instance in which a resolution concerning reports or petitions was adopted by the Council against the vote of the Mandatory Power." Ibid., p. 86.

R. Y. Jennings, criticizing Judge Lauterpacht's view, remarks: "The practice so carefully described and examined in Judge Lauterpacht's opinion is difficult to understand unless one may assume at any rate the possibility of a veto in the mandatory State. A veto does not need to be exercised in order to influence proceedings, and the invariable careful and even elaborate

2) "Has the General Assembly the Power to Proceed by a Voting Procedure other than that laid down in Article 18 of the Charter?"[52]

On this question Judge Lauterpacht held that while absolute unanimity was ruled out as a principle of operation in the United Nations, there was nothing to bar the Assembly from adopting a standard higher than the two-thirds majority rule. Failure to attempt to establish some such specially qualified voting rule might have proved fatal to the validity of rule F, if not for the answer to be provided to the next and final question.

3) "Do the decisions of the General Assembly possess the same legal force in the system of supervision as the decisions of the Council of the League of Nations?"[53]

In reply, Judge Lauterpacht held that General Assembly resolutions "do not possess a degree of legal authority equal to that of the decisions of the Council of the League."[54] The former are merely recommendations which "do not create a legal obligation to comply with them."[55] South Africa was, therefore, not being subjected to a system of supervision more exacting than that which obtained under the League Council whose decisions *were* legally binding. This consideration, Judge Lauterpacht (like Judge Klaestad) regarded as decisive in finding that rule F was consistent with the 1950 opinion.

The separate opinions then, unlike the Court, recognized the inherent difficulties of applying a novel voting procedure to a League mandate and could only reconcile such a move with the 1950 opinion by concluding that no new legal obligations were created, since the General Assembly lacked the power to impart a compulsory quality to its resolutions in any case.

The majority opinion may be said to have adopted the view (implicitly) that it was inaccurate to imagine that the mandate had been continued in force precisely as if the League had never come to an end.

---

avoidance of an adverse vote from the Mandatory seems to support Judge Klaestad's reading of the situation." "Voting Procedure on South West Africa," p. 92.

On the practice of unanimity in the League generally, see Cromwell A. Riches, *The Unanimity Rule and the League of Nations* (Baltimore: The Johns Hopkins Press, 1933). On the unanimity rule in relation to Minorities questions, see Julius Stone, *International Guarantees of Minority Rights* (London: Oxford University Press, 1932), pp. 184-93.

52. *Voting Procedure Opinion* (1955): 106. And see the discussion of this matter, ibid., pp. 106-14.

53. Ibid., p. 114. See discussion, ibid., pp. 114-22.

54. Ibid., p. 123.

55. Ibid., p. 115. They do, however, create "a moral obligation." A state to which a General Assembly resolution is directed is not at liberty to simply ignore the resolution. It is duty-bound to give the resolution "due consideration in good faith." See ibid., pp. 117-22. For a careful analysis of this aspect of the opinion, see D. H. N. Johnson, "The Effect of Resolutions of the General Assembly of the United Nations," *BYB* XXXII (1955-56): 97-122. See also Clive Parry, *The Sources and Evidences of International Law* (Manchester: Manchester University Press, 1965), pp. 20-21.

Such an interpretation was contrary to both fact and logic. What was preserved was the principle of international accountability, as part of the mandate institution. The *mode* of supervision was important, but not absolutely so. It could never be applied *precisely* as it had been under the League, since that organization no longer existed; but this fact could not be allowed to destroy the *essential* principle of the mandate, i.e., international accountability. The obligations assumed under the Mandate were not all equal, and if the central feature was to be preserved, then some measure of adjustment was necessary. This was presumably what the Court meant by its concluding remark that "the expression 'as far as possible' [in the 1950 opinion] was designed to allow for adjustments and modifications necessitated by legal or practical considerations."[56]

## ORAL HEARINGS FOR PETITIONERS QUESTION

Three aspects of the South West Africa question were, according to the agenda, slated for consideration at the Tenth Session of the General Assembly in 1956: (1) the 1955 advisory opinion of the Court; (2) the annual report of the Committee on South West Africa on conditions in the territory; (3) the question of the admissibility of oral hearings by the Committee on South West Africa.

1) A resolution was adopted by the General Assembly whereby it "accepted and endorsed" the advisory opinion of the International Court of Justice on voting procedure on questions relating to reports and petitions concerning the territory of South West Africa.[57] Speaking in support of the draft resolution in the Fourth Committee, the United States delegate said:

> The Assembly could now proceed to deal with the difficult substantive problems surrounding the question of South West Africa with full confidence as to the legality of its voting procedures. . . . The adoption of the draft resolution would once again make clear the importance that the General Assembly attached to proceeding with scrupulous legality in dealing with the unprecedented and difficult case of South West Africa. His delegation hoped that by so doing the Assembly would bring closer the day when the Union of South

---

56. *Voting Procedure Opinion* (1955): 77. R. Y. Jennings, after carefully reviewing the legal implications of the majority and separate opinions, concludes with the following penetrating remark: "The attempt . . . to explore the legal no-man's-land between the Covenant and Charter takes us, I think, to the nub of the difficulty in this case: the virtual impossibility of finding any safe legal bridge between the League Council and the General Assembly of the United Nations in respect of the supervisory functions. . . . The attempts of the 1955 Judges to discover that 'legal ground' and then to compare in terms of degree, supervision by two bodies utterly dissimilar in kind, seems to me only to demonstrate the soundness and the wisdom of the 1950 dissents." "Voting Procedure on South West Africa," pp. 96-97.

57. G.A. Res. 934 (X), Dec. 3, 1955. As noted earlier, the original 1950 opinion was only "accepted" by the General Assembly. See above, chap. VI, n. 11.

Africa would give its full cooperation to the United Nations in the interest of the peoples of South West Africa.[58]

The latter hope appeared rather forlorn, however, as soon as the South African representative delivered his government's views on the matter. The 1955 opinion, he indicated, was quite beside the point, since it merely interpreted the 1950 opinion, which, in the view of his government, was fundamentally mistaken. It was for this reason that South Africa had refrained from participating in the 1955 pleadings.[59]

2) The report of the South West Africa Committee noted that South Africa had been as unwilling to cooperate with the Committee in 1955 as it had been in 1954.[60] South Africa had not furnished any reports or petitions and had declined to enter into further negotiations, since it did not believe that these "would lead to any positive results."[61]

Notwithstanding, the South West Africa Committee had once again compiled a report on the territory, based on all official and general information the Secretary-General could amass for its consideration. The report again dealt with all aspects of administration and covered political, economic, and social conditions in the territory. In its concluding remarks, the report, while noting some positive steps on the part of the Mandatory, was basically very critical of the failure to improve the "moral and material welfare of the Native inhabitants." "It is apparent that the main efforts of the Administration are directed almost exclusively in favour of the European inhabitants . . . often at the expense of the Native population."[62]

The General Assembly adopted a resolution expressing appreciation for the work of the South West Africa Committee and urged the Union government "to give serious consideration to the observations and recommendations of the Committee . . . in order to ensure the fulfillment of its obligations and responsibilities under the Mandate."[63]

3) The 1950 advisory opinion, it will be recalled, had indicated that the examination of petitions (as well as reports) "should conform as far as possible to the procedure followed by the League Council."

58. GAOR, 10th Sess., 4th Ctte., 491st Mtg., Oct. 31, 1955, pp. 129–30. See also the remarks of the representative of Thailand, ibid., p. 130.

59. Ibid., pp. 130–32.

60. Report of Committee on South West Africa, GAOR, 10th Sess., Supp. No. 12 (A/2913) (1955).

61. Ibid., p. 7. Letter dated May 21, 1955.

62. Ibid., p. 32.

63. G.A. Res. 941 (X), Dec. 31, 1955. In response, the South African delegate indicated that, "in view of his Government's contention that the Mandate had lapsed, and in view of the circumstances in which the Committee on South West Africa had been established it was unable to recognize the legality of the Committee, or of its report, or of the resolutions it had submitted for consideration." He charged, moreover, that the report was marked by inaccuracies and untruths. GAOR, 10th Sess., 4th Ctte., 491st Mtg., Oct. 31, 1955, pp. 134–36.

Accordingly, the General Assembly had requested the South West Africa Committee to "examine as far as possible in accordance with the procedure of the former Mandates System, . . . petitions which may be submitted to the Committee or Secretary-General."[64]

Under the Permanent Mandates Commission, petitions would either emanate directly from the mandatory power or would be subject to its prior comments. A similar procedure was instituted by the South West Africa Committee.[65] However, an alternative procedure was also provided for, whereby the Committee could examine a petition once a copy had been transmitted to South Africa and a relatively short interval had elapsed without benefit of reply.[66] Again, under the Mandates Commission there was no provision for consideration of oral presentation of petitions. To receive official consideration a petition had to be in writing.[67] In contrast, the United Nations trusteeship system did not distinguish between written and oral petitions.[68] The Committee on South West Africa, in 1954, when drawing up its rules of procedure, decided that should a request for an oral hearing be made to the Committee, the matter would be referred to the General Assembly for determination.[69] In 1955 a request of this nature was received,[70] and the issue was considered by the Fourth Committee.[71]

The majority of states represented on the South West Africa Committee were of the opinion that it would not be in conformity with the 1950 advisory opinion for the Committee to grant oral hearings. In their view, such a step might jeopardize the legality of the Committee's actions.[72] A majority of the Fourth Committee endorsed this viewpoint. However, a firm minority argued that the rules of the Mandates Commission were always subject to change, and it was doubtful if "that body would adopt the same rules of procedure today, having regard to the considerably changed outlook on such matters."[73] In their view, "the right of oral hearing was part and parcel of the right of petition."[74]

---

64. See above, p. 141.
65. Report of Committee on South West Africa, A/2666 and Corr. 1, Annex II, rule VIII, in GAOR, 9th Sess., Supp. No. 14 (1954).
66. Ibid., rule XXVI, replacing rule VIII; and rule XXVII, replacing rule XII. For further details, see Repertory of Practice of United Nations Organs, Supp. no. 1 (1958), II: 227–29.
67. See above, pp. 47–48.
68. See Goodrich and Hambro, p. 468.
69. Report of Committee on South West Africa (A/2666) in GAOR, 9th Sess., Supp. No. 14, Annex II, Sect. D., p. 11 (1954).
70. U.N. Doc. A/2913/Add.2, Annex I, in GAOR, 10th Sess., Annexes, Agenda Item 30, p. 4 (1955).
71. GAOR, 10th Sess., 4th Ctte., 500th Mtg., Nov. 8, 1955, pp. 180 ff.
72. See the remarks of the representatives of Mexico, the United States, and Thailand, ibid., pp. 180–82.
73. See the remarks of the representatives of Israel and Venezuela, ibid., pp. 181–82.
74. Statement of the representative of the Philippines, ibid., 501st Mtg., Nov. 8, 1955, p. 186.

A draft resolution[75] was presented to the Fourth Committee by the representatives of Mexico, Pakistan, Syria, Thailand, and the United States, whereby the Assembly would decide that the oral hearing of petitioners by the Committee on South West Africa would *not* be in accordance with mandates procedure and was therefore not admissible; members of the Committee would, however, be specifically permitted to accord private audiences to petitioners. This draft resolution was in the end withdrawn because it could not be assured of the necessary two-thirds majority for adoption.[76]

It was clear, therefore, that the Assembly was unable to muster a sufficient majority to provide any clear answer—one way or the other—to the question posed by the Committee on South West Africa. It was resolved, therefore, that the question should be submitted to the International Court of Justice for an advisory opinion. In the words of the Mexican delegate, this was "the only means of surmounting the difficulty . . . since the Court's views commanded universal respect . . . [and] nobody would be able to take exception" to this procedure.[77] The draft resolution for requesting the advisory opinion was adopted by the Fourth Committee[78] and subsequently endorsed by the General Assembly.[79]

The decision of the Fourth Committee to seek judicial guidance on the authority of the South West Africa Committee to admit oral hearings did not, however, prevent the Fourth Committee itself from granting immediately thereafter an oral hearing to the Reverend Michael Scott.[80] Various delegates argued that the two moves were logically inconsistent.[81] If the Court's injunction applied to the South West Africa Committee, it applied equally to the Fourth Committee. After all, the Court had said, "The degree of supervision to be exercised by the *General Assembly* should not therefore exceed that which applied under the Mandates System,"[82] and the Fourth Committee, no less

---

75. U.N. Doc. A/C.4/L.413, in GAOR, 10th Sess., Annexes, Agenda Item 30, p. 9 (1955).

76. GAOR, 10th Sess., 4th Ctte., 505th Mtg., Nov. 10, 1955, p. 201.

77. Ibid., 506th Mtg., Nov. 11, 1955, p. 205. See also the remarks of the representatives of Liberia, Denmark, and Lebanon, ibid., pp. 205-6. But cf. the views of the Uruguayan representative, ibid., p. 205.

78. Ibid., p. 206.

79. Ibid., Plen., 550th Mtg., Dec. 3, 1955, p. 399. G.A. Res. 942 (X). The question posed to the Court read as follows:

   Is it consistent with the advisory opinion of the International Court of Justice of 11 July 1950 for the Committee on South West Africa, established by General Assembly resolution 749 A (VIII) of 28 November 1953, to grant oral hearings to petitioners on matters relating to the Territory of South West Africa?

80. GAOR, 10th Sess., 4th Ctte., 507th Mtg., Nov. 11, 1955, pp. 212-13.

81. See the remarks of the representatives of Israel, Australia, the United States, and New Zealand, ibid., pp. 209-11. See also the remarks of the representatives of Denmark and Belgium, ibid., 504th Mtg., Nov. 10, 1955, p. 197.

82. Emphasis supplied.

than the Committee on South West Africa, was an organ of the General Assembly. The Fourth Committee, however, was not to be deterred. It was not prepared to relinquish its supervisory authority over South West Africa in any manner; nor was it prepared to cast doubt on its decisions on several previous occasions to accord the Reverend Scott an oral hearing.[83] In any case, it was argued, there was an essential difference between a Fourth Committee hearing, which was for purposes of information (relevant to an item on the agenda), and a hearing by the South West Africa Committee, which related to a supervisory function.[84]

## THE 1956 ADVISORY OPINION ON HEARINGS OF PETITIONERS

The Court, in its opinion of June 1, 1956, held, by a vote of 8 to 5, that it would not be inconsistent with the 1950 opinion for the Committee on South West Africa to grant oral hearings.[85]

In contrast to its approach in the 1955 opinion, the Court did not view its task narrowly as one of pure verbal construction of the relevant passage in the 1950 opinion relating to the degree and procedure of supervision. Instead, the Court held that an answer to the question posed could not be attained by examination of one isolated passage, but rather by having "regard to the whole of its previous Opinion and its general purport and meaning."[86] And the Court proceeded to determine:

83. See e.g., above, pp. 104-5, 136 and n. 54.
84. See the remarks of the representative of Thailand, GAOR, 10th Sess., 4th Ctte., 506th Mtg., Nov. 11, 1955, pp. 206-7. But cf. the statement of the United States representative, ibid., 507th Mtg., Nov. 11, 1955, pp. 210-11.
85. *Oral Petitions Opinion* (1956): 32. The pleadings occasioned an about-turn by the United States on the question. In the Assembly, the United States adopted the position that oral petitions were not admissible by the Committee on South West Africa. However, in a written statement before the Court, the United States argued that, since the Assembly is "denied access to direct sources of information concerning the mandated territory ... it ... could properly authorize resort to other sources ... including the oral hearings of petitioners." *1956 Oral Petitions Pleadings*, pp. 26, 36. This surprising development prompted the United Kingdom government to present an oral statement in support of the view that the Assembly could not, in conformity with the 1950 opinion, authorize such hearings. Ibid., pp. 43-54. See also relevant correspondence, ibid., pp. 60-70. As in 1955, South Africa did not participate in the pleadings.
86. *Oral Petitions Opinion* (1956): 27. The Court, incidentally, circumscribed the scope of the question by construing it (a) as relating only to persons who had already presented written petitions and who now wished to supplement those by oral hearings; and (b) as referring to General Assembly power to authorize the South West Africa Committee to grant oral hearings and not to the question whether the Committee can grant hearings independently without prior Assembly authorization. Ibid., pp. 25-26.
For an excellent summary and analysis of the case, see Verzijl, *Jurisprudence of World Court*, II: 231-39; see also Manley O. Hudson, "The Thirty-Fifth Year of the World Court," *AJIL* LI (1957): 1-4; Shabtai Rosenne, "Sir Hersch Lauterpacht's Concept of the Task of the International Judge," *AJIL* LV (1961): 825-62, passim.; Rosenne, *The Law and Practice of the International Court* II: 719-24; Sir Gerald Fitzmaurice, "Hersch Lauterpacht—The Scholar as

The general purport and meaning of the Opinion of the Court of 11 July 1950 is that the paramount purpose underlying the taking over by the General Assembly of the United Nations of the supervisory functions in respect of the Mandate for South West Africa formerly exercised by the Council of the League of Nations was to safeguard the sacred trust of civilization through the maintenance of effective international supervision of the administration of the Mandated Territory.[87]

The General Assembly was, therefore, qualified to exercise all the powers that the League Council possessed in supervising the mandate, whether the Council had actually applied those powers or not. Consequently, the fact that the League Council had never in fact instituted oral hearings as part of the Permanent Mandates Commission procedure was not determinative. The crucial question was whether the League Council had been *"competent"* to authorize the Permanent Mandates Commission to grant oral hearings to petitioners, had it seen fit to do so. The Court, upon examination, concluded that the Council had possessed this power, and as a result, the General Assembly was likewise competent to authorize oral hearings.[88]

In effect, the Court was saying that the 1950 opinion had determined that the General Assembly, although not the successor in title to the League Council, was nonetheless its *de facto* successor and all powers of the Council had automatically devolved upon it.[89] There was therefore no logic in attempting to limit the authority of the Assembly to what the Council had *actually* done. The assumption of supervisory authority by the General Assembly did not have "the effect of crystal-lyzing the Mandates System at the point which it had reached in 1946."[90] The General Assembly was free to develop and to utilize any of the potential sources of authority that were inherent in the mandate.

In reaching this conclusion, the Court was hard put to explain what the 1950 opinion had meant by its limitative sentence: "The degree of supervision . . . should not . . . exceed that which applied under the Mandates System, and should conform as far as possible to [League] procedure." If the General Assembly was simply the Council under a different name, then quite obviously Article 22 of the Covenant and the Mandate, as the governing instruments, defined Assembly power as

---

Judge," part I, *BYB* XXXVII (1961): 1-71, passim.; part II, ibid., XXXVIII (1962): 1-83, passim.; part III, ibid., XXXIX (1963): 133-88, passim.

87. *Oral Petitions Opinion* (1956): 28.

88. Ibid., pp. 29-30.

89. In 1962, in the *South West Africa Cases (Preliminary Objections)*, the Court eschewed basing its jurisdiction on any notion of succession between the League and the United Nations. See above, chap. V, n. 38; and below, chap. IX, n. 43.

90. *Oral Petitions Opinion* (1956): 29.

they did Council power, and what need was there to spell out standards of supervision? Furthermore, why should the Assembly be bound to the Council procedure of 1946? Without doubt the Council could have modified its procedure, and if so, the Assembly, as the *de facto* heir of the Council, could do likewise.

In answer, the Court referred to the qualifying expression "as far as possible" in the latter part of the passage, which indicated that the 1950 opinion had not intended to impose "a rigid limitation" on the supervisory function of the General Assembly. In support, the Court quoted from its 1955 opinion in which it had said "the expression . . . was designed to allow for adjustment and modifications necessitated by legal or practical considerations."[91]

Five judges were unable to accept that the majority's ruling was consistent with the 1950 opinion.[92] That opinion, they recalled, had expressly rejected "the idea of United Nations' succession to the League of Nations, of the transfer of powers from one organization to the other," since the events of 1946 clearly excluded any such conclusion.[93] Discussion, therefore, of the scope of League powers was quite beside the point. The 1950 opinion had based itself "on the objective elements of the situation—the importance of international supervision under the Mandates System as well as the provisions of the Charter," in determining that "the former regime" was maintained.[94] The fundamental notion was one of "continuity, of maintenance of the *status quo*."[95] It was on this basis that the opinion determined that the General Assembly was "legally qualified to exercise the supervisory functions previously exercised by the League." This meant *actually* exercised "and not those which it was entitled to exercise or could have exercised. . . . The established practice is the only criterion."[96] Consequently, since the oral hearing of petitioners was never instituted under the League, the terms of the 1950 opinion did not permit the Assembly to innovate such a practice.[97]

Since the request referred solely to the compatibility of oral hearings with the 1950 opinion, the dissenting judges did not think it permissible for the Court to go outside the terms of the request, by taking into account developments subsequent to the 1950 opinion, such as the refusal of the South African government to submit to United Nations

91. Ibid., p. 31.
92. Ibid., pp. 60–71. Dissenting opinion of Judges Badawi, Basdevant, Hsu Mo, Armand-Ugon, and Moreno Quintana.
93. Ibid., pp. 65–66.
94. Ibid., p. 66.
95. Ibid., p. 63.
96. Ibid., p. 66.
97. Ibid., p. 70.

supervision.[98] Indeed, even if the Court had been expressly requested to consider such issues, it would not be clear that the Court could actually furnish a reply, since the question then would not be one of compatibility with the 1950 opinion, "which is a purely legal question, and as such, one suitable for submission to the Court," but whether South Africa's action "constitutes a ground justifying the supervisory authority in departing . . . from observance" of the 1950 opinion. "Such a question might be asked, but the considerations upon which a reply to it might be based would go beyond the scope of legal considerations and would involve political elements the appraisal of which is not within the domain of the Court."[99] The question would involve "considerations of a political and practical character" which would be within the competence of the General Assembly and not within that of the Court.[100]

Judge Winiarski, in a separate declaration, stated "that as the Opinion of 1950 was not based on the idea of the United Nations as a successor in title of the League of Nations, the question of a devolution of the powers of the Council of the League of Nations to the General Assembly" did not arise. He was in agreement with the minority opinion that "the maintenance of the previously existing situation constitutes the dominant theme of the [1950] Opinion and that the decisive test is to be found in what was formerly done, and . . . any enquiry as to the extent of the powers of the Council and of the General Assembly respectively is pointless." Nonetheless, Judge Winiarski held that the Court was unable to avoid taking judicial notice of the irregular circum-

98. Ibid., p. 61. This was designed to refute the argument presented by Judges Winiarski and Lauterpacht that account should be taken of the circumstances arising from South Africa's refusal to cooperate with the United Nations. See below, pp. 161-62.

99. *Oral Petitions Opinion* (1956): 62.

100. Ibid., p. 70. These comments are especially significant in the light of the question that subsequently arose in the 1962 and 1966 phases of the *South West Africa* cases regarding the scope of Article 7 of the Mandate and whether this provision authorized the Court to exercise judicial supervision of the mandate. See below, Chapters IX, X, and XI. Had the five dissenting judges in the present case held that Article 7 related to judicial supervision and that the 1950 opinion had preserved that supervision in force after the demise of the League, then why would it not be appropriate for the Court to examine violations of the mandate? Why did they consider that a question of departure from the 1950 opinion would be a political question properly to be determined by the General Assembly and not by the Court? The approach of the five minority judges would strongly suggest that they did not find in Article 7 an instrument for judicial consideration of violations of the conduct clauses of the Mandate. In their view (concurring with one that had found frequent expression in the Assembly), the South West Africa dispute in the final analysis was a political and not a legal problem and could be settled ultimately only by political means. (It may be noted incidentally that four out of the five judges were nationals of states generally classified as activist—Egypt, China, Uruguay, and Argentina.) In the 1962 Judgment, three of the five judges were still on the bench. Judges Badawi and Moreno-Quintana sided with the majority while Judge Basdevant (the French judge) dissented on the ground, *inter alia*, that it had not been clearly established that Article 7 envisaged judicial supervision. *SWA Judgment* (1962): 462-64.

stances prompting the request, namely, South Africa's failure to discharge its obligations in accordance with the 1950 opinion. These "imperative considerations" justified the granting of oral hearings by the Assembly if these are "kept within reasonable limits and governed by the rule of good faith."[101] In essence, then, Judge Winiarski predicated authorization of hearings on the grounds of necessity.

Somewhat along similar lines, Judge Lauterpacht based himself on the principle of effectiveness in finding authority for the Assembly to grant oral hearings.[102] In his view, the essence of the 1950 Opinion was the application of this principle of effectiveness to the relevant clauses of the Covenant and the Charter so as to formulate "a regime in the nature of an objective law" and thereby preserve the mandatory system for South West Africa, in so far as that was possible. By interpreting the relevant instruments in light of their basic purpose, the Court was forced to depart from the strict letter of the texts. By the same token, the Court, in 1956, was entitled to modify somewhat the prescription for supervision enunciated by the Court in 1950, so as to preserve its overall effectiveness. Authorization of oral hearings would only serve to compensate for South Africa's failure to cooperate in the international supervision of the mandate. In this manner, "the law—the existing law as judicially interpreted—finds means for removing a clog or filling a lacuna or adopting an alternative device in order to prevent a standstill of the entire system on account of a failure in any particular link or part."[103] For this reason, concluded Judge Lauterpacht, the Assembly could authorize oral hearings since (1) only by this means could the status quo be upheld; and (2) the degree of supervision in the aggregate would not be more stringent than it had been under the League.[104]

The decision of the Court revealed both the strength and weakness of the 1950 opinion. The majority opinion taking into account "the lack of cooperation by the Mandatory,"[105] adopted a maximalist interpretation of the original opinion, in conferring on the General Assembly all the powers—applied and potential—of the League Council. But judicial enlargement of the supervisory powers of the Assembly could not really resolve the basic problem, viz., the absence of South African participation in any scheme of international accountability. The minority judges were perhaps more realistic in holding that South Africa's attitude was something for the political, not the judicial, forum to take account of. South African intransigence could not, in their view, provide

101. *Oral Petitions Opinion* (1956): 33.
102. Ibid., pp. 35–59.
103. Ibid., p. 48.
104. Ibid., pp. 52–53.
105. Ibid., p. 31.

a basis for Court modification of the legal regime established under the 1950 opinion.

By 1956, then, a clear division had developed in the Court over the proper role of the judicial organ in the South West Africa crisis and the degree to which the 1950 opinion could provide all the answers to that sore problem. A significant group of judges (mostly from nonaligned states) looked to the General Assembly itself to find a solution to this problem, which they considered basically political. The clash of outlook in the Court portended a more significant division if and when the question of compulsory jurisdiction should arise.

# IV.

## EFFORTS
## TO OBTAIN
## A BINDING
## COURT
## JUDGMENT

# VIII.

## THE GENERAL ASSEMBLY PROMOTES RECOURSE TO THE COMPULSORY JURISDICTION OF THE COURT

### THE INITIATION OF STUDIES

The activities of the South West Africa Committee during 1956 were as unproductive in finally resolving the crisis as they had been in previous years.[1] South Africa rejected the offer of further negotiations and, needless to say, spurned the opportunity to present either an annual report or petitions.[2] Nonetheless, the Committee, as in previous years, drew up a report on conditions in South West Africa, based on the information at its disposal. South Africa's administration of the territory was criticized as failing totally to meet "in a reasonable way the standards of either endeavour or achievement implicit in the purposes of the Mandates System and in the attitudes prevailing generally today in respect of peoples not yet able to stand by themselves. The 'Native' of South West Africa . . . lives and works in an inferior and subordinate status in relation to a privileged 'European' minority."[3] Added to the Committee's "grave concern over conditions" in the territory were "its profound misgivings as to the future course of the administration of the Territory" arising from the intentions of the Union government to apply its policy of apartheid to the territory and to implement a closer system of political integration with the Union.

South Africa had not, in fact, declared explicitly that it was instituting apartheid in South West Africa. A word of explanation is therefore necessary to appreciate the Committee's misgivings on this score.

---

1. Report of Committee on South West Africa, GAOR, 11th Sess., Supp. No. 12 (A/3151) (1956).
2. Ibid., Annex I.
3. Ibid., Annex II, p. 27.

A policy of racial segregation, as noted earlier, was already current in South West Africa in the period of German rule.[4] Such familiar trappings of discrimination as native reserves and pass laws were even then standard features of life in the territory. For purposes of administration, the Germans had divided South West Africa into two parts. The Police Zone (i.e., the area patrolled by the German police) comprised the southern two-thirds of the territory and was subject to direct white control, while the Northern or Tribal Areas, comprising one-third of the territory, were administered through a system of indirect rule, allowing the tribal chiefs to exercise their traditional form of authority. With the assumption of the mandate in 1920, South Africa accepted the pre-existing pattern of racial segregation, including the reserves system, and developed it further.[5] Thus in 1922 arrangements were instituted for the application of night curfews on Natives where such was requested by local authorities, and in 1924 separate urban areas for Natives were introduced into South West Africa.

Up until 1954 no major modifications were effected in the administration of South West Africa's racial system. However, in that year the South African government undertook a program of tying South West Africa closer to the Union, not only in the political but in the administrative field as well. By the 1954 Native Affairs Administration Act, the following changes were introduced:

a) Native affairs in South West Africa, previously in the charge of the Administrator of the territory, were to come under the direct control of the South African Minister of Bantu Administration and Development.

b) South West Africa Native Reserve Land was to vest henceforth in the general South Africa Native Trust, i.e., the operation of native reserves in the territory would be handled directly from South Africa.[6]

These South African moves to closer administrative integration meant that, as a corollary, native policy in South Africa and South West Africa would be unified and the policy of apartheid applied to the

4. See J. H. Wellington, *South West Africa and Its Human Issues* (Oxford: Clarendon Press, 1967), pp. 344-45; *SWA Pleadings* III: 238-40, 306.
5. Wellington, *South West Africa*, pp. 282-83, 345; *SWA Pleadings* III: 201, 240, 308 ff.
6. These provisions in the 1954 Act were cited by the Applicants in the *South West Africa* cases as evidence that South Africa was intent on unilaterally modifying the international status of the territory in violation of the Mandate. This statute was one of four South African actions which, it was said, revealed an intention to incorporate or annex the territory. Submissions 5 and 9. See *SWA Pleadings* I: 194-95; IV: 583-86. South Africa rejected the charges and claimed that the steps taken were merely changes in the form of administration which it was fully authorized to institute as part of its authority to administer South West Africa "as an integral portion" of South Africa. The international status of the territory, if such existed, remained unaffected by any of the actions taken. See ibid., pp. 119-131, and VI: 414-18.

territory. Thus, the issue of apartheid in the context of South West Africa was now for the first time squarely before the United Nations.

The significance of this development was two-fold. First, it added a major new facet to the conflict between the United Nations and South Africa over South West Africa. Previously, that conflict had centered on the issues of international accountability to the United Nations and the right of South Africa to modify the status of the territory. Now a further and more critical matter had arisen before the world body—the charge that South Africa, by its implementation of apartheid, was in violation of its duty "to promote to the utmost the material and moral well-being" of the population of the territory. Second, the introduction of apartheid into South West Africa meant that the *"apartheid* front" was that much further extended and that much more vulnerable to challenge. If racial policies within South Africa were not so open to attack because of the principle of domestic jurisdiction (Article 2[7] of the Charter), this was not the case with regard to racial matters in South West Africa, a territory stamped with an indubitable international character. Subsequent moves toward the institution of contentious proceedings before the International Court were in no small measure connected with the foregoing considerations.

In concluding its report, the South West Africa Committee asserted that the situation in the territory was

> neither in conformity with the principles of the Mandates System nor with the Universal Declaration of Human Rights, nor with the advisory opinions of the International Court of Justice, nor with the resolutions of the General Assembly. Accordingly, the Committee considers that the situation of South West Africa requires close re-examination at the present time by the Assembly, particularly in respect of the failure of the Union Government to cooperate in the implementation of the advisory opinion of the Court of 11 July 1950, as endorsed by the Assembly in resolution 449A (V) of 13 December 1950.[7]

The final sentence reflected the growing frustration of the Committee, and of the United Nations generally, over the organization's inability to bring South Africa to accept, and apply, standards of international accountability in regard to South West Africa. South Africa was not only uncooperative it was openly defiant. The discussions in the Fourth Committee at the Eleventh Assembly Session bore witness to the new mood of impatience. The Philippine delegate asked "why the

---

7. Report of Committee on South West Africa, GAOR, 11th Sess., Supp. No. 12 (A/3151) (1956), Annex II, p. 27.

Committee should go on discussing the question, as it had been doing for eleven years, seeing that the South African Government turned a deaf ear to the recommendations of the General Assembly and the advisory opinions of the International Court of Justice." He called upon the United Nations "to take measures to enforce its authority." In the light of the almost intolerable situation in the territory, he felt "there was a danger that the problem might be solved by other than peaceful means."[8] The sense of urgency was heightened by a warning delivered by South West African petitioners, who, in appearances before the Committee, stressed that "it was natural for an oppressed and frustrated people to resort to violence."[9] Delegates of newly independent states, admitted to the United Nations that same year, launched bitter attacks on South Africa's "backward and inhuman policy."[10] Even the representative of the United States referred to the situation as one that represented "a probable cause of what might well be one of the ugliest explosions of violence in history."[11]

All of these considerations prompted Assembly search for a new course of action. Toward that end, an Indian-sponsored draft resolution was adopted, which requested the Committee on South West Africa, in addition to its regular functions, to study and report to the Twelfth Assembly Session on the following question:

> What legal action is open to the organs of the United Nations, or to the Members of the United Nations, or to the former Members of the League of Nations, acting either individually or jointly, to ensure that the Union of South Africa fulfils the obligations assumed by it under the Mandate, pending the placing of the Territory of South West Africa under the International Trusteeship System?[12]

As explained by the Indian representative, the ineffectiveness of the Court's pronouncements to date resulted from their advisory nature. "The United Nations should now try to determine what legal remedies were open to it."[13] The 1950 Court had stated that Article 7, the compulsory jurisdiction clause of the Mandate, was still in force. Action could therefore be taken under that provision to obtain a Court judgment against South Africa. In effect, this would convert the operative part of the advisory opinion into a judicial determination legally bind-

---

8. GAOR, 11th Sess., 4th Ctte., 572nd Mtg., Dec. 11, 1956, pp. 113–14.
9. Ibid.
10. See the remarks of the representatives of Sudan and Morocco, ibid., 575th Mtg., Dec. 14, 1956, p. 125.
11. Ibid., 576th Mtg., Dec. 17, 1956, p. 131.
12. G.A. Res. 1060 (XI), Feb. 26, 1957.
13. GAOR, 11th Sess., 4th Ctte., 580th Mtg., Dec. 20, 1956, p. 155.

ing on South Africa. In the event that the Union government refused to comply, the Security Council could be called upon to enforce the judgment in accordance with Article 94 of the Charter.[14] Despite the hesitations of certain delegates who claimed that the problem of South West Africa was essentially political and should be handled by the Assembly itself,[15] the proposal for studying possibilities of legal action was overwhelmingly adopted by the General Assembly.[16]

At the same time the Assembly also adopted a number of other resolutions bearing on the subject of South West Africa.[17] The most important of these was a request to the Secretary-General "to explore ways and means of solving satisfactorily the question of South West Africa."[18] It was envisaged that the Secretary-General might visit South Africa and negotiate on the matter. It will be recalled that 1956 was the year in which the "Leave it to Dag" slogan was in vogue, in the aftermath of the Suez crisis. Presumably, the Assembly hoped that Mr. Hammarskjold's personal intervention might provide the healing touch to the perennial South West Africa problem. For his part, however, the Secretary-General was decidedly reluctant to undertake single-handed the resolution of a crisis that had plagued the world organization since its inception. He informed the Fourth Committee that "in view of the many pressing and onerous tasks now entrusted to him . . . he would not be able to do full justice to such an important request."[19]

Another resolution provided for an increase in the membership of the South West Africa Committee from 7 to 9, with annual replacement of one-third of the Committee.[20] The latter move demonstrated Assembly belief that the "siege" would not be a short one.[21]

In August 1957 the Committee on South West Africa, in addition to its regular report on conditions in the territory, furnished the Assem-

14. Ibid., p. 156. Article 94, paragraph 2, provides: "If any party to a case fails to perform the obligations incumbent upon it under a judgment rendered by the Court, the other party may have recourse to the Security Council, which may, if it deems necessary, make recommendations or decide upon measures to be taken to give effect to the judgment."

15. See, e.g., the remarks of the Uruguayan representative, GAOR, 11th Sess., 4th Ctte., 580th Mtg., Dec. 20, 1956, p. 156.

16. The vote was 40 to 4, with 23 abstentions. Ibid., Plen., 661st Mtg., Feb. 26, 1957, p. 1224.

17. Earlier, the Assembly "accepted and endorsed" the 1956 advisory opinion. G.A. Res. 1047 (XI), Jan. 23, 1957.

18. G.A. Res. 1059 (XI), Feb. 26, 1957.

19. Statement by Under-Secretary Cohen, GAOR, 11th Sess., 4th Ctte., 579th Mtg., Dec. 20, 1956, p. 152.

20. G.A. Res. 1061 (XI), Feb. 26, 1957.

21. Other resolutions related to receipt of petitions (G.A. Res. 1056, 1057, 1058 [XI], Feb. 26, 1957); reiteration of the Assembly view that the normal way to modify the international status of South West Africa would be to place it under the trusteeship system (G.A. Res. 1055 [XI], Feb. 26, 1957); and, finally, endorsement of the recommendations of the Committee for South West Africa for improving conditions in the territory (G.A. Res. 1054 [XI], Feb.

bly with a special report on possible legal action.[22] Three possible courses of action were outlined:

1) Further Assembly requests for advisory opinions from the Court. These opinions, the report indicated, while not binding, "may be a factor in influencing a State to fulfill its obligations."[23]
2) Institution of contentious proceedings by one or more members of the United Nations, regarding South Africa's failure to submit annual reports to the United Nations.[24]
3) Institution of contentious proceedings by one or more members of the United Nations (or parties to the Statute of the Court) who had been members of the League of Nations at the time of its dissolution in 1946.[25]

Any contentious proceedings, the report noted, would need to be based on Article 7 of the Mandate. The 1950 opinion had stated that that provision was in force, but it had not indicated which parties were eligible to invoke it. Some members of the Committee argued that the Court had in effect ruled that "international supervision had passed from one organization to another organization" and this included judicial supervision. Therefore, all present members of the United Nations were qualified to invoke Article 7. Other Committee members noted, however, that even Judges McNair and Read—who, in contrast to the majority, explicitly endorsed the notion of judicial supervision and undertook to define the scope and operation of Article 7—did not extend the right to invoke the provision beyond the membership of the League. In sum, then, the report found that former members of the League currently members of the United Nations were in the strongest position to invoke the compulsory jurisdiction of the Court.[26]

The regular report of the South West Africa Committee recommended "as a matter of urgency that the Mandatory Power take steps to repeal all racially discriminatory legislation and practices."[27] It stated that it had, however, "found no evidence that the Mandatory Power intends to change the course of the administration of the Terri-

26, 1957). These last-mentioned recommendations advised (a) abolition of apartheid; (b) a greater measure of self-government for all people in the territory; (c) a common educational system for the entire population; and (d) separate governmental institutions for South Africa and South West Africa.
22. GAOR, 12th Sess., Supp. No. 12A (A/3625) (1957).
23. Ibid., p. 3.
24. Ibid., pp. 4–5.
25. Ibid., pp. 5–7.
26. The report noted that states, members of the League, that were not completely independent in 1946 (e.g., India) would have to overcome difficult questions of succession before they could invoke the Court's jurisdiction. Ibid., p. 5, n. 24.
27. GAOR, 12th Sess., Supp. No. 12 (A/3626) (1957), p. 11.

tory to bring it into conformity with the Mandates System. The Committee therefore considers that the General Assembly should weigh the gravity of the present situation and consider the need for acting without further delay in the matter."[28]

The two reports laid the groundwork for a firmer stand by the General Assembly at its Twelfth Session, with the distinct possibility that direct legal action would be advocated. It was indeed in this direction that the Fourth Committee began to move, when discussions on South West Africa commenced. Liberia submitted a severely condemnatory draft resolution for adoption.[29] However, at this point, a new conciliatory move, proposing a fresh attempt at negotiations, was initiated by the Chairman of the Fourth Committee, Mr. Thanat Khoman, of Thailand, and, as a result, the Assembly was deflected from a more vigorous course.[30] All the critical phrases in the Liberian draft resolution were now eliminated, and the Assembly simply "approved" the South West Africa Committee's report.[31] In similar fashion, the Assembly resolved that detailed consideration of the legal report would be deferred until the Thirteenth Session. Nevertheless, although the "carrot" was being held out once again, the "stick" was not totally abandoned. The General Assembly, at the same time, drew the attention of member states "to the failure of the Union of South Africa to render annual reports to the United Nations and to the legal action provided for in Article 7 of the Mandate read with Article 37 of the Statute of the International Court of Justice."[32]

## THE GOOD OFFICES COMMITTEE

The efforts of Mr. Thanat Khoman led to the creation of a Good Offices Committee, composed of representatives of the United States, the United Kingdom, and Brazil, which was empowered to discuss with the Union government "a basis for an agreement which would continue to accord to the Territory of South West Africa an international

28. Ibid., p. 26.
29. U.N. Doc. A/C.4/L.487, in Report of 4th Ctte., Part 1 (A/3701), GAOR, 12th Sess., Annexes, Agenda Item 38, p. 5.
30. GAOR, 12th Sess., 4th Ctte., 664th Mtg., Oct. 8, 1957, p. 59. Apparently, Mr. Khoman had been assured by the Union government that it would be responsive to this endeavor.
31. See Report of Fourth Committee, A/3701, Part 1, pp. 5–6. At the same time, however, a Canadian attempt to have the Fourth Committee simply "note" rather than "approve" the report, was defeated. Ibid., p. 6.
32. G.A. Res. 1142 (XII), Oct. 25, 1957, Part A. The resolution also requested the South West Africa Committee to consider further the question of advisory opinions "and to make recommendations in its next report concerning acts of the administration on which a reference to the Court may usefully be made as to their compatibility or otherwise with Article 22 of the Covenant," the Mandate and the Charter. Ibid., Part B.

status." These terms of reference were deliberately broader than those accorded previous committees, and it was hoped that this would result in a reconciliation between United Nations claims for an effective role in supervising the administration of the territory and South Africa's insistence that its obligations under the Mandate not be increased.[33]

During 1958 the Good Offices Committee conducted extensive talks with the South African government.[34] The Committee initially proposed that a quasi-mandates system be created within the framework of the United Nations.[35] According to this plan, to parallel the League Council, a select South West Africa Council would be established, composed of France, the United Kingdom, and the United States as permanent members, with two additional nonpermanent members; and in place of the Permanent Mandates Commission, there would be a South West Africa Commission, composed of experts. Reports on the territory would not be transmitted directly to the General Assembly, but rather through the circuitous route of Commission to Council and then to Assembly. South Africa, however, remained totally uninterested, since it persisted in its refusal to contemplate accountability to the United Nations in any form or manner.[36] Nor was it prepared to accept the world body as the second party to any proposed agreement. In its turn, South Africa resubmitted its earlier proposal for a special and direct agreement with France, the United Kingdom, and the United States to revive the provisions of the sacred trust. This proposal, the Committee indicated, had already been rejected by the United Nations and could not be entertained anew.

One proposal, however, attracted the attention of both South Africa and the Good Offices Committee.[37] This involved a scheme for partitioning South West Africa, so that the southern section would be annexed by the Union, while the northern section would be placed under the trusteeship system, with South Africa as the trust authority. South Africa's willingness to consider this proposal, the Committee report indicated, derived largely from the fact that "the area to be placed under a trusteeship agreement . . . would probably contain only

---

33. During the debate, certain delegates expressed fears that the terms of reference of the Good Offices Committee were, in fact, too liberal and might allow negotiations to range too far from basic Charter principles and the views of the Assembly with regard to the territory. Report of 4th Ctte., Part I (A/3701) in GAOR, 12th Sess., Annexes, Agenda Item 38, pp. 6–8. The issue of terms of reference assumed special significance after the Committee presented its report to the 13th Assembly Session. See below, p. 175.

34. Report of Good Offices Committee (A/3900), GAOR, 13th Sess., Annexes, Agenda Item 39, pp. 2–10 (1958).

35. Ibid., pp. 6–7.

36. Ibid.

37. Ibid., pp. 8–10.

Bantu races. This would obviate [United Nations] discussions on the multi-racial situation existing in the Union."[38] The Committee report expressed the hope that the General Assembly would "encourage" the Union government "to carry out an investigation of the practicability of partition."[39]

The Assembly's reaction, however, was one of violent opposition to the whole suggestion. Delegates charged the Good Offices Committee with having far exceeded its terms of reference.[40] The United Nations, it was made clear, could not allow the practice of apartheid in any part of the territory. And, furthermore, the obligations arising out of the international status of the territory could not be seriously compromised, either with respect to geographical area or with respect to the measure of international accountability. By a vote of 61 to 8, with 7 abstentions, the Assembly adopted a resolution deciding "not to accept the suggestions contained in the report of the Good Offices Committee that envisage partition and annexation of any part of the Territory."[41] Nonetheless, the Committee was invited to renew discussions with the South African government "to find a basis for an agreement which would continue to accord to the... Territory... *as a whole* an international status, and which would be in conformity with the purposes and principles of the Charter."[42] The Committee was bidden "to bear fully in mind the discussions held at the thirteenth session."[43]

In the meantime, the Assembly decided to postpone, once again, consideration of possible legal action.[44] In the words of the Indian delegate, it was hoped that by the next session "a reasonable and just settlement would be in sight and that... forms of legal action... would not have to be considered further."[45] At the same time, however, the standard resolution recommending to South Africa that it conclude a trusteeship agreement for South West Africa was adopted,[46] as was a resolution "approving" the annual report of the Committee on South West Africa and expressing the Assembly's "deep concern regarding the social, economic and political situations... prevailing in the Territory."[47]

38. Ibid., p. 9.
39. Ibid., p. 10.
40. See discussions in GAOR, 13th Sess., 4th Ctte., 756th–763rd Mtgs., Oct. 10–16, 1958, pp. 57–97.
41. G.A. Res. 1243 (XIII), Oct. 30, 1958. Par. 1.
42. Ibid., par. 2 (emphasis supplied).
43. Ibid., par. 3.
44. G.A. Res. 1247 (XIII), Oct. 30, 1958.
45. GAOR, 13th Sess., 4th Ctte., 771st Mtg., Oct. 23, 1958, p. 132.
46. G.A. Res. 1246 (XIII), Oct. 30, 1958.
47. G.A. Res. 1245 (XIII), Oct. 30, 1958.

## ENDORSEMENT OF LEGAL ACTION BY ETHIOPIA AND LIBERIA

During 1959 the efforts of the Good Offices Committee proved to be totally unproductive.[48] No basis for agreement was discovered. This event signaled the end of the road for the path of conciliation and marked a drastic turning point in United Nations efforts to induce South Africa to hold itself accountable to the world organization. All avenues of negotiation had now been exhausted by the world organization. The efforts of the *Ad Hoc* Committee had been fruitless; the attempts of the South West Africa Committee to even initiate talks had been spurned; and now, the Good Offices Committee, with the most liberal terms of reference of any committee, had failed to produce any reasonable solution to the problem. (The solution which the Committee had proposed was not deemed "reasonable" by the Assembly.) After thirteen years of persistent effort, the United Nations was reminded that it was still totally excluded from any supervisory role in reference to South West Africa—a territory which had been impressed with an international status since 1919.

In the meantime, the number of South West Africa petitioners hammering at the doors of the world organization had increased immensely. From an isolated petition or two in the early period, the number of petitioners annually now reached into the tens and scores. The charges leveled at South Africa with reference to its treatment of the native population had also grown steadily more serious. It was at this time, too, that the ranks of the United Nations began to swell, with the advent of newly independent African states. All of the foregoing factors promoted the rise of a new, more determined, impatient mood, with respect to the South West Africa question. The move for legal proceedings before the Court, which had been forestalled by the efforts of the Good Offices Committee, now returned to center stage.

The new mood was reflected in the 1959 report of the South West Africa Committee.[49] After presenting its annual review of political, economic, social, and educational conditions, and after noting South Africa's persistent failure to remedy matters in these areas, in disregard of Assembly recommendations, the report concluded:

> The administration of the Territory [must] be altered without undue delay in order to ensure the political, social and educational development of the *whole* of the population and the application of the principle of equal rights and opportunities for *all* of the inhab-

---

48. Report of Good Offices Committee (A/4224), in GAOR, 14th Sess., Annexes, Agenda Item 38, pp. 1-5 (1959).

49. Report of Committee on South West Africa (A/4191) in GAOR, 14th Sess., Supp. No. 12 (1959).

itants. . . . However such an essential change in the administration is not likely to occur owing to the intransigence of the Mandatory Power. . . . The Committee accordingly recommends . . . that the General Assembly *should consider means of ensuring the fulfilment by the Union Government of its obligations under the Mandate and the Charter.*[50]

The last sentence was specifically directed "to the possibility of legal action against South Africa before the International Court of Justice."[51] A special subcommittee had undertaken, during 1959, an extensive and detailed examination of possible parties and issues in any such contentious proceedings, and its results were now presented for General Assembly consideration.

The new and more militant mood of United Nations members, bent on some course of "action," apparently had some effect in Pretoria, and for the first time in several years, South Africa participated fully in the Assembly discussions on South West Africa.[52] In the Fourth Committee the South African delegate announced that his government intended participating not only in the current Fourteenth Session but at the Fifteenth Session as well and, moreover, would furnish the United Nations with public documents on South West Africa.[53] This data, however, would not be presented in the form of a report; nor would it be supplemented by any further information upon request. It was merely designed to remedy serious factual errors in the reports of the Committee on South West Africa. At the same time, the South African representative indicated his government's desire "to keep the door open for future discussions,"[54] and its willingness "to enter into discussions with an appropriate United Nations *ad hoc* body that might be appointed after prior consultation with the Union Government," to undertake "the fullest exploration of all possibilities."[55]

Despite the more positive attitude reflected in the South African statements, the Assembly was not prone to give them much attention.

50. Ibid., p. 33 (emphasis supplied).
51. Ibid., pp. 1–2, par. 8. During 1958, the Committee had reviewed, in accordance with a General Assembly request, the possibility of securing further advisory opinions from the International Court. The 1958 report stated that advisory opinions could be sought with reference to two main categories of acts committed by South Africa: (a) acts affecting the international status of the territory, e.g., moves for closer integration; (b) acts affecting the moral and material well-being of the population, e.g., apartheid and restrictions on freedom of movement. The report questioned, however, the "usefulness" of any further advisory opinions. Report of Committee on South West Africa (A/3906), in GAOR, 13th Sess., Supp. No. 12, Part II, pp. 6–8 (1958). In 1959 the Committee focused its attention on possible contentious proceedings.
52. These discussions commenced on October 8, 1959.
53. GAOR, 14th Sess., 4th Ctte., 900th Mtg., Oct. 8, 1959, pp. 84–87.
54. Ibid., p. 85.
55. Ibid., 924th Mtg., Oct. 26, 1959, p. 221.

It entertained little hope for fruitful negotiations, nor was it prepared to procrastinate any longer. The African states, and particularly those recently admitted to United Nations membership, staunchly opposed any tendency toward moderation. As expressed by the delegate from Ghana: "The time for action had come, and the Committee could no longer evade its obligations after fourteen years of frustrated efforts at negotiation. The next step, and one that had to be taken, was recourse to the compulsory jurisdiction of the International Court of Justice."[56] Oddly enough, those states that had, to date, been consistently in the forefront of United Nations endeavors with reference to South West Africa attempted, but were unable, to restrain the surge for "action." Thus, Mr. Carpio, the Philippine representative and chairman of the Sub-Committee on Legal Questions, counseled the Assembly not to take "precipitate action which it might afterwards regret," but to "confine itself to more moderate action such as seeking advisory opinions, to which no one could raise any objection."[57] Similarly, Mr. Krishna Menon, the Indian delegate, "urged the members of the Committee not to be led by impatience into putting forward a proposal which might smack of an ultimatum." "The function of the United Nations," he declared, "was reconciliation."[58] But the hour for moderation had passed, and the demand for action was too powerful, too sweeping, and too pervasive to be restrained.[59]

Two resolutions gave voice to the Assembly's new attitude. In the preambular part of the first resolution,[60] which dealt with the report of the South West Africa Committee, the General Assembly, *inter alia*, noted with grave concern that the administration of the territory in recent years had been conducted increasingly in a manner contrary to the Mandate, the Charter, the Universal Declaration of Human Rights, the advisory opinions of the International Court of Justice, and the resolutions of the General Assembly. In the operative part of the resolution, the Assembly: (1) noted the statement of the South African representative expressing the readiness of the Union government to enter into discussions with the United Nations; (2) invited the Union government to enter into negotiations through the Committee on South

56. Ibid., 923rd Mtg., Oct. 23, 1959, p. 216. See also the remarks of the representative of Sudan, ibid., 918th Mtg., Oct. 21, 1959, p. 188.
57. Ibid., 919th Mtg., Oct. 21, 1959, p. 195.
58. Ibid., 923rd Mtg., Oct. 23, 1959, pp. 218–19.
59. The Assembly's attitude was measurably hardened by hearings conducted by the Fourth Committee. Various petitioners described in graphic detail conditions within the territory and appealed for legal action against South Africa. They asked for consideration of sanctions against the Union. Ibid., 904th to 913th Mtgs., Oct. 12–16, 1959, pp. 110–55, passim.
60. G.A. Res. 1360 (XIV), Nov. 17, 1959.

West Africa "with a view to placing the Mandated Territory under the International Trusteeship System"; and (3) requested the Union government in the meantime, "to formulate for the consideration of the General Assembly at its Fifteenth Session proposals which will enable the . . . Territory . . . to be administered in accordance with the principles and purposes of the Mandate, the supervisory functions being exercised by the United Nations according to the terms and intent of the Charter."

This was a forceful demonstration of United Nations intent to put an end, once and for all, to the incessant delays and sidetracking that had prevented South West Africa from coming under United Nations jurisdiction to date. Negotiation, if there was to be negotiation, would be directed toward the only goal acceptable to the United Nations, namely, a trusteeship agreement. In the meantime, the authority of the United Nations was to be established in accordance with the advisory opinion. But the procedures for the exercise of this United Nations authority were no longer a suitable subject for negotiation. South Africa was to acknowledge without delay the right of the United Nations to supervise and was itself to submit proposals to the Fifteenth Assembly Session which would give effect to the principle of international accountability. This resolution was certainly not designed to "appease" South Africa.[61] An attempt by four Scandinavian states to promote a draft resolution calling for general negotiations not limited specifically to achieving a trusteeship agreement was unable to muster significant support in the Fourth Committee and was withdrawn.[62]

The second Assembly resolution[63] drew

> the attention of Member States to the conclusions of the special report of the Committee on South West Africa covering the legal action open to Member States to refer any dispute with the Union of South Africa concerning the interpretation or application of the

61. See the remarks of the South African representative, GAOR, 14th Sess., 4th Ctte., 931st Mtg., Oct. 29, 1959, p. 254.

62. See Report of the 4th Ctte. (A/4272), in GAOR, 14th Sess., Annexes, Agenda Item 38, p. 18 (1959). Attempts to achieve a similar result by the introduction of amendments into the draft resolution were defeated. Ibid., pp. 18–19.

63. G.A. Res. 1361 (XIV), Nov. 17, 1959. The draft resolution had been sponsored by Liberia, Ethiopia, and eleven other states.

In the roll-call vote in the Fourth Committee the United States voted with the majority. Only the United Kingdom, Australia, Portugal, and South Africa voted against the resolution, while seventeen states abstained. GAOR, 14th Sess., 4th Ctte., 932nd Mtg., Oct. 30, 1959, p. 260.

The Soviet delegate, despite his belief that "in accordance with the Charter, it was the General Assembly alone which could decide the problem," supported the resolution "out of a desire to help the African delegations to attempt the approach to the International Court." Rather prophetically, he added that "it was difficult to guarantee that any concrete results would emerge from that approach." Ibid., pp. 260–62.

Mandate for South West Africa to the International Court of Justice for adjudication in accordance with Article 7 of the Mandate read in conjunction with Article 37 of the Statute of the Court.

A joint Colombian-Iranian amendment to the original draft resolution, calling for postponement of the issue to the Fifteenth Assembly Session so as to allow time for further study, was withdrawn for lack of support.[64] The amendment had been intended to promote the chances of success of negotiations to be undertaken under Resolution 1360 (XIV). As explained by the Colombian delegate: "Negotiations and legal action represented two different and consecutive steps; if they were taken simultaneously, the result might be to stultify negotiations."[65] The Assembly, however, was unwilling to accept this viewpoint, since it did not consider that one course of action necessarily excluded the other. To the contrary, it was presumably believed that reference to possible legal action would enhance rather than inhibit the prospects of negotiations.[66] Moreover, certain delegates, in particular the United States representative, were of the opinion that only the International Court of Justice could satisfactorily resolve the difficult South West Africa problem which, it was held, was "susceptible to adjudication."[67] In any case, states would wait and see: if negotiations were moving ahead with reasonable progress, no legal action would be initiated. If not, the way was open for recourse to the compulsory jurisdiction of the International Court of Justice.[68]

In June 1960 the Second Conference of Independent African States, meeting at Addis Ababa, adopted a resolution endorsing the intention of Ethiopia and Liberia to submit the question of South West Africa before the International Court of Justice for adjudication in a contentious proceeding.[69] As expressed by the Liberian delegate, it was his government's "determination on behalf of all the African States, to pursue further action to get this territory placed under the Trusteeship provisions of the Charter." His government was "pleased to know that . . . [it had] the support and co-operation of other African States."[70]

64. Ibid., p. 259.
65. Ibid., 930th Mtg., Oct. 29, 1959, p. 244.
66. See the remarks of the United States representative, ibid., 931st Mtg., Oct. 29, 1959, p. 254.
67. Ibid.
68. See the remarks of the Liberian delegate, ibid., 930th Mtg., Oct. 29, 1959, pp. 246-47.
69. "Second Conference of Independent African States, Addis Ababa, 14-26 June, 1960," published by the Ministry of Information of the Imperial Ethiopian Government (1960), pp. 101-2.
70. Ibid., p. 32.

In the same month, the United Nations Committee on South West Africa invited the South African government to enter into negotiations with it, in accordance with General Assembly Resolution 1360 (XIV).[71] In its reply, the South African government stated that it "could not see any possibility of fruitful results flowing from negotiations which required the Union to place 'South West Africa under the International Trusteeship System'—terms of reference which prescribe the end result in advance."[72] South Africa, however, indicated readiness to enter into negotiations with an appropriate United Nations *ad hoc* body which would have an opportunity to explore "all possibilities."[73]

The Committee on South West Africa, in its report to the Assembly, noted the resolution adopted in Addis Ababa and "commended" Ethiopia and Liberia for their intention to institute judicial proceedings "as one of the practical approaches for the implementation of resolution 1361 (XIV)." In addition, the report reviewed once again conditions in South West Africa and expressed sharp criticism of the administration, which, it declared, was "marked by an increasingly rigid application of *apartheid* laws."[74]

The Fifteenth Assembly Session commenced discussions on the topic of South West Africa on November 4, 1960. Upon that occasion the representative of Liberia announced to the Fourth Committee that the Liberian and Ethiopian governments had, that very day, instituted proceedings against the Union of South Africa before the International Court of Justice.[75] This announcement drew forth an immediate request from the South African representative that the Assembly suspend further debate on the South West Africa issue on the ground that the question was now *sub judice*.[76] He presented various legal arguments in support of his proposal, but it was overwhelmingly rejected by the Assembly.[77] The attitude of the delegates was reflected in the comments of the Guinean representative, who maintained that the South African arguments were "inadmissible in the context of the sufferings of the people of South West Africa. . . . At the current session," he said, "the anti-colonialist tide was carrying all before it. The African States had placed the question of South West Africa before the International

71. Report of Committee on South West Africa (A/4464), in GAOR, 15th Sess., Supp. No. 12, Annex II, pp. 57–58 (1960).
72. Ibid.
73. Ibid., p. 4.
74. Ibid., p. 56. The report also took note of serious disturbances that had erupted in Windhoek on December 10, 1959, and which resulted in the deaths of eleven Africans.
75. GAOR, 15th Sess., 4th Ctte., 1037th Mtg., Nov. 4, 1960, p. 228.
76. Ibid., pp. 296–97.
77. Ibid., p. 298. The vote was 67 to 1, with 11 abstentions. The United States representative, it may be noted, voted with the majority.

Court of Justice because they wished to make use of any procedure whereby South Africa would be compelled to abide by its obligations."[78] He denied that anything in the Charter supported the South African argument on the *sub judice* rule.

Two dramatic events during the course of the year 1960 had given fresh impetus to the campaign against South Africa. The first was the Sharpeville shooting incident on March 21, 1960, in which some sixty-eight Africans were killed in clashes with the police outside Johannesburg. This serious outburst of violence within South Africa marked a turning point in the history of South African race relations and initiated a new pattern of active concern in the matter on the part of the international community. For the first time, the issue of apartheid, notwithstanding its ostensible "domestic jurisdictional" character, came before the Security Council. That body, on April 1, 1960, adopted a resolution which declared "that the situation in . . . South Africa is one that has led to international friction and if continued might endanger international peace and security," and called on South Africa to "abandon the policies of apartheid and discrimination."[79]

For the first time, the major powers, as permanent members of the Security Council, were directly involved in the issue of racial conflict in the southern part of Africa. Even France and the United Kingdom did no more than abstain. In point of fact, the United Kingdom henceforth adopted a critical attitude on the whole issue and generally endorsed United Nations protests (if not every action) against South African racial policies.[80]

The second noteworthy event to take place in 1960 was the dramatic entry of seventeen newly independent states into the United Nations. Sixteen of these states were from Africa. Henceforth, two issues close to the hearts of African states were to receive renewed

78. Ibid., p. 298. An attempt by the representative of the Philippines to postpone the vote, so as to allow more time for consideration of the question raised by the South African delegate, was disallowed. Ibid.

For a discussion of the General Assembly's treatment of the *sub judice* question, see Shabtai Rosenne, *The Law and Practice of the International Court* (Leyden: Sijthoff, 1965), I: 83–87; and Leo Gross, "The International Court of Justice and the United Nations," Hague Academy, *Recueil des Cours* CXXI (II–1967): 328–30. See also D. H. N. Johnson, "Sanctions Against South Africa? The Legal Aspect," in Ronald Segal (ed.), *Sanctions Against South Africa* (Baltimore: Penguin Books, 1964), pp. 69–70.

79. S.C. Res. 134. On the significance of the Sharpeville incident generally, see Vernon McKay, *Africa in World Politics* (New York: Harper and Row, 1963), pp. 68–70; Leo Marquard, *The Peoples and Policies of South Africa* (4th ed.; London: Oxford University Press, 1969), pp. 24–26; Amelia C. Leiss (ed.), *Apartheid and United Nations Collective Measures: An Analysis* (New York: Carnegie Endowment for International Peace, 1965), pp. 8–9; Rupert Emerson, *Africa and United States Policy* (Englewood Cliffs, N.J.: Prentice-Hall, 1967), p. 90.

80. On February 3, 1960, it will be recalled, Prime Minister MacMillan had delivered his famous "wind of change" speech in the South African Parliament.

On the change in the United Kingdom's position, see Johnson, "Sanctions Against South Africa," p. 72. See also Waldemar A. Nielsen, *African Battleline* (New York: Harper and Row, 1965), pp. 64–65.

emphasis—the elimination of colonialism and the elimination of racial discrimination. South West Africa, which combined in extraordinary manner both of these critical issues, became a focal point of active United Nations endeavors. The first step along the road to a more vigorous, and even aggressive, policy was United Nations endorsement of recourse to the Court.

On December 18, 1960, the General Assembly adopted a resolution in which, after recalling its resolution 1361 (XIV) of November 7, 1959, whereby it drew the attention of member states to the possibility of legal action against South Africa, and after noting the failure of all United Nations efforts to negotiate with South Africa, addressed itself to the action undertaken by Ethiopia and Liberia, and declared, *inter alia*, that it:

> 2. *Concludes* that the dispute which has arisen between Ethiopia, Liberia and other Member States on the one hand, and the Union of South Africa on the other, relating to the interpretation and application of the Mandate has not been and cannot be settled by negotiation;
> 3. *Notes* that Ethiopia and Liberia, on 4 November 1960, filed concurrent applications in the International Court of Justice instituting contentious proceedings against the Union of South Africa;
> 4. *Commends* the Governments of Ethiopia and Liberia upon their initiative in submitting such dispute to the International Court of Justice for adjudication and declaration in a contentious proceeding in accordance with article 7 of the Mandate.[81]

This resolution of the General Assembly confirmed the representative nature of the Ethiopian and Liberian action. After fifteen years of persistent effort to reach an understanding with South Africa, the United Nations had finally resolved to refer the matter to the Court in the form of contentious proceedings. In lieu of its own appearance in Court as a litigant—which, in view of Article 34 of the Court's Statute, was impossible[82]—the United Nations had urged member states to initiate contentious proceedings; and this suggestion having been taken up by two of its members, the United Nations proceeded to endorse it.[83]

---

81. G.A. Res. 1565 (XV), Dec. 18, 1960. The vote was 86 to 0, with 6 abstentions. The states abstaining were Luxembourg, Portugal, United Kingdom, Australia, Belgium, and France.
82. Article 34 provides that "only States may be parties in cases before the Court."
83. This action of the United Nations, in promoting in advance recourse to the Court and endorsing the step once it was taken, demonstrated, it was later argued, that no real dispute existed between South Africa and Ethiopia and Liberia. The dispute was really one between South Africa and the United Nations, and the Applicants therefore lacked standing to sue. Dissenting opinion of Judges Spender and Fitzmaurice, *SWA Judgment* (1962); 548-49. See also dissenting opinion of Judge Winiarski, ibid., p. 457. But cf. dissenting opinion of Judge Jessup, *SWA Judgment* (1966): 413-14.

By this action, the Assembly was instituting its third attempt to bring about a measure of international accountability for South West Africa. In its first attempt it had endeavored to induce South Africa to place the territory under the trusteeship system. Without really abandoning this first line, the second effort of the Assembly centered on obtaining South Africa's voluntary compliance with the 1950 opinion, which called for the continuation of the international obligations of the mandate. All these efforts having failed, the Assembly was now resorting to the compulsory jurisdiction of the Court to compel South Africa to submit to international accountability and to compel it to abandon its racial policies in South West Africa. The expectation was that an affirmative Court judgment would provide a firm basis for forceful action against South Africa—if such were needed. Moreover, it would possibly provide a judicial opinion on the general incompatibility of apartheid with international law, and would thereby fortify the United Nations campaign to eliminate racial discrimination from South Africa itself.

# THE JURISDICTIONAL PHASE: THE 1962 JUDGMENT— THE COURT ADVANCES

## INSTITUTION OF PROCEEDINGS

On November 4, 1960, the governments of Ethiopia and Liberia separately instituted proceedings against the government of the Union of South Africa relating to "the continuing existence of the Mandate of South West Africa and the duties and performance of the Union, as Mandatory, thereunder."[1] Both actions were initiated by unilateral Applications submitted on behalf of the two governments by their common agent, Ernest A. Gross, a member of a New York law firm and former deputy United States representative to the United Nations, who conducted the Applicants' case from 1960 to 1966.[2]

The Memorials of Ethiopia and Liberia were submitted on April 15, 1961, and contained in brief the following nine submissions[3] (i.e., claims advanced by the parties and issues which they wished the Court to adjudge or declare):

1. South West Africa is a territory under Mandate.

2. The Union continues to have the international obligations stated in Article 22 of the Covenant and in the Mandate, with supervisory

1. *SWA Pleadings* I: 4. In the proceedings Ethiopia and Liberia are referred to as the Applicants and South Africa as the Respondent. Ethiopia and Liberia, it might be noted, were the only two African states south of the Sahara (aside from the Union itself) which were members of the United Nations and had been members of the League at the date of its dissolution. Elements of geographical proximity and racial affinity were therefore present in their case and made them the best candidates to institute proceedings.

2. Both governments separately requested the right to choose judges *ad hoc* to join the bench, in accordance with Article 31(3) of the Court's Statute. The Court, however, considering the two applicant governments to be in the same interest and, so far as the choice of a judge *ad hoc* was concerned, to be reckoned as one party only, joined the proceedings in the two cases, in accordance with Article 31(5) of the Statute. The Applicants chose Sir Louis Mbanefo of Nigeria as their judge *ad hoc*, and the Respondent chose Judge J. T. van Wyk of South Africa as its judge *ad hoc*. *SWA Judgment* (1962): 321-22.

3. Ibid., pp. 324-26. For the full text of the submissions, see Appendix IV.

functions to be exercised by the United Nations to which annual reports and petitions are to be submitted.

3. The Union has practised apartheid, in violation of Article 2 of the Mandate and Article 22 of the Covenant, and it has the duty forthwith to cease such practice.

4. The Union has violated Article 2 of the Mandate and Article 22 of the Covenant by failing to promote to the utmost the material and moral well-being and social progress of the inhabitants of the territory and has the duty forthwith to proceed to carry out these obligations.

5. The Union has, by word and action, treated the territory in a manner inconsistent with its international status and has impeded opportunities for self-determination and has the duty to desist from such acts.

6. The Union has established military bases in the territory in violation of Article 4 of the Mandate, and has the duty to remove such bases forthwith.

7. The Union has failed to submit annual reports to the General Assembly, in violation of Article 6 of the Mandate.

8. The Union has failed to transmit petitions to the General Assembly, in violation of its obligations as Mandatory, and has the duty to submit same to the General Assembly.

9. The Union has attempted to modify substantially the terms of the Mandate without Assembly consent, in violation of Article 7 of the Mandate.

As can be seen, the submissions revolved around three fundamental issues: (1) the continued existence of the mandate; (2) international accountability; and (3) the promotion of the well-being of the inhabitants of the territory. As regards the first two issues the Applicants were, in effect, asking the Court to confirm the legal conclusions it had reached in the 1950 advisory opinion—that the mandate continued in force, the General Assembly replacing the League Council both with reference to such supervisory functions as reports and petitions and with regard to modification of the international status of the territory (Submissions 1, 2, 5, 7, 8, and 9). Submissions 3 and 4 related to alleged violations of the welfare clauses of the Mandate and involved essentially a factual determination.[4] The fundamental issue of apartheid was presented to the Court for the first time in this action and was, of course, dependent on determination of the first point, regarding the continued operation of the mandate. Essentially, Ethiopia and Liberia were, at one and the same time, acting on behalf of the United Nations in seeking to obtain an "order of specific performance" with regard to the principle of international accountability, and also on be-

4. There was also the specific charge of militarization of the territory (Submission 6).

half of the inhabitants of South West Africa in seeking to obtain a "cease and desist order" with reference to violations of the welfare provisions of the Mandate. The strategy was, therefore, a two-fold one. The United Nations would be confirmed in contentious proceedings in its supervisory powers and, at the same time, South Africa would be required to desist from certain conduct, primarily its practice of apartheid. In the event that South Africa would not hold itself accountable to the United Nations, and/or if it failed to desist from its unlawful conduct, the Applicants/United Nations would be able to enforce the judgment by means of Security Council action under Article 94 of the Charter.[5] The key to everything was the transformation of the legal conclusions of the 1950 advisory opinion into legally binding decisions of the Court. And the antecedent key to this, of course, was assumption of jurisdiction by the Court in these proceedings.

The Applicants, in asking the Court to assume jurisdiction, based themselves four-square on the 1950 pronouncement of the Court, and simply asked the Court to reaffirm its earlier stand on the subject.[6]

With reference to jurisdiction, the 1950 opinion had stated:

> According to Article 7 of the Mandate, disputes between the mandatory State and another Member of the League of Nations relating to the interpretation or the application of the provisions of the Mandate, if not settled by negotiation, should be submitted to the Permanent Court of International Justice. Having regard to Article 37 of the Statute of the International Court of Justice, and Article 80, paragraph 1, of the Charter, the Court is of opinion that this clause in the Mandate is still in force and that, therefore, the Union of South Africa is under an obligation to accept the compulsory jurisdiction of the Court according to those provisions.[7]

The Court, however, did not delineate the scope of the compulsory jurisdiction to which South Africa was subject. Did the Court mean that Article 7 related to the exercise of judicial supervision of the mandate, as Judge McNair held, or was the Court's authority limited to cases of actual material interest in dispute between the parties? But, more significantly, the Court gave no indication of how it reached the conclusion that Article 7 of the Mandate was still in force. Article 37 of the Statute only confers jurisdiction on the International Court of Justice if the treaty is "still in force." Did the Court mean that Article

5. On the strategy of the litigation generally, see Ernest A. Gross, "The South West Africa Cases: On the Threshold of Decision," *Columbia Journal of Transnational Law* III (1964): 19-25; Anthony D'Amato, "Legal and Political Strategies of the South West Africa Litigation," *Law in Transition Quarterly* IV (1967): 8-43.

6. *SWA Pleadings* I: 103; VII: 301-2, 316-17, 319, 325-26, 368.

7. *Status Opinion* (1950): 138. The Court also included the duty to submit to the compulsory jurisdiction of the Court in its *dispositif*. See above, chap. V, n. 8.

7 of the Mandate alone constituted a treaty? Or did it mean that the entire Mandate agreement was still in force as a treaty? In either case, who were the respective parties after the demise of the League? And who qualified as "another Member of the League," entitled to invoke Article 7? If the Court meant that the United Nations had fully replaced the League in the terms of the mandate, did this mean that all present and future members of the United Nations were entitled to invoke Article 7 of the Mandate?

These and other questions remained unclarified by the 1950 pronouncement. The respective pleadings in 1950 had directed very little attention to this issue;[8] and in the absence of any detailed reasoning in the opinion, the Court's pronouncement appeared as bare assertion.[9]

Some of these difficulties were emphasized in 1959 by Mr. Carpio, the Philippine representative and chairman of the Sub-Committee on Legal Questions to the Committee on South West Africa. The 1950 opinion, he noted,

> from . . . passing reference to Article 7 of the Mandate and Article 37 of the Court's Statute, concluded that this clause of the Mandate is still in force and that therefore South Africa is bound to accept the Court's compulsory jurisdiction. Article 37 . . . however, refers only to a treaty "in force" on which to base compulsory jurisdiction. It would seem, therefore, that before we can maintain compulsory jurisdiction of the Court, it must first be established that Article 7 of the Mandate, or for that matter the entire Mandate or Article 22 of the League Covenant, is "in force." The Advisory Opinion seems to beg this question rather than prove it.[10]

Further doubts, of a rather prophetic nature, on the jurisdictional issue were expressed by the representative of Mexico, in 1960, during Fourth Committee discussions.[11] He said:

> Considering the wording of the Mandate, it seems to my delegation that Article 7, on which the application is based, refers rather to

---

8. In all, only a few sentences were directed at the topic by the United States and South Africa, respectively. See *1950 Status Pleadings*, pp. 139, 288–90.

9. Only Judges McNair and Read, as indicated, considered, in their separate opinions, some of the foregoing questions to some extent. In their view, Article 7 provided for a system of judicial review of the conduct of the mandate; the term "Member of the League" was descriptive and not conditional; and the Mandate, as a treaty, was still in force. Every member of the United Nations (or party to the Statute of the Court) that was a member of the League at the date of its dissolution was entitled to invoke the compulsory jurisdiction of the Court under Article 7, so as to ensure fulfillment of the substantive obligations of the mandate. *Status Opinion* (1950): 158–59, 166, 169. The majority opinion did not consider these issues at all.

10. U.N. Doc. A/AC.73/2, Annex I, p. 2, Jan. 27, 1959.

11. U.N. Doc. A/C.4/459. The Fourth Committee decided that the remarks of the Mexican delegate warranted publication as a separate document. GAOR, 15th Sess., 4th Ctte., 1063rd Mtg., Nov. 24, 1960, p. 374. As indicated, later developments added to the significance of these remarks, and it is for this reason that they are quoted here *in extenso*.

specific violations by the Mandatory Power which may injure the defined interests of one or more Members of the League of Nations. My delegation has carefully studied the report of the Committee on South West Africa concerning the legal action open to Member States. It entirely shares the opinion of the Liberian and Ethiopian Governments that this action was recommended; it joins in the praise expressed in the Committee for their initiative in bringing this difficult matter before the Court.

Nevertheless, I have grave doubts regarding . . . the procedure itself. . . .

It is extremely difficult for a jurist to bridge the gap between the representation of the international community and the representation of Member States. Under the Statute of the Court, it is impossible for the international community, as such, to be a party. Consequently, except in the matter of advisory opinions, the United Nations cannot act directly. . . . Liberia and Ethiopia could have brought suit as parties injured by the Government of the Union because that Government does not carry out the purposes and principles of the Mandate. It is clear, however, from the application to the Court by the Liberian Government . . . that it is alleging before the Court all the violations committed by the Government of the Union which this Committee has discussed in past years.

Thus the Government of Liberia is bringing suit, not as a party injured by the Union Government's faulty exercise of the Mandate, but as a representative of the international community. This point is extremely difficult for me to understand. *And I am afraid that it might constitute an insurmountable obstacle, even for independent jurists with the best possible will.*[12]

Secondly, a study of the application made by the Government of Liberia leads me to conclude that there is no formal evidence of the injuries sustained by the Liberian Government directly, or through its citizens, as a result of the wrongful exercise of the Mandate. It is therefore quite possible that this may be grounds for another demurrer which would lead the Court to declare itself incompetent.

Lastly . . . there is the problem of negotiations. Liberia and Ethiopia state that the negotiations conducted with the Union Government have had no result whatsoever; the negotiations in question, however, are those in connection with the many proposals made and the numerous debates held in this Committee on the question of South West Africa.

It is also necessary to establish a connection which, while quite logical, is not necessarily legal. We wonder to what extent the Court can accept the proposition that negotiations are tantamount to

12. Emphasis supplied.

participating in discussions held in the United Nations; this is an extremely delicate point on which my delegation has serious reservations.

All of these jurisdictional issues were summed up in the four Preliminary Objections submitted by South Africa contesting the right of the Court to exercise jurisdiction.[13] In brief these were:

1. The Mandate for South West Africa (or, at least Article 7 thereof) never was, or is, at least since the dissolution of the League, no longer, "a treaty in force," within the meaning of Article 37 of the Court's Statute.

2. Neither Ethiopia nor Liberia is any longer, "another Member of the League of Nations," as required by Article 7 of the Mandate.

3. Ethiopia and Liberia lack any material interest in the alleged conflict and therefore no "dispute" is present within the meaning of Article 7.

4. It cannot be said that the alleged dispute "cannot be settled by negotiation," as required by Article 7.

These Objections were supported by lengthy and involved written and oral pleadings. Underlying all of the arguments was the basic premise that no sovereign state can be subjected to the jurisdiction of an international tribunal without its consent. This consent, the Respondent claimed, did not exist, and it was up to the Applicants to prove otherwise. In other words, the onus of proof for the existence of jurisdiction was upon the Applicants. The Applicants countered with their own Observations and oral arguments, and argued that the original consent to jurisdiction given by South Africa when it assumed the mandate continued in force and was fully applicable to the issue presented to the Court. They called upon the Court to dismiss the Preliminary Objections of the Respondent.

## THE 1962 JUDGMENT

The judgment of the Court on the Preliminary Objections was handed down on December 21, 1962. The Court concluded that

Article 7 of the Mandate is a treaty or convention still in force within the meaning of Article 37 of the Statute of the Court and

13. *SWA Judgment* (1962): 326–27. For full text, see Appendix IV. There had been considerable speculation whether South Africa would actually appear in Court to fight the case. It had not participated in either the 1955 or 1956 advisory proceedings, and perhaps it would boycott the present action as well. It was for this reason that the Applicants specifically requested the Court to "adjudge and declare" on their submissions, "whether the Government of the Union of South Africa is present or absent." Ibid., p. 322. See also Gross, "South West Africa Cases," p. 22; D'Amato, "Legal and Political Strategies," pp. 21–22. Under Article 62 of the Rules of Court, the filing of preliminary objections suspends the proceedings on the merits, until a decision is handed down on the objections.

that the dispute is one which is envisaged in the said Article 7 and cannot be settled by negotiation. Consequently the Court is competent to hear the dispute on the merits.
For these reasons,
THE COURT,
by eight votes to seven,
finds that it has jurisdiction to adjudicate upon the merits of the dispute.[14]

The Court reached this conclusion after rejecting each of the Respondent's Preliminary Objections in turn.

By way of introduction, the Court first established that a dispute in fact existed between the parties[15] and then proceeded to analyze the general nature of the mandates system. One of the essential principles of that system, said the Court, was the "recognition of 'a sacred trust of civilization' laid upon the League as an organized international community and upon its Member States."[16] The rights of the Mandatory in relation to the mandated territory and the inhabitants had "their foundation in the obligations of the Mandatory" and were, so to speak,

14. *SWA 1962 Judgment*, p. 347. Those voting with the majority were: Judges Alfaro (Panama), Badawi (U.A.R.), Moreno Quintana (Argentina), Wellington Koo (China), Koretsky (Soviet Union), Bustamante (Peru), Jessup (United States) and Sir Louis Mbanefo (Nigeria—Applicants' judge *ad hoc*). Those voting with the minority were: the President of the Court, Judge Winiarski (Poland) and Judges Basdevant (France), Spiropoulos (Greece), Sir Percy Spender (Australia), Sir Gerald Fitzmaurice (United Kingdom), Morelli (Italy), and van Wyk (South Africa—Respondent's judge *ad hoc*).
For discussion of the case, see J. H. W. Verzijl, *The Jurisprudence of the World Court* (Leyden: Sijthoff, 1965), II: 495–521; Elizabeth S. Landis, "South West Africa in the International Court: Act II, Scene I," *Cornell Law Quarterly* XLIX (1964): 179–227; Gerald M. Feder, David A. Rice, and Aaron Etra, "The South West Africa Cases: A Symposium," *Columbia Journal of Transnational Law* IV (1965): 47–118; C. Wilfred Jenks, *The Prospects of International Adjudication* (London: Stevens, 1964), pp. 490–95; R. B. Ballinger, "The International Court of Justice and the South West Africa Cases: Judgment of 21st December, 1962," *South African Law Journal* LXXX (1964): 35–62; Louis Favoreau, "L'Arrêt du 21 Decembre Sur Le Sud-Ouest Africain et L'Evolution du Droit Des Organisations Internationales," *Annuaire Francais De Droit International* IX (1963): 303–57; Leo Gross, "The International Court of Justice and the United Nations," Hague Academy, *Recueil des Cours* CXXI (II-1967): 315–439; G. Wynne, "Grounds for Revision of the Judgment of the International Court of Justice of 21 Dec. 1962, on Jurisdiction in the South West Africa Case," *South African Law Journal* LXXXI (1964): 449–57; C. J. R. Dugard, "Objections to the Revision of the 1962 Judgment of the International Court of Justice in the South West African Case," *South African Law Journal* LXXXII (1965): 178–91; Charles de Visscher, *Aspects Récents Du Droit Procédural De La Cour Internationale De Justice* (Paris: Pedone, 1966), passim. See also Leo Gross, "Limitations upon the Judicial Function," *AJIL* LVIII (1964): 415–31; and D. H. N. Johnson, "The Case Concerning the Northern Cameroons," *ICLQ* XIII (1964): 1143–58.
15. *SWA Judgment*(1962): 328. The Court considered that a dispute was clearly present, since the claim of one party, relating to the performance of mandatory obligations, was positively opposed by the other. It thus rejected the contrary view of Judge Morelli, who argued that no real dispute had existed between the parties before proceedings were instituted—a fact attested to by the lack of any claim or protest on the part of Ethiopia and Liberia, and of rejection of same by South Africa. Ibid., pp. 564–73.
16. Ibid., p. 329. This raised the question subsequently whether the "organized international community" was separate and distinct from the League, or identified with it. See below, pp. 220 and 263.

"mere tools given to enable it to fulfill its obligations." These features were "inherent in the Mandates System as conceived by its authors and as entrusted to the respective organs of the League *and* the Member States for application."[17]

These opening remarks provided the conceptual framework for the Court's subsequent detailed consideration of the specific issues.

*First Objection—Part I:*
*The Mandate never was a treaty.*

The First Objection centered on Article 37 of the Statute of the International Court of Justice.[18] According to the Applicants, this provision operated in conjunction with Article 7 of the Mandate[19] to confer jurisdiction on the International Court of Justice.

The Respondent, in the first half of its First Objection, maintained that Article 37 was inapplicable, because the Mandate never bore the character of a "treaty or convention"—having been constituted by a resolution of the League Council.[20] While the Mandate could, and did, qualify (in its time), as an international instrument with resultant rights and obligations, it could not come within the ambit of the *particular* type of international instrument required by Article 37, viz., a "treaty or convention." In support, Respondent pointed to the following considerations: (1) The Mandate was called a "declaration," not a treaty or convention. (2) It was not signed by any parties. (3) It was never ratified by any state. (4) It was never registered as a treaty, as required by Article 18 of the Covenant. (5) The League Council is not presumed to have possessed a treaty-making power in any case. (6) Moreover no agreement, in the form of a treaty, was ever concluded between the Mandatory and the Principal Powers, since the original plans for such an

17. *SWA Judgment* (1962): 329 (emphasis supplied). The Court hereby stressed that guardianship for the mandates system was placed not only upon the League as an entity but upon the members in their individual capacity as well. It was on this critical issue that the minority, and ultimately the 1966 Court, differed.

18. Article 37 of the Court's Statute reads as follows: "Whenever a treaty or convention in force provides for reference of a matter . . . to the Permanent Court of International Justice, the matter shall, as between the parties to the present Statute, be referred to the International Court of Justice."

19. Article 7, paragraph 2, of the Mandate for South West Africa reads as follows: "The Mandatory agrees that, if any dispute whatever should arise between the Mandatory and another Member of the League of Nations relating to the interpretation or the application of the provisions of the Mandate, such dispute, if it cannot be settled by negotiation, shall be submitted to the Permanent Court of International Justice."

20. See discussion above, pp. 39–42. Actually this particular submission arose out of questions put to the parties by Judge Spender. *SWA Pleadings* VII: 326–28. The Respondent had previously accepted as "common cause" that the Mandate had operated as a treaty during the life-time of the League. Ibid., p. 376. But in providing answers to the questions posed, the Respondent elected to amend its submissions. Ibid., p. 382. See also *SWA Judgment* (1962): 330.

arrangement were abandoned, and the Mandate was instead adopted in the form of a Council resolution.[21]

In rejecting this part of the First Objection, the Court held that the Mandate was not *only* the product of an executive action of the League Council. It was "in fact and in law . . . an international agreement having the character of a treaty or convention."[22] It incorporated the provisional terms of the Mandate agreed upon by the Mandatory and the Principal Powers, which were simply formally confirmed by the action of the Council. As a result, the Mandate was "a special type of instrument composite in nature and instituting a novel international regime."[23] The fact that it was titled a Declaration rather than a treaty was not crucial since "terminology" was not a determinant factor as to the character of an international agreement.[24] Nor was the fact of nonregistration of the Mandate under Article 18 of the Covenant significant. First, registration was required only for international engagements entered into "hereafter"—i.e., after January 10, 1920, when the Covenant took effect—and the conferral, acceptance, and provisional agreement on the terms of the Mandate had all occurred prior to that date. Second, the provision for registration was designed to secure publicity and avoid secret treaties, a consideration which obviously did not apply to an international instrument of an institutional character, to which the League, as represented by the Council, was itself a party.[25]

21. Respondent's argument on the nontreaty nature of the original Mandate had to overcome two major hurdles. First, both the parties and the Permanent Court in the *Mavrommatis* case in 1924 had proceeded on the necessary assumption that the Mandate (the Palestine Mandate in that case) was a treaty, and that the Court could exercise jurisdiction on the basis of Article 36 (1) of the Statute, which limited jurisdiction to "all cases which the parties refer to it and all matters specially provided for in *treaties and conventions* in force" (emphasis supplied). See the statement of Mr. Gross, *SWA Pleadings* VII: 380; and the separate opinion of Judge Jessup, *SWA Judgment* (1962): 406. But cf. the joint dissenting opinion of Judges Spender and Fitzmaurice, p. 494, n. 1. Second, if the Mandate had never been a treaty or convention, then the attempt to confer compulsory jurisdiction on the Permanent Court by means of Article 7 was totally meaningless and abortive *ab initio*. For in a concrete case arising even in the lifetime of the Permanent Court it would have been open to the Mandatory as Respondent to object that jurisdiction had never been provided for in a *treaty or convention*, as required by Article 36. The framers of the Mandate, who one day before its adoption signed the Protocol of Signature of the Court's Statute, would certainly have been surprised to learn of the nugatory effect of Article 7. This writer has not discovered any reference to this latter consideration, either in the pleadings or in any of the opinions.
22. *SWA Judgment* (1962): 330.
23. Ibid., p. 331. According to Judge Jessup, the adjudicatory clause, Article 7, constituted a separate agreement or treaty, between the Mandatory and the Principal Powers. Moreover, the League Council "defined" the Mandate (as per the preamble) only in the sense that it made the earlier agreements "definite" by approving them. Ibid., pp. 397–98, 401.
24. Ibid., p. 331. This point is particularly emphasized by Judge Jessup in his separate opinion. "Nothing in the form—or formlessness—or novelty of the Mandate, militates against its being considered a 'treaty'." Ibid., p. 405. "The notion that there is a clear and ordinary meaning of the word 'treaty' is a mirage." Ibid., p. 402.
25. Ibid., p. 332. Moreover, if nonregistration of the Mandate made it null and void *ab initio*, then South Africa lacked title over the territory in the first place. Ibid.

Judges Spender and Fitzmaurice, in their joint dissent, sought to prove that the Mandate had never been in force as a "treaty." It was, they said, merely a unilateral undertaking by South Africa expressed in the form of a League Council resolution. Whatever earlier intentions might have existed for formulating the Mandate as a treaty were abandoned in favor of constituting it in the form of a League resolution. As such, it was simply a quasi-legislative act but not a treaty (an "international agreement in written form . . . concluded between two or more States or other subjects of international law").[26]

*First Objection—Part 2:*
*In any case the Mandate was no longer "in force."*

In this submission, South Africa argued that the Mandate was no longer a "treaty in force," since the only possible second parties to the Mandate—the League of Nations and/or the members of the League, in their capacity as members—no longer existed.[27] As a *contractual arrangement*, then, the Mandate necessarily lapsed. This did not bear on the question whether the mandate survived as an institution or status. The holding in the 1950 advisory opinion regarding survival of the objective or "real" aspect of the mandate might be conceded. But the obligation in Article 7 to submit to jurisdiction was clearly a contractual obligation and, thus, of necessity came to an end with the extinction of the other party.[28]

Respondent recognized that its argument was contrary to the finding of the Court in 1950 that Article 7 was still in force. But this conclusion of the Court, Respondent maintained, had been based on the assumption that in 1946 South Africa had tacitly consented to the continuation of the mandate together with all its contractual obligations. Certain "new facts" not brought to the attention of the 1950 Court, however, contradicted any such assumption of tacit consent. Furthermore, South Africa contended that the views expressed in the advisory opinion on the question of jurisdiction could not be determinative in the instant contentious case; for the issue of jurisdiction was now for the first time squarely before the Court.[29]

In response, the Applicants stood by the 1950 conclusions. Respondent's arguments on the lapse of the Mandate as a contract, it was

---

Cf., in the matter of registration, the joint dissent of Judges Spender and Fitzmaurice, ibid., p. 494.

26. Ibid., pp. 474–94. See also the dissenting opinion of Judge Basdevant, ibid., pp. 460–61.

27. *SWA Pleadings* I: 298–360; VII: 29–156.

28. Ibid., I: 360; VII: 152–53.

29. Ibid., I: 345–46; VII: 91–106. For a review of Respondent's "new facts," see above, pp. 66–68, 71–72; and see below, p. 217.

said, had been presented to the Court at that time and had been rejected. The so-called "new facts" were neither new nor crucial. The essence of the 1950 opinion was the indivisibility of the mandate—with all the appurtenant rights and duties surviving the dissolution of the League. This fact enabled the United Nations to succeed to the supervisory powers of the League, and this same principle operated so as to sustain Article 7 in force.[30]

This, in essence was also the approach adopted by the Court. The contentions of the Respondent on the lapse of contractual obligations, it was said, were already advanced in 1950 and found untenable. South Africa's position had been viewed as an attempt to retain rights without at the same time assuming the concurrent obligations. "To exclude the obligations connected with the Mandate would be to exclude the very essence of the Mandate." As part of these obligations, the Court in 1950 had unanimously held that South Africa was subject to the compulsory jurisdiction of the Court. "The unanimous holding of the Court in 1950 on the survival and continuing effect of Article 7 of the Mandate, continues to reflect the Court's opinion today. Nothing has since occurred which would warrant the Court reconsidering it. All important facts were stated or referred to in the [1950] proceedings."[31] The Court further noted that each of the parties had subscribed to the Charter before the demise of the League and, therefore (as a result of the combined operation of Article 37 of the Court's Statute and Articles 92 and 93 of the Charter),[32] had "bound itself . . . to accept the compulsory jurisdiction of this Court in lieu of that of the Permanent Court." "The validity of Article 7 . . . was not affected by the dissolution of the League, just as the Mandate as a whole is still in force for the reasons stated above."[33]

Judges Spender and Fitzmaurice objected to the basic approach of the majority opinion. They considered (in line with the Respondent's views) that the 1950 pronouncement on the issue of jurisdiction was of "no real assistance . . . since no jurisdictional issue . . . was before the Court in 1950. Assumptions apparently made without any reasoning as to, or consideration of, the specific underlying issues involved, in an

30. *SWA Pleadings* I: 425–36; VII: 283–315.
31. *SWA Judgment* (1962): 334.
32. Article 92 stipulates that the Statute "forms an integral part of the . . . Charter." By Article 93, "All Members of the United Nations are *ipso facto* parties to the Statute of the International Court of Justice."
33. *SWA Judgment* (1962): 335. It might be noted that in the final summation preceding the *dispositif*, the Court concluded "that *Article 7 of the Mandate* is a treaty or convention still in force" (emphasis supplied); the Court did not speak of the mandate as a whole continuing in existence. This perhaps lends weight to the conclusion of the Court in 1966 that the 1962 judgment had not in any way intended to rule with finality on the question of the survival of the mandate, which was properly a matter for the merits. See *SWA Judgment* (1966): 19. But cf. the dissenting opinion of Judge Jessup, ibid., p. 337.

Advisory Opinion directed chiefly to other matters not involving any concrete jurisdictional question, clearly do not constitute a sufficient basis on which to found jurisdiction in subsequent contentious proceedings in which these issues are now directly raised."[34]

The Mandate had not, in their view *ever* been a treaty; but if it had, the only possible parties were South Africa and the League. "Since neither League nor Council exist now, the number of parties is less than two, and therefore, as a *treaty or convention*, the Mandate is no longer in force."[35] The continuation of the mandate "on an *institutional* basis," they stressed, could not affect the lapse of the Mandate as "*a treaty or convention*" in force as required by Article 37.[36] The Court was therefore not entitled to exercise jurisdiction.

*Second Objection:*
*Neither Ethiopia nor Liberia has* locus standi
*since neither is "another Member of the League*
*of Nations."*

South Africa maintained that even assuming Article 7 of the Mandate still to be in force it could only be applied in accordance with its terms. To invoke the compulsory jurisdiction of the Court, a state had to be "another Member of the League of Nations." Once the League was dissolved, no state could be described as "a Member of the League," and Article 7 could not be invoked for lack of *locus standi.*[37] This interpretation of the provision, it was said, accorded with the natural and ordinary meaning of the words. Any alternative interpretation would require the importation of words, e.g., a change from "Members of the League" to "*former* Members of the League."[38] Any such modification would have produced quite extraordinary results even in the time of the League: any state formerly a member would have been entitled to invoke the compulsory jurisdiction of the Court in reference to the mandate, despite present nonmembership in the international organization charged with supervision; that state might have even been ejected from the League; and its very action in instituting proceedings might be in direct conflict with the interests and policy of the international organization.[39] Such a result would be man-

---

34. *SWA Judgment* (1962): 472.
35. Ibid., p. 503 (emphasis in original).
36. Ibid., p. 495 (emphasis in original).
37. *SWA Pleadings* I: 361–65; VII: 156–99.
38. Ibid., I: 367–68.
39. Ibid., pp. 357, 371; VII: 165–66. In support, Respondent referred to an article by Manley O. Hudson in which he criticized Judge McNair's view that the term "another Member of the League" was descriptive, and not conditional. Hudson asked how such an interpretation would affect a state such as Brazil, which had left the League in 1923. Hudson concluded that "the meaning [of the term] is so imprecise that perhaps the Court might have shown more

ifestly absurd and contrary to the intention of the framers of the provision. Only present members of the League were entitled to invoke the
provision, and neither Applicant possessed this qualification.

In rejecting this approach, the Court indicated that the normal rule
of interpretation, whereby words are given their natural and ordinary
meaning, could not be applied in this instance, since it would result in a
meaning "incompatible with the spirit, purpose and context of the
clause or instrument in which the words are contained."[40] Three considerations dictated application of a nonliteral interpretation to the
words "another Member of the League of Nations."

> In the first place, judicial protection of the sacred trust . . . was
> an essential feature of the Mandates System . . . . The administra-
> tive supervision by the League constituted a normal security to
> ensure full performance . . . of the "sacred trust" . . . but the
> specially assigned role of the Court was even more essential, since it
> was to serve as the final bulwark of protection by recourse to the
> Court against possible abuse or breaches of the Mandate.[41]

The capacity of the mandatory power to block League action, as a
result of the unanimity principle operative in the League, high-lighted
the function of the Court as a guarantor that the obligations assumed
by the Mandatory would be faithfully fulfilled. Article 7 was of pivotal
importance in the successful functioning of the mandates system.

> In the second place, besides the essentiality of judicial protec-
> tion for the sacred trust and for the rights of Member States under
> the Mandates, . . . the right to implead the Mandatory Power before
> the Permanent Court was . . . conferred on the Members of the
> League, evidently also because it was the most reliable procedure of
> ensuring protection by the Court, whatever might happen to or
> arise from the machinery of administrative supervision.[42]

Finally, Article 7, with particular reference to the term "another
Member of the League of Nations" continued to be applicable because
"an agreement was reached among all the Members of the League at the
Assembly session in April 1946 to continue the different Mandates as
far as it was practically feasible or operable with reference to the obligations of the Mandatory Powers and therefore to maintain the rights of

---

hesitance in declaring the replacement to be made in the second paragraph of Article 7." *AJIL*
XLV (1951): 16. Cited in *SWA Pleadings* I: 371-72.
40. *SWA Judgment* (1962): 336.
41. Ibid.
42. Ibid., pp. 337-38. Why it should be assumed that in 1920, the states engaged in
creating the mandates system would have thought that the Court would outlive the League, is
not readily grasped. Cf. the separate opinion of Judge van Wyk, *SWA Judgment* (1966): 76.

the Members of the League, notwithstanding the dissolution of the League itself."[43] In support of this conclusion, the Court adduced both the contents of the final League resolution, as well as the various statements made by the mandatory powers during that session. Citing the statement made by the South African representative,[44] the Court stated:

There could be no clearer recognition on the part of the Government of South Africa of the continuance of its obligations under the Mandate for South West Africa, including Article 7, after the dissolution of the League of Nations.[45]

The common intention was to maintain, in treaty form, the force of the obligations assumed under the Mandate until other arrangements were agreed upon by the United Nations and the mandatory powers.[46]

43. *SWA Judgment* (1962): 338. This third point of the Court was the second of two arguments presented by the Applicants for according the term "another Member of the League" a broad interpretation. As presented by the Applicants, the events surrounding adoption of the resolution at the final session of the League Assembly demonstrated an intention that members be qualified to "carry over" the responsibilities of the League for as long as necessary. This arrangement was analogous to the power conveyed to parties to wind up a corporation.

The other argument, which the Court implicitly refused to accept, was a "succession" argument—whereby the United Nations replaced the League, and the members of the one organization replaced the members of the other in reference to mandates, so that the term "another Member of the League," now read, "another Member of the United Nations." See *SWA Pleadings* I: 429, 443, 445–49; VII: 319. For Respondent's comments see ibid., VII: 110–22, 355. Judge Bustamante, in his separate opinion, expressly declared that the events of 1945–46 clearly ruled out any possibility of automatic succession between the two world organizations. *SWA Judgment* (1962): 364. And see the joint dissenting opinion of Judges Spender and Fitzmaurice, ibid., pp. 515–16. Subsequently, Applicants abandoned any notion of automatic succession. See *SWA Pleadings* VIII: 132–33; and see Respondent's comment, ibid., pp. 311–12.

It is also noteworthy that the Court made no reference to Article 80(1) of the Charter, although this had been a mainstay of the 1950 opinion. On this point, see the dissenting opinion of Judge Basdevant, *SWA Judgment* (1962): p. 459; and the Spender—Fitzmaurice joint dissent, ibid., pp. 515–16. For Applicants' initial reliance upon Article 80(1) and the modification of their stand in the light of the 1962 judgment, see above, Chap. V, n. 16, and the citations there noted. But cf. the revival of Article 80(1) in *Namibia Opinion* (1971): 33–37, and the critical comments of Judge Fitzmaurice in his dissenting opinion, ibid., pp. 238–41.

44. See above, pp. 68–69.

45. *SWA Judgment* (1962): 340. The 1950 Court, it may be noted, did not find in the South African statement any intent to continue supervision of the mandate—administrative or judicial—beyond the demise of the League. At most, it was evidence of a desire to continue administrative obligations of the sacred trust, but implied nothing with regard to submission to external supervision. It is for this reason that, although that Court cited the South African statement with regard to the sacred trust, it did not refer to it in connection either with the supervision of the United Nations or the operation of Article 7. See *Status Opinion* (1950): 134–36, 137, 138.

46. The Court also rejected the argument which sought to confirm the nonessentiality of an adjudicatory clause to the functioning of a sacred trust from the fact that three out of four trusteeship agreements for former "C" mandates contained no adjudicatory clause. Judicial supervision was not as urgent in the trusteeship system, precisely because the League's unanimity rule had been replaced by a voting rule requiring, as a maximum, a qualified majority of

Judges Spender and Fitzmaurice rejected the Court's reasoning by contending that "the Court could not . . . both rely on the presence of Article 7 in the Mandate instrument, and refuse to apply it in accordance with the terms in which it figures there."[47] In their view, it was "in disregard of legal principle" to postulate "for certain States a right they only had in a capacity they have lost."[48] Could it be said that Brazil, once it left the League in 1923, still retained a right to invoke the compulsory jurisdiction of the Court with reference to the mandate? The cessation of League membership in 1946 by all of the members was as voluntary and deliberate as Brazil's, and they were no more entitled than Brazil to the rights of membership.[49] If Article 7 was indeed intended as a provision for "policing the Mandate," as the Court held, "could it seriously be suggested in everyday life that if a police force is disbanded, its ex-members can still go on exercising their former police functions?"[50] Moreover, the substantive differences introduced by the advent of Article 94 of the Charter had so drastically changed the burden of consequences on the Mandatory resulting from Article 7, that it was impermissible to extend or perpetuate the obligations under Article 7, "above and beyond its actual language."[51] The suggested modifications in Articles 7 and 37, to grant capacity where no capacity existed, would amount to "quasi-legislative 'rectification' " rather than "legitimate 'interpretation.' "[52]

The dissenting judges challenged each of the basic considerations employed by the majority opinion for not according the term "another Member of the League" a literal interpretation.

1) **The institution argument.** The fact that the mandate is held to survive as an institution cannot dictate that a particular article, which according to its terms has fallen, must also survive. It could only do so if the whole institution is dependent for its survival on this one clause.[53]

2) **The necessity argument.** The reasoning of the Court regarding the necessity of judicial supervision as a "last bulwark of protection" of the sacred trust was untenable. It was never intended that the League

---

two-thirds. *SWA Judgment* (1962): 342. Judges Spender and Fitzmaurice argued, however, that the explanation was inadequate, since General Assembly resolutions, in the final analysis, were at most recommendations. Judicial machinery to deal with a recalcitrant state, then, was no less urgent under the United Nations than under the League of Nations. Ibid., p. 523.

47. Ibid., p. 517.
48. Ibid., p. 504. But cf. the comment of Verzijl, *Jurisprudence of World Court*, II: 518.
49. *SWA Judgment* (1962): 509.
50. Ibid., p. 510.
51. Ibid., p. 511.
52. Ibid., p. 512.
53. Ibid., pp. 516–18.

should impose its views on a Mandatory. "The existence of the unanimity rule shows the exact reverse." The whole system was designed to operate through "discussion, negotiation, and common understanding," rather than through compulsion.[54] Moreover, the whole "necessity" argument regarding judicial supervision was really an application of the principle of "hindsight." Only Article 94 of the Charter could provide a coercive quality to Article 7 so as to control the mandatory power. But in 1920, when no corresponding Article existed, how crucial a provision could Article 7 have been in the operation of the mandates system? And how valid was it to give a broad and expansive interpretation to that provision now, on the basis of necessity?[55] Finally, if the concept of judicial supervision was regarded as absolutely essential to the operation of the mandates system, then why was it not included in Article 22 of the Covenant as one of the "securities" of the sacred trust?[56]

3) **The events of 1945–46.** The final ground of the Court for extending the effect of Article 7 was the alleged agreement of South Africa in 1946 to prolong the life of the mandate, including its obligation to submit to the jurisdiction of the Court. In the estimation of Judges Spender and Fitzmaurice, the Court's interpretation of the events of that time were at variance with the facts.[57] (a) The final League resolution only *"took note"* of certain expressions of *"intention"*; it did not "purport to impose or record any obligations."[58] (b) South Africa's statement regarding future intentions was clearly directed to administrative obligations relative to the welfare of the inhabitants, not to collateral obligations owed to members of the League. (c) South Africa had made abundantly clear at the final session of the League Assembly and during the founding conference of the United Nations at San Francisco that it intended to incorporate South West Africa into the Union. It was, therefore, "quite inconceivable" that South Africa was willing "simultaneously to perpetuate, possibly indefinitely, an obligation of compulsory jurisdiction."[59] (d) The United Nations, as is evident from the actions of its Preparatory Commission, deliberately refrained from taking over any supervision of the mandates, *per se*. Instead, the General Assembly called upon mandatory powers to conclude trusteeship agreements. Moreover, the fact that the original Chinese proposal at the

54. Ibid., p. 520.
55. Ibid., p. 521. The learned judges might have noted that even if a counterpart to Article 94 of the Charter had been incorporated in the Covenant, enforcement of judgments might, in any case, have been subject to the unanimity rule.
56. Ibid. They also rejected the Court's explanation for the absence of an adjudicatory clause in a number of trusteeship agreements. See above, n. 46.
57. *SWA Judgment* (1962): 526–41.
58. Ibid., p. 527 (emphasis in original).
59. Ibid., p. 530.

final session of the League Assembly calling for a transfer of super-visory powers from League to United Nations was replaced by a resolu-tion which did not more than *note* "that Chapters XI, XII and XIII of the Charter . . . embody principles corresponding to those declared in Article 22 of the Covenant," proved conclusively that the two Assem-blies were "unwilling to provide in *any* specific way for the conse-quences of the termination of the League."[60] In short, the events at the last League Assembly did not warrant implying "any undertaking, ex-press or implied, by the Mandatory, or any general agreement, in rela-tion to Article 7."[61]

*Third Objection:*
*There was no "dispute" as envisaged by Article 7.*

South Africa contended that the Applicants could not invoke Article 7 so as to confer jurisdiction on the Court, since the supposed conflict related to the general conduct of the mandate and did "not affect any material interest of the Applicants or their nationals."[62] But such a direct material interest was a necessary prerequisite for resort to Article 7. That Article does not itself create legal rights; it merely confers jurisdiction where legal rights are already in dispute. Nor can the words "any" and "whatever" flanking the word "dispute" in Article 7 in any way broaden the scope of the term "dispute," which relates only to a conflict involving rights and interests. The desire of a state to ensure observance of the sacred trust does not, in itself, consti-tute a legal interest, since the mandates system did not confer a right of this nature upon any individual state. Mandatory powers were answer-able to the League as an entity, not to each state individually. This is confirmed by the fact that Article 22 of the Covenant does not list "judicial supervision" (to be instituted by individual states) as one of the "securities" of the sacred trust.[63] Indeed, had "judicial supervision" been adopted, the Mandatory might well have been caught up in con-flicting demands made upon it by the Council, on the one hand, and an individual state bringing an action before the Court, on the other. And since every single state could press separate demands, pure chaos might result.[64] Significantly, too, the League Council alone (without consulta-

---

60. Ibid., p. 539. The two judges noted that this resolution included a reference to Chapter XI of the Charter. This indicated quite clearly that the members of the League had in mind that if mandates would not come under the trusteeship system by the conclusion of trusteeship agreements, Chapter XI would automatically apply to such mandated territories. In their view, the 1950 Court had wrongly disregarded the applicability of Chapter XI to the South West Africa situation. Ibid., pp. 541–44. See also ibid., pp. 532, 533.

61. Ibid., p. 544.

62. *SWA Pleadings* I: 376–94; VII: 200–39.

63. Ibid., I: 382; VII: 209, 213.

64. Ibid., I: 384–86; VII: 210.

tion with, or the agreement of, individual League members) was empowered by Article 7(1) of the Mandate to consent to modifications in the Mandate.[65] For all these reasons, Article 7 could not be said to refer to judicial supervision, and the Applicants therefore lacked *locus standi.*[66]

In response, the Applicants denied that the provision required a material, legal interest before it could be invoked.[67] The term "any dispute whatever" clearly covered the instant dispute, and the Respondent's interpretation was merely an attempt "to import . . . an unstated requirement" into the clause.[68] But furthermore, even if a "material interest" was indeed required, the Applicants were unquestionably endowed with such an interest. The design of the Covenant was to give all states, members of the League, a vested interest "in the welfare of the inhabitants of [mandated] areas." A legal interest could be based on humanitarian, moral, or political considerations, as much as on economic ones. Judicial supervision allowed for expression of this vested interest of member states in the observance of the sacred trust and in this respect the Court was "an integral part of the System's supervisory machinery."[69]

65. Ibid., I: 381; VII: 206.
66. Respondent noted that the 1950 majority opinion, although it held that Article 7 was still in force, made no reference to any concept of "judicial supervision" (in contradistinction to Judges McNair and Read). Ibid., I: 393; VII: 232.
67. Ibid., I: 450–73; VII: 323–25.
68. Ibid., I: 471.
69. Ibid., p. 459. As evidence that Article 7 related to judicial supervision, to be invoked by individual states, the Applicants cited a statement of the South African representative before the Fourth Committee in 1952. Upon that occasion, the representative noted that his government, in the course of negotiations with the *Ad Hoc* Committee that year, "had offered to submit to judicial supervision and to accept in that connection the compulsory jurisdiction of the International Court of Justice" so as to satisfy the *Ad Hoc* Committee's desire for "international supervision." "By equating 'judicial supervision' with 'international supervision' Respondent displayed an understanding of what 'judicial supervision' means in the context of Mandates." Ibid., p. 469. Counsel for Respondent denied that the quotation lent any support to the Applicants' interpretation of Article 7. The discussions in 1952 related purely to judicial supervision of a very restricted nature, connected with the proposed agreement between South Africa and the three powers. Ibid., VII: 233–34. The Applicants omitted to pursue the matter any further or to refer to the record of the *Ad Hoc* Committee itself.

However, an examination of the actual discussions as they took place between the South African representative and the *Ad Hoc* Committee reveal quite clearly, it is submitted, that that representative did, in fact, attribute a role of judicial supervision to the Court in the period of the League. The following excerpts from the record of his statement might be cited. "The former mandate had contained two forms of international supervision: the Permanent Mandates Commission and judicial supervision. In deference to the Committee's views his Government had agreed to submit to judicial supervision, accepting the compulsory jurisdiction of the International Court of Justice with regard to the administration of South West Africa. . . . His Government had agreed to revive the clauses in the first category. [Articles 2 to 5 of the Mandate, relating to the sacred trust.] As for clauses 6 and 7, his Government had agreed to accept judicial supervision. Thus, it had agreed to revive the basic principles of the entire mandate, with the sole exception of the question of reporting dealt with in clause 6." U.N. Doc. A/AC.49/SR.23, pp. 3–4.

The Court placed principal emphasis on the first part of the Applicant's argument, in rejecting the Third Objection of the Respondent.[70] Article 7 did not, in the Court's view, require the Applicant state to be acting in defense of a material right or interest.

> The Respondent's contention runs counter to the natural and ordinary meaning of . . . Article 7 . . . which mentions "any dispute whatever." . . . The language used is broad, clear and precise: it gives rise to no ambiguity and it permits of no exception.[71]
>
> . . . . . . . . . . . . . . . . . . . . . . . . . . . . . . . . . . . .
> The right to take legal action conferred by Article 7 on Member States of the League . . . is an essential part of the Mandate itself and inseparable from its exercise.[72]
>
> . . . . . . . . . . . . . . . . . . . . . . . . . . . . . . . . . . . .
> Protection of the material interests of the Members or their nationals is of course included within its compass, but the well-being and development of the inhabitants of the Mandated territory are not less important.[73]

Judge Jessup, in his separate opinion, centered chiefly on the second part of the Applicants' argument, in confirming their right to bring the action before the Court.[74] "International law has long recognized that States may have legal interests in matters which do not affect their financial, economic, or other 'material,' or, say, 'physical' or 'tangible' interests."[75] This principle of international law was illustrated by the right of a state to concern itself, on general humanitarian grounds, with atrocities in foreign countries, and by international efforts directed at suppression of the slave trade and the prevention of acts of genocide. The mandates system was one of at least four great manifestations in

---

This statement reveals very clearly that South Africa understood that Article 7 related to a system of judicial supervision in the period of the League. No doubt, this statement in itself could hardly provide conclusive evidence as to the correct meaning of Article 7, but it does at least indicate that Respondent, perhaps in an unguarded moment, did interpret the provision in accordance with the interpretation submitted by the Applicants. Had it been brought to the attention of the Court, it is respectfully submitted, it might have qualified as something of probative value, which the 1962 majority might have cited and the 1966 majority would have had to overcome.

70. *SWA Judgment* (1962): 342–44. As for the second of Applicants' arguments, see p. 343, the sentence beginning: "For the manifest scope and purport" etc.

71. Ibid., p. 343.

72. Ibid., p. 344.

73. Ibid. Rosenne supports the broad view adopted by the Court. "Conflict of legal interests is only one type of controversy which can be brought before the Court. Indeed, it is probably true to say that the objective of the settlement of international disputes is more prominent in the theory of international litigation than the mere protection of legal rights and interests." *The Law and Practice of the International Court* (Leyden: Sijthoff, 1965), II: 518–19.

74. *SWA Judgment* (1962): 422–33.

75. Ibid., p. 425.

1919-20 of the recognition of the interest of all states in matters occurring in any quarter of the globe.[76] These were: (1) Article 11 of the Covenant, which recognized "that peace was indivisible"; (2) the protection of minorities; (3) the recognition in the Constitution of the International Labor Organization of a general interest in humane conditions of labor in all countries; and (4) the mandates system, which recognized the principle of the "sacred trust of civilization." Each of the last three arrangements contained provision for the exercise of the Court's jurisdiction, and in each instance no "material" interest was required for a state to invoke such jurisdiction. The common conviction was "that just as peace was indivisible, so too was the welfare of mankind."[77]

Judge Jessup referred also to the Tanganyika clause for support of his broad interpretation of Article 7.[78] The Tanganyika Mandate, it will be recalled,[79] contained an adjudicatory clause composed of two paragraphs. The first paragraph was identical to the adjudicatory clause in Article 7 of the South West Africa Mandate; the second paragraph empowered states, members of the League, to bring actions "on behalf of their nationals for infraction of their rights." Obviously, then, the first paragraph "must mean something different from, or more than," claims on behalf of citizens. Very clearly it referred to the right of states to initiate action in relation to the welfare of the mandate population.[80]

The broad interpretation of the term "dispute" adopted by the majority opinion was vigorously criticized by the minority judges. On no other of the Respondent's Objections were the dissenting judges as much in unison as they were in according Article 7 a restrictive scope of operation.[81]

In a sharp and lucid opinion,[82] Judge Winiarski stated the basic rule as: "no interest, no action." An applicant state basing itself upon

76. Ibid., pp. 429-31.
77. Ibid., p. 431.
78. Ibid. For the contrary view, see below, n. 93; and chap. XI, n. 38. For a consideration of the opposing viewpoints regarding the Tanganyika clause, see Aaron Etra, "Justiciable Disputes: A Jurisdictional and Jurisprudential Issue," *Columbia Journal of Transnational Law* IV (1965): 100-3.
79. See above, pp. 43-44.
80. Respondent subsequently endeavored to suggest an interpretation of the Tanganyika clause different from Judge Jessup's. *SWA Pleadings* II: 191-92. See above Chap. II, n. 13.
81. See the dissenting opinions of Judges Winiarski, *SWA Judgment* (1962): 458; Basdevant, ibid., pp. 462-64; Spender and Fitzmaurice, ibid., pp. 547-60; Morelli, ibid., pp. 569-70; and van Wyk, ibid., pp. 658-62. The only dissenting judge who did not express a clear view on the Third Objection was Judge Spiropoulos. However, from his short Declaration (ibid., pp. 347-48), it would appear that his dissent was not based on the Third Objection; and this would be consistent with his stand in the *Northern Cameroons* case that the application of Cameroon should have been held admissible. (See *ICJ Reports* [1963]: 39.) Nevertheless, he concurred with the 1966 *South West Africa* judgment.
82. *SWA Judgment* (1962): 449-58.

Article 7, as upon any other compromissory clause, must possess "a subjective right, a real and existing individual interest which is legally protected."[83] In support of the restrictive view, he cited historical considerations, League practice, the terms of Article 7, and legal and judicial authority.

1) **Historical background.** The mandates system, it is well known, was only reluctantly accepted by the mandatory powers. It would be totally unreasonable, therefore, to assume that they had accepted a duty of "judicial accountability . . . towards any Member of the League which might take exception to their administration of the Mandate."

> This *actio popularis* would have been such a novelty in international relations, going far beyond the novelty of the Mandates system itself in its implications, that, if the drafters of these instruments had all agreed on the self-imposition of such a responsibility, they would not have failed to say so explicitly, as they did in the case of certain States subjected to the minorities régime.[84]

2) **League practice.** The League Council never regarded Article 7 as an ancillary aid in its supervision of the mandate. Rather, supervision was considered to be preeminently a political function, to be exercised with the cooperation of the mandatory power.[85] The Council never entertained the idea of coercing a mandatory power through the instrumentality of a member of the League appearing before the Court in the capacity of "agent," and never even requested an advisory opinion on any matter related to the mandates system. The idea of "judicial supervision" was alien to the spirit and practice of the mandates system. Certainly, no one seems to have regarded it, as the Court would have it, "as an essential security in the Mandates System."[86]

3) **The terms of Article 7.** In accordance with the terms of Article 7, the Court was only qualified to assume jurisdiction "if it [the dispute] cannot be settled by negotiation." This condition denoted that the dispute had to be of a type which was amenable to settlement by negotiation. But in the present case, "the three States are unable to settle by negotiation between themselves the questions which are the subject-matter of the submissions of the Applicants because they do not involve their rights and interests." The Applicants were merely acting in a representative capacity and were incapable of negotiating on such

83. Ibid., p. 455.
84. Ibid., p. 453. Even in the case of the minorities treaties, *imposed* by the Principal Allied and Associated Powers upon the "new States" and certain other states, judicial accountability was established only toward members of the Council (not of the League as a whole). Ibid., p. 452.
85. Ibid., p. 454.
86. Ibid., p. 458.

matters as annual reports, petitions, preparations for self-government, etc. "They do not have control over these problems, over these duties and these interests." They were powerless to make either concessions or demands with reference to these matters.[87]

**4) Judicial and scholarly authority.** In the *Mavrommatis* case, the interpretation suggested by the Applicants was endorsed by only two members of the Court. The remainder of the Court, however, was unable to accept such a broad and sweeping interpretation of what was a standard compromissory clause.[88] In 1950, again, only two judges, McNair and Read, regarded Article 7 as a provision relating to judicial supervision, but the Court was unable to subscribe to that view.[89] So far as scholarly authority was concerned, Professor Feinberg in 1937 had said: "I consider that the judicial settlement clause does not confer on Members of the League of Nations the right unilaterally to bring a Mandatory Power before the Court except in cases where they can allege the violation of some right of their own or some injury to the interests of their nationals."[90]

Judge Winiarski concluded that the Applicants "lack capacity to take legal action."[91]

Many of the points referred to by Judge Winiarski were also stressed by Judges Spender and Fitzmaurice. However, additionally, they devoted attention both to the original intentions of the framers of Article 7 of the Mandate, and the chaotic consequences that could arise from according each and every individual state the right to implead a mandatory (or trust) power before the Court. The Mandate, they noted, contained two categories of provisions. One class related to the welfare of the people of the territory (the "conduct" provisions), while the other related to the commercial, missionary, and other interests of League members (the "State rights and interests" class).[92] From the *travaux préparatoires* it was clear that the adjudication clause was designed to protect the states' interests only and was never intended "to enable them to intervene in matters affecting solely the conduct of the Mandate in relation to the peoples of the mandated territory."[93]

87. Ibid., pp. 457–58. Judge Winiarski also referred to Article 62 of the Court Statute to demonstrate that a state required "an interest of a legal nature" to intervene in, or initiate, an action before the Court. Ibid., pp. 455–56.

88. Ibid., p. 451.

89. Ibid. It may be noted that Judge Winiarski was a member of the 1950 Court.

90. Ibid., p. 455. The view of Professor Feinberg is also cited approvingly by Judges Spender and Fitzmaurice, ibid., p. 558, n. 1.

91. Ibid., p. 457.

92. Ibid., pp. 549–50.

93. Ibid., p. 559. The Tanganyika clause was dismissed as "one of those drafting quirks that constantly occur at international conferences." "There was simply a failure to drop the second part, as being superfluous." And "no useful information as to the meaning of the first

Furthermore, it was impossible to reconcile the view that Article 7 related to disputes about the general conduct of the mandate with the supervisory functions given to the League Council. The Mandatory could be subject to contrary directives from Court and Council, and moreover, could always be faced with innumerable demands from individual states.[94] Quite obviously, supervision of the general conduct of the mandate was entrusted exclusively to the Council and was not connected with Article 7 at all.

For this conclusion Judges Spender and Fitzmaurice (in their introductory remarks) found strong confirmation in the very nature of the task confronting the Court on the merits. It was apparent from the Memorials that the principal issue would be whether the respondent state was in breach of its obligation under Article 2 of the Mandate to "promote to the utmost the material and moral well-being and the social progress of the inhabitants of the territory." They went on to state:

> There is hardly a word in this sentence which has not now become loaded with a variety of overtones and associations. There is hardly a term which would not require prior objective definition, or redefinition, before it could justifiably be applied to the determination of a concrete legal issue. There is hardly a term which could not be applied in widely different ways to the same situation or set of facts, according to differing subjective views as to what is meant, or ought to mean in the context; and it is a foregone conclusion that, in the absence of objective criteria, a large element of subjectivity must enter into any attempt to apply these terms to the facts of a given case. They involve questions of appreciation rather than of objective determination. As at present advised we have serious misgivings as to the legal basis on which the necessary objective criteria can be founded. . . .
>
> The above considerations . . . strongly reinforce the view which, on other grounds, we have taken as to the third preliminary objection, namely that disputes about the conduct of the Mandate in relation to the "sacred trust" . . . are not the kind of disputes to which the compulsory adjudication clause of the Mandate was intended to, or did, apply.[95]

In short, if the task of supervision was inherently nonjusticiable, then very clearly it could not have been meant that individual states

---

part can be derived" from this. Ibid., p. 560, and n. 1. See also the comment of Judge Winiarski: "No one has been able to explain how this paragraph, which seems completely unnecessary, got into the Mandate for Tanganyika and that Mandate alone, but this is not of the slightest importance." Ibid., p. 454.

94. Ibid., p. 552.

95. Ibid., pp. 466–67.

would be entitled to invoke the Court's jurisdiction in the matter of supervision.

*Fourth Objection:*
*There have been no negotiations.*

South Africa pointed out that Ethiopia and Liberia were not claiming that direct diplomatic intercourse had ever taken place between the parties on the issues in dispute. The Applicants argued that their participation in General Assembly discussions and endorsement of United Nations efforts at negotiation had amply satisfied the implicit requirement of Article 7 for prior efforts at settlement of the dispute by negotiation. South Africa, for its part, did not deny that such negotiations had taken place. It claimed, however, that various factors operated to make these negotiations less than meaningful.[96] In short, they had never been conducted with "no holds barred." These factors were:

1) The terms of reference of the various United Nations committees were overly restrictive.

2) Negotiating committees were simultaneously authorized to supervise—a duality of function which could only inhibit negotiations.

3) South African acceptance of United Nations supervision as a basis for negotiation was made a prior condition of negotiations.

4) Persistent urging by a majority of the Assembly, expressed by means of Assembly resolutions, that South Africa bring South West Africa under the trusteeship system, suggested that nothing less would be ultimately acceptable.

Until the Respondent "has been afforded a real and genuine opportunity to negotiate it can *not* be said that the dispute is one which cannot be settled by negotiation."[97]

The Court approached the question of negotiations by considering the relevant section of Article 7.[98] The phrase, "if it cannot be settled by negotiation," it was said, assumed that an attempt to settle the dispute by negotiation had at least been made, and that further negotiations would most likely be fruitless.

The dispute between the parties to the present action, the Court noted, was matched by a similar dispute between the Respondent and the members of the United Nations as a whole. And though they were

---

96. *SWA Pleadings* I: 395–405; VII: 239–59. See also above, Chap. VI, n. 24.
97. *SWA Pleadings* VII: 248 (emphasis in original).
98. *SWA Judgment* (1962): 344–46.

two different disputes, the questions at issue were identical.[99] "The fact that a deadlock was reached in the collective negotiations in the past and the further fact that . . . the present proceedings . . . confirmed the continuance of this deadlock,[100] compel a conclusion that no reasonable probability exists that further negotiations would lead to a settlement."[101]

As for Respondent's claim that "collective negotiations in the United Nations are one thing and direct negotiations between it and the Applicants are another," the Court remarked:

> Diplomacy by conference or parliamentary diplomacy has come to be recognized . . . as one of the established modes of international negotiation. . . . If . . . [a dispute] is one of mutual interest to many States, whether in an organized body or not, there is no reason why each of them should go through the formality and pretence of direct negotiation with the common adversary State after they have already fully participated in the collective negotiations with the same State in opposition.[102]

It was clear, therefore, that negotiation had in fact taken place between the parties and that it had not resolved the dispute.

Judges Spender and Fitzmaurice denied that any negotiations at all had taken place.[103] It was not sufficient to say that a *similar* dispute existed with the United Nations and that negotiations relative to *that* dispute had taken place. The parties before the Court had never themselves engaged in any direct negotiations and, manifestly, the requirement of Article 7 remained unfulfilled. Negotiations confined to the floor of an international assembly could not be deemed meaningful negotiations. Such public discussions "are, and necessarily must be, of too general and diffused a character to constitute a negotiation between the specific parties who eventually come before the Court in relation to

99. Rosenne is of the view that the Court purposely stressed the fact that the two disputes were distinct and separate, so as "to preserve the independence of the fields of activity of the General Assembly and the Court, and prevent any possible plea of *litispendance* (or its political equivalent) from interfering with the freedom of action of either organ." *Law and Practice of International Court*, II: 516.

100. Leo Gross, "The International Court of Justice and the United Nations," p. 384, n. 182, very correctly asks what relevance proceedings before the Court could have for confirming a deadlock in negotiations, when the Court itself acknowledged that the crucial date was "the time when the applications were filed." See *SWA Judgment* (1962): 344.

101. Ibid., p. 345. This point was summed up by Judge Jessup in these words: "In this respect States are not eternally bound by the old adage: 'If at first you don't succeed, try, try again.'" Ibid., p. 435.

102. Ibid., p. 346. Cf. Leo Gross "The International Court of Justice and the United Nations," p. 379, on the question whether an "interpolation" of the terms "international" or "collective" negotiations into Article 7 was desirable, in the light of a general "interest in preserving the integrity of adjudication clauses."

103. *SWA Judgment* (1962): 560–63.

a specific dispute between them as States."[104] It was consequently untenable to "hold *and adjudge* that the dispute (that *any* dispute) 'cannot' be settled, when no recourse at all has been had" to the normal procedure of settling a dispute by means of diplomatic negotiation.[105]

It has been justly observed that the majority view rests essentially upon "far-reaching considerations of international public policy"[106] —an approach which the dissenting judges rejected. In essence, the difference of opinion centered on the applicability of the principle of effectiveness to the relevant instruments and whether jurisdiction of the Court could be affirmed on this basis alone. The 1950 opinion had indicated that Article 7 was still in force and that the Court was qualified to exercise jurisdiction. But, as the Philippine delegate had said, this assertion seemed "to beg this question rather than prove it."[107] The Court considered, however, that in postulating the survival of the mandate as an international regime or institution, the 1950 opinion had effectively confirmed the indivisibility of the mandate, so that it remained intact in all its parts. This meant that the obligations of the Mandatory to submit to international supervision could not be severed from its continued authority to administer the territory. As a result, the technical terminology of the adjudicatory clause could not be allowed to frustrate the authority of the Court to exercise judicial supervision. It was only by having regard to the integrity of the institution as a whole that one could assess whether a particular provision, such as Article 7, continued in force. In 1950 the Court had emphasized the role of the General Assembly in the continued survival of the mandate institution. But ten years of effort demonstrated the futility of that line of endeavor, and so, in 1962, the need to ensure the continued viability of the mandate required the Court to assert fully its own role of judicial supervision. The common concept underlying both pronouncements of the Court was that international obligations freely assumed should not be permitted to be lightly abandoned; the institution of the mandate must therefore be effectively preserved.

The minority was unable to accept this teleological approach. In its view, jurisdiction could only rest on clearly manifested consent, and this had to be proved, in Lauterpacht's words, "up to the hilt."[108] In

104. Ibid., p. 562.
105. Ibid. (emphasis in original).
106. Jenks, *International Adjudication*, p. 491.
107. See above, p. 188.
108. Sir Hersch Lauterpacht, *The Development of International Law by the International Court* (London: Stevens, 1958), p. 91. Judge Spiropoulos, in his short declaration, said: "To be upheld, the Court's jurisdiction must be very clearly and unequivocally established, and that does not seem . . . to be the case here." *SWA Judgment* (1962): 348. See also remarks of Judges

view of the principle of state sovereignty, the Court, in case of doubt, was not permitted to exercise jurisdiction. The survival of an international institution was not, in itself, sufficient to confirm jurisdiction if the particular adjudicatory provision failed to confer such authority.

But more fundamental than the difference between effective or restrictive interpretation of specific provisions was the more general difference of opinion over the nature of the mandates system—its design and mode of functioning, and the role of the Court within the overall scheme. As noted above, although each of the dissenting judges supported one or another of the Respondent's Preliminary Objections, they were most united in upholding the Third Objection and in confirming that the Court did not possess a power of judicial supervision. It was here that the critical issue between majority and minority was most sharply defined—reflected in the narrow 8 to 7 division in the Court. The minority held that the operation of the mandates system was at base a political matter, to be resolved by political means, through political organs. The system functioned in an atmosphere of cooperation and conciliation, not coercion.

The majority, however, considered that the mandates system was, notwithstanding its political attributes, a legal institution in which judicial authority played a crucial role. The obligations of the Mandatory were not just political commitments but legally enforceable duties. In this arrangement, the Court was indeed "the final bulwark of protection" for the sacred trust. Furthermore, the majority—again undoubtedly with considerations of international public policy in mind—deemed it essential for the Court, as the principal judicial organ of the United Nations, to sustain the "constitutional document" established by the 1950 opinion.

In a situation where the political organs were stymied, it was doubly urgent for the Court to assume a more active role in ensuring the preservation of the "rule of law" in international affairs. The Mandate conferred authority on the Court, and the Court should not avoid or evade this responsibility. The sacred trust could not be allowed to go by default and just disappear into thin air. If the Court was powerless, then this meant that virtually no international institution could exercise any supervision over South West Africa, and the *de facto* annexation of the territory would be more than complete. If it was questionable whether the Court could extend its legal net over the territory, it was even more questionable whether South Africa should be permitted to abscond from any international control.

---

Winiarski, ibid., p. 458; Basdevant, ibid., pp. 459-60, 463; Spender and Fitzmaurice, ibid., pp. 467, 472-74; van Wyk, ibid., p. 575.

The minority judges, however, implied that the very considerations underlying the Court's reasons for intervening should have led the Court to refrain from such action. The whole mandates question was a political not a legal issue, and the South West Africa question pre-eminently so. This was not the occasion for the Court—an institution devoted strictly to making judicial, i.e., legally grounded, decisions—to intervene.

The sharp and close division over the proper role of the Court, it could have been expected, would bear heavily on the Court's consideration of the issue on the merits. In the event, it was crucial.

# THE COURT
# BATTLE:
# THE METAMORPHOSIS
# OF NUREMBERG INTO
# *BROWN V. BOARD OF EDUCATION*

## THE ISSUES ON THE MERITS

The merits phase of the proceedings commenced with the submission by South Africa of its Counter-Memorial on January 10, 1964. In contrast to Applicants' one-volume Memorial of 180 pages, the Counter-Memorial consisted of some ten volumes and supplement totaling over 1,400 pages. It contained extensive arguments on the legal issues involved (including a renewed challenge to the standing of the Applicants) along with a detailed exposition of conditions in South West Africa designed to refute the charges of violations of the welfare clauses of the Mandate. All in all the forensic struggle on the merits ran on for a period of some three years and produced a veritable mountain of legal material from both written and oral pleadings, as well as the testimony and cross-examination of experts and witnesses.

Normally, the pleadings in a case—the arguments presented, as well as the tactics adopted, by the contending parties—provide a vital key to understanding the result reached by the Court. But in the *South West Africa* cases, since in 1966 the Court denied Ethiopia and Liberia the right to obtain a decision on the merits, one might assume that for an appreciation of the judgment a study of the voluminous pleadings is totally irrelevant and wholly misplaced. Nothing, however, could be more misplaced than this assumption itself. For, in fact, it is only by seeing how the case evolved and what was asked of the Court that one can gain proper perspective on the refusal of the Court to make any determination on the merits. The formulation of Applicants' case, the tergiversations of the Applicants in the case, and the radical bases upon which the challenge to apartheid was ultimately premised all had direct implications for the "antecedent question" raised by the Court in 1966, viz., whether Applicants were, indeed, entitled to obtain a Court ruling on the merits. The legal disputation surrounding the apartheid issue served to throw into sharp relief the more fundamental issue of the place of "judicial supervision" in the functioning of the mandates system. Such doubts as were already expressed within the Court in 1962 regarding the justiciability of Article 2(2) of the Mandate received their most dramatic confirmation by the manner in which the case on the merits was unfolded before the Court.

The 1966 judgment of the Court has been variously labeled by its critics as unjust,[1] politically grounded,[2] or, even worse, racially motivated.[3] How far these charges accord with the facts and the degree to which the Court conformed to, or strayed from, the judicial function can only be assessed on the basis of a careful examination of the positions adopted by the parties in the course of the pleadings on the merits.

Three main issues on the merits were presented to the Court by the Applicants in their Memorials.[4] These were:

1) whether the mandate for South West Africa remained in existence or had lapsed;

2) whether the United Nations had succeeded to the supervisory powers of the League with respect to both annual reports and petitions, so that South Africa, by refusing to submit to United Nations supervision, was in violation of the mandate; and

3) whether the application of apartheid to South West Africa constituted a violation of Article 2 of the Mandate and Article 22 of the Covenant.[5]

1. Thus, in the view of Keith Highet, one of the Counsel for Ethiopia and Liberia, "the judgment does not appear to be 'just.' . . . The maxim that not only must justice be done, but must appear to be done, should apply to international tribunals as well as to domestic courts." "The South West Africa Cases," *Current History* LII (1967): 160.

2. Wolfgang Friedmann has described the judgment as "probably the most 'political' ever rendered by the International Court or its predecessor." "The Jurisprudential Implications of the South West Africa Case," *Columbia Journal of Transnational Law* VI (1967): 10.

3. Representatives of the Afro-Asian bloc in the United Nations have unabashedly charged the members of the 1966 majority with bias. But even the United States representative to the United Nations Human Rights Commission, Mrs. Rita Hauser, has said that the International Court of Justice is "prejudiced by the taint of colonialism." *Proceedings of the American Society of International Law, AJIL* LXIV (1970): 124.

4. The text of Applicants' formal submissions are to be found in *SWA Judgment* (1966): 12–13, and are reproduced in Appendix IV, below.

5. Six of the nine formal submissions (nos. 1, 2, 3, 4, 7 and 8) may be subsumed under the three main issues outlined above. Submissions 5 and 9 raised the further issue of the international status of the territory and submission 6 related to the question of the establishment of military bases in South West Africa. But these latter issues never assumed more than tangential significance in the forensic struggle and will not be singled out for special consideration. It should, however, be noted that the changes which the Applicants were subsequently

As against Applicants' request for an affirmative Court ruling on these issues, South Africa contended in its submissions that:

1) the whole mandate had lapsed upon the dissolution of the League, and, consequently, South Africa no longer had any obligations under the Mandate;

2) alternatively, even if the mandate as such endured after the dissolution of the League,

a) no supervisory power relative to South West Africa, with respect to either reports or petitions, had passed to the United Nations; and

b) South Africa had not, "in any of the respects alleged, violated its obligations as stated in the Mandate or in Article 22 of the Covenant."[6]

## THE MANDATE AND UNITED NATIONS SUCCESSION

The issues of the continuance of the mandate and United Nations succession to the supervisory powers of the League had, of course, both been dealt with in the proceedings on the Preliminary Objections. Nonetheless, Respondent now reargued *in extenso* various aspects of those earlier pleadings. Applicants, contending that Respondent had already "had its day in Court on these issues," complained about this seemingly needless repetition.[7] However, it must be recognized that a decision at the preliminary objection stage, even as an earlier advisory opinion, can not preclude the Court from considering the issues afresh at the merits stage.[8] Moreover, technically at least, the issues argued before and after 1962 were different. Before 1962, the central question debated was the continued existence of the Mandate *as a contractual relationship*; after 1962, it was the continuation of the mandate *as an institution*. Furthermore, while certain of Respondent's arguments were similar to those presented earlier, these were now directed toward developing a very different thesis. The new approach was analytically the inverse of the earlier. Previously, South Africa's major premise had been that the mandate had lapsed automatically upon the disappearance of the other party—the League; and the absence of supervision

---

induced to make in their case on apartheid affected the other charges as well and resulted in a series of amendments to the submissions. For further discussion of this topic, see below, pp. 260-61.

6. *SWA Judgment* (1966): 14. For text, see below, Appendix IV.

7. *SWA Pleadings* IV: 552.

8. See Applicants' Reply, ibid., p. 522, and comment of Respondent, ibid., V: 15-16. See also ibid., II: 98-103; VIII: 582-83. For the view of the Court, see *SWA Judgment* (1966): 19, 36-38, 42-43. Even Judge Tanaka, while dissenting from the 1966 judgment, acknowledged the Court's right to consider anew at the merits stage the substantive issue of the existence of the mandate. Ibid., p. 261. But cf. the view of Judge Jessup, ibid., p. 337. For further discussion of this topic, see below, pp. 292-94.

(judicial or administrative) followed as a corollary from this major premise. But now the starting point was the absence of United Nations succession to the League's supervisory powers; and the conclusion was that without the element of international supervision, regarded as "essential" to the operation of the mandate by both the 1950 and 1962 Courts, the mandate as a whole must be deemed to have lapsed.[9]

The initiative in defining the case on the continuance of the mandate and on United Nations supervision rested, in considerable measure, with the Respondent. In their Memorials, Applicants did not present any substantive arguments on these issues, but merely requested the Court to reaffirm the conclusions of the 1950 advisory opinion.[10] It was only during the course of the pleadings and at each stage, in reaction to Respondent's challenge to the 1950 opinion, that Applicants were forced to come to grips with the underlying questions involved. And in their reactive role, Applicants in the end came to rest much of their case on South African consent to United Nations supervision—something upon which they initially denied placing any reliance.

In presenting its thesis, South Africa, as noted, focused first on the question of United Nations succession.[11] The supervisory arrangements instituted under the mandates system, it was stressed, related exclusively to a specific international body composed in a defined manner and endowed with limited and precise powers and functions. There was no commitment to "international accountability" in the abstract, which could attach itself to any general international organization that happened to be operating at the time. International law knew of no such vague nebulous body as the "organized international community" toward which rights and obligations could accrue.[12] The texts of the basic instruments and their *travaux préparatoires* were cited to confirm the very restricted nature of the compromise worked out at Versailles between President Wilson and the Dominion ministers.[13]

9. See *SWA Pleadings* V: 25-26.
10. Ibid., I: 95, 103. The only argument presented was directed at persuading the Court that the opinion should be regarded as having settled these issues since "an advisory opinion as to a dispute is 'substantially equivalent to deciding the dispute'," a thesis allegedly derived from the *Eastern Carelia* case. Ibid., p. 98. Respondent denied that any such thesis could be derived from the *Eastern Carelia* case. See ibid., II: 99-102. For an analysis of the *Eastern Carelia* case, see Michla Pomerance, *The Advisory Function of the International Court in the League and United Nations Eras: A Comparative Study* (Baltimore: The Johns Hopkins University Press, 1973), Chap. V.
11. South Africa's arguments on the issues of the existence of the mandate and United Nations supervision are to be found in *SWA Pleadings* II: 97-257; V: 15-99; VIII: 281-584; IX: 377-480.
12. It was doubtful whether the League itself was endowed with personality in international law. Ibid., II: 207-8; V: 52.
13. See above, chap. I. Particular emphasis was placed on the views expressed by the South African prime minister, General Botha, at that Conference. See above, p. 31.

With the demise of the League in 1946 the supervisory functions of the relevant organs ceased automatically. No other international body was entitled to assume those supervisory functions unless South Africa in some way consented to the new arrangement or unless some rule of law operated to transfer supervisory authority regardless of South Africa's lack of consent.[14] But no such rule could be cited, for in fact, the founding fathers of the United Nations had deliberately avoided making the new organization successor in title to the old. And for its part, South Africa had never granted express consent to a United Nations supervisory role with regard to South West Africa, a fact which had been recognized by the Court in 1950. Thus, if the 1950 Court nevertheless affirmed the United Nations' right to supervise, it could have done so only by assuming tacit South African consent to such supervision. However, such an assumption could only have been made in unawareness of certain critical "new facts" which had first come to light subsequent to delivery of the Court's opinion, and the present Court was, therefore, fully entitled to depart from the 1950 ruling. The facts alluded to were: (a) the decision not to set up a temporary trusteeship committee to supervise the mandates or arrange for transfer to the United Nations of supervisory functions over mandates; (b) withdrawal of the original Chinese proposal at the final session of the League Assembly in 1946 which would have provided for annual reports on the mandates to be submitted to the United Nations; and (c) subsequent practice in the United Nations demonstrating that supervision of the mandate had not been transferred from the League to any other body. Respondent also pointed to the fact that the 1950 opinion had been made in reliance upon a special interpretation of Article 80(1) which subsequent analysis demonstrated could not be sustained. In conclusion, South Africa respectfully asked the Court to consider the 1950 conclusions *de novo* and rule that the United Nations had not succeeded to the supervisory powers of the League in reference to South West Africa.

As for the 1962 judgment, Respondent claimed that the major premises of this decision, so far from supporting Applicants' thesis,

---

14. South Africa referred to the decision of the Court in the *Barcelona Traction* case (Preliminary Objections), *ICJ Reports* (1964): 38–39, for evidence that South African consent to the substitution of one supervisory organ for another would always be necessary, even if Applicants' thesis regarding an "organized international community" could be accepted. In that case it was held that the inoperation of a clause in an instrument due to the absence of an appropriate tribunal could be remedied "if for instance the parties agree on another tribunal, or if another is supplied by the automatic operation of some other instrument by which both parties are bound." In the present case dissolution of the League certainly made inoperable the machinery for supervision, but no subsequent agreement was ever reached on the substitution of one supervisory organ for another. *SWA Pleadings* V: 47–48.

actually confirmed South Africa's view that Article 6 of the Mandate (relating to annual reports) had lapsed. This, South Africa claimed, arose from the judgment's "necessity" argument regarding judicial supervision—that the mandate would be without international supervision unless the Court was qualified to supervise. But, argued South Africa, had the Court posited United Nations succession to the supervisory powers of the League, then the whole basis for assuming the necessity of judicial supervision would have fallen away.

Having established to its satisfaction that Article 6 of the Mandate relating to supervision had lapsed, South Africa contended that the entire mandate must be presumed to have lapsed, since international supervision was the "heart and soul" of the mandates system. Article 6 was not severable from the rest of the Mandate articles. Without this crucial provision, the mandate could not possibly survive in any manner, not even as an institution or status. South Africa, therefore, retained no obligations under the Mandate, either with respect to accountability to the United Nations or in the matter of its racial policies in South West Africa.

But could not the mandate continue to survive even without administrative supervision, so long as *judicial* supervision remained in force beyond the dissolution of the League? This question raised the basic issues encompassed in the first three of South Africa's preliminary objections, and particularly the third objection—viz., whether Applicants were entitled to obtain a judgment on the merits in the absence of a material interest in the case. For if Ethiopia and Liberia were not entitled to obtain a judgment, then no power of judicial supervision resided in the Court. South Africa could then continue to premise the lapse of the mandate on the absence of any international supervision—administrative, because it had lapsed; and judicial, because it had never existed. At first glance the issue of Applicants' right to a judgment on the merits might appear to have been settled by the 1962 judgment. Recognizing this, South Africa stressed the limited scope of the 1962 decision which, it said, related solely to the question of jurisdiction, not admissibility. In the words of Mr. de Villiers, counsel for South Africa:

> The scope of Article 7, paragraph 2—that is its scope as opposed to the question whether it is still in existence—is also relevant to the question which arises in regard to justiciability of Article 2, paragraph 2, of the Mandate. Consequently, quite apart from the relevance which those questions had to the issue of the Court's jurisdiction, they are also relevant, I submit, in relation to the validity of these various contentions—these various submissions—which are advanced to the Court by the Applicants. . . . Article 7, paragraph 2 . . . covers, in our submission, only questions of

disputes regarding matters in which League Members had legal rights or interests of their own, and not matters of the kind which have been brought before the Court in these proceedings. If a Member of the Court should be of the opinion that that contention of the Respondent is a sound one, that may well lead that Member of the Court to decide that on that basis, . . . [he] ought not to give any consideration to any of the other questions raised in this case, because they must all be regarded as inadmissible. . . . The mere fact, . . . that the Court has, on that question, come to a decision, for purposes of the Preliminary Objections alone, by a very narrow majority—if I may refer to it, with respect—of eight to seven, surely cannot, in principle, bind any judge as to the significance which he should attach to that question in regard to the admissibility of the claims now before the Court, particularly in view of the fact that the Court is now differently constituted, that it was divided almost on a half-and-half basis on that very question, and that the question is one that goes to the very root of the admissibility of all the claims in the case.[15]

On the basis of all the foregoing, Respondent asked the Court to rule that the mandate as a whole had lapsed; or, in the alternative, that even if the mandate survived as an international status or institution, no supervisory power with regard to South West Africa vested in the United Nations.

In response, Applicants challenged South Africa's entire thesis.[16] Conceding Respondent's premise that international accountability was, indeed, of the essence of the mandate, Applicants deduced the reverse conclusion: international accountability "must survive so long as rights or powers over the Territory are asserted, as the Court has twice made clear [i.e., in 1950 and 1962]."[17] Applicants denied that the founders of the mandates system had intended to endorse a very restricted regime of international accountability. It was "the common intention of the parties to [the relevant] instruments that international super-

15. Ibid., VIII: 582-83. For discussion of this issue in the written pleadings, see ibid., II: 170-93; V: 85-99.

De Villiers' statement is of particular importance in denoting the nature of Respondent's claim regarding the lapse of the mandate. Subsequently, in the 1966 judgment, it was a matter of debate between the Court majority and, most notably, Judge Jessup, whether the decision was actually based upon any one of Respondent's submissions. See SWA Judgment (1966): 19, 328. From the foregoing analysis it would appear evident that the final submission relating to lapse of the mandate clearly incorporated within itself, as was argued in the above quotation, the thesis that the Applicants were not entitled to a judgment on the merits for lack of a material interest—the precise basis of the 1966 decision.

For further discussion of this topic, see below pp. 291-92.

16. For Applicants' arguments, see SWA Pleadings IV: 520-52; VIII: 124-231; IX: 124-242. Concise summaries are to be found at ibid., VIII: 229-31; IX: 173-74, 240-42.

17. Ibid., IV: 524. "So long as Respondent retains rights over the Territory it is, by that very fact, manifesting consent to international supervision." Ibid., VIII: 229.

vision should continue so long as the mandate itself endures."[18] International accountability was owed not to one specific international body, but to the "organized international community," as the 1962 judgment had made clear. There was no lapse of international accountability or of the mandate, since the competent international body, representing or constituting the organized international community, was at all times present and prepared to carry out the responsibility of supervision. Initially the League fulfilled that function and subsequently "the United Nations . . . replaced the League of Nations as such 'organized international community,' and Respondent's obligation of international accountability, accordingly, is owed to the United Nations in that capacity."[19]

The Applicants, however, had to face the fact that the United Nations was not the successor in title to the League, nor, as the 1950 opinion had indicated, was any express transfer ever effected between the two organizations with reference to mandates. Moreover, even if the "organized international community" was a constant, as Applicants alleged, there might still be need to demonstrate that the "dormant" obligation of international accountability had been "revived" or "kept in operation" by South Africa's acceptance of the new supervisory organ.[20] To this end, Applicants, in their later pleadings,[21] asserted that South Africa had, indeed, manifested its consent to United Nations supervision of the South West Africa mandate.[22] This consent was evidenced by: the position adopted by South Africa (in common with other mandatory powers) in the 1945 discussions of the United Nations Preparatory Commission with respect to the creation of trusteeship machinery; South Africa's statements before the League Assembly in April 1946; and South Africa's endorsement of the resolution relating to mandates adopted at that final League session.

In the last stage of their oral arguments, Applicants singled out and relied very heavily upon the following statement of the South African representative, Mr. Nicholls, during the 1945 Preparatory Commission deliberations: "It seems reasonable to create an interim body as the Mandates Commission was now in abeyance and the countries holding mandates should have a body to which they could report."[23] Clearly,

18. Ibid., p. 130.
19. Ibid., IV: 539; and see ibid., VIII: 197–201.
20. The reasoning of the *Barcelona Traction* case (Preliminary Objections) seemed to require this. See above, n. 14.
21. In their earlier pleadings, Applicants had claimed that their case was not based on any element of consent on South Africa's part in the period 1945–46. See *SWA Pleadings* VII: 299; VIII: 131. And see comment of Respondent, ibid., pp. 309–19.
22. *SWA Pleadings* VIII: 123, 131–32, 208, 212; IX: 240. The 1962 Court lent support for such a line of reasoning. It held that in 1946 South Africa, together with the other mandatory powers, had agreed to the continuation (as far as feasible) of all the obligations of the mandate (including judicial supervision). *SWA Judgment* (1962): 338–41.
23. Quoted in *SWA Pleadings* VIII: 152; IX: 141.

Applicants claimed, in the South African view, "the mandatory powers were obligated to subject their administration of mandated territories to the supervision of the United Nations."[24] On this basis, Applicants proceeded to enunciate a very novel interpretation of the events of 1945–46,[25] according to which a system of pledges was adopted as a compromise between the positions of mandatory and nonmandatory powers. It was the former group of states (including South Africa) that actually favored United Nations supervision of the mandates by means of a temporary trusteeship council, until the conclusion of other arrangements. Most other states, fearing that such a temporary set-up would only delay creation of a permanent trusteeship council, insisted that the mandatory powers pledge themselves to convert the mandates into trust territories.

> What occurred historically, upon the Applicants' careful analysis, was a compromise between these two positions. That is, pledges were made but not pledges to place the mandated territories under the trusteeship system: rather, the pledges were to carry out all the obligations of the mandate, including the obligation to submit to international supervision, the essence of the mandate, until other agreed arrangements could be made.
>
> This is the answer to the problem posed by the Respondent's suggestion that 1945 and 1946 events are consistent only with, or even reasonably consistent with, the proposition that the essence of the mandate somehow became excluded along the road.[26]

In the light of their historical analysis, Applicants declared, nothing at all remained of Respondent's "new facts" arguments:

1) The discussions in the United Nations Preparatory Commission, far from evidencing failure to transfer supervision over mandates to the United Nations, demonstrated, in accordance with Mr. Nicholls' statement, that the mandatory powers regarded the United Nations as the proper supervisory body.

2) Replacement of one Chinese draft proposal by another at the last session of the League Assembly was not meant to deny United Nations supervisory power over mandates, but was designed to promote the system of "pledges" endorsed earlier in the United Nations Preparatory Commission.

> The first draft Chinese resolution was an attempt to revive the approach of the mandatories in the Preparatory Commission, which envisaged the establishment of a temporary trusteeship procedure, and was not accepted. . . .

24. Ibid., p. 142.
25. See generally, ibid., pp. 140–50, 159–61, 187–90, 241.
26. Ibid., p. 146.

The second Chinese resolution, which was adopted, followed the pledging technique, . . . a procedure which the Preparatory Commission itself had considered more appropriate in order to avoid the possibility of . . . delay in the . . . conclusion of trusteeship agreements.[27]

While Respondent apparently "would have preferred the first Chinese draft to the second,"[28] the majority of states at the League Assembly session favored the pledging system. But no one denied the capacity of the United Nations to supervise mandates or the obligation of the mandatory powers to submit to such United Nations supervision pending the institution of "other arrangements."[29]

3) Subsequent conduct in the General Assembly in 1945-46 could not be cited as evidence, since the discussions at that time reflected doubt, ambiguity, and confusion among member states. Precisely because of the prevailing uncertainty the question was submitted to the International Court of Justice in 1950 for legal clarification.[30]

In summation, Applicants submitted that the mandate had never lapsed, since the duty of international accountability to the organized international community remained constant throughout, with the United Nations ready and qualified to supervise in place of the League. Furthermore, South African consent to the assumption of that supervisory role was manifested by its actions in the critical period 1945-47.[31]

In response, Mr. de Villiers, counsel for South Africa, dismissed Applicants' newly discovered interpretation of the events of 1945-46 as "a figment of their imagination."[32] In support of their theory of a "pledges" compromise, Applicants were, he said, unable to cite any evidence to show "that there was such a compromise, that anybody was aware of it, that anybody spoke of it, that there is any kind of record of it whatsoever."[33] The suggestion that the mandatory powers, including

27. Ibid., pp. 188-89.
28. Ibid., p. 160.
29. In Applicants' estimation, the "full story" was so persuasive, that had Judges McNair and Read been aware of it, they might well have joined their colleagues in 1950 in confirming United Nations authority to supervise the mandate for South West Africa. Ibid. IX: 189-90.
30. Ibid., pp. 198-99, 224. For Respondent's comment, see ibid., pp. 446-47.
31. Among the 1946-47 actions cited were the submission to the General Assembly in 1946 of the proposal to incorporate South West Africa into the Union; and the inclusion, in a 1947 letter addressed to the United Nations Secretary-General, of a resolution adopted by the House of Assembly of the Union Parliament directing the Union government to "continue to render reports to the United Nations . . . as it has done heretofore under the Mandate." Ibid., VIII: 158-59; IX: 168-74. For Respondent's reaction, see ibid., VIII: 449-53, 462-63; IX: 418-24. It may be noted that Respondent's attempt to minimize the importance of the House resolution fails to account for the fact that the resolution was included by the government in an official communication to the United Nations.
32. Ibid., p. 405. See, generally, ibid., pp. 384-416.
33. Ibid., p. 405.

South Africa, actually sought United Nations supervision "when regard is had to the true factual position ... [was] entirely ludicrous."[34] South Africa had explicitly reserved its position all along with reference to South West Africa and the United Kingdom had also done so with reference to Palestine. It was, therefore, inconceivable that either power could have agreed to, much less sought, United Nations supervision.[35] Furthermore, Applicants' reliance on Mr. Nicholls' statement was entirely misplaced.[36] The statement contained no element of commitment on South Africa's part to submit to United Nations supervision with respect to South West Africa; it merely noted that establishment of an interim body would permit continued supervision for those states desirous thereof.

The arguments on the mandate and United Nations supervisory authority over South West Africa had brought to the fore two fundamental questions:

1) Did the mandates system entail supervision by a specific organ of a particular organization, composed and operated in a defined manner, or did it involve a general commitment to the "organized international

34. Ibid., p. 414. In corroboration of its claim that no arrangements for United Nations supervision had ever been effected, Respondent referred to two newly discovered documents revealed after a search of United Nations archives. They were two United States draft proposals (PC/EX/92/Add.1., Oct. 14, 1945 and PC/TC/11, Dec. 4, 1945) to specifically empower the proposed Temporary Trusteeship Committee, and later the Trusteeship Council, "to receive the reports which the mandatory powers are now obligated to make to the Permanent Mandates Commission." SWA Pleadings IX: 401-2, and 393-94. Both proposals, however, were simply dropped, and "the inference is inescapable," declared Mr. de Villiers, that this was due to the opposition of the mandatory powers. Ibid., p. 403; and see p. 394.

In the view of the Applicants, "no special provision was required" for United Nations supervision of mandates. The authority could be assumed without it. See ibid., pp. 148-50.

Judge Fitzmaurice in his 1971 dissenting opinion adopted the interpretation of the Respondent. Namibia Opinion (1971): 245-46.

35. It may be noted that Applicants' interpretation of events was also open to challenge on several other grounds. First, if the United Nations in 1945-46 totally rejected the idea of a temporary trusteeship council and adopted a "pledging" system in its stead, what purpose was there in the mandatory powers attempting to promote the idea of a United Nations temporary supervisory body in the forum of the League Assembly? Second, and more importantly, can one assume that China would act on behalf of mandatory powers engaged in a struggle with an anticolonial lobby, when all along China stood at the forefront of that very lobby? The remarks of the Chinese delegate negative any such suggestion. In submitting his second draft proposal, he noted that the functions of the League in respect of mandates "were not transferred automatically to the United Nations ... [and] the League would wish to be assured as to the future of the mandated territories." League of Nations, Official Journal, 1946, Spec. Suppl. No. 194, pp. 78-79. If the mandatory powers were, as Applicants alleged, actively campaigning for United Nations supervision, one wonders what need there was for assurances. Particularly is this surprising if all the mandatories had already pledged themselves in the United Nations "to carry out all the obligations of the mandate, including the obligation to submit to international supervision."

It is perhaps not unworthy of note that Applicants' novel interpretation of the events of 1945-46 was not endorsed by any of the separate or dissenting opinions in the 1966 judgment. In a telling footnote Judge Jessup commented: "Counsel for Applicants attached undue weight ... to the statement by Mr. Nicholls of South Africa." SWA Judgment (1966): 345, n. 1.

36. See SWA Pleadings IX: 395-400.

community" to submit to supervision by one or another international organization endowed with authority in the sphere of dependent territories?

2) Had South Africa in the years 1945–47 manifested consent to the assumption by the United Nations of supervisory authority over South West Africa?

The first of these questions clearly revolved around the meaning of the principle of international accountability in the functioning of the mandates system. Closely related to it was the further matter posed in the course of the pleadings on apartheid: what was the content of international accountability? Did it endow the international organization with authority to establish binding standards to which the Mandatory must adhere in its administration of the territory? But this question was only formulated at the ultimate stage of the pleadings on apartheid after a long and protracted court battle.

## APARTHEID

Applicants' case against apartheid—the issue which was indisputably the "heart" of the entire proceedings—underwent far-reaching and dramatic changes in the course of the forensic struggle.[37] There is no denying that South Africa, despite its position as defendant, skilfully led the way in shaping the legal issues presented to the Court and compelled the Applicants to shift ground repeatedly and to introduce radical amendments into their final submissions. From a case resting on a broad basis of factual evidence relating to oppression, Applicants' case was transformed into one resting on a single untried legal thesis of dubious authority in international law—an "international legal norm of non-discrimination."

### The Oppression Issue

In the Memorials, Applicants charged that apartheid was deliberately applied in South West Africa as a means of oppressing the non-White majority for the benefit of the White minority; and that the practice of apartheid violated Article 22 of the Covenant (which declares that "the well-being and development of such peoples form a

---

37. Even on the issue of the mandate and United Nations succession, Applicants' case, as noted, underwent some important changes. Thus earlier reliance upon Article 80(1) of the Charter and a law of automatic succession was abandoned, and despite earlier disavowal of any need to prove South African consent, Applicants' case became premised upon evidence of just such consent to United Nations supervision. But these changes related only to matters of interpretation (of the 1950 opinion basically) and could not be regarded as fundamental or crucial modifications of their case. The same, however, could not be said with reference to the case on apartheid.

sacred trust of civilization") and Article 2 of the Mandate (which obligates the Mandatory "to promote to the utmost the material and moral well-being and the social progress of the inhabitants of the territory").[38]

In the view of the Applicants, the meaning of the foregoing provisions was clear and their application to the issue of apartheid unquestionable. But if any doubts persisted, these might be resolved by interpretation in the light of "currently accepted standards as reflected in Chapters XI, XII and XIII of the Charter of the United Nations."[39] These Charter provisions were said to be in *pari materia*[40] with the relevant provisions of the Covenant and Mandate and served to construe the latter instruments so as to establish "clear and meaningful norms marking the duties of the Mandatory." Indisputably, those duties included advancement of the native welfare in the economic, political, legal, and educational spheres. Yet, in each of these areas, Respondent's apartheid policies had served to retard and stifle rather than promote the "material and moral well-being," the "social progress," and the "development" of the territory's population.[41]

Thus, in the economic sphere, Applicants pointed, *inter alia*, to the following conditions in the territory:[42] Natives are totally barred from holding land, and even such land as they are permitted to occupy is frequently alienated from them for the benefit of the White population. The result is that "less than 12 per cent of the population, being 'White,' enjoys the use of some 45 per cent of the total land area; while over 88 per cent of the population, being 'Native' or 'Coloured,' is confined to 27 per cent." Within the reserves, agricultural development has not been promoted and subsistence farming continues; and outside

---

38. These charges are set forth in Submissions 3 and 4, which read as follows: "3. the Union, in the respects set forth in Chapter V of this Memorial and summarized in Paragraphs 189 and 190 thereof, has practised *apartheid*, i.e., has distinguished as to race, color, national or tribal origin in establishing the rights and duties of the inhabitants of the Territory; that such practice is in violation of its obligations as stated in Article 2 of the Mandate and Article 22 of the Covenant of the League of Nations; and that the Union has the duty forthwith to cease the practice of *apartheid* in the Territory;

"4. the Union, by virtue of the economic, political, social and educational policies applied within the Territory, which are described in detail in Chapter V of this Memorial and summarized at Paragraph 190 thereof, has failed to promote to the utmost the material and moral well-being and social progress of the inhabitants of the Territory; that its failure to do so is in violation of its obligations as stated in the second paragraph of Article 2 of the Mandate and Article 22 of the Covenant; and that the Union has the duty forthwith to cease its violations as aforesaid and to take all practicable action to fulfill its duties under such Articles."

39. *SWA Pleadings* I: 104.

40. In support of the doctrine of "*in pari materia*," Applicants cited the Permanent Court's opinion in *Interpretation of the 1919 Convention on Employment of Women during the Night* (PCIJ, Ser. A/B, No. 50 [1932]), in which the Court took into account "the terms of another Convention . . . relating to a comparable subject-matter and problems." *SWA Pleadings* I: 105-6.

41. Ibid., pp. 105-8.

42. Ibid., pp. 110-31.

the reserves the Natives engage in agriculture mainly as farm laborers or domestic servants. In industry, the Native is essentially confined to unskilled labor. He is barred from participating in mining and industry in the role of prospector, entrepreneur, operator, or owner. He is barred from occupying an executive, managerial, or technical position in White-owned industries. And even in his role as laborer, he is not given the opportunity to improve his lot, since he is prohibited from partici- pating in the processes of collective bargaining. The pattern of "con- straint and compulsion that consistently subordinates" his interests to the interests of his European employer is vividly illustrated by the fact that he can be held guilty of a criminal offence for, among other acts, absenting himself from work "without leave or other lawful cause"; becoming intoxicated during working hours; neglecting to perform "any work which it is his duty to perform"; and refusing "to obey any order of his master."

In the political sphere[43] Applicants noted that the Natives were denied the right of suffrage and any participation in the governing organs of the territory. Even on the administrative level, Native partici- pation was minimal and restricted basically to the lowest levels of employment involving neither skill nor responsibility.

As for the legal sphere—the realm of "Security of the Person, Rights of Residence and Freedom of Movement"[44]—"a pattern of com- prehensive, pervasive and tight control over the lives of the 'Native' population" results from a series of "interlocking statutes, decrees, regulations, and administrative policies and practices." Natives are sub- ject to arbitrary arrest, often without warrant. For purposes of resi- dence they are confined within sharply defined areas under prescribed conditions, either in the Native reserves or Native urban areas within the Police Zone, and are permitted to move out of these areas only with special passes. The search for suitable employment is usually dependent on the issuance of an appropriate permit. Many Native urban areas are subjected to frequent night curfews. Thus, freedom of movement is almost completely denied the Native population.

In the area of education,[45] Applicants contended that the Manda- tory's policies and practices were designed to "restrict and shape the education of the young so as to perpetuate the denial of possibilities for self-improvement and the relegation to a status of imposed inferiority to which the 'Native' population is now subject." Thus, in contrast with the provision of compulsory education for White children, only a small fraction of Native children received any schooling at all; secondary

43. Ibid., pp. 131–43.
44. Ibid., pp. 143–52.
45. Ibid., pp. 152–61.

education was almost totally absent; and, apart from some limited opportunities for teacher training, the Natives had no access to higher education. The explanation of the Minister of Bantu Education "that he did not want 'frustrated people' to be turned out by the Bantu universities," provided "a grim insight into the quality of education" offered the Bantu.

All of the Mandatory's policies and practices in the territory combined to paint a picture summarized by the Applicants in the following terms:

187. The factual record of the Mandatory's conduct, . . . has a desolate but remarkable consistency. Whatever segment or sector of the life of the Territory may be examined, the import of the facts is identical. . . .

188. It might be possible for the Mandatory to explain or extenuate this or that detail of the factual record. . . . Taken as a whole, the weight of the factual record cannot be materially diminished by attempts at extenuation. . . .

189. The policy and practice of *apartheid* has shaped the Mandatory's behavior and permeates the factual record. . . . Under *apartheid*, the status, rights, duties, opportunities and burdens of the population are fixed and allocated arbitrarily on the basis of race, color and tribe, without any regard for the actual needs and capacities of the groups and individuals affected. Under *apartheid*, the rights and interests of the great majority of the people of the Territory are subordinated to the desires and conveniences of a minority. We here speak of *apartheid*, as we have throughout this Memorial, as a fact and not as a word, as a practice and not as an abstraction. *Apartheid*, as it actually is and as it actually has been in the life of the people of the Territory is a process by which the Mandatory excludes the "Natives" of the Territory from any significant participation in the life of the Territory except insofar as the Mandatory finds it necessary to use the "Natives" as an indispensable source of common labor or menial service.

190. Deliberately, systematically and consistently, the Mandatory has discriminated against the "Native" population of South West Africa, which constitutes overwhelmingly the larger part of the population of the Territory. In so doing, the Mandatory has not only failed to promote *"to the utmost"* the material and moral well-being, the social progress and the development of the people of South West Africa, but it has failed to promote such well-being and social progress in any significant degree whatever. To the contrary, the Mandatory has thwarted the well-being, the social progress and the development of the people of South West Africa throughout varied aspects of their lives. . . . The grim past and present reality in the condition of the "Natives" is unrelieved by promise of future

amelioration. The Mandatory offers no horizon of hope to the "Native" population.[46]

Clearly, the *leitmotif* of Applicants' case on apartheid was the charge of deliberate oppression of the population of the territory. The essence of this charge (as formulated in paragraphs 189 and 190, above) was expressly incorporated in Applicants' submissions to the Court;[47] and South Africa's response, naturally enough, was geared primarily to meeting this charge.[48]

The arguments employed by South Africa in its Counter-Memorial in order to refute the accusation of oppression leveled against it were developed along the following lines:

First, South Africa attempted to prove the inaccuracy of a number of Applicants' specific allegations.

Second, and more important, South Africa sought to demonstrate that the very measures and policies cited by Applicants were designed not to oppress but to promote the "material and moral well-being" of *all* the inhabitants of South West Africa, as the mandate required. Apartheid—or separate development, as Respondent preferred to call it—far from being an instrument to subjugate the non-White population, was a sophisticated and elaborate program for instituting self-government and self-determination for each of the peoples or nations in the territory. Moreover, the alternative policy advocated by Applicants and their supporters in the United Nations would result in utter disaster for the population of South West Africa and the very negation of all that the mandates system was intended to achieve.

Since South Africa's goals in the territory were precisely those enunciated in the Mandate and the Covenant, the only bone of contention between the litigants, Respondent asserted, was the question of means. But the choice of means was clearly within the discretion of the Mandatory; and the sole possible basis on which such discretion was challengeable before the Court was on the grounds of "bad faith." The Court was neither empowered nor equipped to adjudge on any other basis.

---

46. Ibid., pp. 161–62.
47. See Submissions 3 and 4. Ibid., p. 197. In their Applications initiating the litigation, Ethiopia and Liberia charged that the Mandatory's policies were "arbitrary, unreasonable, unjust and detrimental to human dignity"; and that those policies "suppress the rights and liberties of inhabitants of the Territory." Paragraphs G and H, ibid., pp. 21–22. Reproduced also in the 1962 and 1966 judgments.

It should be noted that the submissions, rather than the supportive arguments, are decisive in defining the issues placed before the Court. The Court is always free to uphold a submission on grounds of its own choosing. See Shabtai Rosenne, *The Law and Practice of the International Court* (Leyden: Sijthoff, 1965), II: 585–89.

48. South Africa's arguments on apartheid were, of course, presented only in the alternative. Were the Court to accept its basic plea that the mandate had lapsed, the arguments on apartheid would become irrelevant and superfluous.

The attempt to show the compatibility of apartheid with the goals of the mandate involved Respondent in a comprehensive historical review, analysis, and rationalization of the policy.

The policy of apartheid, of course, had its origin in South Africa itself; and although Respondent repeatedly stressed that South Africa's own racial policies were not at issue before the Court,[49] nevertheless, a rather detailed exposition of the practice of apartheid in South Africa was contained in Respondent's own pleadings.[50] It is, therefore, illuminating, by way of introduction and comparison, to consider the rationale which South Africa has standardly offered for its own racial system.

Although racial segregation had been endemic to southern Africa throughout much of its modern history,[51] the policy of apartheid (Afrikaans for "separateness"), instituted after the Nationalists' advent to power in 1948, represented a new species of the old genre:[52] a comprehensive, ubiquitous, system of racial segregation, based on a distinct philosophy, and aimed at keeping White and Black apart, not only politically and socially, but territorially as well. Apartheid, with its territorial segregation, is in turn seen as but an intermediate stage to the ultimate stage (allegedly already begun) of "separate development": of providing "for each of the major ethnic groups to achieve an increasing measure of self-government and to develop toward self-determination in a political and territorial entity of its own."[53]

The justification of apartheid presented by its proponents is comprised of both a "negative" and a "positive" aspect.

The "negative" aspect relates to the desire of the White community to preserve its identity, "its institutions, its culture [and] its heritage,"[54] and to do so in the face of "a numerically preponderant and aggressively nationalistic Bantu population."[55] The Whites, it is emphasized, are entitled to preserve their civilization in South Africa, since they did not arrive there as colonial conquerors. They reached South Africa no later than the Bantu and settled a vacant land, dis-

49. See, for example, *SWA Pleadings* II: 461.
50. Ibid., pp. 457 ff.
51. On the tradition of racial discrimination in South Africa generally, see K. L. Roskam, *Apartheid and Discrimination* (Leyden: Sijthoff, 1960), chaps. I, II, and III; N. J. Rhoodie and H. J. Venter, *Apartheid* (Cape Town: Haum, 1960); parts II and III; Eugene P. Dvorin, *Racial Separation in South Africa* (Chicago: University of Chicago Press, 1952), chap. II. The consensus underlying South Africa's racial policies ever since it became independent in 1910 was summed up by Smuts in 1945 as follows: "A fixed policy to maintain white supremacy is agreed upon by all parties in South Africa except those quite mad." Cited in J. H. Wellington, *South West Africa and Its Human Issues* (Oxford: Clarendon Press, 1967), p. 406.
52. For an analysis of the distinction between earlier segregation in South Africa and the policy of apartheid, see D. V. Cowen, *The Foundations of Freedom* (Cape Town: Oxford University Press, 1961), pp. 23–30.
53. *SWA Pleadings* II: 460.
54. J. S. F. Botha, "Aspects of the Nations of South Africa," in Phillip W. Quigg (ed.), *South Africa: Problems and Prospects* (New York: Council on Religion and International Affairs, 1965), p. 25.
55. Rhoodie and Venter, *Apartheid*, p. 36.

placing no one.[56] There is no other homeland to which they can return.[57] Assimilation would mean "the constitutional and national suicide of the Whites";[58] and multi-racialism is nothing but a myth, particularly where a White minority is involved.[59] The only solution, then, is a policy of separation or apartheid.

But if the Whites are entitled to preserve their separate identity, they must accord a similar right to the Blacks. In the words of Dr. Verwoerd: "We don't want for ourselves what we are not prepared to cede to others."[60] This, then, is the "positive" aspect of the apartheid rationale: the granting of full opportunity to each racial group to develop to the maximum its separate social, economic, and political institutions, in accordance with its distinctive culture and civilization. To this end, mother-tongue instruction for the children of the tribe is encouraged, as is the development of political institutions based on traditional forms of tribal authority. The ultimate goal is separate nationhood for each racial group, with the Native reserves transformed into economically viable permanent homelands, or Bantustans. The Natives will then have greater opportunities for employment at home and greater scope for leadership in an environment free of frustrating competition with Whites.[61] Even while working, or residing, outside the Bantustan, the Native will be only a migrant, retaining legal and political ties exclusively to his homeland, with no claim to participate in the White man's councils.[62] (The first operating Bantustan was established in the Transkei in 1963, and was intended to serve as the model for future ones.)[63] Despite the pledge of ultimate independence to the various racial groups, the goal envisaged is not the "Balkanization" of

56. *SWA Pleadings* II: 462. But cf. Leo Marquard, *The Peoples and Policies of South Africa* (4th ed.; London: Oxford University Press, 1969), p. 1. For Applicants' views on this historical question, see *SWA Pleadings* IV: 459; and see South Africa's response, ibid., V: 464 ff.

57. See the testimony of Mr. Cillie, ibid., X: 511.

58. Rhoodie and Venter, *Apartheid*, p. 27.

59. Quigg, *South Africa*, p. 7. The failure of such schemes for racial partnership as were attempted in the Congo, Kenya, Tanganyika, and Nyasaland is cited by South Africa in confirmation of its thesis. See, e.g., *SWA Pleadings* II: 469-70.

60. Cited in ibid., p. 464.

61. Ibid., pp. 463, 475.

62. Applicants claimed that it was "now hardly open to question that the principal object aimed at in introducing the Bantustan policy was to neutralize the call for an extension of the franchise to non-whites." Ibid., IV: 318. For Respondent's acknowledgment of this intention, see ibid., II: 463.

63. Ibid., pp. 479-81. On the subject of the Transkei and Bantustans generally, see Thomas Karis, "South Africa," in Gwendolen M. Carter (ed.), *Five African States* (Ithaca: Cornell University Press, 1963), pp. 556-71; Christopher R. Hill, *Bantustans* (London: Oxford University Press, 1964); Gwendolen M. Carter, Thomas Karis, and Newell M. Stultz, *South Africa's Transkei: The Politics of Domestic Colonialism* (Evanston, Ill.: Northwestern University Press, 1967); Wellington, *South West Africa*, pp. 356-61. For the report of a United Nations study group on the issue of the Transkei, see United Nations Docs. S/5426, Sept. 16, 1963, and S/5621, March 25, 1964, both reproduced in *SWA Pleadings* IV: 349-61.

southern Africa, but the creation of a kind of "commonwealth" or "economic association" combining political independence with economic interdependence.[64]

South Africa emphatically rejects the argument that the policy of separate development is a scheme for ensuring the permanent dominance of the White man by means of a "divide and conquer" process, or that it is a statutory caste system involving "education for subservience" for the Natives.[65] Rather, South Africa insists, its policy is the most effective method of resolving its multiracial problem, while taking into account the rights of each group. It is based on notions not of racial superiority and inferiority, but of difference; and it enables people to live, in Dr. Verwoerd's words, "next to one another as good neighbors and not as people who are continually quarrelling over supremacy."[66]

The explanation for applying apartheid in South West Africa is not identical with the rationale outlined above. In particular, the "negative" aspect of the rationale, the self-preservation argument, is far less tenable in South West Africa.[67] It is hardly consistent with the facts to assert that the Whites arrived in South West Africa no later than the Bantu and that, therefore, their civilization has as much right to exist as does that of the Bantu. The pattern of settlement in the territory followed, in fact, the classical colonial pattern, with the White settlers, be they German or South African, arriving much later than the non-Whites. Nor can one argue with the same force that South West Africa is the only territory the Whites have known for countless generations. The protection of the rights and status of the Whites in South West Africa is, therefore, premised on different grounds—on the essentiality of the Whites in the development of the territory,[68] and on the Mandatory's obligation to promote the well-being of *all* the inhabitants of the territory, White and non-White alike.[69]

On the other hand, the "positive" side of the apartheid rationale, if accepted, obviously has equal validity for South West Africa. In fact, South Africa argues, the territory's peculiar demographic pattern—with the Ovambo tribe in the North constituting 45 percent of the total population—and its pre-mandate history of incessant and devastating

64. Ibid., II: 466.
65. Ibid., pp. 466–72.
66. Ibid., p. 472.
67. On this point, see the comment by Philip Mason, quoted by Applicants in ibid., IV: 329: "The argument that separate development is necessary for national survival has much less force in South West Africa." See also ibid., p. 337.
68. Ibid., II: 410–11, 419–21.
69. Ibid., p. 459. See also ibid., XII: 243–44. Cf. above, p. 51, for consideration of this question in the Permanent Mandates Commission.

tribal warfare heighten the importance of a policy of separate development. A system of universal adult suffrage based on "one man, one vote" would probably lead in a short time to an Ovambo-dominated dictatorial regime which could suppress the minority groups in the territory, or even (in the case of the Whites) expel them altogether. Alternatively, fierce tribal strife would erupt resulting in continuous internecine violence. In either case, self-determination for the tribal units of South West Africa would be a vain dream and the concept of the "sacred trust" rendered meaningless.[70]

South Africa's own program for the territory is designed instead to advance the separate groups, each at its own pace, to the stage where they can be recognized as free self-governing units at liberty to determine "whether, and in what form and to what extent" they wished to cooperate in matters of common concern.[71] And during the transitional stage South Africa, as guardian, must "retain control over the various groups until they have reached a level of sufficient maturity for the exercise of self-determination."[72]

On the strength of the foregoing rationalization of apartheid, South Africa proceeded to explain and justify those features of life in South West Africa—whether in the economic, political, legal, or educational sphere—of which Applicants complained. Many of these features had their roots in the distinctive patterns of the Natives' communal life; and separate development did not aim to discard the prevailing patterns, but rather to develop political and economic institutions based on the existing infrastructures of the Native societies. Furthermore, certain of the restrictions and inequalities cited by Applicants were said to be but a result of the initial backwardness of the Natives and the need for European protection and assistance. These were to give way, in time, to expanded opportunities within the Natives' self-governing units or homelands.

Thus, in the economic area it was the initial backwardness of the Natives which accounted for the disproportionate amount of land occupied by Europeans. White settlement was necessary for the economic development of the territory and was therefore encouraged.[73]

70. *SWA Pleadings* II: 472–73. Outbursts of tribal conflict in various newly independent African states (such as Congo, Sudan, and Rwanda) are cited by South Africa in confirmation of its thesis. Ibid., V: 198–201; XII: 248.

71. Ibid., pp. 245–46. See ibid., pp. 244–46 for a concise summary of the suggested advantages of the policy of separate development.

72. Ibid., II:474. For its part, South Africa said, the peoples of South West Africa had already by 1946 reached a stage of sufficient maturity to exercise self-determination and decide that they wished to have the territory incorporated into South Africa. But the General Assembly had ruled that the people had not yet reached such "a stage of political development"; and it was in accordance with this stand that South Africa continued to exercise its tutelage over the territory. Ibid., p. 459.

73. Ibid., pp. 410–11; 419–21; III: 30–31.

But no Native land had ever been taken for White settlement.[74] The absence of private ownership of land by the Natives and the continuation of subsistence farming in the Native reserves were due not at all to Respondent's discriminatory policies, but to tribal practice. Land was traditionally vested in the chiefs who allotted plots to individual members of the tribe for their lifetimes.[75] And subsistence farming was "an aspect of the traditional lives of these people, which they lead out of preference, not necessity."[76] They are thus free to remain independent of the money economy. At the same time, however, since "labour is the normal way in which underdeveloped peoples enter the money economy," such Natives as choose to work in the White agricultural sector naturally do so as laborers.[77] As for the Natives who work in the industrial sector, there was no statutory bar to their forming trade unions. But most Native workers were illiterate migrants whose interests would only suffer if unscrupulous individuals sought to handle their affairs. Consequently, protection of their interests was not left to collective bargaining; instead, government officials represented the Natives at Conciliation Boards when matters affecting their welfare were discussed.[78]

Restrictions on Native employment in various managerial, executive, or technical positions were merely temporary "unpopular control measures" which took account of the factual situation, and which aimed at avoiding racial friction and other "deleterious consequences."[79] Once Bantu homelands and Bantu enterprises are developed, opportunities for Native employment and leadership will assuredly be expanded.[80]

Prospecting for minerals in the Police Zone was reserved for Whites, not as a matter of discrimination or privilege, but because the Police Zone was earmarked for White settlement. By the same token, only Natives could prospect within the reserves. The basic principle was that "as far as is practicable, rights of priority should be reserved to particular groups in separate parts of the Territory."[81]

In the political sphere, Respondent contended, the Natives were denied participation only in the White man's institutions. They were encouraged to participate in indigenous political institutions, and self-

74. Ibid., p. 38.
75. Ibid., pp. 243–45.
76. Ibid., p. 23.
77. Ibid.
78. Ibid., pp. 92–93.
79. Ibid., pp. 55–56, 65. "Certain kinds of contact" between Europeans and Natives "tend to create friction." And "most Europeans would refuse to serve in positions where Natives might be placed in authority over them." Ibid., p. 55.
80. Ibid., pp. 56, 65–66.
81. Ibid., p. 51.

government was promoted at each level of authority, local, tribal, and territorial.[82] Furthermore, in accordance with the expected conclusions of the Odendaal Commission,[83] territorial autonomy was anticipated for the more "advanced" tribal units.[84]

Respondent's policies in the matters of residence, freedom of movement, and the like, represented but effective means to safeguard the identity of each group and to promote the goal of separate development. The function of these policies was protective and not at all arbitrary or discriminatory.[85]

In the field of education, too, the goal of differentiation and separate development guided Respondent's policies.[86] Mother-tongue instruction, the formulation of special syllabi, and the creation of local school committees all were essential if auto-development in education was to materialize. Comparisons of education statistics and expenditures between White and non-White were unrealistic and inappropriate. Tribal conditions militated against instituting a system of universal compulsory education at this stage. (Indeed, in many tribes it was difficult enough to secure acceptance of *any* degree of education for the young.) Nevertheless, Respondent noted, a significant increase in the proportion of Native children attending school had been recorded. From 30 percent in 1951, the figure had risen to 46 percent by 1962, with a target of 60 percent set for 1970. These figures, Respondent stressed, compared very favorably with Ethiopia's 5 percent and Liberia's 23 percent in the year 1960–61.[87]

The ultimate goal of the stage of separate development was, as noted earlier, the creation of a system of Bantustans. In the course of the proceedings before the Court it appeared that South Africa was intent on instituting such a system in South West Africa even before the delivery of the final Court judgment.

A commission, known as the Odendaal Commission,[88] had been set up in September 1962 "to enquire thoroughly into further promoting the material and moral welfare and the social progress of the inhabitants of South West Africa, and more particularly its non-White inhabitants" and pursuant to such inquiry to prepare "a comprehensive five-

82. Ibid., pp. 105–7.
83. See below, pp. 234–35.
84. *SWA Pleadings* III: 131.
85. See ibid., pp. 195–339.
86. See ibid., pp. 341–540.
87. Ibid., pp. 444–46.
88. Officially it was designated the Commission of Enquiry into South West Africa Affairs.

year plan for the accelerated development of the various non-White groups" of South West Africa.[89] While the Commission's report had not been available in time for inclusion in the Counter-Memorial, South Africa had served notice that it intended subsequently to supplement the Counter-Memorial with relevant portions of the projected report.[90]

On January 27, 1964, the Commission's report, containing some 475 recommendations, was laid before the South African Parliament. The most important recommendations related to a vast five-year economic and social plan estimated to cost some £ 75 million, and early establishment of Bantustans in South West Africa. (The territory would be divided into eleven separate entities, ten of which would be earmarked for non-Whites.)[91]

Hints that South Africa (intent on proving the *bona fides* of its racial policies in South West Africa) might move toward rapid implementation of the Odendaal recommendations sent shock waves through the United Nations, echoes of which reverberated in the legal proceedings at the Hague. Applicants claimed that if apartheid was illegal, then the Bantustan scheme, representing but "an extreme application" of the apartheid policy, was "incontrovertibly and by hypothesis . . . *a fortiori* . . . in violation of . . . Article 2 of the Mandate."[92] And to head off any drastic steps by South Africa, Applicants, in a letter to the Court of February 25, 1964, intimated that they would request interim

89. *SWA Pleadings* IV: 201–2. It will be noted that the terms of reference of the Commission correspond to the terms employed in Article 2 of the Mandate to define the general obligations of the mandatory power. It is not unlikely that the proceedings at the Hague influenced the creation of the Commission in 1962. The expected report would not only affirm South Africa's policy of promoting the welfare of the population in such matters as health, economic development, and social progress, but would also demonstrate the enlightened motive underlying the apartheid policy (namely, self-determination for *each* of the peoples of South West Africa). See, in this connection, Wellington, *South West Africa*, p. 378; and Anthony A. D'Amato, "Legal and Political Strategies of the South West Africa Litigation," *Law in Transition Quarterly* IV (1967): 30–31. See also the comments of Judge Jessup, *SWA Judgment* (1966): 330.

90. *SWA Pleadings* II: 476–77. See also ibid., IV: 197.

91. Extracts of the Commission's report together with comments by the South African government were presented to the Court in the form of a supplement to the Counter-Memorial, on May 28, 1964. Ibid., pp. 197–219.

For a detailed and critical review of the report, see Wellington, *South West Africa*, chap. XVII. See also Anthony A. D'Amato, "The Bantustan Proposal for South West Africa," *Journal of Modern African Studies* IV (1966): 177–92; D'Amato, "Apartheid in South West Africa: Five Claims of Equality," *Portia Law Journal* I (1966): 59–76; Philip Mason, "Separate Development and South West Africa: Some Aspects of the Odendaal Report," *Race* V (1964): 83–97, excerpts of which are reproduced in *SWA Pleadings* IV: 328–40; Mburumba Kerina, "South-West Africa, the United Nations, and the International Court of Justice," *African Forum* II (1966): 15–16. For a working paper prepared by the United Nations Secretariat on the Odendaal Report, see U.N. Doc. A/AC.109/L.108, Apr. 8, 1964, an extract of which is reproduced in *SWA Pleadings* IV: 341–48.

The main criticism of the Bantustan proposal related to the inequitable distribution of land as between Whites and non-Whites and the lack of economic viability of the projected homelands.

92. Ibid., p. 319.

measures of protection from the Court "in the event Respondent should proceed with measures of implementation" of the Odendaal Commission's Report.[93] In the light of this very real threat, and in the face of considerable Anglo-American pressure to desist, the South African government relented and announced postponement of any action on the Bantuastan proposals. This step was taken, South Africa said, in accordance with the *sub judice* principle and "to obviate unnecessary further complication of the case through proceedings concerning possible interim measures."[94]

As has been seen, Respondent, in its Counter-Memorial sought to establish that apartheid—or separate development—was an instrument designed to promote the well-being of all elements of South West Africa's population and to advance each of the territory's groups to self-determination. On this basis, South Africa now proceeded to narrow down the issue between the litigants to the question of good or bad faith. Its arguments were, in brief, as follows.[95]

There was no dispute between Applicants and Respondent over the goals to be pursued in the territory. All conceded that the ideals enunciated in the Mandate were to be followed, and all admitted the right of the people of South West Africa to self-determination. They differed only in regard to the appropriate means to achieve the desired ends. But as to means, the Mandatory's discretion (assuming the mandate to be still in existence) was very wide. Article 2, while bidding the Mandatory in its second paragraph, to "promote to the utmost the material and moral well-being" of the inhabitants, granted the Mandatory, in its first paragraph, "full power of administration and legislation over the territory." The juxtaposition in the same provision of the power and the purpose signified that "the particular methods whereby this purpose was sought to be attained were left to the discretion of the Mandatory."[96] The wide latitude conferred with respect to promotion of native welfare in Article 2 contrasted with the very specific obligations concerning slavery, arms traffic, liquor, etc., enumerated in Articles 3 to 5.

93. Ibid., XII: 552–53.
94. See ibid., IV: 215–16; see also ibid., p. 198. Work on the noncontroversial five-year economic plan was to begin immediately.
95. The arguments are summarized from *SWA Pleadings*, II: 384–98; V: 157–74; VIII: 612–34; IX: 492–510, 519–20.
96. Ibid., II: 387. Both the source and scope of the discretionary power claimed were more precisely defined by Respondent in reply to a question posed on the subject by Judge Fitzmaurice, ibid., VIII: 30–31; IX: 492–506. In answer to a further question, Respondent agreed that paragraph 1 of Article 2 (the power) was, in essence, subordinated to paragraph 2 (the obligation). See ibid., pp. 519–20.

As long as its purpose is genuinely and in good faith to promote the welfare of the inhabitants of the territory, the Mandatory has near-absolute freedom in the selection of appropriate legislative and administrative policies. Only if an "act or omission" of the Respondent can be shown to have been guided by an illegal *intention* or directed at an illegal *purpose* will a breach of Article 2 have been established, for such an act or omission would represent not a valid exercise of discretion, but an abuse of power.

The Court, then, is not free to determine whether the policy of apartheid is the best, or even a good, system to achieve the desired goal of promoting the well-being of the South West African population. It cannot do so because it is not entitled to substitute its own discretion for that of the Mandatory. The sole question upon which the Court may rule is whether South Africa was genuine in its purported desire to achieve the purposes of the mandate.

Respondent supported this conclusion by a second line of argument.[97] The Court, as a judicial organ, could only reach decisions on the basis of legal norms. A determination whether a particular policy fulfilled the broad obligation of Article 2—of promoting "to the utmost the material and moral well-being and the social progress" of the inhabitants—would have to be based upon social, ethnological, economic, and political considerations, since there were no appropriate legal norms which could be utilized for this purpose. Even the Applicants, Respondent stressed, "do not suggest any such norms. . . . or indicate what standards ought to have been achieved" under Article 2(2) of the Mandate.[98] In the absence of legal criteria it would be impossible for the Court to undertake the task of judging the merits of apartheid over any other given policy, as a means of fulfilling the obligations under Article 2(2), since such a task would be inherently nonjudicial. Manifestly, then, "the question before the Court can . . . only be one of intentions, or purpose, or good faith"—[99] a traditional judicial function.

Respondent's attempt to thus reduce the case against apartheid to the question of South Africa's motives might have been countered by Applicants in various ways. One option, of course, would have been to

97. Ibid., II: 391–95.

98. Ibid., p. 394. In this connection, it is pertinent to recall the doubts regarding the justiciability of Article 2, expressed by Judges Spender and Fitzmaurice at the beginning of their 1962 dissent. They entertained "serious misgivings as to the legal basis on which the necessary objective criteria can be found." *SWA Judgment* (1962): 466–67. For a more complete quotation of their views on the topic, see above, p. 207. Respondent did not refer to these remarks of the dissenting judges; but its arguments on the nonjusticiability of the apartheid question reflected similar reasoning.

99. *SWA Pleadings* II: 391.

accept Respondent's challenge and adduce evidence of evil intent—proof that the real motive for the system was not at all promotion of the welfare of the population but rather the desire to perpetuate White supremacy interminably. However, such "subjective intent" would be immensely difficult to establish. The motives of an individual are difficult enough to prove, and those of a series of governments of fluctuating composition, literally impossible. Moreover, it would, as Mr. Gross, Agent for Applicants, declared, involve the Court "in passing upon the conscience, rather than upon the conduct, of the authorities concerned . . . [and] such a task is neither an appropriate nor feasible one, on the terrestrial level at any rate, for any tribunal."[100]

An alternative approach might have led Applicants to argue that the discretion—however wide—granted the Mandatory must be exercised within the bounds of *reasonableness*; and apartheid fell outside these bounds.[101] The Court would be asked to assess whether a policy which, as Applicants asserted, entailed in its parts and totality such oppressive and inhuman consequences for such a vast number of people over such a lengthy period of tutelage could be viewed as a reasonable means of fulfilling the Mandatory's obligation to "promote to the utmost" the well-being of the South West African population. Would the "reasonable man" of the common law, so to speak, see in such appurtenances of apartheid as pass laws, native reserves, curfew regulations, detention laws, and influx control provisions (resulting in the splitting of families) tolerable measures to advance the inhabitants' welfare? Could a system in which "the accident of birth imposes a mandatory life sentence to discrimination, repression and humiliation"[102] be deemed a reasonable mode of administration? Or would such a system rather be adjudged repugnant to the Mandate, regardless of the intentions or purposes involved?

100. Ibid., VIII: 245.
101. This general approach was adopted by several of the dissenting judges in 1966. See further, below, pp. 299–302. The test of "reasonableness" would also seem to be implied by the following question posed to Respondent by Judge Fitzmaurice: "Admitting that the Mandatory must possess a certain latitude, can there be more than an initial presumption in its favour? Suppose a prima facie case were made out for the view that certain measures . . . were in fact detrimental to well-being or social progress—would . . . the Court . . . [be] incompetent to assess . . . the matter, except on the basis of the Mandatory's good or bad faith, . . . ?" *SWA Pleadings* VIII:32. Respondent, in answer to this question (and even earlier) acknowledged that total unreasonableness, if proven, would constitute adequate grounds upon which to challenge the Mandatory's policy. But the policy in question would have to be shown to be so unreasonable that "*no* reasonable person . . . could have . . . adopted" it (emphasis supplied). In such an event, however, the illegality of the action would be so manifest that the holder of power would certainly have realized that he was acting unlawfully; in other words, he would, in effect, be acting *mala fides.* Ibid., IX: 500, 504, 506; and V: 158–59.
   The "reasonableness test" as formulated by Respondent would appear to be unduly strict. For the purpose of challenging a policy, it should be sufficient to show that *the* reasonable man regarded the policy as unreasonable without having to establish that "*no* reasonable person" could have adopted such a policy.
102. Ibid., IV: 274.

The approach just outlined would have offered scope for powerful testimony by petitioners from South West Africa (as, e.g., those who had appeared before United Nations committees) and by others, such as the Reverend Scott[103] and Allard K. Lowenstein,[104] who had personal acquaintance with conditions in the territory. The numerous United Nations resolutions condemning apartheid would also have been very much in place in such a line of argument—not because these resolutions possessed binding or quasi-legislative authority, but because by reflecting current attitudes on race relations they could serve as one of several indicators of what, at the present time, would be regarded as "reasonable" in the interpretation and application of Article 2(2) of the Mandate.[105]

The reasonableness test was, however, not adopted by the Applicants, and instead they presented two alternative theses to defeat the "good faith" challenge of the Respondent.

In their first line of argument Applicants asserted that intentions and professions of "good faith" were beside the point. According to "a universally accepted axiom . . . in the absence of evidence to the contrary, the predictable consequences of conduct are presumed to be intended." The issue of Respondent's fulfillment of its obligations under Article 2 of the Mandate hinges, therefore, "upon an objective evaluation of its conduct" rather than upon its "good or bad faith."[106] In other words, Respondent's intentions need not be independently proven since the facts and effects of apartheid speak for themselves in establishing that intention. And "if the policy of apartheid is unacceptable, a 'good' intention to apply a 'bad' policy would be a contradiction in terms and, in any event, irrelevant."[107]

This line of argument was not, however, developed or pursued with any consistency. It was not clear, even at the outset, whether Applicants meant that Respondent's intentions were totally beside the point

103. See above, chap IV, n. 79.

104. After visiting South West Africa, Lowenstein described conditions in the territory in a book whose title aptly sums up his impressions: *Brutal Mandate: A Journey to South West Africa* (New York: Macmillan, 1962).

105. As will be seen, however, Applicants sought to impart a totally different quality to Assembly resolutions, viz., the force of a rule of law capable of binding an objecting state. It is submitted that Judge Jessup, in his 1966 dissent, contemplated employment of the Assembly resolutions, not in the way suggested by Applicants, but rather in the manner outlined above. *SWA Judgment* (1966): 439–41; and see below, pp. 300–2. Judge Jessup cited Respondent's own acknowledgment (see *SWA Pleadings* V: 135–36) that the "general philosophical views prevalent in the world" had to be considered by the Mandatory in its administration of the mandated territory; and in Judge Jessup's opinion, these "general philosophical views" undoubtedly encompassed Articles 1, 55, and 73 of the United Nations Charter and "the world-wide condemnation of *apartheid*." *SWA Judgment* (1966): 439.

106. *SWA Pleadings* IV: 257. As to the relevance of "good faith," Applicants noted elsewhere that "without any purpose or intimation of comparison . . . history teaches that the most reprehensible doctrines, frequently are propounded and executed with professions of good faith and lofty purpose." Ibid., VIII: 245.

107. Ibid., IV: 260–61.

and only the consequences of its actions need be considered, or that intentions were decisive, but could be established by means of the consequences of the actions undertaken. In the second alternative, the objective evaluation of Respondent's conduct would establish, at most, only a presumption of intention which would remain open to rebuttal.

More importantly, Applicants never indicated what, exactly, they intended to do with this particular argument. What might have been a promising lead—a thesis related to empirical standards of administration by which to judge the *effects* of apartheid[108] (i.e., a form of reasonableness test based on the facts)—never did get off the ground. In the Reply, Applicants made but a brief reference to the thesis (although they separately discussed the existence of "generally accepted political and moral standards of the international community").[109] At the commencement of the oral pleadings, they promised to elaborate upon the legal reasoning involved during Part D of their oral argument.[110] When Part D was reached the legal exposition was postponed to a later stage,[111] only to be abandoned entirely as irrelevant at the ultimate stage of the pleadings. It became irrelevant precisely because the second line of argument, that of an "international legal norm of non-discrimination" came to be the sole mainstay of Applicants' case against apartheid.

## The International Legal Norm

Respondent's good-faith challenge, it will be recalled, was premised on a two-faceted argument: (1) that under the terms of Article 2(1) of the Mandate, the Court was not empowered to question the Mandatory's discretion on any basis other than that of good faith; and (2) that no legal criteria existed wherewith to adjudge the consistency of apartheid with Article 2(2) of the Mandate, so that the apartheid issue was nonjusticiable, except on a basis of good or bad faith.

In response, Applicants now asserted that Article 2(2) was indeed endowed with at least one legal norm having a "specific content and objective meaning," viz., the "international human rights norm of non-discrimination or non-separation."[112] Article 2(2) was thus as fully justiciable as, e.g., Articles 3 and 4, which contained specific prohibitions against the slave trade, arms traffic, the supply of liquor to the Natives, and the military training of the Natives. Moreover, the sug-

---

108. In regard to this possible line of development, see D'Amato, "Legal and Political Strategies of the South West Africa Litigation," pp. 28-29.

109. *SWA Pleadings*, IV: 257, 271.

110. Ibid., VIII: 121.

111. Ibid., p. 246.

112. Ibid., IV: 493.

gested norm served to set an absolute limit to Respondent's discretion as Mandatory.[113]

In defining the norm, Applicants declared:

> The terms "non-discrimination" or "non-separation" are used in their prevalent and customary sense: stated negatively the terms refer to the absence of governmental policies or actions which allot status, rights, duties, privileges or burdens on the basis of membership in a group, class or race rather than on the basis of individual merit, capacity or potential: stated affirmatively, the terms refer to governmental policies and actions the objective of which is to protect equality of opportunity and equal protection of the laws to individual persons as such.[114]

The norm had "evolved over the years" and was now "generally accepted as a *minimum* norm of official policy and practice on the part of a government toward persons subject to its jurisdiction." "Failure to apply the *minimum* norm, accordingly, involves, *a fortiori*, failure to comply with the more demanding standard of the Mandate," which requires promotion of the inhabitants' welfare *"to the utmost."*[115]

Among the sources for the alleged international norm were the following:[116] the standards developed and applied by the Permanent Mandates Commission and those reflected in the post-World War I minorities treaties; the United Nations Charter; the Universal Declaration of Human Rights; the 1949 Draft Declaration on the Rights and Duties of States; United Nations Trusteeship Agreements; various resolutions of the General Assembly and Security Council; the draft Human Rights Covenants; the 1963 United Nations Declaration on the Elimination of all Forms of Racial Discrimination and the draft convention adopted pursuant thereof; the Constitution and Conventions of the International Labor Organization; and various regional treaties and declarations, as, e.g., the European Convention for the Protection of Human Rights.

In what way was this "norm of non-discrimination" applicable to the case at bar?[117] First, it was said, the norm was binding on the Mandatory as a rule of customary international law having universal application. The policy and practice of apartheid was *"ipso facto,* a violation of international law, in terms of Article 38, paragraphs 1(b) and (c) of the Statute of the International Court of Justice."[118] Second,

---

113. See ibid., IX: 342.
114. Ibid., IV: 493.
115. Ibid. (emphasis in original).
116. Ibid., pp. 493–510.
117. See generally, ibid., pp. 510–19.
118. Ibid., p. 518. For the text of Article 38 of the Court's Statute, see Appendix III.

and in the alternative, the norm was of sufficiently widespread acceptance to impart a "specific and objective content to Article 2, paragraph 2, of the Mandate," wherewith to adjudge the repugnance of apartheid to the Mandate.[119] (As originally formulated, this alternative to the assertion of a binding legal norm seems close to a reasonableness argument, and perhaps it was meant to be linked to the empirical standards of administration approach mentioned earlier. Subsequently, however, it emerged as a "standard of non-discrimination" possessing "a content similar to" the norm, "but not an equivalent degree of legal authoritativeness.")[120]

Applicants rejected the view that only "standards or criteria . . . deemed applicable or acceptable at the time the Mandate was conferred or undertaken" were relevant. Rather, Respondent's obligations under Article 2(2) were to be judged by reference to "the relevant norms currently and generally accepted."[121] "Discharge of the obligation to *promote* well-being and social progress necessarily involves continuous, dynamic and ascending growth." To measure this obligation by Respondent's "so-called 'intentions' as of 1920 is manifestly incompatible with, and repugnant to, the essence and purpose of the obligation itself."[122]

With the introduction of the international legal norm of nondiscrimination, a new facet was added to the previous specific allegations regarding apartheid. South Africa's racial policies were now objectionable not only because of their oppressive effects, but because the very existence of separate arrangements constituted a direct violation of the mandate obligations.

Thus, for example, in the sphere of educational apartheid, although reference had been made in the Memorials to the existence of separate schools for each racial group, the complaint was not directed at this fact but at the unequal and discriminatory treatment of the non-White population. South Africa was charged with having taken "positive action which drastically restricts opportunities for education for 'Native' children and 'Native' young men and women."[123]

In the Reply, however, Applicants, while continuing to elaborate the original charge of oppression, contended that apartheid in education "is incompatible with the meaning of education itself," and that "the principle of non-discrimination is essential to and is an essential part of education." The goal of equal opportunity in education dictated

119. Ibid., pp. 510–11 and 519.
120. Ibid., IX: 261.
121. Ibid., IV: 518.
122. Ibid., p. 512.
123. Ibid., I: 160.

"equal treatment, not separate treatment."[124] Separation in education could only mean ignoring entirely the needs of the individual members of the group.[125]

In addition, then, to the accusation that South Africa had failed to fulfill the "separate but equal standard," Applicants were now charging that "separate is inherently unequal."[126] In the light of this new turn in Applicants' case, it is not surprising that reference was made to the famous 1954 United States Supreme Court decision of *Brown* v. *Board of Education*, which first gave judicial imprimatur to the "separate is not equal" doctrine.[127] The Supreme Court's reasoning, Applicants maintained, was directly relevant to the case at bar.

> This holding by the United States Supreme Court was made on the basis of a clause in the Fourteenth Amendment to the United States Constitution which prohibited state action depriving persons of "the equal protection of the laws." The present Mandate is a constitutional-type document, and the obligations contained in Article 2 are more affirmative and explicit than the general injunction of the "equal protection" clause of the Fourteenth Amendment. Moreover, Respondent's policy of racial segregation in the educational system of the Territory is more affirmative, explicit and far-reaching than was the racial bar struck down by the *Brown* decision.[128]

Clearly, the Applicants hoped that the judgment in the present case would represent the counterpart of *Brown* v. *Board of Education* in the international arena. Applicants were certainly not unaware that acceptance of the norm thesis would have implications for the question of apartheid within South Africa itself, although the Court was in no sense being asked to rule upon race relations in that country. In this regard it is illuminating to refer to an address by Mr. Ernest Gross, Agent for Ethiopia and Liberia, delivered in 1963 prior to submission of Applicants' Reply to the Court. He said:

> The South West Africa litigation is widely regarded by many who are aware of its scope as the key to the question of *apartheid* within the Union itself, even though, juridically, the two issues are separate. . . . It is very difficult to believe that if the Court should

124. Ibid., IV: 398.
125. Ibid., p. 370.
126. Ibid., pp. 372–74; and p. 518, n. 1.
127. 347 U.S. 483 (1954). The Supreme Court overturned an 1896 Supreme Court decision (*Plessy* v. *Ferguson*, 163 U.S. 537), which had declared that the maintenance of separate facilities for different races did not violate the "equal protection" clause of the Constitution so long as the separate facilities were equal in standard. The 1954 Court held that "separate educational facilities are inherently unequal." 347 U.S. 495.
128. *SWA Pleadings* IV: 373.

adjudge that *apartheid* is not in the interest of the inhabitants of the territory, the policies could nevertheless be carried on in South Africa.[129]

It is a historic coincidence that at the same time in history these most sensitive and aggrevated [sic] racial issues were remitted, both in the United States and before the court of the international community, for what we may hope will be final solution through the judicial process.[130]

The manner in which Applicants sought to transpose *Brown* v. *Board of Education* from the American to the international sphere played, it is submitted, a not insignificant role in determining the final outcome of the *South West Africa* cases.

## The Inspection Proposal

As initially expounded, the international legal norm was designed to supplement Applicants' charge of oppression and provide a concrete and objective basis upon which the Court might adjudge apartheid incompatible with Article 2 of the Mandate. During the course of the oral proceedings, the international legal norm advanced from this essentially supportive role to become the central and, in fact, solitary issue in the entire litigation on apartheid.

The occasion for this revolutionary change in Applicants' case was South Africa's "inspection proposal," presented to the Court by Mr. de Villiers at the commencement of his oral argument on March 30, 1965.[131] The Court was asked to conduct an on-site inspection of South West Africa, and, for purposes of comparison, to visit other

129. Ernest A. Gross, "*The South West Africa Cases*: On the Threshold of Decision," *Columbia Journal of Transnational Law* III (1964): 24–25.

130. Ibid., p. 20.

131. *SWA Pleadings* VIII: 270 ff. The suggestion was first raised by Respondent at a conference between the parties and the President in advance of the oral proceedings, on March 12, 1965. Ibid., XII: 571. But, in view of the scope of the proposal, Applicants were not willing to grant Respondent's request to yield the floor temporarily on the opening day of the oral hearings so as to permit formal presentation of the proposal at that time. Respondent, therefore, had to wait its turn in the pleadings before presenting its proposal. Ibid., pp. 571, 576–78. At the aforementioned conference with the President, two matters with reference to the further conduct of the case were agreed upon. (1) The legal and factual aspects of the dispute were to be argued separately, the Respondent being given the opportunity to reply on the "law" before Applicants' presentation on the facts. Ibid., VIII: 110, 271. (2) In order to clarify just which facts were actually in dispute between the parties (something which at times was not an easy task, given the rather desultory style of Applicants' pleadings), Applicants agreed to admit all averments of fact ("as distinct from inferences which may be drawn therefrom") set out in Respondent's pleadings, save those that Applicants denied. Ibid., XII: 572, 576, 577. This second point was embodied in a formal agreement between the parties. Ibid., p. 577.

The Court deferred a decision on the inspection proposal until all arguments by the parties were completed. Ultimately, on November 24, 1965, by a vote of 8 to 6, the Court decided not to accede to the request to visit South Africa or South West Africa. (The vote on other parts of the proposed trip was nine to five.) See *SWA Judgment* (1966): 9; and *South West Africa, Order of 29 November 1965, I.C.J. Reports 1965*, p. 9.

African territories as well. The itinerary envisaged for the Court would have embraced South Africa itself, Ethiopia, Liberia, and one or two other sub-Saharan African states (at least one of which, preferably, would be a former mandated and trusteeship territory). By this means the Court would gain vital perspective on "African reality."[132] It would "form a general impression of comparable conditions and standards of the material and moral well-being and social progress of the inhabitants" of other parts of Africa.[133] And this was "absolutely essential for a just and proper adjudication upon the factual aspects" of the case.[134] In the same vein, South Africa announced its intention to present oral testimony by witnesses and experts "in order to assist the Court in coming to a just conclusion."[135]

This turn of events, it is clear, had an enormous impact upon Applicants' further conduct of their case. It was evidently decided that the inspection proposal must be defeated at all costs, even if this entailed a total restructuring of Applicants' case.[136] Despite their earlier intention to announce which facts in Respondent's pleadings they contested,[137] Applicants now declared:

> All facts set forth in this record, which upon the Applicants' theory of the case are relevant to its contentions of law, are undisputed. There have been certain immaterial, in our submission, allegations of facts, data or other materials which have been contraverted by the Respondent and such contraversion has been accepted by the Applicants and those facts are not relied upon. The Applicants have gone further in order to obviate any plausible or reasonable basis for an objection that the Applicants have not painted the whole picture in their own written pleadings. The Applicants have advised Respondent as well as this honourable Court that all and any averments of fact in Respondent's written pleadings will be and are accepted as true, unless specifically denied. And the Applicants have not found it necessary and do not find it necessary to controvert any such averments of fact. Hence, for the purposes of these proceedings, such averments of fact, although made by Respondent in a copious and unusually voluminous record, may be treated as if incorporated by reference into the Applicants' pleadings.[138]

132. *SWA Pleadings* VIII: 278.
133. Ibid., p. 279.
134. Ibid., p. 278.
135. Ibid., p. 272. Some thirty-eight witnesses in all were due to appear on behalf of Respondent. Ibid., XII: 573–75, 581, 583.
136. For speculation on the motives underlying this decision of the Applicants, see Anthony A. D'Amato, "Legal and Political Strategies of the South West Africa Litigation," p. 36; and Elizabeth S. Landis, "The South West Africa Cases: Remand to the United Nations," *Cornell Law Quarterly* LII (1967): 640 and 651. See also below, pp. 306–7.
137. See above, n. 131.
138. *SWA Pleadings* IX: 21.

The sole issue in dispute was the existence of an international legal norm which absolutely and categorically prohibited apartheid. But this was a purely legal issue, which "can, and should . . . be resolved upon the basis of the undisputed facts of the record."[139] Consequently, an inspection *in loco* was pointless; it was "unnecessary, expensive, dilatory, cumbersome and unwarranted."[140] Nor, for that matter, was there any purpose in hearing the testimony of witnesses and experts, now that the projected arguments on the facts, reserved for the second half of the pleadings, were themselves quite superfluous. And Applicants did not, therefore, plan to cross-examine any of the proposed witnesses.[141]

Neither South Africa's *motives* in instituting apartheid in South West Africa, nor the *effects* of that policy on the territory's inhabitants were now at issue. South Africa's contravention of Article 2 of the Mandate stemmed purely and simply from the fact that a policy of discrimination and separation was "inherently and *per se* . . . repugnant to . . . the international legal norm."[142] The test was a purely mechanical one in which nothing but the very fact of separation on racial grounds need be established; and this fact was not in dispute between the parties. The issue was joined, therefore, according to Applicants, on the legal level and on that level alone.

Despite the momentous and sweeping nature of Applicants' concession on the facts, neither Respondent nor members of the Court were fully satisfied that the Applicants had indeed eliminated all elements of disputed fact from the litigation. Judge Fitzmaurice wanted to know, first, whether, according to the Applicants, "a policy of group differentiation was in all circumstances, necessarily and in itself, contrary to Article 2 of the Mandate, irrespective of any other steps taken by the Mandatory for promoting the welfare of the inhabitants" of South West Africa. Second, "if the Applicants' contention did not go so far as that, and if there might be circumstances in which measures of group differentiation might have some justification, would the Applicants still wish to maintain that an investigation of the factual situation, by hearing evidence or by local inspection, would be wholly superfluous?"[143] The

---

139. Ibid., pp. 15–16.
140. Ibid., p. 53.
141. Ibid., p. 24. Applicants suggested that any testimony of witnesses deemed essential by Respondent could be taken in the form of depositions. A formal proposal to this effect was, however, rejected by the Court, and Respondent was permitted to present its witnesses and experts in open Court. See ibid., pp. 24, 122–23; XII: 578–79; and VIII: 28 and 42.

Applicants indicated that they had no intention of summoning any witnesses of their own. They even went so far as to state that their earlier citation of petitions to the United Nations was done not in reliance "upon the accuracy of statements in such petitions," but because such petitions were "confirmatory of the reasonably predictable consequences" of the apartheid policy. Ibid., IX: 49. For the comment of Respondent, see ibid., p. 110.

142. Ibid., p. 46.
143. Ibid., VIII: 21–22.

President of the Court requested clarification of the distinction between Submission 3, which mentioned the term "*apartheid*," and Submission 4, which spoke of "the economic, political, social, and educational policies applied within the territory," without referring to apartheid by name.[144] Implicitly, the President was asking whether Submission 4 did not call for a factual investigation.

In reply to Judge Fitzmaurice's question, Applicants distinguished between, on the one hand, a permissible policy of differentiation designed to protect certain segments of society, such as women, minors, etc., and, on the other hand, an impermissible policy of discrimination and separation "which allots rights, burdens, status, privileges, and duties on the basis of membership in a group by reason of race, colour [etc.] . . . on . . . a basis which does not pay regard to the individual quality, capacity, merit or potential." The latter policy was impermissible absolutely "at all times, under all circumstances, and in all places." Nothing the Mandatory might undertake by way of promoting the welfare of the inhabitants can alter this fact. "It is the Applicants' case, rightly or wrongly, that the policy and practices complained of, as a matter of the international legal norm . . . , cannot inherently promote the welfare of individual inhabitants of the Territory. Any contention to the contrary is an attack upon the norm itself."[145] The only factual situation which is to be investigated "is that contained in the body and within the four corners of the written pleadings—that is the factual situation, that is the statement of facts which describes the policies and practices."[146] In answer to the President's question, Mr. Gross, counsel for Applicants, indicated that no substantive distinction was intended between Submissions 3 and 4; both meant to charge Respondent with violation of the international legal norm by its practice of apartheid.[147]

But was there, indeed, no element of factual controversy yet at issue between the parties? Mr. de Villiers pressed for further elucidation.[148] Applicants, he noted, still had on record certain factual allegations (incorporated into the submissions) to the effect that Respondent's policies were arbitrary, that they ignored the needs and capacities of the persons concerned, and that they subordinated the interests of the majority to the preferences of the minority. Unless Applicants could state categorically that their case did not call for any value judgment whatsoever on the part of the Court, then it could not be said that the case was so devoid of any factual element as to make an inspection trip or the presentation of testimony unnecessary. To this,

144. Ibid., pp. 23–24.
145. Ibid., IX: 45.
146. Ibid., pp. 46–47.
147. Ibid., pp. 60–62.
148. See ibid., pp. 54–55, 66–72.

Mr. Gross replied that no value judgment was being asked of the Court since "in the Applicants' view the value judgment whether apartheid is 'good or bad,' . . . already has been made . . . as a normative judgment by the organized international community, acting and speaking . . . through the competent organs, including the United Nations, the International Labour Organization, and other Specialized Agencies."[149] Accordingly, said Mr. Gross, Applicants could concur fully with the following summation made earlier by the Respondent:

> If this alleged norm [that is, the norm asserted by the Applicants] exists as part of the Mandate, it would have the consequence that Respondent's admitted policies of differentiation would constitute a contravention of the Mandate even if the Court were to hold that such policies were intended to enure, and did in fact enure, to the benefit of the population as a whole. Consequently the sole issue between the Parties on this aspect of the case is a legal one, viz., whether or not the Mandate contains such a norm.[150]

As can be seen, the Applicants were compelled, step by step, to reduce the factual content of their original case until nothing but the bare scaffolding of law was left. No factual mortar or bricks remained in the entire edifice of their case. For its part, South Africa sought to exploit to maximum advantage this new turn in Applicants' pleadings. If South Africa could prevail on the inspection proposal, so well and good. It could perhaps hope that a personal visit by the judges to South West Africa might convince them of the untenability of Applicants' charges and of the *bona fide* intentions of the South African government toward the population of the territory. After all, a 1962 visit to South West Africa by Messrs. Carpio and De Alva, respectively chairman and vice-chairman of the United Nations Special Committee for South West Africa, had produced some dramatic developments with regard to certain charges leveled against South Africa at the United Nations.[151] On the other hand, if South Africa could not convince the Court to make the trip because of Applicants' abandonment of all disputed facts, it would exploit to the hilt the new turn in Applicants' case, which it classified as "a new cause of action."[152] It would attempt

149. Ibid., p. 64.
150. Ibid.
151. A communique issued in conjunction with the South African Foreign Minister declared that the United Nations representatives "found no evidence and heard no allegations that there was a threat to international peace and security within South West Africa; that there were signs of militarisation in the territory; or that the indigenous population was being exterminated." U.N. Press Release GA/2501, May 26, 1962.
   For a full review of the episode as seen by South Africa, see *SWA Pleadings* V: 5–12. For Applicants' earlier comment (which did not seek to challenge the fact of the communiqué), see ibid., IV: 225–27.
152. See ibid., V: 105; and VIII: 654–63. Mr. Gross, naturally enough, denied that Applicants' case had undergone any change and asserted that the norm of nondiscrimination,

to high-light the degree to which Applicants had retreated from their original charges and to prove the untenability of the alleged international norm. And in this latter connection South Africa would seek to establish either that the grounds upon which Applicants premised their case were not purely "legal"—that factual considerations, and value judgments based on those considerations continued to be crucial; or, alternatively, that a "pure" international legal norm (which made no allowance for value judgments based on factual considerations) was an "impossible creature," totally untenable in law.

### The Law of the International Norm: The Applicants

The "international legal norm of non-discrimination or non-separation" had been discussed by the Applicants in their written Reply and in their oral argument-in-chief, but, up until the final stage of the oral pleadings, a satisfactory legal analysis of the norm—in terms of its origin, scope, and applicability to South West Africa—had yet to be forthcoming. Small wonder then that at the opening day of Applicants' oral reply, Judge Fitzmaurice found it necessary to pose to Mr. Gross, Applicants' agent, the following question:

> Taking for granted the great importance of the humanitarian and sociological considerations involved, but having regard to the position of the Court as a court of law, what is the purely juridical basis on which the Applicants contend that "the *non-apartheid* norm" amounts to an accepted rule of law, and whence does it derive its obligatory force as such—for instance, does the application of this norm form part of general State practice in such a way as to constitute a rule of customary international law; or in what other way is the norm, considered as a legal norm, said to be derived?[153]

This question clearly raised the crucial issue of the "sources" of the alleged international legal norm—the processes whereby the norm came into existence and assumed a universally mandatory quality, so as to bind even a state steadfastly opposed to its creation. No less crucial was the question of the definition and scope of the norm. How could the definition be sufficiently broad to prohibit all forms of "discrimination" or "separation," yet not so categorical as to bar conventional

---

which first made its formal appearance in the Reply, was implicitly included in "the clear and meaningful norms" mentioned in the Memorials. See ibid., IX: 18, 43, and 65. This, however, was hardly sufficient to dispose of Respondent's claim that the "norms" of the Memorials, as the context made clear, were in the nature of rights and had nothing in common with a legal norm of nondiscrimination.

153. Ibid., VIII: 30. This question was the first of ten posed by Judge Fitzmaurice to one or both of the parties in order to elicit clarification of the legal issues raised in reference to Article 2 of the Mandate. Ibid., pp. 30–33. For Applicants' replies, see ibid., IX: 360–66; for those of Respondent, ibid., pp. 491–523.

patterns of differentiation legitimately applied by states the world over? In other words, how, in the absence of any factual inquiry, could the norm be formulated so as to be truly universal, and not merely a *lex specialis* outlawing apartheid? Finally, there was, too, the fundamental difficulty regarding the applicability of the norm to the present litigation. If the norm did not constitute part of the original Mandate, how could it fall within the ambit of Article 7, the compromissory clause? Belatedly, the Applicants were forced to go beyond the bare assertion that an "international legal norm of non-discrimination" existed and come to grips with some of the inescapable and complex problems which that assertion raised.[154]

The first thing to note is that in the final stage of Applicants' oral pleadings the international legal norm of nondiscrimination emerged under two heads—"standards of non-discrimination" and the norm proper.[155] When the norm first made its appearance in the Reply, it was said that it could apply to the case at hand in two possible ways—either to impart an objective content to Article 2(2) of the Mandate or as a rule of international law.[156] But no reference was made to "standards" in that connection.[157] Elsewhere in the Reply, however, reference was made to objective standards of a political, moral, and scientific character.[158] In the aftermath of the inspection proposal these factual-type standards went by the wayside and in their place there now arose new legal "standards of non-discrimination" as part of the general norm thesis. Thus, the earlier empirical standards were now transformed into legal standards of nondiscrimination linked with the interpretation of Article 2 of the Mandate.[159]

The "norm" and the "standards," Applicants stressed, had the "same scope and content,"[160] and were premised on "the same evi-

154. Applicants frankly acknowledged: "Judge Sir Gerald Fitzmaurice's questions have struck at the central issue and challenged us to expound our views." Ibid., p. 307.
155. Ibid., pp. 242–45.
156. Ibid., IV: 493.
157. Thus, Judge Fitzmaurice, in posing his questions, assumed that only one norm was contended for. Ibid., VIII: 30. Mr. Gross acknowledged that the standards had not been spelled out in the definition offered in the Reply, but emphasized that the norm thesis in fact encompassed two lines of argument. Ibid., IX: 302. For the comment of Respondent see ibid., XII: 82–83.
158. Ibid., IV: 271; and see ibid., VIII: 121, 245–49.
159. See, on this point, the discussion in D'Amato "Legal and Political Strategies of the South West Africa Litigation," p. 35.
It might also be noted that while originally the norm was clearly primary, and the standards (or their counterpart), subsidiary (see *SWA Pleadings* IV: 518–19), at the instant stage of the oral reply the two strands of argument are referred to as "cumulative and alternative" contentions (see ibid., IX: 243, 259, 261). Ultimately, the norm was demoted to a "subsidiary argument," and the standards were elevated to become the "main" or "principal argument." See ibid., X: 187–88, and XI: 647. For Respondent's comments on this change of emphasis, see ibid., XII: 82–83.
160. Ibid., IX: 259.

dence, the same materials, [and] the same sources."[161] They differed only in the absence of "an equivalent degree of legal authoritativeness."[162] Whereas the standards were "rules of conduct ... gov-ern[ing] the interpretation of the Mandate," and therefore binding upon South Africa *qua* Mandatory, the norm was a rule of general international law "created independently of the Mandate," having "universal application," and binding upon South Africa *qua* sovereign state.[163] The standards, Applicants explained, provided the foundation for the norm; and for this reason they sought first to demonstrate the manner in which the standards arose and came to be incorporated in the Mandate for South West Africa.

The Mandate, Applicants argued, was "a unique form of treaty or convention, embodying a commitment to take account of the responsi-bility and the judgment of the international community."[164] By an implied term in the Mandate the mandatory power was required to give effect to the standards laid down by the competent international super-visory organs.[165]

> When Respondent undertook in 1920 the obligation to "pro-mote to the utmost" the well-being and "the social progress" of the inhabitants of the Territory of South West Africa, Respondent thereby undertook an obligation to apply evolving and developing standards in the light of modern conceptions and knowledge with regard to the well-being and development of dependent peoples, as appreciated by the international organs vested with the duty of supervision as a *safeguard* to effectuate the purposes of the sacred trust.[166]

Applicants went yet a step further and postulated a kind of "supremacy clause" in the Mandate which circumscribed absolutely the Mandatory's discretion.

> The organized international community, rather than the Respond-ent, possesses the competence and the responsibility to determine the content of the obligation in the light of its nature and purpose and where the organized international community, through the competent organs, has set such standards in categorical, imperative and unusually clear terms, they take precedence over incompatible exercises of discretion by the Mandatory as a matter of law.[167]

161. Ibid., p. 346.
162. Ibid., p. 261.
163. Ibid.
164. Ibid., p. 316.
165. Ibid., p. 319.
166. Ibid., p. 318.
167. Ibid., p. 320.

Such preemptory standards, Applicants said, had indeed been set by the organized international community. The United Nations Charter and the Constitution of the International Labor Organization (to both of which South Africa subscribed), as interpreted "by an overwhelming consensus of member States, approaching unanimity, . . . establish beyond a possibility of doubt the authority and relevance of the international standard of non-discrimination and non-separation with regard to the interpretation and application of a sacred trust laid upon the organized international community."[168] Although the Charter "does not make explicit the human rights and fundamental freedoms of which it speaks" (in the Preamble and in Articles 1[3], 13[b], 55[c], 56, and 62[2]), "it does make clear that, . . . a fundamental norm lies at its base: official non-discrimination on the basis of membership in a group or race."[169] Furthermore, the Charter provisions had been supplemented by all those resolutions of the General Assembly, the Security Council, and other United Nations organs, which condemned apartheid in no uncertain terms and which thus confirmed the existence of minimal international standards of nondiscrimination or nonseparation.[170] These standards formed part of United Nations law, and the Court, as the "principal judicial organ of the United Nations," was obliged to apply such law in the instant case, since United Nations organs, no less than member states, were committed to fulfilling "the purposes and principles of the United Nations."[171]

Respondent's attempt to deny that a charter drawn up twenty-five years after the Mandate could have any bearing on the question of mandate standards was dismissed by Applicants, who pointed out that South Africa had "supported and voted for" the final League resolution which took note of the existence of Chapters XI, XII, and XIII of the Charter. This resolution "on its face establishes the relevance of the provisions of the Charter to the mandates system."[172]

On the foundation of the "standards of non-discrimination," Applicants proceeded to enunciate their theory of an international legal norm. The standards, Applicants contended, have already "attained the requisite degree of authority so as to qualify as an international legal norm . . . in accordance with, and pursuant to, the several sub-sections of Article 38, paragraph 1, of the Statute."[173] And if this was the case, then South Africa, along with every other sovereign state, was bound by it; a fortiori was South Africa obligated to observe the norm in

168. Ibid., p. 339.
169. Ibid., p. 328 (citing IV: 498).
170. Ibid., IX: 327, 332–33, 339.
171. Ibid., pp. 328–29.
172. Ibid., pp. 329–30.
173. Ibid., p. 342.

respect of a territory in its trust and impressed with an international status. For the Mandate must be read as containing an implied term requiring administration of the mandate in accordance with *current international law*.[174]

But international law was not static; it had a dynamic nature, and many matters previously considered beyond its sphere of operation were now within its ambit.[175] Indeed, not only the content of international law had changed, but the very process of law-creation had been modified in response to far-reaching changes in the international milieu in which the law functioned.[176] In particular, such factors as the expanding nature of the international community; rapid technological developments and the resultant greater interdependence of states; the revolution in attitudes toward human rights and racial equality and toward the centrality of human rights in the maintenance of world peace have led to the modification of the law-creating process, with consensus replacing the requirement of unanimous sovereign consent in the generation of new norms. Furthermore, the heightened needs of international society for dynamic and evolving norms coupled with the absence of any international legislative organs to effect the necessary changes, pointed to the necessity of attributing *quasi*-legislative effect to "official acts of international institutions."[177]

Applicants urged the Court, therefore, to "confirm the role of international consensus as a source of international law within the meaning of Article 38 of the Statute of the Court and *within clear, practical limitations*."[178] "Consensus" referred to "an overwhelming majority, a convergence of international opinion, a predominance of view; it means considerably more than a simple majority, but something less than unanimity."[179] Applicants acknowledged that the law-creating process whose acceptance was now being pressed had "not heretofore been considered or passed upon" by the International Court.[180] However, in the absence of law "only force is left to implement the pre-

---

174. Ibid., p. 302.
175. The oft-quoted passage from the *Tunis–Morocco Nationality Decrees* case (PCIJ, Ser. B, No. 4, p. 24) was cited in support of this proposition. *SWA Pleadings* IX: 342–43. For an excellent discussion of the manner in which the issue of race relations has increasingly come to be regarded as governed by international law, see Rita F. and Howard J. Taubenfeld, *Race, Peace, Law, and Southern Africa* (Dobbs Ferry: Oceana, 1968), pp. 31–79.
176. *SWA Pleadings* IX: 343–45.
177. Ibid., p. 344.
178. Ibid., p. 345 (emphasis supplied). The meaning of the italicized phrase, in the context of Applicants' present case, is somewhat puzzling. For "practical" limitations could, presumably be applied only on the basis of factual investigations or, at least, some kind of value judgment—and introduction of the international legal norm was designed to avoid precisely such investigations and value judgments.
179. Ibid., p. 345.
180. Ibid., p. 262. Cf., however, Applicants' subsequent claim that they were not asking the Court to apply "innovational" principles, but rather "traditional" ones. Ibid., p. 361.

ponderant will of the international community," and such force, in accordance with the relaxation of the unanimity requirement in the United Nations, would not require the consent of all states; *a fortiori*, "the maintenance of peace should rest on no narrower basis."[181]

Turning next to the specific enumeration of the "sources" of international law found in Article 38(1) of the Court's Statute,[182] Applicants attempted to show how an "international legal norm of non-discrimination or non-separation" based on consensus might be confirmed by reference to each of the categories listed in the article.[183]

Thus, it was said, the norm could be viewed as a conventional rule encompassed by Article 38(1) (a). The treaties discussed earlier in reference to the creation of standards, such as the United Nations Charter and the Constitution of the International Labor Organization, were directly in point. In particular, Articles 55(c) and 56 of the Charter, "impose legal duties susceptible of definition by a consensus of the membership of the Organization when such consensus, as in this case, approaches unanimity. . . . Specifically . . . , the formal acts of the constituent organs of the United Nations have produced an authoritative construction of Articles 55(c) and 56 . . . such that the practice of apartheid is legally impermissible."[184] The norm of nondiscrimination could, therefore, be viewed as an obligation emanating from the United Nations Charter.

As for Article 38(1) (b), regarding "international custom," even the language of that provision negates any necessity of unanimous sovereign consent, lending itself more readily to the view that "a preponderant majority of States may in appropriate situations generate norms."[185] Isolated objections cannot prevent the emergence of such a norm. Moreover, it is no longer necessary to rest law-creating procedures on state practice. "With the growth of an organized international community, with constituent organs, it is increasingly reasonable to regard the collective acts of the competent international institutions as evi-

---

181. Ibid., pp. 345–46.
182. The text of Article 38(1) is as follows:
  "The Court, whose function is to decide in accordance with international law such disputes as are submitted to it, shall apply:
  "a) international conventions, whether general or particular, establishing rules expressly recognized by the contesting states;
  "b) international custom, as evidence of a general practice accepted as law;
  "c) the general principles of law recognized by civilized nations;
  "d) subject to the provisions of Article 59, judicial decisions and the teachings of the most highly qualified publicists of the various nations, as subsidiary means for the determination of rules of law."
183. It is to be noted that Applicants' initial reference to the norm, in the Reply (*SWA Pleadings* IV: 518) mentioned only paragraphs (b) and (c) of Article 38(1). At that point they had apparently not yet conceived of the notion that the General Assembly was qualified to give authoritative and binding interpretations of the provisions of the Charter. See above p. 241.
184. Ibid., IX: 346–47.
185. Ibid., p. 347.

dence of general practice accepted as law."[186] True, traditional doctrine required concordant state practice over a period of time, *opinio juris* (the state's conviction that its conduct is obligatory), and general acquiescence in the rule by other states. But this approach overlooked "the centralization of the normative process in international society resulting from the existence and expanding role of . . . international institutions."[187] A liberal view on the generation of custom was especially valid where what was involved was not the "adjustment of directly competing interests of States," but rather "the promotion of common . . . and collective interests of States, and of the organized international community taken as a whole."[188] Apartheid corresponded in this respect to genocide, "and the nature of the law-creating process in response to both has been remarkably similar."[189] Nor could South Africa claim exemption from the international legal norm because of its persistent opposition to the norm's development.[190] Even if such opposition could bar application of the norm to South Africa's own sovereign territory, it could not affect matters with regard to South West Africa, a territory having an international status.[191]

The source of law mentioned in Article 38(1) (c)—"general principles of law recognized by civilized nations"—served, it was said, both "to supplement and reinforce" Applicants' other explanations for the existence of an international legal norm, and as "an independent foundation" for Applicants' theory.[192] Frequently Article 38(1) (c) "had been identified as the manner by which the perspectives of natural law can be most easily accommodated in a developing international

186. Ibid. In support of the view that consensus rather than unanimity was today the true criterion for the generation of custom, Applicants cited the works of Rosalyn Higgins (*The Development of International Law by the Political Organs of the United Nations* [London: Oxford University Press, 1953], pp. 1 and 5), and C. Wilfred Jenks (*The Prospects of International Adjudication* [London: Stevens, 1964], p. 225). See *SWA Pleadings* IX: 347-48, 350.

187. Ibid., p. 350.

188. The dicta of the International Court in the *Fisheries* and *Asylum* cases, reflecting a restrictive view on the generation of custom, were therefore deemed irrelevant to the instant case. For in neither case was the Court faced with a clash between the collective interests of the international community and the interests of a sole dissenter. Ibid., pp. 350-51.

189. Ibid., p. 351.

190. In the Rejoinder (ibid., V: 140-41) South Africa had cited an article by Sir Gerald Fitzmaurice in which the following principle was enunciated: " . . . if (i) at some time in the past . . . any other 'dissenting' State had in fact, under international law as it then stood, enjoyed rights wider than those conferred by international law in its present form, and (ii) on the emergence of a new and more restrictive rule, had openly and consistently made known its dissent, at the time when the new rule came, or was in process of coming, into otherwise general acceptance, then the dissenting State could claim exemption from the rule even though it was binding on the community generally and had become a general rule of international law." "The Law and Procedure of the International Court of Justice, 1951-1954; General Principles and Sources of Law," *BYB* XXX (1953): 25. Furthermore, South Africa had pointed to the recognition of the principle in the *Fisheries* case, in which the Court said: "In any event the ten-mile rule would appear to be inapplicable as against Norway inasmuch as she has always opposed any attempt to apply it to the Norwegian coast." *ICJ Reports* (1951): 131.

191. *SWA Pleadings* IX: 349.

192. Ibid., p. 353.

system." But, in the view of the Applicants, the provision might additionally be used to establish "the role of consensus as manifest in the formal acts and proceedings of the competent organs of the international community as a source or basis of international legal norms."[193] In this regard, it was significant that Article 38(1) (c) was the source "least closely tied to . . . legal positivism." In relation to this source "there is no tradition, as with customary international law, of premising the existence of a general principle of law upon evidence of universality, or the absence of any protest, or upon a sense of obligation."[194] To establish the existence of the "international legal norm" under the terms of Article 38(1) (c), it was sufficient to show that apartheid had come to be condemned by international consensus as no less an international crime than piracy or genocide. The objections of solitary states could not impede the crystallization into law of the manifest collective interest of international society.[195]

Finally, as for Article 38(1) (d), which lists judicial decisions and the teachings of publicists as "subsidiary means for the determination of rules of law," Applicants argued that "the judgments of the international institutions themselves" plus the writings of such international jurists as Rosalyn Higgins, C. Wilfred Jenks, and Oscar Schachter, confirmed "the trend toward legitimizing the normative processes of the organized international community."[196]

In summation, Applicants requested the Court, on the basis of all four grounds listed in Article 38(1), to recognize that a norm of international law had emerged which was binding upon South Africa. In the event the Court was not prepared to go so far, it should still recognize on the basis of "the same evidence, the same sources and the same considerations" as those advanced for the norm, that international standards of nondiscrimination had arisen which outlawed apartheid in the mandated territory of South West Africa.[197]

If the question of the sources of the international norm had led the Applicants to posit "*quasi*-legislative" powers for the organs of the international community, the conceptual difficulties surrounding the

193. Ibid.
194. Ibid.
195. Ibid., pp. 353–57. In support of their conception of Article 38(1) (c), Applicants quoted the following passage from Shabtai Rosenne, *The International Court of Justice* (Leyden: Sijthoff, 1957), p. 423: "The 'general principles of law recognized by civilized nations' are not so much generalizations reached by application of comparative law . . . as particularizations of a common underlying sense of what is just in the circumstances. Having an independent existence, their validity as legal norms does not derive from the consent of the parties as such, provided they are norms which the Court considers civilized States ought to recognize." Quoted in *SWA Pleadings* IX: 354.
196. Ibid., pp. 357–59.
197. Ibid., p. 360.

definition and scope of the asserted norm (in the absence of any factual inquiry) compelled the Applicants to go a step further and endow the organized international community with "*quasi*-judicial" powers as well. The steps leading up to this development were as follows.

In the Rejoinder South Africa had classified the new norm as one of "non-differentiation," and had argued that Articles 55 and 56 of the United Nations Charter, to which Applicants refer, do not relate to *differentiation*, but only to *unfair discrimination* or *oppression*.[198] In their oral arguments, Applicants vigorously objected to Respondent's attempt to label the norm as one of "non-differentiation."[199] In the first place, the Mandate itself differentiated between the non-native and native populations by, for instance, forbidding the military training of the natives or the supply of intoxicating spirits to them. Moreover, such a norm would operate to illegalize special provisions in minority treaties favoring ethnic or racial groups; it would also bar special arrangements for such groups as women and minors. In fact, it would invalidate a great part of routine municipal law, since much of this law is concerned with permitting for "some" what it prohibits for "others." The norm, Applicants had insisted all along, was one of "non-*discrimination*," and a vital distinction existed between "differentiation" which protected and was, therefore, permissible, and "discrimination" which coerced and was, therefore, impermissible. In reaction, South Africa noted that protection and coercion were inherent in every legislative act.[200] But, more important, how can one tell if a measure is protective or coercive in the absence of a factual investigation (specifically excluded by Applicants' present formulation of their case)?[201] The policy of separate development, Respondent insisted, was designed to protect and not to coerce and oppress. The very vagueness of the asserted norm confirmed that the administration of policy was left to the discretion of the Mandatory, who alone was equipped to judge the merits and demerits of any arrangements affecting the various groups in the territory.[202]

In response, Mr. Gross, counsel for Applicants, now elaborated upon his earlier distinction by emphasizing that protective measures focused on the individual as part of a group "which he is free to quit if he so chooses," while apartheid focused on the group at the expense of the individual and was, therefore, coercive.[203] "The individual person is subject to burdens, restrictions or duties precisely because of his membership in a group—a group moreover, of which he is made an irrev-

198. Ibid., V: 131, 141.
199. Ibid., VIII: 261–63; and IX: 45 and 247.
200. Ibid., VIII: 665–67; IX: 540; and XII: 404–5.
201. Ibid., IX: 80, 540–42; XII: 402–8.
202. Ibid., VIII: 666.
203. Ibid., IX: 88, 247–48.

ocable life member."[204] But this distinction was in itself open to objection, since women and minors are hardly free to quit their groups, nor, in the case of a member of a religious minority, was it reasonable to suggest that he was free to abandon his faith.[205] Accordingly, Applicants adopted a sharply radical approach to the whole issue of definition. "The Applicants," declared Mr. Gross,

> attach no particular significance either to the designation or to the precise words used in the definition of the norm and of the international standards having the same content and scope. What is relevant, and what is essential to understanding of the Applicants' case, is the submission that such international standards and such an international legal norm exist; that they have been declared by those responsible for its creation as being applicable to Respondent's policies of group separation in the Territory.[206]

In accordance with this new stance, the Applicants proceeded to indicate the restricted role envisaged for the International Court of Justice in applying the norm contended for.

> The Applicants do not rest their case upon the degree to which the norm-creating process at work in international society has been correct or fair in its appraisal of the incompatibility between apartheid as practised by Respondent and the material welfare of the inhabitants of the Territory.
> Although the Applicants have no doubt that the norm-creating process was fair and correct in its evaluation of the policy complained of, the Applicants do not ask the Court to say so.[207]

Furthermore, Applicants emphasized, in a phrase which was to reverberate throughout the proceedings, that they were not suggesting

> that the Court undertake the task of second-guessing the competent international organs responsible for the development of the norm. . . .
> If the standards and the legal norm for which the Applicants contend do exist, as a matter of law, then they should be applied by the Court as part of its duty to decide this dispute in accordance with international law, and in accordance with the international rule regulating the mandate institution itself.[208]

---

204. Ibid., p. 88.
205. These shortcomings in Applicants' arguments were subsequently noted by Respondent. See ibid., p. 542.
206. Ibid., p. 246.
207. Ibid.
208. Ibid.

In elaboration of this position, Applicants went on to declare: "Standards relevant to interpretation of legal instruments or institutions are not to be attacked as based upon faulty appraisal of the underlying facts; once the standards are established by the competent organs, then in the Applicants' view the Court should accept them as part of 'the legal given' and not as themselves subject to judicial redetermination."[209] This, perhaps, summed up Applicants' argument on defining the norm. Whether or not the norm was susceptible of a precise definition, the Court was bidden to recognize that the norm did, indeed, exist as a product of the organized international community; that it was endowed with a minimum content which, at the least, outlawed apartheid; and that it applied to South West Africa because the organized international community had declared this to be the case. All of these propositions should be accepted as "judicial data," and the Court should rule accordingly.

This conclusion was confirmed by a further consideration. The Court, Applicants claimed, was not expected, and was not really qualified, to undertake an independent evaluation of Respondent's administrative policies. "This Court, and no court, by the very nature of the judicial process, has the facilities or the responsibilities to reach judgments, to formulate standards, of the sort which are uniquely within the competence of administrative organs and which reflect political and moral and social considerations of which they are specially competent to judge and evaluate."[210]

In other words, Applicants acknowledged that the Court could not possibly be asked to formulate its own judicial standards wherewith to adjudge the compatibility of apartheid with the obligation of the sacred trust, for to ask this was to expect the Court to engage in an inherently nonjudicial task. The only basis upon which the Court could exercise supervision with respect to Article 2(2) of the Mandate was that of the norm and/or standards set by the appropriate administrative organs of the organized international community. By clear implication, then, if the Court, for some reason, should find itself unable to accept the "norm/standards" thesis, there would remain, by Applicants' own admission, no other grounds upon which the Court could find apartheid incompatible with the Mandate.[211]

With the legal analysis completed, Applicants now proceeded to present to the Court their amended and final submissions, in which they detailed the charges made against South Africa and what they

209. Ibid., p. 255.
210. Ibid., p. 326.
211. Subsequently, Applicants seemed to argue that the norm/standards thesis was not really the only basis upon which the Court could rule. See below, p. 276.

requested of the Court in the light of these charges.[212] The most significant aspects of these final submissions relate to the amendments introduced in Submissions 3 and 4 dealing with apartheid and to the nature of the supplementary "formal interpretations and explanatory comments."[213] The amendments reflected the changes which had overtaken Applicants' case on apartheid in the course of the pleadings. All references to disputed factual material, such as the references to Chapter V of the Memorials, were now deleted from these submissions. Furthermore, the term "in the light of applicable international standards or international legal norm or both" was expressly incorporated into Submission 4 as a basis for determining that apartheid violated Article 2 of the Mandate. The entire case was now postulated on the undisputed fact of apartheid as a policy which distinguishes between races, and the inconsistency of that policy with the international norm and/or standards which arose under Article 2 of the Mandate and Article 22 of the Covenant. The "explanatory comments" made clear that no difference was intended between Submissions 3 and 4, "the distinction . . . being verbal only." They also confirmed that the "standards and norm" referred to in Submission 4 were employed "in the sense described and defined in the Reply, IV, at page 493,[214] and solely and exclusively as there described and defined."[215]

Besides the apartheid issue, other parts of Applicants' case also bore the marks of the transformation engendered by the inspection proposal. Acceptance of Respondent's facts as part of Applicants' own case meant that the charges on violation of the international status of the territory (Submission 5), unilateral modification of the terms of the Mandate (Submission 9), and militarization of the territory (Submission 6) had to be drastically altered. By the end of the oral proceedings the Applicants were maintaining that South Africa's failure to submit to international supervision, in and of itself, constituted modification of the territory's status; modification of the terms of the Mandate; and violation of the prohibition against militarization, since an unsupervised territory could be utilized for military purposes.[216] In effect, Submis-

---

212. *SWA Pleadings* IX: 374–76. For the text of the original and amended submissions, see Appendix IV, below.

The importance of the formal submissions should be borne in mind. They define "the precise issue on which the Court's decision is required"; and the *final* submissions represent "the ultimate concretization of the difference" between the parties. Rosenne, *The Law and Practice of the International Court* II: 585. Arguments in support of the formal submissions are merely supplementary and elucidating and may be disregarded by the Court should it decide to accept the submissions on different grounds. See, in general, ibid., pp. 584–89.

213. These "interpretations" and "comments" are to be found in *SWA Pleadings* IX: 375–76.

214. See above, p. 241.

215. *SWA Pleadings* IX: 375–76.

216. Applicants' new approach to these issues is outlined at ibid., pp. 235–39. For Respondent's reaction, see ibid., XII: 316–42.

sions 5, 6, and 9 were now subsumed under Submission 2 relating to United Nations supervisory authority. Formally, however, the only change effected in the aforementioned three submissions was the elimination of every reference to disputed facts.

Applicants had gone all the way to satisfy both the Court and Respondent that nothing, but nothing, in their case hinged on a disputed factual element. Every aspect of Applicants' case now reflected the purely legal nature of Applicants' challenge to apartheid. And the key question now was: how formidable a case remained? Respondent's focal aim would be to demonstrate the untenability of the norm theory and its inapplicability to the situation in South West Africa.

*The Law of the International Legal Norm: The Respondent*

South Africa opened its attack on Applicants' case by denying that the organized international community, whatever the concept may entail, possessed authority to establish standards binding upon a mandatory power for the conduct of its mandate.[217] Applicants' entire thesis—which, Respondent stressed, even Applicants recognized as "entirely novel and almost revolutionary"[218]—was premised on several assumptions, all of which Respondent set about to rebut.

At the base of Applicants' thesis, it was said, lay the assertion that an implied term in Article 2 of the Mandate gave the competent international organizations not only the right but the responsibility to provide "objective determination" of the current standards whereby the "concepts of moral well-being and social progress" are to be attained.[219] But all the evidence, Respondent maintained, clearly showed that there was never any intention—either express or implied—to give such authority to the League; and the United Nations, by hypothesis, could not possess greater authority in this respect than the League. Moreover, if the United Nations, as South Africa contended, never succeeded to the supervisory functions of the League with respect to South West Africa, then the "standards of non-discrimination" (which even Applicants admit did not arise before 1945) were never established by any competent international organization in the first place.[220]

Among the evidence cited by Respondent to refute Applicants' claim that the League had the power to prescribe binding standards for the Mandatory were the following:

217. Ibid., IX: 462 ff.
218. Ibid., p. 486.
219. Ibid., pp. 575–77.
220. Ibid., p. 579. Furthermore, Respondent noted, according to Applicants' own argument, the General Assembly alone had succeeded to the supervisory functions of the League Council. This should, then, theoretically have ruled out any reference to such organs as the Security Council, the Trusteeship Council, the Committee on South West Africa, and the Governing Body of the International Labor Office in connection with the suggested "standards." Ibid., pp. 579–80.

1) Any intention to grant such novel and sweeping authority would undoubtedly have been incorporated in an express provision and not left to mere conjecture.[221]

2) The very opposite intention arises from the express terms of Article 2 of the Mandate granting the Mandatory "full power of administration and legislation over the territory . . . as an integral portion of the Union of South Africa." If the League were given standard-setting powers, this would have seriously interfered with the Mandatory's discretion.[222] Furthermore, the power to administer South West Africa as "an integral portion of the Union" was inconsistent with the asserted obligation to abide by prescribed "standards." For if the situation in South Africa conflicted with the "standards," Respondent would either have to violate such standards or be compelled to modify the situation in South Africa itself—something which it was clearly under no obligation to do.[223]

3) The general emphasis in League matters on unanimity and consensus, rather than on dictation, militated strongly against positing any instruction-giving authority for the Permanent Mandates Commission or the League Council.[224]

4) From the history of the compromise hammered out at Versailles in the writing of Article 22 of the Covenant, it is clear that League control over Class C mandates was meant to be restricted to an essential minimum. There was very obviously no intention to allow League organs powers of dictation.[225]

5) In fact, the League organs, in the exercise of their supervisory functions, never deemed themselves qualified, nor attempted, to impose legal standards; they possessed and applied only moral force.[226]

In sum, then, if the League never possessed the authority to set binding standards for mandates, the United Nations (even on the assumption that it succeeded to the supervisory functions of the League) could not possess broader powers than the League in this regard (as the 1950 opinion confirmed). In fact, the United Nations was not given standard-setting powers even with respect to its own trust territories.[227]

221. Ibid., p. 594. In fact (although Respondent fails to refer to this point), the final draft of Article 22(9) went further in the direction of voluntarism and noncompulsion than an earlier draft which it replaced. See above, chap. I, n. 88.
222. *SWA Pleadings* IX: 589.
223. Ibid., p. 522.
224. Ibid., pp. 594-95.
225. Ibid., pp. 597-98.
226. Ibid., pp. 599-607. Respondent cited views of such authorities on the mandates as Wright, Hall, and Bentwich, to confirm the record of League practice. It was also noted that the Permanent Mandates Commission in its supervisory role only reviewed past events and did not prescribe future conduct. Ibid.
227. Ibid., pp. 485, 608-13. In support Respondent cited a lengthy extract from the separate opinion of Judge Lauterpacht in the *Voting Procedure Opinion* (1955): 116, which

But if neither the League nor the United Nations was qualified to create "standards," then *a fortiori* was this the case for the "organized international community," considered as a separate entity lacking any specific institutional existence.[228] The "organized international community" was perhaps a "social phenomenon," but if it was not "real" in that sense "then it must be either just a dream or nothing."[229] Was it conceivable that the authors of the mandates system, while refraining from granting standard-setting powers to such a concrete international organization as the League of Nations, should have bestowed such competence upon so nebulous and vague a concept as the "organized international community"?

Respondent also rejected the argument that by becoming a member of the United Nations and the International Labor Organization South Africa had bound itself to give effect to the standards embodied in the United Nations Charter and in the Constitution of the International Labor Organization and to the "authoritative interpretations" of these two documents. For the vital point was not whether or not South Africa was bound by the alleged obligations, but rather, how, if such obligations existed, were they linked to the *Mandate*, so as to fall within the ambit of the jurisdictional clause. Unless the two instruments cited were constituted *as part of the Mandate*, of what relevance were any possible standards emanating from them to the Mandate, and hence, to the present litigation?[230]

Indeed, this same jurisdictional question, according to Respondent, constituted the fatal shortcoming—the Achilles' heel—of the second leg of Applicants' thesis, the "international legal norm." Even if this norm existed, how did it fall under "the provisions of the Mandate" as required for the purposes of the adjudicatory clause?[231]

The Applicants, Respondent indicated, attempt to overcome the jurisdictional difficulty by postulating that the Mandatory, as part of its obligations under Article 2, "must be conclusively presumed to have undertaken and agreed to comply with international law in the exercise of the Mandate."[232] But which international law was meant? If it was

---

included the following statement: "The Trust Agreements do not provide for a legal obligation of the administering authority to comply with the decisions of the organs of the United Nations. . . . To suggest that any such particular recommendation is binding in the sense that there is a legal obligation to put it into effect is to run counter not only to the paramount rule that the General Assembly has no legal power to legislate or bind its Members by way of recommendations, but, . . . also to cogent considerations of good government and administration." *SWA Pleadings* IX: 609.

228. Ibid., pp. 614–19. Cf. the comments of Judge Fitzmaurice in the *Namibia Opinion* (1971): 241–42. The organized international community argument, he states, "has no basis in concrete international law. . . . It is—an expedient."

229. *SWA Pleadings* IX: 617.

230. Ibid., pp. 619–25.

231. Ibid., pp. 626–28.

232. Ibid., pp. 628–29, citing Applicants at ibid., p. 302.

the international law incumbent upon the Mandatory, regardless of the Mandate, then why was it felt necessary to incorporate this law *as part of the obligations of the Mandate*? And if not binding upon the Mandatory as part of normal international law, then why should it be presumed that the authors of the mandates system would have felt it necessary to relate it to the Mandate? Only if the Applicants could show that South Africa had accepted the relevant international law *as an amendment to the Mandate* could it be said that such law formed part of the terms of the Mandate.[233] "In other words, it would not be enough for the Applicants to show that the Respondent has consented to the imposition of a new obligation: they would have to go further and show that there existed an intention to incorporate that obligation in the Mandate."[234] For this reason alone, it was submitted, there was "no basis in law" for Applicants' reliance upon an international legal norm of nondiscrimination in the proceedings before the Court.

But quite apart from the jurisdictional issue, Respondent set about to prove "independently and alternatively" that Applicants' case on the international legal norm was "totally unsubstantiated."[235] Both the alleged sources and the suggested content or definition of the norm came under attack.

As to the alleged "sources," Respondent, before turning to a detailed examination of the enumeration in Article 38(1) of the Court's Statute, assailed Applicants' fundamental reliance on the *quasi*-legislative powers of international organizations. The "formal acts of international institutions" was a source nowhere listed in Article 38(1); and even the Applicants do not show "that this law-creating process does exist," but only "why it should exist."[236] The fact that scholars have "increasingly urged" acceptance of this new method of norm-making cannot affect the task of the Court, "whose function it is to decide a case in accordance with international law."[237] It is well known that the founders of the United Nations deliberately refrained from conferring legislative, or even *quasi*-legislative, powers upon the world body. "Do the Applicants now contend that by some undefined process, by the need for a *quasi*-legislative body, that that, by itself, has altered the basic nature of the United Nations?"[238] Even more untenable was the suggestion that the Court assume some sort of *quasi*-legislative function to minister to the needs of international society by applying concepts or drawing on sources "other than those traditionally recognized in

233. Ibid., pp. 629–31.
234. Ibid., p. 632.
235. Ibid., pp. 632 ff.
236. Ibid., p. 633.
237. Ibid., p. 634.
238. Ibid., pp. 634–35.

international law." The suggestion that the Court confirm "that international legal obligations may be imposed upon a State without its consent" by a consensus of the General Assembly amounted to a request that the Court "go beyond its normal judicial functions so as to declare that the so-called organized international community . . . possesses normative capacity which it was not intended by its creators to possess."[239] The whole thesis that a "preponderance of votes could, in itself, be normative" truly represented "a revolutionary contention."[240]

Respondent then proceeded to demonstrate that none of the four sources enumerated in Article 38(1) could be used to substantiate the existence of the alleged international norm.

Applicants' reliance on Article 38(1) (a) by reference to the United Nations Charter and the Constitution of the International Labor Organization was said to be entirely misplaced.[241] For, in fact, neither instrument contained any explicit references to the alleged norm; and the interpretation accorded certain provisions in these instruments by "consensus" votes in the respective organizations was in no way binding upon dissentient states. The organs of neither organization were empowered to adopt authoritative interpretations binding upon the member states. And, as far as the United Nations Charter is concerned, the famous Report of Committee IV/2 at San Francisco, on Charter interpretation, made clear that only by the process of Charter amendment could binding interpretations be adopted.[242] The separate opinion of Judge Spender in the *Expenses* case was cited for the proposition that the subsequent practice of a United Nations organ, acting through a majority, could not bind a protesting minority, no matter how large the majority and no matter how often the practice is repeated.[243] In the face of the persistent opposition of South Africa and other states, the norm could not possibly have become part of these conventions—the United Nations Charter or the International Labor Organization—by any so-called process of interpretation.

As for Article 38(1) (b),[244] it was clear that Applicants did not rely upon the activities of states in their inter-state practice as the source for

239. Ibid., p. 635.
240. Ibid., p. 636.
241. Ibid., pp. 636-52.
242. Ibid., pp. 638-39. For a general discussion of the implications of the Report of Committee IV/2, see Goodrich and Hambro, pp. 547-51.
243. *SWA Pleadings* IX: 640-41, citing *ICJ Reports* (1962): 187-97. For a discussion of Judge Spender's views on the subject of the subsequent practice of parties to a treaty, see S. Slonim, "The Advisory Opinion of the International Court of Justice on Certain Expenses of the United Nations: A Critical Analysis," *Howard Law Journal* X (1964): 266-70.
244. For Respondent's discussion of the inapplicability of this source to the alleged norm, see *SWA Pleadings* IX: 652-58; and X: 3-41.

the alleged custom, but upon "the collective acts of the competent international institutions as evidence of general practice accepted as law."[245] But the only practice carried on by these international organizations is that of talking and voting, and this in relation basically to recommendations directed at *ad hoc* situations.[246] Did the repetition of statements and resolutions constitute "practice over a considerable period of time"?[247] Moreover, where could one find an *opinio juris* in the political forum of the General Assembly for a norm of nondiscrimination? Could the affirmative votes of states for a resolution bearing only a recommendatory quality amount to such *opinio juris*?[248] Above all, even assuming that the alleged norm had evolved so as to bind states voting for the relevant resolutions, how could the norm bind South Africa, which had consistently objected to any norm of nondiscrimination?[249] Only if the international institutions concerned were endowed with legislative capacity could such obligatory force be attributed to their resolutions. This involved, however, an argument "for reform, even for revolution . . . but not for application of law."[250] And in any case, such a suggestion would not bring the matter under Article 7 of the Mandate so as to confer jurisdiction on the Court in reference to the proposed norm.

Respondent also rejected Applicants' contention that even if South Africa could bar application of the norm to South Africa it could not do so with reference to South West Africa, a territory imbued with an international status. South Africa argued that since it was accorded full administrative and legislative authority over the territory and was qualified to conclude or terminate treaties applying to the territory, it was no less competent to accept or to bar the application of a developing custom to the territory. Otherwise the mandatory power would not be qualified to determine which elements of international law actually promoted the material and moral well-being of the South West Africa population.[251]

With regard to Article 38(1) paragraphs (c) and (d) postulating "the general principles of law recognized by civilized nations" and judicial decisions and the teachings of publicists as sources of international law, Respondent claimed that these were not meant to serve as independent,

245. Ibid., IX: 653, citing Applicants at ibid., p. 347.
246. Ibid., X: 12-13.
247. Ibid., p. 23.
248. Ibid., pp. 25-28.
249. Ibid., p. 29. Respondent once again quoted the article of Sir Gerald Fitzmaurice (see above, n. 190) which confirms that a state which had "openly and consistently made known its dissent" at the time the new rule was in the process of coming into general acceptance could not be bound thereby. *SWA Pleadings* X: 29.
250. Ibid., p. 30.
251. Ibid., pp. 34-38.

but rather as secondary and subsidiary, sources.[252] Furthermore, these sources, no more than others, could bind a dissentient state. The Applicants, Mr. de Villiers noted, could refer to no authors or judicial pronouncements to establish that the norm of nondiscrimination exists. The few authors cited—Higgins, Schachter, and Jenks—were adduced not in support of the specific norm claimed but rather with reference to the general thesis that consensus is sufficient to give rise to custom (a thesis which Respondent claimed was unsupported even by the authorities cited). For its part, however, Respondent said, it could cite at least one authority—Professor Wilhelm Wengler—in support of the *nonexistence* of the alleged norm.[253] A state, according to Wengler, violated international law if it oppressed or deliberately retarded the progress of ethnic, racial, or religious minorities; it did not violate any rule of international law if it merely differentiated between groups by granting one more rights, even political rights, than another. In this view, then, a norm of nonoppression was recognized by international law, but not a norm of nondifferentiation—i.e., not an absolute norm of nondiscrimination or nonseparation.

Respondent's view, in sum, was that Applicants had not succeeded in demonstrating that their alleged norm of nondiscrimination had arisen to bind South Africa under any of the heads of Article 38(1) of the Court's Statute. Equally vain, in Respondent's opinion, were Applicants' attempts to produce an adequate definition of the norm which would outlaw apartheid without simultaneously striking down permissible forms of differentiation.[254]

Applicants' problem arose from the need to develop a definition free of reference to any disputed factual criteria—an absolutely legal, and even mechanical, rule which would apply automatically without regard to any value judgment. Apartheid would then be stamped as a rank illegality, irrespective of good motive or beneficial effect. But such a peremptory prohibition on policies that distinguish on a group basis meant that, as noted earlier, special arrangements for women, minority groups, etc. would be similarly impermissible. In fact, the source of the alleged norm—Article 55(c) of the Charter—referred to race, sex, language, and religion, indistinguishably.[255]

252. For Respondent's discussion of these two sources, see ibid., pp. 41–52.
253. Ibid., pp. 78–79. The work cited was *Volkerrecht* (Berlin, Göttingen, Heidelberg: Springer Verlag, 1964), pp. 1028–29.
254. For Respondent's discussion of the problem of definition of the norm, see *SWA Pleadings* IX: 524–60; and X: 53–57.
Respondent pointed out that initially the Applicants themselves acknowledged that they could not expect to prevail unless "the nature, scope and content of such an international legal norm and international standards" were satisfactorily defined. Ibid., IX: 549, citing Applicants at ibid., p. 91.
255. See, on this point, ibid., XII: 407–9.

Efforts to overcome this basic difficulty by distinguishing between protective and coercive policies, or by focusing on the freedom of an individual to quit his group, Respondent claimed, had all proved unhelpful and unsupportable. And because of this, it was said, Mr. Gross had been compelled in the end to fall back on the radical assertion that not only was the organized international community qualified to promulgate the alleged norm of nondiscrimination, it was also empowered to declare the norm, undefined as it was, specifically applicable to South West Africa. Indeed, Respondent noted, the Applicants had actually conceded that the Court was not even a suitable organ to determine the merits of any particular administrative policy, and must, of necessity, accept as given the ruling of the relevant international organ.[256] In short, declared Respondent "the organized international community in Applicants' contention would now combine the functions of legislature, witness, judge and jury, and . . . also that of executioner. The Court is interested only in the mechanical function of signing the warrant."[257] Applicants' call for the Court to adopt a "dynamic and flexible" approach constituted an invitation to the Court "to decide this case not on justice in accordance with law, but on what might be termed . . . revolutionary justice."[258]

"They are in effect assigning to this Court a most unworthy role in this whole process, viz., that of a revolutionary tribunal to aid and abet, and to rubber-stamp, the usurpation, by the political majorities in international organs, of legislative powers which have not been granted to them in the constitutive instruments or with the consent of the States which have created them."[259]

In contrast, declared Mr. de Villiers, Respondent was asking the Court to apply the rule of law, which, in this case, meant staying its hand. "Only time can bring a solution to the political aspects of this dispute. . . . It is with respect to finding a political solution that dynamics and flexibility can and will undoubtedly play their part if allowed to take their course."[260]

With this, Respondent concluded its pleadings on the law of the case and proceeded to the presentation of the testimony of witnesses and experts.

*The Oral Testimony*

Having already presented legal arguments denying the competence of international institutions to establish binding norms purely on the

256. Ibid., IX: 556.
257. Ibid., p. 545.
258. Ibid., X: 80.
259. Ibid.
260. Ibid., p. 81.

basis of consensus, Respondent wished now to go further and demonstrate that the actual practice of states—a factor totally omitted in Applicants' analysis—manifestly contradicted the existence of the norm or standards asserted by the Applicants. This was the purpose of the evidence now presented in the form of oral testimony by witnesses and experts. Specifically, Respondent aimed to show the following:[261] (1) the existence of state practice contrary to the norm; (2) the validity (and, in fact, urgent necessity) of pursuing a policy of differentiation in certain circumstances, if peace and order were to be preserved and the goal of promoting the well-being and progress of the inhabitants, successfully fulfilled; and (3) the unsupportability of the international legal norm, even by reference to the Assembly resolutions cited by the Applicants. And in this last connection, the testimony was designed to demonstrate that South Africa's policies in South West Africa were condemned by the United Nations not because those policies failed to adhere to any alleged norm, but because, rightly or wrongly, they were deemed oppressive.

Initially, it will be recalled, South Africa had intended calling some thirty-eight witnesses to testify, but as a result of the changes in Applicants' case, whereby all disputed facts were conceded, Respondent found it had need for only fourteen witnesses.[262] Most of these were experts on South West Africa and its indigenous population and testified as to the seriously adverse consequences which would eventuate if Applicants' alleged norm and/or standards were to be applied to the territory. However, three witnesses—Professors van den Haag, Manning, and, most particularly, Possony—testified on the widespread existence of governmental policies and practices involving group differentiation. Thus, Professor Possony cited some fifty states (among whom, forty, including Ethiopia and Liberia, were members of the United Nations) in which status, rights, duties, and burdens were officially allotted on a basis of group, class, or race—evidence clearly contradicting the existence of any norm of nondiscrimination as alleged by Applicants.[263]

The Applicants, who had vehemently opposed the presentation of oral testimony in the first place, now attempted to discount the significance of the evidence proffered. First, they contended (in the course of their cross-examination of the witnesses[264] and in their final observa-

261. Ibid., pp. 82–85; XII: 84–85.
262. The hearings extended from June 18 to July 14, 1965, and from September 20 to October 21, 1965. For the record of the testimony, see ibid., X: 88–558; XI: 3–708; and XII: 3–66.
263. Ibid., XI: 648 ff.
264. In the arguments on the inspection proposal, it will be recalled (see above, p. 246), Applicants announced they would not undertake any cross-examination of Respondent's witnesses. *SWA Pleadings* IX: 24. Applicants kept to this position with reference to the first witness but proceeded to cross-examine all witnesses from the second one on. See ibid., X: 131, 137, and 182.

tions on the evidence), that the true nature of the "norm" had been distorted by the Respondent, and, as a result, all the evidence to contradict the existence of the norm was inconsequential and totally beside the point.[265] Second, Applicants insisted, while the practice of states might have some bearing on the creation of the "international legal norm," for the "standards of non-discrimination" (which, by this time, had become the "principal" part of the norm thesis), such state practice had no relevance whatsoever. The "standards of non-discrimination" (even as the "standard of negligence," of "reasonable care," of "due process," and the like) could not be contraverted by evidence of practice inconsistent with them.[266]

The latter objection led the President to remind Applicants that their "norm" and "standards" were based on the same sources and had the identical content, even if their legal effect was different. Therefore, state practice might well be relevant, at least to the matter of the content of the standards.[267] For his part, Mr. de Villiers pointed out that the "standards" were said to be a product of the *quasi*-legislative powers of international organizations. But if it could be proved that some forty states members of the United Nations did not themselves adhere to any standards of nondiscrimination, was it logical to assert that the United Nations resolutions for which these states had voted were meant to prescribe such binding standards for South Africa?[268]

Applicants' first objection—that Respondent was distorting the true nature of the "norm"—brought about a running debate between the respective counsel as to just what norm was actually in dispute. Respondent, while posing questions to witnesses, generally adhered to the practice of referring to "a norm and/or standards of non-discrimination or non-separation as contended for by the Applicants";[269] but the clear implication was that the norm under consideration was in essence, one of nondifferentiation. Repeatedly, Mr. Gross protested against this implication, which he considered made a caricature of Applicants' case, and which led to such absurd assertions as that the "norm" would forbid separate public conveniences for men and women. To get away from these absurdities Applicants at times appeared intent on introducing some qualifications into the norm;[270] but they never came around to stating what these qualifications were or what was the essence of the distortion of which Respondent was guilty.[271] Applicants intimated

265. See especially, ibid., pp. 131–33, 138–39; and XII: 347–57.
266. Ibid., XI: 644–47; and XII: 352.
267. Ibid., XI: 647.
268. Ibid., XII: 450.
269. See, e.g., ibid., X: 130; and XII: 582.
270. See, e.g., ibid., XI: 315 and 690–91; and see also X: 183–88.
271. See on this Respondent's comments, ibid., XII: 75–79, and 397–99.

that the definition at Volume IV, page 493,[272] was not final or self-contained but was to be read in conjunction with further material in other parts of the Applicants' pleadings.[273] This raised the question, posed by the President, whether Applicants were not changing their case.[274] Applicants denied any such intention, but went on to imply that the term "discrimination" had a pejorative quality built in to it so that the word implied more than mere differentiation, and, in fact meant something like "unfair discrimination."[275]

Respondent countered this new semantic effort of the Applicants by tendering dictionary definitions of the term "discrimination,"[276] and, more pointedly, by noting that Applicants' norm was officially labeled not only as one of "non-discrimination" but also as one of "non-separation." Since both terms referred to one and the same norm, it was impossible to allege, as Applicants were now attempting to do, that their norm meant something other than a categorical nondifferentiation—"separate is not equal"—rule.[277] As for Applicants' charge that Respondent was misrepresenting their case by high-lighting absurd consequences, it was Respondent's contention that these absurdities only confirmed the untenability of Applicants' case.[278] A purely legal norm of absolute standards, devoid of any factual evaluation, could not possibly exclude the rank absurdities noted, since there was no criterion by which to distinguish permissible from impermissible discrimination.

By the end of the oral testimony, and at the culmination of six years of litigation, Applicants' case against apartheid had come to rest on the worst possible terrain for a forensic struggle—a "semantic swamp."[279]

## FROM NUREMBERG TO *BROWN*

The Applicants in their litigation before the Court initially undertook to challenge apartheid frontally before the tribunal of the world as a

272. See above, p. 241.
273. *SWA Pleadings* XII: 7, 26–29.
274. Ibid., p. 27.
275. See ibid., pp. 5–8, 353, and 375; and for the comments of Respondent, see ibid., pp. 78–79, 172–73, and 399–401.
276. Ibid., p. 72.
277. Ibid., pp. 72–74, and 401. It may be noted that as the pleadings progressed, Applicants tended to hedge on the absolute nature of their norm. Particularly illuminating in this regard was their reply to the President's query as to whether the absence of compulsory education, irrespective of any possible extenuating circumstances, constituted an inherent violation of Article 2 of the Mandate. Applicants answered that "this would be a factor relevant for the Court's consideration in connection with the significance of the educational aspect of apartheid." Ibid., XI: 315. Applicants thereby intimated that the norm was not really absolute.
278. Ibid., XII: 407.
279. The term is borrowed from Judge Jessup, who, in his 1966 dissent, noted that the argument between the parties "frequently bogged down" in a "semantical swamp." *SWA Judgment* (1966): 432.

manifest violation of the mandate. They would marshal all the evidence, all the incriminating material that had been assembled over the years in reference to this invidious system of racial superiority, and would spread it before the Court in all its gory detail. The whole system would be stamped as nothing less than a form of mass genocide, a crime against humanity, and a trespass on the conscience of the world. At this point, very clearly, the goal of the Applicants was a second Nuremberg trial and not at all a *Brown* v. *Board of Education* ruling.

However, as a result of a series of challenges posed by Respondent, the Applicants' case was steadily modified until the entire frontal challenge to apartheid on a factual basis was supplanted by a purely legal concept of doubtful validity in international law. In the end, nothing at all was left of Nuremberg and in its place there stood but a pallid replica of *Brown*.

Respondent's first challenge involved the "good faith" issue. Given the sweeping administrative discretion conferred on the Mandatory by Article 2 of the Mandate, and given, too, the inherent limitations of the judicial function, the Court was said to possess neither the competence nor the available legal criteria wherewith to pass upon the compatibility of apartheid with Article 2 of the Mandate, except by reference to South Africa's good or bad faith in the selection of its administrative policies in South West Africa.

In response, Applicants were led to posit, in their Reply, the existence of an "international legal norm of non-discrimination or non-separation"—a categorical "separate is not equal" rule—as part of Article 2 of the Mandate. The Court would thereby have both the power—since the norm set an absolute limit to the Mandatory's discretion—and the tools—since the norm provided a "legal" criterion—to adjudicate upon the apartheid issue. The matter would thus be rendered fully justiciable; and the very fact of separation between Whites and non-Whites, without further ado, would serve to establish the incompatibility of apartheid with the Mandate. At this stage of the pleadings, however, the Nuremberg aspect of the case was not abandoned; the oppression charge continued to ride in tandem with the norm thesis.

It was Respondent's second major challenge—the inspection proposal raised at the commencement of the oral arguments—that triggered off a complete and radical transformation of Applicants' case. In order to defeat the inspection proposal, Applicants decided to premise their case exclusively on a "legal" basis and to abandon any reliance on disputed facts or on value judgments. To render superfluous any factual enquiry, whether by inspection or personal testimony, Applicants agreed to accept all the facts of the Respondent as part of their own case. The norm thesis, which now incorporated within itself two variants—a "norm of non-discrimination or non-separation" proper, and "standards" having an identical content, but a lesser "degree of legal authoritativeness"—became the crucial and exclusive prop of Applicants' arguments. On the basis of either or both parts of the norm thesis, the Court was asked to adjudge apartheid incompatible *ipso facto* (i.e., regardless of good motives or beneficial effects) with Article 2 of the Mandate—and to do so without engaging in any independent factual enquiry or value judgment.

Applicants indeed won their point on the inspection proposal,[280] but at the expense of their entire legal case. They were now called upon by both Respondent and members of the Court to spell out the sources and content of the asserted norm. How did it arise? How did it come to be binding on the mandatory power? And how, in the absence of a factual enquiry, could the norm prohibit only those forms of separation which the Applicants wished to see prohibited? In attempting to provide answers to these questions, Applicants came to argue that consensus had already replaced consent as the essential element in the generation of new international legal norms and to assert sweeping *quasi*-legislative and even *quasi*-judicial powers for the organized international community. Their search for a definition of the norm led them to become entangled in a series of tautologies. And in the end, Applicants ended up agreeing with Respondent that the Court was not really competent to review independently the administrative discretion of the Mandatory.

The first stumbling block that Applicants had to overcome was the question where the norm and/or standards emanated from and how they came to fall within the ambit of the compromissory clause of the Mandate. They were certainly not present in express form in the original Mandate which itself distinguished in various provisions between the Native and non-Native populations. To surmount this difficulty Applicants were compelled to "rewrite," as it were, two sets of documents. The first comprised the mandate instruments; and it was the Applicants' contention, in the face of contrary *travaux préparatoires* and the full record of League and mandate experience, that the League supervisory organs were from the start empowered to set binding standards for mandatory powers. But, going even further, Applicants asserted that the mandate instruments, by an implied term, obligated the Mandatory to abide, not only by the standards set by the League but also by the standards set by any later embodiment of the "organized international community." The second set of documents to be rewritten encompassed primarily the United Nations Charter itself (and secondarily,

280. See above final paragraph in n. 131.

such instruments as the International Labor Organization Constitution and the Trusteeship Agreements). Applicants were claiming for the United Nations organs such *quasi*-legislative powers and such authority to prescribe binding norms and/or standards upon a dissentient state by force of consensus as were neither contemplated by the founders of the present world organization nor accepted on a general basis by the present membership of the organization. Even with regard to the United Nations' own trust territories, no such broad authority had been asserted. Applicants' thesis of a "norm and/or standards of non-discrimination or non-separation" as a matter of the *quasi*-legislative fiat of the General Assembly, appeared to contradict both general state practice in regard to the generation of new legal norms and specific state practice in regard to the content of the alleged norm. For, in fact, many of the states voting for the relevant resolutions apparently acted, in their own state practice, contrary to the principles said to be embodied in the resolutions.

No less of a stumbling block to the Applicants was the difficulty of defining the scope and content of the alleged norm in the absence of any factual enquiry and value judgment. Here, the Applicants were led, inevitably and fatally, into a semantical bog of tautological dead-ends. The crucial issue, as noted, was how to define the norm so as to bar illegitimate discrimination or separation, while permitting legitimate forms of differentiation. But this was a question which no semantical discussion could possibly solve. At root, the problem was: what constituted *fair*, or *reasonable*, differentiation, as opposed to differentiation which was *unfair*, or *unreasonable*? The issue of reasonableness—related, in turn, to an examination and evaluation of the facts—was unavoidable. It was the yardstick of reasonableness which had allowed the United States Supreme Court in *Brown* v. *Board of Education* to interpret and give meaning to the equal protection clause of the Fourteenth Amendment of the United States Constitution. Thus, the Supreme Court was able in that case to declare that the maintenance of separate schools for different races was "arbitrary" and "unreasonable," while allowing, in other cases, forms of differentiation deemed "reasonable."[281] But Applicants' self-denying gesture of excluding both disputed facts and value judgments also served to deny the Court the essential tools wherewith to make the crucial link between the abstract norm and the concrete case of apartheid. Applicants vainly attempted to read the word "unfair" or "unreasonable" into the norm; and they thus inevitably became embroiled in circular reasoning: the "norm of

---

281. For a succinct review of Supreme Court decisions under the Fourteenth Amendment distinguishing between "reasonable" and "unreasonable" classifications, see Edward S. Corwin and Jack W. Peltason, *Understanding the Constitution* (3rd ed.; New York: Holt, Rinehart and Winston, 1964), pp. 153–56.

non-discrimination or non-separation" encompassed only prohibited forms of differentiation, and apartheid was prohibited because it was a prohibited form of differentiation. There remained one other way that Applicants could relate the norm to apartheid in a value-free vacuum while escaping tautological reasoning: if some *other* body—political or administrative—had already made the crucial link between the abstract norm and the specific case, and if the Court need only confirm the right of that body to do so. This is precisely what the Applicants came around to arguing. The General Assembly was now endowed not only with *quasi*-legislative powers, but also with *quasi*-judicial authority: it was the organ which was qualified both to legislate the norm and to declare it applicable to South West Africa. The Court's role was to adjudge that the judgment of the Assembly had been transformed into, or always had, the force of legal fiat. The Court was then to be the instrumentality by which the General Assembly's *quasi*-legislative, *quasi*-judicial, pronouncements would be up-graded and metamorphosed into judicial, fully binding pronouncements.

Indeed, Applicants ended up by agreeing with an important part of Respondent's argument on the nonjusticiability of the apartheid issue. The Court, Applicants argued, was not even qualified to adjudge independently the compatibility of apartheid with Article 2 of the Mandate, for this would involve the Court in an essentially nonjudicial role; it had to accept the ruling of the General Assembly on this matter. The Court could not engage in "second-guessing the competent international organs responsible for the development of the norm."[282] Respondent, of course, had all along urged that Article 2 of the Mandate was nonjusticiable, except on the basis of the Mandatory's good or bad faith. The Applicants were now arguing that apartheid was nonjusticiable except on the basis of "the international legal norm and/or standards of non-discrimination or non-separation." Apart, then, from the respective totally divergent grounds proffered by each side in the litigation, the Court was, by consensus of the parties, denied any third alternative ground for adjudicating the matter of apartheid.

This fact was high-lighted by a question addressed by the Court to both parties at the end of the oral proceedings. Interrupting the hearing of witnesses, the President, on June 22, 1965, stated:

> These questions bore upon the fact that the Applicants relied upon a certain norm and/or standards as the basis for interpreting compliance with Article 2(2). On the other hand, the Respondent disputed the existence of any such norm or standards and based its case upon the proposition that Article 2(2) could not be shown to have been breached by it unless, in respect to the exercise of its

282. *SWA Pleadings* IX: 246; and see above, p. 259.

authority under Article 2 of the Mandate, it was shown that it had acted in bad faith, or for a purpose other than to give effect to Article 2(2) of the Mandate and that the Article must be interpreted accordingly.

The questions which the Court desired to put to the Parties were the following:

Assuming the Court were to come to the conclusion that there had not been established any such legal norm or standards and were also to come to the conclusion that the interpretation sought to be placed upon Article 2(2) of the Mandate by the Respondent was not the proper interpretation to be placed upon that Article, or did not exhaust the meaning thereof.

Question I. Do the Parties contend that the Court is bound to adjudicate the dispute between the Parties exclusively upon the basis on which they have presented their respective cases and the interpretation they have respectively sought to give to Article 2(2) of the Mandate?

Question 2. Do the Parties contend that it is not open to the Court to place its own interpretation upon the article, having regard to all relevant legal considerations and adjudge between the Parties accordingly?

Question 3. In particular, do the Parties contend that it is not open to the Court to interpret paragraph 2, sub-paragraph 2 thereof, in a manner by which it would examine and evaluate all relevant facts, circumstances and conditions appertaining to the Territory, as they appear before it on the final record in the case, in order to determine whether the Respondent had discharged its obligations under that article and adjudge between the Parties accordingly?[283]

In reply,[284] Applicants indicated, that although in their contention apartheid constituted an *ipso facto* violation of Article 2(2) of the Mandate on the basis of the international legal norm and/or standards of nondiscrimination, they would not object if the Court reached an independent conclusion on the matter, outside the scope of the submissions. The arguments which they had presented regarding the violation of Article 2(2) did "not restrict the discretion of the Court in any way in adjudging upon the dispute . . . in accordance with the Court's conception of the relevant legal and factual considerations."[285]

Respondent, in contrast, took vehement exception to this stance of the Applicants.[286] The Court was entitled to select independent *legal*

283. *SWA Pleadings* VIII: 60, 62. It is to be noted that this set of questions, in contrast to all other questions raised during the proceedings, was posed by the Court as a whole, and not by individual judges. The significance of these questions is noted in the dissenting opinion of Judge Jessup, *SWA Judgment* (1966): 430, n. 1.

284. For the reply of the Applicants, see *SWA Pleadings* X: 183–88 and 228–33.

285. Ibid., p. 185.

286. For Respondent's reply to the Court's questions, see ibid., pp. 188–228, and 233–37.

grounds for its decision; but it could not go outside the ambit of the final submissions as regards the *facts* in dispute. In the present case, Applicants had circumscribed the factual enquiry, had categorically excluded any request for a value judgment from the Court, and had premised their case solely on the existence of the international legal norm and/or standards. With both the motives and effects of apartheid rendered irrelevant, Respondent had abstained from presenting any further evidence regarding the *bona fide* intentions of the Mandatory, or the merits and reasonableness of apartheid. Were the Court to now undertake an independent evaluation of the purpose or reasonableness of apartheid, it would be condemning one party without giving that party a full "opportunity of leading evidence and presenting argument on his own behalf, and that would be contrary to the principles of natural justice which underlie all procedural systems."[287] The Court, Respondent insisted, was not authorized "to conduct any factual enquiry beyond the scope of the Applicants' case, . . . namely the case based upon standards and/or the norm."[288] Applicants could not expect the Court to "try to make a case for them where their own case has failed."[289]

Clearly, the entire course of the pleadings on the merits, as climaxed by the aforementioned questions of the Court and replies of the parties, set strict bounds on the Court's adjudicatory role on the merits. (Despite Applicants' last-minute attempt to allow an independent judgment of the apartheid issue by the Court, their entire norm thesis—incorporated in their final submissions—had led them to *negate* the possibility of any such independent judgment.) But simultaneously, and more importantly, the long forensic struggle spotlighted the question of the justiciability of the apartheid issue. For if a Nuremberg ruling was excluded and a *Brown* decision dependent on the Court assuming a self-denying role in favor of the *quasi*-judicial powers of the organized international community, then how adjudicable could Article 2 of the Mandate have really been in the first place? And if this provision was not adjudicable, then what was the intended role of the Court in the functioning of mandates, and, in particular, with reference to such a dispute as the instant one? And if the Court's role was severely circumscribed, then what did this denote with regard to the place of individual states in the operation of the mandates system and their capacity to serve in a supervisory role through the agency of the Court? These were some of the questions which the lengthy proceedings on the merits had served to project onto center stage.

287. Ibid., p. 198.
288. Ibid., p. 209.
289. Ibid., p. 228.

# XI.

## THE SECOND PHASE: THE 1966 JUDGMENT —THE COURT RETREATS

### ANTICIPATION OF THE JUDGMENT

When the public proceedings in the *South West Africa* cases closed on November 15, 1965, the President of the Court, Sir Percy Spender, summed up the significance of this event in the following terms: "These cases were of great importance, not only for the States directly involved. With the vast amount of evidence and documentation and with the number of issues to be determined, they were, he did not doubt, the heaviest that had been submitted to this Court or its predecessor. Certainly they were the most protracted."[1]

All the crucial issues that had so engaged the attention of the United Nations over the years—international accountability, apartheid, the international status of the territory, and the right of self-determination—were now arrayed before the Court in extraordinary detail for judicial determination. The world looked forward with great impatience to the decision that would pronounce, with finality, upon so many momentous issues.

Few people outside the confines of the Peace Palace of the Hague, however, were aware of the manner in which the case had been unraveled before the Court and what ultimate issues were presented for adjudication. The impression prevailing both in the halls of the United Nations and in the world at large was that the issues before the Court were fairly simple and straightforward. On the one hand, the Court was merely to reaffirm, in the form of a binding judgment, the conclusions regarding international accountability to the United Nations already

---

1. *SWA Pleadings* VIII: 96. The pleadings in the cases had run on for five years (November 4, 1960, to November 15, 1965) and had produced some 6,725 pages of printed record covering both the written and oral pleadings.

embodied in the 1950 opinion; and, on the other hand, it was to rule that apartheid—as a totally oppressive system of administration and unreasonable exercise of discretion—was incompatible with the mandate. As a "principal organ" of the United Nations, the Court could not fail to find for Applicants and thereby, to again serve the General Assembly as in the past.[2]

Clearly, those making this assumption did not know (and could not have been expected to know) that the issue of the oppressiveness of apartheid—the "Nuremberg" aspect of the case—had, in the course of the proceedings, fallen by the wayside; that Applicants' own pleadings had, in effect, barred the application of a reasonableness test by the Court; and that, as a result, the issue of apartheid *per se* was no longer the central element in the litigation, having been superseded by fundamental questions regarding methods of norm-creation in international law (and most particularly questions regarding the *quasi*-legislative and *quasi*-judicial capacity of the organized international community in relation to the generation and application of new norms). What had, then, to be taken into account was not only the role of the Court as a "principal organ" of the United Nations, but also its position as the "principal *judicial* organ." The Court, unlike the political bodies of the United Nations, could not permit itself the liberty of grounding out *ad hoc* decisions;[3] its pronouncements must be principled ones, based on rules capable of *generalized* application.

Those not privy to the pleadings could not know, too, how hard the Court was grappling with the issues as they were ultimately presented to it—something dramatically illustrated by the questions posed to the parties by the full Court in regard to the freedom of the Court to undertake its own independent assessment of apartheid.[4] Nor could it be generally appreciated to what extent the fundamental question of

2. Such doubts as were harbored by even so severe a critic of the 1966 judgment as J. H. W. Verzijl were apparently not entertained by many less knowledgeable persons. Verzijl has stated: "As a judicial body . . . —not being a political organ, nor a body with pseudo-legislative competences—the Court would . . . have met with serious difficulties in finding against South Africa on strictly legal grounds." "The South West Africa Cases: (Second Phase)," *International Relations* III (1966): 97.

As one writer has noted, it was even anticipated in many quarters that the Court would order South Africa to surrender its Mandate, despite the fact that the Applicant states had made no such request of the Court. See D. H. N. Johnson, "The South West Africa Cases (Second Phase)," *International Relations* III (1967): 158.

Illustrative of the attitude prevalent at the United Nations was the argument of the Guinean representative in support of a 1960 move to divest South Africa of its mandate. (See below, chap. XII, n. 5.) The Assembly could take this step, he said, "since it could be assumed *a priori* that the . . . Court . . . would not deliver a judgment contrary to its first advisory opinion in 1950." GAOR, 15th Sess., 4th Ctte., 1063rd Mtg., Nov. 24, 1960, p. 377.

3. On the tendency of the General Assembly to ignore, on occasion, "neutral principles," see Louis Henkin, "The United Nations and the Rules of Law," *Harvard International Law Journal* XI (1970): 428 ff.; and see, especially, ibid., p. 431.

4. See above, pp. 275–76.

the justiciability of Article 2 was thrown into high relief by the entire course of the proceedings on the merits, culminating in the aforementioned questions of the Court and replies of the parties. For, if the Court, as even the Applicants came to concede during the pleadings, was not competent to examine independently the merits of any given administrative policy, but was left with the alternative of "buying" either the near-absolute discretion of the Mandatory, as espoused by Respondent, or the absolute "norm of non-discrimination or non-separation," as espoused by Applicants—then how justiciable was Article 2 of the Mandate in the first place, and how meaningful was the supervisory role of the Court under such circumstances? Had not the tortuous path and final denouement of the pleadings constituted a resounding confirmation and vindication of the doubts regarding the inherent nonjusticiability of Article 2 already adumbrated by Judges Spender and Fitzmaurice in their 1962 joint dissent? As will be recalled,[5] the two judges, linking the question of justiciability with the third preliminary objection, had enunciated a sort of "separation of powers" argument. Supervision of the administration of the mandate, they said, was a "political" function which had been conferred solely upon the political organs of the League and never entrusted to the Court. Individual states, in the absence of a material interest, could not implead the Mandatory before the Court, for if they could, they would involve the Court in a task which was inherently nonjudicial, and which, as the relevant mandate instruments made clear, the Court was never intended to fulfill. The arguments on the merits which had ultimately led each side to posit a less than meaningful role for the Court, conclusively established, in the eyes of the Court, the validity of the thesis that Article 7 of the Mandate, the compromissory clause, was not meant to institute judicial supervision at all. It was this conclusion which was embodied in the 1966 judgment of the Court denying Ethiopia and Liberia any right to obtain a judgment on the merits.

Those who had looked forward with a sense of complete sanguineness to a definitive anti-South African ruling by the Court had undoubtedly also paid insufficient attention to the very closeness of the vote (8 to 7) in the 1962 judgment on the question of the standing of Ethiopia and Liberia in the case, and to certain changes in the composition of the Court which took place between the 1962 and 1966 decisions. While the erstwhile minority of seven was hardly affected at all—with only Judge Basdevant of France being replaced by his countryman, Judge Gros—the 1962 majority underwent certain important changes as follows: Judges Alfaro (Panama) and Moreno Quintana (Argentina)

5. See above, pp. 207-8.

retired[6] in 1964, and Judge Bustamante y Rivero (Peru) was unable to participate in the 1966 decision due to ill health. Of the three judges (other than Judge Gros) newly elected to the Court in 1964, one, Judge Sir Muhammed Zafrulla Khan (Pakistan)[7] was disqualified from participating in the case, due, apparently, to his previous candidature as a judge *ad hoc* on behalf of the Applicants.[8] In August 1965, before the oral proceedings were completed, Judge Badawi (United Arab Republic) died and was subsequently replaced by Judge Ammoun (Lebanon), who, however, could not participate in the 1966 decision, since he had not been present for the first part of the oral hearings. Thus, of the original eight judges of the 1962 majority, only four were left on the bench in 1966.[9] Consequently, even if these were joined by the three remaining judges[10] (other than Judge Gros), and if for some reason the erstwhile minority (with the support of Judge Gros) undertook to examine afresh the question of Applicants' standing in the case, the result would be an evenly divided (7 to 7) Court. In such circumstances the

6. Judge Cordova (Mexico) likewise retired, but since he had been unable to participate in the 1962 decision, his departure did not affect the line-up in the case.

7. The others elected were Judges Forster (Senegal) and Luis Padilla Nervo (Mexico).

8. Press Release of the Pakistan Mission to the United Nations, Aug. 1, 1966. See U.N. Doc. A/6388, Aug. 17, 1966.

It would appear that Judge Zafrulla Khan's nonparticipation was due to the insistence of the President, who informed him that he was speaking on behalf of a majority of the Court. Judge Zafrulla Khan does not seem to have contested the matter or brought it to a vote in the Court.

For a discussion of the provisions of the Court Rules relevant to this matter (Articles 17 and 24), see Bin Cheng, "The 1966 South-West Africa Judgment of the World Court," *Current Legal Problems 1967* XX: 196–99; and Rosalyn Higgins, "The International Court and South West Africa: The Implications of the Judgment," *International Affairs* XLII (1966): 586–88. See also R. P. Anand, *Studies in International Adjudication* (Dobbs Ferry, N.Y.: Oceana, 1969), p. 138, n. 54.

It is to be noted that in the 1970–71 proceedings on the Namibia question, South Africa formally challenged President Zafrulla Khan's right to participate in the case, both on the grounds for which he was disqualified in the *South West Africa* cases and because of the active role which he played in General Assembly deliberations and decisions bearing directly on the subject involved in the advisory proceedings. These objections were rejected by the Court, as were, also, objections to the participation of two other members of the Court (Judges Padilla Nervo and Morozov). See *Namibia Opinion* (1971): 18–19. For the details of South Africa's objections, see *Namibia Pleadings* I: 437–39.

9. In this connection it might be noted that a South African challenge regarding the composition of the Court (made at the opening of the oral proceedings), had it succeeded, would have affected the line-up in the Court even more drastically. Court hearings on this challenge were held in camera, but it is now clear that South Africa objected to the right of Judge Padilla Nervo to sit on the case in view of his active involvement in the General Assembly's adoption of decisions relating to South West Africa, and, most specifically, his reaction to the famed 1962 visit to South West Africa by Messrs. Carpio and de Alva. (Mr. de Alva was a Mexican delegate to the United Nations; Padilla Nervo was, at the time, Mexico's Permanent Representative.) See above, p. 248, n. 151. The Court rejected the South African challenge by a vote of eight to six. See *SWA Judgment* (1966) p. 9; and see *South West Africa, Order of 18 March 1965, I.C.J. Reports 1965*, p. 3. In the Namibia proceedings (as noted in the preceding footnote), South Africa once again objected to the participation of Judge Padilla Nervo.

10. Judges Forster and Padilla Nervo, both newly elected, and Judge Tanaka (Japan), who had been ill during the proceedings on the Preliminary Objections.

question of who, as President of the Court, would be entitled to the casting vote would be crucial. Since 1964 this position was held by the Australian judge, Sir Percy Spender, a member of the 1962 dissenting minority.

It is hardly surprising, in view of the general ignorance of the factors enumerated with regard to both the course of the pleadings and the composition of the Court, that the 1966 pronouncement was greeted with general consternation and dismay. Nor is it surprising that in the torrent of fierce criticism unleashed against the judgment, one factor among those previously overlooked was singled out for blame, namely, the changed composition of the Court. The judgment was thus seen as but a "fluke, an accident, perhaps . . . an anomaly."[11] It is, however, essential to appreciate what the Court actually said in denying Applicants a judgment on the merits, and the strengths and weaknesses of the legal—as against the political or emotional—criticisms leveled against the Court.[12]

## THE COURT JUDGMENT[13]

The final judgment of the Court in the *South West Africa* cases, handed down on July 18, 1966, declared that Ethiopia and Liberia were not

11. Remarks of the Philippines delegate, GAOR, 21st Sess., Plen., 1417th Mtg., Sept. 26, 1966, p. 20.

12. The General Assembly proceedings immediately following delivery of the judgment were characterized by considerable emotional invective against the Court and against individual judges. Even some articles appearing in scholarly journals have been hardly less emotional. For a particularly far-out criticism of this sort, making no reference to the pleadings, see William M. Reisman, "Revision of the South West Africa Cases: An Analysis of the Grounds of Nullity in the Decision of July 18th, 1966 and Methods of Revision," *Virginia Journal of International Law* VII (1966): 1-90.

13. For discussion and analysis of the Court judgment, see (in addition to the works already cited in this chapter): S. Bastid, "L'affaire du Sud-Ouest africain devant la Cour internationale de justice," *Journal du Droit International* XCIV (1967): 571-83; John Carey, Harry Inman, and Clifford J. Hynning, "The World Court's Decision on South West Africa," *International Lawyer* I (1966): 12-38; Anthony A. D'Amato, "Legal and Political Strategies of the South West Africa Litigation," *Law in Transition Quarterly* IV (1967): 8-43; D. P. de Villiers, "The South West Africa Cases: The Moment of Truth," in *Ethiopia and Liberia* vs. *South Africa: The South West Africa Cases* (Occasional Paper No. 5, African Studies Center, University of California, Los Angeles, 1968) (Hereinafter cited as *UCLA Paper*), pp. 13-19; C. J. R. Dugard, "The South West Africa Cases, Second Phase, 1966," *South African Law Journal* LXXXIII (1966): 429-60; Richard A. Falk, "The South West Africa Cases: The Limits of Adjudication," in *UCLA Paper*, pp. 31-41; Richard A. Falk, *The Status of Law in International Society* (Princeton, N.J.: Princeton University Press, 1970), chap. XI (reproduced from *International Organization* XXI [1967]: 1-23); G. Fischer, "Les Réactions devant l'Arrêt de la Cour Internationale de Justice Concernant le Sud-Ouest Africain," *Annuaire Francais de Droit International* XII (1966): 144-54; Brian Fleming, "South West Africa Cases. *Ethiopia v. South Africa*; *Liberia v. South Africa*. Second Phase, *Canadian Yearbook of International Law* V (1967): 241-53; Wolfgang Friedmann, "The Jurisprudential Implications of the South West Africa Case," *Columbia Journal of Transnational Law* VI (1967): 1-16; L. C. Green, "The United Nations, South-West Africa and the World Court," *Indian Journal of International Law* VII (1967): 491-525; Ernest A. Gross, "The South West Africa Cases: An Essay on Judicial Outlook," in *UCLA Paper*, pp. 1-12; Ernest A. Gross, "The South West Africa Case: What

entitled to a decision on the merits, since they lacked a "legal right or interest" in the subject matter of their claim. In effect, the judgment ruled that the right of the Applicants to have the Court exercise jurisdiction in the case did not, of itself, ensure them of a right to a judicial answer to their submissions. To obtain an answer to the various questions bearing on the mandate, the Applicants needed to possess a specific legal interest in the affairs of the mandate, and this, the Court held, they did not possess.

The Court emphasized that its present decision related to a different aspect of the case from that dealt with in the 1962 judgment. That decision was a ruling on the *jurisdiction*, whereas the instant decision was a ruling relating to the *merits*. "The essential point is that a decision on a preliminary objection can never be preclusive of a matter appertaining to the merits, whether or not it has in fact been dealt with in connection with the preliminary objection."[14] But in fact, said the Court, the earlier decision had not even dealt with the same issue that was now being adjudged. The issue of jurisdiction involved a technical consideration of the conditions or requirements arising from the adjudicatory clause itself, and whether these requirements had been fulfilled so as to establish the competence of the Court to assume jurisdiction. This would cover the matters implicitly required by Article 7—that the forum be the correct one, that the parties belong to the relevant category of states, and that the dispute be one which cannot be settled by negotiation, etc. This, however, was very different from confirming a legal claim on the merits. The Applicants, in addition to establishing the

---

Happened?" *Foreign Affairs* XLV (1966): 36–47; Leo Gross, "The International Court of Justice and the United Nations," Hague Academy, *Recueil des Cours* CXXI (II–1967): 314–439; Keith Highet, "The South West Africa Cases," *Current History* LII (1967): 154–61; Milton Katz, *The Relevance of International Adjudication* (Cambridge, Mass.: Harvard University Press, 1968), chap. IV; Elizabeth S. Landis, "The South West Africa Cases: Remand to the United Nations," *Cornell Law Quarterly* LII (1967): 627–71; Edward McWhinney, "The Changing United Nations Constitutionalism: New Arenas and New Techniques for International Law-Making," *Canadian Yearbook of International Law* V (1967): 68–83; Ambassador Endalkachew Makonnen, "The South West Africa Cases: The Case for Rectification," in *UCLA Paper*, pp. 21–29; C. A. W. Manning, "The South West Africa Cases: A Personal Analysis," *International Relations* III (1966): 98–110; Cornelius F. Murphy, Jr., "The South-West Africa Judgment: A Study in Justiciability," *Duquesne University Law Review* V (1966–67): 477–86; Alexander J. Pollock, "The South West Africa Cases and the Jurisprudence of International Law," *International Organization* XXIII (1969): 767–87; Robert W. Scrivner, "The South-West Africa Case: 1962 Revisited," *African Forum* II (1966): 33–50; Julius Stone, "South West Africa and the World Court" I, II, and III, in *The Australian*, Sept. 26–28, 1966; Rita F. and Howard J. Taubenfeld, *Race, Peace, Law, and Southern Africa* (Dobbs Ferry, N.Y.: Oceana, 1968), pp. 16–23, 52–60, and passim.; and J. H. Wellington, *South West Africa and Its Human Issues* (Oxford: Clarendon Press, 1967), chap. XIX.

14. *SWA Judgment* (1966): 37. By this means the Court avoided any question of *res judicata* with reference to the 1962 judgment. As will be seen below (pp. 292–94), where the issue is more fully discussed, the dissenting judges differed strongly from the Court on this question.

right of the Court to *hear* the case, must, on the merits, establish that they had the necessary "right or interest in the carrying out of the provisions which they invoked, such as to entitle them to the pronouncements and declarations they were seeking from the Court."[15] In its formal conclusions the Court found

> that the Applicants cannot be considered to have established any legal right or interest appertaining to them in the subject-matter of the present claims, and that, accordingly, the Court must decline to give effect to them.
>
> For these reasons,
>
> THE COURT,
>
> by the President's casting vote—the votes being equally divided,

decides to reject the claims of the Empire of Ethiopia and the Republic of Liberia.[16]

Despite the disclaimer of the Court, it is quite clear that the 1966 decision, in fact, if not in technical form, represents a reversal of the 1962 judgment. The 1966 majority opinion, without question, reflects basically the thinking of the 1962 minority on the third Preliminary Objection, and, of course, presents an entirely opposite interpretation of the mandates system, and of the role of the Court within that system, from that adopted by the 1962 majority.

The 1966 judgment opened by noting that the Court, in its consideration of the issues, found that

> there was one matter that appertained to the merits of the case but which had an antecedent character, namely the question of the Applicants' standing in the present phase of the proceedings, not, that is to say, of their standing before the Court itself, which was the subject of the Court's decision in 1962, but the question, as a matter of the merits of the case, of their legal right or interest regarding the subject-matter of their claim.[18]

---

15. *SWA Judgment* (1966): 38.

16. Ibid., p. 51. Those voting with the majority were: President of the Court, Sir Percy Spender (Australia), and Judges Winiarski (Poland), Spiropoulos (Greece), Sir Gerald Fitzmaurice (United Kingdom), Morelli (Italy), Gros (France), and van Wyk (South Africa—Respondent's judge *ad hoc*). Those voting with the minority were: Judges Wellington Koo (China), Koretsky (Soviet Union), Tanaka (Japan), Jessup (United States), Padilla Nervo (Mexico), Forster (Senegal), and Sir Louis Mbanefo (Nigeria—Applicants' judge *ad hoc*).

17. See the dissenting opinions of Judges Tanaka and Jessup, ibid., pp. 248 and 330. Judge van Wyk, in his separate opinion, was led to say: "A great deal of the reasoning of the present Judgment is in conflict with the reasoning of the 1962 Judgment . . . —so much so that the inescapable inference is that in 1962 the Court assumed a jurisdiction it does not possess." Ibid., p. 65.

18. Ibid., p. 18.

In answer to the question why the Court was first dealing with this crucial question at such a late stage of the proceedings, the judgment went on to say:

[Despite the antecedent character of this question, the Court was unable to go into it until the Parties had presented their arguments on the other questions of merits involved.]The same instruments are relevant to the existence and character of the Respondent's obligations concerning the Mandate as are also relevant to the existence and character of the Applicants' legal right or interest in that regard. Certain humanitarian principles alleged to affect the nature of the Mandatory's obligations in respect of the inhabitants of the mandated territory were also pleaded as a foundation for the right of the Applicants to claim in their own individual capacities the performance of those same obligations.[19]

(Actually, two questions presented themselves for prior consideration, the Court said, so that "a decision respecting any of them might render unnecessary an enquiry into other aspects of the matter." The questions were: (1) whether the mandate still subsists at all—for if not, there was no point to considering contraventions of the mandate; and (2) the aforementioned question of the Applicants' legal right or interest in the subject matter of their claim. Of the two questions, however, the second was deemed "more fundamental," since the first constituted part of Applicants' submissions and should not be answered unless the Applicants possessed the necessary right or interest to obtain an answer.]For this reason the Court turned its attention to the issue of standing.[20] At the same time, however, the Court stressed that its consideration of this question was undertaken "without pronouncing upon, and wholly without prejudice to, the question of whether [the] Mandate is still in force." Moreover, the Court emphasized that its 1962 decision on the question of competence "was equally given without prejudice to that of the survival of the Mandate, which is a question appertaining to the merits of the case." The 1962 decision only *assumed* the survival of the mandate so as to reach a decision on the

---

19. Ibid.
20. Ibid., pp. 18–19. Judge Morelli, in his separate opinion, regards the selection of the one issue in preference to the other, as being based on considerations not of logic, but of "economy," i.e., the use of the simplest means of reaching the decision. Ibid., pp. 65–66.

More practical reasons may also have dictated the choice of issue. Determination that the mandate had come to an end would have conflicted directly with the 1950 opinion on the question, and it is not clear that a majority could be summoned to overturn the earlier pronouncement. Judge Winiarski, for instance, was a member of the Court majority both in 1950 and 1966. Furthermore, Judges Fitzmaurice and Gros, both members of the 1966 majority, subsequently indicated (in their dissenting opinions in the *Namibia* case) that the mandate, as an institution, had, in their view, not lapsed in 1946. *Namibia Opinion* (1971): 224 and 342. Nevertheless, the very fact that the 1966 Court entered an express reservation on the question of the survival of the mandate served to throw some doubt on the standing of the 1950 opinion on this issue. See the following footnote.

question of jurisdiction; moreover, such a decision on a purely preliminary point could not possibly determine with finality a matter which,
both by its nature and its inclusion in the final submissions of the
Applicants, constituted essentially one of the elements to be determined upon the merits.[21]

21. *SWA Judgment* (1966): 19. This express reservation regarding the survival of the
mandate would seem to discount not only the Court's 1962 pronouncement on the matter
(which, according to the judgment, only amounted to a provisional assumption) but also the
1950 advisory opinion itself, which, of course, was quite definite on the subject. The Court did
not state categorically that the 1950 opinion was wrong on this point; it merely declared that
the question of the survival of the mandate was still an open one. The effect of this reservation
is not easy to assess—particularly since it was not really essential to the judgment of the Court
and might therefore be classified as a mere *obiter dictum*.

Strictly speaking, there is no rule of *stare decisis* to bind the International Court of
Justice. Consequently, the Court is never obligated to follow an earlier decision, even if delivered in a contentious case, so long as the question does not involve the same parties in one
and the same case (in which event the rule of *res judicata* would apply. Articles 59 and 60 of
the Court Statute. See also Shabtai Rosenne, *The Law and Practice of the International Court*
[Leyden: Sijthoff, 1965], II: 612.) *A fortiori*, then, the pronouncement of the Court in an
advisory opinion cannot bind the Court in subsequent contentious proceedings, and the Court
is always free to depart from its earlier pronouncement. The later pronouncement of the Court
delivered in a contentious proceeding might, then, normally be regarded as the more authoritative statement of the law. But in the present case, the Court did no more than cast doubt on the
ruling delivered in the advisory opinion, and one may well query whether this in itself could be
sufficient to undermine the authoritativeness of that ruling, particularly since the 1966 majority was achieved only by means of the casting vote of the President, whereas the 1950 opinion
represented the unanimous view of the Court. Some writers, however, have suggested that the
authority of the 1950 opinion had indeed been weakened by the 1966 Court. See, e.g., Falk,
*The Status of Law*, p. 394, and Landis, "The South West Africa Cases," p. 661.

Judge Jessup, in his dissenting opinion, considered that the strength of the unanimous
1950 opinion on the survival of the mandate remained unimpaired. Furthermore, he specifically
rejects the majority view that the 1962 pronouncement on this matter had been made only on a
hypothetical basis, so as to reach a decision on the question of jurisdiction. *SWA Judgment*
(1966): 331, 338.

In contrast, Judge Tanaka, also a member of the dissenting minority, held specifically that
neither the 1950 nor the 1962 pronouncements bore the character of *res judicata* as regards the
survival of the mandate. He concluded: "What was decided in a finding in the preliminary
objection proceedings as a basis of jurisdiction, must not be prejudicial to the decision on the
merits, therefore may not have binding force *vis-à-vis* the parties; accordingly, . . . it is permissible that the Respondent should deny and continue to deny the survival of the Mandate after
the dissolution of the League, despite the fact that this issue was dealt with by the Court at the
stage on jurisdiction, and despite the fact that the arguments might become repetitive." Ibid.,
p. 261.

The question of the survival of the mandate is, of course, relevant not only to the issue of
South Africa's obligations in the territory but also to the question whether the General Assembly was technically able (even assuming it was legally qualified) to revoke South Africa's
mandate in 1966. For if the mandate lapsed with the demise of the League in 1946, the General
Assembly obviously had nothing to revoke in 1966. In its 1971 Namibia opinion, the Court, it
is to be noted, stated categorically that the mandate survived the League and the 1966 action of
the Assembly was validly taken. *Namibia Opinion* (1971): 32–41.

The upshot of all this would seem to be that for the United Nations itself there is little
doubt that the 1950 opinion remains the authoritative expression of international law on the
subject of the survival of the mandate, since that opinion was formally accepted by the United
Nations and thereby incorporated into United Nations law. Security Council acceptance of the
1971 opinion reinforces this conclusion. However, for South Africa itself, the express reservation of the 1966 Court on the question of the survival of the mandate, since it was embodied in
a contentious judgment, might leave it legally entitled, even after Security Council endorsement
of the 1971 Namibia Opinion, to assert that the mandate lapsed in 1946 with the dissolution of
the League. This issue raises fundamental questions regarding the binding force and authority of

In order to ascertain whether the Applicants possessed any legal right or interest in the subject matter of their claim, the Court proceeded to examine the mandate for South West Africa in the context of the whole mandates system. Essentially, this examination was a more elaborate version of the analysis presented on this point by Judges Spender and Fitzmaurice in their 1962 joint dissent.

The mandates system, as such, was established by Article 22 of the Covenant; the precise terms of each mandate were spelled out by the instruments of mandate. Their substantive provisions were composed of two main categories. "On the one hand . . . there were the articles defining the mandatory's powers and its obligations in respect of the inhabitants of the territory and towards the League and its organs." These constituted the "conduct of the mandate" provisions. "On the other hand, there were articles conferring in different degrees . . . certain rights relative to the mandated territory, directly upon the members of the League as individual States or in favour of their nationals." These constituted the "special interests" provisions. The latter category covered such matters as the open door in the A and B Mandates, and the general right of missionaries, nationals of the League members, to prosecute their calling within the mandated territory.[22]

The instant dispute related exclusively to the "conduct" provisions. In respect of this fact,

> the question which has to be decided is whether, according to the scheme of the mandates and of the mandates system as a whole, any legal right or interest (which is a different thing from a political interest) was vested in the members of the League of Nations, including the present Applicants, individually and each in its own separate right to call for the carrying out of the mandates as regards their "conduct" clauses;—or whether this function must, rather, be regarded as having appertained exclusively to the League itself, and not to each and every member State, separately and independently. In other words, the question is whether the various mandatories had any direct obligation towards the other members of the League individually, as regards the carrying out of the "conduct" provisions of the mandates.[23]

In order to obtain an answer to this question, the Court proceeded to examine the intentions of the framers of the mandates system. Only

---

advisory opinions for individual states under international law, on which, see Leo Gross, "The International Court of Justice and the United Nations," pp. 417–19; but cf. his comments concerning the possible effect of Security Council endorsement of an advisory opinion, ibid., p. 415, and p. 389, n. 199. On the 1971 advisory opinion, see further below, pp. 332 ff.

22. *SWA Judgment* (1966): 20.

23. Ibid., p. 22.

by applying the rule of contemporaneity to the interpretation of the relevant documents could the "juridical notion" of the "sacred trust" be properly ascertained.[24] The mandates system formed part of, and was integrated into, the general framework of the League of Nations. The League, it was emphasized, could only operate through the instrumentality of its defined organs, and as a corollary, "individual member States could not themselves act differently relative to League matters."[25] Mandatories, in assuming their responsibility to exercise "tutelage," did so "on behalf of the League"—and not additionally on behalf of the members of the League in their individual capacity.[26] Article 22, in specifying that "securities for the performance" of the sacred trust were to be "embodied in this Covenant," referred only to the League Council and the Permanent Mandates Commission as the supervisory agents. "Neither by the Covenant nor by the instruments of mandate, was any role reserved to individual League members" in respect of such supervisory functions. "No security taking the form of a right for every member of the League separately and individually to require from the mandatories the due performance of their mandates, or creating a liability for each mandatory to be answerable to them individually—still less conferring a right of recourse to the Court in these regards,—was provided by the Covenant."[27] The individual states were qualified to participate in the supervision of the mandates only through the organs of the League, as such, i.e., operating through the institution as an entity.

The provisions of the mandate instruments confirmed this conclusion. The Mandates were issued by the League Council in the form of resolutions—something which did not admit of separate signature and ratification by member states. These states, therefore, could hardly have been parties to the instruments.[28] This conclusion was also confirmed by the fact that the Council, according to Article 7, paragraph 1, of the Mandate, could authorize modifications in the Mandate without consulting individual members of the League.[29]

[Accountability owed to each and every member of the League separately would hardly have been consistent with the generous freedom of administration accorded to mandatory powers, and particularly to those in charge of class C mandates.[30] Moreover, mandatory powers would have been constantly subjected to a cross-fire of criticism

24. Ibid., p. 23. The principle of contemporaneity of interpretation was also endorsed by Judge Jessup. Ibid., pp. 326 and 389.
25. Ibid., p. 24.
26. Ibid., and see the separate opinion of Judge Morelli, ibid., p. 64.
27. Ibid., p. 25.
28. Ibid., p. 27. The Court did not, however, seek to contravene the conclusion of the 1962 judgment that the Mandate constituted a "treaty."
29. Ibid., p. 28.
30. Ibid., p. 30.

and demands emanating from "some 40 or 50 independent centres of invigilatory rights."[31] Not only would the position of the mandatory power have been impossible, but the authority of the League Council would have been severely undermined. Finally, it would have been quite inconsistent for the mandatories, on the one hand, to be capable of exercising a veto in the League Council, and yet, on the other, to be subject to the demands of each and every individual League member.[32]

The Court thereupon rejected in turn various contentions advanced in opposition to its view. It was claimed that "the sacred trust of civilization" imparted an interest to every civilized state to see that the sacred trust was carried out. This interest, it was said, constituted a legal interest in the conduct of the mandate.[33] The argument was fallacious, said the Court. "Humanitarian considerations may constitute the inspirational basis for rules of law." But unless given "juridical expression" and "clothed in legal form," they cannot "generate legal rights and obligations."[34] The mandates system undoubtedly represented "a moral ideal given form as a juridical regime," but "its legal rights and obligations were those, and those alone, which resulted from the relevant instruments creating the system, and the mandate itself within the framework of the League of Nations."[35] In short, the mandates system had a moral foundation—but such foundation did not permit an open-ended evolutionary system of legal rights and duties.[36]

The fact that there was now no entity "entitled to claim the due performance of the Mandate" was not a ground for postulating the existence of certain rights, so as to avert the resultant consequences. "This would be to engage in an essentially legislative task, in the service of political ends the promotion of which, however desirable in itself, lies outside the function of a court-of-law."[37]

The Court supported its interpretation of the relevant documents by tracing the historical development of the adjudicatory clause in the Mandates instruments. This clause only came up for consideration when

31. Ibid., p. 31.
32. Ibid. "In the last resort, the assent, or non-dissent, of the mandatory had to be negotiated." Ibid. This was of course the obverse of the necessity argument. The 1962 majority had argued that the existence of the veto confirmed the essentiality of judicial supervision. The 1966 majority insisted that the veto proved quite conclusively that any concept of coercion was entirely alien to the mandates system.
33. Ibid., p. 34.
34. Ibid.
35. Ibid., p. 35.
36. The Court also dismissed an analogy that had been made with the minorities treaties, where political supervision was entrusted to the League Council, and simultaneous adjudicatory power was conferred on states, members of the Council. The minorities treaties, in contrast to the mandates system, said the Court, clearly spelled out such an invigilatory function. Ibid., p. 40. Article 7 of the Mandate, however, was no different from any other adjudicatory clause. It was "adjectival not substantive," in its "nature and effect." Ibid., p. 39.
37. Ibid., p. 36. The Court also rejected any "carry-over" notion, whereby the rights formerly vested in the League, devolved upon individual states at the date of dissolution of the

the clauses relating to the "special interests," such as commercial and missionary rights, were introduced—demonstrating the limited role envisioned for the adjudicatory clause.[38]

Finally, the Court dealt with the necessity argument—that in the absence of a legal right or interest in the mandate which each member state of the League could judicially protect, a Mandatory would be able to flout at will the purpose of the mandate. On this, the Court said: "The plain fact is that, in relation to the 'conduct' provisions of the mandates, it was never the intention that the Council should be able to impose its views on the various mandatories—the system adopted was one which deliberately rendered this impossible."[39] Experience demonstrated that "it was by argument, discussion, negotiation and cooperative effort that matters were to be, and were, carried forward."[40] Moreover, the type of *actio popularis* envisaged by the necessity argument was unknown to international law. The whole argument was really "based on considerations of an extra-legal character, the product of a process of after-knowledge."[41] Whatever real necessity exists lies in the political, not the legal, field. The Court, as "implied by the opening phrase of Article 38, paragraph 1, of its Statute, . . . is not a legislative body. Its duty is to apply the law as it finds it, not to make it."[42] For the same reason, the Court was not "entitled to engage in a process of 'filling in the gaps' " by applying a teleological principle of interpretation. Such action in the present case would involve the Court in "a process of rectification or revision" rather than interpretation. And "the Court cannot remedy a deficiency if, in order to do so, it has to exceed the bounds of normal judicial action."[43]

From its review of the relevant constitutional documents governing the operation and functioning of the mandates system, the Court determined that the supervisory function was exclusively a collective political responsibility and not one that was imparted to an individual state to be executed by means of judicial action. For this reason the Applicants were not entitled to a judgment on the merits of their claims.

---

League. See above, p. 198, n. 43. Rights which these states did not possess as members could not suddenly accrue to them upon the cessation of membership. *SWA Judgment* (1966): 35–36.

38. Ibid., pp. 43–44. The Tanganyika clause was dismissed as "a drafting caprice." Ibid., p. 44. See above, pp. 43–44, and 204, nn. 78 and 80. Judge Jessup, on the other hand, once again argued at length the importance of the Tanganyika clause in confirming that protection of the rights of the inhabitants of the mandated territory fell within the ambit of the adjudicatory clause of the South West Africa Mandate. *SWA Judgment* (1966): 356–67.

39. Ibid., p. 46.

40. Ibid., p. 47.

41. Ibid. The Court also referred to the absence of a compromissory clause in a number of trusteeship agreements. Ibid., pp. 49–51. See also above, chap. IX, n. 46.

42. *SWA Judgment* (1966): 48.

43. Ibid.

## THE VIEWS OF THE DISSENT ON THE JUDGMENT

The seven dissenting judges, each in a separate opinion, vigorously protested the Court's decision. In their view, the Applicants were entitled to a ruling on the merits on the basis of the 1962 judgment without need to demonstrate any further right or interest. The Court's present judgment, it was charged, "was completely unfounded in law."[44] More specifically, the Court's ruling was challenged on the following grounds:

1. The decision of the Court was not based upon any theory advanced in the final submissions of Respondent.[45] The gravamen of this complaint is that since neither Respondent nor the Court itself, in the course of the proceedings on the merits, ever raised the question of Applicants' standing, no opportunity was ever given to Applicants to argue the issue.

In answering this complaint the Court noted that "quite apart from the recognized right of the Court, implicit in paragraph 2 of Article 53 of its Statute, to select *proprio motu* the basis of its decision,"[46] Respondent had in the proceedings on the merits (and particularly in the written pleadings) in fact denied "that the Applicants had any legal right or interest in the subject-matter of their claim—a denial which, at this stage of the case, clearly cannot have been intended merely as an argument against the applicability of the jurisdictional clause of the Mandate." And this renewed challenge to Applicants' standing had been incorporated by reference in Respondent's final submissions in which the Court was asked to reject Applicants' submissions, on the basis, *inter alia*, of "the statements of fact and law as set forth in [its] [i.e., Respondent's] pleadings and the oral proceedings."[47]

An examination of the pleadings would seem to confirm the validity of the Court's thesis. It will be recalled that in the oral plead-

44. Dissenting opinion of Judge Jessup, ibid., p. 325.
45. See dissenting opinions of Judges Jessup, ibid., pp. 326 and 328; Koretsky, ibid., p. 240; and Mbanefo, ibid., pp. 493–94. For further criticism along these lines, see Higgins, "The International Court and South West Africa," pp. 581–82; and Falk, *The Status of Law*, pp. 382–83.
46. *SWA Judgment* (1966): 19. Judge Mbanefo questioned the right of the Court to raise "of its own motion" a point for decision not raised by the parties in their submissions. Ibid., p. 494. On the other hand, Judge Tanaka, despite his dissent, acknowledged the power of the Court "to re-examine jurisdictional and other preliminary matters at any stage of proceedings *proprio motu*." Ibid., p. 250.
   For critical discussion of the Court's invocation in this case of its right to raise an issue *proprio motu*, see Higgins, "The International Court and South West Africa," pp. 581–82; and Falk, *The Status of Law*, p. 383, n. 14. But cf. Johnson, "South West Africa Cases," pp. 167–68, and in particular, his discussion of the *Nottebohm* decision in relation to this question.
47. *SWA Judgment* (1966): 19. See also the separate opinion of Judge van Wyk, ibid., pp. 68–69.

ings Respondent specifically argued that the 1962 judgment "cannot, in principle bind any judge . . . [with] regard to the admissibility of the claims now before the Court."[48] Moreover, the entire thrust of Respondent's contention regarding the nonjusticiability of Article 2 of the Mandate was that Applicants, of necessity, lacked standing under Article 7, the compromissory clause.[49] Furthermore, and perhaps most significantly, Respondent's formulation of its case on the lapse of the mandate (Submission 1), according to which the absence of any system of international supervision—administrative *or* judicial—led to the collapse of the entire mandate, actually contained within itself the specific plea that Applicants lacked the right to obtain a judgment in the matter of their claims.[50] Submission 1 thus incorporated within itself (albeit implicitly) the precise grounds upon which the 1966 decision was based.[51]

2. The 1966 judgment constituted, in effect, a reversal of the 1962 decision—or at least of its essential reasoning; as such, it represented a violation of the *res judicata* principle which, in accordance with Articles 59 and 60 of its Statute, binds the Court.[52] Moreover, the 1962 deci-

---

48. *SWA Pleadings* VIII: 583.
49. Ibid.
50. See discussion above, pp. 218–19.
51. Certainly, there is little room for the allegation (made by one of Applicants' counsel) that "even South Africa itself, . . . appeared to acquiesce in the assumption . . . that the prior questions of competence had been fully resolved in the 1962 judgment." Falk, *The Status of Law*, p. 383. Such a comment could only have been made in unawareness of the content and thrust of Respondent's pleadings on the merits. (The dissenting judges, in contrast to Falk, merely held that the plea on standing did not arise under Respondent's final submissions; they never claimed that South Africa refrained from arguing the issue in its pleadings.)
52. See the dissenting opinions of Judges Koretsky, *SWA Judgment* (1966): 239–40, and Jessup, ibid., pp. 331–37. See also the dissenting opinion of Judge Mbanefo, ibid., pp. 490–91, and 495. Both Judges Koretsky and Jessup (who cites Rosenne, *Law and Practice of International Court*, II: 627, in support) maintain that the rule of *res judicata* applies not only to the *dispositif*, but to its underlying reasons as well. In contrast, Judge Tanaka, in his dissenting opinion, considered that the only effect of an affirmative decision on jurisdiction is "that the Court shall proceed to examine the question of the merits. To the preliminary stage must not be attached more meaning than this." Ibid., p. 261. The Court was free, in his view, to dismiss the claim, at the merits stage, for lack of standing. Ibid., p. 250.
It may be noted that even Judge Jessup seemed to harbor some doubts regarding the scope and applicability of the *res judicata* rule in the present case. Thus, he said: "I do not think it would be adequate to rest on the finalities of the 1962 Judgment of this Court." Ibid., p. 331.
For scholarly criticism of the Court on the issue of *res judicata*, see Verzijl, *Jurisprudence of World Court*, pp. 90–96; Higgins, "The International Court and South West Africa," p. 581; Landis, "The South West Africa Cases," pp. 664–65; Scrivner, "The South West Africa Case," p. 36; Cheng, "1966 South-West Africa Judgment," pp. 204–5; and Dugard, "South West Africa Cases," p. 447. Dugard also argues that disregard of the *res judicata* principle violates Article 38(1) (c) of the Court Statute according to which the Court is required to apply "general principles of law recognized by civilized nations." See also a comment by Judge Jessup on this point. *SWA Judgment* (1966): 332–33. But cf. the view expressed by Rosenne, *Law and Practice of International Court*, II: 624 and n. 2.

sion was a ruling not only on the issue of jurisdiction, but also on the admissibility of the claim, and could not be subsequently reversed.[53]

The Court, as noted above, avoided the entire issue of *res judicata* by declaring that the 1962 judgment was strictly a decision on the question of jurisdiction while the present decision was on a matter relating to the merits.

> It may occur that a judgment on a preliminary objection touches on a point of merits, but this it can do only in a provisional way, to the extent necessary for deciding the question raised by the preliminary objection. Any finding on the point of merits therefore, ranks simply as part of the motivation of the decision on the preliminary objection, and not as the object of that decision. It cannot rank as a final decision on the point of merits involved.[54]

This result, the Court said, was confirmed by the fact that according to Article 62(3) of the Rules the introduction of preliminary objections operates to suspend the proceedings on the merits.[55]

The Court also held that the 1962 decision did not constitute a ruling on the admissibility of the claim. The Respondent had not raised the issue of admissibility at the preliminary objection stage, and the Court had not ruled on anything but its own jurisdiction, as is clear from the *dispositif* of the 1962 judgment.[56] Any question of admissibility would have fallen to be decided in 1966 and would have led to

53. Judge Jessup held that all four of the preliminary objections rejected by the 1962 Court constituted objections to the admissibility of the claim as well as to the jurisdiction. *SWA Judgment* (1966): 336. In Judge Mbanefo's view, at least the question of Applicants' legal interest (the third objection) raised an issue of admissibility. Ibid., p. 494. See, further, n. 56, below.

54. *SWA Judgment* (1966): 37.

55. Ibid. Judge Jessup disputed the Court's reliance upon Article 62(3) of the Court's Rules. This provision—as he said, the relevant *travaux préparatoires* made clear—related only to the procedural matter of suspension of the time limits for the presentation of the Counter-Memorial; it was not intended to have the substantive effect of converting anything in the judgment on the preliminary objections which might touch on the merits into mere *obiter dictum*. Ibid., pp. 334-35. To the same effect, see Cheng, "1966 South-West Africa Judgment," pp. 201-3.

Implicitly, the Court majority discounted the importance of the drafting history of the provision. For the Court the essential point was that a decision on the preliminary objection was inherently incapable of pre-empting or prejudging any issue of the merits. And the reference to Article 62(3) was merely supportive of this basic thesis.

56. *SWA Judgment* (1966): 42-43. Judge Fitzmaurice, in his separate opinion in the *Northern Cameroons* case, suggests the following distinction between a plea to the jurisdiction and a plea to the admissibility of the claim: whereas the former "is based on, or arises from, the jurisdictional clause," the latter "is founded on considerations lying outside the ambit of any jurisdictional clause" and does not involve the interpretation or application of such a provision. *ICJ Reports* (1963): 102-3. The 1966 Court, it would seem, had this, or a similar, distinction in mind. However, cf. Dugard, "South West Africa Cases," p. 444, who, basing himself on the Fitzmaurice definition, concludes that the third preliminary objection represented a "forensic hybrid" containing elements of both jurisdiction and admissibility.

precisely the same result reached in the present decision appertaining to the merits of the claim, viz., that the Applicants lacked capacity to advance their claims.[57]

(3) The distinction which the Court enunciates between the right to invoke the Court's jurisdiction and the right to obtain a judgment on the merits rests, as Judge Jessup argued, on a thesis unsupported by any authority, and "suggests a procedure of utter futility." And as Judge Jessup proceeded to query:

> Why should any State institute any proceeding if it lacked standing to have judgment rendered in its favour if it succeeded in establishing its legal or factual contentions on the merits? Why would the Court tolerate a situation in which the parties would be put to great trouble and expense to explore all the details of the merits, and only thereafter be told that the Court would pay no heed to all their arguments and evidence because the case was dismissed on a preliminary ground which precluded any investigation of the merits?[58]

At first glance, this stinging rebuke to the Court would appear to be fully justified. It can therefore be appreciated why this telling comment has been so heartily endorsed by esteemed commentators.[59] Upon second thought, however, it is not clear that Judge Jessup's criticism is really tenable. If the Court in 1962 had taken the not uncommon step of joining one or more of the preliminary objections to the merits—a procedure which a few of the judges[60] and at least one outstanding authority[61] consider should have been followed—and had nonetheless in 1966 decided to dismiss the case on a preliminary ground, would the effort and expense of the parties have been any less? Would this have suggested, to any lesser degree, "a procedure of utter futility"?[62] And in this connection, the fate of the *Barcelona Traction* case—in which one of the preliminary objections joined to the merits in 1964 was

---

57. *SWA Judgment* (1966) p. 43. For further discussion of the issue of *res judicata*, see below, pp. 296–97.

58. *SWA Judgment* (1966): 382.

59. See Verzijl, *Jurisprudence of World Court*, pp. 96–97, who refers to the remarks of Judge Jessup as a "slashing criticism" of the Court. The latter's defense, he declares, "is wholly unsatisfactory and as artificial as its entire juristic edifice of hypotheses and distinctions." See also Katz, *Relevance of International Adjudication*, pp. 101–2; and Taubenfeld and Taubenfeld, *Race, Peace, Law*, pp. 21 and 57.

60. See the dissenting opinion of Judge Basdevant, *SWA Judgment* (1962): 464; and dissenting opinion of Judge Tanaka, *SWA Judgment* (1966): 261.

61. Johnson, "South West Africa Cases," pp. 170–71.

62. This same point is made by even such a critic of the 1966 decision as Rosalyn Higgins. "The International Court and South West Africa," p. 579.

upheld in 1970, after eight years of litigation on the merits—is highly pertinent.[63]

As for authority, the Court, it is true, does not expressly rely upon any precedent, although it does refer to the *Nottebohm* decision with regard to the appropriateness of deciding a question of admissibility at the merits stage.[64] Quite apart from this precedent, however, it is noteworthy that the concept of requiring a distinct and separate right of the Applicants in order to obtain a judgment on the merits was clearly adumbrated by Judge Morelli in his 1962 dissent, in which he stated:

> A question might arise with regard to the interpretation of the substantive provisions of the Mandate, for the purpose of ascertaining what are the interests of States Members of the League of Nations which these provisions are designed to protect by conferring upon those States corresponding subjective rights. This is a question touching the merits of the case: a question which, as such, could not be examined in the present phase of the proceedings.[65]

Furthermore, as one commentator has pointed out,[66] Charles de Visscher, writing in 1965,[67] enunciated a thesis very close to the one ultimately adopted by the Court. De Visscher distinguishes between Applicants' right of action under Article 7 and the admissibility of their claim. The same commentator went so far as to say: "De Visscher's book may . . . have helped pave the way for the 1966 Judgment."[68]

4. Even if a material interest was required in, for instance, a claim for damages, no such interest was necessary to obtain a mere declaratory judgment. Consequently, at least with respect to Submissions 1

63. See *Case Concerning the Barcelona Traction, Light and Power Company Limited (Belgium v. Spain), ICJ Reports* (1970): 3 ff.
On the entire problem of separating antecedent questions, including those of jurisdiction and admissibility, from the merits, see the comments of Leo Gross, "The International Court of Justice and the United Nations," pp. 432–33.
64. *SWA Judgment* (1966): 43. Johnson, "South West Africa Cases," pp. 167–68, regards the *Nottebohm* decision as one of a number of valid precedents for the Court's ruling. For the contrary view on the relevance of the *Nottebohm* decision, see Dugard, "South West Africa Cases," p. 447; and Scrivner, "The South West Africa Case," p. 37.
65. *SWA Judgment* (1966): 569; and see ibid., p. 574. See also the separate opinion of Judge Morelli in the *Northern Cameroons* case, *ICJ Reports* (1963): 131–49, and especially, 149.
Interestingly enough, Judge Jessup himself, in discussing the matter of interest in relation to jurisdiction, pointed out that a question, for example, of whether a treaty is in force and whether rights arise under the treaty, would be "a question for the merits" and not for the jurisdiction, since it would require determination whether the case "rested upon a legal right." *SWA Judgment* (1962): 423–24.
66. Cheng, "1966 South-West Africa Judgment," p. 208, n. 3.
67. Charles de Visscher, *Aspects Récents du Droit Procédural de la Cour Internationale de Justice* (Paris: Pedone, 1966), pp. 22, 36 ff., and 74.
68. Cheng, "1966 South-West Africa Judgment," p. 208, n. 3.

and 2, Applicants were entitled to a declaratory judgment confirming that the mandate subsisted and that the United Nations had succeeded to the supervisory powers of the League.[69]

In the view of the majority, however, Submissions 1 and 2 only provided "the basis" for the remaining submissions; and if the Court found, as it did, that in regard to the latter the Applicants were without standing because of lack of interest, it was "inappropriate and misplaced" for the Court to render a declaratory judgment with regard to the first two submissions.[70]

5. According to the Court only Article 5 in the South West Africa Mandate (relating to missionaries) gave rise to any "special interest," and it was only with reference to that provision that individual states could implead the Court. Why, then, does the compromissory clause, Article 7(2), employ the generic and plural term "provisions of the Mandate," rather than refer simply to Article 5 by name?[71] "Why," in the words of Judge Wellington Koo citing a Chinese proverb, "write such a long and big essay on such a small subject?"[72]

In response, the Court maintained that the compromissory clause was first adopted with regard to Class A and B mandates, where commercial and other rights were also involved; and "once the principle of a jurisdictional clause had been accepted, the clause was then introduced as a matter of course into all the mandates," including the Class C group.[73]

From the foregoing review of the debate between majority and minority opinions it is clear that the fundamental criticism leveled against the 1966 judgment relates to the question of *res judicata* and the propriety of the Court overruling, in effect, its earlier decision. The central difficulty, of course, lies in the need to reconcile the 1966 with the 1962 decision, when both seem to deal with exactly the same subject and yet reach diametrically opposite conclusions. As one writer has said: "The facts on which the 1966 judgment on a matter of an 'antecedent character' are based are facts which from the report appear

---

69. See the dissenting opinions of Judge Jessup, *SWA Judgment* (1966): 327–28; and Judge Mbanefo, ibid., pp. 491, 493, 496–97, and 502.

70. Ibid., pp. 22–23.

71. Dissenting opinions of Judges Wellington Koo and Koretsky, ibid., pp. 219–20, and 247. For criticism along the same lines, see Scrivner, "The South West Africa Case," p. 40.

72. *SWA Judgment* (1966): 220. Falk, *The Status of Law*, p. 384, totally misreads the context in which Judge Wellington Koo employed this proverb. It is the jurisdictional clause, not the Court's judgment, which is the referent of Judge Wellington Koo's statement. The judge's intention was, very clearly, to elucidate the precise meaning of the relevant clause and not at all (as Falk would have it) to cast a disparaging remark at the majority opinion.

73. *SWA Judgment* (1966): 44.

to have been before the Court in 1962."[74] This would suggest two questions: First, were there any new facts or fresh aspects of the issue of interest before the 1966 Court not present before the 1962 Court? Second, even if such facts called for a reversal of the 1962 conclusion, was the Court in 1966 at liberty to take such a step?

It is submitted that a sound appreciation of the pleadings on the merits and of the manner in which the ultimate issues, as analyzed above, were formulated before the Court affords a new perspective on the relationship between 1962 and 1966 decisions. As indicated, the course and conduct of the proceedings served to establish that there was no meaningful way for any individual state to mount an effective challenge to a mandatory power's administrative discretion or for the Court to adjudicate upon such a challenge. This question of the justici- ability of Article 2 of the Mandate was only, and could only have been illuminated fully at the merits stage. In 1962 Judges Spender and Fitzmaurice, while suggesting the nonjusticiability of the apartheid issue as one ground for upholding the third preliminary objection on the matter of Applicants' interest, recognized that this question was, properly speaking, something relating to the merits. In effect, the entire pleadings on the merits served to determine conclusively by 1966 what was mere surmise in 1962: that the matter of apartheid was nonjustici- able; that the Court was not the proper forum for assessing the consist- ency of any given administrative policy with the general goals of the mandate; and, hence, that it was never intended to grant individual states the right to invoke the Court's jurisdiction for the purpose of undertaking such an assessment. In a word, the Mandate had never provided for judicial supervision.

Viewed from this angle, it is clear that the 1966 decision is not simply a reproduction of the 1962 minority viewpoint, but a *genuine conclusion* on the arguments on the merits. As such, there can be no question of a reversal of the 1962 judgment nor a violation of the *res judicata* principle. No doubt the reasoning of the 1966 Court was simi- lar to that of the 1962 Spender–Fitzmaurice dissent—but the Court's conclusions were postulated upon a set of facts not available to the 1962 Court and arose from a new and expanded perspective in the case.

But even if the Court violated no rule of *res judicata*, nonetheless, the Court could not have failed to realize that to the outside world it would appear that the Court had simply overruled its earlier decision. Nor can it be supposed that seven distinguished international jurists, of the eminence of the majority, would be oblivious of the dismay with

74. Dugard, "South West Africa Cases," p. 445.

which their decision would be greeted and of the serious consequences the judgment might have for the future of the Court as an international institution.

Commentators unfamiliar with the pleadings in the *South West Africa* cases have, naturally enough, attributed everything to the set of adventitious events affecting the Court's composition and to the divergence between conservative and teleological schools of international law reflected in the Court. But in truth, it is just a little too facile to attribute the 1966 denouement to the fortuitous circumstance whereby the 1962 minority became a technical majority in 1966 and was able to impose its own restrictive form of interpretation in the case at hand. No Court, it is believed, willingly and blithely overthrows a pattern of precedential authority, even if the earlier pronouncements are not technically binding. Furthermore, and most significantly, to ascribe the 1966 decision to a simple "fluke" is to completely fail to take account of the steady erosion that had taken place within the Court over the attitude reflected in the 1950 opinion that legal answers could provide a full and complete solution to the South West Africa problem. Already by 1956, at least five judges, most of them from states of the Third World, held that the question of South Africa's violation of the mandate was not meet for the Court, since it was essentially a political, not a legal, problem. By 1962 seven judges implicitly (and among these, Judges Spender and Fitzmaurice, expressly) endorsed this view. The pleadings on the merits placed the matter—at least in the eyes of these judges—beyond a shadow of a doubt and established the political, nonjusticiable character of the dispute. As reluctant as the judges must have been to withdraw at this stage, particularly in the light of the 1962 ruling and the expectations built up around the pending judgment, once it was clear from all that had gone on that the Court could not possibly adopt a principled judgment or fulfill an essentially judicial role in the dispute, there was no alternative but to announce this fact before the world and explain the reasons for returning the matter to its proper forum—the international political arena.

In essence, then, the 1966 judgment might be said to have been predicated, no less than the 1962 judgment, upon concepts of "international public policy"[75]—but these were directed at safeguarding the essentially judicial character of the Court rather than attempting to resolve an inherently political conflict.[76]

75. The term was used by Jenks to explain the underlying rationale of the 1962 judgment. See above, p. 210 and n. 106.
76. See, to similar effect, Leo Gross, "The International Court of Justice and the United Nations," p. 379, n. 164; and see also Leo Gross, "Limitations Upon the Judicial Function," *AJIL* LVIII (1964): 427.

## THE VIEWS OF THE DISSENT ON THE MERITS

The Court, as noted, never ruled upon the actual merits[77] since it found that Applicants lacked a legal right or interest in the subject matter of their claim. Despite this fact, and notwithstanding the objections of President Spender,[78] several dissenting opinions (and also the concurring opinion of Judge *ad hoc* van Wyk)[79] entered upon a consideration of the merits. Without venturing into any detailed discussion of the views expressed in these opinions—a discussion which, in the light of the Court's failure to reach the merits, would be somewhat beside the point—it is instructive to examine to what extent Applicants' pleadings "scored" with the judges of the minority.

In this regard, it is significant that not a single judge found his way clear to accept unqualifiedly Applicants' thesis on the power of international consensus alone to generate binding international norms and/or standards. Of the fourteen judges on the Court, only one, Judge Tanaka, came close to adopting Applicants' viewpoint—but with certain crucial differences. In the first place, Judge Tanaka's norm of nondiscrimination is heavily predicated on concepts of natural law and is not simply a product of the *quasi*-legislative powers of international organizations.[80] There is no evidence that Judge Tanaka would be prepared to accept that consensus alone can create norms in the absence of a foun-

77. However, the Court's judgment would seem to be at variance, in its underlying rationale, with Applicants' norm thesis. See, for example, the following points: the need to apply the principle of contemporaneity in the interpretation of the mandate instruments (*SWA Judgment* [1966] : 23); the denial that humanitarian considerations alone can give rise to legal obligations where such obligations are not clearly spelled out in the original instruments (ibid., pp. 34–35); the fact that "in the last resort, the assent, or nondissent, of the mandatory had to be negotiated" (ibid., p. 31); "that, in relation to the 'conduct' provisions of the mandates, it was never the intention that the Council should be able to impose its views on the various mandatories—the system adopted was one which deliberately rendered this impossible" (ibid., p. 46); that at base questions relating to the conduct of the mandate had their place in the political not the legal field; and, finally, that "the persuasive force of [General] Assembly resolutions . . . operates on the political not the legal level" (ibid., pp. 50–51).

78. In a separate declaration, President Spender argued that Article 57 of the Court's Statute, which authorizes separate and dissenting opinions, does not allow such opinions to enter upon a consideration of issues not at all broached by the majority opinion. Ibid., pp. 51–57. Judges Tanaka, ibid., pp. 262–63, and Mbanefo, ibid., pp. 489–90, took issue with the President on this point. Cf. the separate opinion of Judge van Wyk, ibid., p. 65.
For comment on this subject, see Friedmann, "The Jurisprudential Implications," pp. 14–15.

79. In the longest single opinion of the judgment (*SWA Judgment* [1966] : 67–215), Judge van Wyk found for the Respondent on all counts and dismissed each of the Applicants' submissions. He specifically discounted the existence or applicability of any norm and/or standards as alleged by Applicants.

80. In discussing the question how a customary norm which has developed subsequent to the creation of the mandate could yet be held to bind the Mandatory, Judge Tanaka said: "What ought to have been clear 40 years ago has been revealed by the creation of a new customary law which plays the role of authentic interpretation the effect of which is retroactive." Ibid., p. 294. In analyzing the norm as a rule of natural law which comes within the scope of "general principles of law recognized by civilized nations" (Article 38 [1] [c] of the Court Statute), Judge Tanaka declared: "States are not capable of creating human rights by law

300 / EFFORTS TO OBTAIN A BINDING COURT JUDGMENT

dation of natural law. Second, in defining his norm and its application, Judge Tanaka indicates that in each case the factual situation must be examined so as to determine which differentiation is *reasonable* and permitted and which *unreasonable* and forbidden. Thus, in Judge Tanaka's view it may be reasonable to provide for separate schooling for Whites and Natives, so as to allow the latter to receive instruction in the vernacular.[81] This stand is in marked contrast to the views of the Applicants on the subject of separate education—the touchstone of the whole norm thesis. Under the absolute norm and/or standards of the Applicants, such educational separation would be categorically proscribed, since the norm was a product of legislative fiat and made no allowance for the evaluation of facts or for any test of reasonableness.

Of the remaining dissenting judges who dealt with the issues on the merits,[82] three (Judges Wellington Koo, Forster, and Mbanefo) did not base themselves on any norm and/or standards.[83] In their view apartheid, on its face, was incompatible with Article 2(2) of the Mandate because it represented an unreasonable, unjustifiable system of administration.[84]

Judge Jessup, in his dissenting opinion, categorically rejected the assertion that the resolutions of international organizations had given rise to an international legal norm of nondiscrimination.[85] Since the General Assembly and the International Labor Organization "lack a true legislative character, their resolutions alone cannot create law."[86]

---

or by convention; they can only confirm their existence and give them protection. The role of the State is no more than declaratory." Ibid., p. 297.

In this regard it might be mentioned that at the Versailles Peace Conference in 1919 Japan fought vigorously for inclusion of a racial equality clause in the League Covenant. Opposition to this proposal by Australian Prime Minister Hughes, who feared the effect of such a clause on Australia's immigration policies, led to its defeat. See Seth P. Tillman, *Anglo-American Relations at the Paris Peace Conference of 1919* (Princeton, N.J.: Princeton University Press, 1961), pp. 300–4.

For an excellent analysis of the manner in which Judge Tanaka's international norm rests on natural law concepts for its binding quality, see Pollock, ". . . Jurisprudence of International Law," pp. 780–81.

81. *SWA Judgment* (1966): 310.

82. Judge Koretsky limited himself to holding that the 1962 judgment was *res judicata* on the matter of interest. He did not consider any of the issues on the merits.

83. Judge Padilla Nervo in his dissenting opinion states that "racial discrimination . . . is a violation of a norm or rule or standard of the international community." Ibid., p. 464. It is not clear what this is meant to entail in terms of scope or application; nor is it clear what the sources of the principle are.

84. See dissenting opinions of Judges Wellington Koo, ibid., pp. 233–35; Forster, ibid., pp. 482–83; and Mbanefo, ibid., pp. 486, 489–90.

85. Ibid., pp. 432–33, 441.

86. Ibid., p. 432. Richard Falk, in a lengthy treatise, discounts Judge Jessup's opposition to the norm and instead endorses Judge Tanaka's views on the question. *The Status of Law*, chap. V. Falk's preference for the Tanaka stand is quite understandable in view of the fact that Falk was one of the counsel for Applicants (see *SWA Judgment* [1966]: 8) and, taking into account his other writings, was undoubtedly a major architect of the norm thesis. What is, however, somewhat surprising, if not a little disturbing, is the impression conveyed that this

("The literature on this point," Judge Jessup notes, "is abundant.")[87] At the same time, however, Judge Jessup held that "an international standard or criterion *as an aid to interpretation* of the Mandate," existed and *"could have been and should have been* utilized by the Court in performing . . . the purely judicial function of measuring by an objective standard whether the practice of apartheid in the mandated territory of South West Africa was a violation of the Mandatory's obligation" to promote to the utmost the welfare of the inhabitants.[88] The fact that the Mandatory was granted a discretion "in the first instance" to select appropriate means for fulfilling the "sacred trust" did not mean that the Mandatory's choice was not subject to review. And the exercise of such review did not call for "each member of the Court . . . to decide subjectively whether he believes the mandatory has chosen wisely or correctly. The law abounds in examples of standards or criteria which are applied by Courts as tests of human conduct."[89] Thus, "one can trace in many legal fields the judicial applications of tests for the interpretation of constitutions or laws—tests such as *due* process of law, *unreasonable* restraint of trade, *unfair* competition, *equal* protection of the laws, *unreasonable* searches and seizures, *good moral* character, etc."[90] It was not beyond the power of the International Court, declared Judge Jessup, to devise objective standards wherewith to adjudge the conduct of a mandatory. In his view the case involved "a justiciable issue, not just a political question."[91]

This exposition by Judge Jessup is important not only because it high-lights the crucial issue of justiciability which lies at the root of the dichotomy between majority and minority viewpoints but also because of two further considerations. First, it should be noted that Judge Jessup himself does not attempt to reach any conclusion on the matter of the compatibility of apartheid with the mandate. He merely states that this question is measurable by reference to an objective test which the Court might have used had it proceeded to the actual merits. (Earlier in his opinion, Judge Jessup stated quite categorically: "I do not pretend to make a finding on the evidence.")[92] Second, Judge

---

essay was drafted subsequent to the 1966 judgment and provides supplementary or fresh evidence to support the norm thesis and to rebut Judge Jessup's stand. But, in fact, the content, order, detail, and, in numerous places, even the wording, of the Falk essay and of a chapter in Applicants' oral presentation (*SWA Pleadings* IX: 342–59) are so strikingly similar that the inescapable conclusions are first, that both the essay and the chapter are attributable to the same author, and second, that Judge Jessup was fully aware of all the arguments presented in the essay when he adjudged the norm thesis to be totally unsupportable.

87. *SWA Judgment* (1966): 432, n. 2.
88. Ibid., p. 433 (emphasis supplied).
89. Ibid., p. 433–34.
90. Ibid., p. 435 (emphasis in original).
91. Ibid., p. 442.
92. Ibid., p. 330.

Jessup's "standard" is very different from the "standards" of the Applicants. His standard would serve as an "aid to interpretation"—to be employed in conjunction with other "aids to interpretation" in assessing whether the Mandatory's choice of policy complies with the obligations of the "sacred trust." It is clear that Judge Jessup's approach relates to a "reasonableness" test based upon an objective standard enabling the Court to reach a conclusion on the facts. It was in this vein that Judge Jessup argued that the test he was proposing was no different from the commonly applied tests of "due process," "unreasonable searches and seizures," etc., all of which were premised upon an evaluation of the factual situation. There is no hint in Judge Jessup's opinion that even as regards the standard he was prepared to accept Applicants' essential thesis, viz., that the relevant supervisory organs were endowed with the capacity to set binding standards by means of consensus. Judge Jessup's standard was contingent upon an independent consideration of the facts by the Court, while Applicants' "standards" emanated from the *quasi*-legislative fiat of the supervisory organ and excluded any factual enquiry by the Court.

The foregoing reveals that there was, in effect, a three-way split among the dissenting judges on how to handle the issues on the merits, or, more specifically, the question of apartheid. Judge Tanaka held that this policy violated the mandate on the basis of an international legal norm of nondiscrimination derived from principles of natural law. Judges Wellington Koo, Forster, and Mbanefo likewise found that apartheid was incompatible with the mandate not because it violated any norm or standards—a subject which they did not investigate—but simply because on its face this policy ranked as an arbitrary, unreasonable means of fulfilling the "sacred trust." And finally, Judge Jessup did not make any final determination in the matter at all, but held that even though the existence of an international legal norm was excluded, a standard could have been employed by the Court in reaching an objective conclusion in the matter.

In sum, therefore, barely one judge out of fourteen endorsed Applicants' norm thesis, even in part, and each of the dissenting judges who ventured to address himself to the merits found it proper and, in fact, essential to take account of and evaluate the factual situation—something which the Applicants had expressly excluded.[93]

93. From all this it would appear that the majority and minority judges were divided not only on Applicants' standing to receive a judgment on the merits, but, implicitly, also on the underlying issue relating to justiciability (and reflected in the questions posed to the parties by the Court): whether the Court was free to independently evaluate all the relevant facts of apartheid. The majority apparently felt that the door to such an independent judicial examination had been effectively closed by the Applicants—by their amendment of the submissions coupled with their repeated and categorical assertions that they were requesting no finding on

It has been suggested that the *South West Africa* cases provided impressive authority for the "theory that the will of the international community has a law-creating role." "One of the most positive results" of the litigation, it has in fact been said, was "that the authoritative jurisprudence of the ICJ now contains highly respectable support for the argument that the General Assembly and other international institutions are able, through their formal action when supported by a relevant consensus, to evolve binding rules of international law."[94]

Yet, from the actual record, the opposite conclusion is more readily deduced—that the minority opinions, no less than the Court judgment itself, constituted a resounding refutation of the notion that consensus expressed through the resolutions of international bodies is sufficient to establish binding rules of international law.

That Applicants' norm thesis, in the form in which it was presented, remained without "takers" even among the minority judges is not really surprising when one examines more closely what acceptance of this thesis entailed. Quite apart from the very fundamental question of how a new norm could become part of the Mandate so as to figure in the instant litigation, the assertion of the norm, postulated upon the *quasi*-legislative and *quasi*-judicial powers of the General Assembly, entailed multiple difficulties regarding the role of consensus.[95] For Applicants were attempting to carry the theory of consensus to lengths to which it had not been carried before in international litigation or even in the writings of most publicists. Most writers who accord a place to consensus in the formation of international law, see in the resolutions of the General Assembly but a factor in the growth of new norms, or perhaps, a "subsidiary means for the determination of rules of law."[96]

---

disputed facts, no value judgment, and no ruling on motives or consequences and that they were resting their case solely on the existence of the norm and/or standards. (And, in this regard, see the separate opinion of Judge van Wyk, ibid., pp. 149, 153, and 173, n. 1.) In contrast, some of the minority judges, it would seem, did not think that the Court's evaluation of the facts of apartheid would amount to a denial of justice to the Respondent's disadvantage or that Respondent's reliance on Applicants' declarations entailed a suitable matter for estoppel. The matter was therefore fully justiciable on a factual basis, and these judges ruled accordingly.

Since Judge Jessup did not reach any conclusion on the question of apartheid, it is not clear what his attitude was on the propriety of the Court considering the facts as they stood at the conclusion of the pleadings. His claim that a factual standard could have been utilized by the Court does not exclude the possibility that he would have expected further argument on the facts by the parties.

For a discussion by Respondent of the effect of Applicants' admissions of fact, see *SWA Pleadings* XII: 212–25, 414, and 418. For comment by Applicants, see ibid., pp. 354–57.

94. Falk, "The South West Africa Cases: The Limits of Adjudication," *UCLA Paper*, p. 34.

95. It should be noted that the "standards," no less than the norm, were premised upon the *quasi*-legislative and *quasi*-judicial powers of the General Assembly, and hence, presented similar difficulties regarding the role of consensus. See above, pp. 251–52, 256–59.

96. See Leo Gross, "The United Nations and the Role of Law," *International Organization* XIX (1965): 555–57; Leo Gross, "The International Court of Justice and the United

However, for Applicants' purposes this was entirely inadequate. Consensus had to be viewed as having already replaced consent as the key element in the generation of new international law; resolutions of the Assembly had to constitute an independent head or source of law, and such resolutions had to be capable of binding a dissentient state.[97] In a word, international organizatidn, operating through consensus, had to be granted the status of a true world parliament whose legislative enactments were qualified to override contrary state practice.[98]

But where could Applicants cite a consensus of states to accord consensus such a role?[99] That certain writers have advocated endowing Assembly resolutions with greater force may be acknowledged; but which state, and especially which major power, ever agreed, on a generalized basis, to be bound by Assembly resolutions? Which government ever delegated, even by implication, the necessary plenary power to a conference of its peers? How logical was it to argue before a Russian, American, British, or French judge that their respective states, by joining the United Nations, had submitted to the legislative fiat of the General Assembly—and this, despite the retention of a veto in the Security Council? What purpose, it could well be asked, was Article 13 of the Charter meant to serve if the General Assembly was qualified not only to "encourage" "the progressive development of international law and its codification," but actually to determine and even legislate the norms of international law? And how explain the Assembly's practice of following up even a unanimously supported declaration with the adoption of a convention requiring individual state ratifications for entry into force?[100] Even for a state supporting a resolution, could there be inferred "an intention to be bound from what is usually a political vote in a political forum for a political resolution with a politi-

Nations," pp. 374–76; D. H. N. Johnson, "The Effect of Resolutions of the General Assembly," *BYB* XXXII (1955–56): 97, 121–22; Clive Parry, *The Sources and Evidences of International Law* (Manchester: Manchester University Press, 1965), p. 21; and Krzysztof Skubiszewski, "The General Assembly of the United Nations and Its Power to Influence National Action," *Proceedings of the American Society of International Law* (1964): 157.

97. See the highly relevant remarks of N. G. Onuf, "Professor Falk on the Quasi-Legislative Competence of the General Assembly," *AJIL* LXIV (1970): 352.

98. See the discussion by Rosalyn Higgins, who, despite her well-known stand in favor of according a measure of legal authority to Assembly resolutions, nevertheless rejects the view that "practice within the United Nations is paramount in the face of conflicting evidence," i.e., contrary state practice. "The United Nations and Lawmaking: The Political Organs," *Proceedings of the American Society of International Law* (1970): 48.

99. See Onuf, "Professor Falk," pp. 353–54; Pollock, ". . . Jurisprudence of International Law," pp. 781–82; John H. Halderman, *The United Nations and the Rule of Law* (Dobbs Ferry, N.Y.: Oceana, 1966), pp. 67–68; Edward Yemin, *Legislative Powers in the United Nations and Specialized Agencies* (Leyden: Sijthoff, 1969), p. 24; M. Virally, "Droit international et décolonisation devant les Nations Unies," *Annuaire Francais de Droit International* IX (1963): 533–37.

100. See Leo Gross, "The United Nations and the Role of Law," pp. 555–56.

cal purpose"?[101] And, more pointedly, where was the necessary *opinio juris*, if a state's own pattern of behavior contradicted the very resolution for which that state voted? Indeed, what "consensus" was allegedly capable of generating new norms—"consensus in words or consensus in deeds"?[102] Above all, how could consensus bind a dissentient state, when even new customary law arising from the traditional processes of law creation and based on near universal state practice could not, according to most writers and the Court itself,[103] bind a protesting state?

Quite clearly, the consensus theory which the Applicants were proffering to the Court represented a very radical thesis[104] with vast and profound implications for international law—its content, and, more importantly, the processes of its creation. And the inescapable conclusion to be drawn from the *South West Africa* cases is that the consensus theory, as presented by the Applicants, is not part of the corpus of present-day international law.[105]

Perhaps the real tragedy of the *South West Africa* cases lies in the fact that the Court was never allowed to grapple with the realities of apartheid—to adjudge this policy as either an enlightened method of attaining self-determination or as a horrendous system of mass oppression. Instead, the forensic struggle was converted into a gigantic laboratory for testing novel theories regarding the law-creating powers of international organizations as propounded by a few isolated scholars. Given the charge that apartheid was equivalent to genocide, the Applicants could have been expected to develop a case commensurate with the nature of the charge, to present clear evidence of mass exploitation and vile oppression. As reluctant as any group of judges may initially have been to undertake a value judgment of the system, evidence of the total unreasonableness of apartheid might well have convinced them of

101. Louis Henkin, "The United Nations and the Rules of Law," *Harvard International Law Journal* XI (1970): 429. J.H.W. Verzijl, in his work, *International Law in Historical Perspective* (Leyden: Sijthoff, 1968), I: 77, sums up the matter as follows: "It is in any case impossible to acknowledge the validity under the Charter of the proposition that Recommendations of the General Assembly . . . are, as such, clothed with binding force, however limited, as long as they remain the plaything of politics, being either acted upon or neglected according to from what quarter the political wind blows."
102. See Oliver J. Lissitzyn in Richard N. Swift (ed.), *Annual Review of United Nations Affairs, 1963-1964* (Dobbs Ferry, N.Y.: Oceana, 1965), p. 128.
103. The *Fisheries* and *Asylum* cases, and the recent ruling in the *North Sea Continental Shelf* cases are particularly in point. For Applicants' attempt to overcome the clear implications of the Court's jurisprudence, see above, pp. 254-55.
104. See, in this regard, Onuf, "Professor Falk," p. 352.
105. It is also highly revealing that in its Namibia opinion of 1971, the Court, in finding that South Africa had been in breach of the Charter, made no reference whatsoever to any norm and/or standards emanating from the resolutions of international organizations which South Africa could be said to have violated.

its utter incompatibility with the legal obligations assumed under the mandate.[106]

No one has yet adequately explained why the Applicants completely abjured premising their case, even in the alternative, on a consideration of the facts or why they were so bitterly opposed to South Africa's inspection proposal. (Nor has it been explained why the Applicants were not prepared to present witnesses of their own, either South West Africans or others, to establish the validity of their initial oppression charges.) It has been suggested that Applicants' exclusive reliance on the norm thesis may have been motivated by the desire to obtain judicial support for illegalizing apartheid in South Africa no less than in South West Africa.[107] Applicants possibly hoped to institute a universal rule of nondiscrimination as a means of combatting racial discrimination on a global scale. Or perhaps they were simply influenced by a certain progressive school of legal thought in the United States which adopts an apocalyptic view of the integrative processes of international law and accords the organized international community expanding authority in ordering the affairs of states.

Whatever the motive, it remains something of a mystery why the Applicants did not retain a factual basis for their charges in addition to, or as an alternative to, the norm thesis. Professor Richard Falk, one of Applicants' counsels, has sought to dispel the mystery by explaining Applicants' conduct in these terms:

> Ethiopia and Liberia did not, in any way, abandon the original charges about *apartheid*, but rather . . . reformulate[d] the allegations of oppression so as to take account of the judicial setting within which the controversy was taking place. . . . In this regard, it is important to bear in mind that the International Court of Justice had established a jurisprudentially conservative image, an image that placed a burden on the complaining state(s) to establish the existence of legal criteria of decision, as distinct from moral or political criteria. . . . The applicant was not abandoning the charge of oppressiveness; in fact, quite to the contrary, it was contending that the oppressiveness of *apartheid* was so manifest . . . that it could be inferred persuasively by merely reading South Africa's own legislation, and that, therefore, there was no need for the Court to widen the dimensions of inquiry in such a way as to

---

106. In this regard, the question posed by Judge Fitzmaurice to the Respondent in *SWA Pleadings* VIII: 32, is highly pertinent. See above, p. 238, n. 101.

107. For a discussion of this, and other possible reasons, see D'Amato, "Legal and Political Strategies of the South West Africa Litigation," p. 36; and Landis, "The South West Africa Cases," pp. 640 and 651.

endanger its function as a judicial body by calling upon it to pass judgment on a wide range of unverifiable data.[108]

The approach suggested by Falk would indeed have been a perfectly legitimate and even powerful one: to ask the Court to find that the laws of apartheid, *on their face*, were manifestly oppressive and violative of the mandate. But, of course, this is precisely what the Applicants did *not* ask the Court to do. They expressly declared they were not requesting any value judgment on the nature of apartheid. In place of a value judgment they asked the Court to accord recognition to the *quasi*-legislative action of the organized international community in outlawing apartheid by creating a new norm of nondiscrimination. And in regard to the norm Falk is compelled to say: "This feature of the argument called for a rather sharp reappraisal by the Court of its traditional, but quite outmoded, notions that international legal norms presuppose the consent of the state that is subject to their regulation."[109] A moment earlier Falk had asserted that the norm thesis was designed to take account of the Court's "jurisprudentially conservative image"; yet, in the same breath he acknowledges that this very thesis "called for a rather sharp reappraisal by the Court of its traditional, but quite outmoded notions." Either the norm thesis was meant to satisfy a conservative Court or it was meant to provoke it!

In truth, the denouement in the *South West Africa* cases cannot be understood by examining the Court judgment alone, while ignoring the strategy and tactics of the Applicants. The fortuitous circumstances surrounding the composition of the Court apart (and these, as noted earlier, have been unduly emphasized), it would appear that a different strategy and/or tactics might have produced a different result in the case. (All this, of course, proceeds on the assumption that the litigation was well advised in the first place, as a means of promoting a solution to the South West Africa problem—a matter which is by no means free of doubt.)[110] As far as strategy is concerned, rather than presenting a battery of nine submissions, seven of which had never been considered before by the Court and which inevitably would invite a host of factual and evidentiary problems on such matters as apartheid, militarization, incorporation, etc., the Applicants could have simply asked for affirmation of the 1950 opinion on the continued existence of the mandate and the duty of international accountability. These were two straight-

108. Falk, "The South West Africa Cases: The Limits of Adjudication," in *UCLA Paper*, pp. 32–33.
109. Ibid., p. 33.
110. See below, p. 353.

forward issues raising purely legal questions previously considered by the Court. If the Court were to accept jurisdiction it would have been hard-pressed to rule against the Applicants on these two points. With this precedent established, Applicants might at some later date have followed through on the much more difficult and contentious questions of fact. And as for tactics, once the issue was indeed joined on the question of apartheid, Applicants' decision to rely solely on the norm thesis and to exclude, even in the alternative, any reliance on disputed facts or value judgment constituted a damaging and possibly fatal blow to the entire case. Applicants had themselves undercut the juridical grounds upon which the Court might otherwise have given judgment. What is perhaps particularly surprising is the fact that the Applicants, in light of their very close call on the preliminary objections, did not take better account of the conservative nature of the International Court (as it was then composed) in formulating their case on the merits. After all, they could not have failed to appreciate that seven out of fifteen judges held that they had no right to be in Court for lack of standing. Moreover, this question of standing had, at least in the joint dissent of Judges Spender and Fitzmaurice, been closely tied to the question of the actual justiciability of the issues on the merits. Given this early start warning one might have expected that the Applicants would steer their ship on as safe and as least innovative a course as possible and would select traditional and conservative grounds for arguing their case. Instead, they seem to have deliberately selected a line of argument which challenged accepted doctrines all down the line.

But Applicants' actions had not only damaged their own case; they had seriously harmed the Court's prestige and had set back the cause of all those combatting apartheid upon realistic terms. It is to be regretted that Counsel for the Applicants have not been frank and forthright in protecting the honor and prestige of the Court by at least admitting the extraordinary nature of the demands which they had made upon the Court. Instead, they have referred to the Court's decision as "regressive"[111] and have even equated it with the *Dred Scott* case,[112] the infamous pre-Civil War decision of the United States Supreme Court.[113] If the analogy, though unintended, in any way conjures up racial innuendoes, this is, indeed, most unfortunate. For of all the things which the *South West Africa* cases represented, least of all did they represent a test of attitudes on racial matters or apartheid. Not one of the judges, it may be confidently asserted, could regard the racial situation in south-

111. Falk, *The Status of Law*, p. 401.
112. 60 U.S. (19 Howard) 393 (1857).
113. Ernest A. Gross, "The South West Africa Cases: An Essay on Judicial Outlook," pp. 9-10; and see also Highet, "The South West Africa Cases," pp. 154-55.

ern Africa with equanimity, despite the altruistic aims with which South Africa wishes to surround its policies of separate development. But, in fact, what was placed in test in these cases were such matters as the law-making capacity of international organizations, the nature of customary international law, the strength of consensus, the right of one side to an agreement to impose its own revised interpretation of the agreement on the other side, and the assumption of judicial functions where none were initially envisaged.

One authority, after estimating that the Applicants must have reckoned their chances at about fifty-fifty, went on to comment: "It is reasonable for a litigant to take the risk of bringing an action in such circumstances. But if he loses, it is not reasonable that a torrent of one-sided criticism should be let loose upon the tribunal in question and that no examination should be made of the litigant's own conduct."[114] This certainly must rank as one of the most penetrating comments yet made on the South West Africa litigation.

---

114. Johnson, "The South West Africa Cases," p. 159.

# V.
## SOUTH WEST AFRICA OR NAMIBIA?

# XII.

# REVOCATION OF THE MANDATE AND ITS AFTERMATH

## ACTION BY THE ASSEMBLY

The 1966 judgment caused joy in Pretoria;[1] dismay, bewilderment, and anger in the rest of Africa;[2] and general confusion in many of the world's capitals.[3] In effect, the entire fabric of Assembly-Court cooperation—developed and woven through the advisory opinions of 1950, 1955, and 1956 and the Judgment of 1962—was now rent asunder. The General Assembly was, as it were, cast adrift to fend for itself in the political arena, without benefit of a judicial—hence, legally binding and enforceable—determination.

The Court's complete withdrawal from the South West Africa scene marked the effective end of the struggle for international accountability. A new goal—obtaining outright independence for South West Africa—was formally proclaimed on October 27, 1966, by Assembly adoption of Resolution 2145 (XXI), in which the Assembly announced termination of the mandate, and decided that "henceforth South West Africa comes under the direct responsibility of the United Nations."

1. For a critical discussion of South Africa's attempts to exploit the outcome to its own advantage see Vernon McKay, "South African Propaganda on the International Court's Decision," *African Forum* II (1967): 51-64.
2. Thus, the Liberian representative at the United Nations, for example, declared that the decision had been "the object of condemnation and a source of shock and disgust all over the entire world." GAOR, 21st Sess., Plen., 1414th Mtg., Sept. 23, 1966, p. 9. Pouring scorn on the ruling of the Court, he went on to cite the comment of the *Johannesburg Star* of July 23, 1966: "Turning its back firmly on the great questions that move the world of the second half of the twentieth century, such as racial discrimination and the responsibility of the United Nations for the welfare of non-self-governing peoples, the Court cast an eye on the plaintiffs as if seeing them for the first time and asked what right they had to be there at all. None, it decided (though by the narrowest possible majority) and threw the case out without further ceremony."
3. The United States government was totally unprepared for the actual outcome and did not formulate a statement for a number of days. *New York Times*, July 28, 1966, p. 11.

In reality, this action was already foreshadowed in the events of 1960. On December 14 of that year the Assembly had adopted its historic Resolution 1514 (XV), proclaiming the right of all colonial territories to independence. It had declared, *inter alia*:

3. Inadequacy of political, economic, social or educational preparedness should never serve as a pretext for delaying independence.

. . . . . . . . . . . . . . . . . . . . . . . . . . . . . . . . . . . . . .

5. Immediate steps shall be taken, in Trust and Non-Self-Governing Territories or all other territories which have not yet attained independence, to transfer all powers to the peoples of those territories, without any conditions or reservations, in accordance with their freely expressed will and desire.

As part of the drive to confirm independence for all territories, a draft resolution was introduced into the Fourth Committee during the same (fifteenth) session by Guinea, Libya, Mali, Morocco, Togo, and Tunisia, according to which the General Assembly would, *inter alia*, entrust the administrative powers of South West Africa to a special administrative commission which would be charged with leading South West Africa to self-government and independence.[4] As explained by the representative of Guinea, the draft resolution would have had the Assembly withdraw the Union government's "right to administer the territory of South West Africa."[5] A number of delegates pointed out, however, that the General Assembly could not adopt a resolution (then pending before the Committee) commending the legal action brought before the Court, which was premised on the continuance of the mandate, and simultaneously adopt a second resolution which, in effect, revoked the mandate.[6] The United States representative expressed doubt over the competence of the General Assembly to decide that the mandate had ended. It was a legal question, to be adjudged only by the Court.[7] The representatives of Ethiopia and Liberia also voiced fears that the proposed draft resolution might jeopardize their case before the International Court of Justice. As a result, the draft resolution was altered, and instead of creating a new governing body for South West

4. U.N. Doc. A/C.4/L.653, reproduced in GAOR, 15th Sess., Annexes, Agenda Item 43, pp. 4–5 (1960).
5. GAOR, 15th Sess., 4th Ctte., 1063rd Mtg., Nov. 24, 1960, p. 377. See also U.N. Doc. A/C.4/458. The Guinean representative claimed that the Assembly was competent to terminate the mandate, "since it could be assumed *a priori* that the International Court of Justice would not deliver a judgment contrary to its first advisory opinion in 1950." Ibid.
6. See, for instance, the remarks of the representative of Bolivia, GAOR, 15th Sess., 4th Ctte., 1064th Mtg., Nov. 25, 1960, p. 381.
7. Ibid.

Africa it merely invited the South West Africa Committee to visit the territory and investigate the situation there.[8]

The drive to terminate the South West Africa mandate was thus held in abeyance so long as the Court was still adjudicating on the issue. In the period from 1961 to 1965 the Assembly adopted numerous resolutions bearing on South West Africa. Most related to efforts to institute a United Nations presence in the territory; others drew the attention of the Security Council to the critical situation prevailing in South West Africa.[9] All were predicated on the firm recognition that the people of South West Africa possess an "inalienable right . . . to self-government and independence."[10] However, no resolution to terminate South Africa's mandate was ever adopted. Nonetheless, the Assembly, even while awaiting the Court's verdict, was obviously moving away from the concept of continued international account-ability for South West Africa and aiming directly for the ultimate goal of independence.[11]

Briefly, this course of development was marked by the following events: According to Resolution 1568, adopted on December 18, 1960, the Committee on South West Africa was invited to go to South West Africa immediately to investigate the situation, which was described as "a serious threat to international peace and security." South Africa refused to admit the Committee, and upon resumption of the Assembly session in March 1961, the Committee was asked to "discharge the special and urgent tasks entrusted to it . . . as fully and expeditiously as possible with the cooperation of . . . South Africa, if such cooperation is available, and without it if necessary."[12] At the same time the Assembly drew the attention of the Security Council to the situation in South West Africa. Once again South Africa barred the entrance of the Committee. The proposed visit, the South African government said, did

8. G.A. Res. 1568 (XV), Dec. 18, 1960.
9. The attempt to stamp the South West African problem as a threat to the peace was, no doubt, designed to foster Security Council action, independent of any Court judgment. Addi-tionally—although it is doubtful whether this was a conscious consideration—by so stamping the problem, the Security Council's right to act, even in the event of a judgment, would be bolstered. Under one interpretation of Article 94(2), the Security Council might lack the power to enforce a judgment in the absence of a threat to the peace. On this last point, see Goodrich and Hambro, pp. 486–87; Leo Gross, "The International Court of Justice and the United Nations," Hague Academy, *Recueil des Cours*, CXXI (II—1967): 324; and Shabtai Rosenne, *The Law and Practice of the International Court* (Leyden: Sijthoff, 1965), I: 152–54. See also Amelia C. Leiss (ed.), *Apartheid and United Nations Collective Measures: An Analysis* (New York: Carnegie Endowment for International Peace, 1965), pp. 84–85.
10. See G.A. Res. 1702 (XVI), Dec. 19, 1961.
11. In the view of one authority, the Assembly's equivocal attitude on the matter of the continued existence of the mandate was reflected in the "rather uncertain and inconsistent character" of the Ethiopian and Liberian claims in their litigation. D. H. N. Johnson, "The South-West Africa Cases (Second Phase)," *International Relations* III (1967): 164–65.
12. G.A. Res. 1596 (XV), Apr. 7, 1961.

not even "fall within the scope of the supervisory functions envisaged in the 1950 advisory opinion of the International Court."[13]

At the Sixteenth Assembly Session a new Special Committee for South West Africa was created,[14] whose specific task was to visit South West Africa to arrange for the abolition of the system of apartheid and the introduction of complete self-determination into the territory. The efforts of this Special Committee were no more successful than those of its predecessor in gaining entrance to the territory. Matters, in fact, became somewhat confused when the Chairman and Vice-Chairman of the Special Committee, upon completion of a visit to the territory, issued a joint statement in conjunction with the South African Foreign Minister, declaring that they "found no evidence and heard no allegations that there was a threat to international peace and security within South West Africa; that there were signs of militarisation in the territory; or that the indigenous population was being exterminated."[15] The "Carpio incident" only served to enrage members of the Afro–Asian bloc who, once again, moved to have the mandate revoked. The Assembly, however, demurred, since such a step could very well prejudice the case before the Court. Instead, the Assembly adopted a resolution requesting the Secretary-General "to take all necessary steps to establish an effective United Nations presence in South West Africa," and requested him to appoint a United Nations technical assistance resident representative for South West Africa.[16] In response to an inquiry from the Secretary-General on this matter, South Africa indicated its unwillingness to permit any United Nations "presence" in the territory.[17] With reference to the offer of outside expert advice, the reply noted that the South African government had appointed a special Commission to examine the future of the territory and that "until such time as the Odendaal Commission's findings and recommendations have been received and carefully studied," it was not clear whether any such advice would be necessary.[18]

In the meantime, the Assembly during its seventeenth session had transferred the functions of the Special Committee on South West Africa to the Special Committee on the situation with regard to the implementation of the declaration on the granting of independence to colonial countries and peoples (initially the Committee of 17, and later

13. U.N. Doc. S/4854/Add.1, July 18, 1961, Annex V.
14. G.A. Res. 1702 (XVI), Dec. 19, 1961. Throughout the history of the South West Africa issue, the transfer of the problem from one committee to another signaled a new stage in the dispute.
15. U.N. Press Release GA/2501, May 26, 1962. For discussion of this incident in the pleadings of the *South West Africa* cases, see the citations referred to in chap. X, n. 151, above.
16. G.A. Res. 1805 (XVII), Dec. 14, 1962.
17. U.N. Doc. A/AC.109/37, Apr. 3, 1963, p. 3.
18. Ibid.

the Committee of 24).[19] Nothing perhaps could better reveal that in the eyes of the Assembly, South West Africa, notwithstanding the concurrent judicial proceedings on international accountability, was now only one part of the overall drive to bring non-self-governing territories to independence.

In line with this trend of thought, the Assembly, at its eighteenth session, adopted a resolution which labeled any attempt by South Africa to annex the whole or part of South West Africa as "an act of aggression" and stated that the continuation of the "present critical situation" in the territory "constitutes a serious threat to international peace and security."[20] All states were urged to refrain from supplying military equipment, petroleum, and petroleum products to South Africa.

In December 1965,[21] the Assembly, anxiously awaiting the Court's decision, adopted a resolution reaffirming "the inalienable right of the people of South West Africa to freedom and independence" and condemning "the policies of *apartheid* and racial discrimination" which, it charged, constituted a "crime against humanity."[22] It also condemned South Africa for its refusal to cooperate "in implementing the Declaration on the Granting of Independence to Colonial Countries and Peoples."

By late 1965, therefore, the struggle over South West Africa could no longer be viewed in isolation. As a conflict imbued with elements of colonial and racial significance, it had become merged with the overall struggle of the United Nations against the vestiges of colonialism and racialism in southern Africa. The campaign against the White redoubt was, of course, being conducted on a number of fronts—against Portugal for its colonial policies in Angola and Mozambique; against South Africa for its domestic policy of apartheid; and against Rhodesia for its Unilateral Declaration of Independence issued on November 11, 1965. (In connection with this last, the Security Council had, for the first time in its history, taken action under Chapter VII of the Charter.) The Court's judgment in the matter of South West Africa, it was hoped, would provide the United Nations with a powerful new weapon to pierce the wall of White domination erected on the Zambesi River.

But when the *South West Africa* cases were dismissed by the Court, the hope that the Court would be enlisted as a vital ally in the campaign to emancipate southern Africa was shattered. The Court's action

19. G.A. Res. 1805 (XVII), Dec. 14, 1962.
20. G.A. Res. 1899 (XVIII), Nov. 13, 1963.
21. No resolutions on South West Africa were adopted during the famous nineteenth Assembly "non-session" in 1964.
22. G.A. Res. 2074 (XX), Dec. 17, 1965.

equally signified the total abortiveness of the effort to impose a system of international accountability upon South Africa with regard to its administration of South West Africa. At this point the earlier move for divesting South Africa of its mandate was revived, since the Assembly, in any case, was no longer interested in international accountability, as such. Resolution 2145 adopted on October 27, 1966 ushered in the new stage of conflict—a drive for full and unimpeded progress toward independence for South West Africa.

In the preambular part of its resolution,[23] the General Assembly, *inter alia*, reaffirmed the right of the people of South West Africa to freedom and independence; recalled the advisory opinions of 1950, 1955, and 1956, and the Judgment of 1962, "which have established the fact that South Africa continues to have obligations under the Mandate . . . and that the United Nations as the successor to the League of Nations has supervisory powers in respect of South West Africa";[24] and affirmed its right "to revert to itself the administration of the Mandated Territory." On this basis, the Assembly proceeded, in the key provisions of the operative part of the resolution: to reaffirm that "South West Africa is a territory having international status"; to declare that "South Africa has failed to fulfil its obligations in respect of the administration of the Mandated Territory . . . and has, in fact, disavowed the Mandate"; to decide that "the Mandate . . . is therefore terminated, that South Africa has no other right to administer the Territory and that henceforth South West Africa comes under the direct responsibility of the United Nations"; to establish an *Ad Hoc* committee for South West Africa composed of fourteen member states to recommend to a special session of the General Assembly, not later than April 1967, "practical means by which South West Africa should

23. For the full text of the resolution, see Appendix V, below.

24. It is not readily understood how the 1950 opinion could provide authority for termination of the mandate. That opinion ruled that "the competence to determine and modify the international status of the Territory rests with the Union of South Africa acting with the consent of the United Nations." *Status Opinion* (1950): 144. In effect, neither the United Nations nor South Africa could unilaterally modify the status of the territory, if the opinion were to be followed. Only by going beyond the opinion and referring to extra-legal considerations of a political nature could it be maintained that the Assembly was qualified to rescind the mandate. This was, in fact, the contention underlying the minority opinion in the 1956 *Oral Petitioners Opinion*. See above, pp. 160–61. It is also noteworthy that Judge Tanaka, despite his dissent on the merits in 1966, stated: "So long as the Mandate survives . . . the necessity for the future amendment of the Mandate by consent of both parties does subsist." *SWA Judgment* (1966): 323.

For a citation of the views of commentators on the issues of the legality and legal force of the revocation of the mandate, see n. 38, below. These same issues were, of course, before the Court in the *Namibia* case. (See further below, pp. 332–43). Strangely enough, the Court, in finding the action terminating the mandate fully valid, did not advert to the aforementioned question regarding the consistency of the United Nations actions with the 1950 opinion. However, cf. the dissenting opinions of Judges Fitzmaurice and Gros, *Namibia Opinion* (1971): 289–90, and 335–36.

be administered" up until independence, and to call the Security Council's attention to the Assembly's resolution.

The vote on the resolution was 114 to 2, with 3 abstentions. The two negative votes were cast by South Africa and Portugal, and the three states abstaining were France, the United Kingdom, and Malawi. The French delegate expressed doubt with regard to the "legal validity" of the method selected for putting an end to the mandate. If indeed the mandate could be revoked, it was, he said, "advisable to determine first which United Nations bodies would have competence to effect that revocation."[25] The United Kingdom delegate warned that members must not deceive themselves as to the means at their disposal to change matters in South West Africa. He also adverted to "juridical problems" arising from the Assembly action and wondered whether further guidance from the Court might not be sought.[26]

However, the overwhelming majority of the United Nations membership, including the United States and the Soviet Union, did not entertain doubts in the matter—or, in any event, did not permit any remaining doubts to interfere with the adoption of a firm and resolute stand on the South West Africa question. The near unanimity with which the Assembly called for South African withdrawal from the territory might have encouraged the belief that the United Nations was about to take active steps toward attaining its goal. Nothing, however, could have been farther from the truth.

The fourteen-member *Ad Hoc* Committee deliberated for three months, from January through March 1967, but was unable to arrive at a unanimous proposal.[27] Instead, when the special Assembly session convened, in April 1967, three separate proposals were laid before it. The United States, Canada, and Italy advocated further study of the South West Africa question;[28] a Latin American proposal favored immediate steps for bringing South West Africa to independence but made no reference to Security Council action for realizing this goal;[29] and an Afro-Asian proposal called for direct Security Council action.[30] The Soviet Union (and the Soviet bloc generally) endorsed the efforts to have South Africa removed from South West Africa, but maintained

25. GAOR, 21st Sess., Plen., 1439th Mtg., Oct. 12, 1966, p. 17.
26. Ibid., 1448th Mtg., Oct. 19, 1966, p. 5. Subsequently, the United Kingdom delegate raised particular objection to the last preambular paragraph in the draft resolution in which the Assembly asserted the right "to revert to itself the administration of the Mandated Territory." This clause, the United Kingdom deemed as "doubtful in law." Ibid., 1454th Mtg., Oct 27, 1966, p. 6.
27. U.N. Doc. A/6640. Report of the *Ad Hoc* Committee for South West Africa. Apr. 7, 1967.
28. Ibid., pp. 32-33.
29. Ibid., pp. 35-37.
30. Ibid., pp. 16-17, 29-30.

that this was a task for the Organization of African Unity, and not the United Nations, to implement.[31] In short, the Soviet Union, no less than the United States, refused to contemplate Security Council action in the South West Africa dispute.[32] The near unanimity that had been recorded in the theoretical stage of the discussions had evaporated once the practical stage of action was reached. The major powers were simply not prepared to move with force against South Africa.

This fact notwithstanding, the Assembly proceeded to the creation of a United Nations Council for South West Africa to administer the territory.[33] The vote to create this Council was 85 to 2, with 30 abstentions—including, as abstainers, all the major powers except China. Given South Africa's refusal to cooperate and the absence of great power coercion, this latest United Nations move was clearly unavailing.

As if to underscore the lack of realism surrounding adoption of the resolution, the Council's "powers and functions" included the following: "(a) To administer South West Africa until independence, . . . (b) To promulgate such laws, decrees and administrative regulations as are necessary for the administration of the Territory until a legislative assembly is established. . . . " Moreover, the Council was directed "to enter immediately into contact with the authorities of South Africa in order to lay down procedures, . . . for the transfer of the administration of the Territory with the least possible upheaval." It was also decided that June 1968 should be the target date for independence for South West Africa. And finally the Security Council was requested "to take all appropriate measures to enable the United Nations Council for South West Africa to discharge the functions and responsibilities entrusted to it by the General Assembly."

The eleven-member Council for South West Africa set out for the territory in April 1968.[34] It got as far as Lusaka in Zambia, but because South Africa announced that entry would be barred, no suitable transportation was available to complete the last leg of the journey to Windhoek, capital of the territory. As a result, the members of the Council were compelled to return to New York without having advanced very far toward the goal of assuming the administration of the territory.

The frustration of the Afro–Asian bloc at being unable to focus serious attention on the South West Africa problem was reflected in the debates of the resumed 22nd General Assembly session toward the end of April 1968. Although the major powers wanted the Assembly to

31. Ibid., pp. 25–28.
32. France and the United Kingdom, it should be borne in mind, refused to join the Committee in the first place.
33. G.A. Res. 2248 (S–V), May 19, 1967.
34. See the Council's second report, U.N. Doc. A/7088, May 4, 1968.

concentrate on the subject of nuclear nonproliferation, the Afro-Asian bloc succeeded in having this issue relegated to the First Committee while the subject of South West Africa was discussed in Plenary, since the latter problem, it was said, constituted an even more immediate threat to international peace and security than the former.[35] But despite these dramatic efforts the resultant resolution did not effectuate much significant change in the South West Africa situation. South West Africa was renamed Namibia "in accordance with the desires of its people"; the Council on Namibia was authorized to issue passports to Namibians and was directed to set up training programs for Namibians in conjunction with interested governments.[36] (But no funds were voted for these projects.) The situation some two years after Assembly termination of the mandate was summed up in these terms: "Apart from . . . limited and essentially peripheral efforts, United Nations action on the basic political problem of the Namibian situation has been without practical effect."[37]

In view of the impasse reached by the General Assembly, delegates repeatedly urged that the Security Council be brought into the picture to give meaningful effect to the action of the United Nations in terminating the mandate. The involvement of the Security Council had, after all, been the main aim of the litigation strategy. And such involvement was none the less necessary now that direct Assembly action had taken the place of the ill-fated venture into the Court. Without forceful Council intervention, it was recognized, the Assembly's efforts would remain but empty gestures—in fact, if not in law.[38] The Western powers, how-

35. See, for example, the remarks of the delegate of Ghana. U.N. Doc. A/PV.1646, Apr. 30, 1968, p. 22.

36. G.A. Res. 2372 (XXII), June 12, 1968.

37. "Issues Before the 24th General Assembly," International Conciliation, No. 574 (Sept. 1969): 79.

38. Although within the confines of the United Nations, only the United Kingdom and France (apart from South Africa and Portugal) voiced any misgivings regarding the legality of the Assembly's actions, prior to the 1971 Namibia opinion (about which see further below, pp. 332–43) most commentators regarded the Assembly's efforts to terminate the mandate to be inconsistent with the 1950 opinion and/or of doubtful legal force. See Johnson, "The South-West Africa Cases," p. 164, n. 11; Rahmatullah Khan and Satpal Kaur, "The Deadlock over South-West Africa," Indian Journal of International Law VIII (1968): 184–85; Rosalyn Higgins, "The International Court and South West Africa: The Implications of the Judgment," International Affairs XLII (1966): 598; Leo Gross, "The International Court of Justice and the United Nations," pp. 408, 423; Milton Katz, The Relevance of International Adjudication (Cambridge, Mass.: Harvard University Press, 1968), pp. 123–24; and see also the statement of Francis T. P. Plimpton, in Rita F. Taubenfeld and Howard J. Taubenfeld, Race, Peace, Law and Southern Africa (Dobbs Ferry, N.Y.: Oceana, 1968), p. 191. But cf. U. O. Umozurike, "International Law and Self-Determination in Namibia," Journal of Modern African Studies VIII (1970): 585–603.

John Dugard, in "The Revocation of the Mandate for South West Africa," AJIL LXII (1968): 94, argues that the Assembly's act of revocation was constitutionally sound, but, since it possessed only recommendatory force, could "not achieve its desired legal object," except through the endorsement of the Security Council.

ever—the United States, the United Kingdom, and France—showed no signs that they were prepared to see the South West Africa problem elevated to the Security Council. This, in turn, led to severe criticism of these states which were charged with being partial to South Africa's cause because of economic interests in southern Africa—interests, moreover, which they were expanding rather than curtailing.[39] These charges were, of course, the mainstay of the Soviet Union and other Communist states, which attributed all the evil in southern Africa to the greedy monopolies of the Western capitalist states.[40] But despite the severity of their criticism, there is no evidence at this stage that the Communist states favored direct Security Council action. And given the mutual reluctance of both East and West to become involved in the matter it is quite likely that the dispute would have remained at the same low key—in both practical (political) and legal terms—for years to come, if not for a dramatic new development (initiated, interestingly enough, by South Africa itself) which spot-lighted the issue before the conscience of the world and propelled it into the lap of the Security Council.

## THE INTERVENTION OF THE SECURITY COUNCIL

In June 1967 South Africa promulgated a Terrorism Act which provided for the death penalty for a long list of crimes, even if these were committed prior to passage of the Act; and the law was declared applicable to South West Africa as well.[41] Immediately after the Act went into force the South African government announced that thirty-seven persons from South West Africa, some of whom had been held in custody since 1966, would be charged under the Act and tried in Pretoria, capital of South Africa.[42] This proposed trial of inhabitants of an "international territory," coupled with the planned staging of the trial outside the territory where the alleged crimes were committed and the projected application of an *ex post facto* law, set in motion a worldwide storm of protest over what was regarded as a gross violation of every elementary principle of justice.[43] Various bodies, both inter-

---

39. See, for example, the remarks of the representatives of India, A/PV.1737, Dec. 10, 1968, pp. 49–50; Zambia, A/PV.1728, Nov. 27, 1968, pp. 8–12; Nepal, A/PV.1729, Nov. 27, 1968, pp. 7–10; and Tanzania, A/PV.1730, Nov. 29, 1968, pp. 23–25.

40. See, e.g., the remarks of the Soviet representative, A/PV.1734, Dec. 5, 1968, pp. 28, 31–35.

41. According to the *New York Times* of December 9, 1967 (p. 46), the Act also had the effect of holding the accused guilty unless he could prove his innocence beyond a reasonable doubt.

42. For the background to the terrorist trial, see U.N. Doc. A/6700/Add.2, Oct. 31, 1967, pp. 50–54. For a discussion of the trial in relation to the mandate, see John Dugard, "South West Africa and the 'Terrorist Trial'," *AJIL* LXIV (1970): 19–41.

43. See, for example, the protests of 200 United States lawyers, as reported in the *New York Times* of August 8, 1967 and the protest of the New York City Bar Association, as reported in that newspaper on January 22, 1968. For a critical review of the course and

national and national, called on South Africa to desist from the projected trial. These appeals notwithstanding, the trial, which commenced on August 7, 1967, proceeded as planned. After the various organs of the United Nations, including the General Assembly[44] (in a near unanimous vote) had condemned the trial, the matter reached the Security Council in January 1968. Although some of the permanent members were reluctant to have the Council consider the substantive aspects of the South West Africa question, they apparently did not object to the Council—in common with the other instrumentalities of the United Nations—condemning, on purely humanitarian and moral grounds, the injustice of this trial.[45] In fact, as it turned out, the issue of the terrorist trial was merely the thin side of the wedge.

In its unanimously adopted resolution of January 25, 1968,[46] the Security Council, taking note of the 1966 resolution "by which the Assembly terminated South Africa's Mandate over South West Africa," noted "with great concern that the trial is being held under arbitrary laws whose application has been illegally extended to . . . South West Africa in defiance of General Assembly resolutions," condemned South Africa, and called upon it "to discontinue forthwith this illegal trial and to release and repatriate the South West Africans concerned."

After the vote both the French and United Kingdom delegates expressed reservations about certain parts of the resolution just adopted. In particular, the French representative stressed that the 1966 Assembly resolution was "not binding upon the Security Council which therefore remains the master of its own decisions."[47] The United Kingdom delegate took exception to "the unqualified use of the term 'illegal' " in the resolution.[48] Despite these reservations both countries voted in support of the resolution since the law under discussion was objectionable in their eyes.[49]

South Africa remained undeterred by this new involvement of the Security Council in the affairs of South West Africa and allowed the trial to proceed as scheduled. Of the accused who were found guilty, nineteen were sentenced to life imprisonment, while eleven others were sentenced to lengthy prison terms.

In the light of this development the Security Council was reconvened in February 1968. Various Afro–Asian speakers asked for the

conduct of the trial, see Richard A. Falk, "Observer's Report on *The State v. Tuhadeleni and others*," in *Erosion of the Rule of Law in South Africa* (International Commission of Jurists, 1968).

44. Res. 2324 (XXII), Dec. 16, 1967.
45. See the comments of the French and United Kingdom representatives following the vote on the Council resolution. U.N. Doc. S/PV.1387, Jan. 25, 1968, pp. 116–17.
46. Res. 245 (1968).
47. U.N. Doc. S/PV.1387, Jan. 25, 1968, p. 116.
48. Ibid., p. 117.
49. See, e.g., ibid., p. 87.

application of enforcement measures under Chapter VII of the Charter,[50] but the Western powers rejected any such course. In discussing the ultimate resolution adopted, Mr. Goldberg of the United States declared that he had been able to support it since "it falls within the provisions of Chapter VI and . . . there is neither commitment to nor exclusion of any particular Charter approach in any necessary future consideration by the Council of this matter." He welcomed the deletion of a reference to Article 25 of the Charter from the draft since he would have regarded its inclusion "as inappropriate for a resolution . . . under Chapter VI."[51]

In its resolution 246, of March 14, 1968, the Council reaffirmed that the trial and sentencing constituted "an illegal act and a flagrant violation of the rights of the South West Africans concerned, the Universal Declaration of Human Rights and the international status of the Territory now under direct United Nations responsibility"; censured South Africa for its "flagrant defiance" of the earlier Council resolution (245); demanded that South Africa "release and repatriate forthwith" those charged and convicted, and decided that in the event South Africa failed to comply, the Council "will meet immediately to determine effective steps or measures in conformity with the relevant provisions of the Charter."

This last sentence of the resolution, it might be said, served to illustrate both the degree of success which the Afro-Asian states had scored in getting the Security Council to take up the issue of South West Africa and the limits of real advance which this development betokened. The Security Council, in taking over where the General Assembly left off, had already adopted the pattern of issuing dire, but as the event proved, vain, threats in relation to South West Africa. South Africa completely disregarded the resolution, but despite this fact the Council never held any further meetings on the matter of the trial.

The two Security Council resolutions on the terrorist trial, it should be noted, although they had gone far to stamp South Africa's presence in South West Africa as illegal, had not actually endorsed, in formal terms, the Assembly's termination of the mandate. This step was achieved in early 1969 when the Security Council, at the request of forty-six Afro-Asian states,[52] met to consider South Africa's defiance of the United Nations, and adopted resolution 264 on March 20, 1969. South Africa had, at that point, moved to integrate South West Africa

---

50. See, e.g., the remarks of the representatives of India and Algeria, SCOR, 23rd Yr., 1392nd Mtg., Feb. 19, 1968, pp. 4 and 7.
51. Ibid., 1397th Mtg., Mar. 14, 1968, p. 5.
52. U.N. Doc. S/9090 and Add. 1-3.

more closely with South Africa and had taken steps to institute the Bantustan program in the territory.

The Odendaal Commission, it will be recalled,[53] had, *inter alia*, recommended the establishment of eleven homelands in South West Africa—one for Whites and ten for non-Whites. This part of the scheme was deferred by South Africa in 1964, while the litigation in the *South West Africa* cases was still pending. But following the 1966 judgment, South Africa proceeded to the implementation of the Bantustan plan and, as a first step, to the granting of a measure of self-government to Ovamboland.[54]

On June 3, 1968 the South African Parliament passed the Development of Self-Government for Native Nations in South West Africa Act establishing six areas for "self-governing nations" and providing for the establishment therein of legislative councils and executive governments.[55] On October 18, 1968, the first session of the Ovamboland Legislative Council was opened.[56] And in March 1969 the South West Africa Affairs Act was adopted, which effected a closer union between South Africa and South West Africa in the legislative, administrative, and financial fields than had hitherto prevailed.[57] In reaction to all these steps, the Security Council adopted the aforementioned resolution (264) by a vote of 13 to 0, with France and the United Kingdom abstaining.

In the operative part of the resolution the Security Council recognized that the "General Assembly terminated the Mandate of South Africa over Namibia"; considered "that the continued presence of South Africa in Namibia is illegal"; called upon South Africa to withdraw from the Territory immediately; and declared that South Africa was not permitted to proceed with either the establishment of Bantustans or the enactment of the South West Africa Affairs Bill. In the event that South Africa failed to comply with the resolution "the Security Council will meet immediately to determine upon necessary steps or measures in accordance with the relevant provisions of the Charter."

The representatives of both France and the United Kingdom expressed doubts concerning the legal basis of the present Council resolution, since this resolution was premised upon the legal force of the Assembly's purported termination of the mandate.[58] The United Kingdom representative warned against "resort to the easy alternative of

53. See above, pp. 234–36.
54. See U.N. Doc. A/6640, Apr. 7, 1967, pp. 48–49.
55. See Report of the U.N. Council for Namibia, U.N. Doc. A/7624, Oct. 24, 1969, p. 29.
56. Ibid.
57. Ibid., pp. 30–31.
58. U.N. Doc. S/PV.1464, Mar. 20, 1969, pp. 32 and 51.

attempting to escape from reality by passing empty resolutions."[59] He joined the United States delegate in expressing satisfaction that the draft omitted any reference to Chapter VII of the Charter. The United Kingdom, he indicated, "is not and will not be prepared to agree to commitments under Chapter VII."[60]

This resolution marked a new stage in the South West Africa conflict, since henceforth the Security Council was South Africa's direct protagonist in the struggle. More significantly, the intervention of the Security Council added a new measure of legal potency to the actions of the General Assembly.[61] This new sharpening of the United Nations/South Africa confrontation did not, however, serve to induce any change in South Africa's policies.

In August 1969 the Security Council once again convened on the subject of South West Africa (Namibia)[62] and adopted, by a vote of 11 to 0, with 4 abstentions (Finland, France, the United Kingdom, and United States) a resolution[63] which, after referring in its preamble to the Council's role in regard to Articles 25 and 6[64] of the Charter, proceeded, in its operative part, to condemn South Africa for its refusal to comply with the earlier Council resolution; decided that the continued occupation of Namibia by South Africa constituted "an aggressive encroachment on the authority of the United Nations, a violation of the territorial integrity and a denial of the political sovereignty of the people of Namibia"; and called upon South Africa to evacuate the territory "immediately and in any case before 4 October 1969." In the event that South Africa failed to comply "the Security Council will meet immediately to determine upon effective measures in accordance with the appropriate provisions of the relevant Chapters of the Charter."

Once again the debates make clear (as is evident from the text itself) that in adopting this resolution the Security Council was not acting under Chapter VII of the Charter. The representatives of the United Kingdom and the United States in particular emphasized that they would have to vote against (and not merely abstain on) any draft resolution obligating the Council in terms of Chapter VII.[65] And the

59. U.N. Doc. S/PV.1465, Mar. 20, 1969, pp. 39–40.
60. Ibid., p. 41.
61. See above, n. 38. In the *Namibia Opinion* (1971): 51, the Court held that the General Assembly, "lacking the necessary powers to ensure the withdrawal of South Africa from the Territory, . . . enlisted the co-operation of the Security Council."
62. U.N. Doc. S/9359.
63. Res. 269, Aug. 12, 1969.
64. Article 25 reads: "The Members of the United Nations agree to accept and carry out the decisions of the Security Council in accordance with the present Charter."
Article 6 relates to the possibility of expelling a member who persistently violates Charter principles.
65. U.N. Doc. S/PV.1496, Aug. 11, 1969, pp. 6, 9–10.

REVOCATION OF MANDATE AND ITS AFTERMATH / 327

representative of Nepal regretted that "the present draft resolution falls far short of the requirements of the situation in that it fails to commit the Security Council to a specific course of action under Chapter VII of the Charter."[66] Nonetheless, the resolution—with its reference to Articles 25 and 6 of the Charter and its characterization of South Africa's acts as "an aggressive encroachment" on United Nations authority— clearly represents a measure of escalation in the conflict. It was for this reason that the three major Western powers abstained, while cautioning the United Nations against embarking "on an unrealistic course of action"[67] which "will in practice lead nowhere."[68]

Not unexpectedly, the target date set by the Security Council resolution—October 4, 1969—came and went, with South Africa doing nothing to loosen its hold on South West Africa, and with the Security Council taking none of the threatened "effective measures." (In fact, the Council failed altogether to reconvene at the projected time.) In the light of the Security Council's ineffectual record on the Rhodesian question over a five-year period,[69] it is little wonder that its ultimatum—though bearing a time limit—made very little impression on South Africa's leaders. The factor which had prevented the Council from acting forcefully in the Rhodesian crisis, viz., unwillingness to countenance a direct confrontation with South Africa, operated with the same—if not greater—force in the South West Africa situation. It is, of course, no secret that the cost of any possible confrontation for the Western powers generally would be high; and for Great Britain, it would be of astronomical proportions—far, far higher than the price which the African states themselves, either individually or collectively, could be called upon to pay. (United Kingdom investments in South Africa are estimated at some $2.8 billion, with trade valued at ca. $700 million annually each way.)[70] These facts and figures establish a chastening limit to the freedom of operation of the Security Council and provide

66. U.N. Doc. S/PV.1497, Aug. 12, 1969, p. 11. See also the remarks of the delegate of Zambia, ibid., p. 6.
67. Remarks of the United States representative, U.N. Doc. S/PV.1496, Aug. 11, 1969, pp. 9-10.
68. Remarks of the United Kingdom representative, ibid., pp. 3-5.
69. On the ineffectual nature of the Council's sanctions, see Ralph Zacklin, "Challenge of Rhodesia," *International Conciliation*, No. 575 (Nov. 1969).
70. For the United States, the figures are: $650 million of investment in South Africa with an annual trade of some $250 million each way. See Ernest A. Gross, "The South West Africa Case: What Happened?" *Foreign Affairs* XLV (1966): 41-42; and Waldemar A. Nielsen, *The Great Powers and Africa* (New York: Praeger, 1969), pp. 39 and 384.
For a review of Western economic interests in southern Africa and the cost of applying sanctions see the following: Ronald Segal (ed.), *Sanctions Against South Africa* (Baltimore: Penguin Books, 1964); Amelia C. Leiss (ed.), *Apartheid and United Nations Collective Measures: An Analysis* (New York: Carnegie Endowment for International Peace, 1965), chap. VI; Colin and Margaret Legum, *South Africa: Crisis for the West* (London: Pall Mall Press, 1964), chap. XI; William A. Hance (ed.), *Southern Africa and the United States* (New York: Columbia University Press, 1968), pp. 119-24.

an appropriate backdrop to the defiant reply which South Africa delivered to the Council's demands.

In a lengthy letter dated September 26, 1969,[71] the South African Minister for Foreign Affairs challenged the validity of the Security Council resolutions on South West Africa. The fundamental claim was that since the original General Assembly resolution purporting to terminate the mandate was itself invalid, all subsequent resolutions, including those of the Security Council, based on the action of the Assembly were likewise invalid. The Assembly could not legally terminate the mandate, since the United Nations had never succeeded to any supervisory power with respect to South West Africa; and even if it had, it would not possess the requisite competence to effectuate termination. Moreover, the 1950 opinion itself, which posited United Nations supervision, negated any unilateral right for the United Nations to modify the territory's mandate status. Apart from these considerations, the letter also alleged that certain Charter provisions were not adhered to when Security Council Resolution 269 (1969) was adopted. Some permanent members of the Security Council abstained, thus raising the question whether the requirements of Article 27 (3) were fulfilled. Furthermore, certain states had in the past raised the question whether China was correctly represented in the Council. The letter then went on to review the extensive benefits which had accrued to the population of South West Africa from South African administration, including the benefits of separate development. And in conclusion, the South African Minister of Foreign Affairs emphasized that South Africa threatened no country and remained firm in its resolve to stay in South West Africa. "On no account will we abandon the peoples of South West Africa who for half a century have placed their trust in us to lead them on the path of progress, peace and stability."[72]

The action of the Security Council in issuing an ultimatum to South Africa to withdraw from the territory, and South Africa's unyielding response, effectively demonstrated that the United Nations had reached a dead-end on the whole question of South West Africa. The Assembly had succeeded in getting the matter into the lap of the Security Council, only to find that its victory was very hollow indeed. The difficulties encountered by the Assembly had in no way been resolved by their transference to the "executive" arm of the United Nations. South Africa persisted in its intransigence and the Western states continued to refuse categorically to contemplate forceful measures. The matter was

71. The 121-page letter plus annexure was subsequently distributed as U.N. Doc. S/9463, Oct. 3, 1969. Each of the arguments noted in the letter was subsequently adduced and elaborated upon in South Africa's pleadings before the Court in the advisory proceedings on Namibia.

72. Ibid., p. 121.

aptly summed up by the delegate of Finland: "Disagreements on strategy had led the General Assembly to a situation where it seems to have exhausted the means at its disposal to influence the course of events in the Territory. The Security Council now faces the same problem."[73] Viewed in this light, the belligerent tone of Council resolutions must be seen as little more than a means of propitiating growing Afro-Asian pressures, at a time when the Council remains, in realistic terms, unable to induce any change in the existing situation.

The impotence of the Security Council on the question was accentuated when, for the first time in its history, it turned to the International Court of Justice for an advisory opinion in July 1970. After five months of deliberation, an *Ad Hoc* Sub-Committee composed of all the Council members and charged with studying means of implementing the Council's resolutions on Namibia, was unable to produce anything more substantial than this suggestion for recourse to the Court.

The *Ad Hoc* Sub-Committee had been established on January 30, 1970, by Resolution 276. In the same resolution, the Council also confirmed (in paragraph 2) the illegality of South Africa's presence in the territory and declared that consequently "all acts taken by the Government of South Africa on behalf of or concerning Namibia after the termination of the Mandate are illegal and invalid." All states were called upon "to refrain from any dealings with the Government of South Africa which are inconsistent" with the aforementioned paragraph 2.

Upon receiving the report of its *Ad Hoc* Sub-Committee,[74] the Security Council proceeded, on July 29, 1970, to adopt two resolutions based on the committee's recommendations. The first (Resolution 283) spelled out in considerable detail the attitude which states were expected to adopt in the diplomatic, economic, and legal spheres, in reaction to South Africa's "illegal" presence in the territory. In the second resolution (284), the Council, as already noted, decided to request an advisory opinion of the International Court. The question submitted was as follows:

> What are the legal consequences for States of the continued presence of South Africa in Namibia, notwithstanding Security Council resolution 276 (1970)?

That this resort to the Court's advisory function was not motivated by any genuine doubts regarding the legality of United Nations actions on South West Africa appears from a number of considerations.

73. U.N. Doc. S/PV.1494, Aug. 6, 1969, p. 7.
74. U.N. Doc. S/9863, July 7, 1970.

First, as was seen, the resolution adopted immediately prior to the request for judicial clarification elaborated in considerable detail the consequences for states of South Africa's illegal presence in Namibia.

Second, the debates make quite clear that the Court was not expected "to rule on the status of Namibia as such."[75] For this reason the Council rejected a suggestion by France that the phrase "notwithstanding Security Council resolution 276 (1970)" be omitted from the request,[76] so as to enable the judges "to question the legal foundations of the revocation of the Mandate."[77] The members of the Council were not at all interested in casting doubt upon those "foundations"; they wished rather, in the words of the Syrian delegate, "to elicit the scope of legal means at the disposal of States, which may erect a wall of legal opposition to the occupation of Namibia by the Government of South Africa."[78]

Third, several of the explanations adduced for referral of the question to the Court were extraneous to the issue at hand. Thus, for example, it was said that the Court would be given an opportunity to "rehabilitate" itself[79] and to "redeem its impaired image" after the "unfortunate judgement" of 1966.[80] Furthermore, it was stated, the Court was "in danger of atrophy" for lack of business, and "the request for an advisory opinion on a question of great interest to the international community would reactivate the Court at a particularly difficult time in its existence."[81]

Finally, the Council discussions reveal a manifest expectation that the Court's opinion would be, from the Council's standpoint, the "correct" one. It would thereby "expose the false front of legality" presented by South Africa, and "help . . . to mobilize public opinion."[82] It would, in a word, operate as an additional element of pressure in the campaign against South Africa.

It should be borne in mind, in connection with the aforementioned considerations, that the Court to which the present request was being addressed was very different in composition from the one that had delivered the 1966 judgment. Two triennial elections had since intervened (in 1966 and 1969) and had resulted in important changes in

75. Statement of Syrian representative, U.N. Doc. S/PV.1550, July 29, 1970, p. 47. See also the remarks of the Zambian representative, ibid., p. 53.
76. France requested a separate vote on the words in question; and the disputed phrase was adopted by a vote of 11-0, with 4 abstentions (France, Poland, Soviet Union, and United Kingdom). Ibid., pp. 76-80. France nevertheless voted for the final resolution. Ibid., p. 81.
77. Ibid., p. 87.
78. Ibid., p. 47.
79. See the statement of the representative of Burundi, ibid., p. 71.
80. See the statement of the representative of Nepal, ibid., pp. 38-40.
81. Statement of the Finnish representative, ibid., pp. 19-20.
82. Ibid., p. 18.

personnel and representation, with Africa gaining an additional judge at the expense of Europe. Moreover, two of the Asian judges unable to sit in the 1966 judgment,[83] would presumably participate in the present opinion. In its new composition, then, the Court could be expected by the states of the emerging world to better reflect their concept of international law. The "old" international law was seen by these states as the creation of the European state system and the hand-maiden of Western economic interests. It was, in their eyes, unresponsive to the ideals and aspirations of the more universal present-day international community.[84] The Court, it was hoped, would now move to "restore world public confidence in its very existence"[85] by "harmonizing . . . [its] position . . . with the position taken by the General Assembly."[86]

There were, very probably, further unstated and not necessarily consistent reasons for turning to the Court at this particular juncture. Perhaps this move was intended to demonstrate to the Afro-Asian states that "something" was at least being done on the question. Yet, at the same time, recourse to the Court would afford the Council, and especially the Western states, a "breathing spell"; it would allow a bit more procrastination over this insoluble problem. At any rate there would appear to have been few, if any, illusions regarding the ability of any advisory opinion to effectuate a dramatic new departure in this perennial international dispute.

The vote for requesting the question of the Court was 12 to 0, with 3 abstentions—those of Poland, the Soviet Union, and the United Kingdom.[87] The Soviet delegate did not deem the request "an effective measure which could contribute to the withdrawal of the South African racists from Namibia."[88] The United Kingdom delegate, on the other hand, explained that his government was unable to support the resolution since "it is based on certain assumptions about the legal status of South West Africa which . . . ought themselves to be examined by the Court." These assumptions related to the question of the General Assembly's competence to terminate the mandate and its right "to vest in the United Nations responsibility for the Territory."[89] Had the issue of "the status of South West Africa as a whole" been posed to the Court,

83. See above, p. 281.
84. On this topic generally, see Oliver J. Lissitzyn, *International Law Today and Tomorrow* (Dobbs Ferry, N.Y.: Oceana, 1965); and Wolfgang Friedmann, *The Changing Structure of International Law* (New York: Columbia University Press, 1964), passim. See also Julius Stone, "The International Court and World Crisis," *International Conciliation*, No. 536 (Jan. 1962): 36–37, and Louis Henkin, *How Nations Behave* (New York: Praeger, 1968), chap. IX.
85. Statement of the representative of Zambia. U.N. Doc. S/PV.1550, July 29, 1970, pp. 54–55.
86. Remarks of the representative of Burundi, ibid., p. 71.
87. Ibid., p. 81.
88. Ibid., pp. 63–65.
89. Ibid., p. 91.

he would have supported the resolution;[90] but as it was, "the Court might feel itself inhibited from pronouncing on the more fundamental issues" involved.[91] The French delegate entertained similar qualms, but voted for the resolution nonetheless, since even in its present form he believed the Court could examine "the legal position as regards the legality of the revocation."[92] In the event, the British representative was closer to the mark, since although the Court *pro forma* considered the issue of United Nations authority in the matter, it never really came to grips with the basic premises upon which any United Nations power of revocation must perforce rest.

## THE 1971 NAMIBIA OPINION[93]

In its advisory opinion of June 21, 1971, the Court held by 13 votes to 2 (Judges Fitzmaurice of the United Kingdom and Gros of France dissenting) that since South Africa's presence in Namibia was illegal, South Africa was under a duty to withdraw from the territory immediately; and by 11 votes to 4 (Judges Petren of Sweden and Onyeama of Nigeria joining the two other dissenters), that states, whether members of the United Nations or not, are under an obligation to recognize the illegality of South Africa's presence in Namibia and to act accordingly.[94]

90. Ibid., pp. 89-90.
91. Ibid., p. 91.
92. Ibid., p. 87.
93. The following states submitted written statements or letters to the Court in the case: Czechoslovakia, Finland, France, Hungary, India, the Netherlands, Nigeria, Pakistan, Poland, South Africa, the United States, and Yugoslavia. In the oral proceedings, Finland, India, the Netherlands, Nigeria, Pakistan, South Africa, South Vietnam, and the United States were represented. The United Nations Secretary-General took part in both written and oral proceedings, while the Organization of African Unity participated in the oral proceedings. *Namibia Opinion* (1971): 18 and 20.
It may be noted that neither Ethiopia nor Liberia participated in the pleadings.
For discussion of the opinion see John Dugard, "The Opinion on South-West Africa ('Namibia'): The Teleologists Triumph," *South African Law Journal* LXXXVIII (1971): 460-77; John Dugard, "Namibia (South West Africa): The Court's Opinion, South Africa's Response, and Prospects for the Future," *Columbia Journal of Transnational Law* XI (1972): 14-49; Oliver J. Lissitzyn, "International Law and the Advisory Opinion on Namibia," *Columbia Journal of Transnational Law* XI (1972): 50-73; Rosalyn Higgins, "The Advisory Opinion on Namibia: Which UN Resolutions are Binding under Article 25 of the Charter?", *ICLQ* XXI (1972): 270-86.
94. The operative part of the opinion read as follows:

"THE COURT IS OF OPINION,
. . . . . . . . . . . . . . . . . . . . . . . . . . . . . . . . . . . . . . . . . . . . . . . . . . . . . . . . . . . .
"by 13 votes to 2,
"(1) that, the continued presence of South Africa in Namibia being illegal, South Africa is under obligation to withdraw its administration from Namibia immediately and thus put an end to its occupation of the Territory;
"by 11 votes to 4,

The first part of the opinion was devoted to answering objections to the Court's competence to give the opinion and to the propriety of its doing so.

South Africa's challenge to the Court's competence was based on the assertion that the requesting resolution was invalid, *inter alia*, because it was adopted despite the abstentions of France and the United Kingdom (and hence, in contravention of Article 27[3] of the Charter, requiring the *concurring* votes of all permanent Council members), and because South Africa should have been invited to participate in the Council discussions on the dispute, in accordance with the mandatory language of Article 32.[95] The Court dismissed this challenge by referring to the "general practice of the Organization" regarding the voluntary abstentions of permanent members, and by noting that the Namibia question had been treated as a "situation" rather than a "dispute," and no objection had been made at the appropriate time to this aspect of the Council's handling of the matter.[96]

Nor did the Court consider that as a matter of "judicial propriety" it should "refuse to exercise its competence."[97] The charge raised by South Africa that the Court was, or might be, subjected to political pressure was one which could not properly be entertained, since it bore "on the very nature of the Court as the principal judicial organ of the United Nations."[98] And as for South Africa's further argument on propriety—that the issue was at base contentious (as reflected in the 1960 litigation) and that the *Eastern Carelia* precedent should apply—the Court held that incidental consideration of contentious matters does not convert the request of a United Nations organ for advice into a

---

"(2)    that States Members of the United Nations are under obligation to recognize the illegality of South Africa's presence in Namibia and the invalidity of its acts on behalf of or concerning Namibia, and to refrain from any acts and in particular any dealings with the Government of South Africa implying recognition of the legality of, or lending support or assistance to, such presence and administration;

"(3)    that it is incumbent upon States which are not Members of the United Nations to give assistance, within the scope of subparagraph (2) above, in the action which has been taken by the United Nations with regard to Namibia." *Namibia Opinion* (1971): 58.

95. See South Africa's arguments in *Namibia Pleadings* I: 398-425; II: 209-27; and *Namibia Opinion* (1971): 21-22. South Africa contended further that the provision in Article 27(3) on the mandatory abstention of Council members, parties to a dispute, should have been observed. See the aforementioned citations.

96. *Namibia Opinion* (1971): 22-23. The non-"dispute" nature of the matter also rendered irrelevant the proviso regarding mandatory abstention in Article 27(3). Ibid., p. 23.

97. Ibid. For South Africa's arguments on the "propriety" issue, see *Namibia Pleadings* I: 425-50; II: 185ff.

98. *Namibia Opinion* (1971): 23. South Africa had also suggested that the Court was the subject of a calculated "courtpacking" plan. See South Africa's Written Statement to the Court in *Namibia Pleadings* I: 433-37.

dispute. For this and other reasons[99] the *Eastern Carelia* precedent was deemed irrelevant.[100]

In the preliminary part of its opinion, the Court also noted its earlier dismissal (in separate Court orders) of South African objections relating to the participation of three judges in the proceedings,[101] and to its rejection of South Africa's application to seat a judge *ad hoc.*[102]

Turning to the substantive question posed, the Court first reviewed the history and purposes of the mandate, and held (in line with the 1950 opinion) that the mandate survived the dissolution of the League and that the function of supervision was transferred to the United Nations.[103] This legal situation arose from the operation of Article 80(1) of the Charter and the final resolution of the League Assembly, both of which worked to maintain the obligations of the mandatories.[104] South Africa's own statements in the period of transition also confirmed that the mandate survived, and as a corollary, that international accountability, an essential element in the mandate, also survived.[105] For twenty years the United Nations had sought to institute appropriate supervisory arrangements, only to be met by the constant rebuff of South Africa. In the face of this refusal to reach an agreement, the General Assembly finally adopted Resolution 2145(XXI) on the termination of the mandate.[106]

Did the Assembly act *ultra vires* in adopting this resolution? The contention that it did was advanced by both France and South Africa in their respective pleadings.[107] In principle, the Court emphasized, it does not possess any power of judicial review in respect of decisions of the United Nations organs in question; nor, in fact, did the issue of the validity of the Assembly resolution or of the relevant Council resolutions form the subject of the present request. Nonetheless, in the exercise of its judicial function, the Court undertook to consider the objec-

---

99. The Court also noted that South Africa, as a member of the United Nations, was "bound by Article 96 of the Charter, which empowers the Security Council to request advisory opinions on any legal question"; and that South Africa, while objecting to the Court's competence, nonetheless appeared before the Court and dealt with the merits of the question. *Namibia Opinion* (1971): 23–24.

100. Ibid. For the Court's dismissal of a South African claim that Article 96 of the Charter excluded extensive factual enquiry by the Court in advisory proceedings, see ibid., p. 27.

101. Ibid., pp. 18–19; and see above, chap. XI, n. 8 and n. 9.

102. *Namibia Opinion* (1971): 19. The denial of a judge *ad hoc* was, of course, related to the Court's affirmation of the noncontentious nature of the question. Ibid., pp. 24–27.

103. Ibid., pp. 27–43.

104. Ibid., pp. 33–35.

105. Ibid., pp. 36 and 39–40.

106. Ibid., pp. 43–45.

107. See the Written Statement of France, *Namibia Pleadings* I: 326–69, and the arguments of South Africa, ibid., pp. 717–24; II: 397–423, 610.

tions which had been raised before examining the legal consequences of the resolutions.[108]

The Court began by recalling that "with the entry into force of the Charter of the United Nations a relationship was established between all Members of the United Nations on the one side, and each Mandatory Power on the other." The mandatory powers obligated themselves to preserve until the conclusion of trusteeship agreements all the rights resulting from the mandate instruments and accruing to other states and to the peoples of the mandated territories.[109]

The Assembly's action in terminating the mandate was related to the general principle of international law (incorporated in the 1969 Vienna Convention on the Law of Treaties) in accordance with which "a right of termination on account of breach must be presumed to exist in respect of all treaties."[110] (And the mandate, even if viewed as an institution, "depends on those international agreements which created the system and regulated its application.")[111] South Africa had not only repudiated the mandate by disavowing it, it had been in material breach thereof by its refusal to submit to supervision and render reports—a fact uncontroverted by any party. "The resolution in question is therefore to be viewed as the exercise of the right to terminate a relationship in case of a deliberate and persistent violation of obligations which destroys the very object and purpose of that relationship."[112]

The Covenant's silence on the matter of the revocability of the mandate was not relevant, since the right of termination has its source "outside of the treaty, in general international law, and is dependent on the occurrence of circumstances which are not normally envisaged when a treaty is concluded."[113] Nor, "for obvious reasons," can "the consent of the wrongdoer to such a form of termination" be required.[114] Nor again was it necessary, as South Africa had insisted, for a judicial, rather than a political, organ to make determinations of the sort included in Resolution 2145 (XXI). After all, the 1966 judgment had declared that "any divergences of view concerning the conduct of the mandate were . . . matters that had their place in the political field, the settlement of which lay between the mandatory and the competent

108. *Namibia Opinion* (1971): 45.
109. Ibid., pp. 45–46.
110. Ibid., pp. 46–48.
111. Ibid., p. 46. The Court cited approvingly the statement in the 1962 judgment that the Mandate was "a special type of instrument composite in nature and instituting a novel international regime. It incorporates a definite agreement . . ." (*SWA Judgment* [1962]: 331.)
112. *Namibia Opinion* (1971): 47.
113. Ibid.
114. Ibid., p. 49.

organs of the League."[115] "To deny a political organ of the United Nations which is a successor to the League in this respect the right to act, on the argument that it lacks competence to render what is described as a judicial decision, would not only be inconsistent but would amount to a complete denial of the remedies available against fundamental breaches of an international undertaking."[116] The General Assembly, then, did not require a Court ruling before adopting the resolution in question; neither did it need to conduct a factual enquiry regarding South Africa's failure to fulfill its obligations regarding the administration of the territory, since the failure to submit to supervision—an essential part of the mandate—was undisputed.[117]

In stating that with termination of the mandate, "South Africa has no other right to administer the Territory," the resolution did not decide on a transfer of territory. The Assembly's statement was made in reliance on the Court's previous pronouncements and did not constitute "a finding on facts, but the formulation of a legal situation."[118] "For it would not be correct to assume that, because the General Assembly is in principle vested with recommendatory powers, it is debarred from adopting, in specific cases within the framework of its competence, resolutions which make determinations or have operative design."[119]

The Court then proceeded to analyze the place of the Security Council in the dispute.

> By resolution 2145(XXI) the General Assembly terminated the Mandate. However, lacking the necessary powers to ensure the withdrawal of South Africa from the Territory, it enlisted the cooperation of the Security Council by calling the latter's attention to the resolution, thus acting in accordance with Article 11, paragraph 2, of the Charter. . . . The Security Council responded to the call of the General Assembly.[120]

Reviewing the relevant Council resolutions, the Court noted that Resolution 276(1970) reaffirmed and espoused Resolution 2145(XXI), "by referring to the decision, not merely of the General Assembly, but of the United Nations 'that the Mandate of South-West Africa was terminated'."[121] In adopting the resolutions in question, the Security Council "was acting in the exercise of . . . its primary responsibility, the maintenance of peace and security, which, . . . embraces situations

---

115. Ibid., citing *SWA Judgment* (1962): 29.
116. *Namibia Opinion* (1971): 49.
117. Ibid., p. 50.
118. Ibid.
119. Ibid.
120. Ibid., p. 51.
121. Ibid.

which might lead to a breach of the peace."[122] Its authority to act in this case was derived from Article 24 of the Charter. "The reference in paragraph 2 of this Article to specific powers of the Security Council under certain chapters of the Charter does not exclude the existence of general powers to discharge the responsibilities conferred in paragraph 1."[123] Taking into account the terms of the resolutions and all the circumstances surrounding their adoption, it was clear that they were intended to impose legal duties upon states and not to be merely hortatory. The resolutions were adopted "in conformity with the purposes and principles of the Charter and in accordance with its Articles 24 and 25. The decisions are consequently binding on all States Members of the United Nations, which are thus under obligation to accept and carry them out."[124] This obligation covered also those members of the Security Council voting against the relevant resolutions and members of the United Nations who are not members of the Council.[125] In reaching this conclusion, the Court rejected the contention that Article 25 (imposing an obligation on United Nations members "to accept and carry out the decisions of the Security Council") applied only to enforcement measures adopted under Chapter VII of the Charter. The term "decision" covered all decisions, whether or not of an enforcement nature.[126]

Regarding the legal consequences of the situation, the Court declared: "A binding determination made by a competent organ of the United Nations to the effect that a situation is illegal cannot remain without consequences."[127] As a result, "South Africa, being responsible for having created and maintained" the illegal situation, "has the obligation to put an end to it." "Member States of the United Nations are . . . under obligation to recognize the illegality and invalidity of South Africa's continued presence in Namibia [and] . . . to refrain from lending any support or any form of assistance to South Africa with reference to its occupation of Namibia."[128]

Without attempting to spell out the measures that are "available and practicable," and the precise determination of the acts permitted

122. Ibid., pp. 51–52.
123. Ibid., p. 52. Article 24 reads:
1. In order to ensure prompt and effective action by the United Nations, its Members confer on the Security Council primary responsibility for the maintenance of international peace and security, and agree that in carrying out its duties under this responsibility the Security Council acts on their behalf.
2. In discharging these duties the Security Council shall act in accordance with the Purposes and Principles of the United Nations. The specific powers granted to the Security Council for the discharge of these duties are laid down in Chapters VI, VII, VIII, and XII.
124. Ibid., p. 53. For the text of Article 25 of the Charter see above n. 64.
125. Ibid., p. 54.
126. Ibid., pp. 52–53.
127. Ibid., p. 54.
128. Ibid.

338 / SOUTH WEST AFRICA OR NAMIBIA?

and allowed—all of which lay within the competence of the appropriate political organs—the Court nevertheless gave advice "on those dealings with the Government of South Africa which, under the Charter of the United Nations and general international law, should be considered as inconsistent with the declaration of illegality and invalidity made in . . . resolution 276(1970), because they may imply a recognition that South Africa's presence in Namibia is legal."[129] In this context, the Court detailed some of the treaty, diplomatic, consular, and economic relations which in its view were proscribed.[130] Non-member states too, although not bound by Articles 24 and 25 of the Charter, were obligated under general international law to recognize, and to act in accordance with, the illegality of the situation.[131]

Finally, the Court considered both South Africa's offer to supply factual information and its request for a plebiscite in the territory unnecessary. Apartheid was, on its face, "a flagrant violation of the purposes and principles of the Charter," and to determine this the Court needed no factual evidence regarding either the consequences or effects of the policy.[132] And as for the proposal to hold a plebiscite under the joint supervision of the Court and South Africa, this was not entertainable, once South Africa's presence in the territory was confirmed by the Court to be illegal.[133]

From this review of the opinion, it emerges that the Court in furnishing its reply never really came to grips with some of the fundamental issues raised by the Assembly's purported termination of the mandate.

How, for example, could a recommendation of the General Assembly have the dispositive effect of depriving a state of its authority to administer a territory? The Court's suggestion that South Africa's actions had amounted to a repudiation of the mandate, entitling the other

---

129. Ibid., p. 55.
130. Ibid., pp. 55–56.
131. Ibid., p. 56.
132. Ibid., p. 57. There are several noteworthy aspects of this statement by the Court. The first is that it came at the tail end of the opinion and did not constitute a basis for the Court's ruling. Certainly it could not be taken as part of the *ratio decidendi* of the case for confirming the validity of the United Nations resolutions or determining the consequences for states. Second, the Court found that apartheid was a violation of the Charter; it made no finding that this racial system constituted a violation of the mandate. Third, the Court ruled that apartheid violated the purposes and principles of the Charter; it did not rule that the human rights provisions of the Charter (Articles 55 and 56) were violated. Nor did it even hint that General Assembly resolutions had defined such provisions so as to render South Africa's actions illegal. And finally, the Court's ruling represented an independent value judgment and not the automatic acceptance of a judgment made by some other body which the Court was obliged to accept as a legal given. Cf. the approach of the Applicants in the South West Africa litigation, above, pp. 251–59, 273–75.
133. *Namibia Opinion* (1971): 57–58.

party, the General Assembly, to declare the mandate terminated, does nothing to resolve this basic issue. Where did the Assembly derive its competence not only to declare the mandate terminated but to vest administration of the territory in the United Nations?[134] A recommendation of the General Assembly might be acknowledged to possess dispositive effect in relation to non-self-governing territories when the Assembly acts in unison with the administering authority, as in the termination of the Cameroons trusteeship or the Palestine mandate; but if, as in the present case, the Assembly attempts to act unilaterally, how can binding force be attributed to its recommendations?

The 1950 opinion, it will be recalled, had postulated that "the competence to determine and modify the international status of the Territory rests with the Union of South Africa acting with the consent of the United Nations." Neither of the two, then, could act unilaterally: South Africa required the consent of the United Nations for incorporation of the territory; and the United Nations required South African consent for termination of the mandate. Yet, Resolution 2145(XXI), while basing itself on the 1950 opinion in respect of United Nations succession to the League's supervisory powers, totally ignored the 1950 ruling in the matter of termination—a fact which, in the view of many commentators, cast doubt on the legality of this resolution.[135]

The Court, curiously enough, did not even advert to the problem of the consistency of the Assembly's act with the 1950 opinion—though the matter was raised in the pleadings[136] and in the dissenting opinions.[137] The thesis of the Court regarding a "material breach" of the mandate was presumably designed to avoid this particular difficulty.[138] By implication the Court was saying that the 1950 pronouncement was based on the assumption of observance of the mandate, while the termination was premised upon the fact of its breach. And in the latter case, the normal methods of effectuating a change of status must give way to the extraordinary recourse, presumed in respect of all treaties, of termination by the injured party. In fact, however, this thesis of "material breach" raises more difficulties than it solves.

First of all, even if the Assembly is competent to declare the existence of a breach, can such declaration have any greater effect than

134. See the statement of the United Kingdom representative, referred to above, p. 331.
135. See above, n. 38.
136. See, e.g., the Written Statement of the United States in *Namibia Pleadings* I: 862–63. It may be noted that South Africa, at least in its pleadings, studiously avoided any reliance upon the 1950 opinion.
137. See the dissenting opinions of Judges Fitzmaurice and Gros, *Namibia Opinion* (1971): 289–90 and 335–36.
138. The Court may also have accepted (though it nowhere said so explicitly) the United States thesis that revocation of the mandate left intact the international status of the territory. See *Namibia Pleadings* I: 862–63. The United States thesis, of course, only begs the question.

releasing the injured party—in this case, the United Nations—from *its* obligations (whatever they may be) under the agreement? How can it also serve to divest the other party of its right of administration over the territory?

Second, what treaty was being referred to? The Court speaks of a "relationship" which "was established between all Members of the United Nations on the one side, and each mandatory Power on the other."[139] It further states that the Assembly, in the light of South Africa's disavowal of the mandate, exercised the right to terminate the "relationship."[140] But even if such a separate "relationship"—or implied agreement—existed, could it have conveyed to the Assembly a competence not granted to it even in formally adopted trusteeship agreements, viz., the right of unilateral dismissal of the Administering Authority? What connection was there between a breach of the postulated "relationship" and the complete revocation of South Africa's mandate? If, on the other hand, as the Court also seems to imply, it is the original mandate agreement which was breached, then only if the United Nations was a *successor in title* to the League in respect of mandates, could it be deemed a party to this contractual relationship. The Court appears to exhibit some confusion as to whether the Assembly was terminating a "treaty" or a "relationship," and whether the relationship was between the United Nations and the mandatory powers, or that established in the original mandate agreements. But in either case, the 1971 Court was going beyond and, in fact, contradicting its earlier pronouncements of 1950 and 1962. The idea of a separate agreement with the United Nations was not previously asserted by the Court. The 1962 judgment only posited an agreement *among* members of the League of Nations.[141] And the concept of the United Nations as successor in title to the League in a contractual relationship with the mandatories is an idea rejected both in 1950 and 1962. (Indeed, had the United Nations been such a successor, then any of its members, and not only members of the League, might have invoked the jurisdiction of the Court in 1960.) But unless the United Nations is seen as a full-fledged successor to the League, then its inheritance of the League's supervisory role would not grant it any right to terminate the mandate agreement as a whole. (All this is on the assumption that such a right of termination was vested in the League, something not free of doubt, as will be seen below.)

Some of the aforementioned difficulties, along with a host of others, were noted by Judge Fitzmaurice in his vigorous and powerful

139. *Namibia Opinion* (1971): 45.
140. Ibid., p. 47.
141. *SWA Judgment* (1962): 338 and 341.

dissent.[142] "The findings of the Court," he held "involve formidable legal difficulties which the Opinion turns rather than meets, and sometimes hardly seems to notice at all."[143] The validity of the Assembly's termination of the mandate, he noted, was premised by the Court on two kinds of alleged breaches of the mandate—failure to report to the United Nations and failure to promote the welfare of the territory's inhabitants. But how, asked Judge Fitzmaurice, could South Africa be held in breach of the duty to report when the only basis for such duty was the 1950 advisory opinion which was not binding on South Africa?[144] And as for the second form of breach, how could any breach of duty be declared when "*these charges had never, at the critical date of the adoption of Assembly resolution 2145, been the subject of any judicial determination at all*," and when in the present proceedings the Court had even refused to accept South Africa's offer to investigate the facts?[145] As for the Assembly resolution purporting to terminate the mandate, "there is hardly a clause in it," declared Judge Fitzmaurice, "which is not open to challenge on grounds of law or fact."[146] In his view (following the line of Judges McNair and Read in 1950), although the mandate survived the dissolution of the League, no supervisory powers accrued to the United Nations in reference to mandates. But even if the United Nations had succeeded to the League's supervisory authority, this would not have included a power of unilateral revocation of the mandate since no such power resided in the League.[147] Moreover, the General Assembly did not possess executive powers in any case and was limited to discussion and making recommendations.[148] Nor could the involvement of the Security Council remedy the above-listed shortcomings since, in reference to mandates, the powers of the Security Council were no greater than those of the General Assembly and were, in any case, only consequential on the Assembly's act of revocation.[149] Furthermore, from all the surrounding circumstances it was clear that the Security Council's resolutions amounted to recommendations only, since they did not fall within the scope of Chapter VII of the Charter.[150] Article 24 in no way expands the specific peace-keeping powers provided for in the Charter;[151] and "if, under the relevant chapter or article of the Charter, the decision is *not* bind-

142. *Namibia Opinion* (1971): 220–322.
143. Ibid., pp. 223–24.
144. Ibid., pp. 221–22.
145. Ibid., pp. 222–23 (emphasis in original).
146. Ibid., p. 221, n. 1.
147. Ibid., pp. 264–79.
148. Ibid., pp. 280–83.
149. Ibid., pp. 291–92.
150. Ibid., p. 292.
151. Ibid., pp. 292–93.

ing, Article 25 cannot make it so."[152] And, finally, the Security Council, even when acting genuinely for the preservation of peace, is not empowered to effect legal changes "in territorial rights, whether of sovereignty or administration—and a mandate involves, necessarily, a territorial right of administration, without which it could not be operated."[153] "It was to keep the peace, not to change the world order, that the Security Council was set up."[154] On the grounds just outlined, and others, Judge Fitzmaurice concluded that the mandate for South West Africa was never validly revoked and still subsists.[155]

This dissent, despite the fact that it represents the views of a solitary judge,[156] must be regarded as a formidable challenge to the majority opinion, since it high-lights mercilessly the omissions of that opinion, and the extent to which it merely assumes or glosses over what it should establish. At base, the difference between majority and minority opinions lies perhaps, once again, in the judicial philosophy or jurisprudential concepts of the respective judges. For Judge Fitzmaurice the task of interpretation entailed determining "the intentions of those concerned at the time," and the approach of the Court represented to him an "alien philosophy."[157]

The majority, however, while it considered that the interpretation of an instrument should, as a matter of "primary necessity," take account of the original intentions, felt that the concepts embodied in Article 22 of the Covenant "were not static, but were by definition evolutionary," and the parties presumably accepted them as such originally.[158] Consequently, the Court was obliged to consider also the changes which had taken place in the intervening period. "Moreover," declared the Court, "an international instrument has to be interpreted and applied within the framework of the entire legal system prevailing at the time of the interpretation."[159] The Court embraced then, a truly teleological form of interpretation, or even one that was, to borrow a term from Cheng, "hyperteleological."[160]

In effect, the Court had come full circle. It had adopted the broad approach of the 1950 opinion (but not its conclusions or its essential

152. Ibid., p. 293 (emphasis in original).
153. Ibid., p. 226.
154. Ibid., p. 294.
155. Ibid., p. 295.
156. Judge Gros also dissented, though not on all the grounds raised in the Fitzmaurice dissent. He concurred with Judge Fitzmaurice in holding that Resolution 2145(XXI) terminating the mandate lacked any binding legal force since it represented a mere recommendation of the General Assembly. On the question of South Africa's obligations, however, he adopted a radically different view, viz., that South Africa was bound to negotiate toward the conclusion of a trusteeship agreement. See ibid., pp. 331–45.
157. Ibid., p. 223.
158. Ibid., p. 31.
159. Ibid.
160. Bin Cheng, "The 1966 South-West Africa Judgment of the World Court," *Current Legal Problems 1967* XX: 185.

reasoning), thereby reviving in 1971 the pattern of judicial-political cooperation that had marked the early years of the South West Africa dispute. Viewing the matter from the perspective of a quarter of a century of unremitting conflict, the Court concluded that South Africa had betrayed its trust and had been justly and validly deprived thereof. The judicial solution of 1950, of instituting a *sui generis* system of international accountability, had proved abortive, as vividly demonstrated by the introduction of apartheid into the territory. Recourse to the contentious jurisdiction of the Court had proved similarly fruitless, since, as the 1966 decision held, "divergences of view concerning the conduct of a mandate . . . had their place in the political field." To deny now "to a political organ of the United Nations . . . the right to act . . . would amount to a complete denial of the remedies available against fundamental breaches of an international undertaking."[161] And this was a result which the Court, in accordance with its distinctive concept of international public policy, could not allow to eventuate. South Africa's forfeiture of the mandate must be recognized by international law no less than by international politics.

To Judge Fitzmaurice, who reflected the judicial philosophy and concepts of international public policy of the 1966 majority, the Court's conclusions represented merely a product of *a priori*, rather than legally-grounded, reasoning. And if the Court found it necessary on such an *a priori* basis to give sanction to the political decisions of political bodies, then such sanction could hardly be classified as truly judicial.

> Statements to the effect that certain results cannot be accepted because this would be tantamount to admitting that given rights were in their nature imperfect and unenforceable, do not carry conviction as a matter of international law since, at the present stage of its development, this is precisely what that system itself in large measure is, and will, pending changes not at present foreseeable, continue to be. It is not by ignoring this situation that the law will be advanced.[162]

If the purpose of requesting the advisory opinion was to dispel, once and for all, any doubts regarding the validity and legal force of the United Nations action in purporting to terminate the mandate, then it would seem that the Court, by refusing to address itself to the central legal problems involved, has done very little to remove those doubts. Much more than a Court judgment, an advisory opinion depends for its force on the persuasiveness of its underlying reasoning and the absence of any strong and trenchant dissent. In common with several other

161. *Namibia Opinion* (1971): 49.
162. Ibid., p. 224.

advisory opinions, the 1971 opinion may well serve merely to reinforce the convictions of the believers without in any way inducing a change in the attitude of the nonbelievers. In this sense, the prospects of resolving the basic difficulty in the wake of the opinion are no more—and perhaps even less—promising than previously.

South Africa's own views, not unexpectedly, remained unmodified in the opinion's aftermath, as Prime Minister Vorster made clear on the day the Court's pronouncement was handed down.[163] It was, he said "entirely untenable" and represented "the result of political maneuvering instead of objective jurisprudence." This attitude was reaffirmed by South Africa's foreign minister in the subsequent Security Council debates on the advisory opinion. In a lengthy address he challenged the correctness of the opinion and warned of "its alarming implications . . . which stretch well beyond the particular question of South West Africa."[164] The United Kingdom and French representatives similarly found the opinion quite unacceptable both as to its reasoning and its conclusions.[165] They were unable to accept that the General Assembly had been competent to revoke the mandate and rejected the Court's suggestion that despite the studious refusal of the Security Council membership to bring the South West Africa issue within the ambit of Chapter VII of the Charter, the Council's decisions on this question were nonetheless binding. They denied the validity of the Court's interpretation of Articles 24 and 25 and warned members of the consequences of accepting such an interpretation. The warning (also echoed by other members)[166] appears to have been heeded, for while the resultant resolution stated that the Council "agrees with" the Court's conclusions it merely said the Council "takes note with appreciation" of the opinion generally.[167] (The attempt of the Court to impart a more binding quality to the resolutions of the Security Council than its members, and particularly its permanent members, are prepared to acknowledge has brought the Court into a peculiar and rather paradoxical constitutional conflict with a coordinate organ of the United Nations.) The

163. See *New York Times*, June 22, 1971.

164. U.N. Doc. S/PV.1584, Sept. 27, 1971, pp. 38–62.

165. See statements of United Kingdom representative, U.N. Doc. S/PV.1589, Oct. 6, 1971, pp. 23–33 and U.N. Doc. S/PV.1598, Oct. 20, 1971, p. 12 and statements of French representative, U.N. Doc. S/PV.1588, Oct. 5, 1971, pp. 7–15 and U.N. Doc. S/PV.1598, Oct. 20, 1971, pp. 3–7. Prior to the Council vote the French representative indicated that the only reason his state would refrain from casting a veto against the draft resolution on the opinion was because this draft resolution clearly "has no validity as a decision of the Council." Ibid., pp. 4–5.

166. See statements of representatives of Japan, U.N. Doc. S/PV.1589, Oct. 6, 1971, pp. 39–40; Italy, ibid., p. 47; Belgium, U.N. Doc. S/PV.1594, Oct. 14, 1971, p. 21; and United States, U.N. Doc. S/PV.1598, Oct. 20, 1971, p. 11.

167. Res. 301 (1971), Oct. 20, 1971. And see the remarks of the Italian representative U.N. Doc. S/PV.1595, Oct. 15, 1971 pp. 82–83 and the Somalian representative S/PV.1597, Oct. 19, 1971, p. 5.

Security Council in its resolution, besides referring to the Court opinion, called upon states to abstain from any conduct which might imply a measure of legality in South Africa's continued presence in the territory. The resolution was adopted by a vote of 13 to 0 with the United Kingdom and France abstaining.[168] This vote and the debates which preceded it confirmed that for certain states the legal issue, as opposed to the moral question,[169] was by no means resolved. In practical terms this meant that four years of Security Council involvement in the South West Africa problem had done nothing to bring the matter closer to solution. The Court's endorsement of the actions of the Security Council, even as its earlier endorsement of General Assembly actions in the 1950's, did not radically affect the situation. Given the unwillingness of Council members to resort to Chapter VII it was evident that the Council had come close to exhausting all possibilities.

It was perhaps in recognition of this fact that at the conclusion of its special session at Addis Ababa on February 4, 1972, the Security Council invited the Secretary-General "in consultation and close cooperation with a group of the Security Council . . . to initiate as soon as possible contacts with all parties concerned . . . to enable the people of Namibia . . . to exercise their right to self-determination and independence."[170] With all the other organs of the United Nations stymied it was apparently hoped that direct negotiations conducted by the Secretary-General might offer fresh opportunity for a settlement of the problem. In early March 1972 Secretary-General Kurt Waldheim visited South and South West Africa (Namibia) and held discussions with Prime Minister Vorster. This move to initiate direct negotiations over the future of South West Africa by means of the Secretary-General represents a significant development in the long drawn-out conflict between South Africa and the United Nations.

At the same time as the United Nations appeared willing to explore new paths to a solution, dramatic events within the territory itself seemed to offer prospects that South Africa might now be more amenable than previously to some form of negotiated settlement. During December 1971 Ovambo laborers engaged to work in the factories and mines of the Police Zone protested their working conditions, and in particular the recruiting system, and went out on strike. This mass

168. U.N. Doc. S/PV.1598, Oct. 20, 1971, pp. 13-14.
169. See the statement of the United Kingdom representative, U.N. Doc. S/PV.1589, Oct. 6, 1971, pp. 23-25.
170. Res. 309 (1972). The vote was 14 to 0, with China not participating. U.N. Doc. S/PV.1638, Feb. 4, 1972, p. 41. The resolution named Argentina, Somalia, and Yugoslavia as members of the consultative group.
A second resolution adopted the same day declared *inter alia* "that the continued occupation of Namibia by the Government of South Africa . . . creates conditions detrimental to the maintenance of peace and security in the region." Res. 310 (1972), Feb. 4, 1972.

walkout was an unprecedented event in the history of South West Africa, where striking is a criminal offense. It is always possible that the unrest may be limited to the issue of working conditions, but if experience is any guide, a rebellious tension in the economic sphere is only too readily translated into a spirit of protest in the political and social spheres as well. Such a development could have untold consequences for the future of the territory. The South African government is already committed to a right of self-determination for the population of South West Africa, and perhaps these latest events will help convince that government that the exercise of such a right must be meaningful and realistic if the aspirations of the population are to be satisfied. It is perhaps not too late to hope that a sufficient measure of realism will yet be manifest by the parties in the search for a solution to this vexing international problem.

# CONCLUSIONS

## SOUTH WEST AFRICA
## AND THE DRIVE AGAINST
## COLONIALISM AND RACIALISM

The issue of South West Africa, it may be said, symbolizes the drive of the newly independent states of Africa and Asia to combat and illegalize colonialism and racialism.

The fight against colonialism was heralded, and given a strong initial impetus, by Woodrow Wilson's achievement at Versailles in 1919 in barring the outright annexation of conquered colonial territories and in ensuring that the mandates system would have general application in the post-war territorial settlement. But Wilson's achievement was a qualified one, since, in order to accommodate the Dominion ministers, a compromise arrangement was necessary. A novel system of international accountability was instituted, but its ultimate aims were not defined in clear and unambiguous terms. In place of specific goals, such vague general ideals as "tutelage" and "the sacred trust of civilization" were enunciated, designed to satisfy all parties to the compromise; and divergent interpretations were inevitable under the circumstances. Whereas in the eyes of Wilson and other idealists, the mandates—all mandates—were earmarked for self-determination and independence, to the Dominion ministers, the three-way classification in Article 22 of the Covenant confirmed that different goals were envisaged for different territories and that incorporation of their mandates into their respective national territories was to follow within a relatively short time.

These divergent interpretations were not really crucial until the mandates arrangements were disbanded and a new system of international accountability inaugurated with the creation of a new world organization in 1945. It was at this point that South Africa, in contrast

347

to the other mandatory powers, envisaged fulfillment of its own interpretation of the mandates compromise, viz., the incorporation of South West Africa into South Africa.

By 1945, however, dramatic changes had already taken place in the colonial world. Concepts of freedom and self-determination had penetrated into the most remote regions of Africa and Asia and had stirred a new drive for self-assertion among dependent peoples. This new spirit was reflected in the United Nations Charter. Thus, the ideals of "self-government or independence," only vaguely hinted at in the Covenant were now spelled out; the new supervisory body, the Trusteeship Council, was accorded more extensive powers of inspection and supervision; and the pattern of international accountability was expanded, by means of Chapter XI, so as to cover all colonial territories. These Charter provisions undoubtedly owed much to the arrival in the halls of diplomacy of newly independent states bent on eliminating eventually all remaining vestiges of colonialism from the globe. The presence of these newly independent states at San Francisco and thereafter operated like a leavening agent, constantly promoting a process of change in the body politic of the United Nations. Their influence on United Nations policy in the South West Africa controversy rose steadily as their numbers increased in the world organization—in particular, as their representation from Africa grew in the late fifties and early sixties.[1]

A collision between South Africa and the United Nations over the future of South West Africa was clearly foreseeable already in 1945. But the exact form which the conflict in fact assumed changed over the years, in response, largely, to the changing configuration of forces within the United Nations.

Three distinct phases are discernible in the South West Africa dispute, corresponding to the goals set by the organization with respect to the phenomena of colonialism and racialism generally. It was uniquely characteristic of this dispute that at each stage the political organs—the main protagonists in the struggle on the United Nations side—elicited the support and seal of approval of the organization's judicial organ—the International Court of Justice.

The first phase of the conflict centered on the question of international accountability—whether, and in what form, South Africa was obligated to submit its administration of South West Africa to the supervision of the United Nations. This episode matched the early history of United Nations moves on dependent territories—the drive to bring all mandated territories under the trusteeship system and to institute a universal principle of international accountability for *all* colonial territories by means of Article 73 of the Charter. In line with this

1. For a general review of the influence of these states, see David A. Kay, *The New Nations in the United Nations, 1960–1967* (New York: Columbia University Press, 1970).

approach, the General Assembly scored the attempt of South Africa to remove South West Africa, a territory endowed with an international status, from any form of supervision. The basic stand of the Assembly on the question of accountability was affirmed by the Court in its 1950 advisory opinion, in which it ruled that the mandate continued in force, with the supervisory powers of the League Council accruing to the General Assembly. Subsequently, problems arose in regard to the implementation of the 1950 opinion, and, in particular, with regard to what form the supervision should take. The Court was therefore called upon to amplify, in two further advisory opinions, the principles enunciated in the original 1950 pronouncement.

But all of this was unavailing and South Africa continued to deny the United Nations any authority in reference to South West Africa. So ineffectual were the Assembly's efforts that South Africa could, with impunity, introduce into South West Africa its own racial system of apartheid, a system which had already been the subject of near-universal condemnation.

In 1960, therefore, the United Nations, through the agency of Liberia and Ethiopia, opened the second round in the dispute by challenging South Africa before the International Court of Justice in contentious proceedings. The applicant states asked the Court to rule that the Respondent was obligated to accept the supervision of the United Nations, i.e., international accountability, and at the same time to refrain from applying apartheid to the territory. Thus, at this stage the avowed aim was to bar apartheid in the territory, not to deny South Africa a right to be in South West Africa altogether. The basis of the litigation was, after all, the continued existence of the mandate. In short, the action was designed to outlaw racialism (at least in South West Africa), but not colonialism.

In the meantime, in the broader sphere of anticolonial activities, events had overtaken the pattern of developments on the South West Africa issue. In 1960 the General Assembly adopted the Declaration on Colonialism which, basing itself on the need for respect for equal rights and self-determination, declared that "immediate steps shall be taken" to grant independence to all peoples "without any distinction as to race, creed or colour." "The subjection of peoples to alien . . . domination" was proclaimed as "a denial of fundamental human rights" and as "contrary to the Charter of the United Nations."[2] This Declaration, taken together with the 1963 Declaration on the Elimination of All

2. In the view of certain noted authorities this Declaration went beyond, and in fact amounted to an amendment of, the Charter. See Rupert Emerson, "Colonialism, Political Development and the U.N.," *International Organization* XIX (1965): 493; and Charles De Visscher, *Aspects Récents du Droit Procédural de La Cour Internationale de Justice* (Paris: Pedone, 1966), p. 207. See also Michel Virally, "Droit International et Décolonisation Devant les Nations Unies," *Annuaire Francais de Droit International* IX (1963): 541.

Forms of Racial Discrimination, in effect stamped colonialism and racialism as manifest violations of the international legal order. But at this point these proclamations lacked a judicial imprimatur and represented political, more than legal, pronouncements. The subsequent moves of the United Nations in the struggle over South West Africa may be viewed as an endeavor to secure judicial affirmation that the principles enunciated by the Assembly were part of the corpus of binding international law.

Thus, in the ultimate stage of the South West Africa litigation, the Court was requested by the applicant states to adjudge apartheid an *ipso facto* violation of international law. It was called upon to view the "norm of non-discrimination or non-separation" as a universal norm, established by consensus—a new process of law-creation capable of binding even a dissentient state. The norm was, moreover, to be deemed incorporated in a 1920 document, which in its very terms seemed to contradict the alleged new rule. Applicants' approach, however, was unacceptable to, or, at least, unaccepted by, the Court when it ruled that the Applicants lacked the necessary standing for a judgment on the matter of the conduct of the mandate. The move to outlaw racism by means of the Court had proven abortive.

Thereupon the General Assembly opened the third phase of the dispute by proclaiming that South Africa's mandate was terminated and, on the basis of the 1960 Declaration on Colonialism, that South Africa's presence in the territory was illegal; and this position was subsequently endorsed by the Security Council. In effect, the political principle arising under the Declaration, that colonialism was an untenable status in international relations, was in this instance applied by both political organs as a rule of law in order to establish that South Africa, in the absence of the mandate, had no right to remain in South West Africa. The Court, in 1971, provided a measure of legal confirmation for this stand when it ruled that South Africa's presence in the territory is illegal. It also held that apartheid was a violation of the purposes and principles of the Charter. To a degree, therefore, the International Court of Justice in an advisory opinion has found fit to endorse the political proscription of colonialism and racialism—at least in the context of South West Africa. But as of this moment of writing neither the legal grounds nor the legal effects of this opinion are fully clear.

## THE COURT AND SOUTH WEST AFRICA

One of the unique characteristics of the South West Africa dispute, as already noted, was the degree to which the International Court was summoned to the aid of the political organs. Not content to handle the issue exclusively by means of their own political devices, these organs called forth no less than six pronouncements by the International Court of Justice (incidentally providing the Court with a significant proportion of its otherwise slack business in both advisory and contentious spheres).

What was the resultant interrelationship between the political and judicial organs? What did those activating the Court expect to gain, and was their use of the Court realistic and proper? How did the Court fulfill its part of the political-judicial equation? And finally, in what manner did the pronouncements of the Court affect the course of the South West Africa conflict? The answers to these questions undoubtedly have implications not only for the South West Africa issue but also for the broader question of the function of the international judicial process.

The foregoing study would seem to make clear that, in seeking advisory opinions of the Court, neither the General Assembly nor the Security Council were motivated, to any significant extent, by a desire to gain objective clarification of the relevant legal questions as a guide to future action.[3] In the first place, the Assembly and Council, as coordinate organs of the United Nations, considered themselves fully competent to make the necessary legal determinations independently of the Court. Second, both the Assembly and the Council—or a goodly part of their memberships—held that the moral, political, and humanitarian aspects of the problem far outweighed the purely legal elements involved, in any event. It was the spirit of the Charter, rather than the letter of the law, which, it was thought, ought to be determinative. And only a political body representative of the world community of states could adopt an overall perspective on the question—one not anchored to the strict regimen of textual provisions.

As evidence that the political organs were not overly concerned with learning, or adhering to, the strict limits of law on the subject, one need only refer to the repeated occasions when the Assembly took action quite inconsistent with its moves for requesting advisory opinions. Thus, it adopted resolutions on South West Africa by a two-thirds vote at the very time that it was inquiring whether such a majority

3. Note the statement of the Indian representative prior to the 1950 request, that a finding by the Court that South Africa was not under a legal obligation to conclude a trusteeship agreement would not preclude General Assembly insistence that such an agreement be concluded, in accordance with the spirit of the Charter. See above, p. 106. Note also the statement of the representative of Burundi in the 1970 debates on the Security Council request: "At any rate, whatever the result [of the prospective Court opinion], my delegation believes that the political decision of the General Assembly with regard to the status of Namibia is irrevocable." U.N. Doc. S/PV.1550, July 29, 1970, p. 71.

accorded with the 1950 opinion. Similarly, it accorded oral hearings to petitioners, even while it was requesting an advisory opinion on this very subject. The Security Council, in like manner, adopted one resolution spelling out the consequences for states of South Africa's illegal presence in Namibia, while requesting, in a second resolution, an advisory opinion on this selfsame question. Quite obviously there was no over-concern in either organ for legal consistency or legal niceties.

But if the purpose of eliciting opinions was not legal guidance, what, then, was the true purpose? As has been seen, one of the key factors leading the Assembly to make its requests was the pressure which certain key states and, principally, the United States, brought to bear. (Perhaps the most revealing episode in this regard was the see-saw struggle that surrounded the request for the 1955 opinion.) For its part the United States was apparently anxious to ensure that the Assembly was proceeding with scrupulous legality.[4] Initially the United States may have entertained the hope that a legal ruling would actually resolve the issue. Later, however, the prime concern was to obtain the moral backing of a legal opinion for the Assembly's political action. This felt need by the United States for the "judicial review" of the International Court at every stage of the dispute would seem in turn to be strongly linked with elements in the domestic American scene.[5] It may well be but a reflection of the peculiar American tradition, so frequently commented upon by foreign observers, of having Courts umpire and resolve basic political questions. Presumably, too, the United States Executive, when facing the Congress or the electorate, finds it convenient to justify a given position by reference to a Court ruling representing the final word of the law.

As for the Council's 1970 request, various considerations came into play; and many, such as the hope of rehabilitating the Court's image or providing it with some business, were extraneous to the actual question posed to the Court.

In general, then, it may be said that the Court's advisory jurisdiction has been resorted to more as a means of obtaining political support than as a method of gaining legal clarification. Whether or not this employment of the Court is proper, even if legitimate, is perhaps debatable. What is clear, however, is that such use of the Court places subtle pressures upon the tribunal to pronounce itself in the manner desired by the requesting organ. And the Court's prestige is thereby exposed to danger, whatever its substantive ruling and regardless of whether its

4. See above, pp. 147–48. It may be noted that the United States was the only state to participate in the pleadings of all four advisory opinions.

5. See, in general, Louis Henkin, "International Organization and the Rule of Law," *International Organization* XXIII (1969): 669–71.

finding proves to be, from the standpoint of the political organ, "correct" or "incorrect."

The motives prompting recourse to the Court's compulsory jurisdiction were similar in many respects to those already outlined. Any Court ruling favorable to Ethiopia and Liberia, it was realized, would not be voluntarily complied with. The purpose of the litigation was, rather, to involve the Security Council in the South West Africa issue as executor of the verdict which Ethiopia and Liberia would obtain in their role as prosecutors on behalf of the world community. However, no Council enforcement was possible without American support, and no such support would be forthcoming in the absence of the sustaining moral force of a Court decision.

But were the assumptions upon which the litigation was thus premised realistic ones? In the words of Professor Julius Stone, "What was the range of foresight in 1960 as to the effect of litigation on the International Court, . . . in placing the court and its law, however inadvertently, in the position of scapegoats for situations which they could not be expected to resolve?"[6] In his view, "even if judgment had gone against South Africa . . . this would probably have left South Africa's position as hard as ever, without increasing her exposure to enforcement action."[7] The point seems well taken. For if the economic and other interests of the major powers made the price of adopting any meaningful measures against South Africa prohibitive up until 1960, could a Court judgment have in any way reduced the price to non-prohibitive levels? One need hardly be an economic determinist to conclude that in the hierarchy of values of the states concerned the upholding of the rule of law would probably not have ranked so high as to cancel out countervailing material interests.

Indeed, one may well query whether the goals of the litigation were adequately thought through in advance. Was the aim to obtain a ruling restricted in its scope to South West Africa, or was it rather to secure a broad anti-apartheid ruling which would proscribe racial discrimination generally? It would seem that the first goal was initially central, while the second emerged in the course of the litigation. Instead of the strategic aims dictating the tactics, in this instance the tactics would appear to have dictated the strategy. Once the tactical decision was taken to drop the oppression issue, to eliminate from the case all contentious issues of fact, and to rest the case solely on the norm thesis, the objec-

6. Julius Stone, "South West Africa and the World Court," II, *The Australian*, Sept. 27, 1966.
7. Ibid., I, *The Australian*, Sept. 26, 1966. See also Leo Gross, "The International Court of Justice and the United Nations," Hague Academy, *Recueil des Cours* CXXI (II–1967): 423; and D. H. N. Johnson, "The South West Africa Cases (Second Phase)," *International Relations* III (1967): 165.

tives of the litigation were automatically broadened. Acceptance of the thesis, at least in its international law variant, entailed the adoption of a universal rule banning discrimination and separation.

In sum, therefore, while the idea of instituting contentious litigation must have appeared as a very enticing thought at the outset, the assumptions underlying the idea, it would seem, were never adequately plumbed, and neither the design nor even the purpose of the litigation were established in advance, evolving, rather, in the course of the give-and-take of the forensic struggle.

For its part, how has the Court responded to the initiative of the political organs in the South West Africa issue? To what extent has the Court been able to fulfill the desires of these organs by rendering "correct" rulings? What accounts for the swinging of the pendulum from the close Court-Assembly cooperation of the decade of the fifties through the sharp rift between the two organs in the mid-sixties to the restoration, in 1971, of judicial-political harmony?

One explanation for these oscillations—and the explanation perhaps most commonly adverted to—may be found in the dichotomy between two schools of judicial philosophy and the shifting representation of these schools within the Court. The one school favors teleological interpretation and an activist role for the Court, while the second adheres to a more restrictive textual standard of interpretation and emphasizes the limitations inherent in the judicial role.

In the *1950 Status Opinion*, the clash between these two approaches was discernible in the contrast between the views of the Court and those of Judges McNair and Read. On the basis of a broad and constitution-like interpretation of the relevant instruments, the Court majority held that even in the absence of clear consent on South Africa's part the United Nations had succeeded to the supervisory powers of the League over the South West Africa mandate. But to Judge McNair (as also to Judge Read), the suggested succession was "pure inference"[8] and "a piece of judicial legislation" amounting to the imposition of "a new obligation upon the Union Government."[9]

The Court was once again split into two groups in 1956, with a minority of five judges adopting a restrictive form of interpretation and holding that since the succession between the League and the United Nations was a qualified one, the Assembly was not permitted to authorize oral petitions. This same minority also suggested that the question of South Africa's violation of the obligation to submit to international

8. *Status Opinion* (1950): 159.
9. Ibid., p. 162.

supervision "would involve political elements the appraisal of which is not within the domain of the Court."[10]

When, in the 1960 contentious proceedings, the issue of apartheid was added to that of succession, the controversy between the teleological-activist and the restrictive-"judicial restraint" schools became even more acute. A new element, that of justiciability, came into center stage, since the litigation raised the fundamental question whether the Court had been intended to, and was qualified to, fulfill a supervisory role in the operation of the mandates system. The divergency between the two schools was perhaps best illustrated by the antinomy between the Jessup approach, on the one hand, and the Spender-Fitzmaurice approach on the other.[11]

For Judge Jessup—presumably, not uninfluenced by the tradition of American constitutional law and the activist role of the United States Supreme Court—the issue before the Court was fully justiciable. There was no reason for the Court to hesitate in the face of complex issues of human rights and international responsibilities. The Court should not be deterred by the label of "political dispute," rather, it should see the case as an invaluable opportunity to play a vital role in resolving a major international crisis and thus promote the rule of law in international affairs. In accordance with a broad teleological approach, Judge Jessup (along with the 1962 majority) also fully endorsed the interpretation of the 1950 opinion on the succession issue and applied a similar teleological approach in the matter of judicial supervision.

In contrast, Judges Spender and Fitzmaurice, faithful perhaps to their own common law legal training, found the implied analogy with the United States Supreme Court quite inapposite to the position of the International Court of Justice. Indeed, even within the United States Supreme Court itself there were judges, such as Justice Frankfurter and others, who counseled a policy of "judicial restraint" and advised against courts becoming embroiled in "political thickets" which did not lend themselves to adjudication;[12] and in the field of international jurisdiction, grounded as it was in state consent, this was, *a fortiori*, the case.[13]

10. *Oral Petitions Opinion* (1956): 62.
11. The "super-teleological" views of Judge Tanaka were, as noted earlier, isolated ones on the Court.
12. See, for instance, the views of Justice Frankfurter in the famous *Baker* v. *Carr* decision, 369 U.S. 186.
13. It is interesting to note that the difference between Judges Jessup and Fitzmaurice on the question of justiciability is a long-standing one, reflected in their divergent views regarding the *Austro-German Customs Union* case. In 1931 Professor Jessup (as he then was) vigorously upheld the right of the Permanent Court to render a decision in the case, notwithstanding its

In the view of Judges Spender and Fitzmaurice, the whole action before the Court was an endeavor to rectify by judicial means what diplomacy had failed to achieve in 1919 and 1945. The system of international accountability established in 1919 never included the right of the supervisory authority to determine for the mandatory power the particular methods of administration which it must apply in the territory; nor did it entail any notion of judicial supervision. And with reference to the succession issue, the states present at San Francisco had failed to tie South Africa down to a clear commitment to convert the mandate into a trust territory. Applicants' action was designed belatedly to remedy the situation. But a court could only interpret treaties; it was not free to revise them, for that would be to legislate. It was idle to imagine that the function of the Court was to cure every ailment of the international body politic.

To explain the fluctuations in the Court's rulings by reference to divergent judicial philosophies is valid but hardly sufficient. Among the individual judges there has been far from iron-clad consistency in adherence to one or another school of judicial philosophy. Even in the various South West Africa pronouncements one finds, for example, Judge Winiarski among the 1950 and 1956 majorities (i.e., in the "liberal" camp), but later among the 1962 minority and the 1966 majority (i.e., in the "conservative" camp). Again, Judge Basdevant, while associating himself with the teleological 1950 opinion, was in dissent in 1956 and again in 1962. And if one looks beyond the South West Africa issue to other cases, one discovers that even the two key dissenters of 1962—Judges Spender and Fitzmaurice—were members of the "liberal" majority in the *Expenses* case.

A further explanation which goes far to account for some of these inconsistencies and which adds fresh insight into the whole issue of judicial-political relations has been suggested by Professor Leo Gross.[14] In the International Court of Justice, he observes, a dichotomy has arisen between the jurisprudence of the Court in its advisory and contentious functions. In advisory cases, the Court's role as "the principal judicial organ of the United Nations" becomes paramount, with the Court striving for maximal cooperation with its coordinate organs by

---

political implications. "The Customs Union Advisory Opinion," *AJIL* XXXVI (1931): 105–10. In contrast, during 1945 discussions on amendment of the Court Statute, Mr. Fitzmaurice (as he then was) cited the example of the *Customs Union* case—a case which, he said, was among those "referred to the Court by the political organs of the League of Nations to get rid of them"—as grounds for incorporating the word "justiciable" in the text of Article 36(1) of the Statute. "In the long run," he thought, "it would depreciate the value and the prestige of the International Court of Justice if it were used for the settlement of disputes of a non-justiciable character." UNCIO Docs., XIV, 204–5.

14. Leo Gross, "The International Court of Justice and the United Nations," pp. 321, 370–71, 377–80, 404, 418, and 430–31.

means of the application of flexible "United Nations law." On the other hand, in contentious cases the Court sees itself as a completely neutral independent tribunal adjudicating between states "in accordance with international law," i.e., by application of more strictly positivist legal standards.

But in the *South West Africa* cases, the two functions of the Court coalesced or, as it were, crossed paths; and at issue both in 1962 and 1966 was the question whether form or substance should be determinative. Should the case be viewed as a regular inter-state dispute in which the Court adopts a strictly neutral stance between the contenders and applies "international law"? Or should it be regarded as a "United Nations case" in which the ideals and objectives more common to advisory proceedings should predominate? At base, of course, lay the question whether the conclusions reached in 1950 in the service of the General Assembly and in the absence of any real adversary proceedings precluded reconsideration, in a new setting, of the issues in dispute. In both phases of the *South West Africa* cases the Court was split more or less evenly on the question whether the "advisory philosophy" and the conclusions reached on the basis of that philosophy should prevail in a contentious case.

The tension between the two functions of the Court, so perceptively analyzed by Professor Gross, must raise, inevitably, the question whether it is, indeed, desirable for the one institution to be endowed with the both functions. When the advisory jurisdiction of the present Court's predecessor, the Permanent Court of International Justice, was in the process of being established, serious misgivings regarding that jurisdiction were voiced by John Bassett Moore (who was later to become the first American judge on the Permanent Court). He feared that the status and prestige of the Court might be endangered if it engaged in the "nonjudicial" task of giving advisory opinions to the League organs.[15] It would appear that Moore's original misgivings were realized, not in the lifetime of the Permanent Court but only subsequently, with the establishment of the International Court of Justice as a "principal organ" of the new world organization. In the light of the history of political-judicial relations in the United Nations period, might there not, then, be wisdom in restricting the International Court to its primary role of adjudicating inter-state disputes? Legal advice to the political organs of the United Nations and, for that matter, to the Specialized Agencies, might be adequately supplied by the establishment of special committees of jurists—a practice frequently resorted to

15. Cited in Michla Pomerance, *The Advisory Function of the International Court of Justice in the League and United Nations Eras: A Comparative Study* (Baltimore, Md.: The Johns Hopkins University Press, 1973), chap. I.

by League organs.[16] In this manner the independence and neutrality of the International Court would assuredly be enhanced, for the Court would be subjected less to the buffeting winds of political pressure emanating from the other organs of the United Nations.

A proposal of a different sort has frequently been raised, viz., the amendment of Article 34 of the Statute of the Court so as to permit international organizations, including the United Nations, to be parties in contentious proceedings before the Court.[17] And in recent years proponents of such a step have cited in support the final outcome in the *South West Africa* cases.[18] If, so the argument goes, Ethiopia and Liberia lacked standing to sue because they were in fact appearing in a representational capacity on behalf of the General Assembly, and if such representation was necessitated by the inability of the Assembly itself, under Article 34 of the Statute, to appear in contentious proceedings, then the obvious remedy would be to amend this anachronistic provision. Leaving aside the question of the merit of the proposal as a general proposition, it is submitted that in relation to the *South West Africa* cases themselves, the suggested remedy would have been of little avail. As Jenks has pointed out: "The amendment of the Statute would not in itself confer any jurisdiction upon the Court . . . but it would make it possible for the parties concerned to confer such jurisdiction when they thought it appropriate to do so."[19] In the *South West Africa* cases, however, the only compromissory clause in existence was Article 7 of the Mandate, and it is quite clear that the League of Nations, and hence the United Nations, if one assumes succession, was not given any right of action under that provision. Consequently, the United Nations could only appear in conjunction with the Applicants as *amicus curiae*. But in such a case no real improvement would have been effected. The Applicants would have lacked standing, since the dispute was not one between them and the Respondent; the United Nations would have lacked standing, because, even though it was in dispute with the Respondent, it had no claim to the jurisdiction of the Court under any existing compromissory clause.

---

16. On the use of committees of jurists in the League period, see ibid., chap. IV.

17. See, for example, C. Wilfred Jenks, *The Prospects of International Adjudication* (London: Stevens, 1964), pp. 208-24; Leo Gross, "The United Nations and the Role of Law," *International Organization* XIX (1965): 558-59; Leo Gross, "The International Court of Justice and the United Nations," p. 426; and Leo Gross, "The International Court of Justice: Consideration of Requirements for Enhancing its Role in the International Legal Order," *AJIL* LXV (1971): 302-6. And see the discussion in Shabtai Rosenne, *The Law and Practice of the International Court* (Leyden: Sijthoff, 1965), I: 284-90.

18. See Ernest A. Gross, "The South West Africa Case: What Happened?" *Foreign Affairs* XLV (1966): 46-47.

19. Jenks, *International Adjudication*, p. 220.

In assessing the contribution of the Court to the resolution of the South West Africa controversy, one may posit, as a general rule, the existence of two alternative conditions in which adjudication can aid optimally in resolving an international dispute: (1) where both sides agree to abide by the decision; and (2) where the losing party can, within reasonable limits, be compelled to accept the ruling. Neither condition was present in the South West Africa conflict, and it is not surprising, therefore, that resort to law and the Court has not proven a particularly fruitful avenue of approach. In fact, to the contrary, employment of the judicial function in this instance, may well have been misplaced and counterproductive. For where legal pronouncements are inefficacious, they may tend merely to freeze and rigidify positions and to choke off any maneuverability that might otherwise arise from free-wheeling diplomatic negotiations.[20] Thus, in the present case, once the United Nations was confirmed by the 1950 opinion as the appropriate supervisory agency in relation to the mandate, there was little possibility that the United Nations would waive this authority in favor of a supervisory set-up instituted with another body or one that in any way affected the integrity of the international status of the territory. The 1951 proposal for an arrangement between South Africa and the three Principal Allied and Associated Powers was consequently dismissed out-of-hand, as was the 1959 suggestion of the Good Offices Committee for a possible partition of the territory. All of this raises the question whether the ossification of attitudes incident upon judicial pronouncements did not eventuate in the failure to exploit, or at the very least, to explore adequately, such opportunities for resolving the crisis as did present themselves. And, in this regard, it is possible that the Court's latest advisory opinion declaring South Africa's presence in South West Africa illegal may, similarly, serve only to bar any compromise settlement without contributing in any meaningful manner to a final resolution of the dispute.

## REALITIES AND PROSPECTS

The difficulty of finding a middle ground between the main protagonists in the dispute would certainly exist, even in the absence of judicial pronouncements supportive of one or the other disputant. Clearly, each side, from its own standpoint, considers that it has compelling reasons for not countenancing any form of compromise.

To the Afro-Asian majority in the United Nations compromise means, in this instance, permitting the vanishing nightmare of colonial-

---

20. See, on this point, Julius Stone, "The International Court and World Crisis," *International Conciliation*, no. 536 (Jan. 1962): 7 and 9; and Milton Katz, *The Relevance of International Adjudication* (Cambridge, Mass.: Harvard University Press, 1968), passim.

ism to persist in a territory ear-marked for self-determination and independence over fifty years ago. It means suffering the perpetuation in an international territory on the African continent of a degrading system which stamps every Black or Colored person with a badge of permanent inferiority.

To South Africa, on the other hand, any compromise on South West Africa opens the door to endangering the future survival of the Republic itself as a separate and independent White state. South West Africa has been regarded and treated by South Africa as a virtual fifth province for over half a century, and the United Nations campaign to dislodge South Africa from the territory is, therefore, seen as but part of a general conspiracy to displace the White Man's civilization in southern Africa by transferring power to the overwhelming Black majorities. South Africa has, therefore, steadfastly refused to relinquish its control over the territory of South West Africa or to acknowledge any formal accountability to the United Nations.

It is true that South Africa's intransigence has, in one sense perhaps, not been as total as would appear on the surface. Insofar as South Africa has felt constrained to demonstrate by word and—more important—by deed, greater solicitude for the welfare of the indigenous population, it has, thereby, in some measure, acknowledged a kind of "informal international accountability."[21] Thus, for example, the Odendaal Report—leaving aside its more controversial aspects—represented a significant step toward improving the lot of the non-White inhabitants of South West Africa. In this connection, Judge Jessup's comment in his 1966 dissenting opinion is most relevant: "I do not pretend to make a finding on the evidence," he said, "but it appears to me probable that the Court would have found that Respondent, perhaps responsive to the general condemnation of its administration of South West Africa, has introduced numerous improvements and ameliorations."[22] Nevertheless, as Judge Jessup went on to note, "this does not mean that [South Africa] has abandoned the policy of apartheid." Even less does it indicate any weakening of South Africa's basic resolve to retain control of the territory.

On the fundamental issue in dispute between the protagonists, then, failure to compromise has meant only one thing: continued South African occupation of the territory and continued United Nations frustration in its decolonization effort.

Why, it may be asked, have the United Nations efforts been so fruitless in this case, when in the general sphere of decolonization they

21. I am indebted to Dr. Upendra Baxi, of the University of Sydney, for suggesting this distinction between formal and informal modes of international accountability.
22. *SWA Judgment* (1966): 330.

have seemingly been so successful? Why has the tidal wave of anticolonialism been broken, as it were, on the shoals of that territory?[23]

The simple answer is that, contrary to the assumption underlying the question, the role of the United Nations in the general process of decolonization has been a minor one. The independence of the new states of Africa and Asia came as an end-product of a panoply of diverse internal and external forces and pressures which the Organization "neither created nor conjured up."[24] Among these various contributing factors were the following: [25] a vigorous spirit of nationalism within the dependent territory itself, generally operating through a political-action party or parties; the clash and rivalry emanating from the cold war with the Soviet Union on the one hand (conveniently overlooking its own imperialism) constantly prodding and challenging the Western European powers over their domination of alien peoples, and with the United States, on the other hand, quietly pressing its Allies to adopt a more enlightened position on the question of self-determination so as to forestall the violence and revolution which the Soviet Union sought eagerly to exploit; a recognition by the colonial power of the heavy cost entailed in sustaining colonial authority, in the face of increasing hostility, in an area far removed from its own metropolitan territory; renewed skepticism as to the economic benefits of colonialism generally; realization by the colonial power that the colony might be dispensed with without in any way seriously affecting the metropolitan state's existence, vital interests, or basic pattern of life; and increasing domestic pressure arising from liberal humanitarian groups to relinquish control of the colonies. The United Nations served primarily to channel the diplomatic pressures that were extant and to provide the world community with an appropriate forum for focusing these pressures. In this capacity, however, the organization was merely reflecting, not producing, change.

In the case of South West Africa, the organization could not fulfill a similar role because, quite simply, the forces which elsewhere generated change were absent. South Africa, unlike Western Europe, was

23. It is generally acknowledged that South Africa's position of defiance toward the United Nations sustains not only South African control of South West Africa but also bolsters the Portuguese in their retention of control over their African territories and the White minority in Rhodesia in their independence claims.
24. Alf Ross, *The United Nations: Peace and Progress* (Totowa, N.J.: Bedminster, 1966), p. 392. Rupert Emerson makes the same point by declaring that "most of the actions which have been taken to translate non-self-governing territories into independent states have had no direct link whatsoever to the UN save in the sense that they had UN blessing as exemplified most notably after the fact in the speedy acceptance of the new states as Members." "Colonialism," p. 490.
25. For an expanded discussion of this subject, see Thomas Hodgkin, *Nationalism in Colonial Africa* (New York: New York University Press, 1957); and Rupert Emerson, *From Empire to Nation* (Cambridge, Mass.: Harvard University Press, 1960).

remote from the political pressures of the Cold War; no powerful nationalist organization existed within South West Africa itself (such indigenous political organizations as the South West African National Union [SWANU] and the South West African Peoples Organization [SWAPO] were only formed in 1960 and have never exerted any great influence on events); South West Africa was not a remote colony but a territory immediately contiguous to South Africa itself and, moreover, one that, as noted, had been treated, in accordance with Article 22 of the Covenant, as an integral part of South Africa; the South African government was never seriously challenged by any domestic opinion favoring relinquishment of the territory, and, consequently, United Nations resolutions could be defied with impunity without fear of adverse domestic reaction;[26] South African control of South West Africa provided economic profit and vital strategic advantage at almost no extra defense cost; and the racial system governing South West Africa was on all fours with the system operating within South Africa itself, so that a challenge to the system in the territory constituted, in effect, a challenge to South Africa's internal regime (a fact which was confirmed by the overall struggle against apartheid).

With the "normal" factors working for decolonization thus inoperative in South West Africa, South Africa could be displaced only by force; but precisely this element has, in the final analysis, been unavailable to the United Nations in its efforts.[27] The states that are capable have been unwilling, and those that are willing are incapable. There has been no commitment on the part of any of the major powers to do anything more than talk and vote on behalf of resolutions—whether resolutions of the Assembly or the Council. Even the Soviet Union, despite its rhetoric, has steadfastly resisted any suggestion that the world organization itself undertake the task of "liberating" South West Africa. According to the Soviet Union, the Organization of African Unity is the appropriate body to conduct the struggle, with the ex-

26. On the matter of domestic opinion in South Africa with regard to South West Africa, see R. B. Ballinger, "UN Action on Human Rights in South Africa," in Evan Luard (ed.), *The International Protection of Human Rights* (London: Thames and Hudson, 1967), p. 273.

27. Various studies have been made regarding the feasibility of applying sanctions—economic, and, ultimately, military, if necessary—against South Africa. See Ronald Segal (ed.), *Sanctions Against South Africa* (Baltimore, Md.: Penguin Books, 1964); and Amelia C. Leiss (ed.), *Apartheid and United Nations Collective Measures: An Analysis* (New York: Carnegie Endowment for International Peace, 1965). These studies have even included detailed plans on the costs involved for different courses of action, the types and numbers of ships that would be required to enforce a blockade, and the possibility of actually invading South Africa. Both studies conclude that South Africa could not be subjected to duress without the active participation of the Western powers. After presenting extensive material and analysis, one of these studies concludes with a somewhat understated comment by Secretary-General U Thant, who told an audience in June 1963: "The idea that conventional military methods—or, to put it bluntly, war—can be used by or on behalf of the United Nations to counter aggression and secure the peace, seems now to be rather impractical." Ibid., p. 153.

penses to be covered by a tax imposed on the monopoly companies operating in southern Africa. The Soviets have even objected to the broadening of the powers of the Council for Namibia (especially in the matter of issuing passports and visas), since this might tend to give the Council unwarranted executive authority which could possibly impinge on the sovereignty of member states. Quite obviously, the "all-out" war of the Soviet Union is an "all-out" war which should be waged by proxy, even as to its cost!

And as for the Western powers, they remain unalterably opposed to anything likely to lead to a major confrontation in southern Africa. To the extent that Afro–Asian intentions have turned from "the reform of existing policies . . . [to] the overthrow of existing regimes,"[28] a certain degree of displeasure has manifested itself in the Western camp. This fact was strikingly revealed by the joint action of the United Kingdom and the United States in vetoing a 1970 Security Council draft resolution on Southern Rhodesia which hinted at the use of force.

Despite the fact that neither forces within South Africa nor forces without could be marshalled to provide essential backing for United Nations resolutions, the General Assembly and, subsequently, the Security Council have not been deterred from adopting resolutions on South West Africa totally oblivious to international realities. This tendency first became strongly manifest in 1961 when the Assembly directed the Committee on South West Africa to visit South West Africa *with or without South African co-operation.*[29] And in 1962, a resolution was adopted requesting the Secretary-General to establish an effective United Nations presence in South West Africa.[30] (How he was to do this was not indicated in the resolution.) Of course, the directives of neither resolution were fulfilled.

The various moves subsequent to 1966 to terminate the mandate and eject South Africa from the territory, culminating in the hollow demands of the Security Council for immediate withdrawal "or else," added no luster to the authority of the world organization. This pattern of play acting has been aptly commented upon by Rupert Emerson in the following terms: "The U.N. debases its currency and its credibility when it blows thunderous trumpets as in the case of South West Africa which cause no walls to fall down and leave intact what has been destroyed in words."[31]

28. G. E. Goodwin, "The United Nations: Expectations and Experience," *International Relations* III (1970): 750.
29. G. A. Res. 1596 (XV), Apr. 7, 1961 (emphasis supplied).
30. G. A. Res. 1805 (XVII), Dec. 14, 1962.
31. Rupert Emerson, "The United Nations and Colonialism," *International Relations* III (1970): 779. In the same vein, see the following comments by Lord Caradon on the subject of South West Africa: "The road to hopeless frustation is paved with useless resolutions." U.N.

If this is so, then what realistic options are open to both sides of the conflict in order to bridge the gulf between them?

South Africa, for the moment, continues to press on with its own solution: speedy implementation of the Bantustan program. It is South Africa's hope that the creation of African national homelands for the Ovambo and other tribes will give these elements of the indigenous population a vested interest in the retention of South African administration. (A further possible consideration may be that independent Bantustans in the north will decrease the Black population of South West Africa by approximately fifty percent, leaving the Whites in a much stronger demographic position.) Undoubtedly, too, South Africa would wish to receive some form of international endorsement for its plan, so as to fend off the critical charge that the peoples of South West Africa are denied any meaningful opportunity for self-determination. This may well have been one of the motives prompting the plebiscite proposal laid before the International Court of Justice in the proceedings on the Namibia case. But even without international approval, South Africa appears intent on promoting its own concept of "the sacred trust" in South West Africa.

How can the United Nations meaningfully effect any change in South Africa's present program? With direct methods of compulsion apparently barred at this juncture, and the adoption of ever stronger resolutions purposeless, the thought of negotiations as a possible third alternative has begun to find adherents. In relation to apartheid in South Africa itself the idea of conducting a "dialogue" with South Africa has taken hold in some African states. A similar approach may ultimately meet with approval in relation to the South West Africa issue. (The recent visit of Secretary-General Waldheim to Pretoria, under Security Council auspices, to discuss the future of the territory, might be regarded as the harbinger of such a development.) Real diplomacy—which up until now has been given short shrift in the South West Africa case—may hold out the hope of slowly tempering South Africa's solution of separate development and, perhaps, as a realistic goal, replacing it with a form of more equitable partition, such as several opponents of apartheid have suggested for South Africa itself.[32] The

Doc. S/PV.1465, Mar. 20, 1969, p. 31. "The archives of the Assembly will become overcrowded repositories of rotting resolutions." GAOR, 21st Sess., Plen., 1448th Mtg., Oct. 19, 1966, p. 3.

There is, of course, the argument that, unless the Assembly continues to reassert its authority in reference to South West Africa, it will be found to have lost any claim it might have had to intervene in the matter. An assertion of authority, however, is a very different thing from establishing a Council which is empowered to "promulgate . . . laws, decrees and administrative regulations" in the territory. The latter move is nothing less than a flight into fantasy under present-day circumstances.

32. See, for example, Philip Mason, "Separate Development and South West Africa: Some Aspects of the Odendaal Report," *Race* V (1964): 83–97, reprinted in *SWA Pleadings*

recent stirrings of the Ovambo may perhaps spur South Africa to adopt a more flexible and accommodating position than it has previously. But whatever the avenue that diplomatic negotiations may take, the counsel voiced by a distinguished Judge remains pertinent:

> In a situation in which no useful purpose can be served by launching the irresistible force against the immovable object, statesmanship should seek a *modus vivendi*—while there is yet time.[33]

IV: 331–35; Rita F. and Howard J. Taubenfeld, *Race, Peace, Law and Southern Africa* (Dobbs Ferry, N.Y.: Oceana, 1968), pp. 118–23; Colin and Margaret Legum, *South Africa: Crisis for the West* (London: Pall Mall Press, 1964), pp. 221–26. See also Leo Marquard, *A Federation of Southern Africa* (London: Oxford University Press, 1972).

In this regard it is highly relevant to cite the views of a noted authority on Africa, Waldemar A. Nielsen. He writes: "The implicit single goal of the advocates of change has been the transfer of decisive political authority in the existing political units to the black majorities—over some relatively brief period of time. As a goal, such a formulation is reasonable; but as a description of what is likely to happen, it is illusory. . . . [T]here are available a large number of alternative or intermediate forms of concession: . . . in South Africa, the establishment of additional Bantustans on its own territory, and the 'spinning off' of portions of South West Africa into supposedly self-governing units. If and when change comes, it is most likely to be in the form of such murky, controversial compromises. In the end, the Africans themselves will have to decide whether and which of such imperfect solutions they will accept." *The Great Powers and Africa* (New York: Praeger, 1969), p. 361.

33. Dissenting Opinion of Judge Fitzmaurice, *Namibia Opinion* (1971): 298.

# COVENANT
# OF THE LEAGUE
# OF NATIONS

## ARTICLE 22

1. To those colonies and territories which as a consequence of the late war have ceased to be under the sovereignty of the States which formerly governed them and which are inhabited by peoples not yet able to stand by themselves under the strenuous conditions of the modern world, there should be applied the principle that the well-being and development of such peoples form a sacred trust of civilization and that securities for the performance of this trust should be embodied in this Covenant.

2. The best method of giving practical effect to this principle is that the tutelage of such peoples should be entrusted to advanced nations who by reason of their resources, their experience or their geographical position can best undertake this responsibility, and who are willing to accept it, and that this tutelage should be exercised by them as Mandatories on behalf of the League.

3. The character of the mandate must differ according to the stage of the development of the people, the geographical situation of the territory, its economic conditions and other similar circumstances.

4. Certain communities formerly belonging to the Turkish Empire have reached a stage of development where their existence as independent nations can be provisionally recognized subject to the rendering of administrative advice and assistance by a Mandatory until such time as they are able to stand alone. The wishes of these communities must be a principal consideration in the selection of the Mandatory.

5. Other peoples, especially those of Central Africa, are at such a stage that the Mandatory must be responsible for the administration of the territory under conditions which will guarantee freedom of conscience and religion, subject only to the maintenance of public order and morals, the prohibition of abuses such as the slave trade, the arms traffic and the liquor traffic, and the prevention of the establishment of fortifications or military and naval bases and of military training of the natives for other than police purposes and the defence of territory, and will also secure equal opportunities for the trade and commerce of other Members of the League.

6. There are territories, such as South West Africa and certain of the South Pacific Islands, which, owing to the sparseness of their population, or their small

size, or their remoteness from the centres of civilization, or their geographical contiguity to the territory of the Mandatory, and other circumstances, can be best administered under the laws of the Mandatory as integral portions of its territory, subject to the safeguards above mentioned in the interests of the indigenous population.

7. In every case of mandate, the Mandatory shall render to the Council an annual report in reference to the territory committed to its charge.

8. The degree of authority, control, or administration to be exercised by the Mandatory shall, if not previously agreed upon by the Members of the League, be explicitly defined in each case by the Council.

9. A permanent Commission shall be constituted to receive and examine the annual reports of the Mandatories and to advise the Council on all matters relating to the observance of the mandates.

# MANDATE
# FOR GERMAN
# SOUTH WEST AFRICA

*The Council of the League of Nations*:

*Whereas* by Article 119 of the Treaty of Peace with Germany signed at Versailles on June 28th, 1919, Germany renounced in favour of the Principal Allied and Associated Powers all her rights over her oversea possessions, including therein German South-West Africa; and

*Whereas* the Principal Allied and Associated Powers agreed that, in accordance with Article 22 Part I (Covenant of the League of Nations) of the said Treaty, a Mandate should be conferred upon His Britannic Majesty to be exercised on his behalf by the Government of the Union of South Africa to administer the territory aforementioned, and have proposed that the Mandate should be formulated in the following terms; and

*Whereas* His Britannic Majesty, for and on behalf of the Government of the Union of South Africa, has agreed to accept the Mandate in respect of the said territory and has undertaken to exercise it on behalf of the League of Nations in accordance with the following provisions; and

*Whereas*, by the aforementioned Article 22, paragraph 8, it is provided that the degree of authority, control or administration to be exercised by the Mandatory not having been previously agreed upon by the Members of the League, shall be explicitly defined by the Council of the League of Nations:

Confirming the said Mandate, defines its terms as follows: —

## ARTICLE 1

The territory over which a Mandate is conferred upon His Britannic Majesty for and on behalf of the Government of the Union of South Africa (hereinafter called the Mandatory) comprises the territory which formerly constituted the German Protectorate of South-West Africa.

## ARTICLE 2

The Mandatory shall have full power of administration and legislation over the territory subject to the present Mandate as an integral portion of the Union of South Africa, and may apply the laws of the Union of South Africa to the territory, subject to such local modifications as circumstances may require.

The Mandatory shall promote to the utmost the material and moral well-being and the social progress of the inhabitants of the territory subject to the present Mandate.

## ARTICLE 3

The Mandatory shall see that the slave trade is prohibited, and that no forced labour is permitted, except for essential public works and services, and then only for adequate remuneration.

The Mandatory shall also see that the traffic in arms and ammunition is controlled in accordance with principles analogous to those laid down in the Convention relating to the control of the arms traffic, signed on September 10th, 1919, or in any convention amending the same.

The supply of intoxicating spirits and beverages to the natives shall be prohibited.

## ARTICLE 4

The military training of the natives, otherwise than for purposes of internal police and the local defence of the territory, shall be prohibited. Furthermore, no military or naval bases shall be established or fortifications erected in the territory.

## ARTICLE 5

Subject to the provisions of any local law for the maintenance of public order and public morals, the Mandatory shall ensure in the territory freedom of conscience and the free exercise of all forms of worship, and shall allow all missionaries, nationals of any State Member of the League of Nations, to enter into, travel and reside in the territory for the purpose of prosecuting their calling.

## ARTICLE 6

The Mandatory shall make to the Council of the League of Nations an annual report to the satisfaction of the Council, containing full information with regard to the territory, and indicating the measures taken to carry out the obligations assumed under Articles 2, 3, 4 and 5.

## ARTICLE 7

The consent of the Council of the League of Nations is required for any modification of the terms of the present Mandate.

The Mandatory agrees that, if any dispute whatever should arise between the Mandatory and another Member of the League of Nations relating to the interpretation or the application of the provisions of the Mandate, such dispute, if it cannot be settled by negotiation, shall be submitted to the Permanent Court of International Justice provided for by Article 14 of the Covenant of the League of Nations.

The present Declaration shall be deposited in the archives of the League of Nations. Certified copies shall be forwarded by the Secretary-General of the League of Nations to all Powers Signatories of the Treaty of Peace with Germany.

*Made at Geneva the 17th day of December, 1920.*

# CHARTER
# OF THE
# UNITED NATIONS

## CHAPTER V: THE SECURITY COUNCIL

. . . . . . . . . . . . . . . . . . . . . . . . . . . . . . . . . . . . . . . . . . .

*Functions and Powers*

### Article 24

1. In order to ensure prompt and effective action by the United Nations, its Members confer on the Security Council primary responsibility for the maintenance of international peace and security, and agree that in carrying out its duties under this responsibility the Security Council acts on their behalf.

2. In discharging these duties the Security Council shall act in accordance with the Purposes and Principles of the United Nations. The specific powers granted to the Security Council for the discharge of these duties are laid down in Chapters VI, VII, VIII, and XII.

. . . . . . . . . . . . . . . . . . . . . . . . . . . . . . . . . . . . . . . . . . .

### Article 25

The Members of the United Nations agree to accept and carry out the decisions of the Security Council in accordance with the present Charter.

## CHAPTER IX: INTERNATIONAL ECONOMIC AND
## SOCIAL COOPERATION

### Article 55

With a view to the creation of conditions of stability and well-being which are necessary for peaceful and friendly relations among nations based on respect for the principle of equal rights and self-determination of peoples, the United Nations shall promote:

a. Higher standards of living, full employment, and conditions of economic and social progress and development;

b. solutions of international economic, social, health, and related problems; and international cultural and educational co-operation; and

c. universal respect for, and observance of, human rights and fundamental freedoms for all without distinction as to race, sex, language, or religion.

### Article 56

All Members pledge themselves to take joint and separate action in cooperation with the Organization for the achievement of the purposes set forth in Article 55.

## CHAPTER XI: DECLARATION REGARDING NON-SELF-GOVERNING TERRITORIES

### Article 73

Members of the United Nations which have or assume responsibilities for the administration of territories whose peoples have not yet attained a full measure of self-government recognize the principle that the interests of the inhabitants of these territories are paramount, and accept as a sacred trust the obligation to promote to the utmost, within the system of international peace and security established by the present Charter, the well-being of the inhabitants of these territories, and, to this end:

a. to ensure, with due respect for the culture of the peoples concerned, their political, economic, social, and educational advancement, their just treatment, and their protection against abuses;

b. to develop self-government, to take due account of the political aspirations of the peoples, and to assist them in the progressive development of their free political institutions, according to the particular circumstances of each territory and its peoples and their varying stages of advancement;

c. to further international peace and security;

d. to promote constructive measures of development, to encourage research, and to cooperate with one another and, when and where appropriate, with specialized international bodies with a view to the practical achievement of the social, economic, and scientific purposes set forth in this Article; and

e. to transmit regularly to the Secretary-General for information purposes, subject to such limitation as security and constitutional considerations may require, statistical and other information of a technical nature relating to economic, social, and educational conditions in the territories for which they are respectively responsible other than those territories to which Chapters XII and XIII apply.

### Article 74

Members of the United Nations also agree that their policy in respect of the territories to which this Chapter applies, no less than in respect of their metropolitan areas, must be based on the general principle of good-neighborliness, due account being taken of the interests and well-being of the rest of the world, in social, economic, and commercial matters.

## CHAPTER XII: INTERNATIONAL TRUSTEESHIP SYSTEM

### Article 75

The United Nations shall establish under its authority an international trusteeship system for the administration and supervision of such territories as may be placed thereunder by subsequent individual agreements. These territories are hereinafter referred to as trust territories.

### Article 76

The basic objectives of the trusteeship system, in accordance with the Purposes of the United Nations laid down in Article 1 of the present Charter, shall be:

a. to further international peace and security;

b. to promote the political, economic, social, and educational advancement of the inhabitants of the trust territories, and their progressive development towards self-government or independence as may be appropriate to the particular circumstances of each territory and its peoples and the freely expressed wishes of the peoples concerned, and as may be provided by the terms of each trusteeship agreement;

c. to encourage respect for human rights and for fundamental freedoms for all without distinction as to race, sex, language, or religion, and to encourage recognition of the interdependence of the peoples of the world; and

d. to ensure equal treatment in social, economic, and commercial matters for all Members of the United Nations and their nationals, and also equal treatment for the latter in the administration of justice, without prejudice to the attainment of the foregoing objectives and subject to the provisions of Article 80.

### Article 77

1. The trusteeship system shall apply to such territories in the following categories as may be placed thereunder by means of trusteeship agreements:

a. territories now held under mandate;

b. territories which may be detached from enemy states as a result of the Second World War; and

c. territories voluntarily placed under the system by states responsible for their administration.

2. It will be a matter for subsequent agreement as to which territories in the foregoing categories will be brought under the trusteeship system and upon what terms.

. . . . . . . . . . . . . . . . . . . . . . . . . . . . . . . . . . . . . . . . . . . . . . . . . . . . . .

### Article 79

The terms of trusteeship for each territory to be placed under the trusteeship system, including any alteration or amendment, shall be agreed upon by the states directly concerned, including the mandatory power in the case of territories held under mandate by a Member of the United Nations, and shall be approved as provided for in Articles 83 and 85.

### Article 80

1. Except as may be agreed upon in individual trusteeship agreements, made under Articles 77, 79, and 81, placing each territory under the trusteeship system, and until such agreements have been concluded, nothing in this Chapter shall be construed in or of itself to alter in any manner the rights whatsoever of any states or any peoples or the terms of existing international instruments to which Members of the United Nations may respectively be parties.

2. Paragraph 1 of this Article shall not be interpreted as giving grounds for delay or postponement of the negotiation and conclusion of agreements for placing mandated and other territories under the trusteeship system as provided for in Article 77.

### Article 81

The trusteeship agreement shall in each case include the terms under which the trust territory will be administered and designate the authority which will exercise the administration of the trust territory. Such authority, hereinafter called the administering authority, may be one or more states or the Organization itself.

. . . . . . . . . . . . . . . . . . . . . . . . . . . . . . . . . . . . . . . . . . . . . . .

### Article 85

1. The functions of the United Nations with regard to trusteeship agreements for all areas not designated as strategic, including the approval of the terms of the trusteeship agreements and of their alteration or amendment, shall be exercised by the General Assembly.

2. The Trusteeship Council, operating under the authority of the General Assembly, shall assist the General Assembly in carrying out these functions.

### CHAPTER XIV: THE INTERNATIONAL COURT OF JUSTICE

. . . . . . . . . . . . . . . . . . . . . . . . . . . . . . . . . . . . . . . . . . . . . . .

### Article 94

1. Each Member of the United Nations undertakes to comply with the decision of the International Court of Justice in any case to which it is a party.

2. If any party to a case fails to perform the obligations incumbent upon it under a judgment rendered by the Court, the other party may have recourse to the Security Council, which may, if it deems necessary, make recommendations or decide upon measures to be taken to give effect to the judgment.

### STATUTE OF THE INTERNATIONAL COURT OF JUSTICE

### Article 37

Whenever a treaty or convention in force provides for reference of a matter to a tribunal to have been instituted by the League of Nations, or to the Permanent Court of International Justice, the matter shall, as between the parties to the present Statute, be referred to the International Court of Justice.

# SUBMISSIONS
# OF THE
# PARTIES*

*On Behalf of the Governments of Ethiopia and Liberia*
(Essential changes are italicized)

In the Memorials: (April 15, 1961)

"Upon the basis of the foregoing allegations of fact, supplemented by such facts as may be adduced in further testimony before this Court, and the foregoing statements of law, supplemented by such other statements of law as may be hereinafter made, may it please the Court to adjudge and declare, whether the Government of the Union of South Africa is present or absent, that:

1. South West Africa is a territory under the Mandate conferred upon His Britannic Majesty by the Principal Allied and Associated Powers, to be exercised on his behalf by the Government of the Union of South Africa, accepted by his Britannic Majesty for and on behalf of the Government of the Union of South Africa, and confirmed by the Council of the League of Nations on December 17, 1920;

2. the Union of South Africa continues to have the international obligations stated in Article 22 of the Covenant of the League of Nations and in the Mandate for South West Africa as

At the conclusion of the oral proceedings: (May 19, 1965)

"Upon the basis of allegations of fact, and statements of law set forth in the written pleadings and oral proceedings herein, may it please the Court to adjudge and declare, whether the Government of the Republic of South Africa is present or absent, that:

1. South West Africa is a territory under the Mandate conferred upon His Britannic Majesty by the Principal Allied and Associated Powers, to be exercised on his behalf by the Government of the Union of South Africa, accepted by his Britannic Majesty for and on behalf of the Government of the Union of South Africa, and confirmed by the Council of the League of Nations on December 17, 1920;

2. *Respondent continues to have* the international obligations stated in Article 22 of the Covenant of the League of Nations and in the Mandate for South West Africa as well as the

*Submissions of the parties as cited in the 1962 and 1966 South West Africa Judgments.

well as the obligation to transmit petitions from the inhabitants of that Territory, the supervisory functions to be exercised by the United Nations, to which the annual reports and the petitions are to be submitted;

3. the Union, *in the respects set forth in Chapter V of this Memorial and summarized in Paragraphs 189 and 190 thereof,* has practised *apartheid,* i.e., has distinguished as to race, colour, national or tribal origin in establishing the rights and duties of the inhabitants of the Territory; that such practice is in violation of its obligations as stated in Article 2 of the Mandate and Article 22 of the Covenant of the League of Nations; and that the Union has the duty forthwith to cease the practice of *apartheid* in the Territory;

4. the Union, by virtue of the economic, political, social and educational policies applied within the Territory, *which are described in detail in Chapter V of this Memorial and summarized at Paragraph 190 thereof,* has failed to promote to the utmost the material and moral well-being and social progress of the inhabitants of the Territory; that its failure to do so is in violation of its obligations as stated in the second paragraph of Article 2 of the Mandate and Article 22 of the Covenant; and that the Union has the duty forthwith to cease its violations as aforesaid and to take all practicable action to fulfil its duties under such Articles;

5. the Union, by word and by action, *in the respects set forth in Chapter VIII of this Memorial,* has treated the Territory in a manner inconsistent with the international status of the Territory, and has thereby impeded opportunities for self-determination by the inhabitants of the Territory; that such treatment is in violation of the Union's obligations as stated in the first paragraph of Arti-

obligation to transmit petitions from the inhabitants of that Territory, the supervisory functions to be exercised by the United Nations, to which the annual reports and the petitions are to be submitted;

3. Respondent, *by laws and regulations, and official methods and measures, which are set out in the pleadings herein,* has practised apartheid, i.e., has distinguished as to race, colour, national or tribal origin in establishing the rights and duties of the inhabitants of the Territory; that such practice is in violation of its obligations as stated in Article 2 of the Mandate and Article 22 of the Covenant of the League of Nations; and that Respondent has the duty forthwith to cease the practice of apartheid in the Territory;

4. Respondent, by virtue of economic, political, social and educational policies applied within the Territory, *by means of laws and regulations, and official methods and measures, which are set out in the pleadings herein, has, in the light of applicable international standards or international legal norm, or both,* failed to promote to the utmost the material and moral well-being and social progress of the inhabitants of the Territory; that its failure to do so is in violation of its obligations as stated in Article 2 of the Mandate and Article 22 of the Covenant; and that Respondent has the duty forthwith to cease its violations as aforesaid and to take all practicable action to fulfil its duties under such Articles;

5. Respondent, by word and by action, has treated the Territory in a manner inconsistent with the international status of the Territory, and has thereby impeded opportunities for self-determination by the inhabitants of the Territory; that such treatment is in violation of Respondent's obligations as stated in the first paragraph of Article 2 of the Mandate and Article 22 of the Covenant; that Respond-

cle 2 of the Mandate and Article 22 of the Covenant; that the Union has the duty forthwith to cease *the actions summarized in Section C of Chapter VIII herein*, and to refrain from similar actions in the future; and that the Union has the duty to accord full faith and respect to the international status of the Territory;

6. the Union, *by virtue of the acts described in Chapter VII herein*, has established military bases within the Territory in violation of its obligations as stated in Article 4 of the Mandate and Article 22 of the Covenant; that the Union has the duty forthwith to remove all such military bases from within the Territory; and that the Union has the duty to refrain from the establishment of military bases within the Territory;

7. the Union has failed to render to the General Assembly of the United Nations annual reports containing information with regard to the Territory and indicating the measures it has taken to carry out its obligations under the Mandate; that such failure is a violation of its obligations as stated in Article 6 of the Mandate; and that the Union has the duty forthwith to render such annual reports to the General Assembly;

8. the Union has failed to transmit to the General Assembly of the United Nations petitions from the Territory's inhabitants addressed to the General Assembly; that such failure is a violation of its obligations as Mandatory; and that the Union has the duty to transmit such petitions to the General Assembly;

9. the Union, *by virtue of the acts described in Chapters V, VI, VII and VIII of this Memorial coupled with its intent as recounted herein*, has attempted to modify substantially the terms of the Mandate, without the consent of the United Nations; that such attempt is in violation of its duties as stated in Article 7 of the

ent has the duty forthwith to cease such actions, and to refrain from similar actions in the future; and that Respondent has the duty to accord full faith and respect to the international status of the Territory;

6. Respondent has established military bases within the Territory in violation of its obligations as stated in Article 4 of the Mandate and Article 22 of the Covenant; that Respondent has the duty forthwith to remove all such military bases from within the Territory; and that Respondent has the duty to refrain from the establishment of military bases within the Territory;

7. Respondent has failed to render to the General Assembly of the United Nations annual reports containing information with regard to the Territory and indicating the measures it has taken to carry out its obligations under the Mandate; that such failure is a violation of its obligations as stated in Article 6 of the Mandate; and that Respondent has the duty forthwith to render such annual reports to the General Assembly;

8. Respondent has failed to transmit to the General Assembly of the United Nations petitions from the Territory's inhabitants addressed to the General Assembly; that such failure is a violation of its obligations as Mandatory; and that Respondent has the duty to transmit such petitions to the General Assembly;

9. Respondent has attempted to modify substantially the terms of the Mandate, without the consent of the United Nations; that such attempt is in violation of its duties as stated in Article 7 of the Mandate and Article 22 of the Covenant; and that the consent of the United Nations is a necessary prerequisite and condition precedent to

Mandate and Article 22 of the Covenant; and that the consent of the United Nations is a necessary prerequisite and condition precedent to attempts on the part of the Union directly or indirectly to modify the terms of the Mandate.

The Applicant reserves the right to request the Court to declare and adjudge in respect to events which may occur subsequent to the date this Memorial is filed, including any event by which the Union's juridical and constitutional relationship to Her Britannic Majesty undergoes any substantial modification.

May it also please the Court to adjudge and declare whatever else it may deem fit and proper in regard to this Memorial, and to make all necessary awards and orders, including an award of costs, to effectuate its determinations."

attempts on the part of Respondent directly or indirectly to modify the terms of the Mandate.

May it also please the Court to adjudge and declare whatever else it may deem fit and proper in regard to these submissions, and to make all necessary awards and orders, including an award of costs, to effectuate its determinations."

### On Behalf of the Government of South Africa

In the Preliminary Objections Stage, Oct. 11, 1962:

"For all or any one or more of the reasons set out in its written and oral statements, the Government of the Republic of South Africa submits that the Governments of Ethiopia and Liberia have no *locus standi* in these contentious proceedings, and that the Court has no jurisdiction to hear or adjudicate upon the questions of law and fact raised in the Applications and Memorials, more particularly because:

*Firstly*, the Mandate for South West Africa has never been, or at any rate is since the dissolution of the League of Nations no longer, a 'treaty or convention in force' within the meaning of Article 37 of the Statute of the Court, this Submission being advanced

(a) with respect to the Mandate as a whole, including Article 7 thereof; and

(b) in any event, with respect to Article 7 itself;

*Secondly*, neither the Government of Ethiopia nor the Government of Liberia is 'another Member of the League of Nations,' as required for *locus standi* by Article 7 of the Mandate for South West Africa;

*Thirdly*, the conflict or disagreement alleged by the Governments of Ethiopia and Liberia to exist between them and the Government of the Republic of South Africa, is by reason of its nature and content not a 'dispute' as envisaged in Article 7 of the Mandate for South West Africa, more particularly in that no material interests of the Governments of Ethiopia and/or Liberia or of their nationals are involved therein or affected thereby;

*Fourthly*, the alleged conflict or disagreement is as regards its state of development not a 'dispute' which 'cannot be settled by negotiation' within the meaning of Article 7 of the Mandate for South West Africa."

In the Merits Stage, Nov. 5, 1965:

"Upon the basis of the statements of fact and law as set forth in Respondent's pleadings and the oral proceedings, may it please the Court to adjudge and declare that the submissions of the Governments of Ethiopia and Liberia, as recorded at pages 69-72 of the verbatim record of 19 May 1965, C.R. 65/35, are unfounded and that no declaration be made as claimed by them. In particular, Respondent submits—

1. That the whole Mandate for South West Africa lapsed on the dissolution of the League of Nations and that Respondent is, in consequence thereof, no longer subject to any legal obligations thereunder.

2. In the alternative to 1 above, and in the event of it being held that the Mandate as such continued in existence despite the dissolution of the League of Nations;

(a) Relative to Applicants' submissions numbers 2, 7 and 8, that the Respondent's former obligations under the Mandate to report and account to, and to submit to the supervision, of the Council of the League of Nations, lapsed upon the dissolution of the League, and have not been replaced by any similar obligations relative to supervision by any organ of the United Nations or any other organization or body. Respondent is therefore under no obligation to submit reports concerning its administration of South West Africa, or to transmit petitions from the inhabitants of that Territory, to the United Nations or any other body;

(b) Relative to Applicants' submissions numbers 3, 4, 5, 6 and 9, that the Respondent has not, in any of the respects alleged, violated its obligations as stated in the Mandate or in Article 22 of the Covenant of the League of Nations."

APPENDIX **V.**

# RESOLUTIONS
# ADOPTED BY
# THE GENERAL
# ASSEMBLY

1514 (XV). *Declaration on the Granting of Independence to
Colonial Countries and Peoples*

*The General Assembly,*

*Mindful* of the determination proclaimed by the peoples of the world in the Charter of the United Nations to reaffirm faith in fundamental human rights, in the dignity and worth of the human person, in the equal rights of men and women and of nations large and small and to promote social progress and better standards of life in larger freedom,

*Conscious* of the need for the creation of conditions of stability and well-being and peaceful and friendly relations based on respect for the principles of equal rights and self-determination of all peoples, and of universal respect for, and observance of, human rights and fundamental freedoms for all without distinction as to race, sex, language or religion,

*Recognizing* the passionate yearning for freedom in all dependent peoples and the decisive role of such peoples in the attainment of their independence,

*Aware* of the increasing conflicts resulting from the denial of or impediments in the way of the freedom of such peoples, which constitute a serious threat to world peace,

*Considering* the important role of the United Nations in assisting the movement for independence in Trust and Non-Self-Governing Territories,

*Recognizing* that the peoples of the world ardently desire the end of colonialism in all its manifestations,

*Convinced* that the continued existence of colonialism prevents the development of international economic co-operation, impedes the social, cultural and economic development of dependent peoples and militates against the United Nations ideal of universal peace,

*Affirming* that peoples may, for their own ends, freely dispose of their natural wealth and resources without prejudice to any obligations arising out of international economic co-operation, based upon the principle of mutual benefit, and international law,

*Believing* that the process of liberation is irresistible and irreversible and that, in order to avoid serious crises, an end must be put to colonialism and all practices of segregation and discrimination associated therewith,

*Welcoming* the emergence in recent years of a large number of dependent territories into freedom and independence, and recognizing the increasingly powerful trends towards freedom in such territories which have not yet attained independence,

*Convinced* that all peoples have an inalienable right to complete freedom, the exercise of their sovereignty and the integrity of their national territory,

*Solemnly proclaims* the necessity of bringing to a speedy and unconditional end colonialism in all its forms and manifestations;

And to this end

*Declares* that:

1. The subjection of peoples to alien subjugation, domination and exploitation constitutes a denial of fundamental human rights, is contrary to the Charter of the United Nations and is an impediment to the promotion of world peace and co-operation.

2. All peoples have the right to self-determination; by virtue of that right they freely determine their political status and freely pursue their economic, social and cultural development.

3. Inadequacy of political, economic, social or educational preparedness should never serve as a pretext for delaying independence.

4. All armed action or repressive measures of all kinds directed against dependent peoples shall cease in order to enable them to exercise peacefully and freely their right to complete independence, and the integrity of their national territory shall be respected.

5. Immediate steps shall be taken, in Trust and Non-Self-Governing Territories or all other territories which have not yet attained independence, to transfer all powers to the peoples of those territories, without any conditions or reservations, in accordance with their freely expressed will and desire, without any distinction as to race, creed or colour, in order to enable them to enjoy complete independence and freedom.

6. Any attempt aimed at the partial or total disruption of the national unity and the territorial integrity of a country is incompatible with the purposes and principles of the Charter of the United Nations.

7. All States shall observe faithfully and strictly the provisions of the Charter of the United Nations, the Universal Declaration of Human Rights and the present Declaration on the basis of equality, non-interference in the internal affairs of all States, and respect for the sovereign rights of all peoples and their territorial integrity.

(G.A. Res. 1514 [XV], Dec. 14, 1960, in GAOR, 15th Sess., Supp. No. 16 [A/4684], pp. 66-67.)

### 2145 (XXI). *Question of South West Africa*

*The General Assembly,*

*Reaffirming* the inalienable right of the people of South West Africa to freedom and independence in accordance with the Charter of the United Nations, General Assembly resolution 1514 (XV) of 14 December 1960 and earlier Assembly resolutions concerning the Mandated Territory of South West Africa,

*Recalling* the advisory opinion of the International Court of Justice of 11 July 1950, which was accepted by the General Assembly in its resolution 449 A (V) of 13 December 1950, and the advisory opinions of 7 June 1955 and 1 June 1956 as well as the judgement of 21 December 1962, which have established the fact that South Africa continues to have obligations under the Mandate which was entrusted to it on 17 December 1920 and that the United Nations as the successor to the League of Nations has supervisory powers in respect of South West Africa,

*Gravely concerned* at the situation in the Mandated Territory, which has seriously deteriorated following the judgement of the International Court of Justice of 18 July 1966,

*Having studied* the reports of the various committees which had been established to exercise the supervisory functions of the United Nations over the administration of the Mandated Territory of South West Africa,

*Convinced* that the administration of the Mandated Territory by South Africa has been conducted in a manner contrary to the Mandate, the Charter of the United Nations and the Universal Declaration of Human Rights,

*Reaffirming* its resolution 2074 (XX) of 17 December 1965, in particular paragraph 4 thereof which condemned the policies of apartheid and racial discrimination practised by the Government of South Africa in South West Africa as constituting a crime against humanity,

*Emphasizing* that the problem of South West Africa is an issue falling within the terms of resolution 1514 (XV),

*Considering* that all the efforts of the United Nations to induce the Government of South Africa to fulfil its obligations in respect of the administration of the Mandated Territory and to ensure the well-being and security of the indigenous inhabitants have been of no avail,

*Mindful* of the obligations of the United Nations towards the people of South West Africa,

*Noting with deep concern* the explosive situation which exists in the southern region of Africa,

*Affirming* its right to take appropriate action in the matter, including the right to revert to itself the administration of the Mandated Territory,

1. *Reaffirms* that the provisions of General Assembly resolution 1514 (XV) are fully applicable to the people of the Mandated Territory of South West Africa and that, therefore, the people of South West Africa have the inalienable right to self-determination, freedom and independence in accordance with the Charter of the United Nations;

2. *Reaffirms further* that South West Africa is a territory having international status and that it shall maintain this status until it achieves independence;

3. *Declares* that South Africa has failed to fulfil its obligations in respect of the administration of the Mandated Territory and to ensure the moral and material well-being and security of the indigenous inhabitants of South West Africa, and has, in fact, disavowed the Mandate;

4. *Decides* that the Mandate conferred upon His Britannic Majesty to be exercised on his behalf by the Government of the Union of South Africa is therefore terminated, that South Africa has no other right to administer the Territory and that henceforth South West Africa comes under the direct responsibility of the United Nations;

5. *Resolves* that in these circumstances the United Nations must discharge those responsibilities with respect to South West Africa;

6. *Establishes* an *Ad Hoc* Committee for South West Africa—composed of fourteen Member States to be designated by the President of the General Assembly—to recommend practical means by which South West Africa should be administered, so as to enable the people of the Territory to exercise the right of self-determination and to achieve independence, and to report to the General Assembly at a special session as soon as possible and in any event not later than April 1967;

7. *Calls upon* the Government of South Africa forthwith to refrain and desist from any action, constitutional, administrative, political or otherwise, which will in any manner whatsoever alter or tend to alter the present international status of South West Africa;

8. *Calls the attention* of the Security Council to the present resolution;

9. *Requests* all States to extend their whole-hearted co-operation and to render assistance in the implementation of the present resolution;

10. *Requests* the Secretary-General to provide all assistance necessary to implement the present resolution and to enable the *Ad Hoc* Committee for South West Africa to perform its duties.

(G.A. Res. 2145 [XXI], Oct. 27, 1966, in GAOR, 21st Sess., Supp. No. 16 [A/6316], pp. 2-3.)

# BIBLIOGRAPHY

## OFFICIAL PUBLICATIONS

1. *League of Nations*

*Minutes of the Council*, 1920.

*Official Journal*, I, No. 1 (February 1920)–XXI, No. 2/3 (January/March 1940).

*Records of the Assembly*, 1920–46.

*Minutes of the Permanent Mandates Commission*, 1921–39.

*The Mandates System: Origin–Principles–Application.* Geneva, League of Nations Series, 1945. VI. A.1.

*The League Hands Over.* Geneva: League of Nations Series, 1946. 1.

2. *United Nations*

*Documents of the United Nations Conference on International Organization, San Francisco, 1945.* New York and London: United Nations Information Organizations, 1945–46, 16 vols.

Preparatory Commission of the United Nations. *Journal.* London, 1945.

———. *Report . . .* London, Doc. PC/20, December 23, 1945.

———. *Report by the Executive Committee . . .* London, Doc. PC/EX/113/Rev. 1. November 12, 1945.

———. Committees 1–8. *Summary Records of Meetings November 24–December 24, 1945.* 1946.

*General Assembly Official Records.*

*Security Council Official Records.*

*Trusteeship Council Official Records.*

*Repertory of Practice of United Nations Organs.* New York. 1955. Vol. IV.

———. Supplement, No. 1, Vol. II. New York, 1958.

———. Supplement No. 2, Vol. III. New York, 1963.

3. *Permanent Court of International Justice*, Publications, Series A, No. 2, 1924.

4. *International Court of Justice.*

International Court of Justice, Reports of Judgments, Advisory Opinions and Orders.

_____. Pleadings, Oral Arguments and Documents.
_____. Yearbooks.
_____. Bibliographies. (1965–)

5. *South Africa.*
*Report of South West Africa Commission.* Pretoria, 1936.
*Report of Union of South Africa to the Council of the League of Nations
   Concerning the Administration of South West Africa, for Year 1936.* Pre-
   toria, 1937.
*Report by the Government of the Union of South Africa on the Administration
   of South West Africa for the Year 1946.* Pretoria, 1947.
*Report of the Commission of Enquiry into South West Africa Affairs 1962–63.*
   Pretoria, 1964.
*South West Africa Survey 1967.* Department of Foreign Affairs of the Republic
   of South Africa, March 1967.


6. *Other.*
United States, Department of State, *Papers Relating to the Foreign Relations of
   the United States, 1919, The Paris Peace Conference.* 13 vols. Washington:
   United States Government Printing Office, 1942–47.
*Conférence de la Paix 1919–1920*, Recueil des Actes de la Conférence. Paris:
   Impr. Nationale, 1934.
Woodward, E. L., and Butler, Rohan (eds.). *Documents on British Foreign
   Policy, 1919–1939*, First series. 8 vols. London: His Majesty's Stationery
   Office, 1947–58.
Second Conference of Independent African States, Addis Ababa 14–26 June,
   1960. Published by the Ministry of Information of the Imperial Ethiopian
   Government, 1960.


## BOOKS

Anand, R. P. *Compulsory Jurisdiction of the International Court of Justice.*
   London: Asia Publishing House, 1961.
_____. *Studies in International Adjudication.* Dobbs Ferry, N.Y.: Oceana, 1969.
Asamoah, Obed Y. *The Legal Significance of the Declarations of the United
   Nations.* The Hague: Nijhoff, 1966.
Baker, Ray Stannard. *Woodrow Wilson and World Settlement*, 3 vols. New York:
   Doubleday, Page, 1922.
Beer, George Louis. *African Questions at the Peace Conference*, ed. Louis
   Herbert Gray. New York: Macmillan, 1923.
Bemis, Samuel Flagg. *A Diplomatic History of the United States.* 4th ed. rev.
   New York: Holt, Rinehart and Winston, 1955.
Bentwich, Norman. *The Mandates System.* London: Longman's, Green and Co.,
   1930.
Bentwich, Norman, and Martin, Andrew. *A Commentary on the Charter of the
   United Nations.* London: Routledge and Kegan Paul Ltd., 1951.
Birdsall, Paul. *Versailles Twenty Years After.* London: Allen and Unwin, 1941.
Bonsal, Stephen, *Unfinished Business.* New York: Doubleday, Doran, 1944.
Borden, Henry (ed.). *Robert Laird Borden: His Memoirs*, 2 vols. New York:
   Macmillan, 1938.

Brierly, J. L. *The Law of Nations*, 4th ed. New York and Oxford: Oxford University Press, 1949.

Carroll, Faye. *South West Africa and the United Nations.* Lexington, Ky.: University of Kentucky Press, 1967.

Carter, Gwendolen M. *The Politics of Inequality: South Africa Since 1948.* London: Thames and Hudson, 1958.

Carter, Gwendolen M., Karis, Thomas, and Stultz, Newell M. *South Africa's Transkei: The Politics of Domestic Colonialism.* Evanston, Ill.: Northwestern University Press, 1967.

Castañeda, Jorge. *Legal Effects of United Nations Resolutions* (transl. by Alba Amoia). New York: Columbia University Press, 1969.

Cheng, Bin. *General Principles of Law as Applied by International Courts and Tribunals.* London: Stevens, 1953.

Chowdhuri, R. N. *International Mandates and Trusteeship Systems: A Comparative Study.* The Hague: Nijhoff, 1955.

Claude, Inis L., Jr. *Swords into Plowshares*, 3rd. ed., rev. New York: Random House, 1964.

Cobban, Alfred. *National Self-Determination.* London: Oxford University Press, 1945.

Cocks, Frederick Seymour. *The Secret Treaties and Understandings.* London: Union of Democratic Control, 1918.

Comissetti, Louis. *Mandats et Souvraineté.* Paris: Sirey, 1934.

Corwin, Edward S., and Peltason, Jack W. *Understanding the Constitution*, 3rd. ed. New York: Holt, Rinehart, and Winston, 1964.

Cowen, D. V. *The Foundations of Freedom.* Capetown: Oxford University Press, 1961.

Dubisson, Michel. *La Cour Internationale de Justice.* Paris: Pichon et Durand-Auzias, 1964.

Dugard, John (ed.). *The South West Africa/Namibia Dispute: Documents and Scholarly Writings on the Controversy between South Africa and the United Nations.* Berkeley, Calif.: University of California Press, 1973.

Dvorin, Eugene P. *Racial Separation in South Africa.* Chicago: University of Chicago Press, 1952.

Emerson, Rupert. *From Empire to Nation: The Rise to Self-Assertion of Asian and African Peoples.* Cambridge, Mass.: Harvard University Press, 1960.

_____. *Africa and United States Policy.* Englewood Cliffs, N.J.: Prentice-Hall, 1967.

Falk, Richard A. *The Status of Law in International Society.* Princeton, N.J.: Princeton University Press, 1970.

Feinberg, Nathan. *La Juridiction de la Cour Permanente de Justice Internationale dans le Système des Mandats.* Paris: Rousseau, 1930.

Fifield, Russell H. *Woodrow Wilson and the Far East: The Diplomacy of the Shantung Question.* New York: Crowell, 1952.

First, Ruth. *South West Africa.* Baltimore, Md.: Penguin Books, 1963.

Friedmann, Wolfgang. *The Changing Structure of International Law.* New York: Columbia University Press, 1964.

Gelfand, Lawrence E. *The Inquiry: American Preparations for Peace, 1917–1919.* New Haven: Yale University Press, 1963.

Goldblatt, I. *The Conflict between the United Nations and the Union of South Africa in Regard to South West Africa.* By the author, 1960.

_____. *The Mandated Territory of South West Africa in Relation to the United Nations.* Capetown: C. Struik, 1961.

_____. *History of South West Africa From the Beginning of the Nineteenth Century*. Cape Town: Juta, 1971.

Goodrich, Leland M. *The United Nations*. New York: Crowell, 1959.

Goodrich, Leland M., and Hambro, Edvard. *Charter of the United Nations: Commentary and Documents*, 2nd rev. ed. Boston: World Peace Foundation, 1949.

Goodrich, Leland M., and Hambro, Edvard, and Simons, Anne P. *Charter of the United Nations: Commentary and Documents*, 3rd rev. ed. New York: Columbia University Press, 1969.

Gottlieb, W. W. *Studies in Secret Diplomacy during the First World War*. London: Allen and Unwin, 1957.

Halderman, John H. *The United Nations and the Rule of Law*. Dobbs Ferry, N.Y.: Oceana, 1966.

Hall, H. Duncan. *Mandates, Dependencies and Trusteeship*. Washington, D.C.: Carnegie Endowment for International Peace, 1948.

Hance, William A. (ed.). *Southern Africa and the United States*. New York: Columbia University Press, 1968.

Henkin, Louis. *How Nations Behave*. New York: Praeger, 1968.

Higgins, Rosalyn. *The Development of International Law by the Political Organs of the United Nations*. London: Oxford University Press, 1953.

Hill, Christopher R. *Bantustans*. London: Oxford University Press, 1964.

Hodgkin, Thomas. *Nationalism in Colonial Africa*. New York: New York University Press, 1957.

House, Edward Mandell, and Seymour, Charles (eds.). *What Really Happened at Paris*. New York: Scribner's, 1921.

Hudson, Manley O. *The Permanent Court of International Justice 1920-1942*. New York: Macmillan, 1943.

_____. *International Tribunals Past and Future*. Washington: The Brookings Institution and Carnegie Endowment for International Peace, 1944.

Imishue, R. W. *South West Africa: An International Problem*. London: Pall Mall Press, 1965.

Jenks, C. Wilfred. *The Prospects of International Adjudication*. London: Stevens, 1964.

Jessup, Philip C. *A Modern Law of Nations*. New York: Macmillan, 1948.

Kahng, Tae Jin. *Law, Politics, and the Security Council*. The Hague: Martinus Nijhoff, 1964.

Katz, Milton. *The Relevance of International Adjudication*. Cambridge, Mass.: Harvard University Press, 1968.

Kay, David A. *The New Nations in the United Nations*. New York: Columbia University Press, 1970.

Kelsen, Hans. *The Law of the United Nations*. London: Stevens, 1950.

Lakshminarayan, C. V. *Analysis of the Principles and System of International Trusteeship in the Charter*. Geneva: Imprimeries Populaires, 1951.

Lauterpacht, Hersch. *An International Bill of Rights of Man*. New York: Columbia University Press, 1945.

_____. *International Law and Human Rights*. London: Stevens, 1949.

_____. *The Development of International Law by the International Court*. London: Stevens, 1958.

Legum, Colin and Margaret. *South Africa: Crisis for the West*. London: Pall Mall Press, 1964.

Leiss, Amelia C. (ed.). *Apartheid and United Nations Collective Measures: An Analysis*. New York: Carnegie Endowment for International Peace, 1965.

Lipsky, George A. (ed.). *Law and Politics in the World Community.* Berkeley and Los Angeles: University of California Press, 1953.

Lissitzyn, Oliver J. *The International Court of Justice: Its Role in the Maintenance of International Peace and Security* (United Nations Studies: No. 6). New York: Carnegie Endowment for International Peace, 1951.

_____. *International Law Today and Tomorrow.* Dobbs Ferry, N.Y.: Oceana, 1965.

Lloyd George, David. *The Truth About the Peace Treaties,* 2 vols. London: Gollancz, 1938.

Louis, W. R. *Great Britain and Germany's Lost Colonies, 1914-1919.* Oxford: Clarendon Press, 1967.

Lowenstein, Allard K. *Brutal Mandate: A Journey to South West Africa.* New York: Macmillan, 1962.

van Maanen-Helmer, Elizabeth. *The Mandates System in Relation to Africa and the Pacific Islands.* London: King, 1929.

de Madariaga, Salvador. *The World's Design.* London: Allen and Unwin, 1938.

Margalith, Aaron M. *The International Mandates.* Baltimore, Md.: The Johns Hopkins Press, 1930.

Marquard, Leo. *South Africa's Colonial Policy.* Johannesburg: South African Institute of Race Relations, 1957.

_____. *The Peoples and Policies of South Africa,* 4th ed. London: Oxford University Press, 1969.

_____. *A Federation of Southern Africa.* London: Oxford University Press, 1972.

Mayer, Arno J. *Political Origins of the New Diplomacy 1917-1918.* New Haven: Yale University Press, 1959.

McKay, Vernon. *Africa in World Politics.* New York: Harper and Row, 1963.

McNair, Arnold D. *The Law of Treaties.* Oxford: The Clarendon Press, 1961.

McWhinney, Edward. *International Law and World Revolution.* Leyden: A. W. Sijthoff, 1967.

Miller, David Hunter. *My Diary at the Conference of Paris,* privately printed, 21 vols. New York: Appeal Printing Company, 1924.

_____. *The Drafting of the Covenant,* 2 vols. New York: G. P. Putnam's Sons, 1928.

Millot, Albert. *Les Mandats Internationaux.* Paris: Larose, 1924.

Molnar, Thomas. *South West Africa: The Last Pioneer Country.* New York: Fleet Publishing Corporation, 1966.

Murray, James N., Jr. *The United Nations Trusteeship System.* Urbana, Ill.: University of Illinois Press, 1957.

Nielsen, Waldemar A. *African Battleline: American Policy Choices in Southern Africa.* New York: Harper and Row, 1965.

_____. *The Great Powers and Africa.* New York: Praeger, 1969.

O'Brien, William V. (ed.). *The New Nations in International Law and Diplomacy.* Vol. III, *The Yearbook of World Polity.* New York: Praeger, 1965.

Oppenheim, L. *International Law,* 2 vols. (ed.). H. Lauterpacht. 8th ed. London: Longmans, Green, 1955.

Parry, Clive. *The Sources and Evidences of International Law.* Manchester: Manchester University Press, 1965.

Pomerance, Michla. *The Advisory Function of the International Court in the League and UN Eras.* Baltimore, Md.: The Johns Hopkins Press, 1973.

Van Rees, D. F. W. *Les Mandats Internationaux: Le controle international de l'administration.* Paris: Rousseau, 1927.

Rhoodie, N. J., and Venter, H. J. *Apartheid.* Capetown: Haum, 1960.

Riches, Cromwell A. *The Unanimity Rule and the League of Nations.* Baltimore, Md.: The Johns Hopkins Press, 1933.

Riddell, Lord George. *Lord Riddell's Intimate Diary of the Peace Conference and After, 1918-1923.* London: Gollancz, 1937.

Rosenne, Shabtai. *The International Court of Justice.* Leyden: Sijthoff, 1957.

_____. *The Law and Practice of the International Court,* 2 vols. Leyden: Sijthoff, 1965.

Roskam, K. L. *Apartheid and Discrimination.* Leyden: Sijthoff, 1960.

Ross, Alf. *The United Nations: Peace and Progress.* Totowa, N.J.: Bedminster, 1966.

Russell, Ruth B., and Muther, Jeannette E. *A History of the United Nations Charter.* Washington, D.C.: The Brookings Institution, 1958.

Sandhaus, Edith. *Les Mandats C dans l'Empire Britannique.* Grenoble: Imprimerie Saint-Bruno, 1931.

Schwarzenberger, George. *International Law,* 3rd ed. London: Stevens, 1957.

Scott, Ernest. *Australia During the War.* Vol. XI of *The Official History of Australia in the War of 1914-1918,* 12 vols. Sydney: Angus and Robertson, 1936.

Scott, James Brown (ed.). *Official Statements of War Aims and Peace Proposals, December 1916 to November 1918.* Washington, D.C.: Carnegie Endowment for International Peace, 1921.

Scupin, Ernst-Ottomar. *Die Völkerrechtliche Stellung Der Sudafrikanishen Union Hintsichlich Sudwestafrikas.* Munich: Drukerei Charlotte Schon, 1963.

Segal, Ronald (ed.). *Sanctions Against South Africa.* Baltimore, Md.: Penguin Books, 1964.

Seymour, Charles (ed.). *The Intimate Papers of Colonel House,* 4 vols. Boston and New York: Houghton Mifflin, 1926-28.

_____. *American Diplomacy during the World War.* Baltimore, Md.: The Johns Hopkins Press, 1934.

Shihata, Ibrahim F. I. *The Power of the International Court to Determine Its Own Jurisdiction, Compétence de la Compétence.* The Hague: Nijhoff, 1965.

Shotwell, James T. *At the Paris Peace Conference.* New York: Macmillan, 1937.

Smuts, J. C. *The League of Nations: A Practical Suggestion.* London: Hodder and Stoughton, 1918.

Stone, Julius. *International Guarantees of Minority Rights.* London: Oxford University Press, 1932.

_____. *Legal Controls of International Conflict.* London: Stevens, 1954.

Stoyanovsky, J. *La Théorie Générale Des Mandats Internationaux.* Paris: Presses Universitaires de France, 1925.

Taubenfeld, Rita F., and Howard J. *Race, Peace, Law, and Southern Africa.* Dobbs Ferry, N.Y.: Oceana, 1968.

Temperley, H. W. V. (ed.). *A History of the Peace Conference of Paris,* 6 vols. London: Frowde, Hodder and Stoughton, 1920-24.

Thompson, Leonard M. *Politics in the Republic of South Africa.* Boston: Little Brown and Company, 1966.

Tillman, Seth P. *Anglo-American Relations at the Paris Peace Conference of 1919.* Princeton, N.J.: Princeton University Press, 1961.

Toussaint, Charmian Edwards. *The Trusteeship System of the United Nations.* New York: Praeger, 1956.

Verzijl, J. H. W. *The Jurisprudence of the World Court*, 2 vols. Leyden: Sijthoff, 1965.
_____. *International Law in Historical Perspective.* Leyden: Sijthoff, 1968-.
de Visscher, Charles. *Théories et Réalites en Droit International Public*, 2nd ed. Paris: Pedone, 1955.
_____. *Aspects Récents du Droit Procédural de La Cour Internationale de Justice.* Paris: Pedone, 1966.
Wainhouse, David W. *Remnants of Empire: The United Nations and the End of Colonialism.* New York: Harper and Row, 1964.
Walker, Eric A. *A History of Southern Africa*, 3rd ed. London: Longmans, Green, 1957.
Walters, F. P. *A History of the League of Nations*, 2 vols. London: Oxford University Press, 1952.
Walworth, Arthur. *Woodrow Wilson*, 2 vols. New York: Longmans, Green, 1958.
Wellington, J. H. *South West Africa and its Human Issues.* Oxford: Clarendon Press, 1967.
Wengler, Wilhelm. *Völkerrecht.* Berlin, Göttingen, Heidelberg: Springer Verlag, 1964.
White, Freda. *Mandates.* London: Jonathan Cape, 1926.
Whiteman, Marjorie M. *Digest of International Law.* Washington: U.S. Department of State, 1963-.
Wright, Quincy. *Mandates Under the League of Nations.* Chicago: University of Chicago Press, 1930.
Yemin, Edward. *Legislative Powers in the United Nations and Specialized Agencies.* Leyden: Sijthoff, 1969.
Zimmern, Alfred. *The League of Nations and the Rule of Law 1918-1935.* London: Macmillan, 1936.

## ARTICLES

Asamoah, Obed. "The Legal Effect of Resolutions of the General Assembly," *Columbia Journal of Transnational Law* 3 (1965): 210-30.
Ballinger, R. B. "The International Court of Justice and the South West Africa Cases: Judgment of 21st December, 1962," *South African Law Journal* 81 (1964): 35-62.
_____. "UN Action on Human Rights in South Africa." In *The International Protection of Human Rights*, edited by Evan Luard. London: Thames and Hudson, 1967.
Bastid, Suzanne. "Les Problèmes Territoriaux dans la Jurisprudence de la Cour Internationale de Justice," Hague Academy, *Recueil des Cours* 107 (1962-III): 365-495.
_____. "L'affaire du Sud-Ouest Africain devant la Cour Internationale de Justice," *Journal du Droit International* 94 (1967): 571-83.
Baty, I. "Protectorates and Mandates," *British Year Book of International Law* 2 (1921-22): 109-21.
Bentwich, Norman. "The Jurisdiction of the International Court of Justice over Concessions in a Mandated Territory," *Law Quarterly Review* 44 (1928): 450-63.
_____. "Colonial Mandates and Trusteeships," *Transactions of the Grotius Society* 32 (1946): 121-34.
Berthoud, Paul. "Des Mandats aux Accords de Tutelle: La Publicité des Travaux de la Commission Permanente des Mandats," *Die Friedens-Warte* 47 (1947): 233-54.

Borchard, Edwin M. "The Mavrommatis Concessions Cases," *American Journal of International Law* 19 (1925): 728–38.

———. "The Customs Union Advisory Opinion," *American Journal of International Law* 25 (1931): 711–16.

Botha, J. S. F. "Aspects of the Nations of South Africa." In *South Africa: Problems and Prospects*, edited by Phillip W. Quigg. New York: Council on Religion and International Affairs, 1965.

Bowett, D. W. "Estoppel Before International Tribunals and Its Relation to Acquiescence," *British Year Book of International Law* 33 (1957): 176–202.

Brown, Philip Marshall. "The Anschluss and the Permanent Court of International Justice," *American Journal of International Law* 25 (1931): 508–12.

Brownlie, Ian. "The Justiciability of Disputes and Issues in International Relations," *British Year Book of International Law* 42 (1967): 123–44.

Carey, John, Inman, Harry, and Hynning, Clifford J. "The World Court's Decision on South West Africa," *International Lawyer* 1 (1966): 12–38.

Cheng, Bin. "The 1966 South-West Africa Judgment of the World Court," *Current Legal Problems 1967* 20 (1967): 181–212.

Crawford, John F. "South West Africa: Mandate Termination in Historical Perspective," *Columbia Journal of Transnational Law* 6 (1967): 91–137.

Dale, Richard. "South Africa and the International Community," *World Politics* 18 (1966): 297–313.

D'Amato, Anthony A. "Apartheid in South West Africa: Five Claims of Equality," *Portia Law Journal* 1 (1966): 59–76.

———. "The Bantustan Proposal for South West Africa," *Journal of Modern African Studies* 4 (1966): 177–92.

———. "Legal and Political Strategies of the South West Africa Litigation," *Law in Transition Quarterly* 4 (1967): 8–43.

Dugard, C. J. R. "Objections to the Revision of the 1962 Judgment of the International Court of Justice in the South West African Case," *South African Law Journal* 82 (1965): 178–91.

———. "The South West Africa Cases, Second Phase, 1966," *South African Law Journal* 83 (1966): 429–60.

———. "The Revocation of the Mandate for South West Africa," *American Journal of International Law* 62 (1968): 78–97.

———. "South West Africa and the 'Terrorist Trial'," *American Journal of International Law* 64 (1970): 19–41.

———. "The Opinion on South West Africa ('Namibia'): The Teleologists Triumph," *South African Law Journal* 88 (1971): 460–77.

———. "Namibia (South West Africa): The Court's Opinion, South Africa's Response, and Prospects for the Future," *Columbia Journal of Transnational Law* 11 (1972): 14–49.

Emerson, Rupert. "Colonialism, Political Development and the U.N.," *International Organization* 19 (1965): 484–503.

———. "The New Higher Law of Anti-Colonialism." In *The Relevance of International Law*, edited by Karl Deutsch and Stanley Hoffmann. Cambridge, Mass.: Schenkman, 1968.

———. "The United Nations and Colonialism," *International Relations* 3 (1970): 766–81.

———. "Self-Determination," *American Journal of International Law* 65 (1971): 459–75.

Engel, Salo. "The Compulsory Jurisdiction of the International Court of Justice," *Georgetown Law Journal* 40 (1951-52): 40-66.

_____. " 'Living' International Constitutions and the World Court (The Subsequent Practice of International Organs Under Their Constituent Instruments)," *International and Comparative Law Quarterly* 16 (1967): 865-910.

Etra, Aaron. "Justiciable Disputes: A Jurisdictional and Jurisprudential Issue," *Columbia Journal of Transnational Law* 4 (1965): 86-118.

Evans, Luther Harris. "Some Legal and Historical Antecedents of the Mandatory System," *Proceedings of the Southwestern Political Science Association* 5 (1924): 143-61.

_____. "Are 'C' Mandates Veiled Annexations?," *Southwestern Political and Social Science Quarterly* 7 (1927): 381-400.

_____. "The General Principles Governing the Termination of a Mandate," *American Journal of International Law* 26 (1932): 735-58.

_____. "Would Japanese Withdrawal from the League Affect the Status of the Japanese Mandate?" *American Journal of International Law* 27 (1933): 140-42.

"An Examination of Certain Criticisms of the South West Africa Cases Judgment," *Australian Year Book of International Law* 2 (1966): 143-48.

Falk, Richard A. "The South West Africa Cases: An Appraisal," *International Organization* 21 (1967): 1-23.

_____. "The South West Africa Cases: The Limits of Adjudication." In *Ethiopia and Liberia* vs. *South Africa: The South West Africa Cases.* Occasional Paper No. 5, African Studies Center, University of California, Los Angeles, 1968.

_____. "Observer's Report on *The State* v. *Tuhadeleni and Others.*" In *Erosion of the Rule of Law in South Africa.* International Commission of Jurists, 1968.

Favoreau, Louis. "L'Arrêt du 21 Decembre sur le Sud-Ouest Africain et L'Évolution du Droit Des Organisations Internationales," *Annuaire Francais De Droit International*, 9 (1963): 303-57.

Feder, Gerald M., Rice, David A., Etra, Aaron. "The South West Africa Cases: A Symposium," *Columbia Journal of Transnational Law* 4 (1965): 47-118.

Feinberg, Nathan. "La Juridiction et la Jurisprudence de la Cour Permanente de Justice Internationale en Matière de Mandats et la Minorités," Hague Academy, *Recueil des Cours* 59 (1937-I): 591-703.

Fischer, G. "Les Réactions devant l'Arrêt de la Cour Internationale de Justice Concernant le Sud-Ouest Africain," *Annuaire Francais de Droit International* 12 (1966): 144-54.

Fitzmaurice, G. G. "The Law and Procedure of the International Court of Justice: Treaty Interpretation and Certain Other Treaty Points," *British Year Book of International Law* 28 (1951): 1-28.

_____. "The Law and Procedure of the International Court of Justice: International Organizations and Tribunals," *British Year Book of International Law* 29 (1952): 1-62.

_____. "The Law and Procedure of the International Court of Justice, 1951-1954: General Principles and Sources of International Law," *British Year Book of International Law* 30 (1953): 183-231.

_____. "Hersch Lauterpacht—The Scholar as Judge. Part I," *British Year Book of International Law* 37 (1961): 1-71.

_____. "Hersch Lauterpacht—The Scholar as Judge. Part II," *British Year Book of International Law* 38 (1962): 1-83.

———. "Hersch Lauterpacht—The Scholar as Judge. Part III," *British Year Book of International Law* 39 (1963): 133–88.

———. "Judicial Innovation—Its Uses and its Perils—As Exemplified in Some of the Work of the International Court of Justice during Lord McNair's Period of Office." In *Cambridge Essays in International Law.* London: Stevens, 1965.

Friedmann, Wolfgang. "The Jurisprudential Implications of the South West Africa Case," *Columbia Journal of Transnational Law* 6 (1967): 1–16.

"The Future of South West Africa (Namibia)": A Symposium, *1971 Proceedings of the American Society of International Law, American Journal of International Law* 65 (1971): 144–68.

"The Future of the Mandates: A Symposium," *African Affairs* 43 (1944): 159–71.

Gilchrist, H. "The United Nations: Colonial Questions at the San Francisco Conference," *American Political Science Review* 39 (1945): 982–92.

———. "Trusteeship and the Colonial System," *Proceedings of the Academy of Political Science* 22 (1947): 203–17.

Goodwin, G. L. "The United Nations: Expectations and Experience," *International Relations* 3 (1970): 729–55.

Green, L. C. "United Nations General Assembly, 1950: South West Africa," *International Law Quarterly* 4 (1951): 219–21.

———. "South West Africa and the World Court," *International Journal* 22 (1966–67): 39–67.

———. "The United Nations, South-West Africa and the World Court," *Indian Journal of International Law* 7 (1967): 491–525.

Gross, Ernest A. "The South West Africa Cases: On the Threshold of Decision," *Columbia Journal of Transnational Law* 3 (1964): 19–25.

———. "The South West Africa Case: What Happened?" *Foreign Affairs* 45 (1966): 36–47.

———. "The South West Africa Cases: An Essay on Judicial Outlook." In *Ethiopia and Liberia* vs. *South Africa: The South West Africa Cases.* Occasional Paper No. 5, African Studies Center, University of California, Los Angeles, 1968.

Gross, Leo. "Limitations upon the Judicial Function," *American Journal of International Law* 58 (1964): 415–31.

———. "The United Nations and the Role of Law," *International Organization* 19 (1965): 537–61.

———. "The International Court of Justice and the United Nations," Hague Academy, *Recueil des Cours* 121 (1967–II): 315–439.

———. "The International Court of Justice: Consideration of Requirements for Enhancing its Role in the International Legal Order," *American Journal of International Law* 65 (1971): 253–326.

———. "The Right of Self-Determination in International Law." In *New States in the Modern World,* edited by Martin Kilson. Cambridge, Mass.: Harvard University Press, 1972.

Haas, Ernest B. "The Reconciliation of Conflicting Colonial Policy Aims: Acceptance of the League of Nations Mandate System," *International Organization* 6 (1952): 521–36.

———. "The Attempt to Terminate Colonialism: Acceptance of the United Nations Trusteeship System," *International Organization* 7 (1953): 1–21.

Hales, James C. "Some Legal Aspects of the Mandate System: Sovereignty—Nationality—Termination and Transfer," *Transactions of the Grotius Society* 23 (1937): 85–126.

_____. "The Creation and Application of the Mandate System," *Transactions of the Grotius Society* 25 (1939): 185–284.

Hall, H. Duncan. "The Trusteeship System and the Case of South West Africa," *British Year Book of International Law* 24 (1947): 385–89.

Hauser, Mrs. Rita. "United Nations Law on Racial Discrimination." *Proceedings of the American Society of International Law, American Journal of International Law* 64 (1970): 114–25.

Henkin, Louis. "International Organization and the Rule of Law," *International Organization* 22 (1969): 656–82.

_____. "The United Nations and the Rules of Law," *Harvard International Law Journal* 11 (1970): 428–35.

Higgins, Rosalyn. "The International Court and South West Africa: The Implications of the Judgment," *International Affairs* 42 (1966): 573–99.

_____. "The United Nations and Lawmaking: The Political Organs," *Proceedings of the American Society of International Law, American Journal of International Law* 64 (1970): 37–48.

Highet, Keith. "The South West Africa Cases," *Current History* 52 (1967): 154–61.

Hudson, Manley O. "The Twenty-Ninth Year of the World Court," *American Journal of International Law* 45 (1951): 11–19.

_____. "The Common Interpretation of the Mandates of International Law," *Proceedings of the American Society of International Law* 45 (1951): 44–55.

_____. "The Thirty-Fourth Year of the World Court," *American Journal of International Law* 50 (1956): 1–17.

_____. "The Thirty-Fifth Year of the World Court," *American Journal of International Law* 51 (1957): 1–17.

Jennings, R. Y. "The International Court's Advisory Opinion on the Voting Procedure on Questions Concerning South West Africa," *Transactions of the Grotius Society* 42 (1956) 85–97.

Jessup, Philip C. "The Customs Union Advisory Opinion," *American Journal of International Law* 26 (1932): 105–10.

Johnson, D. H. N. "The Effect of Resolutions of the General Assembly of the United Nations," *British Year Book of International Law* 32 (1955–56): 97–122.

_____. "The Case Concerning the Northern Cameroons," *International and Comparative Law Quarterly* 13 (1964): 1143–92.

_____. "Sanctions Against South Africa? The Legal Aspect." In *Sanctions Against South Africa*, edited by Ronald Segal. Baltimore: Penguin Books, 1964.

_____. "The South West Africa Cases (Second Phase)," *International Relations* 3 (1967): 157–76.

Jully, Laurent. "La question du Sud-Ouest africain devant la Cour internationale de Justice," *Friedens-Warte* 50 (1950–51): 207–26.

Kahn, Ellison. "The International Court's Advisory Opinion on the International Status of South West Africa," *International Law Quarterly* 4 (1951): 78–99.

Karis, Thomas. "South Africa." In *Five African States*, edited by Gwendolen M. Carter. Ithaca, N.Y.: Cornell University Press, 1963.

Kerina, Mburumba. "South-West Africa, the United Nations, and the International Court of Justice," *African Forum* 2 (1966): 5–32.

Khan, Rahmatullah, and Kaur, Satpal. "The Deadlock over South West Africa," *Indian Journal of International Law* 8 (1968): 179–200.

Landis, Elizabeth S. "South West Africa in the International Court: Act II, Scene 1," *Cornell Law Quarterly* 49 (1964): 179-227.

_____. "The South West Africa Cases: Remand to the United Nations," *Cornell Law Quarterly* 52 (1967): 627-71.

Lipton, Merle. "Independent Bantustans?," *International Affairs* 48 (1972): 1-19.

Lissitzyn, Oliver J. "International Law and the Advisory Opinion on Namibia," *Columbia Journal of Transnational Law* 11 (1972): 50-73.

Louis, Wm. Roger. "The United States and the African Peace Settlement of 1919: The Pilgrimage of George Louis Beer," *Journal of African History* 4 (1963): 413-33.

_____. "African Origins of the Mandates Idea," *International Organization* 19 (1965): 20-36.

MaKonnen, Ambassador Endalkachew. "The South West Africa Cases: The Case for Rectification." In *Ethiopia and Liberia* vs. *South Africa: The South West Africa Cases.* Occasional Paper No. 5, African Studies Center, University of California, Los Angeles, 1968.

Manning, Charles A. W. "South Africa and the World: In Defense of Apartheid," *Foreign Affairs* 43 (1964): 135-49.

_____. "The South West Africa Cases: A Personal Analysis," *International Relations* 3 (1966): 98-110.

Mason, Philip. "South Africa and the World: Some Maxims and Axioms," *Foreign Affairs* 43 (1964): 150-64.

_____. "Separate Development and South West Africa: Some Aspects of the Odendaal Report," *Race* 5 (1964): 83-97.

McKay, Vernon. "South African Propaganda on the International Court's Decision," *African Forum* 2 (1967): 51-64.

McKean, W. A. " 'Legal Right or Interest' in the South West Africa Cases: A Critical Comment," *Australian Year Book of International Law* 2 (1966): 135-41.

McNair, Arnold D. "Mandates," *Cambridge Law Journal* 3 (1928): 149-60.

McWhinney, Edward. "The Changing United Nations Constitutionalism: New Arenas and New Techniques for International Law-Making," *Canadian Year Book of International Law* 5 (1967): 68-83.

Miller, David Hunter. "The Origin of the Mandates System," *Foreign Affairs* 6 (1928): 277-89.

Morley, Jeremy D. "Relative Incompatibility of Functions in the International Court," *International and Comparative Law Quarterly* 19 (1970): 316-27.

Murphy, Cornelius F., Jr. "The South West Africa Judgment: A Study in Justiciability," *Duquesne University Law Review* 5 (1966-67): 477-86.

Nisot, Joseph. "The Advisory Opinion of the International Court of Justice on the International Status of South West Africa," *South African Law Journal* 68 (1951): 274-85.

_____. "La question du Sud-Ouest africain devant la Cour internationale de Justice," *Revue Belge de droit international* 1 (1967): 24-36.

Nyerere, Julius K. "Rhodesia in the Context of Southern Africa," *Foreign Affairs* 44 (1966): 373-86.

Onuf, N. G. "Professor Falk on the Quasi-Legislative Competence of the General Assembly," *American Journal of International Law* 64 (1970): 349-55.

Parry, Clive. "The Legal Nature of the Trusteeship Agreements," *British Year Book of International Law* 27 (1950): 164-85.

Pollock, Alexander J. "The South West Africa Cases and the Jurisprudence of International Law," *International Organization* 23 (1969): 767-87.

Potter, Pitman B. "Origin of the System of Mandates Under the League of Nations," *American Political Science Review* 16 (1922): 563-83.

_____. "Further Notes," *American Political Science Review* 20 (1926): 842-46.

Prott, Lyndel V. "Some Aspects of Judicial Reasoning in the South West Africa Case of 1962," *Revue Belge de droit internationale* 1 (1967): 37-51.

Rappard, William E. "The Mandates and the International Trusteeship Systems," *Political Science Quarterly* 61 (1946): 408-19.

Reisman, William M. "Revision of the South West Africa Cases: An Analysis of the Grounds of Nullity in the Decision of July 18th, 1966 and Methods of Revision," *Virginia Journal of International Law* 7 (1966): 1-90.

Rolin, H. "La Pratique des Mandats Internationaux," Hague Academy, *Recueil des Cours* 19 (1927-IV): 493-628.

Rosenne, Shabtai. "The International Court and the United Nations: Reflections on the Period 1946-1954," *International Organization* 9 (1955): 244-56.

_____. "Sir Hersch Lauterpacht's Concept of the Task of the International Judge," *American Journal of International Law* 55 (1961): 825-62.

Sayre, Francis B. "Legal Problems Arising from the United Nations Trusteeship System," *American Journal of International Law* 42 (1948): 263-98.

Schachter, Oscar. "The Relation of Law, Politics and Action in the United Nations," Hague Academy, *Recueil des Cours* 109 (1963-II): 169-256.

_____. "Legal Problems." In *Annual Review of United Nations Affairs 1963-1964,* edited by Richard N. Swift. Dobbs Ferry, N.Y.: Oceana, 1965.

Scott, Michael. "The International Status of South West Africa," *International Affairs* 34 (1958): 318-29.

Scrivner, Robert W. "The South West Africa Case: 1962 Revisited," *African Forum* 2 (1966): 33-50.

Skubiszewski, Krzysztot. "The General Assembly of the United Nations and Its Power to Influence National Action," *Proceedings of the American Society of International Law* (1964): 153-62.

Sloan, F. Blaine. "The Binding Force of a 'Recommendation' of the General Assembly of the United Nations," *British Year Book of International Law* 25 (1948): 1-33.

Slonim, S. "The Advisory Opinion of the International Court of Justice on Certain Expenses of the United Nations: A Critical Analysis," *Howard Law Journal* 10 (1964): 226-70.

_____. "The Origins of the South West Africa Dispute: The Versailles Peace Conference and the Creation of the Mandates System," *Canadian Yearbook of International Law* 6 (1968): 115-43.

Sohn, Louis B. "Exclusion of Political Disputes from Judicial Settlement," *American Journal of International Law* 38 (1944): 694-700.

"South West Africa Cases. Ethiopia v. South Africa; Liberia v. South Africa, Second Phase," *Canadian Year Book of International Law* 5 (1967): 241-53.

Stone, Julius. "The International Court and World Crisis," *International Conciliation*, No. 536, Jan. 1962.

_____. "South West Africa and the World Court," *The Australian* Sept. 26-28, 1966.

_____. "Reflections on Apartheid after the South West Africa Cases," *Washington Law Review* 42 (1967): 1069.

Umozurike, U. O. "International Law and Self-Determination in Namibia," *Journal of Modern African Studies* 8 (1970): 585–603.

Verzijl, J. H. W. "The South West Africa Cases (Second Phase)," *International Relations* 3 (1966): 87–97.

de Villiers, D. P. "The South West Africa Cases: The Moment of Truth." In *Ethiopia and Liberia* vs. *South Africa: The South West Africa Cases.* Occasional Paper No. 5, African Studies Center, University of California, Los Angeles, 1968.

Virally, Michel, "Droit International et Décolonisation devant les Nations Unies," *Annuaire Français De Droit International* 9 (1963): 508–41.

Wynne, George. "Grounds for Revision of the Judgment of the International Court of Justice of 21st December 1962, That It Had Jurisdiction to Adjudicate Upon the South West Africa Case: *Ad Hoc* Judge Improperly Chosen As Liberia Had No *Locus Standi*," *South African Law Journal* 81 (1964): 449–57.

Zacklin, Ralph. "Challenge of Rhodesia," *International Conciliation* No. 575, Nov. 1969..

## UNPUBLISHED MATERIAL

Dale, Richard. "The Evolution of the South West African Dispute Before the United Nations, 1945–1950." Ph.D. dissertation, Princeton University, 1962. (University Microfilms)

Evans, Luther Harris. "The Mandates System and the Administration of Territories Under C Mandate." Ph.D. dissertation, Stanford University, 1927. (University Microfilms)

Gottlieb, Paul Herbert. "The Commonwealth of Nations at the United Nations." Ph.D. dissertation, Boston University Graduate School, 1962. (University Microfilms)

Hedrich, Richard Henry. "Conservative and Progressive Attitudes Manifested by Members of the International Court of Justice." Ph.D. dissertation, University of Maryland, 1959.

Jahanbani, Mansour Elddin. "The Question of South West Africa." Masters thesis, Columbia University, 1956. (Copy available in United Nations Reference Library.)

Menges, Hans Eberhard. "Die Rechtstellung von Sud-West-Afrika nach dem 2 Weltkrieg." Ph.D. dissertation, der Rheinischen Friedrich-Wilhelm, University of Bonn, 1955. (Copy available in United Nations Reference Library.)

# INDEX

sions); and succession argument, 120 n.38, 198 n.43, 219–22; summary of arguments on merits, 271–77; and survival of mandate, 96 n.94, 194–95, 219–24; and witnesses, 239, 246, 269–70, 306. *See also* Apartheid; Norm of nondiscrimination; Respondent; *SWA* cases

Applicants' submissions: No. 1, 185, 295–96; No. 2, 185–86, 261, 295–96; No. 3, 186, 225 n.38, 260; No. 4, 186, 225 n.38, 260; No. 5, 100 n.117, 168 n.6, 186, 260–61; No. 6, 186, 260–61; No. 7, 186; No. 8, 186; No. 9, 168 n.6, 186, 260–61

Arab-Asian bloc, 81–83, 86

Armand-Ugon, E. C. (Judge), in joint dissent (1956), 160–61

*Asylum* case (1949), 255 n.188, 305 n.103

Australia: and Pacific islands, 15, 17–20, 23, 27, 29, 31, 32; and anticolonialism, 60 n.4; and racial equality clause in Covenant, 229 n.80. *See also* Dominions

*Austro-German Customs Union* case (1931), 355 n.13

Badawi, A. H. (Judge): implications of death of upon 1966 Court, 281; in joint dissent (1950), 111 n.4; in joint dissent (1956), 160–61; and 1962 judgment, 191 n.14

Baker, Ray Stannard, 22 n.44

*Baker v. Carr,* 369 U.S. 186 (1962), 355

Balfour, Lord (Arthur), 24 n.51, 25, 37 n.95

Bantustans. *See* Apartheid; Odendaal Commission; Racial discrimination; Separate development

*Barcelona Traction* case (Preliminary Objections) (1964), 217 n.14

*Barcelona Traction* case (Second Phase) (1970), 294–95

Basdevant, J. (Judge), 191 n.14, 280, 356; on Article 80(1) of Charter, 198 n.43; in joint dissent (1956), 160–61, 356; in separate opinion (1950), 151 n.44

Baxi, Upendra, 360 n.21

Beer, George Louis: and mandates proposal, 13–14, 19; on mandates system, 33, 36; proposes annexation of SWA, 14, 19; views of, cited by South Africa, 79 n.14

Berlin, Treaty of (1885), 11, 24

Bolshevik Revolution, and self-determination, 12

Bonar Law, Andrew, 18

Bondelzwarts incident, 50

Borden, Robert L., 23

Botha, Louis, 2; at Paris Peace Conference, 31–32; statement of, cited by South Africa, 32 n.78, 79 n.14, 216 n.13

Bourgeois, Léon, 35

*Brown v. Board of Education,* 347 U.S. 483 (1954), 243–44, 271–72, 274

Bustamante y Rivero, J. L. (Judge), 191 n.14, 280–81; denies rule of automatic succession between League and UN, 198 n.43

Caradon, Lord, 363 n.31

Carpio, Victorio D., counsels Assembly restraint, 178; expresses doubt on legal proceedings, 188; and visit to SWA, 248, 281 n.9, 316

de Castro, F. (Judge), 35 n.90, 47 n.22

Cecil, Lord Robert, 21, 27 n.66, 35

Chamberlain, Sir Austen, 46

Charter of United Nations. *See* United Nations Charter

China: and drafting of Charter, 59, 61 n.14; proposals of, at final session of League Assembly, 69–71, 128–29, 200–1, 217, 221–22, 223 n.35; and representation in UN issue, 328

Claude, Inis L., Jr., 62 n.17

Clemenceau, Georges, 25–26

Colonialism, struggle against, 4–6, 183, 317, 347–50, 359–63

Color-bar legislation: in SWA, in period of League, 51–52; as issue in *SWA* cases, 225–28, 232–34

Committee on SWA (1953–61): creation of, 141; functions and purposes of, 141–43; membership increased, 171; and negotiations with South Africa, 143–44, 155, 181; operation of, 143–44, 167–70, 176–77, 315–16; and oral petitions, 154–58; on possible legal action, 171–73; reports of, 144, 155, 167, 169, 175, 176, 181

Committee of 24, 316–17

Contentious litigation: first advocated, 139 n.69; steps leading up to, 142–43, 170–73, 175, 176–84. *See also SWA* cases

Cordova, R. (Judge), 281 n.6

Covenant. *See* League of Nations Covenant

Declaration on Colonialism (1960), 6, 314, 317, 349, 350

Declaration on the Elimination of All Forms of Racial Discrimination (1963), 349–50

Declaration on the Granting of Independence to Colonial Countries and Peoples. *See* Declaration on Colonialism (1960)

Decolonization, 183, 317, 347–50, 359–63

Dominions: against mandates principle, 15, 16, 19–20, 22–28, 31; and mandates compromise, 11, 29–32, 36–38, 57, 347. *See also* Australia, and Pacific islands; Hughes, William M.; Lloyd George, David; Wilson, President Woodrow

*Dred Scott* case (*Scott* v. *Sanford*), 19 Howard 393 (1857), 309

Dugard, John, 292 n.52, 293 n.56, 295 n.64, 296–97, 321 n.38

*Eastern Carelia* case (1923), 216 n.10, 333–34

Egypt: and Charter provisions, 59, 62 n.18, 70 n.43

Emerson, Rupert, 59, 361 n.24, 363

THE JOHNS HOPKINS UNIVERSITY PRESS

This book was composed in Baskerville text and Melior display type
by Jones Composition Company, Inc. from a design by Laurie Jewell.
It was printed by Universal Lithographers, Inc. on S. D. Warrens
60-lb. Sebago, text color, regular finish and bound by L. H. Jenkins, Inc.
in Columbia Bayside linen cloth.

Library of Congress Cataloging in Publication Data

Slonim, Solomon.
    South West Africa and the United Nations.

    Bibliography: p.
    1. Mandates—Africa, Southwest.  2. United
Nations—Africa, Southwest.  I. Title.
JX1586.S64S55        341.2'7        72-4020
ISBN 0-8018-1430-8